MW01240881

Copyright

All rights reserved.

MEDITERRANEAN DIET COOKBOOK FOR BEGINNERS

Mediterranean Diet Cookbook For Beginners: The Only Guide That Teaches You How To Reproduce Over 1200 Tasty Recipes In Just 7 Easy Steps To Enjoy A Daily Healthy Lifestyle | Included 16-Week Meal Plan

Sarah Marino

The Mediterranean Culinary Academy

Table of Contents

INTRODUCTION.. 1
CHAPTER 1. YOUR NEW JOURNEY THROUGH THE MEDITERRANEAN DIET................................ 4
BENEFITS OF MEDITERRANEAN DIET........... 8
CHAPTER 2. BREAKFAST RECIPES................ 10
1. ITALIAN BREAKFAST SAUSAGE WITH BABY POTATOES AND VEGETABLES.................. 10
2. CAULIFLOWER FRITTERS WITH HUMMUS.... 10
3. OVERNIGHT BERRY CHIA OATS.................. 11
4. RASPBERRY VANILLA SMOOTHIE............... 11
5. BLUEBERRY BANANA PROTEIN SMOOTHIE.. 11
6. CHOCOLATE BANANA SMOOTHIE................ 11
7. MOROCCAN AVOCADO SMOOTHIE.............. 11
8. GREEK YOGURT WITH FRESH BERRIES, HONEY AND NUTS.................................... 11
9. MEDITERRANEAN EGG MUFFINS WITH HAM........... 11
10. QUINOA BAKE WITH BANANA................... 12
11. SUN-DRIED TOMATOES, DILL AND FETA OMELET CASSEROLE................................ 12
12. BREAKFAST TACO SCRAMBLE................. 12
13. GREEK BEANS TORTILLAS...................... 13
14. BAKED CAULIFLOWER HASH................... 13
15. EGGS, MINT AND TOMATOES.................. 13
16. BACON, SPINACH AND TOMATO SANDWICH... 13
17. COTTAGE CHEESE AND BERRIES OMELET... 13
18. SALMON FRITTATA............................... 13
19. CORIANDER MUSHROOM SALAD............. 14
20. CINNAMON APPLE AND LENTILS PORRIDGE..... 14
21. LENTILS AND CHEDDAR FRITTATA.......... 14
22. SEEDS AND LENTILS OATS..................... 14
23. ORZO AND VEGGIE BOWLS.................... 14
24. LEMON PEAS QUINOA MIX..................... 15
25. WALNUTS YOGURT MIX.......................... 15
26. STUFFED PITA BREADS.......................... 15
27. FARRO SALAD..................................... 15
28. CRANBERRY AND DATES SQUARES......... 15
29. CHEESY EGGS RAMEKINS...................... 16
30. LEEKS AND EGGS MUFFINS................... 16
31. ARTICHOKES AND CHEESE OMELET......... 16
32. QUINOA AND EGGS SALAD.................... 16
33. CORN AND SHRIMP SALAD.................... 16
34. TOMATO AND LENTILS SALAD................ 17
35. COUSCOUS AND CHICKPEAS BOWLS....... 17
36. ZUCCHINI AND QUINOA PAN................... 17
37. CHEESY YOGURT................................. 17
38. BAKED OMELET MIX.............................. 17
39. STUFFED SWEET POTATO...................... 18
40. CAULIFLOWER FRITTERS...................... 18
41. VEGGIE QUICHE.................................. 18
42. POTATO HASH.................................... 19
43. SCRAMBLED EGGS.............................. 19
44. WATERMELON PIZZA............................ 19
45. HAM MUFFINS.................................... 19
46. AVOCADO CHICKPEA PIZZA.................. 19
47. BANANA AND QUINOA CASSEROLE........ 20
48. AVOCADO SPREAD.............................. 20

49. AVOCADO TOAST................................ 20
50. MINI FRITTATAS................................. 20
51. BERRY OATS...................................... 20
52. SUN-DRIED TOMATOES OATMEAL........... 20
53. QUINOA MUFFINS................................ 21
54. QUINOA AND EGGS PAN....................... 21
55. STUFFED TOMATOES........................... 21
56. SUNNY-SIDE UP BAKED EGGS WITH SWISS CHARD, FETA, AND BASIL................ 21
57. POLENTA WITH SAUTÉED CHARD AND FRIED EGGS........... 22
58. SMOKED SALMON EGG SCRAMBLE WITH DILL AND CHIVES............................ 22
59. BANANA OATS.................................... 22
60. SLOW-COOKED PEPPERS FRITTATA....... 22
61. AVOCADO AND APPLE SMOOTHIE.......... 22
62. GREEK QUINOA BREAKFAST BOWL......... 23
63. MUSHROOM GOAT CHEESE FRITTATA..... 23
64. MEDITERRANEAN FRITTATA.................. 23
65. HONEY-CARAMELIZED FIGS WITH GREEK YOGURT..................................... 24
66. SAVORY QUINOA EGG MUFFINS WITH SPINACH.. 24
67. AVOCADO TOMATO GOUDA SOCCA PIZZA..... 24
68. SHAKSHUKA WITH FETA....................... 24
69. PEANUT BUTTER BANANA GREEK YOGURT.... 25
70. VEGGIE MEDITERRANEAN QUICHE......... 25
71. SPINACH, FETA AND EGG BREAKFAST QUESADILLAS..................................... 26
72. MEDITERRANEAN QUINOA AND FETA EGG MUFFINS....................................... 26
73. GREEN SHAKSHUKA............................ 26
74. APPLE QUINOA BREAKFAST BARS......... 27
75. BLUEBERRIES QUINOA........................ 27
76. ENDIVES, FENNEL AND ORANGE SALAD... 27
77. RASPBERRIES AND YOGURT SMOOTHIE.. 27
78. HOMEMADE MUESLI............................. 27
79. TANGERINE AND POMEGRANATE BREAKFAST FRUIT SALAD..................... 28
80. HUMMUS AND TOMATO BREAKFAST PITTAS... 28
81. BAKED RICOTTA & PEARS..................... 28
82. CRUMBLED FETA AND SCALLIONS......... 29
83. GNOCCHI HAM OLIVES......................... 29
84. SPICY EARLY MORNING SEAFOOD RISOTTO..... 29
85. ROCKET TOMATOES AND MUSHROOM FRITTATA 29
86. CHEESY OLIVES BREAD........................ 30
87. SWEET POTATO TART........................... 30
88. FULL EGGS IN A SQUASH...................... 30
89. BARLEY PORRIDGE.............................. 31
90. TOMATO AND DILL FRITTATA................. 31
91. STRAWBERRY AND RHUBARB SMOOTHIE.. 31
92. BACON AND BRIE OMELET WEDGES....... 31
93. COCONUT PORRIDGE........................... 32
94. MEDITERRANEAN FETA AND QUINOA EGG MUFFINS....................................... 32
95. MEDITERRANEAN EGGS........................ 32

96. PASTRY-LESS SPANAKOPITA........................ 32
97. DATE AND WALNUT OVERNIGHT OATS................. 33
98. PEAR AND MANGO SMOOTHIE......................... 33
99. ARTICHOKE FRITTATA.............................. 33
100. FETA FRITTATA................................... 33
101. SMOKED SALMON AND POACHED EGGS ON
TOAST.. 33
102. HONEY ALMOND RICOTTA SPREAD WITH   34
PEACHES...
103. MEDITERRANEAN EGGS CUPS........................ 34
104. LOW-CARB BAKED EGGS WITH AVOCADO AND
FETA.. 34
105. MEDITERRANEAN EGGS WHITE BREAKFAST
SANDWICH WITH ROASTED TOMATOES.................... 35
106. GREEK YOGURT PANCAKES......................... 35
107. FETA & QUINOA EGG MUFFINS.....................35
108. 5-MINUTE HEIRLOOM TOMATO & CUCUMBER
TOAST... 35
109. GREEK YOGURT WITH WALNUTS AND HONEY.....36
110. TAHINI PINE NUTS TOAST........................36
111. FETA - AVOCADO & MASHED CHICKPEA TOAST... 36
112. MANGO PEAR SMOOTHIE...........................36
113. MEDITERRANEAN SMOOTHIE........................36
114. FRUIT SMOOTHIE................................36
115. STRAWBERRY-RHUBARB SMOOTHIE..................37
116. CHIA-POMEGRANATE SMOOTHIE....................37
117. EGG WHITE SCRAMBLE WITH CHERRY
TOMATOES & SPINACH................................ 37
118. BLUEBERRY, HAZELNUT, AND LEMON
BREAKFAST GRAIN SALAD............................. 37
119. BLUEBERRY GREEK YOGURT PANCAKES.............37
120. MEDITERRANEAN BREAKFAST EGG WHITE
SANDWICH.. 38
CHAPTER 3. SALADS............................. 39
121. TUNA SALAD....................................39
122. VEGGIE SALAD..................................39
123. SALMON AND BULGUR SALAD......................39
124. HERBED QUINOA AND ASPARAGUS..................39
125. POTATO AND PANCETTA BOWLS....................39
126. QUINOA SALAD..................................40
127. CORN SALAD....................................40
128. BROWN LENTILS SALAD..........................40
129. QUICK ZUCCHINI BOWL..........................40
130. HEALTHY BASIL PLATTER........................40
131. SPICED CHICKPEAS BOWLS.......................41
132. EGGPLANT SALAD................................41
133. GARBANZO BEAN SALAD..........................41
134. PEARL COUSCOUS SALAD.........................41
135. MEDITERRANEAN BREAKFAST SALAD...............42
136. BROWN RICE SALAD.............................42
137. RAINBOW MANGO SALAD..........................42
138. SATISFYING SPRING SALAD......................42
139. THE RAW GREEN DETOX SALAD....................43
140. DANDELION SALAD..............................43
141. SPICY WAKAME SALAD...........................43
142. AVO-ORANGE SALAD DISH........................43

143. NOURISHING ELECTRIC SALAD....................43
144. SUPERFOOD FONIO SALAD........................44
145. VEGGIE BOWLS..................................44
146. HEALTHY CHICKPEA ROAST SALAD.................44
147. AMARANTH TABBOULEH SALAD.....................44
148. ZUCCHINI AND MUSHROOM BOWL...................44
149. PEAR & STRAWBERRY SALAD......................45
150. RASPBERRY & ARUGULA SALAD....................45
151. MIXED BERRIES SALAD..........................45
152. APPLE & KALE SALAD...........................45
153. MANGO & ARUGULA SALAD........................45
154. ORANGE & KALE SALAD..........................45
155. ZUCCHINI & TOMATO SALAD......................46
156. TOMATO & ARUGULA SALAD.......................46
157. WARM AVO AND QUINOA SALAD....................46
158. CHICKPEAS & QUINOA SALAD.....................46
159. QUINOA, TOMATO & MANGO SALAD.................46
160. ZESTY CITRUS SALAD...........................46
161. ZUCCHINI HUMMUS WRAP.........................47
162. BASIL AND AVOCADO SALAD......................47
163. GRILLED ROMAINE LETTUCE SALAD...............47
164. KALE AND SPROUTS SALAD.......................47
165. DANDELION AND STRAWBERRY SALAD..............47
166. BASIL SALAD..................................48
167. CITRUS SALAD.................................48
168. MANGO SALAD..................................48
169. CUCUMBER AND ARUGULA SALAD...................48
170. GREEK SALAD WRAPS............................49
171. DILL SALMON SALAD WRAPS......................49
172. CHICKEN PARMESAN WRAPS.......................49
173. DELICIOUS QUINOA & DRIED.....................50
174. KOREAN BEEF AND ONION TACOS..................50
175. CHEESY SWEET POTATO AND BEAN BURRITOS... 50
176. GOLDEN CHICKEN AND YOGURT TAQUITOS..........51
177. COD TACOS WITH SALSA.........................51
178. GOLDEN SPRING ROLLS..........................51
179. TUNA AND LETTUCE WRAPS.......................52
180. GOLDEN CABBAGE AND MUSHROOM SPRING
ROLLS... 52
181. CRUNCHY CHICKEN EGG ROLLS....................53
182. FAST CHEESY BACON AND EGG WRAPS.............53
183. CHICKEN-LETTUCE WRAPS........................53
184. VEGGIE SALSA WRAPS...........................54
185. NUGGET AND VEGGIE TACO WRAPS.................54
186. LETTUCE FAJITA MEATBALL WRAPS...............54
187. CHICKEN PITA.................................54
188. BACON AND EGG WRAPS WITH SALSA..............54
189. CHICKEN WRAPS WITH RICOTTA CHEESE...........55
190. AVOCADO AND TOMATO WRAPS.....................55
191. SWEET POTATO AND SPINACH BURRITOS...........55
192. CABBAGE AND PRAWN WRAPS......................56
CHAPTER 4. STARTERS........................... 57
193. STUFFED CELERY...............................57
194. BUTTERNUT SQUASH FRIES.......................57
195. DRIED FIG TAPENADE...........................57
196. CHICKPEA PATTIES IN PITAS....................57

197. ROAST ASPARAGUS.................................58
198. ZA'ATAR FRIES.....................................58
199. SUMMERTIME VEGETABLE CHICKEN WRAPS.......58
200. SPEEDY SWEET POTATO CHIPS...................58
201. NACHOS WITH HUMMUS (MEDITERRANEAN INSPIRED)...58
202. HUMMUS AND OLIVE PITA BREAD................58
203. MARGHERITA OPEN-FACE SANDWICHES..........59
204. ROASTED VEGGIE PANINI.........................59
205. PREMIUM ROASTED BABY POTATOES............59
206. FIG WITH YOGURT AND HONEY...................60
207. GREEK SHRIMP SAGANAKI........................60
208. GREEK FAVA.......................................60
209. HUMMUS, FETA & BELL PEPPER CRACKERS......60
210. TOMATO & BASIL BRUSCHETTA...................60
211. LEMON-PEPPER CUCUMBERS.......................61
212. FALAFEL...61
213. WALNUT-FETA YOGURT DIP........................61
214. DATE WRAPS.......................................61
215. CLEMENTINE & PISTACHIO RICOTTA..............61
216. SERRANO-WRAPPED PLUMS........................62
217. CLASSIC APPLE OATS.............................62
218. PEACH & CHIA SEED..............................62
219. ALMOND BUTTER AND BLUEBERRY SMOOTHIE...62
220. SALMON AND EGG MUFFINS.......................62
221. NACHOS..63
222. TOMATO CREAM CHEESE SPREAD.................63
223. ITALIAN FRIES....................................63
224. TEMPEH SNACK....................................63
225. AVOCADO DIP......................................63
226. FETA AND ROASTED RED PEPPER BRUSCHETTA..63
227. MEAT-FILLED PHYLLO (SAMBOOSEK)............64
228. TASTY BLACK BEAN DIP..........................64
229. ZUCCHINI CAKES..................................64
230. PARSLEY NACHOS.................................64
231. PLUM WRAPS.......................................65
232. PARMESAN CHIPS..................................65
233. CHICKEN BITES....................................65
234. CHICKEN KALE WRAPS............................65
235. SAVORY PITA CHIPS..............................65
236. ARTICHOKE SKEWERS.............................66
237. KIDNEY BEAN SPREAD............................66
238. MEDITERRANEAN POLENTA CUPS.................66
239. TOMATO TRIANGLES...............................66
240. CHILI MANGO AND WATERMELON SALSA.........66
241. BLUEBERRY FAT BOMBS...........................67
242. CHEESY ZUCCHINI TRIANGLES WITH GARLIC MAYO DIP..67
243. HERBED CHEESE CHIPS...........................67
244. CAULIFLOWER POPPERS...........................67
245. CRISPY PARMESAN CHIPS.........................67
246. TEX-MEX QUESO DIP..............................68
247. SWEET ONION DIP.................................68
248. TRAIL MIX...68
249. COLD CUTS AND CHEESE PINWHEELS............68
250. ZUCCHINI BALLS WITH CAPERS AND BACON......68
251. STRAWBERRY FAT BOMBS.........................69
252. KALE CHIPS..69
253. PLANTAINS WITH TAPIOCA PEARLS..............69
254. BROWN RICE PUDDING WITH PUMPKIN SPICE..69
255. MANGO CASHEW CAKE.............................70
256. SWEET ORANGE AND LEMON BARLEY RISOTTO 70
257. HOMEMADE APPLESAUCE..........................70
258. BOILED PEANUTS..................................71
259. HOMEMADE BEET HUMMUS........................71
260. COCONUT PUDDING WITH TROPICAL FRUIT.......71
261. SWEET COCONUT CASSAVA........................71
262. TOFU WITH SALTED CARAMEL PEARLS...........72
263. HOMEMADE HUMMUS...............................72
264. CORN COCONUT PUDDING.........................72
265. RASPBERRY CHOCOLATE PARFAIT................73
266. BERRY JAM WITH CHIA SEEDS...................73
267. APPLE RISOTTO....................................73
268. NECTARINES WITH DRIED CLOVES...............73
269. CHOCOLATE RASPBERRY PARFAIT................74
270. PATBINGSU – IN MODERATION...................74
271. COCONUT BROWN RICE CAKE.....................74
272. RICE DUMPLINGS IN COCONUT SAUCE...........74
273. ROASTED CAULIFLOWER WITH PROSCIUTTO, CAPERS, AND ALMONDS.................................75
274. BUTTERY SLOW-COOKER MUSHROOMS...........75
275. ROASTED RADISHES WITH BROWN BUTTER SAUCE...75
276. PARMESAN AND PORK RIND GREEN BEANS......76
277. PESTO CAULIFLOWER STEAKS....................76
278. TOMATO, AVOCADO, AND CUCUMBER SALAD......76
279. CRUNCHY PORK RIND ZUCCHINI STICKS........76
280. CHEESE CHIPS AND GUACAMOLE................77
281. CAULIFLOWER POTATO SALAD....................77
282. LOADED CAULIFLOWER MASHED POTATOES......77
283. ALMOND BREAD....................................78
284. CHEESE STUFFED MUSHROOMS..................78
285. DELICIOUS CHICKEN ALFREDO DIP..............78
286. PERFECT CUCUMBER SALSA......................78
287. CREAMY AVOCADO SAUCE........................78
288. ZUCCHINI TOTS...................................79
289. AVOCADO YOGURT DIP............................79
290. MACADAMIA HUMMUS..............................79
291. EASY & PERFECT MEATBALLS....................79
292. EGGPLANT CHIPS..................................79
293. CREAMY CRAB DIP.................................79
294. HEALTHY CHICKEN FRITTERS.....................80
295. CREAMY MUSHROOMS WITH GARLIC AND THYME...80
296. EASY ROASTED BROCCOLI.........................80
297. ZUCCHINI STRIPS WITH MARINARA DIP.........80
298. ROASTED GARLIC DIP.............................80
299. KOHLRABI CHIPS..................................80
300. DAIKON CHIPS.....................................81
301. KALE DIP..81
302. JALAPENO CHEESE DIP............................81

303. SPICY DIP..81
304. ONION DIP..81
305. EASY CARROT DIP....................................81
306. PANKO TOFU WITH MAYO SAUCE..........81
307. LEMON AVOCADO SALAD DRESSING......82
308. CREAMY AVOCADO CILANTRO LIME DRESSING 82
309. CREAMY AVOCADO DRESSING..............82
310. SOUTHWESTERN AVOCADO SALAD DRESSING 82
311. MANGO SALSA...82
312. ROASTED TOMATO SAUCE.....................83

CHAPTER 5. PASTA/MAIN COURSE.............84
313. CREAMY CHICKEN BREAST.....................84
314. INDIAN CHICKEN STEW...........................84
315. CHICKEN, BAMBOO, AND CHESTNUTS MIX...84
316. SALSA CHICKEN......................................84
317. QUINOA CHICKEN SALAD.......................84
318. RICE WITH CHICKEN................................85
319. TOMATO SOUP..85
320. COD SOUP..85
321. TUNA CROQUETTES.................................85
322. SWEET POTATOES AND ZUCCHINI SOUP......86
323. LEMONGRASS AND CHICKEN SOUP.........86
324. EASY LUNCH SALMON STEAKS...............86
325. LIGHT BALSAMIC SALAD..........................86
326. PURPLE POTATO SOUP............................87
327. LEEKS SOUP...87
328. CAULIFLOWER LUNCH SALAD..................87
329. SHRIMP COCKTAIL...................................87
330. QUINOA AND SCALLOPS SALAD..............87
331. SQUID AND SHRIMP SALAD......................88
332. PARSLEY SEAFOOD COCKTAIL.................88
333. SHRIMP AND ONION GINGER DRESSING......88
334. FRUIT SHRIMP SOUP...............................89
335. MUSSELS AND CHICKPEA SOUP...............89
336. LEMON AND GARLIC FETTUCINE..............89
337. SHRIMP AND BROCCOLI SOUP.................90
338. COCONUT TURKEY MIX............................90
339. LIME SHRIMP AND KALE..........................90
340. PARSLEY COD MIX...................................90
341. SALMON AND CABBAGE MIX.....................90
342. TOFU & GREEN BEAN STIR-FRY................90
343. PEANUT VEGETABLE PAD THAI................91
344. SPICY TOFU BURRITO BOWLS WITH CILANTRO AVOCADO SAUCE...91
345. SWEET POTATO CAKES WITH CLASSIC GUACAMOLE...91
346. CHICKPEA CAULIFLOWER TIKKA MASALA......
347. EGGPLANT PARMESAN STACKS................92
348. ROASTED VEGETABLE ENCHILADAS.........93
349. LENTIL AVOCADO TACOS.........................93
350. TOMATO & OLIVE ORECCHIETTE WITH BASIL PESTO...93
351. ITALIAN STUFFED PORTOBELLO MUSHROOM BURGERS..94
352. GNOCCHI WITH TOMATO BASIL SAUCE........94
353. CREAMY PUMPKIN PASTA........................94

354. MEXICAN-STYLE POTATO CASSEROLE.......95
355. BLACK BEAN STEW WITH CORNBREAD......95
356. MUSHROOM FLORENTINE.........................96
357. HASSELBACK EGGPLANT.........................96
358. VEGETARIAN KEBABS...............................96
359. WHITE BEANS STEW.................................96
360. VEGETARIAN LASAGNA............................96
361. CARROT CAKES.......................................96
362. VEGAN CHILI...97
363. AROMATIC WHOLE GRAIN SPAGHETTI.......97
364. BAKED FALAFEL......................................97
365. PAELLA...97
366. CHUNKY TOMATOES................................97
367. MUSHROOM CAKES.................................97
368. GLAZED EGGPLANT RINGS.......................98
369. SWEET POTATO BALLS.............................98
370. CHICKPEA CURRY...................................98
371. PAN-FRIED SALMON WITH SALAD............98
372. VEGGIE VARIETY.....................................98
373. VEGETABLE PASTA..................................99
374. VEGETABLE NOODLES WITH BOLOGNESE......99
375. HARISSA BOLOGNESE WITH VEGETABLE NOODLES...99
376. CURRY VEGETABLE NOODLES WITH CHICKEN....100
377. SWEET AND SOUR VEGETABLE NOODLES...100
378. FARRO CUCUMBER-MINT SALAD.............100
379. CHORIZO-KIDNEY BEANS QUINOA PILAF......100
380. GOAT CHEESE 'N RED BEANS SALAD.......101
381. GREEK FARRO SALAD.............................101
382. WHITE BEAN AND TUNA SALAD...............101
383. SPICY SWEET RED HUMMUS...................102
384. BLACK BEAN CHILI WITH MANGOES.........102
385. ISRAELI STYLE EGGPLANT AND CHICKPEA SALAD..102
386. ITALIAN SAUTÉED CANNELLINI BEANS......102
387. LENTIL AND VEGETABLE CURRY STEW.....103
388. LUSH MOROCCAN CHICKPEA, VEGETABLE, AND FRUIT STEW..103
389. SIMPLE PORK STIR FRY...........................103
390. PORK AND LENTIL SOUP.........................104
391. SIMPLE BRAISED PORK...........................104
392. PORK AND CHICKPEA STEW....................104
393. PORK AND GREENS SALAD......................105
394. PORK STRIPS AND RICE.........................105
395. PORK AND BEAN STEW...........................105
396. PORK WITH COUSCOUS.........................105
397. GRILLED STEAK, MUSHROOM, AND ONION KEBABS...105
398. KALE SPROUTS & LAMB..........................106
399. SHRIMP WITH GARLIC AND MUSHROOMS...106
400. PISTACHIO-CRUSTED WHITEFISH...........106
401. CRISPY HOMEMADE FISH STICKS RECIPE....107
402. SAUCED SHELLFISH IN WHITE WINE........107
403. PISTACHIO SOLE FISH............................107
404. SPEEDY TILAPIA WITH RED ONION AND AVOCADO..107
405. STEAMED MUSSELS IN WHITE WINE SAUCE......108

406. ORANGE AND GARLIC SHRIMP..................108
407. ROASTED SHRIMP-GNOCCHI BAKE..................108
408. TUNA SANDWICH..................109
409. FRUITED QUINOA SALAD..................109
410. TURKEY WRAP..................109
411. CHICKEN WRAP..................109
412. VEGGIE WRAP..................110
413. SALMON WRAP..................110
414. DILL CHICKEN SALAD..................110
415. DILL CHUTNEY SALMON..................110

CHAPTER 6. DRESSINGS, SAUCES AND SEASONINGS..................111
416. PASTA WITH CHICKPEA SAUCE..................111
417. ZOODLES WITH BASIL & AVOCADO SAUCE..................111
418. MANGO & APPLE SAUCE..................111
419. COTTAGE CHEESE SALAD DRESSING..................111
420. SIMPLE SPINACH DIP..................111
421. AVOCADO MAYO..................112
422. APPLESAUCE..................112
423. BEEF ROASTED WINE SAUCE..................112
424. BEET SALAD DRESSING..................112
425. SHORT RIBS AND BEER SAUCE..................112
426. SHORT RIBS AND SPECIAL SAUCE..................112
427. BEEF PATTY IN MUSHROOM SAUCE..................113
428. BEEF BRISKET AND ONION SAUCE..................113
429. TURKEY WRAPS WITH SAUCE..................113
430. COD STEAKS AND PLUM SAUCE..................114
431. STEAMED SALMON AND SAUCE..................114
432. SALMON AND COCONUT SAUCE..................114
433. SALMON AND SAUCE..................114
434. LOBSTER TAILS WITH WHITE WINE SAUCE..................114
435. BEET SALAD WITH PARSLEY DRESSING..................115
436. CHICKEN WINGS WITH ALFREDO SAUCE..................115
437. SMALL PASTA AND BEANS POT..................115
438. WILD RICE, CELERY, AND CAULIFLOWER PILAF..................115

CHAPTER 7. FISH AND SEAFOOD RECIPES..................117
439. BAKED COD FILLETS WITH GHEE SAUCE..................117
440. AVOCADO PEACH SALSA ON GRILLED SWORDFISH..................117
441. BREADED AND SPICED HALIBUT..................117
442. BERRIES AND GRILLED CALAMARI..................117
443. COCONUT SALSA ON CHIPOTLE FISH TACOS..................118
444. BAKED COD CRUSTED WITH HERBS..................118
445. CAJUN GARLIC SHRIMP NOODLE BOWL..................118
446. CRAZY SAGANAKI SHRIMP..................119
447. CREAMY BACON-FISH CHOWDER..................119
448. TROUT AND PEPPERS MIX..................119
449. CRISPED COCO-SHRIMP WITH MANGO DIP..................119
450. CUCUMBER-BASIL SALSA ON HALIBUT POUCHES..................120
451. CURRY SALMON WITH MUSTARD..................120
452. DIJON MUSTARD AND LIME MARINATED SHRIMP..................120
453. DILL RELISH ON WHITE SEA BASS..................121
454. GARLIC ROASTED SHRIMP WITH ZUCCHINI PASTA..................121
455. EASY SEAFOOD FRENCH STEW..................121

456. FRESH AND NO-COOK OYSTERS..................121
457. EASY BROILED LOBSTER TAILS..................122
458. GINGER SCALLION SAUCE OVER SEARED AHI.....122
459. HEALTHY POACHED TROUT..................122
460. LEFTOVER SALMON SALAD POWER BOWLS.....122
461. LEMON-GARLIC BAKED HALIBUT..................122
462. MINTY-CUCUMBER YOGURT TOPPED GRILLED FISH..................123
463. ONE-POT SEAFOOD CHOWDER..................123
464. ORANGE ROSEMARY SEARED SALMON..................123
465. ORANGE HERBED SAUCED WHITE BASS..................123
466. PAN FRIED TUNA WITH HERBS AND NUT..................124
467. PAPRIKA SALMON AND GREEN BEANS..................124
468. PECAN CRUSTED TROUT..................124
469. PESTO AND LEMON HALIBUT..................125
470. RED PEPPERS & PINEAPPLE TOPPED MAHI-MAHI..................125
471. ROASTED HALIBUT WITH BANANA RELISH..................125
472. ROASTED POLLOCK FILLET WITH BACON AND LEEKS..................125
473. SCALLOPS IN WINE 'N OLIVE OIL..................126
474. SEAFOOD STEW CIOPPINO..................126
475. SIMPLE COD PICCATA..................126
476. SMOKED TROUT TARTINE..................126
477. STEAMED MUSSELS THAI STYLE..................127
478. TASTY TUNA SCALOPPINE..................127
479. THYME AND LEMON ON BAKED SALMON..................127
480. WARM CAPER TAPENADE ON COD..................127
481. YUMMY SALMON PANZANELLA..................128
482. FISH AND ORZO..................128
483. BAKED SEA BASS..................128
484. FISH AND TOMATO SAUCE..................128
485. HALIBUT AND QUINOA MIX..................129
486. LEMON AND DATES BARRAMUNDI..................129
487. FISH CAKES..................129
488. CATFISH FILLETS AND RICE..................129
489. HALIBUT PAN..................130
490. BAKED SHRIMP MIX..................130
491. SHRIMP AND LEMON SAUCE..................130
492. SHRIMP AND BEANS SALAD..................130
493. PECAN SALMON FILLETS..................131
494. SALMON AND BROCCOLI..................131
495. SALMON AND PEACH PAN..................131
496. TARRAGON COD FILLETS..................131
497. SALMON AND RADISH MIX..................131
498. SMOKED SALMON AND WATERCRESS SALAD....131
499. SALMON AND CORN SALAD..................132
500. COD AND MUSHROOMS MIX..................132
501. SESAME SHRIMP MIX..................132
502. CREAMY CURRY SALMON..................132
503. MAHI MIDSOLO AND POMEGRANATE SAUCE.....132
504. SMOKED SALMON AND VEGGIES MIX..................132
505. SALMON AND MANGO MIX..................133
506. SALMON AND CREAMY ENDIVES..................133
507. TROUT AND TZATZIKI SAUCE..................133
508. PARSLEY TROUT AND CAPERS..................133

509. BAKED TROUT AND FENNEL..................... 133
510. LEMON RAINBOW TROUT......................... 133
511. FAVORITE GREEK SALMON........................ 134
512. CITRUS FLAVORED SALMON...................... 134
513. LIVELY FLAVORED SALMON....................... 134
514. SIMPLY DELICIOUS TILAPIA...................... 134
515. AROMATIC TILAPIA.................................. 134
516. RICHLY DELICIOUS TILAPIA...................... 134
517. NO-FUSS SARDINE.................................. 135
518. SPANISH STYLE SARDINE......................... 135
519. MOUTH WATERING TUNA......................... 135
520. SATISFYING HALIBUT MEAL...................... 135
521. BOLD FLAVORED HALIBUT........................ 135
522. MIDWEEK DINNER HALIBUT...................... 135
523. DELICATE COD DISH............................... 136
524. VERSATILE COD..................................... 136
525. FANCY BRAESIDE SHRIMP........................ 136
526. ENJOYABLE SHRIMP............................... 136
527. OUTSTANDING SHRIMP MEAL................... 136
528. BUTTERED SHRIMP................................. 137
529. FLAVORFUL SHRIMP CURRY...................... 137
530. MAHI TACO WRAPS................................. 137
531. SALMON... 137
532. SHRIMP TACOS...................................... 137
533. FISH CURRY... 138
534. SALMON WITH CREAMY LEMON SAUCE...... 138
535. SALMON WITH LEMON-CAPER SAUCE......... 138
536. SPICY BARBECUE SHRIMP........................ 139
537. LEMON DILL HALIBUT.............................. 139
538. COCONUT CILANTRO CURRY SHRIMP......... 139
539. SHRIMP IN MARINARA SAUCE................... 139
540. GARLIC SHRIMP..................................... 140
541. POACHED SALMON................................. 140
542. LEMON PEPPER TILAPIA.......................... 140
543. CLAM CHOWDER................................... 140
544. SOY-GINGER STEAMED POMPANO............ 141
545. VIETNAMESE BRAISED CATFISH................ 141
546. CHILI PRAWNS....................................... 141
547. TUNA SALPICAO..................................... 141
548. SOY-GINGER BRAISED SQUID................... 141
549. SEA BASS IN COCONUT CREAM SAUCE...... 142
550. COD CHOWDER..................................... 142
551. TUNA IN POTATOES................................ 142
552. SHRIMP SCAMPI.................................... 142
553. SHRIMP BOIL... 143
554. SHRIMP & SAUSAGE GUMBO.................... 143
555. FISH STEW.. 143
556. SALMON WITH LEMON & DILL................... 143
557. ASPARAGUS SMOKED SALMON................. 143
558. SALMON WITH CAPER SAUCE................... 144
559. HERBED SALMON LOAF WITH SAUCE......... 144
CHAPTER 8. POULTRY AND MEAT RECIPES..... 144
560. BEEF CORN CHILI................................... 145
561. BALSAMIC BEEF DISH............................. 145
562. SOY SAUCE BEEF ROAST......................... 145
563. ROSEMARY BEEF CHUCK ROAST.............. 145

564. PORK CHOPS AND TOMATO SAUCE........... 146
565. PORK POTATO.. 146
566. COFFEE FLAVORED PORK RIBS.................. 146
567. SLOW COOKER MEATLOAF RECIPE............ 146
568. SLOW COOKER MEDITERRANEAN BEEF
HOAGIES... 147
569. BEEF, ARTICHOKE & MUSHROOM STEW..... 147
570. BEEF & TAPIOCA STEW........................... 148
571. BEEF PIZZA... 148
572. BEEF & BULGUR MEATBALLS.................... 148
573. TASTY BEEF AND BROCCOLI..................... 149
574. TOMATO PORK PASTE............................. 149
575. GARLIC PULLED PORK............................. 149
576. BUTTERED PORK CHOPS.......................... 149
577. QUICK AND EASY PORK LOIN ROAST......... 150
578. CHEESE AND HAM ROLL-UPS.................... 150
579. MEAT CUP SNACKS................................. 150
580. PORK AND CHEESE STUFFED PEPPERS...... 151
581. PEPPERED PORK RACK............................ 151
582. PORK BELLY.. 151
583. EASY PORK CHOPS................................. 151
584. COFFEE BBQ PORK BELLY........................ 151
585. MUSTARD AND ROSEMARY PORK
TENDERLOIN.. 152
586. STUFFED PORK LOIN WITH SUN-DRIED
TOMATO AND GOAT CHEESE........................... 152
587. MEATBALLS IN CREAMY ALMOND SAUCE... 152
588. FLANK STEAK WITH ORANGE-HERB PISTOU... 153
589. BRAISED SHORT RIBS WITH RED WINE....... 153
590. BEEF KOFTA.. 154
591. SPICY BEEF WITH OLIVES AND FETA.......... 154
592. BEST EVER BEEF STEW............................ 154
593. ONE-POT MEDITERRANEAN SPICED BEEF AND
MACARONI.. 154
594. BEEF AND CHEESE GRATIN...................... 155
595. BEEF CACCIATORE................................. 155
596. GREEK BEEF AND VEGGIE SKEWERS......... 155
597. PORK TENDERLOIN WITH ORZO................ 155
598. GRILLED PORK CHOPS WITH TOMATO SALAD 156
599. BONELESS PORK CHOPS WITH SUMMER
VEGGIES... 156
600. ONE-SKILLET MEDITERRANEAN PORK AND
RICE.. 156
601. PORK TENDERLOIN WITH ROASTED
VEGETABLES.. 157
602. MARINATED BALSAMIC PORK LOIN SKILLET... 157
603. GROUND PORK AND BEEF CHILI WITH TOMATO
AND BASIL... 157
604. MEATBALLS IN FRESH TOMATO SAUCE...... 158
605. PORK MEDALLIONS WITH ROASTED FENNEL... 158
606. STUFFED BELL PEPPERS WITH BEEF AND
MUSHROOMS.. 159
607. SEASONED BEEF KEBABS........................ 159
608. GRILLED SKIRT STEAK OVER TRADITIONAL
MEDITERRANEAN HUMMUS............................ 159
609. SPANISH PEPPER STEAK......................... 159

610. GRILLED KEFTA..160
611. TAHINI BEEF AND POTATOES......................160
612. MEDITERRANEAN PORK CHOPS.................160
613. PORK SOUVLAKI..160
614. CORIANDER AND COCONUT CHICKEN.......161
615. SAFFRON CHICKEN THIGHS AND GREEN BEANS..161
616. BOLD CHORIZO PAELLA..............................161
617. MOIST SHREDDED BEEF...............................161
618. HEARTY BEEF RAGU....................................161
619. DILL BEEF BRISKET......................................162
620. TASTY BEEF STEW..162
621. MEATLOAF..162
622. FLAVORFUL BEEF BOURGUIGNON.............162
623. DELICIOUS BEEF CHILI.................................163
624. BASIC MEATBALLS.......................................163
625. OLIVE AND FETA BURGERS........................163
626. MEATLOAF IN A PINCH................................163
627. SKIRT STEAK FAJITAS..................................164
628. GRILLED STEAK WITH HERB SAUCE.........164
629. BEEF TENDERLOIN WITH RED WINE REDUCTION..164
630. SLOW COOKER SHREDDED BARBECUE BEEF...165
631. SLOW COOKER BEEF WITH BELL PEPPERS.....165
632. PORK LARB..165
633. HERBED PORK MEATBALLS.........................165
634. ASIAN-SPICED PORK LOIN..........................166
635. PORK TENDERLOIN WITH APPLE-TARRAGON SAUCE...166
636. MISO-GARLIC PORK CHOPS........................167
637. SLOW COOKER HONEY MUSTARD PORK WITH PEARS..167
638. SLOW COOKER CRANBERRY PORK CHOPS.....167
639. CHICKEN AND OLIVES.................................168
640. CHICKEN BAKE...168
641. CHICKEN AND ARTICHOKES.......................168
642. CHICKEN KEBABS...168
643. CHILI CHICKEN MIX.....................................168
644. CHICKEN PILAF...169
645. CHICKEN AND SWEET POTATOES..............169
646. CHICKEN AND CASHEWS MIX......................169
647. CHICKEN, CORN AND PEPPERS...................169
648. WALNUT TURKEY AND PEACHES................170
649. BALSAMIC TURKEY BITES AND APRICOTS......170
650. CHIPOTLE TURKEY AND TOMATOES...........170
651. PARMESAN CHICKEN AND CREAM..............170
652. OREGANO CHICKEN AND ZUCCHINI PAN....171
653. CREAMY CHICKEN AND GRAPES................171
654. TOMATO CHICKEN AND LENTILS................171
655. TURKEY, LEEKS AND CARROTS...................171
656. HERBED CHICKEN...171
657. CHIVES CHICKEN AND RADISHES...............172
658. FETA CHICKEN AND CABBAGE....................172
659. GARLIC CHICKEN AND ENDIVES.................172
660. TURKEY AND CHICKPEAS............................172
661. LIME TURKEY AND AVOCADO MIX..............172

662. TURKEY AND SALSA VERDE.........................173
663. BASIL TURKEY AND ZUCCHINIS..................173
664. HERBED ALMOND TURKEY..........................173
665. DUCK AND TOMATO SAUCE.......................173
666. CHICKEN AND MUSTARD SAUCE................173
667. CINNAMON DUCK MIX.................................174
668. TURKEY, ARTICHOKES AND ASPARAGUS......174
669. ORANGE DUCK AND CELERY......................174
670. DUCK AND BLACKBERRIES.........................174
671. GINGER DUCK MIX.......................................174
672. DUCK, CUCUMBER AND MANGO SALAD......175
673. DUCK AND ORANGE WARM SALAD...........175
674. CREAMY CORIANDER CHICKEN...................175
675. LEMONY TURKEY AND PINE NUTS..............175
676. CREAMY CHICKEN AND MUSHROOMS.......175
677. OREGANO TURKEY AND PEPPERS..............176
678. CHICKEN AND MINT SAUCE........................176
679. CURRY CHICKEN, ARTICHOKES AND OLIVES......176
680. TURKEY AND CRANBERRY SAUCE..............176
CHAPTER 9. SIDE DISHES..................................177
681. CHERRY TOMATO GRATIN..........................177
682. FENNEL-PARMESAN FARRO.......................177
683. CREAMY ZOODLES......................................177
684. BLACK BEAN VEGGIE BURGER....................177
685. RED CURRY..178
686. SWEET-AND-SOUR TEMPEH.......................178
687. MEXICAN CASSEROLE WITH BLACKBEANS......178
688. BAKED ZUCCHINI GRATIN..........................179
689. VEGGIE GREEK MOUSSAKA.......................179
690. GOUDA CAULIFLOWER CASSEROLE..........179
691. SPINACH AND ZUCCHINI LASAGNA...........180
692. LEMON CAULIFLOWER COUSCOUS WITH HALLOUMI..180
693. SPICY CAULIFLOWER STEAKS WITH STEAMED GREEN BEANS..180
694. CHEESY CAULIFLOWER FALAFEL...............180
695. TOFU SESAME SKEWERS WITH WARM KALE SALAD..181
696. BRUSSEL SPROUTS WITH SPICED HALLOUMI.....181
697. VEGETABLE PATTIES...................................181
698. VEGAN SANDWICH WITH TOFU & LETTUCE SLAW..182
699. PUMPKIN AND CAULIFLOWER CURRY.......182
700. CAULIFLOWER EGG BAKE..........................182
701. ZUCCHINI CASSEROLE.................................182
702. CHINESE CAULIFLOWER RICE WITH EGGS......183
703. MUSHROOM STROGANOFF.........................183
704. ZUCCHINI FRITTERS.....................................183
705. CHEESE STUFFED SPAGHETTI SQUASH......183
706. COTTAGE KALE STIR-FRY............................184
707. HERBED EGGPLANT AND KALE BAKE.........184
708. BROCCOLI AND CAULIFLOWER MASH.......184
709. CHEESY STUFFED PEPPERS........................184
710. CREAMY SPINACH......................................185
711. FRIED CABBAGE..185
712. CUMIN GREEN CABBAGE STIR-FRY............185

713. GREEK VEGGIE BRIAM................................185
714. BRAISED CREAM KALE................................186
715. WHITE WINE-DIJON BRUSSELS SPROUTS.........186
716. PAPRIKA RICED CAULIFLOWER....................186
717. WAX BEANS WITH TOMATO-MUSTARD SAUCE....186
718. LEEK, MUSHROOM, AND ZUCCHINI STEW........187
719. ALMOND AND RIND CRUSTED ZUCCHINI
FRITTERS................................187
720. SPICED CAULIFLOWER CHEESE BAKE..............187
721. ROASTED ASPARAGUS................................187
722. MOZZARELLA ITALIAN PEPPERS....................187
723. QUESO FRESCO AVOCADO SALSA..................188
724. INDIAN WHITE CABBAGE STEW....................188
725. BAKED EGGPLANT ROUNDS........................188
726. FENNEL AVGOLEMONO................................188
727. SPINACH AND BUTTERNUT SQUASH STEW.......189
728. BROCCOLI CHEESE................................189
729. ZA'ATAR CHANTERELLE STEW......................189
730. DUO-CHEESE BROCCOLI CROQUETTES............190
731. BELL PEPPER AND TOMATO SATARA..............190
732. PROVEN AL RATATOUILLE..........................190
733. MOZZARELLA ROASTED PEPPERS..................190
734. ITALIAN TOMATO AND CHEESE STUFFED
PEPPERS................................190
735. MUSHROOM MÉLANGE................................191
736. GREEN CABBAGE WITH TOFU......................191
737. MUSHROOM AND BELL PEPPER OMELET...........191
738. PARMIGIANO-REGGIANO CHEESE BROILED
AVOCADOS................................191
739. ROMAINE LETTUCE BOATS..........................192
740. GRUYÈRE CELERY BOATS............................192
741. PEASANT STIR-FRY................................192
742. CAULIFLOWER SOUP................................192
743. AVOCADO SAUCED CUCUMBER NOODLES..........192
744. ZUCCHINI NOODLES WITH MUSHROOM SAUCE 193
745. GOAT CHEESE EGGPLANT CASSEROLE............193
746. MUSHROOM RED WINE CHILI........................193
747. MINUTES VEGETARIAN PASTA......................193
748. CHIPOTLE, PINTO, AND GREEN BEAN AND
CORN SUCCOTASH................................194
749. BROCCOLI SALAD................................194
750. POTATO CARROT SALAD............................194
751. MIXED VEGETABLE MEDLEY........................194
752. SPICY LENTILS WITH SPINACH....................195
753. PARMESAN ASPARAGUS............................195
754. GREEK VEGETABLES................................195
755. LEMON GARLIC CAULIFLOWER......................195
756. BALSAMIC BRUSSELS SPROUTS....................196
757. FLAVORFUL BUTTERNUT SQUASH..................196
758. CRISPY GREEN BEANS................................196
759. ROASTED ZUCCHINI................................196
760. AIR FRIED CARROTS, ZUCCHINI & SQUASH......196
761. CRISPY & SPICY EGGPLANT........................196
762. CURRIED EGGPLANT SLICES........................197
763. SPICED GREEN BEANS................................197
764. AIR FRYER BASIL TOMATOES......................197

765. AIR FRYER RATATOUILLE............................197
766. GARLICKY CAULIFLOWER FLORETS................197
767. PARMESAN BRUSSELS SPROUTS....................197
768. FLAVORFUL TOMATOES..............................198
769. HEALTHY ROASTED CARROTS......................198
770. CURRIED CAULIFLOWER WITH PINE NUTS........198
771. THYME SAGE BUTTERNUT SQUASH................198
772. GRILLED CAULIFLOWER............................198
773. STUFFED ZUCCHINI................................199
774. VINEGAR VEGGIES................................199
775. GARLICKY MIXED VEGGIES........................199
776. MEDITERRANEAN VEGGIES........................200
777. MARINATED VEGGIE SKEWERS......................200
778. PINEAPPLE & VEGGIE SKEWERS....................201
779. BUTTERED CORN................................201
780. GUACAMOLE................................201
781. POTATO LATKE................................202
782. BROCCOLI RABE................................202
783. SHRIMP VEGGIE PASTA SALAD....................202
784. PEA SALAD................................202
785. SNAP PEA SALAD................................202
786. PINTO AND GREEN BEAN FRY WITH
COUSCOUS................................203
787. INDONESIAN-STYLE SPICY FRIED TEMPEH STR
IPS................................203
788. CUCUMBER TOMATO CHOPPED SALAD............203
789. ZUCCHINI PASTA SALAD............................203
790. FRIED RICE AND VEGETABLES......................204
791. SPANISH-STYLE SAFFRON RICE WITH BLACK
BEANS................................204
792. EGG AVOCADO SALAD..............................204
793. PEPPER TOMATO SALAD............................205
794. SIMPLE LEMON DAL................................205
795. CAULIFLOWER LATKE................................205
796. PENNE WITH VEGGIES..............................205
797. MARINATED VEGGIE SALAD........................206
798. ROASTED BRUSSELS SPROUTS....................206
799. BRUSSELS SPROUTS & CRANBERRIES............206
800. ARUGULA SALAD................................206
801. MEDITERRANEAN SALAD............................206
CHAPTER 10. VEGETARIAN DISHES....................207
802. VEGETARIAN CHILI WITH AVOCADO CREAM......207
803. EGGS WITH ZUCCHINI NOODLES..................207
804. ROASTED ROOT VEGGIES..........................207
805. RUSTIC VEGETABLE AND BROWN RICE BOWL...207
806. ROASTED BRUSSELS SPROUTS AND PECANS....208
807. ROASTED VEGETABLES AND ZUCCHINI PASTA...208
808. SAUTÉED COLLARD GREENS........................208
809. BALSAMIC BULGUR SALAD........................208
810. SAVOY CABBAGE WITH COCONUT CREAM SAU
CE................................208
811. SLOW COOKED BUTTERY MUSHROOMS............208
812. RADISH AND CORN SALAD..........................209
813. ARUGULA AND CORN SALAD......................209
814. STEAMED SQUASH CHOWDER......................209
815. STEAMED ZUCCHINI-PAPRIKA......................209

816. ORANGE AND CUCUMBER SALAD................ 209
817. PARSLEY AND CORN SALAD................ 209
818. STIR FRIED BRUSSELS SPROUTS AND CARROTS................ 210
819. STIR FRIED EGGPLANT................ 210
820. TOMATO AND AVOCADO SALAD................ 210
821. CORN AND TOMATO SALAD................ 210
822. SUMMER VEGETABLES................ 210
823. STIR FRIED BOK CHOY................ 211
824. BEANS AND CUCUMBER SALAD................ 211
825. MINTY OLIVES AND TOMATOES SALAD................ 211
826. SUMMER VEGGIES IN INSTANT POT................ 211
827. SUMPTUOUS TOMATO SOUP................ 212
828. SUPERFAST CAJUN ASPARAGUS................ 212
829. SWEET AND NUTRITIOUS PUMPKIN SOUP................ 212
830. SWEET POTATO PUREE................ 212
831. SWEET POTATOES OVEN FRIED................ 212
832. TASTY AVOCADO SAUCE OVER ZOODLES................ 213
833. TOMATO BASIL CAULIFLOWER RICE................ 213
834. VEGAN SESAME TOFU AND EGGPLANTS................ 213
835. VEGETARIAN COCONUT CURRY................ 213
836. VEGGIE LO MEIN................ 213
837. VEGGIE JAMAICAN STEW................ 214
838. VEGETABLE SOUP MOROCCAN STYLE................ 214
839. VEGGIE RAMEN MISO SOUP................ 214
840. YUMMY CAULIFLOWER FRITTERS................ 215
841. ZUCCHINI GARLIC FRIES................ 215
842. ZUCCHINI PASTA WITH MANGO-KIWI SAUCE................ 215
843. QUINOA WITH ALMONDS AND CRANBERRIES.... 215
844. MEDITERRANEAN BAKED CHICKPEAS................ 215
845. FALAFEL BITES................ 216
846. QUICK VEGETABLE KEBABS................ 216
847. TORTELLINI IN RED PEPPER SAUCE................ 216
848. FREEKEH, CHICKPEA, AND HERB SALAD................ 216
849. KATE'S WARM MEDITERRANEAN FARRO BOWL   217
850. CREAMY CHICKPEA SAUCE WITH WHOLE-WHEAT FUSILLI................ 217
851. LINGUINE AND BRUSSELS SPROUTS................ 217
852. PEPPERS AND LENTILS SALAD................ 218
853. CASHEWS AND RED CABBAGE SALAD................ 218
854. APPLES AND POMEGRANATE SALAD................ 218
855. CRANBERRY BULGUR MIX................ 218
856. CHICKPEAS, CORN AND BLACK BEANS SALAD... 218
857. OLIVES AND LENTILS SALAD................ 218
858. LIME SPINACH AND CHICKPEAS SALAD................ 219
859. WHIPPED POTATOES................ 219
860. JALAPENO RICE NOODLES................ 219
861. SAUTÉED CABBAGE................ 219
862. SOUTHWEST STYLE SALAD................ 219
863. RAINBOW SOBA NOODLES................ 220
864. GRILLED FAJITAS WITH JALAPEÑO SAUCE................ 220
865. SHAVED BRUSSEL SPROUT SALAD................ 220
866. COLORFUL PROTEIN POWER SALAD................ 221
867. GRILLED RATATOUILLE KEBABS................ 221
868. TOFU HOAGIE ROLLS................ 221
869. EDAMAME & GINGER CITRUS SALAD................ 222

870. TACO TEMPEH SALAD................ 222
871. BLACK BEAN WRAP WITH HUMMUS................ 222
872. BLACK-EYED PEAS AND CORN SALAD................ 222
873. GRILLED AVOCADO WITH TOMATOES................ 223
874. GRILLED TOFU WITH CHIMICHURRI SAUCE................ 223
875. LEBANESE POTATO SALAD................ 223
876. CHICKPEA AND SPINACH SALAD................ 224
877. INDIAN TOMATO AND GARBANZO STEW................ 224
878. SIMPLE BAKED NAVY BEANS................ 224
879. BLACK BEAN BUDA BOWL................ 224
880. GRILLED SEITAN WITH CREOLE SAUCE................ 225
881. GREEN BEANS GREMOLATA................ 225
882. SPINACH & DILL PASTA SALAD................ 225
883. VINEGARY BLACK BEANS................ 225
884. SPICED LENTIL BURGERS................ 226
885. MIDDLE EASTERN CHICKPEA STEW................ 226
886. LENTIL AND TOMATO DIP................ 226
887. MINTED PEAS................ 226
888. SWEET AND SPICY BRUSSELS SPROUT HASH... 227
889. ITALIAN VEGGIE SALAD................ 227
890. PECAN-MAPLE GRANOLA................ 227
891. BEAN AND SUMMER SQUASH SAUTÉ................ 227
892. CREAMED GREEN PEA SALAD................ 227
893. MIDDLE EASTERN ZA'ATAR HUMMUS................ 228
894. GLAZED CURRIED CARROTS................ 228
895. PEPPER MEDLEY................ 228
896. SPINACH AND MASHED TOFU SALAD................ 228
897. PEPPERY BLACK BEANS................ 228
898. WALNUT, COCONUT, AND OAT GRANOLA................ 229
899. TRADITIONAL INDIAN RAJMA DAL................ 229
900. RED KIDNEY BEAN SALAD................ 229
901. GARLICKY RED WINE MUSHROOMS................ 230
902. SAUTÉED CITRUS SPINACH................ 230
903. SUPER SUMMER SALAD................ 230
904. RITZY FAVA BEAN RATATOUILLE................ 230
905. PEPPERS AND BLACK BEANS WITH BROWN RICE................ 231
906. ANASAZI BEAN AND VEGETABLE STEW................ 231
907. EASY AND HEARTY SHAKSHUKA................ 231
908. LEMON BROCCOLI RABE................ 231
909. SPICY SWISS CHARD................ 232
910. ROASTED ALMOND PROTEIN SALAD................ 232
911. BLACK-EYED PEA, BEET, AND CARROT STEW   232
912. KOSHARI................ 232
913. OLD-FASHIONED CHILI................ 233
914. EASY RED LENTIL SALAD................ 233
915. QUINOA AND CHICKPEA VEGETABLE BOWLS................ 233
916. PAPAYA, JICAMA, AND PEAS RICE BOWL................ 234
917. ITALIAN BAKED BEANS................ 234
918. CANNELLINI BEAN LETTUCE WRAPS................ 234
919. ISRAELI EGGPLANT, CHICKPEA, AND MINT SAUTÉ................ 235
920. MEDITERRANEAN LENTILS AND RICE................ 235
921. SPRING SOUP WITH GOURMET GRAINS................ 235
922. MINESTRONE CHICKPEAS AND MACARONI CASSEROLE................ 236

923. SPICED SOUP WITH LENTILS & LEGUMES........... 236
924. BROWN RICE PILAF WITH GOLDEN RAISINS........ 237
925. RITZY VEGGIE CHILI... 237
926. SPICY ITALIAN BEAN BALLS WITH MARINARA..... 237
927. BAKED ROLLED OAT WITH PEARS AND PECANS 238
928. BROWN RICE PILAF WITH PISTACHIOS AND
RAISINS... 238
CHAPTER 11. SOUP RECIPES............................... 239
929. BASIC RECIPE FOR VEGETABLE BROTH................ 239
930. CUCUMBER DILL GAZPACHO............................... 239
931. RED LENTIL SOUP... 239
932. SPINACH AND KALE SOUP.................................. 239
933. COCONUT AND GRILLED VEGETABLE SOUP......... 239
934. CELERY DILL SOUP... 240
935. BROCCOLI FENNEL SOUP..................................... 240
936. TOFU GOULASH SOUP.. 240
937. PESTO PEA SOUP... 240
938. TOFU AND MUSHROOM SOUP.............................. 241
939. MOROCCAN VERMICELLI VEGETABLE SOUP........ 241
940. MOROCCAN VEGETABLE STEW............................. 241
941. AVOCADO CUCUMBER SOUP................................ 242
942. GARDEN VEGETABLE STEW.................................. 242
943. LEMON AND EGG PASTA SOUP............................ 242
944. ROASTED VEGETABLE SOUP................................ 243
945. MEDITERRANEAN TOMATO SOUP......................... 243
946. TOMATO AND CABBAGE PUREE SOUP.................. 243
947. ATHENIAN AVGOLEMONO SOUR SOUP................. 243
948. ITALIAN BEAN SOUP.. 244
949. RED SOUP, SEVILLE STYLE................................... 244
950. GARLIC SOUP.. 244
951. DALMATIAN CABBAGE, POTATO, AND PEA SOUP 245
952. GREEN CREAMY SOUP.. 245
953. ORZO AND LEMON CHICKEN SOUP...................... 245
954. CHILLED AVOCADO SOUP..................................... 246
955. BROCCOLI AND POTATO SOUP.............................. 246
956. TORTELLINI AND VEGETABLE SOUP...................... 246
957. TRADITIONAL OYSTER SOUP................................. 247
958. EGGPLANT SOUP.. 247
959. TORTELLINI AND SPINACH SOUP......................... 247
960. SPICY VEGETABLE SOUP...................................... 247
961. CHEESY KETO ZUCCHINI SOUP............................ 248
962. SPRING SOUP WITH POACHED EGG...................... 248
963. MINT AVOCADO CHILLED SOUP........................... 248
964. EASY BUTTERNUT SQUASH SOUP......................... 248
965. CAULIFLOWER, LEEK & BACON SOUP................... 249
966. SWISS CHARD EGG DROP SOUP........................... 249
967. MUSHROOM SPINACH SOUP................................ 249
968. DELICATE SQUASH SOUP..................................... 249
969. BROCCOLI SOUP.. 249
970. APPLE PUMPKIN SOUP.. 250
971. KETO FRENCH ONION SOUP................................. 250
972. CAULIFLOWER AND THYME SOUP......................... 250
973. HOMEMADE THAI CHICKEN SOUP........................ 250
974. CHICKEN KALE SOUP... 250
975. CHICKEN VEGGIE SOUP....................................... 250
976. CHICKEN MULLIGATAWNY SOUP.......................... 251

977. BUFFALO RANCH CHICKEN SOUP......................... 251
978. TRADITIONAL CHICKEN SOUP.............................. 251
979. CHICKEN NOODLE SOUP...................................... 251
980. CHICKEN CABBAGE SOUP.................................... 252
981. CARROT AND RED LENTIL SOUP........................... 252
982. WHITE BEAN SOUP.. 252
983. PEAS SOUP... 252
984. SWEET POTATO SOUP.. 253
985. WHITE MUSHROOMS SOUP.................................. 253
986. LAMB SOUP.. 253
987. LEMON ZEST SOUP.. 253
988. PUMPKIN SOUP.. 253
989. BACON & POTATO SOUP...................................... 253
990. LEMON CHICKEN SOUP....................................... 254
991. ARTICHOKE SOUP... 254
992. DALMATIAN POTATO SOUP.................................. 254
993. PUMPKIN SOUP WITH RICE AND SPINACH.......... 254
994. NETTLE SOUP.. 255
995. WILD MUSHROOM SOUP...................................... 255
996. TOMATO AND ALIMENTARY PASTE SOUP............. 255
997. SORREL SOUP... 256
998. SUMMER VEGETABLE SOUP................................. 256
999. TUSCAN BLACK CABBAGE SOUP.......................... 256
1000. POTATO LEEK SOUP.. 257
1001. LENTIL BEET SOUP... 257
CHAPTER 12. SNACKS AND SMOOTHIES............. 258
1002. TOMATO OLIVE SALSA....................................... 258
1003. THIN-CRUST FLATBREAD.................................... 258
1004. SMOKED SALMON GOAT CHEESE ENDIVE BIT
ES.. 258
1005. HUMMUS PEPPERS.. 258
1006. LOADED MEDITERRANEAN HUMMUS................. 258
1007. WARM BEEF AND LENTIL SALAD........................ 258
1008. LIGHTER LASAGNA.. 259
1009. SMOKY LOADED EGGPLANT DIP......................... 259
1010. PEANUT BUTTER BANANA GREEK YOGURT BO
WL... 259
1011. ROASTED CHICKPEAS.. 260
1012. SAVORY FETA SPINACH AND SWEET RED
PEPPER MUFFINS.. 260
1013. BAKED WHOLE-GRAIN LAVASH CHIPS WITH DI
P.. 260
1014. QUINOA GRANOLA.. 260
1015. GREEK YOGURT SPINACH ARTICHOKE DIP......... 260
1016. FIG SMOOTHIE WITH CINNAMON....................... 261
1017. SMOKED SALMON, AVOCADO AND CUCUMBER
BITES... 261
1018. BAKED ROOT VEGETABLE CHIPS WITH
BUTTERMILK-PARSLEY DIPPING SAUCE....................... 261
1019. SPICY RED LENTIL DIP....................................... 261
1020. CUCUMBER HUMMUS SANDWICHES.................. 261
1021. FIG & HONEY YOGURT.. 261
1022. PEACH CAPRESE SKEWERS................................ 261
1023. TOMATO-BASIL SKEWERS.................................. 262
1024. FIG & RICOTTA TOAST....................................... 262
1025. MEATBALLS PLATTER.. 262

1026. ARTICHOKE FLATBREAD.................................. 262
1027. TRIPLE BERRY BANANA SMOOTHIE.................. 262
1028. RASPBERRY, PEACH AND WALNUTS
SMOOTHIE.. 262
1029. SMOOTHIE WITH STRAWBERRIES AND
COCONUT... 263
1030. NUTTY DATE PAPAYA SMOOTHIE.................. 263
1031. CUCUMBER AND COCONUT SMOOTHIE.......... 263
1032. HEARTY BERRY SMOOTHIE.......................... 263
1033. DANDELION GREEN SMOOTHIE.................... 263
1034. CANTALOUPE SMOOTHIE............................ 263
1035. WATERMELON REFRESHER.......................... 264
1036. SMOOTHIE SNACK...................................... 264
1037. SMOOTHIE WITH NUTS.............................. 264
1038. WATERCRESS DETOX SMOOTHIE................. 264
1039. MANGO AND ORANGE SMOOTHIE............... 264
1040. GREEN SMOOTHIE WITH APPLE AND
BLUEBERRIES.. 264
1041. NUTTY SEA MOSS SMOOTHIE..................... 265
1042. ZUCCHINI AND AVOCADO SMOOTHIE.......... 265
1043. BLUEBERRY-PIE SMOOTHIE........................ 265
1044. CUCUMBER AND BASIL CLEANSING DRINK.... 265
1045. BANANA, PEAR AND COCONUT SMOOTHIE.... 265
1046. WATERMELON AND RASPBERRIES SMOOTHIE 265
1047. PAPAYA AND QUINOA SMOOTHIE................ 266
1048. AVOCADO AND CUCUMBER SMOOTHIE........ 266
1049. ORANGE AND BANANA DRINK..................... 266
1050. LETTUCE, BANANA AND BERRIES SMOOTHIE... 266
CHAPTER 13. PIZZA RECIPES.............................. 267
1051. PIZZA BIANCA... 267
1052. EGGPLANT PIZZA WITH TOFU..................... 267
1053. NAAN BREAD PIZZA................................... 267
1054. THIN CRUST LOW CARB PIZZA.................... 267
1055. BBQ CHICKEN PIZZA................................. 267
1056. BUFFALO CHICKEN CRUST PIZZA................ 268
1057. FRESH BELL PEPPER BASIL PIZZA................ 268
1058. CARAMELIZED ONION AND GOAT CHEESE
PIZZA... 268
1059. VEGETARIAN SPINACH-OLIVE PIZZA............ 268
1060. CHICKEN BACON RANCH PIZZA.................. 269
1061. CHICKEN PIZZA... 269
1062. SHRIMP PIZZA.. 269
1063. VEGGIE PIZZA.. 270
1064. BREAD MACHINE PIZZA DOUGH................. 270
1065. PIZZA CRUST... 270
1066. PIZZA BUNS... 270
1067. BRICK OVEN PIZZA (BROOKLYN STYLE)....... 271
1068. VALENTINE PIZZA..................................... 271
1069. PIZZA MUFFINS.. 271
1070. PUB PIZZA.. 272
1071. ALFREDO CHICKEN PITA PIZZA................... 272
1072. MINIATURE PIZZAS.................................... 272
1073. EASY PIZZA WITH A PINCH........................ 272
1074. BASIL & ARTICHOKE PIZZA........................ 273
1075. BALSAMIC-GLAZED PIZZA WITH ARUGULA &
OLIVES... 273

1076. PEPPERONI FAT HEAD PIZZA..................... 273
1077. EXTRA CHEESY PIZZA............................... 274
1078. SPANISH-STYLE PIZZA DE JAMON.............. 274
1079. SPICY & SMOKY PIZZA.............................. 274
1080. TURKEY PIZZA WITH PESTO TOPPING.......... 275
1081. BABY SPINACH PIZZA WITH SWEET ONION.... 275
1082. ITALIAN MUSHROOM PIZZA....................... 275
1083. BROCCOLI-PEPPER PIZZA.......................... 276
1084. WHITE PIZZA WITH PROSCIUTTO AND
ARUGULA.. 276
1085. ZA'ATAR PIZZA... 276
1086. BROCCOLI CHEESE BURST PIZZA............... 277
1087. MOZZARELLA BEAN PIZZA......................... 277
1088. PIZZA DOUGH WITHOUT YEAST IN MILK...... 277
1089. IDEAL PIZZA DOUGH (ON A LARGE BAKING SH
EET).. 277
1090. VEGETABLE OIL PIZZA DOUGH.................. 278
1091. PIZZA DOUGH ON YOGURT....................... 278
1092. EGGPLANT PIZZA..................................... 278
1093. MEDITERRANEAN WHOLE WHEAT PIZZA..... 278
1094. FRUIT PIZZA... 278
1095. SPROUTS PIZZA....................................... 278
1096. CHEESE PINWHEELS................................. 279
1097. GROUND MEAT PIZZA.............................. 279
1098. QUINOA FLOUR PIZZA.............................. 279
1099. ARTICHOKE PIZZA.................................... 279
CHAPTER 14. DESSERT RECIPES......................... 280
1100. TRADITIONAL OLIVE OIL CAKE WITH FIGS.... 280
1101. MASCARPONE AND FIG CROSTINI.............. 280
1102. TRADITIONAL MEDITERRANEAN LOKUM...... 280
1103. MIXED BERRY AND FIG COMPOTE.............. 280
1104. CREAMED FRUIT SALAD............................ 281
1105. ALMOND COOKIES................................... 281
1106. CRUNCHY SESAME COOKIES..................... 281
1107. MINI ORANGE TARTS................................ 281
1108. TRADITIONAL KALO PRAMA....................... 281
1109. TURKISH-STYLE CHOCOLATE HALVA.......... 282
1110. RICE PUDDING WITH DRIED FIGS............... 282
1111. FRUIT KABOBS WITH YOGURT DEEP.......... 282
1112. STUFFED DRIED FIGS............................... 282
1113. FETA CHEESECAKE.................................. 282
1114. NO-BAKE CHOCOLATE SQUARES............... 283
1115. GREEK PARFAIT WITH MIXED BERRIES........ 283
1116. GREEK-STYLE CHOCOLATE SEMIFREDDO.... 283
1117. TRADITIONAL ITALIAN CAKE WITH ALMONDS... 283
1118. PEAR CROUSTADE................................... 284
1119. LOUKOUMADES (FRIED HONEY BALLS)....... 284
1120. CRÈME CARAMEL.................................... 284
1121. GALAKTOBOUREKO................................... 284
1122. KOURABIEDES ALMOND COOKIES............. 285
1123. REVANI SYRUP CAKE................................ 285
1124. ALMONDS AND OATS PUDDING................ 285
1125. MEDITERRANEAN TOMATO SALAD WITH FETA
AND FRESH HERBS... 285
1126. QUINOA BOWL WITH YOGURT, DATES, AND
ALMONDS.. 286

1127. ALMOND BUTTER BANANA CHOCOLATE SMOOTHIE..........286
1128. EKMEK KATAIFI..........286
1129. STRAWBERRY RHUBARB SMOOTHIE..........287
1130. WALNUT & DATE SMOOTHIE..........287
1131. VANILLA APPLE COMPOTE..........287
1132. APPLE DATES MIX..........287
1133. LEMON PEAR COMPOTE..........287
1134. STRAWBERRY STEW..........287
1135. OAT AND FRUIT PARFAIT..........288
1136. WATERMELON FETA & BALSAMIC PIZZA..........288
1137. BANANA DESSERT WITH CHOCOLATE CHIPS..........288
1138. CRANBERRY AND PISTACHIO BISCOTTI..........288
1139. MINTY WATERMELON SALAD..........288
1140. DATE AND NUT BALLS..........289
1141. CREAMY RICE PUDDING..........289
1142. RICOTTA-LEMON CHEESECAKE..........289
1143. BLUEBERRY-BLACKBERRY ICE POPS..........289
1144. STRAWBERRY-LIME ICE POPS..........290
1145. CROCKPOT KETO CHOCOLATE CAKE..........290
1146. CHOCOLATE LAVA CAKE..........290
1147. SEMOLINA CAKE WITH ALMONDS..........290
1148. ROMANTIC MUG CAKES..........290
1149. PISTACHIO AND TAHINI HALVA..........291
1150. AUTHENTIC GREEK RIZOGALO..........291
1151. GREEK FROZEN YOGURT DESSERT..........291
1152. SALTED PISTACHIO AND TAHINI TRUFFLES..........291
1153. APPLE AND BERRIES AMBROSIA..........292
1154. BANANA, CRANBERRY, AND OAT BARS..........292
1155. BERRY AND RHUBARB COBBLER..........292
1156. CITRUS CRANBERRY AND QUINOA ENERGY BITES..........292
1157. CHOCOLATE, ALMOND, AND CHERRY CLUSTERS..........292
1158. CHOCOLATE AND AVOCADO MOUSSE..........293
1159. COCONUT BLUEBERRIES WITH BROWN RICE..........293
1160. EASY BLUEBERRY AND OAT CRISP..........293
1161. GLAZED PEARS WITH HAZELNUTS..........293
1162. LEMONY BLACKBERRY GRANITA..........293
1163. YOGURT DIP..........294
1164. STUFFED AVOCADO..........294
1165. WRAPPED PLUMS..........294
1166. MINI NUTS AND FRUITS CRUMBLE..........294
1167. MINT BANANA CHOCOLATE SORBET..........294
1168. PECAN AND CARROT CAKE..........295
1169. RASPBERRY YOGURT BASTED CANTALOUPE..........295
1170. SIMPLE APPLE COMPOTE..........295
1171. PEANUT BUTTER AND CHOCOLATE BALLS..........295
1172. SPICED SWEET PECANS..........295
1173. LEMON CROCKPOT CAKE..........295
1174. LEMON AND WATERMELON GRANITA..........296
1175. CRAZY CHOCOLATE CAKE..........296
1176. CHUNKY CHOCOLATE PEANUT BUTTER BALLS..........296
1177. CHOCOLATE PEANUT BUTTER CRISPY BARS..........297
1178. CRANBERRY ORANGE POUND CAKE..........297
1179. STRAWBERRY RHUBARB COFFEE CAKE..........297
1180. APPLE CRUMBLE..........298

1181. CASHEW-CHOCOLATE TRUFFLES..........298
1182. BANANA CHOCOLATE CUPCAKES..........298
1183. MINTY FRUIT SALAD..........299
1184. MANGO COCONUT CREAM PIE..........299
1185. CHERRY-VANILLA RICE PUDDING..........299
1186. LIME IN THE COCONUT CHIA PUDDING..........299
1187. MINT CHOCOLATE CHIP SORBET..........300
1188. PEACH-MANGO CRUMBLE..........300
1189. ZESTY ORANGE-CRANBERRY ENERGY BITES..........300
1190. FROSTY CHOCOLATE SHAKE..........300
1191. FRENCH VANILLA ICE CREAM WITH HOT FUDGE..........301
1192. ALMOND-DATE ENERGY BITES..........301
1193. COCONUT AND ALMOND TRUFFLES..........301
1194. CHOCOLATE MACAROONS..........301
1195. CHOCOLATE PUDDING..........301
1196. LIME AND WATERMELON GRANITA..........302
1197. MINT CHOCOLATE FAT BOMBS..........302
1198. SPICED APPLE CHIA PUDDING..........302
1199. GRAHAM PANCAKES..........302
1200. BELGIAN GOLD WAFFLES..........302
1201. PEACH AND RASPBERRY CRISP..........303
1202. CHIA PUDDING WITH COCONUT AND FRUITS..........303
1203. ORANGE AND CRANBERRY QUINOA BITES..........303
1204. ORANGE GLAZED BANANAS..........303
1205. PEAR SQUARES..........304
1206. PRUNE, GRAPEFRUIT, AND ORANGE COMPOTE..........304
1207. PUMPKIN PIE SQUARES..........304
1208. APPLE CRISP..........304
1209. SECRET INGREDIENT CHOCOLATE BROWNIES..........305
1210. CHOCOLATE CHIP PECAN COOKIES..........305
1211. PEANUT BUTTER CHIP COOKIES..........305
1212. NO-BAKE CHOCOLATE COCONUT ENERGY BALLS..........306
CHAPTER 15. ADDITIONAL RECIPES..........307
1213. DUCK AND ORANGE SAUCE..........307
1214. BROWN RICE, CHICKEN AND SCALLIONS..........307
1215. PEANUT AND CHIVES CHICKEN MIX..........307
1216. CHICKEN AND GINGER CUCUMBERS MIX..........307
1217. CHICKEN WINGS AND DATES MIX..........308
1218. SAGE TURKEY MIX..........308
1219. CHICKEN AND APPLES MIX..........308
1220. TURMERIC CHICKEN AND EGGPLANT MIX..........308
1221. TURKEY AND ASPARAGUS MIX..........308
1222. CHICKEN SALAD AND MUSTARD DRESSING..........309
1223. THYME CHICKEN AND POTATOES..........309
1224. CHICKEN AND CELERY QUINOA MIX..........309
1225. PESTO CHICKEN MIX..........309
1226. SLOW-COOKED CHICKEN AND CAPERS MIX..........310
1227. YOGURT CHICKEN AND RED ONION MIX..........310
1228. PAPRIKA CHICKEN AND PINEAPPLE MIX..........310
1229. CHICKEN AND SAUSAGE MIX..........310
1230. CREAMY PEPPERCORN RANCH DRESSING..........310
1231. SWEET PEACH JAM..........310
1232. WARM PEACH COMPOTE..........311
16-WEEKS MEAL PLAN..........312
CONCLUSION..........318
INDEX OF RECIPES..........319

Introduction

Welcome to the Mediterranean Diet Cookbook for Beginners by the Mediterranean Diet Culinary Academy!

The Mediterranean Diet Culinary Academy is an organization made up of foodies, chefs and nutritionists who believe in the health benefits of following the Mediterranean Diet. We will share all of the recipes we have collected over time while cooking traditional Mediterranean dishes for friends and families - from tapenades to soups, pasta and fresh raw vegetables. In addition to conventional cooking methods, we also explore ways to make these dishes vegan or gluten-free, with tips and tricks that will make your cooking experience both easy and professional!

This book aims to provide a complete and accurate cookbook on the Mediterranean Diet and introduce the reader to the healthy and flavorful lifestyle that distinguishes the Mediterranean diet approach.

The Mediterranean diet is a specific diet that removes processed foods and high in saturated fats. It is not just oriented to lose weight: it is also a healthy lifestyle choice. You will indeed use traditional ingredients consumed in the Mediterranean area. It is a diet rich in fruits, vegetables, and fish. Olive oil is a fundamental ingredient and an ideal replacement for saturated fats and trans fats. Vegetables and fruits grow well in the climate near the

Mediterranean see, so it's not surprising that they represent an important component of the entire diet. Studies show that the people who live in these regions live longer and better: changing your eating habits to one that is proven to be healthy is a good enough reason to start your new culinary experience.

Many studies on the Mediterranean diet offered promising results and benefits. Here follow some of them.

Blood pressure tends to drop significantly on the Mediterranean diet; in other words, it is a natural way to lower the risk of cardiovascular disease. Researchers have found that the Mediterranean diet can reduce your chances of having a stroke and other vascular diseases.

The Mediterranean diet emphasizes eating plant-based foods and limiting red meat, harmful oils, and processed foods. Hence, these eating habits may provide some protection against malignant diseases. People in Mediterranean countries are overall less likely to die from cancer.

The Mediterranean diet may also improve brain and cogitative functions in older adults (by 15 percent). Clinical trials have shown that those who followed this dietary regimen were less likely to develop Alzheimer's, dementia, or insomnia. A new study has found that antioxidants in the Mediterranean diet plan may protect the brain and nerves, cutting the risk of neurological disorders by almost 50 percent.

Furthermore, the Mediterranean diet is the most natural and most delicious way to lose weight and maintain an ideal body fat percentage. Low-calorie foods such as fruits, vegetables, yogurt, and fish are widely used in the Mediterranean Sea countries. Natural appetite suppressants include beans, legumes, fatty fish, plain dairy products, and high-fiber foods (almost all vegetables, whole grains, apples, avocado, chia seeds). Ginger may control the hunger hormone **"ghrelin,"** too. Consuming a small amount of honey has been shown to reduce appetite. And you will become one step closer to dropping severe pounds!

The basics of this dietary plan are also vital to longevity and healthy living. Other unexpected benefits include reduced risk of developing depression, diabetes management, improved gut health, and better mood.

Vitamins and minerals can be found in plants and animals, but more often than not, fruits and vegetables are much stronger sources. When we consume another animal, we are finishing all of the energy and nutrition that the animal has also consumed. On the other hand, plants are first-hand sources of calcium, vitamin K, and vitamin C, which our bodies require daily doses of.

So, how can the Mediterranean Diet help you achieve your dreams of a slimmer body?

For a start, the diet requires you to limit processed and sugary foods that are high in calories. Just making this small change will already help you get your calorie intake under control.

Another contributing factor is the healthy fats you'll be eating daily. I know we've been told over and over again that fat makes you fat. To that, I say nonsense, and I have the science to back me! A group of doctors decided to compare weight loss results between low-carb, Mediterranean, and low-fat diets (Shai, 2008). They discovered that those who followed the Mediterranean Diet lost more weight than those on a low-fat diet. Better yet, they maintained their weight loss afterward.

The fact of the matter is that fat makes you feel fuller for longer, and when you're sated, gone is the temptation to stick your hand in the cookie jar! Talking about cookies, the healthy fats combined with the protein you'll be consuming while on the Mediterranean Diet will keep your glucose level in check. This means you won't get those nagging cravings for sugary foods.

Over the past ten years, numerous health researchers have forces doctors and dieticians to change the notion of a healthy diet. As a result, discoveries have been made that talk more about the true causes and mechanisms of harmful ailments like cancer, diabetes, and coronary diseases. For this reason, the previous concept for healthy food has been disregard.

Chapter 1. Your New Journey Through the Mediterranean Diet

The Mediterranean diet is a plant-based diet that incorporates healthy fats and proteins. Things like fruits, vegetables, beans, whole grains, nuts, and seeds are essential parts of this diet. This type of eating plan is also rich in olive oil, which is believed to be one reason why this diet is so healthy. This diet was created way before vegan or vegetarian diets became popular. However, plenty of vegans and vegetarians use this as their eating plan because it's so beneficial to the body.

The Mediterranean diet has been touted as the healthiest and most delicious way to eat. It differs from other popular diets in that it is primarily plant-based and includes vegetables, fruits, whole grains, legumes, nuts, seeds and olive oil instead of animal products such as dairy or meat. This diet is also free from smoking and alcohol. It's also been thought of as having positive effects on mental health conditions like depression through its nutritional content. How does it compare to other popular diets, though? Read on to find out.

The Mediterranean diet is based on eating lots of fruits and vegetables, high-quality proteins, whole grains and olive oil. It also limits unhealthy fats and sugars. While the

Mediterranean diet includes dairy products, meat and fish in addition to plant-based foods, it has been linked with lower risks for heart disease, certain cancers, metabolic wellness and improved mental health

A common misconception is that the Mediterranean Diet consists solely of pasta and pizza. The actual advice given in the diet has more to do with portion control and sticking to unprocessed foods with less added salt, sugar and fat. As a result of this healthy eating pattern, there are decreased risks for cardiovascular disease, type 2 diabetes, and certain cancers, among other chronic diseases.

Many Mediterranean countries have a diet in their name. This is because they are a part of the Mediterranean Diet Pyramid. The pyramid is split up into different levels. Each level has a certain number of daily servings based on your calorie intake and your age.

The goal of this diet is to eat a variety of whole foods and limit the number of processed foods you take in. The Mediterranean Diet is broken down into three categories based on geographical areas and local cultures. 4 other types include food staples such as olive oil, legumes, fish, red wine, and nuts typical throughout the Mediterranean.

Pasta does exist, however, only in small quantities, focusing on whole grains rather than refined grains like white rice or flour. Bread can be replaced with a whole-grain roll. Pita bread and pitas are also available, but I would avoid them as they are full of added fats and oils. Many different vegetables can be used in pasta, such as zucchini, eggplant, broccoli, etc. Spaghetti is one example of this.

A study of a few hundred volunteers conducted in 2003 suggested that a diet based on the Mediterranean diet would lead to more weight loss and better results in keeping off weight than any other diet. The study also showed that even light changes to food habits could make a difference.

For many people, the Mediterranean diet is the holy grail of healthy living. This diet is one of the most well-known and popular diets in the world. It's rich in fruits, vegetables, nuts, olive oil and other foods under this category. But what do these foods have to say for themselves?

The Mediterranean Diet Components

Fruit: Fruits are great for making up most of your daily intake, but they're also an excellent source of fiber and antioxidants. Studies have shown that eating fruit can decrease risk factors such as heart disease and stroke (Cohn et al., 1992; Peloso et al., 2003). It's also been known to help combat obesity-related metabolic disorders such as diabetes (Tidbinbika et al., 2004).

Nuts: Nuts have long been known to be good in the fight against heart disease and diabetes (Lacson et al., 2003). A study done on young men evaluated for the risk factors of heart disease showed that those who ate about 1.5 ounces of nuts or 6 ounces of nuts consumed every day had a much lower risk factor than those without this type of consumption (Erickson et al., 2001).

Olive Oil: According to nutritional researchers, olive oil should only be used as a flavoring agent in cooking or as part of the cooking mix within the food. Consuming olive oil for its nutritional value is too high of a risk for the body to deal with (Spiller & England, 2011).

Fish: Fish consumption has been proven to be an excellent source of Omega-3 fatty acids. These fatty acids are known to help reduce the risk factor of heart disease and stroke. Smaller studies have also shown that eating fish twice a week can reduce the risk factor of death from cardiovascular diseases (He et al., 2009).

Poultry: Poultry is another good source of Omega-3 fatty acids. It's also another food that helps lower the risk factors for cardiovascular diseases, especially if eaten in moderation (He et al., 2009).

Nuts & Seeds: Nuts and seeds are other excellent sources of Omega-3 fatty acids. They're also known to protect the heart, lower cholesterol, reduce joint pain and improve the body's ability to use insulin (He et al., 2009).

Vegetables: Vegetables are an excellent source of fiber. For this reason, they're known to lower blood pressure and cholesterol as well as help treat diabetes (He et al., 2009; Lacson et al., 2003)

Legumes: Legumes are a great source of fiber. For this reason, they're known to lower cholesterol and blood pressure and help treat diabetes (Lacson et al., 2003).

The Mediterranean Diet Nutritional Breakdown

As above, the Mediterranean diet is the most well-known and popular dietary regime. This type of diet is based mainly on the traditional foods of this region. It shows that different food groups should make up most if not all of their daily intake (the exceptions being meat and dairy). The Mediterranean diet contains very little saturated fat, interesting heavy amounts of fiber and essential amino acids. As a result, it has one of the lowest rates of body fat storage in the world. For this reason, many people believe that this is an excellent dietary regime for anybody wishing to lose weight or keep their weight low.

These antioxidants have been proven to help fight free radicals and prevent cellular damage. Like other diets, the Mediterranean diet is known to be loaded with Omega-3 fats, which increase circulation and improve cardiac health. Omega-3 is also known for its ability to calm inflammation within the body and reduce joint pain (Spiller & England, 2011).

Benefits of Mediterranean Diet

The Mediterranean diet helps with many conditions such as diabetes, heart disease, and hypertension. It also has many other benefits for both physical and mental health. Some of these benefits include improved weight loss, reduced risk of heart disease, improved skin health, and reduced body fat.

It's hard enough to stick to a diet, but the Mediterranean Diet is worth making the extra effort. Studies show that this eating plan can significantly reduce your chance of developing cardiovascular disease, cancer, and dementia. The Mediterranean Diet is also known for its weight-loss benefits and its ability to lower stroke and heart attack odds. Read on to find out how adopting this diet can benefit you.

Reduced Risk of Heart Disease

The Mediterranean Diet was inspired by the diet of people living in the Mediterranean area who had lower rates of chronic illness and heart disease than people living in most of the western world.

Combining a high intake of unsaturated fats with a decreased amount of red meat and saturated fat reduces your risk of developing hypertension. Studies have shown that unsaturated fats can bring down blood pressure more than any other type of fat.

Reduced Risk of Type 2 Diabetes

The Mediterranean diet is associated with a reduced risk of developing type 2 diabetes. Studies show that using a Mediterranean diet and regular exercise can reduce the risk of developing diabetes by 70% for people who are obese, 30% for those with average weight, and even up to 50% for those who are overweight. People who follow this eating plan are at a higher risk of diabetes because they have lower rates of body fat, lower waist circumference, and exercise regularly. The combination of lowering your risk factors and adding in healthy fats means you have fewer calories to gain weight in the first place.

Lower Risk of Cancer

It's been shown that following a Mediterranean Diet can reduce your risk of developing cancer. In addition to the high consumption of fruits, vegetables, and healthy fats in this diet also lowers your intake of meats and dairy products. The high fiber content in these foods has been shown to reduce your chances of developing bowel cancer. This is also because carbohydrates fuel cancer and cancer cells feed off glucose. Foods such as whole grains are low on the glycemic index, meaning they are less likely to raise glucose levels or encourage the growth of cancer cells.

These three items show just how powerful a diet like the Mediterranean Food Plan can be for you. It cuts out all the processed foods that are commonly consumed, but it can also be tailored to your specific needs.

Other Health Benefits of the Mediterranean Diet

Lower Blood Pressure Levels: This diet has been shown to help people lower their blood pressure levels and keep them at healthy amounts. By combining rich antioxidants with exercise, you can improve your heart health and reduce your chances of developing heart disease.

Reduced Risk of Stroke: An increased intake of fiber has been shown to lower stroke risks by 30%. A Mediterranean diet is full of fiber which means you're less likely to develop problems with high cholesterol.

Reduced Risk of Dementia: A healthy diet can reduce your risk of dementia by up to 46%! Studies have shown that people who have a diet rich in fruits, vegetables, and nuts are less likely to develop Alzheimer's or Parkinson's.

Reduced Risk of Depression: The Mediterranean Diet has also been linked with a lower risk of depression. Combining whole grains, legumes, and high-fiber foods improves gut health and reduces inflammation in the body. This leads to better mental health by reducing stress levels as well as a better mood overall.

Boosts Brain Health: Studies show that a Mediterranean-style diet can improve your brain health by reducing your risk of developing Alzheimer's or dementia. This is because it is high in antioxidants and contains a lot of plant foods.

The Bottom Line

The Mediterranean Diet can bring about many different benefits, and it's worth giving it a try if you want to live a longer, better life. You may find that this dietary plan improves your mood, reduces your risk of heart disease and stroke and lowers your chances of developing several other disorders.

Enjoy your recipes!

Chapter 2. Breakfast Recipes

2. Italian Breakfast Sausage with Baby Potatoes and Vegetables

Preparation Time: 15 minutes
Cooking Time: 30 minutes
Servings: 4
Ingredients:

- 1-pound sweet Italian sausage links, sliced on the bias (diagonal)
- 2 cups baby potatoes, halved
- 2 cups broccoli florets
- 1 cup onions cut into 1-inch chunks
- 2 cups small mushrooms - half or quarter the large ones for uniform size
- 1 cup baby carrots
- 2 tablespoons olive oil
- ½ teaspoon garlic powder
- ½ teaspoon Italian seasoning
- 1 teaspoon salt & ½ teaspoon pepper

Directions:

1. Preheat the oven to 400°F. In a large bowl, add the baby potatoes, broccoli florets, onions, small mushrooms, and baby carrots.
2. Add in the olive oil, salt, pepper, garlic powder and Italian seasoning and toss to evenly coat. Spread the vegetables onto a sheet pan in one even layer.
3. Arrange the sausage slices on the pan over the vegetables. Bake for 30 minutes – make sure to sake halfway through to prevent sticking. Allow to cool.
4. Distribute the Italian sausages and vegetables among the containers and store in the fridge for 2-3 days

Nutrition: Calories: 321 Fat: 16 g Carbs: 23 g Protein: 22 g

3. Cauliflower Fritters with Hummus

Preparation Time: 15 minutes
Cooking Time: 15 minutes
Servings: 4
Ingredients:

- 2 (15-oz.) cans chickpeas, divided
- 2½ tablespoons olive oil, divided, plus more for frying
- 1 cup onion, chopped, about ½ a small onion
- 2 tablespoons garlic, minced
- 2 cups cauliflower, cut into small pieces, about ½ a large head
- ½ teaspoon salt
- Black pepper

Topping:

- Hummus, of choice
- Green onion, diced

Directions:

1. Preheat oven to 400°F. Rinse and drain 1 can of the chickpeas, place them on a paper towel to dry off well.
2. Then place the chickpeas into a large bowl, removing the loose skins that come off, and toss with 1 tablespoon of olive oil, spread the chickpeas onto a large pan, and sprinkle with salt and pepper.
3. Bake for 20 minutes, then stir and then bake an additional 5-10 minutes until very crispy.
4. Once the chickpeas are roasted, transfer them to a large food processor and process until broken down and crumble - Don't over process them and turn it into flour, as you need to have some texture. Place the mixture into a small bowl, set aside.
5. In a large pan over medium-high heat, add the remaining 1½ tablespoons of olive oil. Once heated, add in the onion and garlic, cook until

lightly golden brown, about 2 minutes.
6. Then add in the chopped cauliflower, cook for an additional 2 minutes, until the cauliflower is golden.
7. Turn the heat down to low and cover the pan, cook until the cauliflower is fork tender and the onions are golden brown and caramelized, stirring often, about 3-5 minutes.
8. Transfer the cauliflower mixture to the food processor, drain and rinse the remaining can of chickpeas and add them into the food processor, along with the salt and a pinch of pepper.
9. Blend until smooth, and the mixture starts to ball, stop to scrape down the sides as needed
10. Transfer the cauliflower mixture into a large bowl and add in ½ cup of the roasted chickpea crumbs, stir until well combined.
11. In a large bowl over medium heat, add in enough oil to lightly cover the bottom of a large pan. Working in batches, cook the patties until golden brown, about 2-3 minutes, flip and cook again. Serve.

Nutrition: Calories: 333 Carbohydrates: 45 g Fat: 13 g Protein: 14 g

4. Overnight Berry Chia Oats

Preparation Time: 15 minutes
Cooking Time: 5 minutes
Servings: 1
Ingredients:

- ½ cup Quaker Oats rolled oats
- ¼ cup chia seeds
- 1 cup milk or water
- pinch of salt and cinnamon
- maple syrup, or a different sweetener, to taste

- 1 cup frozen berries of choice or smoothie leftovers

Toppings:

- Yogurt
- Berries

Directions:

1. In a jar with a lid, add the oats, seeds, milk, salt, and cinnamon, refrigerate overnight. On serving day, puree the berries in a blender.
2. Stir the oats, add in the berry puree, and top with yogurt and more berries, nuts, honey, or garnish of your choice. Enjoy!

Nutrition: Calories: 405 Carbs: 65 g Fat: 11 g Protein: 17 g

5. Raspberry Vanilla Smoothie

Preparation Time: 5 minutes
Cooking Time: 5 minutes
Servings: 2 cups
Ingredients:

- 1 cup frozen raspberries
- 6-ounce container of vanilla Greek yogurt
- ½ cup of unsweetened vanilla almond milk

Directions:

1. Take all of your ingredients and place them in a blender. Process until smooth and liquified.

Nutrition: Calories: 155 Protein: 7 g Fat: 2 g Carbohydrates: 30 g

6. Blueberry Banana Protein Smoothie

Preparation Time: 5 minutes
Cooking Time: 5 minutes
Servings: 1
Ingredients:

- ½ cup frozen and unsweetened blueberries
- ½ banana slices up
- ¾ cup plain nonfat Greek yogurt
- ¾ cup unsweetened vanilla almond milk
- 2 cups of ice cubes

Directions:

1. Add all of the ingredients into a blender. Blend until smooth.

Nutrition: Calories: 230 Protein: 19.1 g Fat: 2.6 g Carbohydrates: 32.9 g

7. Chocolate Banana Smoothie

Preparation Time: 5 minutes
Cooking Time: 0 minutes
Servings: 2
Ingredients:

- 2 bananas, peeled
- 1 cup unsweetened almond milk, or skim milk
- 1 cup crushed ice
- 3 tablespoons unsweetened cocoa powder
- 3 tablespoons honey

Directions:

1. In a blender, combine the bananas, almond milk, ice, cocoa powder, and honey. Blend until smooth.

Nutrition: Calories: 219 Protein: 2 g Carbohydrates: 57 g Fat: 2 g

8. Moroccan Avocado Smoothie

Preparation Time: 5 minutes
Cooking Time: 0 minutes
Servings: 4
Ingredients:

- 1 ripe avocado, peeled and pitted
- 1 overripe banana
- 1 cup almond milk, unsweetened
- 1 cup of ice

Directions:

1. Place the avocado, banana, milk, and ice into your blender. Blend until smooth with no pieces of avocado remaining.

Nutrition: Calories: 100 Protein: 1 g Fat: 6 g Carbohydrates: 11 g

9. Greek Yogurt with Fresh Berries, Honey and Nuts

Preparation Time: 5 minutes
Cooking Time: 0 minutes
Servings: 1
Ingredients:

- 6 ounces nonfat plain Greek yogurt
- ½ cup fresh berries of your choice

- 1 tablespoon crushed walnuts
- 1 tablespoon honey

Directions:

1. In a jar with a lid, add the yogurt. Top with berries and a drizzle of honey. Top with the lid and store in the fridge for 2-3 days.

Nutrition: Calories: 250 Carbs: 35 Fat: 4 g Protein: 19 g

10. Mediterranean Egg Muffins with Ham

Preparation Time: 15 minutes
Cooking Time: 15 minutes
Servings: 6
Ingredients:

- 9 Slices of thin cut deli ham
- ½ cup canned roasted red pepper, sliced + additional for garnish
- ⅓ cup fresh spinach, minced
- ¼ cup feta cheese, crumbled
- 5 large eggs
- Pinch of salt
- Pinch of pepper
- 1½ tablespoons Pesto sauce
- Fresh basil for garnish

Directions:

1. Preheat oven to 400°F. Spray a muffin tin with cooking spray, generously. Line each of the muffin tin with 1½ pieces of ham - making sure there aren't any holes for the egg mixture to come out.
2. Place some of the roasted red pepper in the bottom of each muffin tin. Place 1 tablespoon of minced spinach on top of each red pepper. Top the pepper and spinach off with a large ½ tbsp of crumbled feta cheese.
3. In a medium bowl, whisk together the eggs salt and pepper, divide the egg mixture evenly among the 6 muffin tins.
4. Bake for 15 to 17 minutes until the eggs are puffy and set. Remove each cup from

the muffin tin. Allow to cool completely

5. Distribute the muffins among the containers, store in the fridge for 2 - 3days or in the freezer for 3 months.

Nutrition: Calories: 109 Carbs: 2 g Fat: 6 g Protein: 9 g

11. Quinoa Bake with Banana

Preparation Time: 15 minutes
Cooking Time: 1 hour & 10 minutes
Servings: 8
Ingredients:

- 3 cups medium over-ripe Bananas, mashed
- ¼ cup molasses
- ¼ cup pure maple syrup
- 1 tablespoon cinnamon
- 2 teaspoons raw vanilla extract
- 1 teaspoon ground ginger
- 1 teaspoon ground cloves
- ½ teaspoon ground allspice
- ½ teaspoon salt
- 1 cup quinoa, uncooked
- 2½ cups unsweetened vanilla almond milk
- ¼ cup slivered almonds

Directions:

1. In the bottom of a 2½-3-quart casserole dish, mix together the mashed banana, maple syrup, cinnamon, vanilla extract, ginger, cloves, allspice, molasses, and salt until well mixed.
2. Add in the quinoa, stir until the quinoa is evenly in the banana mixture. Whisk in the almond milk, mix until well combined, cover and refrigerate overnight, or bake immediately.
3. Heat oven to 350°F. Whisk the quinoa mixture making sure it doesn't settle to the bottom.
4. Cover the pan with tinfoil and bake until the liquid is absorbed, and the top of the quinoa is set, about 60 to 90 minutes.

5. Turn the oven to high broil, uncover the pan, sprinkle with sliced almonds, and lightly press them into the quinoa.
6. Broil until the almonds just turn golden brown, about 2-4 minutes, watching closely, as they burn quickly. Allow to cool for 10 minutes then slice the quinoa bake
7. Distribute the quinoa bake among the containers, store in the fridge for 3-4 days.

Nutrition: Calories: 213 Carbs: 41 g Fat: 4 g Protein: 5 g

12. Sun-Dried Tomatoes, Dill and Feta Omelet Casserole

Preparation Time: 15 minutes
Cooking Time: 40 minutes
Servings: 6
Ingredients:

- 12 large eggs
- 2 cups whole milk
- 8 ounces fresh spinach
- 2 cloves garlic, minced
- 12 ounces artichoke salad with olives and peppers, drained and chopped
- 5 ounces sun-dried tomato feta cheese, crumbled
- 1 tablespoon fresh chopped dill or 1 teaspoon dried dill
- 1 teaspoon dried oregano
- 1 teaspoon lemon pepper
- 1 teaspoon salt
- 4 teaspoons olive oil, divided

Directions:

1. Preheat oven to 375°F. Chop the fresh herbs and artichoke salad. In a skillet over medium heat, add 1 tablespoon olive oil.
2. Sauté the spinach and garlic until wilted, about 3 minutes. Oil a 9x13 inch baking dish, layer the spinach and artichoke salad evenly in the dish
3. In a medium bowl, whisk together the eggs, milk, herbs, salt and lemon pepper. Pour the egg

mixture over vegetables, sprinkle with feta cheese.

4. Bake in the center of the oven for 35-40 minutes until firm in the center. Allow to cool, slice a and distribute among the storage containers. Store for 2-3 days or freeze for 3 months.

Nutrition: Calories: 196 Carbohydrates: 5 g Fat: 12 g Protein: 10 g

13. Breakfast Taco Scramble

Preparation Time: 15 minutes
Cooking Time: 1 hour & 25 minutes
Servings: 4
Ingredients:

- 8 large eggs, beaten
- ¼ teaspoon seasoning salt
- 1 pound 99% lean ground turkey
- 2 tablespoons Greek seasoning
- ½ small onion, minced
- 2 tablespoons bell pepper, minced
- 4 ounces can tomato sauce
- ¼ cup water
- ¼ cup chopped scallions or cilantro, for topping

For the potatoes:

- 12 (1 pound) baby gold or red potatoes, quartered
- 4 teaspoon olive oil
- ¾ teaspoon salt
- ½ teaspoon garlic powder
- Fresh black pepper, to taste

Directions:

1. In a large bowl, beat the eggs, season with seasoning salt. Preheat the oven to 425°F. Spray a 9x12 or large oval casserole dish with cooking oil.
2. Add the potatoes 1 tablespoon oil, ¾ teaspoon salt, garlic powder and black pepper and toss to coat. Bake for 45 minutes to 1 hour, tossing every 15 minutes.
3. In the meantime, brown the turkey in a large skillet over medium heat, breaking it up

while it cooks. Once no longer pink, add in the Greek seasoning.
4. Add in the bell pepper, onion, tomato sauce and water, stir and cover, simmer on low for about 20 minutes. Spray a different skillet with nonstick spray over medium heat.
5. Once heated, add in the eggs seasoned with ¼ teaspoon of salt and scramble for 2–3 minutes, or cook until it sets.
6. Distribute ¾ cup turkey and 2/3 cup eggs and divide the potatoes in each storage container, store for 3-4 days.

Nutrition: Calories: 450 Fat: 19 g Carbs: 24.5 g Protein: 46 g

14. Greek Beans Tortillas

Preparation Time: 5 minutes
Cooking Time: 20 minutes
Servings: 4
Ingredients:
- 1 red onion, chopped
- 2 garlic cloves, minced
- 1 tablespoon olive oil
- 1 green bell pepper, sliced
- 3 cups canned pinto beans, drained and rinsed
- 2 red chili peppers, chopped
- 4 tablespoon parsley, chopped
- 1 teaspoon cumin, ground
- A pinch of salt and black pepper
- 4 whole wheat Greek tortillas
- 1 cup cheddar cheese, shredded

Directions:
1. Heat up a pan with the oil over medium heat, add the onion and sauté for 5 minutes.
2. Add the rest of the ingredients except the tortillas and the cheese, stir and cook for 15 minutes.
3. Divide the beans mix on each Greek tortilla, also divide the cheese, roll the tortillas and serve for breakfast.

Nutrition: Calories 673, Fat 14.9, Fiber 23.7, Carbs 75.4, Protein 39

15. Baked Cauliflower Hash

Preparation Time: 10 minutes
Cooking Time: 25 minutes
Servings: 4
Ingredients:
- 4 cups cauliflower florets
- 1 tablespoon olive oil
- 2 cups white mushrooms, sliced
- 1 cup cherry tomatoes, halved
- 1 yellow onion, chopped
- 2 garlic cloves, minced
- ¼ teaspoon garlic powder
- 3 tablespoons basil, chopped
- 3 tablespoons mint, chopped
- 1 tablespoon dill, chopped

Directions:
1. Spread the cauliflower florets on a baking sheet lined with parchment paper, add the rest of the ingredients, introduce to the oven at 350°F and bake for 25 minutes.
2. Divide the hash between plates and serve for breakfast.

Nutrition: Calories 367, Fat 14.3, Fiber 3.5, Carbs 16.8, Protein 12.2

16. Eggs, Mint and Tomatoes

Preparation Time: 10 minutes
Cooking Time: 15 minutes
Servings: 2
Ingredients:
- 2 eggs, whisked
- 2 tomatoes, cubed
- 2 teaspoons olive oil
- 1 tablespoon mint, chopped
- 1 tablespoon chives, chopped
- Salt and black pepper to the taste

Directions:
1. Heat up a pan with the oil over medium heat, add the tomatoes and the rest of the ingredients except the eggs, stir and cook for 5 minutes.
2. Add the eggs, toss, cook for 10 minutes more, divide between plates and serve.

Nutrition: Calories 300, Fat 15.3, Fiber 4.5, Carbs 17.7, Protein 11

17. Bacon, Spinach and Tomato Sandwich

Preparation Time: 5 minutes
Cooking Time: 0 minutes
Servings: 1
Ingredients:
- 2 whole-wheat bread slices, toasted
- 1 tablespoon Dijon mustard
- 3 bacon slices
- Salt and black pepper to the taste
- 2 tomato slices
- ¼ cup baby spinach

Directions:
1. Spread the mustard on each bread slice, divide the bacon and the rest of the ingredients on one slice, top with the other one, cut in half and serve for breakfast.

Nutrition: Calories 246, Fat 11.2, Fiber 4.5, Carbs 17.5, Protein 8.3

18. Cottage Cheese and Berries Omelet

Preparation Time: 5 minutes
Cooking Time: 4 minutes
Servings: 1
Ingredients:
- 1 egg, whisked
- ½ teaspoon olive oil
- 1 teaspoon cinnamon powder
- 1 tablespoon almond milk
- 3 ounces cottage cheese
- 4 ounces blueberries

Directions:
1. In a bowl, mix the egg with the rest of the ingredients except the oil and toss.
2. Heat up a pan with the oil over medium heat, add the eggs mix, spread, cook for 2 minutes on each side, transfer to a plate and serve.

Nutrition: calories

19. Salmon Frittata

Preparation Time: 5 minutes
Cooking Time: 27 minutes
Servings: 4
Ingredients:
- 1-pound gold potatoes, roughly cubed
- 1 tablespoon olive oil
- Cooking spray

- 2 salmon fillets, skinless and boneless
- 8 eggs, whisked
- 1 teaspoon mint, chopped
- A pinch of salt and black pepper

Directions:

1. Put the potatoes in a pot, add water to cover, bring to a boil over medium heat, cook for 12 minutes, drain and transfer to a bowl.
2. Arrange the salmon on a baking sheet lined with parchment paper, grease with cooking spray, broil over medium-high heat for 5 minutes on each side, cool down, flake, and put in a separate bowl.
3. Heat up a pan with the oil over medium heat, add the potatoes, salmon, and the rest of the ingredients except the eggs and toss.
4. Add the eggs on top, put the lid on and cook over medium heat for 10 minutes.
5. Divide the salmon between plates and serve.

Nutrition: calories

20. Coriander Mushroom Salad

Preparation Time: 5 minutes
Cooking Time: 7 minutes
Servings: 6
Ingredients:

- ½ pound white mushrooms, sliced
- 1 tablespoon olive oil
- 3 garlic cloves, minced
- Salt and black pepper to the taste
- 1 tomato, diced
- 1 avocado, peeled, pitted and cubed
- 3 tablespoons lime juice
- ½ cup chicken stock
- 2 tablespoons coriander, chopped

Directions:

1. Heat up a pan with the oil over medium heat, add the mushrooms and sauté them for 4 minutes.

2. Add the rest of the ingredients, toss, cook for 3-4 minutes more, divide into bowls and serve for breakfast.

Nutrition: calories

21. Cinnamon Apple and Lentils Porridge

Preparation Time: 5 minutes
Cooking Time: 10 minutes
Servings: 4
Ingredients:

- ½ cup walnuts, chopped
- 2 green apples, cored, peeled and cubed
- 3 tablespoons maple syrup
- 3 cups almond milk
- ½ cup red lentils
- ½ teaspoon cinnamon powder
- ½ cup cranberries, dried
- 1 teaspoon vanilla extract

Directions:

1. Put the milk in a pot, heat it up over medium heat, add the walnuts, apples, maple syrup and the rest of the ingredients, toss, simmer for 10 minutes, divide into bowls and serve.

Nutrition: Calories 150, Fat 2, Fiber 1, Carbs 3, Protein 5

22. Lentils and Cheddar Frittata

Preparation Time: 10 minutes
Cooking Time: 15 minutes
Servings: 4
Ingredients:

- 1 red onion, chopped
- 2 tablespoons olive oil
- 1 cup sweet potatoes, boiled and chopped
- ¾ cup ham, chopped
- 4 eggs, whisked
- ¾ cup lentils, cooked
- 2 tablespoons Greek yogurt
- Salt and black pepper to the taste
- ½ cup cherry tomatoes, halved
- ¾ cup cheddar cheese, grated

Directions:

1. Heat up a pan with the oil over medium heat, add the onion, stir and sauté for 2 minutes.

2. Add the rest of the ingredients except the eggs and the cheese, toss and cook for 3 minutes more.
3. Add the eggs, sprinkle the cheese on top, cover the pan and cook for 10 minutes more.
4. Slice the frittata, divide between plates and serve.

23. Seeds and Lentils Oats

Preparation Time: 10 minutes
Cooking Time: 50 minutes
Servings: 4
Ingredients:

- ½ cup red lentils
- ¼ cup pumpkin seeds, toasted
- 2 teaspoons olive oil
- ¼ cup rolled oats
- ¼ cup coconut flesh, shredded
- 1 tablespoon honey
- 1 tablespoon orange zest, grated
- 1 cup Greek yogurt
- 1 cup blackberries

Directions:

1. Spread the lentils on a baking sheet lined with parchment paper, introduce in the oven, and roast at 370°F for 30 minutes.
2. Add the rest of the ingredients except the yogurt and the berries, toss and bake at 370°F for 20 minutes more.
3. Transfer this to a bowl, add the rest of the ingredients, toss, divide into smaller bowls and serve for breakfast.

Nutrition: Calories 204, Fat 7.1, Fiber 10.4, Carbs 27.6, Protein 9.5

24. Orzo and Veggie Bowls

Preparation Time: 10 minutes
Cooking Time: 0 minutes
Servings: 4
Ingredients:

- 2½ cups whole-wheat orzo, cooked
- 14 ounces canned cannellini beans, drained and rinsed
- 1 yellow bell pepper, cubed

- 1 green bell pepper, cubed
- A pinch of salt and black pepper
- 3 tomatoes, cubed
- 1 red onion, chopped
- 1 cup mint, chopped
- 2 cups feta cheese, crumbled
- 2 tablespoons olive oil
- ¼ cup lemon juice
- 1 tablespoon lemon zest, grated
- 1 cucumber, cubed
- 1¼ cup kalamata olives, pitted and sliced
- 3 garlic cloves, minced

Directions:
1. In a salad bowl, combine the orzo with the beans, bell peppers and the rest of the ingredients, toss, divide the mix between plates and serve for breakfast.

Nutrition: Calories 411, Fat 17, Fiber 13, Carbs 51, Protein 14

25. Lemon Peas Quinoa Mix

Preparation Time: 10 minutes
Cooking Time: 20 minutes
Servings: 4
Ingredients:

- 1½ cups quinoa, rinsed
- 1-pound asparagus, steamed and chopped
- 3 cups water
- 2 tablespoons parsley, chopped
- 2 tablespoons lemon juice
- 1 teaspoon lemon zest, grated
- ½ pound sugar snap peas, steamed
- ½ pound green beans, trimmed and halved
- A pinch of salt and black pepper
- 3 tablespoons pumpkin seeds
- 1 cup cherry tomatoes, halved
- 2 tablespoons olive oil

Directions:
1. Put the water in a pot, bring to a boil over medium heat,

add the quinoa, stir and simmer for 20 minutes.
2. Stir the quinoa, add the parsley, lemon juice and the rest of the ingredients, toss, divide between plates and serve for breakfast.

Nutrition: Calories 417, Fat 15, Fiber 9, Carbs 58, Protein 16

26. Walnuts Yogurt Mix

Preparation Time: 10 minutes
Cooking Time: 0 minutes
Servings: 6
Ingredients:

- 2½ cups Greek yogurt
- 1½ cups walnuts, chopped
- 1 teaspoon vanilla extract
- ¾ cup honey
- 2 teaspoons cinnamon powder

Directions:
1. In a bowl, combine the yogurt with the walnuts and the rest of the ingredients, toss, divide into smaller bowls and keep in the fridge for 10 minutes before serving for breakfast.

Nutrition: Calories 388, Fat 24.6, Fiber 2.9, Carbs 39.1, Protein 10.2

27. Stuffed Pita Breads

Preparation Time: 5 minutes
Cooking Time: 15 minutes
Servings: 4
Ingredients:

- 1½ tablespoons olive oil
- 1 tomato, cubed
- 1 garlic clove, minced
- 1 red onion, chopped
- ¼ cup parsley, chopped
- 15 ounces canned fava beans, drained and rinsed
- ¼ cup lemon juice
- Salt and black pepper to the taste
- 4 whole-wheat pita bread pockets

Directions:
1. Heat up a pan with the oil over medium heat, add the onion, stir and sauté for 5 minutes.
2. Add the rest of the ingredients, stir and cook for 10 minutes more
3. Stuff the pita pockets with this mix and serve for breakfast.

Nutrition: Calories 382, Fat 1.8, Fiber 27.6, Carbs 66, Protein 28.5

28. Farro Salad

Preparation Time: 5 minutes
Cooking Time: 4 minutes
Servings: 2
Ingredients:

- 1 tablespoon olive oil
- A pinch of salt and black pepper
- 1 bunch baby spinach, chopped
- 1 avocado, pitted, peeled and chopped
- 1 garlic clove, minced
- 2 cups farro, already cooked
- ½ cup cherry tomatoes, cubed

Directions:
1. Heat up a pan with the oil over medium heat, add the spinach, and the rest of the ingredients, toss, cook for 4 minutes, divide into bowls and serve.

Nutrition: Calories 157, Fat 13.7, Fiber 5.5, Carbs 8.6, Protein 3.6

29. Cranberry and Dates Squares

Preparation Time: 30 minutes
Cooking Time: 0 minutes
Servings: 10
Ingredients:

- 12 dates, pitted and chopped
- 1 teaspoon vanilla extract
- ¼ cup honey
- ½ cup rolled oats
- ¾ cup cranberries, dried
- ¼ cup almond avocado oil, melted
- 1 cup walnuts, roasted and chopped
- ¼ cup pumpkin seeds

Directions:
1. In a bowl, mix the dates with the vanilla, honey and the rest of the ingredients, stir well and press everything on a baking sheet lined with parchment paper.
2. Keep in the freezer for 30 minutes, cut into 10 squares and serve for breakfast.

Nutrition: Calories 263, Fat 13.4, Fiber 4.7, Carbs 14.3, Protein 3.5

30. Cheesy Eggs Ramekins

Preparation Time: 10 minutes
Cooking Time: 10 minutes
Servings: 2
Ingredients:

- 1 tablespoon chives, chopped
- 1 tablespoon dill, chopped
- A pinch of salt and black pepper
- 2 tablespoons cheddar cheese, grated
- 1 tomato, chopped
- 2 eggs, whisked
- Cooking spray

Directions:

1. In a bowl, mix the eggs with the tomato and the rest of the ingredients except the cooking spray and whisk well.
2. Grease 2 ramekins with the cooking spray, divide the mix into each ramekin, bake at 400°F for 10 minutes and serve.

Nutrition: Calories 104, Fat 7.1, Fiber 0.6, Carbs 2.6, Protein 7.9

31. Leeks and Eggs Muffins

Preparation Time: 10 minutes
Cooking Time: 20 minutes
Servings: 2
Ingredients:

- 3 eggs, whisked
- ¼ cup baby spinach
- 2 tablespoons leeks, chopped
- 4 tablespoons parmesan, grated
- 2 tablespoons almond milk
- Cooking spray
- 1 small red bell pepper, chopped
- Salt and black pepper to the taste
- 1 tomato, cubed
- 2 tablespoons cheddar cheese, grated

Directions:

1. In a bowl, combine the eggs with the milk, salt, pepper and the rest of the ingredients except the cooking spray and whisk well.
2. Grease a muffin tin with the cooking spray and divide the eggs mixture in each muffin mold.
3. Bake at 380°F for 20 minutes and serve them for breakfast.

Nutrition: Calories 308, Fat 19.4, Fiber 1.7, Carbs 8.7, Protein 24.4

32. Artichokes and Cheese Omelet

Preparation Time: 10 minutes
Cooking Time: 8 minutes
Servings: 1
Ingredients:

- 1 teaspoon avocado oil
- 1 tablespoon almond milk
- 2 eggs, whisked
- A pinch of salt and black pepper
- 2 tablespoons tomato, cubed
- 2 tablespoons kalamata olives, pitted and sliced
- 1 artichoke heart, chopped
- 1 tablespoon tomato sauce
- 1 tablespoon feta cheese, crumbled

Directions:

1. In a bowl, combine the eggs with the milk, salt, pepper and the rest of the ingredients except the avocado oil and whisk well.
2. Heat up a pan with the avocado oil over medium-high heat, add the omelet mix, spread into the pan, cook for 4 minutes, flip, cook for 4 minutes more, transfer to a plate and serve.

Nutrition: Calories 303, Fat 17.7, Fiber 9.9, Carbs 21.9, Protein 18.2

33. Quinoa and Eggs Salad

Preparation Time: 5 minutes
Cooking Time: 0 minutes
Servings: 4
Ingredients:

- 4 eggs, soft boiled, peeled and cut into wedges
- 2 cups baby arugula
- 2 cups cherry tomatoes, halved
- 1 cucumber, sliced
- 1 cup quinoa, cooked
- 1 cup almonds, chopped
- 1 avocado, peeled, pitted and sliced
- 1 tablespoon olive oil
- ½ cup mixed dill and mint, chopped
- A pinch of salt and black pepper
- Juice of 1 lemon

Directions:

1. In a large salad bowl, combine the eggs with the arugula and the rest of the ingredients, toss, divide between plates and serve for breakfast.

Nutrition: Calories 519, Fat 32.4, Fiber 11, Carbs 43.3, Protein 19.1

34. Corn and Shrimp Salad

Preparation Time: 10 minutes
Cooking Time: 10 minutes
Servings: 4
Ingredients:

- 4 ears of sweet corn, husked
- 1 avocado, peeled, pitted and chopped
- ½ cup basil, chopped
- A pinch of salt and black pepper
- 1-pound shrimp, peeled and deveined
- 1½ cups cherry tomatoes, halved
- ¼ cup olive oil

Directions:

1. Put the corn in a pot, add water to cover, bring to a boil over medium heat, cook for 6 minutes, drain, cool down, cut corn from the cob, and put it in a bowl.
2. Thread the shrimp onto skewers and brush with some of the oil.
3. Place the skewers on the preheated grill, cook over medium heat for 2 minutes on each side, remove from skewers and add over the corn.
4. Add the rest of the ingredients to the bowl, toss, divide between plates and serve for breakfast.

Nutrition: Calories 371, Fat 22, Fiber 5, Carbs 25, Protein 23

35. Tomato and Lentils Salad

Preparation Time: 10 minutes
Cooking Time: 35 minutes
Servings: 4
Ingredients:

- 2 yellow onions, chopped
- 4 garlic cloves, minced
- 2 cups brown lentils
- 1 tablespoon olive oil
- A pinch of salt and black pepper
- ½ teaspoon sweet paprika
- ½ teaspoon ginger, grated
- 3 cups water
- ¼ cup lemon juice
- ¾ cup Greek yogurt
- 3 tablespoons tomato paste

Directions:

1. Heat up a pot with the oil over medium-high heat, add the onions and sauté for 2 minutes.
2. Add the garlic and the lentils, stir and cook for 1 minute more.
3. Add the water, bring to a simmer and cook covered for 30 minutes.
4. Add the lemon juice and the remaining ingredients except for the yogurt. toss, divide the mix into bowls, top with the yogurt and serve.

Nutrition: Calories 294, Fat 3, Fiber 8, Carbs 49, Protein 21

36. Couscous and Chickpeas Bowls

Preparation Time: 10 minutes
Cooking Time: 6 minutes
Servings: 4
Ingredients:

- ¾ cup whole wheat couscous
- 1 yellow onion, chopped
- 1 tablespoon olive oil
- 1 cup water
- 2 garlic cloves, minced
- 15 ounces canned chickpeas, drained and rinsed
- A pinch of salt and black pepper

- 15 ounces canned tomatoes, chopped
- 14 ounces canned artichokes, drained and chopped
- ½ cup Greek olives, pitted and chopped
- ½ teaspoon oregano, dried
- 1 tablespoon lemon juice

Directions:

1. Put the water in a pot, bring to a boil over medium heat, add the couscous, stir, take off the heat, cover the pan, leave aside for 10 minutes and fluff with a fork.
2. Heat up a pan with the oil over medium-high heat, add the onion and sauté for 2 minutes.
3. Add the rest of the ingredients, toss and cook for 4 minutes more.
4. Add the couscous, toss, divide into bowls and serve for breakfast.

Nutrition: Calories 340, Fat 10, Fiber 9, Carbs 51, Protein 11

37. Zucchini and Quinoa Pan

Preparation Time: 10 minutes
Cooking Time: 20 minutes
Servings: 4
Ingredients:

- 1 tablespoon olive oil
- 2 garlic cloves, minced
- 1 cup quinoa
- 1 zucchini, roughly cubed
- 2 tablespoons basil, chopped
- ¼ cup green olives, pitted and chopped
- 1 tomato, cubed
- ½ cup feta cheese, crumbled
- 2 cups water
- 1 cup canned garbanzo beans, drained and rinsed
- A pinch of salt and black pepper

Directions:

1. Heat up a pan with the oil over medium-high heat, add the garlic and quinoa, and brown for 3 minutes.

2. Add the water, zucchinis, salt and pepper, toss, bring to a simmer, and cook for 15 minutes.
3. Add the rest of the ingredients, toss, divide everything between plates and serve for breakfast.

Nutrition: Calories 310, Fat 11, Fiber 6, Carbs 42, Protein 11

38. Cheesy Yogurt

Preparation Time: 4 hours and 5 minutes
Cooking Time: 0 minutes
Servings: 4
Ingredients:

- 1 cup Greek yogurt
- 1 tablespoon honey
- ½ cup feta cheese, crumbled

Directions:

1. In a blender, combine the yogurt with the honey and the cheese and pulse well.
2. Divide into bowls and freeze for 4 hours before serving for breakfast.

Nutrition: Calories 161, Fat 10, Fiber 0, Carbs 11.8, Protein 6.6

39. Baked Omelet Mix

Preparation Time: 10 minutes
Cooking Time: 45 minutes
Servings: 12
Ingredients:

- 12 eggs, whisked
- 8 ounces spinach, chopped
- 2 cups almond milk
- 12 ounces canned artichokes, chopped
- 2 garlic cloves, minced
- 5 ounces feta cheese, crumbled
- 1 tablespoon dill, chopped
- 1 teaspoon oregano, dried
- 1 teaspoon lemon pepper
- A pinch of salt
- 4 teaspoons olive oil

Directions:

1. Heat up a pan with the oil over medium-high heat, add the garlic and the spinach and sauté for 3 minutes.
2. In a baking dish, combine the eggs with the artichokes

and the rest of the ingredients.

3. Add the spinach mix as well, toss a bit, bake the mix at 375°F for 40 minutes, divide between plates and serve for breakfast.

Nutrition: Calories 186, Fat 13, Fiber 1, Carbs 5, Protein 10

40. Stuffed Sweet Potato

Preparation Time: 10 minutes
Cooking Time: 40 minutes
Servings: 8
Ingredients:

- 8 sweet potatoes, pierced with a fork
- 14 ounces canned chickpeas, drained and rinsed
- 1 small red bell pepper, chopped
- 1 tablespoon lemon zest, grated
- 2 tablespoons lemon juice
- 3 tablespoons olive oil
- 1 teaspoon garlic, minced
- 1 tablespoon oregano, chopped
- 2 tablespoons parsley, chopped
- A pinch of salt and black pepper
- 1 avocado, peeled, pitted and mashed
- ¼ cup water
- ¼ cup tahini paste

Directions:

1. Arrange the potatoes on a baking sheet lined with parchment paper, bake them at 400°F for 40 minutes, cool them down, and cut a slit down the middle in each.
2. In a bowl, combine the chickpeas with the bell pepper, lemon zest, half of the lemon juice, half of the oil, half of the garlic, oregano, half of the parsley, salt and pepper, toss and stuff the potatoes with this mix.
3. In another bowl, mix the avocado with the water, tahini, the rest of the lemon

juice, oil, garlic and parsley, whisk well and spread over the potatoes.

4. Serve cold for breakfast.

Nutrition: Calories 308, Fat 2, Fiber 8, Carbs 38, Protein 7

41. Cauliflower Fritters

Preparation Time: 10 minutes
Cooking Time: 50 minutes
Servings: 4
Ingredients:

- 30 ounces canned chickpeas, drained and rinsed
- 2½ tablespoons olive oil
- 1 small yellow onion, chopped
- 2 cups cauliflower florets chopped
- 2 tablespoons garlic, minced
- A pinch of salt and black pepper

Directions:

1. Spread half of the chickpeas on a baking sheet lined with parchment pepper, add 1 tablespoon oil, season with salt and pepper, toss and bake at 400°F for 30 minutes.
2. Transfer the chickpeas to a food processor, pulse well and put the mix into a bowl.
3. Heat up a pan with ½ tablespoon oil over medium-high heat, add the garlic and the onion and sauté for 3 minutes.
4. Add the cauliflower, cook for 6 minutes more, transfer this to a blender, add the rest of the chickpeas, pulse, pour over the crispy chickpeas mix from the bowl, stir and shape medium fritters out of this mix.
5. Heat up a pan with the rest of the oil over medium-high heat, add the fritters, cook them for 3 minutes on each side and serve for breakfast.

Nutrition: Calories 333, Fat 12.6, Fiber 12.8, Carbs 44.7, Protein 13.6

42. Veggie Quiche

Preparation Time: 6 minutes
Cooking Time: 55 minutes
Servings: 8
Ingredients:

- ½ cup sun-dried tomatoes, chopped
- 1 prepared pie crust
- 2 tablespoons avocado oil
- 1 yellow onion, chopped
- 2 garlic cloves, minced
- 2 cups spinach, chopped
- 1 red bell pepper, chopped
- ¼ cup kalamata olives, pitted and sliced
- 1 teaspoon parsley flakes
- 1 teaspoon oregano, dried
- ⅓ cup feta cheese, crumbled
- 4 eggs, whisked
- 1½ cups almond milk
- 1 cup cheddar cheese, shredded
- Salt and black pepper to the taste

Directions:

1. Heat up a pan with the oil over medium-high heat, add the garlic and onion and sauté for 3 minutes.
2. Add the bell pepper and sauté for 3 minutes more.
3. Add the olives, parsley, spinach, oregano, salt and pepper, and cook everything for 5 minutes.
4. Add tomatoes and the cheese, toss and take off the heat.
5. Arrange the pie crust in a pie plate, pour the spinach and tomatoes mix inside and spread.
6. In a bowl, mix the eggs with salt, pepper, milk and half of the cheese, whisk and pour over the mixture in the pie crust.
7. Sprinkle the remaining cheese on top and bake at 375°F for 40 minutes.
8. Cool the quiche down, slice and serve for breakfast.

Nutrition: Calories 211, Fat 14.4, Fiber 1.4, Carbs 12.5, Protein 8.6

43. Potato Hash

Preparation Time: 10 minutes
Cooking Time: 15 minutes
Servings: 4
Ingredients:

- A drizzle of olive oil
- 2 gold potatoes, cubed
- 2 garlic cloves, minced
- 1 yellow onion, chopped
- 1 cup canned chickpeas, drained
- Salt and black pepper to the taste
- 1½ teaspoons allspice, ground
- 1-pound baby asparagus, trimmed and chopped
- 1 teaspoon sweet paprika
- 1 teaspoon oregano, dried
- 1 teaspoon coriander, ground
- 2 tomatoes, cubed
- 1 cup parsley, chopped
- ½ cup feta cheese, crumbled

Directions:

1. Heat up a pan with a drizzle of oil over medium-high heat, add the potatoes, onion, garlic, salt and pepper and cook for 7 minutes.
2. Add the rest of the ingredients except the tomatoes, parsley and cheese, toss, cook for 7 more minutes and transfer to a bowl.
3. Add the remaining ingredients, toss and serve for breakfast.

Nutrition: Calories 535, Fat 20.8, Fiber 6.6, Carbs 34.5, Protein 26.6

44. Scrambled Eggs

Preparation Time: 10 minutes
Cooking Time: 10 minutes
Servings: 2
Ingredients:

- 1 yellow bell pepper, chopped
- 8 cherry tomatoes, cubed
- 2 spring onions, chopped
- 1 tablespoon olive oil
- 1 tablespoon capers, drained
- 2 tablespoons black olives, pitted and sliced
- 4 eggs
- A pinch of salt and black pepper
- ¼ teaspoon oregano, dried
- 1 tablespoon parsley, chopped

Directions:

1. Heat up a pan with the oil over medium-high heat, add the bell pepper and spring onions and sauté for 3 minutes.
2. Add the tomatoes, capers and the olives and sauté for 2 minutes more.
3. Crack the eggs into the pan, add salt, pepper and oregano, and scramble for 5 minutes more.
4. Divide the scramble between plates, sprinkle the parsley on top and serve.

Nutrition: Calories 249, Fat 17, Fiber 3.2, Carbs 13.3, Protein 13.5

45. Watermelon "Pizza"

Preparation Time: 10 minutes
Cooking Time: 0 minutes
Servings: 4
Ingredients:

- 1 watermelon slice cut 1-inch thick and then from the center cut into 4 wedges resembling pizza slices
- 6 kalamata olives, pitted and sliced
- 1-ounce feta cheese, crumbled
- ½ tablespoon balsamic vinegar
- 1 teaspoon mint, chopped

Directions:

1. Arrange the watermelon "pizza" on a plate, sprinkle the olives and the rest of the ingredients on each slice, and serve right away for breakfast.

Nutrition: Calories 90, Fat 3, Fiber 1, Carbs 14, Protein 2

46. Ham Muffins

Preparation Time: 10 minutes
Cooking Time: 15 minutes
Servings: 6
Ingredients:

- 9 ham slices
- 5 eggs, whisked
- ⅓ cup spinach, chopped
- ¼ cup feta cheese, crumbled
- ½ cup roasted red peppers, chopped
- A pinch of salt and black pepper
- 1½ tablespoons basil pesto
- Cooking spray

Directions:

1. Grease a muffin tin with cooking spray and line each muffin mold with 1½ ham slices.
2. Divide the peppers and the rest of the ingredients except the eggs, pesto, salt and pepper into the ham cups.
3. In a bowl, mix the eggs with the pesto, salt and pepper, whisk and pour over the peppers mix.
4. Bake the muffins in the oven at 400°F for 15 minutes and serve for breakfast.

Nutrition: Calories 109, Fat 6.7, Fiber 1.8, Carbs 1.8, Protein 9.3

47. Avocado Chickpea Pizza

Preparation Time: 20 minutes
Cooking Time: 20 minutes
Servings: 2
Ingredients:

- 1¼ cups chickpea flour
- A pinch of salt and black pepper
- 1¼ cups water
- 2 tablespoons olive oil
- 1 teaspoon onion powder
- 1 teaspoon garlic, minced
- 1 tomato, sliced
- 1 avocado, peeled, pitted and sliced
- 2 ounces gouda, sliced
- ¼ cup tomato sauce
- 2 tablespoons green onions, chopped

Directions:

1. In a bowl, mix the chickpea flour with salt, pepper, water, oil, onion powder and garlic, stir well until you obtain a dough, knead a bit, put in a bowl, cover and leave aside for 20 minutes.
2. Transfer the dough to a working surface, shape a bit circle, transfer it to a baking sheet lined with parchment

paper and bake at 425°F for 10 minutes.

3. Spread the tomato sauce over the pizza, also spread the rest of the ingredients, and bake at 400°F for 10 minutes more.

4. Cut and serve for breakfast.

Nutrition: Calories 416, Fat 24.5, Fiber 9.6, Carbs 36.6, Protein 15.4

48. Banana and Quinoa Casserole

Preparation Time: 10 minutes
Cooking Time: 1 hour and 20 minutes
Servings: 8
Ingredients:

- 3 cups bananas, peeled and mashed
- ¼ cup pure maple syrup
- ¼ cup molasses
- 1 tablespoon cinnamon powder
- 2 teaspoons vanilla extract
- 1 teaspoon cloves, ground
- 1 teaspoon ginger, ground
- ½ teaspoon allspice, ground
- 1 cup quinoa
- ¼ cup almonds, chopped
- 2½ cups almond milk

Directions:

1. In a baking dish, combine the bananas with the maple syrup, molasses and the rest of the ingredients, toss and bake at 350°F for 1 hour and 20 minutes.

2. Divide the mix between plates and serve for breakfast.

Nutrition: Calories 213, Fat 4.1, Fiber 4, Carbs 41, Protein 4.5

49. Avocado Spread

Preparation Time: 5 minutes
Cooking Time: 0 minutes
Servings: 8
Ingredients:

- 2 avocados, peeled, pitted and roughly chopped
- 1 tablespoon sun-dried tomatoes, chopped
- 2 tablespoons lemon juice
- 3 tablespoons cherry tomatoes, chopped
- ¼ cup red onion, chopped

- 1 teaspoon oregano, dried
- 2 tablespoons parsley, chopped
- 4 kalamata olives, pitted and chopped
- A pinch of salt and black pepper

Directions:

1. Put the avocados in a bowl and mash with a fork.

2. Add the rest of the ingredients, stir to combine and serve as a morning spread.

Nutrition: Calories 110, Fat 10, Fiber 3.8, Carbs 5.7, Protein 1.2

50. Avocado Toast

Preparation Time: 10 minutes
Cooking Time: 0 minutes
Servings: 2
Ingredients:

- 1 tablespoon goat cheese, crumbled
- 1 avocado, peeled, pitted and mashed
- A pinch of salt and black pepper
- 2 whole-wheat bread slices, toasted
- ½ teaspoon lime juice
- 1 persimmon, thinly sliced
- 1 fennel bulb, thinly sliced
- 2 teaspoons honey
- 2 tablespoons pomegranate seeds

Directions:

1. In a bowl, combine the avocado flesh with salt, pepper, lime juice and the cheese and whisk.

2. Spread this onto toasted bread slices, top each slice with the remaining ingredients and serve for breakfast.

Nutrition: Calories 348, Fat 20.8, Fiber 12.3, Carbs 38.7, Protein 7.1

51. Mini Frittatas

Preparation Time: 5 minutes
Cooking Time: 15 minutes
Servings: 12
Ingredients:

- 1 yellow onion, chopped
- 1 cup parmesan, grated
- 1 yellow bell pepper, chopped
- 1 red bell pepper, chopped
- 1 zucchini, chopped

- Salt and black pepper to the taste
- 8 eggs, whisked
- A drizzle of olive oil
- 2 tablespoons chives, chopped

Directions:

1. Heat up a pan with the oil over medium-high heat, add the onion, the zucchini and the rest of the ingredients except the eggs and chives and sauté for 5 minutes stirring often.

2. Divide this mix on the bottom of a muffin pan, pour the eggs mixture on top, sprinkle salt, pepper and the chives, and bake at 350°F for 10 minutes.

3. Serve the mini frittatas for breakfast right away.

Nutrition: Calories 55, Fat 3, Fiber 0.7, Carbs 3.2, Protein 4.2

52. Berry Oats

Preparation Time: 5 minutes
Cooking Time: 0 minutes
Servings: 2
Ingredients:

- ½ cup rolled oats
- 1 cup almond milk
- ¼ cup chia seeds
- A pinch of cinnamon powder
- 2 teaspoons honey
- 1 cup berries, pureed
- 1 tablespoon yogurt

Directions:

1. In a bowl, combine the oats with the milk and the rest of the ingredients except the yogurt, toss, divide into bowls, top with the yogurt and serve cold for breakfast.

Nutrition: Calories 420, Fat 30.3, Fiber 7.2, Carbs 35.3, Protein 6.4

53. Sun-Dried Tomatoes Oatmeal

Preparation Time: 10 minutes
Cooking Time: 25 minutes
Servings: 4
Ingredients:

- 3 cups water
- 1 cup almond milk
- 1 tablespoon olive oil
- 1 cup steel-cut oats
- ¼ cup sun-dried tomatoes, chopped

- A pinch of red pepper flakes

Directions:
1. In a pan, mix the water with the milk, bring to a boil over medium heat.
2. Meanwhile, heat up a pan with the oil over medium-high heat, add the oats, cook them for about 2 minutes and transfer m to the pan with the milk.
3. Stir the oats, add the tomatoes and simmer over medium heat for 23 minutes.
4. Divide the mix into bowls, sprinkle the red pepper flakes on top and serve for breakfast.

Nutrition: Calories 170, Fat 17.8, Fiber 1.5, Carbs 3.8, Protein 1.5

54. Quinoa Muffins

Preparation Time: 10 minutes
Cooking Time: 30 minutes
Servings: 12
Ingredients:

- 1 cup quinoa, cooked
- 6 eggs, whisked
- Salt and black pepper to the taste
- 1 cup Swiss cheese, grated
- 1 small yellow onion, chopped
- 1 cup white mushrooms, sliced
- ½ cup sun-dried tomatoes, chopped

Directions:
1. In a bowl, combine the eggs with salt, pepper and the rest of the ingredients and whisk well.
2. Divide this into a silicone muffin pan, bake at 350°F for 30 minutes and serve for breakfast.

Nutrition: Calories 123, Fat 5.6, Fiber 1.3, Carbs 10.8, Protein 7.5

55. Quinoa and Eggs Pan

Preparation Time: 10 minutes
Cooking Time: 23 minutes
Servings: 4
Ingredients:

- 4 bacon slices, cooked and crumbled
- A drizzle of olive oil

- 1 small red onion, chopped
- 1 red bell pepper, chopped
- 1 sweet potato, grated
- 1 green bell pepper, chopped
- 2 garlic cloves, minced
- 1 cup white mushrooms, sliced
- ½ cup quinoa
- 1 cup chicken stock
- 4 eggs, fried
- Salt and black pepper to the taste

Directions:
1. Heat up a pan with the oil over medium-low heat, add the onion, garlic, bell peppers, sweet potato and mushrooms, toss and sauté for 5 minutes.
2. Add the quinoa, toss and cook for 1 more minute.
3. Add the stock, salt and pepper, stir and cook for 15 minutes.
4. Divide the mix between plates, top each serving with a fried egg, sprinkle some salt, pepper and crumbled bacon, and serve for breakfast.

Nutrition: Calories 304, Fat 14, Fiber 3.8, Carbs 27.5, Protein 17.8

56. Stuffed Tomatoes

Preparation Time: 10 minutes
Cooking Time: 15 minutes
Servings: 4
Ingredients:

- 2 tablespoons olive oil
- 8 tomatoes, insides scooped
- ¼ cup almond milk
- 8 eggs
- ¼ cup parmesan, grated
- Salt and black pepper to the taste
- 4 tablespoons rosemary, chopped

Directions:
1. Grease a pan with the oil and arrange the tomatoes inside.
2. Crack an egg in each tomato, divide the milk and the rest of the ingredients, introduce the pan in the

oven and bake at 375°F for 15 minutes.
3. Serve for breakfast right away.

Nutrition: Calories 276, Fat 20.3, Fiber 4.7, Carbs 13.2, Protein 13.7

57. Sunny-Side Up Baked Eggs with Swiss Chard, Feta, and Basil

Preparation Time: 15 minutes
Cooking Time: 10 minutes
Servings: 4
Ingredients:

- 4 bell peppers, any color
- 1 tablespoon extra-virgin olive oil
- 8 large eggs
- ¾ teaspoon kosher salt, divided
- ¼ teaspoon freshly ground black pepper, divided
- 1 avocado, peeled, pitted, and diced
- ¼ cup red onion, diced
- ¼ cup fresh basil, chopped
- Juice of ½ lime

Directions:
1. Stem and seed the bell peppers. Cut 2 (2-inch-thick) rings from each pepper. Chop the remaining bell pepper into small dice and set aside.
2. Heat the olive oil in a large skillet over medium heat. Add 4 bell pepper rings, then crack 1 egg in the middle of each ring.
3. Season with ¼ teaspoon of salt and ⅛ teaspoon of black pepper. Cook until the egg whites are mostly set, but the yolks are still runny for 2 to 3 minutes.
4. Gently flip and cook for 1 additional minute for an over easy. Move the egg–bell pepper rings to a platter or onto plates and repeats with the remaining 4 bell pepper rings.
5. In a medium bowl, combine the avocado, onion, basil, lime juice, reserved diced bell pepper, the remaining ¼ teaspoon kosher salt, and the remaining ⅛ teaspoon

black pepper. Divide among the 4 plates.

Nutrition: Calories: 270 Protein: 15 g Fat: 19 g Carbs: 12 g

58. Polenta with Sautéed Chard and Fried Eggs

Preparation Time: 5 minutes
Cooking Time: 20 minutes
Servings: 4
Ingredients:

- 2½ cups water
- ½ teaspoon kosher salt
- ¾ cups whole-grain cornmeal
- ¼ teaspoon freshly ground black pepper
- 2 tablespoons grated Parmesan cheese
- 1 tablespoon extra-virgin olive oil
- 1 bunch (about 6-oz.) Swiss chard, leaves and stems chopped and separated
- 2 garlic cloves, sliced
- ¼ teaspoon kosher salt
- ⅛ teaspoon freshly ground black pepper
- Lemon juice (optional)
- 1 tablespoon extra-virgin olive oil
- 4 large eggs

Directions:

1. For the polenta, bring the water and salt to a boil in a medium saucepan over high heat. Slowly add the cornmeal, whisking constantly.
2. Decrease the heat to low, cover, and cook for 10 to 15 minutes, stirring often to avoid lumps. Stir in the pepper and Parmesan and divide among 4 bowls.
3. For the chard, heat the oil in a large skillet over medium heat. Add the chard stems, garlic, salt, and pepper; sauté for 2 minutes. Add the chard leaves and cook until wilted, about 3 to 5 minutes.
4. Add a spritz of lemon juice (if desired), toss together, and divide evenly on top of the polenta.
5. For the eggs, heat the oil in the same large skillet over medium-high heat. Crack

each egg into the skillet, taking care not to crowd the skillet and leaving space between the eggs.

6. Cook until the whites are set and golden around the edges, about 2 to 3 minutes. Serve sunny-side up or flip the eggs over carefully and cook 1 minute longer for over easy. Place one egg on top of the polenta and chard in each bowl.

Nutrition: Calories: 310 Protein: 17 g Fat: 18 g Carbs: 21 g

59. Smoked Salmon Egg Scramble with Dill and Chives

Preparation Time: 5 minutes
Cooking Time: 5 minutes
Servings: 2
Ingredients:

- 4 large eggs
- 1 tablespoon milk
- 1 tablespoon fresh chives, minced
- 1 tablespoon fresh dill, minced
- ¼ teaspoon kosher salt
- ⅛ teaspoon freshly ground black pepper
- 2 teaspoons extra-virgin olive oil
- 2 ounces smoked salmon, thinly sliced

Directions:

1. In a large bowl, whisk together the eggs, milk, chives, dill, salt, and pepper. Heat the olive oil in a medium skillet or sauté pan over medium heat.
2. Add the egg mixture and cook for about 3 minutes, stirring occasionally. Add the salmon and cook until the eggs are set but moist for about 1 minute.

Nutrition: Calories: 325 Protein: 23 g Fat: 26 g Carbs: 1 g

60. Banana Oats

Preparation Time: 10 minutes
Cooking Time: 0 minutes
Servings: 2
Ingredients:

- 1 banana, peeled and sliced
- ¾ cup almond milk
- ½ cup cold-brewed coffee

- 2 dates, pitted
- 2 tablespoons cocoa powder
- 1 cup rolled oats
- 1½ tablespoons chia seeds

Directions:

1. In a blender, combine the banana with the milk and the rest of the ingredients, pulse, divide into bowls and serve for breakfast.

Nutrition: Calories: 451 Protein: 9 g Fat: 25 g Carbs: 55 g

61. Slow-Cooked Peppers Frittata

Preparation Time: 10 minutes
Cooking Time: 3 hours
Servings: 6
Ingredients:

- ½ cup almond milk
- 8 eggs, whisked
- Salt and black pepper to the taste
- 1 teaspoon oregano, dried
- 1½ cups roasted peppers, chopped
- ½ cup red onion, chopped
- 4 cups baby arugula
- 1 cup goat cheese, crumbled
- Cooking spray

Directions:

1. In a bowl, combine the eggs with salt, pepper, and oregano and whisk. Grease your slow cooker with the cooking spray, arrange the peppers and the remaining ingredients inside and pour the egg mixture over them.
2. Put the lid on and cook on Low for 3 hours. Divide the frittata between plates and serve.

Nutrition: Calories: 259 Protein: 16 g Fat: 20 g Carbs: 4.4 g

62. Avocado and Apple Smoothie

Preparation Time: 5 minutes
Cooking Time: 0 minutes
Servings: 2
Ingredients:

- 3 cups spinach
- 1 green apple, cored and chopped
- 1 avocado, peeled, pitted and chopped

- 3 tablespoons chia seeds
- 1 teaspoon honey
- 1 banana, frozen and peeled
- 2 cups coconut water

Directions:
1. In your blender, combine the spinach with the apple and the rest of the ingredients, pulse, divide into glasses and serve.

Nutrition: Calories 168, Fat 10.1, Fiber 6, Carbs 21, Protein 2.1

63. Greek Quinoa Breakfast Bowl

Preparation Time: 15 minutes
Cooking Time: 20 minutes
Servings: 6
Ingredients:

- 12 eggs
- ¼ cup plain Greek yogurt
- 1 teaspoon onion powder
- 1 teaspoon granulated garlic
- ½ teaspoon salt
- ½ teaspoon pepper
- 1 teaspoon olive oil
- 1 (5-oz.) bag baby spinach
- 1-pint cherry tomatoes, halved
- 1 cup feta cheese
- 2 cups cooked quinoa

Directions:
1. In a large bowl whisk together eggs, Greek yogurt, onion powder, granulated garlic, salt, and pepper, set aside.
2. In a large skillet, heat olive oil and add spinach, cook the spinach until it is slightly wilted, about 3-4 minutes.
3. Add in cherry tomatoes, cook until tomatoes are softened, 3-4 minutes. Stir in egg mixture and cook until the eggs are set, about 7-9 minutes, stir in the eggs as they cook to scramble.
4. Once the eggs have set stir in the feta and quinoa, cook until heated through. Distribute evenly among the containers, store for 2-3 days.

Nutrition: Calories: 357 Carbohydrates: 8 g Fat: 20 g Protein: 23 g

64. Mushroom Goat Cheese Frittata

Preparation Time: 15 minutes
Cooking Time: 35 minutes
Servings: 4
Ingredients:

- 1 tablespoon olive oil
- 1 small onion, diced
- 10 ounces cremini or your favorite mushrooms, sliced
- 1 garlic clove, minced
- 10 eggs
- 2/3 cup half and half
- ¼ cup fresh chives, minced
- 2 teaspoon fresh thyme, minced
- ½ teaspoon kosher salt
- ½ teaspoon black pepper
- 4 ounces goat cheese

Directions:
1. Preheat the oven to 375°F. In an oven-safe skillet or cast-iron pan over medium heat, olive oil. Add in the onion and sauté for 3-5 mins until golden.
2. Add in the sliced mushrooms and garlic, continue to sauté until mushrooms are golden brown, about 10-12 minutes.
3. In a large bowl, whisk together the eggs, half and half, chives, thyme, salt and pepper. Place the goat cheese over the mushroom mixture and pour the egg mixture over the top.
4. Stir the MIXTURE in the pan and cook over medium heat until the edges are set but the center is still loose, about 8-10 minutes
5. Put the pan in the oven and finish cooking for an additional 8-10 minutes or until set. Allow to cool completely before slicing.

Nutrition: Calories: 243 Carbohydrates: 5 g Fat: 17 g Protein: 15 g

65. Mediterranean Frittata

Preparation Time: 8 minutes
Cooking Time: 6 minutes
Servings: 4
Ingredients:

- 2 teaspoons of olive oil
- ¾ cup of baby spinach, packed
- 2 green onions
- 4 white eggs, large
- 6 large eggs
- ⅓ cup of crumbled feta cheese, (1.3-oz.) along with sun-dried tomatoes and basil
- 2 teaspoons of salt-free Greek seasoning
- ¼ teaspoon of salt

Directions:
1. Take a boiler and preheat it. Take a ten-inch ovenproof skillet and pour the oil into it and keep the skillet on a medium flame.
2. While the oil gets heated, chop the spinach roughly and the onions. Put the eggs, egg whites, Greek seasoning, cheese, as well as salt in a large mixing bowl and mix it thoroughly using a whisker.
3. Add the chopped spinach and onions into the mixing bowl and stir it well.
4. Pour the mixture into the pan and cook it for 2 minutes or more until the edges of the mixture set well.
5. Lift the edges of the mixture gently and tilt the pan so that the uncooked portion can get underneath it. Cook for another two minutes so that the whole mixture gets cooked properly.
6. Broil for two to three minutes till the center gets set. Your Frittata is now ready. Serve it hot by cutting it into four wedges.

Nutrition: Calories: 178 Protein: 16 g Fat: 12 g Carbs: 2.2 g

66. Honey-Caramelized Figs with Greek Yogurt

Preparation Time: 5 minutes
Cooking Time: 5 minutes
Servings: 4
Ingredients:

- 4 fresh halved figs
- 2 tablespoons of melted butter, 30ml
- 2 tablespoons of brown sugar, 30ml
- 2 cups of Greek yogurt 500ml
- ¼ cup of honey, 60ml

Directions:

1. Take a non-stick skillet and preheat it over a medium flame. Put the butter on the pan and toss the figs into it and sprinkle in some brown sugar over it.
2. Put the figs on the pan and cut off the side of the figs. Cook the figs on a medium flame for 2-3 minutes until they turn a golden brown.
3. Turn over the figs and cook them for 2-3 minutes again. Remove the figs from the pan and let it cool down a little.
4. Take a plate and put a scoop of Greek yogurt on it. Put the cooked figs over the yogurts and drizzle the honey over it

Nutrition: Calories: 350 Protein: 6 g Fat: 19 g Carbs: 40 g

67. Savory Quinoa Egg Muffins with Spinach

Preparation Time: 15 minutes
Cooking Time: 20 minutes
Servings: 2
Ingredients:

- 1 cup of quinoa
- 2 cups of water/ vegetable broth
- 4 ounces of spinach which is about one cup
- ½ chopped onion
- 2 whole eggs
- ¼ cup of grated cheese
- ½ teaspoon of oregano or thyme
- ½ teaspoon of garlic powder
- ½ teaspoon of salt

Directions:

1. Take a medium saucepan and put water in it. Add the quinoa to the water and bring the whole thing to a simmer.
2. Cover the pan and cook it for 10 minutes till the water gets absorbed by the quinoa. Remove the saucepan from the heat and let it cool down.
3. Take a nonstick pan and heat the onions till they turn soft and then add spinach. Cook all of them together till the spinach gets a little wilted and then remove it from the heat.
4. Preheat the oven to 176°C. Take a muffin pan and grease it lightly.
5. Take a large bowl and add the cooked quinoa along with the cooked onions, spinach, and add cheese, eggs, thyme or oregano, salt, garlic powder, pepper and mix them together.
6. Put a spoonful of the mixture into a muffin tin. Make sure it is ¼ of a cup. In the preheated pan, put it in the pan and bake it for around 20 minutes.

Nutrition: Calories: 61 Protein: 4 g Fat: 3 g Carbs: 6 g

68. Avocado Tomato Gouda Socca Pizza

Preparation Time: 20 minutes
Cooking Time: 20 minutes
Servings: 2
Ingredients:

- 1¼ cups of chickpea or garbanzo bean flour
- 1¼ cups of cold water
- ¼ teaspoon of pepper and sea salt each
- 2 teaspoons of avocado or olive oil + 1 teaspoon extra for heating the pan
- 1 teaspoon of minced garlic which will be around two cloves
- 1 teaspoon of onion powder/other herb seasoning powder
- 10 to 12-inch cast iron pan
- 1 sliced tomato
- ½ avocado
- 2 ounces of thinly sliced Gouda
- ¼-⅓ cup of tomato sauce
- 2 or 3 teaspoons of chopped green scallion/onion
- Sprouted greens for green
- Extra pepper/salt for sprinkling on top of the pizza
- Red pepper flakes

Directions:

1. Mix the flour with two teaspoons of olive oil, herbs, water, and whisk it until a smooth mixture form. Keep it at room temperature for around 15-20 minutes to let the batter settle.
2. In the meantime, preheat the oven and place the pan inside the oven and let it get heated for around 10 minutes. When the pan gets preheated, chop up the vegetables into fine slices.
3. Remove the pan after ten minutes using oven mitts. Put one teaspoon of oil and swirl it all around to coat the pan.
4. Pour the batter into the pan and tilt the pan so that the batter spreads evenly throughout the pan. Turn down the oven to 425°F and place back the pan for 5-8 minutes.
5. Remove the pan from the oven and add the sliced avocado, tomato and on top of that, add the gouda slices and the onion slices.
6. Put the pizza back into the oven and wait till the cheese gets melted or the sides of the bread get crusty and brown.
7. Remove the pizza from the pan and add the microgreens on top, along with the toppings.

Nutrition: Calories: 416 Protein: 15 g Fat: 10 g Carbs: 37 g

69. Shakshuka With Feta

Preparation Time: 15 minutes
Cooking Time: 41 minutes
Servings: 4-6
Ingredients:

- 6 large eggs
- 3 tablespoons extra-virgin olive oil
- 1 large onion, halved and thinly sliced
- 1 large red bell pepper, seeded and thinly sliced
- 3 garlic cloves, thinly sliced
- 1 teaspoon ground cumin
- 1 teaspoon sweet paprika
- ⅛ teaspoons cayenne, or to taste
- 1 (28-oz.) can whole plum tomatoes with juices, coarsely chopped
- ¾ teaspoon salt, more as needed
- ¼ teaspoon black pepper, more as needed
- 5 ounces feta cheese, crumbled, about 1¼ cups

To Serve:

- Chopped cilantro
- Hot sauce

Directions:

1. Preheat oven to 375°F. In a large skillet over medium-low heat, add the oil. Once heated, add the onion and bell pepper, cook gently until very soft, about 20 minutes.
2. Add in the garlic and cook until tender, 1 to 2 minutes, then stir in cumin, paprika and cayenne, and cook 1 minute.
3. Pour in tomatoes, season with ¾ teaspoon salt and ¼ teaspoon pepper, simmer until tomatoes have thickened, about 10 minutes. Then stir in crumbled feta.
4. Gently crack eggs into skillet over tomatoes, season with salt and pepper. Transfer skillet to oven. Bake until eggs have just set, 7 to 10 minutes. Serve.

Nutrition: Calories: 337 Carbs: 17 g Fat: 25 g Protein: 12 g

70. Peanut Butter Banana Greek Yogurt

Preparation Time: 15 minutes
Cooking Time: 0 minutes
Servings: 4
Ingredients:

- 3 cups vanilla Greek yogurt
- 2 medium bananas sliced
- ¼ cup creamy natural peanut butter
- ¼ cup flaxseed meal
- 1 teaspoon nutmeg

Directions:

1. Divide yogurt between four jars with lids. Top with banana slices.
2. In a bowl, melt the peanut butter in a microwave-safe bowl for 30-40 seconds and drizzle one tbsp on each bowl on top of the bananas. Store in the fridge for up to 3 days.
3. When ready to serve, sprinkle with flaxseed meal and ground nutmeg. Enjoy!

Nutrition: Calories: 370 Carbs: 47 g Fat: 10 g Protein: 22 g

71. Veggie Mediterranean Quiche

Preparation Time: 15 minutes
Cooking Time: 55 minutes
Servings: 8
Ingredients:

- ½ cup sundried tomatoes - dry or in olive oil
- Boiling water
- 1 prepared pie crust
- 2 tablespoons vegan butter
- 1 onion, diced
- 2 cloves garlic, minced
- 1 red pepper, diced
- ¼ cup sliced Kalamata olives
- 1 teaspoon dried oregano
- 1 teaspoon dried parsley
- ⅓ cup crumbled feta cheese
- 4 large eggs
- 1¼ cups milk
- 2 cups fresh spinach or ½ cup frozen spinach, thawed and squeezed dry
- Salt, to taste
- Pepper, to taste
- 1 cup shredded cheddar cheese, divided

Directions:

1. If you're using dry sundried tomatoes - In a measuring cup, add the sundried tomatoes and pour the boiling water over until just covered, allow to sit for 5 minutes or until the tomatoes are soft. The drain and chop tomatoes, set aside.
2. Preheat oven to 375°F. Fit a 9-inch pie plate with the prepared pie crust, then flute edges, and set aside. In a skillet over medium-high heat, melt the butter.
3. Add in the onion and garlic, and cook until fragrant and tender, about 3 minutes. Add in the red pepper, cook for an additional 3 minutes, or until the peppers are just tender.
4. Add in the spinach, olives, oregano, and parsley, cook until the spinach is wilted (if you're using fresh) or heated through (if you're using frozen), about 5 minutes.
5. Remove the pan from heat, stir in the feta cheese and tomatoes, spoon the mixture into the prepared pie crust, spreading out evenly, set aside.
6. In a medium-sized mixing bowl, whisk together the eggs, ½ cup of the cheddar cheese, milk, salt, and pepper. Pour this egg and cheese mixture evenly over the spinach mixture in the pie crust.
7. Sprinkle top with the remaining cheddar cheese. Bake for 50-55 minutes, or until the crust is golden brown and the egg is set. Allow to cool completely before slicing.

Nutrition: Calories: 239 Carbs: 19 g Fat: 15 g Protein: 7 g

72. Spinach, Feta and Egg Breakfast Quesadillas

Preparation Time: 15 minutes
Cooking Time: 15 minutes
Servings: 5
Ingredients:

- 8 eggs (optional)
- 2 teaspoons olive oil
- 1 red bell pepper
- ½ red onion
- ¼ cup milk
- 4 handfuls of spinach leaves
- 1½ cup mozzarella cheese
- 5 sun-dried tomato tortillas
- ½ cup feta
- ¼ teaspoon salt
- ¼ teaspoon pepper
- Spray oil

Directions:

1. In a large non-stick pan over medium heat, add the olive oil. Once heated, add the bell pepper and onion, cook for 4-5 minutes until soft.
2. In the meantime, whisk together the eggs, milk, salt and pepper in a bowl. Add in the egg/milk mixture into the pan with peppers and onions, stirring frequently, until eggs are almost cooked through.
3. Add in the spinach and feta, fold into the eggs, stirring until spinach is wilted and eggs are cooked through. Remove the eggs from heat and plate.
4. Spray a separate large non-stick pan with spray oil, and place over medium heat. Add the tortilla, on one half of the tortilla, spread about ½ cup of the egg mixture.
5. Top the eggs with around ⅓ cup of shredded mozzarella cheese. Fold the second half of the tortilla over, then cook for 2 minutes, or until golden brown.
6. Flip and cook for another minute until golden brown. Allow the quesadilla to cool completely, divide among the container, store for 2

days or wrap in plastic wrap and foil, and freeze for up to 2 months.

Nutrition: Calories: 213 Fat: 11 g Carbs: 15 g Protein: 15 g

73. Mediterranean Quinoa and Feta Egg Muffins

Preparation Time: 15 minutes
Cooking Time: 30 minutes
Servings: 12
Ingredients:

- 8 eggs
- 1 cup cooked quinoa
- 1 cup crumbled feta cheese
- ¼ teaspoon salt
- 2 cups baby spinach finely chopped
- ½ cup finely chopped onion
- 1 cup chopped or sliced tomatoes, cherry or grape tomatoes
- ½ cup chopped and pitted Kalamata olives
- 1 tablespoon chopped fresh oregano
- 2 teaspoons high oleic sunflower oil plus optional extra for greasing muffin tins

Directions:

1. Preheat oven to 350°F. Prepare 12 silicone muffin holders on a baking sheet or grease a 12-cup muffin tin with oil, set aside.
2. In a skillet over medium heat, add the vegetable oil and onions, sauté for 2 minutes. Add tomatoes, sauté for another minute, then add spinach and sauté until wilted, about 1 minute.
3. Remove from heat and stir in olives and oregano, set aside. Place the eggs in a blender or mixing bowl and blend or mix until well combined.
4. Pour the eggs into a mixing bowl (if you used a blender) then add quinoa, feta cheese, veggie mixture, and salt, and stir until well combined.
5. Pour mixture into silicone cups or greased muffin tins, dividing equally, and bake

for 30 minutes, or until eggs have set and muffins are a light golden brown. Allow to cool completely.

Nutrition: Calories: 113 Carbohydrates: 5 g Fat: 7 g Protein: 6 g

74. Green Shakshuka

Preparation Time: 15 minutes
Cooking Time: 15 minutes
Servings: 2
Ingredients:

- 1 tablespoon olive oil
- 1 onion, peeled and diced
- 1 clove garlic, peeled and finely minced
- 3 cups broccoli rabe, chopped
- 3 cups baby spinach leaves
- 2 tablespoons whole milk or cream
- 1 teaspoon ground cumin
- ¼ teaspoon black pepper
- ¼ teaspoon salt (or to taste)
- 4 Eggs

Garnish:

- 1 pinch sea salt
- 1 pinch red pepper flakes

Directions:

1. Preheat the oven to 350°F. Add the broccoli rabe to a large pot of boiling water, cook for 2 minutes, drain and set aside.
2. In a large oven-proof skillet or cast-iron pan over medium heat, add in the tablespoon of olive oil along with the diced onions, cook for about 10 minutes or until the onions become translucent.
3. Add the minced garlic and continue cooking for about another minute. Cut the par-cooked broccoli rabe into small pieces, stir into the onion and garlic mixture.
4. Cook for a couple of minutes, then stir in the baby spinach leaves, continue to cook for a couple more minutes, stirring often, until the spinach begins to wilt. Stir in the ground cumin, salt,

ground black pepper, and milk.

5. Make four wells in the mixture, crack an egg into each well – be careful not to break the yolks. Also, note that it's easier to crack each egg into a small bowl and then transfer them to the pan.

6. Place the pan with the eggs into the pre-heated oven, cook for 10 to 15 minutes until the eggs are set to preference. Sprinkle the cooked eggs with a dash of sea salt and a pinch of red pepper flakes.

Nutrition: Calories: 278 Carbs: 18 g Fat: 16 g Protein: 16 g

75. Apple Quinoa Breakfast Bars

Preparation Time: 15 minutes
Cooking Time: 40 minutes
Servings: 12
Ingredients:

- 2 eggs
- 1 apple peeled and chopped into ½ inch chunks
- 1 cup unsweetened apple sauce
- 1½ cups cooked & cooled quinoa
- 1½ cups rolled oats
- ¼ cup peanut butter
- 1 teaspoon vanilla
- ½ teaspoon cinnamon
- ¼ cup coconut oil
- ½ teaspoon baking powder

Directions:

1. Heat oven to 350°F. Spray an 8x8 inch baking dish with oil, set aside. In a large bowl, stir together the apple sauce, cinnamon, coconut oil, peanut butter, vanilla and eggs.

2. Add in the cooked quinoa, rolled oats and baking powder, mix until completely incorporated. Fold in the apple chunks.

3. Spread the mixture into the prepared baking dish, spreading it to each corner. Bake for 40 minutes, or until a toothpick comes out

clean. Allow to cool before slicing.

Nutrition: Calories: 230 Fat: 10 g Carbs: 31 g Protein: 7 g

76. Blueberries Quinoa

Preparation Time: 5 minutes
Cooking Time: 0 minutes
Servings: 4
Ingredients:

- 2 cups almond milk
- 2 cups quinoa, already cooked
- ½ teaspoon cinnamon powder
- 1 tablespoon honey
- 1 cup blueberries
- ¼ cup walnuts, chopped

Directions:

1. In a bowl, mix the quinoa with the milk and the rest of the ingredients, toss, divide into smaller bowls and serve for breakfast.

Nutrition: Calories 284 Fat: 14.3 g Carbs: 15.4 g Protein: 4.4 g

77. Endives, Fennel and Orange Salad

Preparation Time: 5 minutes
Cooking Time: 0 minutes
Servings: 4
Ingredients:

- 1 tablespoon balsamic vinegar
- 2 garlic cloves, minced
- 1 teaspoon Dijon mustard
- 2 tablespoons olive oil
- 1 tablespoon lemon juice
- Sea salt and black pepper to taste
- ½ cup black olives, pitted and chopped
- 1 tablespoon parsley, chopped
- 7 cups baby spinach
- 2 endives, shredded
- 3 medium navel oranges, peeled and cut into segments
- 2 bulbs fennel, shredded

Directions:

1. In a salad bowl, combine the spinach with the endives, oranges, fennel, and the rest of the

ingredients, toss and serve for breakfast.

Nutrition: Calories 97 Fat: 9.1 g Carbs: 3.7 g Protein: 1.9 g

78. Raspberries and Yogurt Smoothie

Preparation Time: 5 minutes
Cooking Time: 0 minutes
Servings: 2
Ingredients:

- 2 cups raspberries
- ½ cup Greek yogurt
- ½ cup almond milk
- ½ teaspoon vanilla extract

Directions:

1. In your blender, combine the raspberries with the milk, vanilla, and the yogurt, pulse well, divide into 2 glasses and serve for breakfast.

Nutrition: Calories 245 Fat: 9.5 g Carbs: 5.6 g Protein: 1.6 g

79. Homemade Muesli

Preparation Time: 15 minutes
Cooking Time: 20 minutes
Servings: 8
Ingredients:

- 3½ cups rolled oats
- ½ cup wheat bran
- ½ teaspoon kosher salt
- ½ teaspoon ground cinnamon
- ½ cup sliced almonds
- ¼ cup raw pecans, coarsely chopped
- ¼ cup raw pepitas (shelled pumpkin seeds)
- ½ cup unsweetened coconut flakes
- ¼ cup dried apricots, coarsely chopped
- ¼ cup dried cherries

Directions:

1. Take a medium bowl and combine the oats, wheat bran, salt, and cinnamon. Stir well. Place the mixture onto a baking sheet.

2. Next place the almonds, pecans, and pepitas onto another baking sheet and toss. Pop both trays into the oven and heat to 350°F. Bake for 10-12 minutes.

Remove from the oven and pop to one side.

3. Leave the nuts to cool but take the one with the oats, sprinkle with the coconut, and pop back into the oven for 5 minutes more. Remove and leave to cool.

4. Find a large bowl and combine the contents of both trays then stir well to combine. Throw in the apricots and cherries and stir well. Pop into an airtight container until required.

Nutrition: Calories 250 Fat: 10 g Carbs: 36 g Protein: 7 g

80. Tangerine and Pomegranate Breakfast Fruit Salad

Preparation Time: 15 minutes
Cooking Time: 40 minutes
Servings: 5
Ingredients:
For the grains:
- 1 cup pearl or hulled barley
- 3 cups of water
- 3 tablespoons olive oil, divided
- ½ teaspoon kosher salt

For the fruit:
- ½ large pineapple, peeled and cut into 1½" chunks
- 6 tangerines
- 1¼ cups pomegranate seeds
- 1 small bunch of fresh mint

For the dressing:
- ⅓ cup honey
- Juice and finely grated zest of 1 lemon
- Juice and finely grated zest of 2 limes
- ½ teaspoon kosher salt
- ¼ cup olive oil
- ¼ cup toasted hazelnut oil (olive oil is fine too)

Directions:
1. Place the grain into a strainer and rinse well. Grab 2 baking sheets, line with paper, and add the grain. Spread well to cover then leave to dry.

2. Next, place the water into a saucepan and pop over medium heat. Place a skillet over medium heat, add 2 tablespoons of the oil then add the barley. Toast for 2 minutes.

3. Add the water and salt and bring to a boil. Reduce to simmer and cook for 40 minutes until most of the liquid has been absorbed. Turn off the heat and leave to stand for 10 minutes to steam cook the rest.

4. Meanwhile, grab a medium bowl and add the honey, juices, zest, and salt, and stir well. Add the olive oil then nut oil and stir again. Pop until the fridge until needed.

5. Remove the lid from the barley then place it onto another prepared baking sheet and leave to cool. Drizzle with oil and leave to cool completely then pop into the fridge.

6. When ready to serve, divide the grains, pineapple, orange, pomegranate, and mint between the bowls. Drizzle with the dressing then serve and enjoy.

Nutrition: Calories 400 Fat: 23 g Carbs: 50 g Protein: 3 g

81. Hummus and Tomato Breakfast Pittas

Preparation Time: 5 minutes
Cooking Time: 10 minutes
Servings: 4
Ingredients:
- 4 large eggs, at room temperature
- Salt, to taste
- 2 whole-wheat pita bread with pockets, cut in half
- ½ cup hummus
- 1 medium cucumber, thinly sliced into rounds
- 2 medium tomatoes, large dice
- A handful of fresh parsley leaves, coarsely chopped
- Freshly ground black pepper
- Hot sauce (optional)

Directions:
1. Grab a large saucepan, fill with water, and pop over medium heat until it boils. Add the eggs and cook for 7 minutes.

2. Immediately drain the water and place the eggs under cool water until they cool down. Pop to one side until you can handle them comfortably.

3. Peel the eggs and cut them into ¼" slices, sprinkle with salt, and pop to one side.

4. Grab a pitta pocket and spread with hummus, fill with cucumber and tomato, season well then add an egg. Sprinkle with parsley and hot sauce then serve and enjoy.

Nutrition: Calories 377 Fat: 31 g Carbs: 17 g Protein: 11 g

82. Baked Ricotta & Pears

Preparation Time: 15 minutes
Cooking Time: 30 minutes
Servings: 4
Ingredients:
- ¼ cup White whole wheat flour
- 1 tablespoon Sugar
- ¼ teaspoon Nutmeg
- Ricotta cheese
- 16 ounces container whole-milk
- 2 large eggs
- 1 diced pear
- 2 tablespoons Water
- 1 teaspoon Vanilla extract
- 1 tablespoon Honey
- Also Needed: 4 - 6 ounces ramekins

Directions:
1. Warm the oven to 400°F. Lightly spritz the ramekins with a cooking oil spray. Whisk the flour, nutmeg, sugar, vanilla, eggs, and ricotta together in a large mixing container.

2. Spoon the fixings into the dishes. Bake them for 20 to 25 minutes or until they're firm and set. Transfer them to the countertop and wait for them to cool.

3. In a saucepan, using the medium temperature setting, toss the cored and

diced pear into the water for about ten minutes until it's slightly softened.

4. Take the pan from the burner and stir in the honey. Serve the ricotta ramekins with the warm pear when it's ready.

Nutrition: Calories 312 Protein: 17 g Carbs: 0 g Fat: 17 g

83. Crumbled Feta and Scallions

Preparation Time: 5 minutes
Cooking Time: 15 minutes
Servings: 12
Ingredients:

- 2 tablespoons of unsalted butter (replace with canola oil for full effect)
- ½ cup of chopped up scallions
- 1 cup of crumbled feta cheese
- 8 large-sized eggs
- 2/3 cup of milk
- ½ teaspoon of dried Italian seasoning
- Salt as needed
- Freshly ground black pepper as needed
- Cooking oil spray

Directions:

1. Preheat your oven to 400°F. Take a 3-4-ounce muffin pan and grease with cooking oil. Take a non-stick pan and place it over medium heat.
2. Add butter and allow the butter to melt. Add half of the scallions and stir fry. Keep them to the side. Take a medium-sized bowl and add eggs, Italian seasoning and milk and whisk well.
3. Add the stir-fried scallions and feta cheese and mix. Season with pepper and salt. Pour the mix into the muffin tin. Transfer the muffin tin to your oven and bake for 15 minutes. Serve with a sprinkle of scallions.

Nutrition: Calories: 106 Fat: 8 g Carbohydrates: 2 g Protein: 7 g

84. Gnocchi Ham Olives

Preparation Time: 5 minutes
Cooking Time: 15 minutes

Servings: 4
Ingredients:

- 2 tablespoons of olive oil
- 1 medium-sized onion chopped up
- 3 minced cloves of garlic
- 1 medium-sized red pepper completely deseeded and finely chopped
- 1 cup of tomato puree
- 2 tablespoons of tomato paste
- 1 pound of gnocchi
- 1 cup of coarsely chopped turkey ham
- ½ cup of sliced pitted olives
- 1 teaspoon of Italian seasoning
- Salt as needed
- Freshly ground black pepper
- Bunch of fresh basil leaves

Directions:

1. Take a medium-sized sauce pan and place over medium-high heat. Pour some olive oil and heat it up. Toss in the bell pepper, onion and garlic and sauté for 2 minutes.
2. Pour in the tomato puree, gnocchi, tomato paste and add the turkey ham, Italian seasoning and olives. Simmer the whole mix for 15 minutes, making sure to stir from time to time.
3. Season the mix with some pepper and salt. Once done, transfer the mix to a dish and garnish with some basil leaves. Serve hot and have fun.

Nutrition: Calories: 335 Fat: 12 g Carbohydrates: 45 g Protein: 15 g

85. Spicy Early Morning Seafood Risotto

Preparation Time: 5 minutes
Cooking Time: 25 minutes
Servings: 4
Ingredients:

- 3 cups of clam juice
- 2 cups of water
- 2 tablespoons of olive oil
- 1 medium-sized chopped up onion
- 2 minced cloves of garlic

- 1½ cups of Arborio Rice
- ½ cup of dry white wine
- 1 teaspoon of Saffron
- ½ teaspoon of ground cumin
- ½ teaspoon of paprika
- 1 pound of marinara seafood mix
- Salt as needed
- Ground pepper as needed

Directions:

1. Place a saucepan over high heat and pour in your clam juice with water and bring the mixture to a boil. Remove the heat.
2. Take a heavy bottomed saucepan and stir fry your garlic and onion in oil over medium heat until a nice fragrance comes off.
3. Add in the rice and keep stirring for 2-3 minutes until the rice has been fully covered with the oil. Pour the wine and then add the saffron.
4. Keep stirring constantly until it is fully absorbed. Add in the cumin, clam juice, paprika mixture 1 cup at a time, making sure to keep stirring it from time to time.
5. Cook the rice for 20 minutes until perfect. Finally, add the seafood marinara mix and cook for another 5-7 minutes.
6. Season with some pepper and salt. Transfer the meal to a serving dish. Serve hot.

Nutrition: Calories: 386 Fat: 7 g Carbohydrates: 55 g Protein: 21 g

86. Rocket Tomatoes and Mushroom Frittata

Preparation Time: 5 minutes
Cooking Time: 30 minutes
Servings: 4
Ingredients:

- 2 tablespoons of butter (replace with canola oil for full effect)
- 1 chopped up medium-sized onion
- 2 minced cloves of garlic
- 1 cup of coarsely chopped baby rocket tomato

- 1 cup of sliced button mushrooms
- 6 large pieces of eggs
- ½ cup of skim milk
- 1 teaspoon of dried rosemary
- Salt as needed
- Ground black pepper as needed

Directions:

1. Preheat your oven to 400°F. Take a large oven-proof pan and place it over medium-heat. Heat up some oil.
2. Stir fry your garlic, onion for about 2 minutes. Add the mushroom, rosemary and rockets and cook for 3 minutes. Take a medium-sized bowl and beat your eggs alongside the milk.
3. Season it with some salt and pepper. Pour the egg mixture into your pan with the vegetables and sprinkle some Parmesan.
4. Reduce the heat to low and cover with the lid. Let it cook for 3 minutes. Transfer the pan into your oven and bake for 10 minutes until fully settled.
5. Reduce the heat to low and cover with your lid. Let it cook for 3 minutes. Transfer the pan into your oven and then bake for another 10 minutes. Serve hot.

Nutrition: Calories: 189 Fat: 13 g Carbohydrates: 6 g Protein: 12 g

87.   Cheesy Olives Bread

Preparation Time: 1 hour and 40 minutes
Cooking Time: 30 minutes
Servings: 10
Ingredients:

- 4 cups whole-wheat flour
- 3 tablespoons oregano, chopped
- 2 teaspoons dry yeast
- ¼ cup olive oil
- 1½ cups black olives, pitted and sliced
- 1 cup of water

- ½ cup feta cheese, crumbled

Directions:

1. In a bowl, mix the flour with the water, the yeast, and the oil. Stir and knead your dough very well. Put the dough in a bowl, cover with plastic wrap, and keep in a warm place for 1 hour.
2. Divide the dough into 2 bowls and stretch each ball well. Add the rest of the ingredients to each ball and tuck them inside. Knead the dough well again.
3. Flatten the balls a bit and leave them aside for 40 minutes more. Transfer the balls to a baking sheet lined with parchment paper, make a small slit in each, and bake at 425°F for 30 minutes.
4. Serve the bread as a Mediterranean breakfast.

Nutrition: Calories 251 Fat: 7.3 g Carbs: 39.7 g Protein: 6.7 g

88.   Sweet Potato Tart

Preparation Time: 10 minutes
Cooking Time: 1 hour and 10 minutes
Servings: 8
Ingredients:

- 2 pounds sweet potatoes, peeled and cubed
- ¼ cup olive oil + a drizzle
- 7 ounces feta cheese, crumbled
- 1 yellow onion, chopped
- 2 eggs, whisked
- ¼ cup almond milk
- 1 tablespoon herbs de Provence
- A pinch of salt and black pepper
- 6 phyllo sheets
- 1 tablespoon parmesan, grated

Directions:

1. In a bowl, combine the potatoes with half of the oil, salt, and pepper, toss, spread on a baking sheet lined with parchment paper, and roast at 400°F for 25 minutes.

2. Meanwhile, heat a pan with half of the remaining oil over medium heat, add the onion, and sauté for 5 minutes.
3. In a bowl, combine the eggs with the milk, feta, herbs, salt, pepper, onion, sweet potatoes, and the rest of the oil and toss.
4. Arrange the phyllo sheets in a tart pan and brush them with a drizzle of oil. Add the sweet potato mix and spread it well into the pan.
5. Sprinkle the parmesan on top and bake covered with tin foil at 350°F for 20 minutes. Remove the tin foil, bake the tart for 20 minutes more, cool it down, slice, and serve for breakfast.

Nutrition: Calories 476 Fat: 16.8 g Carbs: 68.8 g Protein: 13.9 g

89.   Full Eggs in a Squash

Preparation Time: 15 minutes
Cooking Time: 30 minutes
Servings: 5
Ingredients:

- 2 acorn squash
- 6 whole eggs
- 2 tablespoons extra-virgin olive oil
- Salt and pepper as needed
- 5-6 pitted dates
- 8 walnut halves
- A fresh bunch of parsley

Directions:

1. Preheat your oven to 375°F. Slice squash crosswise and prepare 3 slices with holes. While slicing the squash, make sure that each slice has a measurement of ¾ inch thickness.
2. Remove the seeds from the slices. Take a baking sheet and line it with parchment paper. Transfer the slices to your baking sheet and season them with salt and pepper.
3. Bake in your oven for 20 minutes. Chop the walnuts and dates on your cutting board. Take the baking dish

out of the oven and drizzle slices with olive oil.

4. Crack an egg into each of the holes in the slices and season with pepper and salt. Sprinkle the chopped walnuts on top. Bake for 10 minutes more. Garnish with parsley and add maple syrup.

Nutrition: Calories: 198 Fat: 12 g Carbohydrates: 17 g Protein: 8 g

90. Barley Porridge

Preparation Time: 5 minutes
Cooking Time: 25 minutes
Servings: 4
Ingredients:

- 1 cup barley
- 1 cup wheat berries
- 2 cups unsweetened almond milk
- 2 cups water
- ½ cup blueberries
- ½ cup pomegranate seeds
- ½ cup hazelnuts, toasted and chopped
- ¼ cup honey

Directions:

1. Take a medium saucepan and place it over medium-high heat. Place barley, almond milk, wheat berries, water and bring to a boil. Reduce the heat to low and simmer for 25 minutes.

2. Divide amongst serving bowls and top each serving with 2 tablespoons blueberries, 2 tablespoons pomegranate seeds, 2 tablespoons hazelnuts, 1 tablespoon honey. Serve and enjoy!

Nutrition: Calories: 295 Fat: 8 g Carbohydrates: 56 g Protein: 6 g

91. Tomato and Dill Frittata

Preparation Time: 5 minutes
Cooking Time: 10 minutes
Servings: 4
Ingredients:

- 2 tablespoons olive oil
- 1 medium onion, chopped
- 1 teaspoon garlic, minced
- 2 medium tomatoes, chopped

- 6 large eggs
- ½ cup half and half
- ½ cup feta cheese, crumbled
- ¼ cup dill weed
- Salt as needed
- Ground black pepper as needed

Directions:

1. Preheat your oven to a temperature of 400°F. Take a large-sized ovenproof pan and heat up your olive oil over medium-high heat. Toss in the onion, garlic, tomatoes and stir fry them for 4 minutes.

2. While they are being cooked, take a bowl and beat together your eggs, half and half cream and season the mix with some pepper and salt.

3. Pour the mixture into the pan with your vegetables and top it with crumbled feta cheese and dill weed. Cover it with the lid and let it cook for 3 minutes.

4. Place the pan inside your oven and let it bake for 10 minutes. Serve hot.

Nutrition: Calories: 191 Fat: 15 g Carbohydrates: 6 g Protein: 9 g

92. Strawberry and Rhubarb Smoothie

Preparation Time: 5 minutes
Cooking Time: 3 minutes
Servings: 1
Ingredients:

- 1 rhubarb stalk, chopped
- 1 cup fresh strawberries, sliced
- ½ cup plain Greek strawberries
- Pinch of ground cinnamon
- 3 ice cubes

Directions:

1. Take a small saucepan and fill with water over high heat. Bring to boil and add rhubarb, boil for 3 minutes. Drain and transfer to the blender.

2. Add strawberries, honey, yogurt, cinnamon and pulse

mixture until smooth. Add ice cubes and blend until thick with no lumps. Pour into glass and enjoy chilled.

Nutrition: Calories: 295 Fat: 8 g Carbohydrates: 56 g Protein: 6 g

93. Bacon and Brie Omelet Wedges

Preparation Time: 10 minutes
Cooking Time: 10 minutes
Servings: 6
Ingredients:

- 2 tablespoons olive oil
- 7 ounces smoked bacon
- 6 beaten eggs
- Small bunch chives, snipped
- 3½ ounces brie, sliced
- 1 teaspoon red wine vinegar
- 1 teaspoon Dijon mustard
- 1 cucumber, halved, deseeded and sliced diagonally
- 7 ounces radish, quartered

Directions:

1. Turn your grill on and set it to high. Take a small-sized pan and add 1 teaspoon of oil, allow the oil to heat up. Add lardons and fry until crisp. Drain the lardon on kitchen paper.

2. Take another non-stick cast iron frying pan and place it over the grill, heat 2 teaspoons of oil. Add lardons, eggs, chives, ground pepper to the frying pan. Cook on low until they are semi-set.

3. Carefully lay brie on top and grill until the Brie sets and is a golden texture. Remove it from the pan and cut up into wedges.

4. Take a small bowl and create dressing by mixing olive oil, mustard, vinegar and seasoning. Add cucumber to the bowl and mix, serve alongside the omelet wedges.

Nutrition: Calories: 35 Fat: 31 g Carbohydrates: 3 g Protein: 25 g

94. Coconut Porridge

Preparation Time: 15 minutes

Cooking Time: 0 minutes
Servings: 6
Ingredients:

- Powdered erythritol as needed
- 1½ cups almond milk, unsweetened
- 2 tablespoons vanilla protein powder
- 3 tablespoons Golden Flaxseed meal
- 2 tablespoons coconut flour

Directions:

1. Take a bowl and mix in flaxseed meal, protein powder, coconut flour and mix well. Add mix to the saucepan (placed over medium heat).
2. Add almond milk and stir, let the mixture thicken. Add your desired amount of sweetener and serve. Enjoy!

Nutrition: Calories: 259 Fat: 13 g Carbohydrates: 5 g Protein: 16 g

95. Mediterranean Feta and Quinoa Egg Muffins

Preparation Time: 15 minutes
Cooking Time: 30 minutes
Servings: 12
Ingredients:

- 2 cups baby spinach finely chopped
- 1 cup chopped or sliced cherry tomatoes
- ½ cup finely chopped onion
- 1 tablespoon chopped fresh oregano
- 1 cup crumbled feta cheese
- ½ cup chopped {pitted} kalamata olives
- 2 teaspoons high oleic sunflower oil
- 1 cup cooked quinoa
- 8 eggs
- ¼ teaspoon salt

Directions:

1. Preheat oven to 350°F, and then prepare 12 silicone muffin holders on the baking sheet, or just grease a 12-cup muffin tin with oil and set aside.

2. Finely chop the vegetables and then heat the skillet to medium. After that, add the vegetable oil and onions and sauté for 2 minutes.
3. Then, add tomatoes and sauté for another minute, then add spinach and sauté until wilted, about 1 minute.
4. Place the beaten egg into a bowl and then add lots of vegetables like feta cheese, quinoa, veggie mixture as well as salt, and then stir well until everything is properly combined.
5. Pour the ready mixture into greased muffin tins or silicone cups, dividing the mixture equally. Then, bake it in an oven for 30 minutes or so.

Nutrition: Calories: 113 Protein: 6 g Fat: 7 g Carbs: 5 g

96. Mediterranean Eggs

Preparation Time: 15 minutes
Cooking Time: 20 minutes
Servings: 2
Ingredients:

- 5 tablespoons of divided olive oil
- 2 diced medium-sized Spanish onions
- 2 diced red bell peppers
- 2 minced cloves garlic
- 1 teaspoon cumin seeds
- 4 diced large ripe tomatoes
- 1 tablespoon of honey
- Salt
- Freshly ground black pepper
- ⅓ cup crumbled feta
- 4 eggs
- 1 teaspoon zaatar spice
- Grilled pita during serving

Directions:

1. Add 3 tablespoons of olive oil into a pan and heat it over medium heat. Along with the oil, sauté the cumin seeds, onions, garlic, and red pepper for a few minutes.
2. After that, add the diced tomatoes and salt and pepper to taste and cook them for about 10 minutes

till they come together and form a light sauce.
3. With that, half the preparation is already done. Now you just have to break the eggs directly into the sauce and poach them.
4. However, you must keep in mind to cook the egg whites but keep the yolks still runny. This takes about 8 to 10 minutes.
5. While plating adds some feta and olive oil with za'atar spice to further enhance the flavors. Once done, serve with grilled pita.

Nutrition: Calories: 304 Protein: 12 g Fat: 16 g Carbs: 28 g

97. Pastry-Less Spanakopita

Preparation Time: 5 minutes
Cooking Time: 20 minutes
Servings: 4
Ingredients:

- ⅛ teaspoons black pepper, add as per taste
- ⅓ cup of Extra-virgin olive oil
- 4 lightly beaten eggs
- 7 cups of Lettuce, preferably a spring mix (mesclun)
- ½ cup of crumbled Feta cheese
- ⅛ teaspoon of Sea salt, add to taste
- 1 finely chopped medium yellow onion

Directions:

1. Warm the oven to 180°C and grease the flan dish. Once done, pour the extra-virgin olive oil into a large saucepan and heat it over medium heat with the onions, until they are translucent.
2. Add greens and keep stirring until all the ingredients are wilted. Season it with salt and pepper and transfer the greens to the prepared dish and sprinkle on some feta cheese.

3. Pour the eggs and bake it for 20 minutes till it is cooked through and slightly brown.

Nutrition: Calories: 325 Protein: 11.2 g Fat: 27.9 g Carbs: 7.3 g

98. Date and Walnut Overnight Oats

Preparation Time: 5 minutes
Cooking Time: 20 minutes
Servings: 2
Ingredients:

- ¼ cup Greek yogurt, plain
- ⅓ cup of yogurt
- 2/3 cup of oats
- 1 cup of milk
- 2 teaspoons date syrup or you can also use maple syrup or honey
- 1 mashed banana
- ¼ teaspoon cinnamon
- ¼ cup walnuts
- pinch of salt (approx. ⅛ teaspoon)

Directions:

1. Firstly, get a mason jar or a small bowl and add all the ingredients. After that stir and mix all the ingredients well. Cover it securely, and cool it in a refrigerator overnight.
2. After that, take it out the next morning, add more liquid or cinnamon if required, and serve cold. (However, you can also microwave it for people with a warmer palate.)

Nutrition: Calories: 350 Protein: 14 g Fat: 12 g Carbs: 49 g

99. Pear and Mango Smoothie

Preparation Time: 5 minutes
Cooking Time: 0 minutes
Servings: 1
Ingredients:

- 1 ripe mango, cored and chopped
- ½ mango, peeled, pitted and chopped
- 1 cup kale, chopped
- ½ cup plain Greek yogurt
- 2 ice cubes

Directions:

1. Add pear, mango, yogurt, kale, and mango to a blender and puree. Add ice and blend until you have a smooth texture. Serve and enjoy!

Nutrition: Calories: 293 Fat: 8 g Carbohydrates: 53 g Protein: 8 g

100. Artichoke Frittata

Preparation Time: 5 minutes
Cooking Time: 10 minutes
Servings: 4
Ingredients:

- 8 large eggs
- ¼ cup Asiago cheese, grated
- 1 tablespoon fresh basil, chopped
- 1 teaspoon fresh oregano, chopped
- Pinch of salt
- 1 teaspoon extra-virgin olive oil
- 1 teaspoon garlic, minced
- 1 cup canned artichokes, drained
- 1 tomato, chopped

Directions:

1. Preheat your oven to broil. Take a medium bowl and whisk in eggs, Asiago cheese, oregano, basil, sea salt and pepper. Blend in a bowl.
2. Place a large ovenproof skillet over medium-high heat and add olive oil. Add garlic and sauté for 1 minute. Remove the skillet from heat and pour in the egg mix.
3. Return skillet to heat and sprinkle artichoke hearts and tomato over eggs. Cook frittata without stirring for 8 minutes.
4. Place skillet under the broiler for 1 minute until the top is lightly browned. Cut frittata into 4 pieces and serve. Enjoy!

Nutrition: Calories: 199 Fat: 13 g Carbohydrates: 5 g Protein: 16 g

101. Feta Frittata

Preparation Time: 15 minutes

Cooking Time: 25 minutes
Servings: 2
Ingredients:

- 1 small clove garlic
- 1 green onion
- 2 large eggs
- ½ cup egg substitute
- 4 tablespoons crumbled feta cheese - divided
- ⅓ cup plum tomato
- 4 thin avocado slices
- 2 tablespoons reduced-fat sour cream
- Also Needed: 6-inch skillet

Directions:

1. Thinly slice/mince the onion, garlic, and tomato. Peel the avocado before slicing. Heat the pan using the medium temperature setting and spritz it with cooking oil.
2. Whisk the egg substitute, eggs, and feta cheese. Add the egg mixture into the pan. Cover and simmer for four to six minutes.
3. Sprinkle it using the rest of the feta cheese and tomato. Cover and continue cooking until the eggs are set or about two to three more minutes.
4. Wait for about five minutes before cutting it into halves. Serve with avocado and sour cream.

Nutrition: Calories: 460 Carbs: 8 g Fat: 37 g Protein: 24 g

102. Smoked Salmon and Poached Eggs on Toast

Preparation Time: 10 minutes
Cooking Time: 4 minutes
Servings: 4
Ingredients:

- 2 ounces avocado smashed
- 2 slices of bread toasted
- Pinch of kosher salt and cracked black pepper
- ¼ teaspoon freshly squeezed lemon juice
- 2 eggs see notes, poached
- 3.5 ounces smoked salmon

- 1 tablespoon thinly sliced scallions
- Splash of Kikkoman soy sauce optional
- Microgreens are optional

Directions:

1. Take a small bowl and then smash the avocado into it. Then, add the lemon juice and also a pinch of salt into the mixture. Then, mix it well and set aside.
2. After that, poach the eggs and toast the bread for some time. Once the bread is toasted, you will have to spread the avocado on both slices and after that, add the smoked salmon to each slice.
3. Thereafter, carefully transfer the poached eggs to the respective toasts. Add a splash of Kikkoman soy sauce and some cracked pepper; then, just garnish with scallions and microgreens.

Nutrition: Calories: 459 Protein: 31 g Fat: 22 g Carbs: 33 g

103. Honey Almond Ricotta Spread with Peaches

Preparation Time: 5 minutes
Cooking Time: 8 minutes
Servings: 4
Ingredients:

- ½ cup Fisher Sliced Almonds
- 1 cup whole milk ricotta
- ¼ teaspoon almond extract
- zest from an orange, optional
- 1 teaspoon honey
- hearty whole-grain toast
- English muffin or bagel
- extra Fisher sliced almonds
- sliced peaches
- extra honey for drizzling

Directions:

1. Cut peaches into a proper shape and then brush them with olive oil. After that, set it aside. Take a bowl; combine the ingredients for the filling. Set aside.

2. Then just preheat the grill to medium. Place peaches cut side down onto the greased grill. Close lid cover and then just grill until the peaches have softened, approximately 6-10 minutes, depending on the size of the peaches.
3. Then you will have to place peach halves onto a serving plate. Put a spoon of about 1 tablespoon of ricotta mixture into the cavity (you are also allowed to use a small scooper).
4. Sprinkle it with slivered almonds, crushed amaretti cookies, and honey. Decorate with the mint leaves.

Nutrition: Calories: 187 Protein: 7 g Fat: 9 g Carbs: 18 g

104. Mediterranean Eggs Cups

Preparation Time: 10 minutes
Cooking Time: 20 minutes
Servings: 8
Ingredients:

- 1 cup spinach, finely diced
- ½ yellow onion, finely diced
- ½ cup sliced sun-dried tomatoes
- 4 large basil leaves, finely diced
- Pepper and salt to taste
- ⅓ cup feta cheese crumbles
- 8 large eggs
- ¼ cup milk (any kind)

Directions:

1. Warm the oven to 375°F. Then, roll the dough sheet into a 12x8-inch rectangle. Then, cut in half lengthwise.
2. After that, you will have to cut each half crosswise into 4 pieces, forming 8 (4x3-inch) pieces of dough. Then, press each into the bottom and up sides of the ungreased muffin cup.
3. Trim dough to keep the dough from touching, if essential. Set aside. Then, you will have to combine the eggs, salt, pepper in the bowl and beat it with a

whisk until well mixed. Set aside.
4. Melt the butter in a 12-inch skillet over medium heat until sizzling; add bell peppers. You will have to cook it, stirring occasionally, 2-3 minutes or until crisply tender.
5. After that, add spinach leaves; continue cooking until spinach is wilted. Then just add egg mixture and prosciutto.
6. Divide the mixture evenly among prepared muffin cups. Finally, bake it for 14-17 minutes or until the crust is golden brown.

Nutrition: Calories: 240 Protein: 9 g Fat: 16 g Carbs: 13 g

105. Low-Carb Baked Eggs with Avocado and Feta

Preparation Time: 10 minutes
Cooking Time: 15 minutes
Servings: 2
Ingredients:

- 1 avocado
- 4 eggs
- 2-3 tablespoons crumbled feta cheese
- Nonstick cooking spray
- Pepper and salt to taste

Directions:

1. First, you will have to preheat the oven to 400°F. After that, when the oven is at the proper temperature, you will have to put the gratin dishes right on the baking sheet.
2. Then, leave the dishes to heat in the oven for almost 10 minutes After that process, you need to break the eggs into individual ramekins.
3. Then, let the avocado and eggs come to room temperature for at least 10 minutes. Then, peel the avocado properly and cut it each half into 6-8 slices.
4. You will have to remove the dishes from the oven and spray them with non-stick spray. Then, you will have to arrange all the sliced

avocados in the dishes and tip two eggs into each dish. Sprinkle with feta, add pepper and salt to taste, serve.

Nutrition: Calories: 280 Protein: 11 g Fat: 23 g Carbs: 10 g

106. Mediterranean Eggs White Breakfast Sandwich with Roasted Tomatoes

Preparation Time: 15 minutes
Cooking Time: 25 minutes
Servings: 2
Ingredients:

- Salt and pepper to taste
- ¼ cup egg whites
- 1 teaspoon chopped fresh herbs like rosemary, basil, parsley,
- 1 whole-grain seeded ciabatta roll
- 1 teaspoon butter
- 1-2 slices Muenster cheese
- 1 tablespoon pesto
- About ½ cup roasted tomatoes
- 10 ounces grape tomatoes
- 1 tablespoon extra-virgin olive oil
- Black pepper and salt to taste

Directions:

1. First, you will have to melt the butter over medium heat in the small nonstick skillet. Then, mix the egg whites with pepper and salt.
2. Then, sprinkle it with fresh herbs. After that cook it for almost 3-4 minutes or until the eggs are done, then flip it carefully.
3. Meanwhile, toast ciabatta bread in the toaster. Place the egg on the bottom half of the sandwich rolls, then top with cheese
4. Add roasted tomatoes and the top half of the roll. To make a roasted tomato, preheat the oven to 400°F. Then, slice the tomatoes in half lengthwise.
5. Place on the baking sheet and drizzle with olive oil. Season it with pepper and salt and then roast in the

oven for about 20 minutes. Skins will appear wrinkled when done.

Nutrition: Calories: 458 Protein: 21 g Fat: 24 g Carbs: 51 g

107. Greek Yogurt Pancakes

Preparation Time: 10 minutes
Cooking Time: 5 minutes
Servings: 2
Ingredients:

- 1 cup all-purpose flour
- 1 cup whole-wheat flour
- ¼ teaspoon salt
- 4 teaspoons baking powder
- 1 tablespoon sugar
- 1½ cups unsweetened almond milk
- 2 teaspoons vanilla extract
- 2 large eggs
- ½ cup plain 2% Greek yogurt
- Fruit, for serving
- Maple syrup, for serving

Directions:

1. First, you will have to pour the curds into the bowl and mix them well until creamy. After that, you will have to add egg whites and mix them well until combined.
2. Then take a separate bowl, pour the wet mixture into the dry mixture. Stir to combine. The batter will be extremely thick.
3. Then, simply spoon the batter onto the sprayed pan heated too medium-high. The batter must make 4 large pancakes.
4. Then, you will have to flip the pancakes once when they start to bubble a bit on the surface. Cook until golden brown on both sides.

Nutrition: Calories: 166 Protein: 14 g Fat: 5 g Carbs: 52 g

108. Feta & Quinoa Egg Muffins

Preparation Time: 20 minutes
Cooking Time: 30 minutes
Servings: 12
Ingredients:

- 1 cup cooked quinoa
- 2 cups baby spinach, chopped
- ½ cup Kalamata olives
- 1 cup tomatoes

- ½ cup white onion
- 1 tablespoon fresh oregano
- ½ teaspoon salt
- 2 teaspoons. + more for coating pans olive oil
- 8 eggs
- 1 cup crumbled feta cheese
- Also Needed: 12-cup muffin tin

Directions:

1. Heat the oven to reach 350°F. Lightly grease the muffin tray cups with a spritz of cooking oil.
2. Prepare a skillet using the medium temperature setting and add the oil. When it's hot, toss in the onions to sauté for two minutes.
3. Dump the tomatoes into the skillet and sauté for one minute. Fold in the spinach and continue cooking until the leaves have wilted (1-minute).
4. Transfer the pot to the countertop and add the oregano and olives. Set it aside.
5. Crack the eggs into a mixing bowl, using an immersion stick blender to mix them thoroughly. Add the cooked veggies in with the rest of the fixings.
6. Stir until it's combined and scoop the mixture into the greased muffin cups. Set the timer to bake the muffins for 30 minutes until browned, and the muffins are set. Cool for about ten minutes. Serve.

Nutrition: Calories: 295 Carbs: 3 g Fat: 23 g Protein: 19 g

109. 5-Minute Heirloom Tomato & Cucumber Toast

Preparation Time: 10 minutes
Cooking Time: 6-10 minutes
Servings: 1
Ingredients:

- 1 small Heirloom tomato
- 1 Persian cucumber
- 1 teaspoon olive oil
- 1 pinch oregano

- Kosher salt and pepper as desired
- 2 teaspoons low-fat whipped cream cheese
- 2 pieces trader Joe's whole grain crispbread or your choice
- 1 teaspoon balsamic glaze

Directions:
1. Dice the cucumber and tomato. Combine all the fixings except for the cream cheese. Smear the cheese on the bread and add the mixture. Top it off with the balsamic glaze and serve.

Nutrition: Calories: 239 Carbs: 32 g Fat: 11 g Protein: 7 g

110. Greek Yogurt with Walnuts and Honey

Preparation Time: 5 Minutes
Cooking Time: 0 minutes
Servings: 4
Ingredients:
- 4 cups Greek yogurt, fat-free, plain or vanilla
- ½ cup California walnuts, toasted, chopped
- 3 tablespoons honey or agave nectar
- Fresh fruit, chopped or granola, low-fat (both optional)

Directions:
1. Spoon yogurt into 4 individual cups. Sprinkle 2 tablespoons of walnuts over each and drizzle 2 teaspoons of honey over each. Top with fruit or granola, whichever is preferred.

Nutrition: Calories 300 Fat: 10 g Carbs: 25 g Protein: 29 g

111. Tahini Pine Nuts Toast

Preparation Time: 5 minutes
Cooking Time: 0 minutes
Servings: 2
Ingredients:
- 2 whole-wheat bread slices, toasted
- 1 teaspoon water
- 1 tablespoon tahini paste
- 2 teaspoons feta cheese, crumbled
- Juice of ½ lemon

- 2 teaspoons pine nuts
- A pinch of black pepper

Directions:
1. In a bowl, mix the tahini with the water and the lemon juice, whisk well, and spread over the toasted bread slices. Top each serving with the remaining ingredients and serve for breakfast.

Nutrition: Calories 142 Fat: 7.6 g Carbs: 13.7 g Protein: 5.8 g

112. Feta - Avocado & Mashed Chickpea Toast

Preparation Time: 10 minutes
Cooking Time: 15 minutes
Servings: 4
Ingredients:
- 15 ounces can Chickpeas
- 2 ounces - ½ cup diced feta cheese
- 1 pitted avocado

Fresh juice:
- 2 teaspoons lemon (or 1 tablespoon orange)
- ½ teaspoon Black pepper
- 2 teaspoons honey
- 4 slices Multigrain toast

Directions:
1. Toast the bread. Drain the chickpeas in a colander. Scoop the avocado flesh into the bowl. Use a large fork/potato masher to mash them until the mix is spreadable.
2. Pour in the lemon juice, pepper, and feta. Combine and divide onto the four slices of toast. Drizzle using the honey and serve.

Nutrition: Calories: 337 Carbs: 43 g Fat: 13 g Protein: 13 g

113. Mango Pear Smoothie

Preparation Time: 5 minutes
Cooking Time: 0 minute
Servings: 1
Ingredients:
- 2 ice cubes
- ½ cup Greek yogurt, plain
- ½ mango, peeled, pitted & chopped
- 1 cup kale, chopped

- 1 pear, ripe, cored & chopped

Directions:
1. Take all ingredients and place them in your blender. Blend together until thick and smooth. Serve.

Nutrition: Calories 350 Protein 40 g Fats 12 g Carbohydrates: 11 g

114. Mediterranean Smoothie

Preparation Time: 5 minutes
Cooking Time: 5 minutes
Servings: 2
Ingredients:
- 2 cups of baby spinach
- 1 teaspoon fresh ginger root
- 1 frozen banana, pre-sliced
- 1 small mango
- ½ cup beet juice
- ½ cup of skim milk
- 4-6 ice cubes

Directions:
1. Take all ingredients and place them in your blender. Blend together until thick and smooth. Serve.

Nutrition: Calories: 168 Protein: 4 g Fat: 1 g Carbohydrates: 39 g

115. Fruit Smoothie

Preparation Time: 5 minutes
Cooking Time: 0 minutes
Servings: 2
Ingredients:
- 2 cups blueberries (or any fresh or frozen fruit, cut into pieces if the fruit is large)
- 2 cups unsweetened almond milk
- 1 cup crushed ice
- ½ teaspoon ground ginger (or other dried ground spice such as turmeric, cinnamon, or nutmeg)

Directions:
1. In a blender, combine the blueberries, almond milk, ice, and ginger. Blend until smooth.

Nutrition: Calories: 125 Protein: 2 g Carbohydrates: 23 g Fat: 4 g

116. Strawberry-Rhubarb Smoothie

Preparation Time: 5 minutes
Cooking Time: 3 minutes
Servings: 1
Ingredients:

- 1 rhubarb stalk, chopped
- 1 cup sliced fresh strawberries
- ½ cup plain Greek yogurt
- 2 tablespoons honey
- Pinch ground cinnamon
- 3 ice cubes

Directions:

1. Place a small saucepan filled with water over high heat and bring to a boil. Add the rhubarb and boil for 3 minutes. Drain and transfer the rhubarb to a blender.
2. Add the strawberries, yogurt, honey, and cinnamon and pulse the mixture until it is smooth. Add the ice and blend until thick, with no ice lumps remaining. Pour the smoothie into a glass and enjoy cold.

Nutrition: Calories: 295 Fat: 8 g Carbohydrates: 56 g Protein: 6 g

117. Chia-Pomegranate Smoothie

Preparation Time: 5 minutes
Cooking Time: 0 minutes
Servings: 2
Ingredients:

- 1 cup pure pomegranate juice (no sugar added)
- 1 cup frozen berries
- 1 cup coarsely chopped kale
- 2 tablespoons chia seeds
- 3 Medjool dates, pitted and coarsely chopped
- Pinch ground cinnamon

Directions:

1. In a blender, combine the pomegranate juice, berries, kale, chia seeds, dates, and cinnamon and pulse until smooth. Pour into glasses and serve.

Nutrition: Calories: 275 Fat: 5 g Carbohydrates: 59 g Protein: 5 g

118. Egg White Scramble with Cherry Tomatoes & Spinach

Preparation Time: 5 minutes
Cooking Time: 8-10 minutes
Servings: 4
Ingredients:

- 1 tablespoon olive oil
- 1 whole egg
- 10 white eggs
- ¼ teaspoon black pepper
- ½ teaspoon salt
- 1 garlic clove, minced
- 2 cups cherry tomatoes, halved
- 2 cups packed fresh baby spinach
- ½ cup light cream or Half & Half
- ¼ cup finely grated parmesan cheese

Directions:

1. Whisk the eggs, pepper, salt, and milk. Prepare a skillet using the med-high temperature setting. Toss in the garlic when the pan is hot to sauté for approximately 30 seconds.
2. Pour in the tomatoes and spinach and continue to sauté it for one additional minute. The tomatoes should be softened, and the spinach wilted.
3. Add the egg mixture into the pan using the medium heat setting. Fold the egg gently as it cooks for about two to three minutes. Remove from the burner, and sprinkle with a sprinkle of cheese.

Nutrition: Calories 142 Protein: 15 g Fat: 2 g Carbs 4 g

119. Blueberry, Hazelnut, and Lemon Breakfast Grain Salad

Preparation Time: 5 minutes
Cooking Time: 10 minutes
Servings: 8
Ingredients:

- 1 cup steel-cut oats
- 1 cup dry golden quinoa
- ½ cup dry millet
- 3 tablespoons olive oil, divided
- ¾ teaspoon salt
- 1 x 1" piece fresh ginger, peeled and cut into coins
- 2 large lemons, zest and juice
- ½ cup maple syrup
- 1 cup Greek yogurt
- ¼ tsp nutmeg
- 2 cups hazelnuts, roughly chopped and toasted
- 2 cups blueberries or mixed berries
- 4½ cups water

Directions:

1. Grab a mesh strainer and add the oats, quinoa, and millet. Wash well then pop to one side. Find a 3-quart saucepan, add a tbsp of the oil, and pop over medium heat.
2. Add the grains and cook for 2-3 minutes to toast. Pour in the water, salt, ginger coins, and lemon zest. Bring to the boil then cover and turn down the heat. Leave to simmer for 20 minutes.
3. Turn off the heat and leave to sit for five minutes. Fluff with a fork, remove the ginger then leave to cool for at least an hour. Grab a large bowl and add the grains.
4. Take a medium bowl and add the remaining olive oil, lemon juice, maple syrup, yogurt, and nutmeg. Whisk well to combine. Pour this over the grains and stir well.
5. Add the hazelnuts and blueberries, stir again then pop into the fridge overnight. Serve and enjoy.

Nutrition: Calories 363 Fat: 11 g Carbs: 60 g Protein: 7 g

120. Blueberry Greek Yogurt Pancakes

Preparation Time: 15 minutes
Cooking Time: 15 minutes
Servings: 6
Ingredients:

- 1¼ cup all-purpose flour

- 2 teaspoons baking powder
- 1 teaspoon baking soda
- ¼ teaspoon salt
- ¼ cup sugar
- 3 eggs
- 3 tablespoons vegan butter unsalted, melted
- ½ cup milk
- 1½ cups Greek yogurt plain, non-fat
- ½ cup blueberries optional

Toppings:
- Greek yogurt
- Mixed berries – blueberries, raspberries and blackberries

Directions:
1. In a large bowl, whisk together the flour, salt, baking powder and baking soda. In a separate bowl, whisk together butter, sugar, eggs, Greek yogurt, and milk until the mixture is smooth.
2. Then add in the Greek yogurt mixture from step to the dry mixture in step 1, mix to combine, allow the batter to sit for 20 minutes to get a smooth texture – if using blueberries fold them into the pancake batter.
3. Heat the pancake griddle, spray with non-stick butter spray or just brush with butter. Pour the batter, in ¼ cupfuls, onto the griddle.
4. Cook until the bubbles on top burst and create small holes, lift up the corners of the pancake to see if they're golden browned on the bottom
5. With a wide spatula, flip the pancake and cook on the other side until lightly browned. Serve.

Nutrition: Calories: 258
Carbohydrates: 33 g Fat: 8 g Protein: 11 g

121. Mediterranean Breakfast Egg White Sandwich

Preparation Time: 15 minutes
Cooking Time: 30 minutes
Servings: 1
Ingredients:
- 1 teaspoon vegan butter
- ¼ cup egg whites
- 1 teaspoon chopped fresh herbs such as parsley, basil, rosemary
- 1 whole-grain seeded ciabatta roll
- 1 tablespoon pesto
- 1-2 slices muenster cheese (or other cheese such as provolone, Monterey Jack, etc.)
- About ½ cup roasted tomatoes
- Salt, to taste
- Pepper, to taste

Roasted Tomatoes:
- 10 ounces grape tomatoes
- 1 tablespoon extra-virgin olive oil
- Kosher salt, to taste
- Coarse black pepper, to taste

Directions:
1. In a small nonstick skillet over medium heat, melt the vegan butter. Pour in egg whites, season with salt and pepper, sprinkle with fresh herbs, cook for 3-4 minutes or until egg is done, flip once.
2. In the meantime, toast the ciabatta bread in the toaster. Once done, spread both halves with pesto.
3. Place the egg on the bottom half of the sandwich roll, folding, if necessary, top with cheese, add the roasted tomatoes, and top half of roll sandwich.
4. For the roasted tomatoes, preheat the oven to 400°F. Slice tomatoes in half lengthwise. Then place them onto a baking sheet and drizzle with the olive oil, toss to coat.
5. Season with salt and pepper and roast in the oven for about 20 minutes, until the skin appears wrinkled

Nutrition: Calories: 458
Carbohydrates: 51g Fat: 0g Protein: 21g

Chapter 3. Salads

122. Tuna Salad
Preparation Time: 10 minutes
Cooking Time: 0 minutes
Servings: 2
Ingredients:
- 12 ounces canned tuna in water, drained and flaked
- ¼ cup roasted red peppers, chopped
- 2 tablespoons capers, drained
- 8 kalamata olives, pitted and sliced
- 2 tablespoons olive oil
- 1 tablespoon parsley, chopped
- 1 tablespoon lemon juice
- A pinch of salt and black pepper

Directions:
1. In a bowl, combine the tuna with roasted peppers and the rest of the ingredients, toss, divide between plates and serve for breakfast.

Nutrition: Calories 250, Fat 17.3, Fiber 0.8, Carbs 2.7, Protein 10.1

123. Veggie Salad
Preparation Time: 5 minutes
Cooking Time: 0 minutes
Servings: 4
Ingredients:
- 2 tomatoes, cut into wedges
- 2 red bell peppers, chopped
- 1 cucumber, chopped
- 1 red onion, sliced
- ½ cup kalamata olives, pitted and sliced
- 2 ounces feta cheese, crumbled
- ¼ cup lime juice
- ½ cup olive oil
- 2 garlic cloves, minced
- 1 tablespoon oregano, chopped
- Salt and black pepper to the taste

Directions:
1. In a large salad bowl, combine the tomatoes with the peppers and the rest of the ingredients except the cheese and toss.
2. Divide the salad into smaller bowls, sprinkle the cheese on top and serve for breakfast.

Nutrition: Calories 327, Fat 11.2, Fiber 4.4, Carbs 16.7, Protein 6.4

124. Salmon and Bulgur Salad
Preparation Time: 25 minutes
Cooking Time: 30 minutes
Servings: 4
Ingredients:
- 1-pound salmon fillet, skinless and boneless
- 1 tablespoon olive oil
- 1 cup bulgur
- 1 cup parsley, chopped
- ¼ cup mint, chopped
- 3 tablespoons lemon juice
- 1 red onion, sliced
- Salt and black pepper to the taste
- 2 cup hot water

Directions:
1. Heat up a pan with half of the oil over medium heat, add the salmon, some salt and pepper, cook for 5 minutes on each side, cool down, flake and put in a salad bowl.
2. In another bowl, mix the bulgur with hot water, cover, leave aside for 25 minutes, drain and transfer to the bowl with the salmon.
3. Add the rest of the ingredients, toss and serve for breakfast.

Nutrition: Calories 321, Fat 11.3, Fiber 7.9, Carbs 30.8, Protein 27.6

125. Herbed Quinoa and Asparagus
Preparation Time: 10 minutes
Cooking Time: 0 minutes
Servings: 4
Ingredients:
- 3 cups asparagus, steamed and roughly chopped
- 1 tablespoon olive oil
- 3 tablespoons balsamic vinegar
- 1 and ¾ cups quinoa, cooked
- 2 teaspoons mustard
- Salt and black pepper to the taste
- 5 ounces baby spinach
- ½ cup parsley, chopped
- 1 tablespoon thyme, chopped
- 1 tablespoon tarragon, chopped

Directions:
1. In a salad bowl, combine the asparagus with the quinoa, spinach and the rest of the ingredients, toss and keep in the fridge for 10 minutes before serving for breakfast.

Nutrition: Calories 323, Fat 11.3, Fiber 3.4, Carbs 16.4, Protein 10

126. Potato and Pancetta Bowls
Preparation Time: 10 minutes
Cooking Time: 15 minutes
Servings: 4
Ingredients:
- 1-pound sweet potatoes, peeled and cut into small wedges
- 1 red onion, chopped
- 3 ounces pancetta, chopped
- 2 garlic cloves, minced
- 2 tablespoons olive oil
- 2 eggs, whisked
- 2 ounces goat cheese, crumbled
- 1 tablespoon parsley, chopped
- A pinch of salt and black pepper

Directions:
1. Put potatoes in a pot, add water to cover, add salt and pepper, bring to a boil over medium heat, simmer for 15 minutes, drain and put them in a bowl.
2. Heat up a pan with half of the oil over medium heat,

add the onion, the potatoes, the eggs and the rest of the ingredients, toss and cook for 15 minutes.

3. Divide between plates and serve for breakfast.

Nutrition: calories

127. Quinoa Salad
Preparation Time: 5 minutes
Cooking Time: 0 minutes
Servings: 4
Ingredients:

- 4 eggs, soft boiled, peeled and cut into wedges
- 2 cups baby arugula
- 2 cups cherry tomatoes, halved
- 1 cucumber, sliced
- 1 cup quinoa, cooked
- 1 cup almonds, chopped
- 1 avocado, peeled, pitted and sliced
- 1 tablespoon olive oil
- ½ cup mixed dill and mint, chopped
- A pinch of salt and black pepper
- Juice of 1 lemon

Directions:

1. In a large salad bowl, combine the eggs with the arugula and the rest of the ingredients, toss, divide between plates and serve for breakfast.

Nutrition: Calories 519, Fat 32.4, Fiber 11, Carbs 43.3, Protein 19.1

128. Corn Salad
Preparation Time: 10 minutes
Cooking Time: 10 minutes
Servings: 4
Ingredients:

- 4 ears of sweet corn, husked
- 1 avocado, peeled, pitted and chopped
- ½ cup basil, chopped
- A pinch of salt and black pepper
- 1-pound shrimp, peeled and deveined
- 1½ cups cherry tomatoes, halved
- ¼ cup olive oil

Directions:

1. Put the corn in a pot, add water to cover, bring to a boil over medium heat, cook for 6 minutes, drain, cool down, cut corn from the cob and put it in a bowl.
2. Thread the shrimp onto skewers and brush with some of the oil.
3. Place the skewers on the preheated grill, cook over medium heat for 2 minutes on each side, remove from skewers and add over the corn.
4. Add the rest of the ingredients to the bowl, toss, divide between plates and serve for breakfast.

Nutrition: calories 371

129. Brown Lentils Salad
Preparation Time: 10 minutes
Cooking Time: 35 minutes
Servings: 4
Ingredients:

- 2 yellow onions, chopped
- 4 garlic cloves, minced
- 2 cups brown lentils
- 1 tablespoon olive oil
- A pinch of salt and black pepper
- ½ teaspoon sweet paprika
- ½ teaspoon ginger, grated
- 3 cups water
- ¼ cup lemon juice
- ¾ cup Greek yogurt
- 3 tablespoons tomato paste

Directions:

1. Heat up a pot with the oil over medium-high heat, add the onions and sauté for 2 minutes.
2. Add the garlic and the lentils, stir and cook for 1 minute more.
3. Add the water, bring to a simmer and cook covered for 30 minutes.
4. Add the lemon juice and the remaining ingredients except for the yogurt. toss, divide the mix into bowls, top with the yogurt and serve.

Nutrition: Calories 294, Fat 3, Fiber 8, Carbs 49, Protein 21

130. Quick Zucchini Bowl
Preparation Time: 10 minutes
Cooking Time: 10 minutes
Servings: 4
Ingredients:

- ½ pound of pasta
- 2 tablespoons of olive oil
- 6 crushed garlic cloves
- 1 teaspoon of red chili
- 2 finely sliced spring onions
- 3 teaspoons of chopped rosemary
- 1 large zucchini cut up in half, lengthways and sliced
- 5 large portabella mushrooms
- 1 can of tomatoes
- 4 tablespoons of Parmesan cheese
- Fresh ground black pepper

Directions:

1. Cook the pasta.
2. Take a large-sized frying pan and place over medium heat.
3. Add oil and allow the oil to heat up.
4. Add garlic, onion and chili and sauté for a few minutes until golden.
5. Add zucchini, rosemary and mushroom, and sauté for a few minutes.
6. Increase the heat to medium-high and add tinned tomatoes to the sauce until thick.
7. Drain your boiled pasta and transfer to a serving platter.
8. Pour the tomato mix on top and mix using tongs.
9. Garnish with Parmesan cheese and freshly ground black pepper.
10. Enjoy!

Nutrition: Calories: 361 Fat: 12 g Carbohydrates: 47 g Protein: 14 g

131. Healthy Basil Platter
Preparation Time: 25 minutes
Cooking Time: 15 minutes
Servings: 4
Ingredients:

- 2 pieces of red pepper seeded and cut up into chunks

- 2 pieces of red onion cut up into wedges
- 2 mild red chilies, diced and seeded
- 3 coarsely chopped garlic cloves
- 1 teaspoon of golden caster sugar
- 2 tablespoons of olive oil (plus additional for serving)
- 2 pounds of small ripe tomatoes quartered up
- 12 ounces of dried pasta
- Just a handful of basil leaves
- 2 tablespoons of grated Parmesan

Directions:
1. Preheat the oven to 392°F.
2. Take a large-sized roasting tin and scatter pepper, red onion, garlic and chilies.
3. Sprinkle sugar on top.
4. Drizzle olive oil then season with pepper and salt.
5. Roast the veggies in your oven for 15 minutes.
6. Take a large-sized pan and cook the pasta in boiling, salted water until Al Dente.
7. Drain them.
8. Remove the veggies from the oven and tip the pasta into the veggies.
9. Toss well and tear basil leaves on top.
10. Sprinkle Parmesan and enjoy!

Nutrition: Calories: 452 Fat: 8 g Carbohydrates: 88 g Protein: 14 g

132. Spiced Chickpeas Bowls

Preparation Time: 10 minutes
Cooking Time: 30 minutes
Servings: 4
Ingredients:
- 15 ounces canned chickpeas, drained and rinsed
- ¼ teaspoon cardamom, ground
- ½ teaspoon cinnamon powder
- 1½ teaspoons turmeric powder
- 1 teaspoon coriander, ground
- 1 tablespoon olive oil

- A pinch of salt and black pepper
- ¾ cup Greek yogurt
- ½ cup green olives, pitted and halved
- ½ cup cherry tomatoes, halved
- 1 cucumber, sliced

Directions:
1. Spread the chickpeas on a lined baking sheet, add the cardamom, cinnamon, turmeric, coriander, oil, salt and pepper, toss and bake at 375°F for 30 minutes.
2. In a bowl, combine the roasted chickpeas with the rest of the ingredients, toss and serve for breakfast.

Nutrition: Calories 519, Fat 34.5, Fiber 13.3, Carbs 49.8, Protein 12

133. Eggplant Salad

Preparation Time: 20 minutes
Cooking Time: 15 minutes
Servings: 8
Ingredients:
- 1 large eggplant, washed and cubed
- 1 tomato, seeded and chopped
- 1 small onion, diced
- 2 tablespoons parsley, chopped
- 2 tablespoons extra-virgin olive oil
- 2 tablespoons distilled white vinegar
- ½ cup feta cheese, crumbled
- Salt as needed

Directions:
1. Preheat your outdoor grill to medium-high. Pierce the eggplant a few times using a knife/fork. Cook the eggplants on your grill for about 15 minutes until they are charred.
2. Keep it on the side and allow them to cool. Remove the skin from the eggplant and dice the pulp. Transfer the pulp to a mixing bowl and add parsley, onion, tomato, olive oil, feta cheese and vinegar.

3. Mix well and chill for 1 hour. Season with salt and enjoy!

Nutrition: Calories: 99 Fat: 7 g Carbohydrates: 7 g Protein: 3.4 g

134. Garbanzo Bean Salad

Preparation Time: 10 minutes
Cooking Time: 0 minutes
Servings: 4
Ingredients:
- 1½ cups cucumber, cubed
- 15 ounces canned garbanzo beans, drained and rinsed
- 3 ounces black olives, pitted and sliced
- 1 tomato, chopped
- ¼ cup red onion, chopped
- 5 cups salad greens
- A pinch of salt and black pepper
- ½ cup feta cheese, crumbled
- 3 tablespoons olive oil
- 1 tablespoon lemon juice
- ¼ cup parsley, chopped

Directions:
1. In a salad bowl, combine the garbanzo beans with the cucumber, tomato, and the rest of the ingredients except the cheese and toss.
2. Divide the mix into small bowls, sprinkle the cheese on top, and serve for breakfast.

Nutrition: Calories 268 Fat: 16 g Carbs: 24 g Protein: 9 g

135. Pearl Couscous Salad

Preparation Time: 15 minutes
Cooking Time: 0 minutes
Servings: 6
Ingredients:
For Lemon Dill Vinaigrette:
- Juice of 1 large-sized lemon
- ⅓ cup of extra-virgin olive oil
- 1 teaspoon of dill weed
- 1 teaspoon of garlic powder
- Salt as needed
- Pepper

For Israeli Couscous:
- 2 cups of Pearl Couscous
- Extra-virgin olive oil
- 2 cups of halved grape tomatoes
- Water as needed

- ⅓ cup of finely chopped red onions
- ½ of a finely chopped English cucumber
- 15 ounces of chickpeas
- 14 ounce can of artichoke hearts (roughly chopped up)
- ½ cup of pitted Kalamata olives
- 15-20 pieces of fresh basil leaves, roughly torn and chopped up
- 3 ounces of fresh baby mozzarella

Directions:
1. Prepare the vinaigrette by taking a bowl and add the ingredients listed under vinaigrette. Mix them well and keep aside. Take a medium-sized heavy pot and place it over medium heat.
2. Add 2 tablespoons of olive oil and allow it to heat up. Add couscous and keep cooking until golden brown. Add 3 cups of boiling water and cook the couscous according to the package instructions.
3. Once done, drain in a colander and keep aside. Take another large-sized mixing bowl and add the remaining ingredients except for the cheese and basil.
4. Add the cooked couscous and basil to the mix and mix everything well. Give the vinaigrette a nice stir and whisk it into the couscous salad. Mix well.
5. Adjust the seasoning as required. Add mozzarella cheese. Garnish with some basil. Enjoy!

Nutrition: Calories: 393 Fat: 13 g Carbohydrates: 57 g Protein: 13 g

136. Mediterranean Breakfast Salad

Preparation Time: 15 minutes
Cooking Time: 10 minutes
Servings: 2
Ingredients:
- 4 eggs (optional)
- 10 cups arugula

- ½ seedless cucumber, chopped
- 1 cup cooked quinoa, cooled
- 1 large avocado
- 1 cup natural almonds, chopped
- ½ cup mixed herbs like mint and dill, chopped
- 2 cups halved cherry tomatoes and/or heirloom tomatoes cut into wedges
- Extra-virgin olive oil
- 1 lemon
- Sea salt, to taste
- Freshly ground black pepper, to taste

Directions:
1. Cook the eggs by soft-boiling them - Bring a pot of water to a boil, then reduce heat to a simmer. Gently lower all the eggs into the water and allow them to simmer for 6 minutes.
2. Remove the eggs from water and run cold water on top to stop the cooking, process set aside and peel when ready to use.
3. In a large bowl, combine the arugula, tomatoes, cucumber, and quinoa. Divide the salad into 2 containers, store in the fridge for 2 days.

Nutrition: Calories: 252 Carbs: 18 g Fat: 16 g Protein: 10 g

137. Brown Rice Salad

Preparation Time: 10 minutes
Cooking Time: 0 minutes
Servings: 4
Ingredients:
- 9 ounces brown rice, cooked
- 7 cups baby arugula
- 15 ounces canned garbanzo beans, drained and rinsed
- 4 ounces feta cheese, crumbled
- ¾ cup basil, chopped
- A pinch of salt and black pepper
- 2 tablespoons lemon juice

- ¼ teaspoon lemon zest, grated
- ¼ cup olive oil

Directions:
1. In a salad bowl, combine the brown rice with the arugula, the beans, and the rest of the ingredients, toss and serve cold for breakfast.

Nutrition: Calories 473 Fat: 22 g Carbs: 53 g Protein: 13 g

138. Rainbow Mango Salad

Preparation Time: 10 minutes
Cooking Time: 0 minutes
Servings: 2
Ingredients:
- 1 mango, peeled, destoned, cubed
- ¼ of onion, chopped
- ½ cup cherry tomatoes halved
- ½ of cucumber, deseeded, sliced
- ½ of green bell pepper, deseeded, sliced

Extra:
- ⅓ teaspoon salt
- ¼ teaspoon cayenne pepper
- ¼ of key lime, juiced

Directions:
1. Take a medium bowl, place the mango pieces in it, add onion, tomatoes, cucumber, and bell pepper, and then drizzle with lime juice.
2. Season with salt and cayenne pepper, toss until combined, and let the salad rest in the refrigerator for a minimum of 20 minutes.

Nutrition: 108 Calories; 0.5 g Fats; 1 g Protein; 28.1 g Carbohydrates; 3.3 g Fiber;

139. Satisfying Spring Salad

Preparation Time: 5 minutes
Cooking Time: 10 minutes
Servings: 2
Ingredients:
- 4 ounces arugula
- ½ cup cherry tomatoes halved
- ¼ cup basil leaves
- ½ key lime, juiced
- 2 tablespoons walnuts

Extra:

- ¼ teaspoon salt
- ⅛ teaspoon cayenne pepper
- ½ tablespoon tahini butter

Directions:

1. Prepare the dressing and for this, take a small bowl, place key lime juice in it, add tahini butter, salt, and cayenne pepper and then whisk until combined.
2. Take a medium bowl, place arugula, tomatoes, and basil leaves in it, pour in the dressing and then massage using your hands.
3. Let the salad rest for 20 minutes, then taste to adjust seasoning and then serve.

Nutrition: 87.3 Calories; 7 g Fats; 1.4 g Protein; 6 g Carbohydrates; 1.3 g Fiber;

140. The Raw Green Detox Salad

Preparation Time: 5 minutes
Cooking Time: 0 minutes
Servings: 2
Ingredients:

- ½ of cucumber, deseeded
- 4 ounces arugula
- ⅛ teaspoon salt
- 1 tablespoon key lime juice
- 1 tablespoon olive oil

Extra:

- ⅛ teaspoon cayenne pepper

Directions:

1. Cut the cucumber into slices, add to a salad bowl, and then add arugula in it.
2. Mix lime juice and oil until combined, pour over the salad, and then season with salt and cayenne pepper.
3. Toss until mixed and then serve.

Nutrition: 142 Calories; 12.5 g Fats; 1.6 g Protein; 7.8 g Carbohydrates; 1 g Fiber;

141. Dandelion Salad

Preparation Time: 10 minutes
Cooking Time: 7 minutes
Servings: 2
Ingredients:

- ½ of onion, peeled, sliced
- Five strawberries, sliced

- 2 cups dandelion greens, rinsed
- 1 tablespoon key lime juice
- 1 tablespoon grapeseed oil

Extra:

- ¼ teaspoon salt

Directions:

1. Take a medium skillet pan, place it over medium heat, add oil and let it heat until warm.
2. Add onion, season with ⅛ teaspoon salt, stir until mixed and then cook for 3 to 5 minutes until tender and golden brown.
3. Meanwhile, take a small bowl, place slices of strawberries in it, drizzle with ½ tablespoon lime juice and then toss until coated.
4. When onions have turned golden brown, stir in remaining lime juice, stir until mixed, and then cook for 1 minute.
5. Remove pan from heat, transfer onions into a large salad bowl, add strawberries and juices and dandelion greens, and then sprinkle with the remaining salt. Toss until mixed and then serve.

Nutrition: 204 Calories; 16.1 g Fats; 7 g Protein; 10.6 g Carbohydrates; 2.8 g Fiber;

142. Spicy Wakame Salad

Preparation Time: 15 minutes
Cooking Time: 0 minutes
Servings: 2
Ingredients:

- 1 cup wakame stems
- ½ tablespoon chopped red bell pepper
- ½ teaspoon onion powder
- ½ tablespoon key lime juice

Extra:

- ½ tablespoon agave syrup
- ½ tablespoon sesame seeds
- ½ tablespoon sesame oil

Directions:

1. Place wakame stems in a bowl, cover with water, let them soak for 10 minutes, and then drain.
2. Meanwhile, prepare the dressing and for this, take a

small bowl, add lime juice, onion, agave syrup, and sesame oil in it and then whisk until blended.
3. Place drained wakame stems in a large dish, add bell pepper, pour in the dressing, and then toss until coated.
4. Sprinkle sesame seeds over the salad and then serve.

Nutrition: 106 Calories; 7.3 g Fats; 3 g Protein; 8 g Carbohydrates; 1.7 g Fiber;

143. Avo-Orange Salad Dish

Preparation Time: 5 minutes
Cooking Time: 0 minutes
Servings: 2
Ingredients:

- 1 orange, peeled, sliced
- 4 cups greens
- ½ of avocado, peeled, pitted, diced
- 2 tablespoons slivered red onion
- ½ cup cilantro

Extra:

- ¼ teaspoon salt
- ¼ cup olive oil
- 2 tablespoons lime juice
- 2 tablespoons orange juice

Directions:

1. Prepare the dressing and for this, place cilantro in a food processor, pour in orange juice, lime juice, and oil, add salt and then pulse until blended.
2. Tip the dressing into a mason jar. Add remaining ingredients, toss until coated, add to a salad bowl, or serve in the jar.

Nutrition: 228 Calories; 18.9 g Fats; 3.3 g Protein; 14.7 g Carbohydrates; 7 g Fiber;

144. Nourishing Electric Salad

Preparation Time: 5 minutes
Cooking Time: 0 minutes
Servings: 2
Ingredients:

- ½ of a medium cucumber, deseeded, chopped
- 6 leaves of lettuce, broke into pieces
- 4 mushrooms, chopped
- 6 cherry tomatoes, chopped

- 10 olives

Extra:
- ½ of lime, juiced
- 1 teaspoon olive oil
- ¼ teaspoon salt

Directions:
1. Take a medium salad bowl, place all the ingredients in it and then toss until mixed.

Nutrition: 129 Calories; 7 g Fats; 2 g Protein; 14 g Carbohydrates; 4 g Fiber;

145. Superfood Fonio Salad
Preparation Time: 10 minutes
Cooking Time: 5 minutes
Servings: 2
Ingredients:
- ½ cup cooked chickpeas
- ¼ cup chopped cucumber
- ½ cup chopped red pepper
- ½ cup cherry tomatoes halved
- ½ cup fonio

Extra:
- ⅓ teaspoon salt
- 1 tablespoon grapeseed oil
- ⅛ teaspoon cayenne pepper
- 1 key lime, juiced
- 1 cup spring water

Directions:
1. Take a medium saucepan, place it over high heat, pour in water, and bring it to boil.
2. Add fonio, switch heat to the low level, cook for 1 minute, and then remove the pan from heat.
3. Cover the pan with its lid, let fonio rest for 5 minutes, fluff by using a fork, and then let it cool for 15 minutes.
4. Take a salad bowl, place lime juice and oil in it and then stir in salt and cayenne pepper until combined.
5. Add remaining ingredients including fonio, toss until mixed, and then serve.

Nutrition: 145 Calories; 3 g Fats; 6 g Protein; 24.5 g Carbohydrates; 5.5 g Fiber;

146. Veggie Bowls
Preparation Time: 10 minutes
Cooking Time: 5 minutes
Servings: 4
Ingredients:
- 1 tablespoon olive oil

- 1-pound asparagus, trimmed and roughly chopped
- 3 cups kale, shredded
- 3 cups Brussels sprouts, shredded
- ½ cup hummus
- 1 avocado, peeled, pitted and sliced
- 4 eggs, soft boiled, peeled and sliced

For the dressing:
- 2 tablespoons lemon juice
- 1 garlic clove, minced
- 2 teaspoons Dijon mustard
- 2 tablespoons olive oil
- Salt and black pepper to the taste

Directions:
1. Heat up a pan with 2 tablespoons of oil over medium-high heat, add the asparagus and sauté for 5 minutes stirring often.
2. In a bowl, combine the other 2 tablespoons of oil with the lemon juice, garlic, mustard, salt and pepper and whisk well.
3. In a salad bowl, combine the asparagus with the kale, sprouts, hummus, avocado and eggs and toss gently.
4. Add the dressing, toss and serve for breakfast.

Nutrition: Calories 323, Fat 21, Fiber 10.9, Carbs 24.8

147. Healthy Chickpea Roast Salad
Preparation Time: 10 minutes
Cooking Time: 20 minutes
Servings: 2
Ingredients:
- ½ of cucumber, deseeded, sliced
- 2 avocados, peeled, pitted, cubed
- 1 medium white onion, peeled, diced
- 2 cups cooked chickpeas
- ¼ cup chopped coriander

Extra:
- 1 teaspoon onion powder
- ½ teaspoon cayenne pepper
- 1 teaspoon of sea salt
- 2 tablespoons hemp seeds, shelled
- 1 key lime, juiced

- 1 tablespoon olive oil

Directions:
1. Switch on the oven, then set it to 425°F and let it preheat.
2. Meanwhile, take a baking sheet, place chickpeas on it, season with salt, onion powder, and pepper, drizzle with oil and then toss until combined.
3. Bake the chickpeas for 20 minutes or until golden brown and crisp, then let them cool for 10 minutes.
4. Transfer chickpeas to a bowl, add remaining ingredients and stir until combined.

Nutrition: 208.3 Calories; 8 g Fats; 6.4 g Protein; 30 g Carbohydrates; 8 g Fiber;

148. Amaranth Tabbouleh Salad
Preparation Time: 5 minutes
Cooking Time: 10 minutes
Servings: 2
Ingredients:
- 1 small white onion, peeled, chopped
- 1 cup cooked amaranth
- ½ of cucumber, deseeded, chopped
- 1 cup cooked chickpeas
- ½ of medium red bell pepper, chopped

Extra:
- ⅓ teaspoon sea salt
- ⅛ teaspoon cayenne pepper
- 2 tablespoons key lime juice

Directions:
1. Take a small bowl, place lime juice in it, add salt and stir until combined.
2. Place remaining ingredients in a salad bowl, drizzle with lime juice mixture, toss until mixed, and then serve.

Nutrition: 214 Calories; 4.5 g Fats; 6.5 g Protein; 37 g Carbohydrates; 9 g Fiber;

149. Zucchini and Mushroom Bowl
Preparation Time: 5 minutes
Cooking Time: 8 minutes
Servings: 2
Ingredients:
- 2 zucchini, spiralized

- ½ of medium red bell pepper, sliced
- ½ cup sliced mushrooms
- ½ of medium green bell pepper, sliced
- ½ of medium white onion, peeled, sliced

Extra:
- ⅓ teaspoon salt
- ⅛ teaspoon cayenne pepper
- 1 tablespoon grapeseed oil

Directions:
1. Take a large skillet pan, place it over medium-high heat, add oil, and when hot, add onion, mushrooms, and bell peppers, and then cook for 3 to 5 minutes until tender-crisp.
2. Add zucchini noodles, toss until mixed, and then cook for 2 minutes until warm.

Nutrition: 168 Calories; 2 g Fats; 0.9 g Protein; 36 g Carbohydrates; 6 g Fiber;

150. Pear & Strawberry Salad

Preparation Time: 15 minutes
Cooking Time: 0 minutes
Servings: 4
Ingredients:
- 4 cups romaine lettuce, torn
- 2 pears, cored and sliced
- 1 cup fresh strawberries, hulled and sliced
- ¼ cup walnuts, chopped
- 3 tablespoons olive oil
- 2 tablespoons fresh key lime juice
- 1 tablespoon agave nectar

Directions:
1. In a salad bowl, place all ingredients and toss to coat well.
2. Serve immediately.

Nutrition: Calories 8 g, Fats 1.8 g, Cholesterol 0 mg, Carbohydrates 25.2 g, Fiber 5.1 g, Protein 2.8g

151. Raspberry & Arugula Salad

Preparation Time: 15 minutes
Cooking Time: 0 minutes
Servings: 2
Ingredients:
Salad:
- 3 cups fresh baby arugula
- 1 cup fresh raspberries

- ¼ cup walnuts, chopped

Dressing:
- 1 tablespoon olive oil
- 1 tablespoon fresh key lime juice
- ½ teaspoon agave nectar
- Sea salt, as needed

Directions:
For the salad:
1. Place all ingredients in a salad bowl and mix.

For the dressing:
1. Place all ingredients in another bowl and beat until well combined.
2. Pour the dressing over the salad and toss to coat well.
3. Serve immediately.

Nutrition: Calories 202, Fats 1.6 g, Cholesterol 0 mg, Carbohydrates 11.4 g, Fiber 5.6 g, Protein 5.3g

152. Mixed Berries Salad

Preparation Time: 15 minutes
Cooking Time: 15 minutes
Servings: 4
Ingredients:
- 1 cup fresh strawberries, hulled and sliced
- ½ cup fresh blackberries
- ½ cup fresh blueberries
- ½ cup fresh raspberries
- 6 cups fresh arugula
- 2 tablespoons olive oil
- Sea salt, as needed

Directions:
1. In a salad bowl, place all ingredients and toss to coat well.
2. Serve immediately.

Nutrition: Calories 105, Fats 1 g, Cholesterol 0 mg, Carbohydrates 10.1 g, Fiber 3.6 g., Protein 1.6 g

153. Apple & Kale Salad

Preparation Time: 15 minutes
Cooking Time: 15 minutes
Servings: 4
Ingredients:
- 3 large apples, cored and sliced
- 6 cups fresh baby kale
- ¼ cup walnuts, chopped
- 2 tablespoons olive oil
- 1 tablespoon agave nectar
- Sea salt, as needed

Directions:
1. In a salad bowl, place all ingredients and toss to coat well.

2. Serve immediately

Nutrition: Calories 260, Fats 1.3 g, Cholesterol 0 mg, Carbohydrates 38.4 g, Fiber 6.3 g, Protein 5.3g

154. Mango & Arugula Salad

Preparation Time: 15 minutes
Cooking Time: 15 minutes
Servings: 6
Ingredients:
- 2½ cups mangoes; peeled, pitted and sliced
- 2½ cups avocados; peeled, pitted and sliced
- 1 red onion, sliced
- 6 cups fresh baby arugula
- ¼ cup fresh mint leaves, chopped
- 2 tablespoons fresh orange juice
- Sea salt, as needed

Directions:
1. Place all ingredients in a salad bowl and gently toss to combine.
2. Cover and refrigerate to chill before serving.

Nutrition: Calories 182, Fats 2.6 g, Cholesterol 0 mg, Carbohydrates 18.8 g, Fiber 6.2 g, Protein 2.6g

155. Orange & Kale Salad

Preparation Time: 10 minutes
Cooking Time: 10 minutes
Servings: 2
Ingredients:
Salad:
- 3 cups fresh kale, tough ribs removed and torn
- 2 oranges, peeled and segmented
- 2 tablespoons fresh cranberries

Dressing:
- 2 tablespoons olive oil
- 2 tablespoons fresh orange juice
- ½ teaspoon agave nectar
- Sea salt, as needed

Directions:
For the salad:
1. Place all ingredients in a salad bowl and mix.

For the dressing:
1. Place all ingredients in n another bowl and beat until well combined.
2. Pour the dressing over the salad and toss to coat well.

3. Serve immediately.

Nutrition: Calories 272, Fats 2 g, Cholesterol 0 mg, Carbohydrates 35.7 g, Fiber 6.3 g, Protein 4.8 g

156. Zucchini & Tomato Salad

Preparation Time: 15 minutes
Cooking Time: 15 minutes
Servings: 4
Ingredients:

- 2 medium zucchinis, sliced thinly
- 2 cups plum tomatoes, sliced
- 2 tablespoons olive oil
- 2 tablespoons fresh key lime juice
- Pinch of sea salt

Directions:

1. In a salad bowl, place all ingredients and gently toss to combine.
2. Serve immediately.

Nutrition: Calories 93, Fats 1.1 g, Cholesterol 0 mg, Carbohydrates 6.9 g, Fiber 2.2 g, Protein 2 g

157. Tomato & Arugula Salad

Preparation Time: 15 minutes
Cooking Time: 15 minutes
Servings: 4
Ingredients:

- 6 cups fresh baby arugula
- 2 cups cherry tomatoes
- 2 scallions, chopped
- 2 tablespoons olive oil
- 2 tablespoons fresh orange juice
- Sea salt, as needed

Directions:

1. In a salad bowl, place all ingredients and toss to combine.
2. Cover the bowl and refrigerate for about 6–8 hours.
3. Remove from the refrigerator and toss well before serving.

Nutrition: Calories 90, Fats 1.1 g, Cholesterol 0 mg, Carbohydrates 6 g, Fiber 1.8 g, Protein 1.8 g

158. Warm Avo and Quinoa Salad

Preparation Time: 5 minutes
Cooking Time: 12 minutes
Servings: 4
Ingredients:

- 4 ripe avocados, quartered
- 1 cup quinoa
- 1-pound Chickpeas, drained
- 1-ounce flat-leaf parsley

Directions:

1. Add quinoa to a pot with 2 cups of water. Bring to boil then simmer for 12 minutes or until all the water has evaporated. The grains should be glassy and swollen.
2. Toss the quinoa with all other ingredients and season with salt and pepper to taste.
3. Serve with olive oil and lemon wedges. Enjoy.

Nutrition: Calories: 354, Fat: 16 g, Carbohydrates: 31 g, Protein: 15 g, Fiber: 15 g

159. Chickpeas & Quinoa Salad

Preparation Time: 20 minutes
Cooking Time: 20 minutes
Servings: 8
Ingredients:

- 1¾ cups spring water
- 1 cup quinoa, rinsed
- Sea salt, as needed
- 2 cups cooked chickpeas
- 1 medium red bell pepper, seeded and chopped
- 1 medium green bell pepper, seeded and chopped
- 2 large cucumbers, chopped
- ½ cup onion, chopped
- 3 tablespoons olive oil
- 4 tablespoons fresh basil leaves, chopped

Directions:

1. In a pan, add the water over high heat and bring to a boil.
2. Add the quinoa and salt and cook until boiling.
3. Now, adjust the heat to low and simmer, covered for about 15–20 minutes or

until all the liquid is absorbed.

4. Remove from the heat and set aside, covered for about 5–10 minutes.
5. Uncover and with a fork, fluff the quinoa.
6. In a salad bowl, place quinoa with the remaining ingredients and gently toss to coat.
7. Serve immediately.

Nutrition: Calories 215, Fats 1 g, Cholesterol 0 mg, Carbohydrates 30.5 g, Fiber 5.6 g, Protein 7.5 g

160. Quinoa, Tomato & Mango Salad

Preparation Time: 15 minutes
Cooking Time: 0 minutes
Servings: 4
Ingredients:

- 2 cups mango; peeled, pitted, and chopped
- 1 cup cooked quinoa
- 1 green bell pepper, seeded and chopped
- 1 cup cherry tomato, halved
- ½ cup fresh parsley, chopped
- ¼ cup onion, sliced
- 2 garlic cloves, minced
- 2 tablespoons fresh key lime juice
- 1½ tablespoons olive oil
- Pinch of sea salt

Directions:

1. In a salad bowl, place all ingredients and gently stir to combine.
2. Refrigerate for about 1–2 hours before serving.

Nutrition: Calories 270, Fats 1.2 g, Cholesterol 0 mg, Carbohydrates 45.3 g, Fiber 5.7 g, Protein 7.8g

161. Zesty Citrus Salad

Preparation Time: 5 minutes
Cooking Time: 0 minutes
Servings: 2
Ingredients:

- 4 slices of onion
- ½ of avocado, peeled, pitted, sliced
- 4 ounces arugula
- 1 orange, zested, peeled, sliced

- 1 teaspoon agave syrup

Extra:

- ⅛ teaspoon salt
- ⅛ teaspoon cayenne pepper
- 2 tablespoons key lime juice
- 2 tablespoons olive oil

Directions:

1. Distribute avocado, oranges, onion, and arugula between two plates.
2. Mix together oil, salt, cayenne pepper, agave syrup and lime juice in a small bowl and then stir until mixed.
3. Drizzle the dressing over the salad and then serve.

Nutrition: 265 Calories; 24 g Fats; 3.8 g Protein; 11.6 g Carbohydrates; 6.4 g Fiber;

162. Zucchini Hummus Wrap

Preparation Time: 10 minutes
Cooking Time: 8 minutes
Servings: 2
Ingredients:

- ½ cup iceberg lettuce
- 1 zucchini, sliced
- 2 cherry tomatoes, sliced
- 2 spelled flour tortillas
- 4 tablespoons homemade hummus

Extra:

- ¼ teaspoon salt
- ⅛ teaspoon cayenne pepper
- 1 tablespoon grapeseed oil

Directions:

1. Take a grill pan, grease it oil and let it preheat over medium-high heat setting.
2. Meanwhile, place zucchini slices in a large bowl, sprinkle with salt and cayenne pepper, drizzle with oil and then toss until coated.
3. Arrange zucchini slices on the grill pan and then cook for 2 to 3 minutes per side until developed grill marks.
4. Assemble tortillas and for this, heat the tortilla on the grill pan until warm and develop grill marks and spread 2 tablespoons of hummus over each tortilla.

5. Distribute grilled zucchini slices over the tortillas, top with lettuce and tomato slices, and then wrap tightly.

Nutrition: 264.5 Calories; 5.1 g Fats; 8.5 g Protein; 34.5 g Carbohydrates; 5 g Fiber;

163. Basil and Avocado Salad

Preparation Time: 10 minutes
Cooking Time: 0 minutes
Servings: 2
Ingredients:

- ½ cup avocado, peeled, pitted, chopped
- ½ cup basil leaves
- ½ cup cherry tomatoes
- 2 cups cooked spelled noodles

Extra:

- 1 teaspoon agave syrup
- 1 tablespoon key lime juice
- 2 tablespoons olive oil

Directions:

1. Take a large bowl, place pasta in it, add tomato, avocado, and basil in it and then stir until mixed.
2. Take a small bowl, add agave syrup and salt in it, pour in lime juice and olive oil, and then whisk until combined.
3. Pour lime juice mixture over pasta, toss until combined, and then serve.

Nutrition: 387 Calories; 16.6 g Fats; 9.4 g Protein; 54.3 g Carbohydrates; 8.6 g Fiber;

164. Grilled Romaine Lettuce Salad

Preparation Time: 10 minutes
Cooking Time: 10 minutes
Servings: 2
Ingredients:

- 2 small heads of romaine lettuce, cut in half
- 1 tablespoon chopped basil
- 1 tablespoon chopped red onion
- ¼ teaspoon onion powder
- ½ tablespoon agave syrup

Extra:

- ½ teaspoon salt
- ¼ teaspoon cayenne pepper
- 2 tablespoons olive oil
- 1 tablespoon key lime juice

Directions:

1. Take a large skillet pan, place it over medium heat and when warmed, arrange lettuce heads in it, cut-side down, and then cook for 4 to 5 minutes per side until golden brown on both sides.
2. When done, transfer lettuce heads to a plate and then let them cool for 5 minutes.
3. Meanwhile, prepare the dressing and for this, place the remaining ingredients in a small bowl and then stir until combined.
4. Drizzle the dressing over lettuce heads and then serve.

Nutrition: 130 Calories; 2 g Fats; 2 g Protein; 24 g Carbohydrates; 4 g Fiber;

165. Kale and Sprouts Salad

Preparation Time: 5 minutes
Cooking Time: 0 minutes
Servings: 2
Ingredients:

- 2 cups kale leaves
- 1 cup sprouts
- 1 cup cherry tomato
- ½ of avocado, peeled, pitted, diced
- 1 key lime, juiced

Extra:

- 1 teaspoon agave syrup
- ½ tablespoon olive oil
- ⅛ teaspoon cayenne pepper

Directions:

1. Take a small bowl, place lime juice in it, add oil and agave syrup and then stir until mixed.
2. Take a salad bowl, place remaining ingredients in it, drizzle with the lime juice mixture and then toss until mixed.

Nutrition: 179.2 Calories; 14.1 g Fats; 3.7 g Protein; 13.5 g Carbohydrates; 6.1 g Fiber;

166. Dandelion and Strawberry Salad

Preparation Time: 10 minutes
Cooking Time: 7 minutes
Servings: 2
Ingredients:

- ½ of onion, peeled, sliced
- 5 strawberries, sliced

- 2 cups dandelion greens, rinsed
- 1 tablespoon key lime juice
- 1 tablespoon grapeseed oil

Extra:
- ¼ teaspoon salt

Directions:
1. Take a medium skillet pan, place it over medium heat, add oil and let it heat until warm.
2. Add onion, season with ⅛ teaspoon salt, stir until mixed and then cook for 3 to 5 minutes until tender and golden brown.
3. Meanwhile, take a small bowl, place slices of strawberries in it, drizzle with ½ tablespoon lime juice and then toss until coated.
4. When onions have turned golden brown, stir in remaining lime juice, stir until mixed, and then cook for 1 minute.
5. Remove pan from heat, transfer onions into a large salad bowl, add strawberries along with their juices and dandelion greens and then sprinkle with remaining salt.
6. Toss until mixed and then serve.

Storage Directions:
1. Divide the salad evenly between two meal prep containers, cover with a lid, and then store the containers in the refrigerator for up to 5 days.

Nutrition: 204 Calories; 16.1 g Fats; 7 g Protein; 10.6 g Carbohydrates; 2.8 g Fiber;

167. Basil Salad
Preparation Time: 10 minutes
Cooking Time: 0 minutes
Servings: 2
Ingredients:
- ½ cup avocado, peeled, pitted, chopped
- ½ cup basil leaves
- ½ cup cherry tomatoes
- 2 cups cooked spelled noodles

Extra:
- 1 teaspoon agave syrup
- 1 tablespoon key lime juice
- 2 tablespoons olive oil

Directions:
1. Take a large bowl, place pasta in it, add tomato, avocado, and basil in it and then stir until mixed.
2. Take a small bowl, add agave syrup and salt in it, pour in lime juice and olive oil, and then whisk until combined.
3. Pour lime juice mixture over pasta, toss until combined, and then serve.

Storage Directions:
1. Divide the salad evenly between two meal prep containers, cover with a lid, and then store the containers in the refrigerator for up to 5 days.

Nutrition: 387 Calories; 16.6 g Fats; 9.4 g Protein; 54.3 g Carbohydrates; 8.6 g Fiber;

168. Citrus Salad
Preparation Time: 5 minutes
Cooking Time: 0 minutes
Servings: 2
Ingredients:
- 4 slices of onion
- ½ of avocado, peeled, pitted, sliced
- 4 ounces arugula
- 1 orange, zested, peeled, sliced
- 1 teaspoon agave syrup

Extra:
- ⅛ teaspoon salt
- ⅛ teaspoon cayenne pepper
- 2 tablespoons key lime juice
- 2 tablespoons olive oil

Directions:
1. Distribute avocado, oranges, onion, and arugula between two plates.
2. Mix together oil, salt, cayenne pepper, agave syrup and lime juice in a small bowl and then stir until mixed.
3. Drizzle the dressing over the salad and then serve.

Storage Directions:
1. Divide the salad evenly between two meal containers, cover with a lid, and then store the containers in the refrigerator for up to 5 days.

Nutrition: 265 Calories; 24 g Fats; 3.8 g Protein; 11.6 g Carbohydrates; 6.4 g Fiber;

169. Mango Salad
Preparation Time: 10 minutes
Cooking Time: 0 minutes
Servings: 2
Ingredients:
- 1 mango, peeled, destoned, cubed
- ¼ of onion, chopped
- ½ cup cherry tomatoes, halved
- ½ of cucumber, deseeded, sliced
- ½ of green bell pepper, deseeded, sliced

Extra:
- ⅓ teaspoon salt
- ¼ teaspoon cayenne pepper
- ¼ of key lime, juiced

Directions:
1. Take a medium bowl, place the mango pieces in it, add onion, tomatoes, cucumber, and bell pepper and then drizzle with lime juice.
2. Season with salt and cayenne pepper, toss until combined, and let the salad rest in the refrigerator for a minimum of 20 minutes.

Storage Directions:
1. Divide salad between two meal prep containers, cover with a lid and then store the containers in the refrigerator for up to 3 days.

Nutrition: 108 Calories; 0.5 g Fats; 1 g Protein; 28.1 g Carbohydrates; 3.3 g Fiber;

170. Cucumber and Arugula Salad
Preparation Time: 5 minutes
Cooking Time: 0 minutes
Servings: 2
Ingredients:
- ½ of cucumber, deseeded
- 4 ounces arugula

- ⅛ teaspoon salt
- 1 tablespoon key lime juice
- 1 tablespoon olive oil

Extra:
- ⅛ teaspoon cayenne pepper

Directions:
1. Cut the cucumber into slices, add to a salad bowl and then add arugula in it.
2. Mix together lime juice and oil until combined, pour over the salad, and then season with salt and cayenne pepper.
3. Toss until mixed and then serve.

Storage Directions:
1. Divide the salad evenly between two containers, cover with a lid, and then store the containers in the refrigerator for up to 5 days.

Nutrition: 142 Calories; 12.5 g Fats; 1.6 g Protein; 7.8 g Carbohydrates; 1 g Fiber;

171. Greek Salad Wraps
Preparation Time: 15 minutes
Cooking Time: 10 minutes
Servings: 2
Ingredients:
- 1½ cups seedless cucumber, peeled and chopped (about 1 large cucumber)
- 1 cup chopped tomato (about 1 large tomato)
- ½ cup finely chopped fresh mint
- 1 (2.25-ounce) can sliced black olives (about ½ cup), drained
- ¼ cup diced red onion (about ¼ onion)
- 2 tablespoons extra-virgin olive oil
- 1 tablespoon red wine vinegar
- ¼ teaspoon freshly ground black pepper
- ¼ teaspoon kosher or sea salt
- ½ cup crumbled goat cheese (about 2 ounces)
- 4 whole-wheat flatbread wraps or soft whole-wheat tortillas

Directions:
1. In a large bowl, mix together the cucumber, tomato, mint, olives, and onion until well combined.
2. In a small bowl, whisk together the oil, vinegar, pepper, and salt. Drizzle the dressing over the salad, and mix gently.
3. With a knife, spread the goat cheese evenly over the four wraps. Spoon a quarter of the salad filling down the middle of each wrap.
4. Fold up each wrap: Start by folding up the bottom, then fold one side over and fold the other side over the top. Repeat with the remaining wraps and serve.

Nutrition: Calories: 262; Total Fat: 15g; Saturated Fat: 5g; Cholesterol: 15mg; Sodium: 529mg; Total Carbohydrates: 23g; Fiber: 4g; Protein: 7g

172. Dill Salmon Salad Wraps
Preparation Time: 20 minutes
Cooking Time: 60 minutes
Servings: 2
Ingredients:
- 1-pound salmon filet, cooked and flaked, or 3 (5-ounce) cans salmon
- ½ cup diced carrots (about 1 carrot)
- ½ cup diced celery (about 1 celery stalk)
- 3 tablespoons chopped fresh dill
- 3 tablespoons diced red onion (a little less than ⅛ onion)
- 2 tablespoons capers
- 1½ tablespoons extra-virgin olive oil
- 1 tablespoon aged balsamic vinegar
- ½ teaspoon freshly ground black pepper
- ¼ teaspoon kosher or sea salt
- 4 whole-wheat flatbread wraps or soft whole-wheat tortillas

Directions:
1. In a large bowl, mix together the salmon, carrots, celery, dill, red onion, capers, oil, vinegar, pepper, and salt.
2. Divide the salmon salad among the flatbreads. Fold up the bottom of the flatbread, then roll up the wrap and serve.

Nutrition: Calories: 336; Total Fat: 16g; Saturated Fat: 2g; Cholesterol: 67mg; Sodium: 628mg; Total Carbohydrates: 23g; Fiber: 5g; Protein: 32g

173. Chicken Parmesan Wraps
Preparation Time: 10 minutes
Cooking Time: 20 minutes
Servings: 2
Ingredients:
- Nonstick cooking spray
- 1-pound boneless, skinless chicken breasts
- 1 large egg
- ¼ cup buttermilk
- 2/3 cup whole-wheat panko or whole-wheat bread crumbs
- ½ cup grated Parmesan cheese (about 1½ ounces)
- ¾ teaspoon garlic powder, divided
- 1 cup canned low-sodium or no-salt-added crushed tomatoes
- 1 teaspoon dried oregano
- 6 (8 inch) whole-wheat tortillas, or whole-grain spinach wraps
- 1 cup fresh mozzarella cheese (about 4 ounces), sliced
- 1½ cups loosely packed fresh flat-leaf (Italian) parsley, chopped

Directions:
1. Preheat the oven to 425°F. Line a large, rimmed baking sheet with aluminum foil. Place a wire rack on the aluminum foil, and spray the rack with nonstick cooking spray. Set aside.

2. Put the chicken breasts in a large, zip-top plastic bag. With a rolling pin or meat mallet, pound the chicken so it is evenly flattened, about ¼ inch thick.

3. Slice the chicken into six portions. (It's fine if you have to place 2 smaller pieces together to form six equal portions.)

4. In a wide, shallow bowl, whisk together the egg and buttermilk. In another wide, shallow bowl, mix together the panko crumbs, Parmesan cheese, and ½ teaspoon of garlic powder.

5. Dip each chicken breast portion into the egg mixture and then into the Parmesan crumb mixture, pressing the crumbs into the chicken so they stick. Place the chicken on the prepared wire rack.

6. Bake the chicken for 15 to 18 minutes, or until the internal temperature of the chicken reads 165°F on a meat thermometer and any juices run clear.

7. Transfer the chicken to a cutting board, and slice each portion diagonally into ½-inch pieces.

8. In a small, microwave-safe bowl, mix together the tomatoes, oregano, and the remaining ¼ teaspoon of garlic powder.

9. Cover the bowl with a paper towel and microwave for about 1 minute on high, until very hot. Set aside.

10. Wrap the tortillas in a damp paper towel or dishcloth and microwave for 30 to 45 seconds on high, until warmed.

11. To assemble the wraps, divide the chicken slices evenly among the six tortillas and top with the cheese.

12. Spread 1 tablespoon of the warm tomato sauce over the cheese on each tortilla, and top each with about ¼ cup of parsley.

13. To wrap each tortilla, fold up the bottom of the tortilla, then fold one side over and fold the other side over the top. Serve the wraps immediately, with the remaining sauce for dipping.

Nutrition: Calories: 373; Total Fat: 10g; Saturated Fat: 4g; Cholesterol: 95mg; Sodium: 591 mg; Total Carbohydrates: 33g; Fiber: 8g; Protein: 30g

174. Delicious Quinoa & Dried

Preparation Time: 10 minutes
Cooking Time: 17 minutes
Servings: 2
Ingredients:

- 3 cup water
- ¼ cup cashew nut
- 8 dried apricots
- 4 dried figs
- 1 teaspoon cinnamon

Directions:

1. In a pot, mix water and quinoa and
2. Let simmer for 15 minutes, until the water evaporates.
3. Chop dried fruit.
4. When quinoa is cooked, stir in all other ingredients.
5. Serve cold. Add milk, if desired.

Nutrition: 44g Carbs, 7g Fat, 13g Protein, 285 Calories 65

175. Korean Beef and Onion Tacos

Preparation Time: 1 hour and 15 minutes
Cooking Time: 12 minutes
Servings: 6
Ingredients:

- 2 tablespoons gochujang
- 1 tablespoon soy sauce
- 2 tablespoons sesame seeds
- 2 teaspoons minced fresh ginger
- 2 cloves garlic, minced
- 2 tablespoons toasted sesame oil
- 2 teaspoons sugar
- ½ teaspoon kosher salt
- 1½ pounds (680 g) thinly sliced beef chuck
- 1 medium red onion, sliced
- 6 corn tortillas, warmed
- ¼ cup chopped fresh cilantro
- ½ cup kimchi
- ½ cup chopped green onions

Directions:

1. Combine the ginger, garlic, gochujang, sesame seeds, soy sauce, sesame oil, salt, and sugar in a large bowl. Stir to mix well.

2. Dunk the beef chunk in the large bowl. Press to submerge, then wrap the bowl in plastic and refrigerate to marinate for at least 1 hour.

3. Remove the beef chunk from the marinade and transfer to the Air Fry basket. Add the onion to the basket.

4. Place the basket on the Air Fry position.

5. Select Air Fry, set temperature to 400°F (205°C) and set Time to 12 minutes. Stir the mixture halfway through the cooking time.

6. When cooked, the beef will be well browned.

7. Unfold the tortillas on a clean work surface, divide the fried beef and onion on the tortillas. Spread the green onions, kimchi, and cilantro on top.

8. Serve immediately.

Nutrition: Calories: 181 Protein: 3 g. Fat: 98 g. Carbs: 42 g.

176. Cheesy Sweet Potato and Bean Burritos

Preparation Time: 15 minutes
Cooking Time: 30 minutes
Servings: 6
Ingredients:

- 2 sweet potatoes, peeled and cut into a small dice
- 1 tablespoon vegetable oil
- Kosher salt and ground black pepper, to taste
- 6 large flour tortillas
- 1 (16-oz. / 454-g.) can refried black beans, divided

- 1½ cups baby spinach, divided
- 6 eggs, scrambled
- ¾ cup grated Cheddar cheese, divided
- ¼ cup salsa
- ¼ cup sour cream
- Cooking spray

Directions:

1. Put the sweet potatoes in a large bowl, then drizzle with vegetable oil and sprinkle with salt and black pepper. Toss to coat well.
2. Place the potatoes in the Air Fry basket.
3. Place the basket on the Air Fry position.
4. Select Air Fry, set temperature to 400ºF (205ºC) and set Time to 10 minutes. Flip the potatoes halfway through the cooking time.
5. When done, the potatoes should be lightly browned. Remove the potatoes from the Air Fryer grill.
6. Unfold the tortillas on a clean work surface. Divide the Air Fried sweet potatoes, black beans, spinach, scrambled eggs, and cheese on top of the tortillas.
7. Fold the long side of the tortillas over the filling, then fold in the shorter side to wrap the filling to make the burritos.
8. Wrap the burritos in aluminum foil and put in the basket.
9. Place the basket on the Air Fry position.
10. Select Air Fry, set temperature to 350ºF (180ºC) and set Time to 20 minutes. Flip the burritos halfway through the cooking time.
11. Remove the burritos from the Air Fryer grill and spread with sour cream and salsa. Serve immediately.

Nutrition: Calories 133 Fat 19 g Protein 8 g

177. Golden Chicken and Yogurt Taquitos

Preparation Time: 15 minutes
Cooking Time: 12 minutes
Servings: 4
Ingredients:

- 1 cup cooked chicken, shredded
- ¼ cup Greek yogurt
- ¼ cup salsa
- 1 cup shredded Mozzarella cheese
- Salt and ground black pepper, to taste
- 4 flour tortillas
- Cooking spray

Directions:

1. Spritz the Air Fry basket with cooking spray.
2. Combine all the ingredients, except for the tortillas, in a large bowl. Stir to mix well.

Make the taquitos:

1. Unfold the tortillas on a clean work surface, then scoop up 2 tablespoons of the chicken mixture in the middle of each tortilla. Roll the tortillas up to wrap the filling.
2. Arrange the taquitos in the basket and spritz with cooking spray.
3. Place the basket on the Air Fry position.
4. Select Air Fry, set temperature to 380ºF (193ºC) and set Time to 12 minutes. Flip the taquitos halfway through the cooking time.
5. When cooked, the taquitos should be golden brown and the cheese should be melted.
6. Serve immediately.

Nutrition: Calories 153 Fat 15 g Protein 9 g

178. Cod Tacos with Salsa

Preparation Time: 5 minutes
Cooking Time: 15 minutes
Servings: 4
Ingredients:

- 2 eggs
- 1¼ cups Mexican beer
- 1½ cups coconut flour

- 1½ cups almond flour
- ½ tablespoon chili powder
- 1 tablespoon cumin
- Salt, to taste
- 1 pound (454-g.) cod fillet, slice into large pieces
- 4 toasted corn tortillas
- 4 large lettuce leaves, chopped
- ¼ cup salsa
- Cooking spray

Directions:

1. Spritz the Air Fry basket with cooking spray.
2. Break the eggs in a bowl, then pour in the beer. Whisk to combine well.
3. Combine the almond flour, coconut flour, cumin, chili powder, and salt in a separate bowl. Stir to mix well.
4. Dunk the cod pieces in the egg mixture, then shake the excess off and dredge into the flour mixture to coat well. Arrange the cod in the basket.
5. Place the basket on the Air Fry position.
6. Select Air Fry, set temperature to 375ºF (190ºC) and set Time to 15 minutes. Flip the cod halfway through the cooking time.
7. When cooking is complete, the cod should be golden brown.
8. Unwrap the toasted tortillas on a large plate, then divide the cod and lettuce leaves on top. Baste with salsa and wrap to serve.

Nutrition: Calories 133 Fat 19g Protein 8g

179. Golden Spring Rolls

Preparation Time: 10 minutes
Cooking Time: 18 minutes
Servings: 4
Ingredients:

- 4 spring roll wrappers
- ½ cup cooked vermicelli noodles
- 1 teaspoon sesame oil

- 1 tablespoon freshly minced ginger
- 1 tablespoon soy sauce
- 1 clove garlic, minced
- ½ red bell pepper, deseeded and chopped
- ½ cup chopped carrot
- ½ cup chopped mushrooms
- ¼ cup chopped scallions
- Cooking spray

Directions:
1. Spritz the Air Fry basket with cooking spray and set aside.
2. Heat the sesame oil in a saucepan on medium heat. Sauté the garlic and ginger in the sesame oil for 1 minute, or until fragrant. Add soy sauce, carrot, red bell pepper, mushrooms and scallions. Sauté for 5 minutes or until the vegetables become tender. Mix in vermicelli noodles. Turn off the heat and remove them from the saucepan. Allow to cool for 10 minutes.
3. Lay out one spring roll wrapper with a corner pointed toward you. Scoop the noodle mixture on the spring roll wrapper and fold the corner up over the mixture. Fold left and right corners toward the center and continue to roll to make firmly sealed rolls.
4. Arrange the spring rolls in the basket and spritz with cooking spray.
5. Place the basket on the Air Fry position.
6. Select Air Fry, set temperature to 340°F (171°C) and set Time to 12 minutes. Flip the spring rolls halfway through the cooking time.
7. When done, the spring rolls will be golden brown and crispy.
8. Serve warm.

Nutrition: Calories 137 Fat 15 g Protein 10 g

180. Tuna and Lettuce Wraps

Preparation Time: 10 minutes
Cooking Time: 4 to 7 minutes
Servings: 4
Ingredients:

- 1 pound (454-g.) fresh tuna steak, cut into 1-inch cubes
- 1 tablespoon grated fresh ginger
- 2 garlic cloves, minced
- ½ teaspoon toasted sesame oil
- 2 low-sodium whole-wheat tortillas
- ¼ cup low-fat mayonnaise
- 1 cup shredded romaine lettuce
- 1 red bell pepper, thinly sliced

Directions:
1. In a medium bowl, mix the tuna, ginger, garlic, and sesame oil. Let it stand for 10 minutes.
2. Transfer the tuna to the Air Fryer basket.
3. Select the Air Fry function and cook at 390°F (199°C) for 4 to 7 minutes, or until lightly browned.
4. Make the wraps with tuna, tortillas, mayonnaise, lettuce, and bell pepper.
5. Serve immediately.

Nutrition: Calories 485 Carbohydrates 6.3 g Protein 47.6 g Fat 29.9 g

181. Golden Cabbage and Mushroom Spring Rolls

Preparation Time: 20 minutes
Cooking Time: 14 minutes
Servings: 14
Ingredients:

- 2 tablespoons vegetable oil - 4 cups sliced Napa cabbage
- 5 ounces (142-g.) shiitake mushrooms, diced
- 3 carrots, cut into thin matchsticks
- 1 tablespoon minced fresh ginger
- 1 tablespoon minced garlic
- 1 bunch scallions, white and light green parts only, sliced
- 2 tablespoons soy sauce

- 1 (4-oz. / 113-g.) package cellophane noodles
- ¼ teaspoon cornstarch
- 1 (12-oz. / 340-g.) package frozen spring roll wrappers, thawed
- Cooking spray

Directions:
1. Heat the olive oil in a nonstick skillet over medium-high heat until shimmering.
2. Add the cabbage, carrots, and mushrooms, and sauté for 3 minutes or until tender.
3. Add the garlic, scallions, and ginger and sauté for 1 minute or until fragrant.
4. Mix in the soy sauce and turn off the heat. Discard any liquid that remains in the skillet and allow to cool for a few minutes.
5. Bring a pot of water to a boil, then turn off the heat and pour in the noodles. Let sit for 10 minutes or until the noodles are al dente. Transfer 1 cup of the noodles to the skillet and toss with the cooked vegetables. Reserve the remaining noodles for other use.
6. Dissolve the cornstarch in a small water dish, then place the wrappers on a clean work surface. Dab the edges of the wrappers with cornstarch.
7. Scoop up 3 tablespoons of filling in the center of each wrapper, then fold the corner in front of you over the filling. Tuck the wrapper under the filling, then fold the corners on both sides into the center. Keep rolling to seal the wrapper. Repeat with remaining wrappers. Spritz the Air Fry basket with cooking spray. Arrange the wrappers in the basket and spritz with cooking spray.
8. Place the basket on the Air Fry position.

9. Select Air Fry, set temperature to 400°F (205°C) and set Time to 10 minutes. Flip the wrappers halfway through the cooking time.
10. When cooking is complete, the wrappers will be golden brown.
11. Serve immediately.

Nutrition: Calories: 161 Protein: 8 g. Fat: 88 g. Carbs: 32 g.

182. Crunchy Chicken Egg Rolls

Preparation Time: 10 minutes
Cooking Time: 24 minutes
Servings: 4
Ingredients:

- 1 pound (454-g.) ground chicken
- 2 teaspoons olive oil
- 2 garlic cloves, minced
- 1 teaspoon grated fresh ginger
- 2 cups white cabbage, shredded
- 1 onion, chopped
- ¼ cup soy sauce
- 8 egg roll wrappers
- 1 egg, beaten
- Cooking spray

Directions:

1. Spritz the Air Fry basket with cooking spray.
2. Heat olive oil in a saucepan over medium heat. Sauté the garlic and ginger in the olive oil for 1 minute, or until fragrant. Add the ground chicken to the saucepan. Sauté for 5 minutes, or until the chicken is cooked through. Add the cabbage, onion and soy sauce and sauté for 5 to 6 minutes, or until the vegetables become soft. Remove the saucepan from the heat.
3. Unfold the egg roll wrappers on a clean work surface. Divide the chicken mixture among the wrappers and brush the edges of the wrappers with the beaten egg. Tightly roll up the egg rolls, enclosing

the filling. Arrange the rolls in the basket.
4. Place the basket on the Air Fry position.
5. Select Air Fry, set temperature to 370°F (188°C) and set Time to 12 minutes. Flip the rolls halfway through the cooking time.
6. When cooked, the rolls will be crispy and golden brown.
7. Transfer to a platter and let cool for 5 minutes before serving.

Nutrition: Calories: 181 Protein: 3 g. Fat: 98 g. Carbs: 42 g.

183. Fast Cheesy Bacon and Egg Wraps

Preparation Time: 15 minutes
Cooking Time: 10 minutes
Servings: 3
Ingredients:

- 3 corn tortillas
- 3 slices bacon, cut into strips
- 2 scrambled eggs
- 3 tablespoons salsa
- 1 cup grated Pepper Jack cheese
- 3 tablespoons cream cheese, divided
- Cooking spray

Directions:

1. Spritz the Air Fry basket with cooking spray.
2. Unfold the tortillas on a clean work surface, divide the bacon and eggs in the middle of the tortillas, and then spread with scatter and salsa with cheeses. Fold the tortillas over.
3. Arrange the tortillas in the basket.
4. Place the basket on the Air Fry position.
5. Select Air Fry, set temperature to 390°F (199°C) and set Time to 10 minutes. Flip the tortillas halfway through the cooking time.
6. When cooking is complete, the cheeses will be melted and the tortillas will be lightly browned.

7. Serve immediately.

Nutrition: Calories 133 Fat 19 g Protein 8 g

184. Chicken-Lettuce Wraps

Preparation Time: 15 minutes
Cooking Time: 12 to 16 minutes
Servings: 2 to 4
Ingredients:

- 1 pound (454-g.) boneless, skinless chicken thighs, trimmed
- 1 teaspoon vegetable oil
- 2 tablespoons lime juice
- 1 shallot, minced
- 1 tablespoon fish sauce, plus extra for serving
- 1 teaspoon packed brown sugar
- 1 garlic clove, minced
- ⅛ teaspoon red pepper flakes
- 1 mango, peeled, pitted, and cut into ¼inch pieces
- ⅓ cup chopped fresh mint
- ⅓ cup chopped fresh cilantro
- ⅓ cup chopped fresh Thai basil
- 1 head Bibb lettuce, leaves separated (8-oz. / 227-g.)
- ¼ cup chopped dry-roasted peanuts
- Thai chiles, stemmed and sliced thin

Directions:

1. Pat the chicken dry with paper towels and rub with oil. Place the chicken in the Air Fryer basket. Select the Air Fry function and cook at 400°F (204°C) for 12 to 16 minutes, or until the chicken registers 175°F (79°C), flipping and rotating chicken halfway through cooking.
2. Meanwhile, whisk lime juice, shallot, fish sauce, sugar, garlic, and pepper flakes together in a large bowl; set aside.
3. Transfer chicken to cutting board, let cool slightly, then shred into bite-size pieces using 2 forks. Add the shredded chicken, mango,

mint, cilantro, and basil to bowl with dressing and toss to coat.

4. Serve the chicken in the lettuce leaves, passing peanuts, Thai chiles, and extra fish sauce separately.

Nutrition: Calories 311 Fat 11 g Carbohydrate 22 g Protein 31 g

185. Veggie Salsa Wraps

Preparation Time: 5 minutes
Cooking Time: 7 minutes
Servings: 4
Ingredients:

- 1 cup red onion, sliced
- 1 zucchini, chopped
- 1 poblano pepper, deseeded and finely chopped
- 1 head lettuce
- ½ cup salsa
- 8 ounces (227-g.) Mozzarella cheese

Directions:

1. Place the red onion, zucchini, and poblano pepper in the Air Fryer basket. Select the Air Fry function and cook at 390°F (199°C) for 7 minutes, or until they are tender and fragrant.
2. Divide the veggie mixture among the lettuce leaves and spoon the salsa over the top. Finish off with Mozzarella cheese. Wrap the lettuce leaves around the filling.
3. Serve immediately.

Nutrition: Calories 140 Fat 4 g Fiber 3 g Carbohydrates 5 g Protein 7 g

186. Nugget and Veggie Taco Wraps

Preparation Time: 5 minutes
Cooking Time: 15 minutes
Servings: 4
Ingredients:

- 1 tablespoon water
- 4 pieces commercial vegan nuggets, chopped
- 1 small yellow onion, diced
- 1 small red bell pepper, chopped
- 2 cobs grilled corn kernels
- 4 large corn tortillas
- Mixed greens, for garnish

Directions:

1. Over a medium heat, sauté the nuggets in the water with the onion, corn kernels and bell pepper in a skillet, then remove from the heat.
2. Fill the tortillas with the nuggets and vegetables and fold them up. Transfer to the Air Fryer basket. Select the Air Fry function and cook at 400°F (204°C) for 15 minutes.
3. Once crispy, serve immediately, garnished with the mixed greens.

Nutrition: Calories 140 Fat 4 g Fiber 3 g Carbohydrates 5 g Protein 7 g

187. Lettuce Fajita Meatball Wraps

Preparation Time: 10 minutes
Cooking Time: 10 minutes
Servings: 4
Ingredients:

- 1 pound (454-g.) 85% lean ground beef
- ½ cup salsa, plus more for serving
- ¼ cup chopped onions
- ¼ cup diced green or red bell peppers
- 1 large egg, beaten
- 1 teaspoon fine sea salt & ½ teaspoon chili powder
- ½ teaspoon ground cumin
- 1 clove garlic, minced
- Cooking spray

For Serving:

- 8 leaves Boston lettuce
- Pico de gallo or salsa
- Lime slices

Directions:

1. Spray the Air Fryer basket with cooking spray.
2. In a large bowl, mix together all the ingredients until well combined.
3. Shape the meat mixture into eight 1-inch balls. Place the meatballs in the Air Fryer basket, leaving a little space between them.
4. Select the Air Fry function and cook at 350°F (177°C) for 10 minutes, or until cooked through and no longer pink inside and the internal temperature reaches 145°F (63°C).

5. Serve each meatball on a lettuce leaf, topped with pico de gallo or salsa. Serve with lime slices.

Nutrition: Calories 576 Fat 49 g Total Carbohydrates 8 g Fiber 2 g Protein 25 g

188. Chicken Pita

Preparation Time: 10 minutes
Cooking Time: 9 to 11 minutes
Servings: 4
Ingredients:

- 2 boneless, skinless chicken breasts, cut into 1-inch cubes
- 1 small red onion, sliced
- 1 red bell pepper, sliced
- ⅓ cup Italian salad dressing, divided
- ½ teaspoon dried thyme
- 4 pita pockets, split
- 2 cups torn butter lettuce
- 1 cup chopped cherry tomatoes

Directions:

1. Select the Bake function and preheat Maxx to 380°F (193°C).
2. Place the chicken, onion, and bell pepper in the Air Fryer basket. Drizzle with 1 tablespoon of the Italian salad dressing, add the thyme and toss.
3. Bake for 9 to 11 minutes, or until the chicken is 165°F (74°C) on a food thermometer, stirring once during cooking time.
4. Transfer the chicken and vegetables to a bowl and toss with the remaining salad dressing.
5. Assemble sandwiches with pita pockets, butter lettuce, and cherry tomatoes. Serve immediately.

Nutrition: Calories 311 Fat 11 g Carbohydrate 22 g Protein 31 g

189. Bacon and Egg Wraps with Salsa

Preparation Time: 15 minutes
Cooking Time: 10 minutes
Servings: 3
Ingredients:

- 3 corn tortillas
- 3 slices bacon, cut into strips

- 2 scrambled eggs
- 3 tablespoons salsa
- 1 cup grated Pepper Jack cheese
- 2 tablespoons cream cheese, divided
- Cooking spray

Directions:

1. Spritz the perforated pan with cooking spray.
2. Unfold the tortillas on a clean work surface, divide the bacon and eggs in the middle of the tortillas, then spread with salsa and scatter with cheeses. Fold the tortillas over.
3. Arrange the tortillas in the pan.
4. Select Air Fry. Set temperature to 390°F (199°C) and set Time to 10 minutes. Press Start to begin preheating.
5. Once the oven has preheated, place the pan into the oven. Flip the tortillas halfway through the cooking time.
6. When cooking is complete, the cheeses will be melted and the tortillas will be lightly browned.
7. Serve immediately.

Nutrition: Calories 290 Total Fat 10.5 g Total Carbohydrates 23.2 g Protein 27.3 g

190. Chicken Wraps with Ricotta Cheese

Preparation Time: 30 minutes
Cooking Time: 5 minutes
Servings: 12
Ingredients:

- 2 large-sized chicken breasts, cooked and shredded
- 2 spring onions, chopped
- 10 ounces (284-g.) Ricotta cheese
- 1 tablespoon rice vinegar
- 1 tablespoon molasses
- 1 teaspoon grated fresh ginger
- ¼ cup soy sauce
- ⅓ teaspoon sea salt

- ¼ teaspoon ground black pepper, or more to taste
- 48 wonton wrappers
- Cooking spray

Directions:

1. Spritz the perforated pan with cooking spray.
2. Combine all the ingredients, except for the wrappers in a large bowl. Toss to mix well.
3. Unfold the wrappers on a clean work surface, then divide and spoon the mixture in the middle of the wrappers.
4. Dab a little water on the edges of the wrappers, then fold the edge close to you over the filling. Tuck the edge under the filling and roll up to seal.
5. Arrange the wraps in the pan.
6. Select Air Fry. Set temperature to 375°F (190°C) and set Time to 5 minutes. Press Start to begin preheating.
7. Once preheated, place the pan into the oven. Flip the wraps halfway through the cooking time.
8. When cooking is complete, the wraps should be lightly browned.
9. Serve immediately.

Nutrition: Calories 250 Total Fat 10.1g Total Carbohydrates 4.9g Protein 34.2g

191. Avocado and Tomato Wraps

Preparation Time: 10 minutes
Cooking Time: 5 minutes
Servings: 5
Ingredients:

- 10 egg roll wrappers
- 3 avocados, peeled and pitted
- 1 tomato, diced
- Salt and ground black pepper, to taste
- Cooking spray

Directions:

1. Spritz the perforated pan with cooking spray.

2. Put the tomato and avocados in a food processor. Sprinkle with salt and ground black pepper. Pulse to mix and coarsely mash until smooth.
3. Unfold the wrappers on a clean work surface, then divide the mixture in the center of each wrapper. Roll the wrapper up and press to seal.
4. Transfer the rolls to the pan and spritz with cooking spray.
5. Select Air Fry. Set temperature to 350°F (180°C) and set Time to 5 minutes. Press Start to begin preheating.
6. Once the oven has preheated, place the pan into the oven. Flip the rolls halfway through the cooking time.
7. When cooked, the rolls should be golden brown.
8. Serve immediately.

Nutrition: Calories 419 Total Fat 14 g Total Carbohydrates 39 g Protein 33 g

192. Sweet Potato and Spinach Burritos

Preparation Time: 15 minutes
Cooking Time: 30 minutes
Servings: 6 burritos
Ingredients:

- 2 sweet potatoes, peeled and cut into a small dice
- 1 tablespoon vegetable oil
- Kosher salt and ground black pepper, to taste
- 6 large flour tortillas
- 1 (16-oz.) can refried black beans, divided
- 1½ cups baby spinach, divided
- 6 eggs, scrambled
- ¾ cup grated Cheddar cheese, divided
- ¼ cup salsa
- ¼ cup sour cream
- Cooking spray

Directions:

1. Put the sweet potatoes in a large bowl, then drizzle with

vegetable oil and sprinkle with salt and black pepper. Toss to coat well.

2. Place the potatoes in the perforated pan.

3. Select Air Fry. Set temperature to 400°F (205°C) and set Time to 10 minutes. Press Start to begin preheating.

4. Once preheated, place the pan into the oven. Flip the potatoes halfway through the cooking time.

5. When done, the potatoes should be lightly browned. Remove the potatoes from the oven.

6. Unfold the tortillas on a clean work surface. Divide the black beans, spinach, Air Fried sweet potatoes, scrambled eggs, and cheese on top of the tortillas.

7. Fold the long side of the tortillas over the filling, then fold in the shorter side to wrap the filling to make the burritos.

8. Wrap the burritos in aluminum foil and put in the pan.

9. Select Air Fry. Set temperature to 350°F (180°C) and set Time to 20 minutes. Place the pan into the oven. Flip the burritos halfway through the cooking time.

10. Remove the burritos from the oven and spread with sour cream and salsa. Serve immediately.

Nutrition: Calories 385 Total Fat 9 g Total Carbohydrates 32 g Protein 13 g

193. Cabbage and Prawn Wraps

Preparation Time: 20 minutes
Cooking Time: 18 minutes
Servings: 4
Ingredients:

- 2 tablespoons olive oil
- 1 carrot, cut into strips
- 1-inch piece fresh ginger, grated
- 1 tablespoon minced garlic
- 2 tablespoons soy sauce
- ¼ cup chicken broth
- 1 tablespoon sugar
- 1 cup shredded Napa cabbage
- 1 tablespoon sesame oil
- 8 cooked prawns, minced
- 8 egg roll wrappers
- 1 egg, beaten
- Cooking spray

Directions:

1. Spritz the perforated pan with cooking spray. Set aside.

2. Heat the olive oil in a nonstick skillet over medium heat until shimmering.

3. Add the carrot, ginger, and garlic and sauté for 2 minutes or until fragrant.

4. Pour in the soy sauce, broth, and sugar. Bring to a boil. Keep stirring.

5. Add the cabbage and simmer for 4 minutes or until the cabbage is tender.

6. Turn off the heat and mix in the sesame oil. Let sit for 15 minutes.

7. Use a strainer to remove the vegetables from the liquid, then combine with the minced prawns.

8. Unfold the egg roll wrappers on a clean work surface, then divide the prawn mixture in the center of the wrappers.

9. Dab the edges of a wrapper with the beaten egg, then fold a corner over the filling and tuck the corner under the filling. Fold the left and right corners into the center. Roll the wrapper up and press to seal. Repeat with remaining wrappers.

10. Arrange the wrappers in the pan and spritz with cooking spray.

11. Select Air Fry. Set temperature to 370°F (188°C) and set Time to 12 minutes. Press Start to begin preheating.

12. Once the oven has preheated, place the pan into the oven. Flip the wrappers halfway through the cooking time.

13. When cooking is complete, the wrappers should be golden.

14. Serve immediately.

Nutrition: Calories 339 Total Fat 15.9 g Total Carbohydrates 27.5 g Protein 24.2 g

Chapter 4. Starters

194. Stuffed Celery
Preparation Time: 15 minutes
Cooking Time: 20 minutes
Servings: 3
Ingredients:

- Olive oil
- 1 clove garlic, minced
- 2 tablespoons Pine nuts
- 2 tablespoons dry-roasted sunflower seeds
- ¼ cup Italian cheese blend, shredded
- 8 stalks celery leaves
- 1 (8-oz.) fat-free cream cheese
- Cooking spray

Directions:

1. Sauté garlic and pine nuts over a medium setting for the heat until the nuts are golden brown. Cut off the wide base and tops from celery.
2. Remove two thin strips from the round side of the celery to create a flat surface.
3. Mix Italian cheese and cream cheese in a bowl and spread into cut celery stalks.
4. Sprinkle half of the celery pieces with sunflower seeds and a half with the pine nut mixture. Cover mixture and let stand for at least 4 hours before eating.

Nutrition: Calories: 64 Carbs: 2 g Fat: 6 g Protein: 1 g

195. Butternut Squash Fries
Preparation Time: 5 minutes
Cooking Time: 10 minutes
Servings: 2
Ingredients:

1 Butternut squash
1 tablespoon Extra-virgin olive oil
½ tablespoon Grapeseed oil
⅛ teaspoon Sea salt

Directions:

1. Remove seeds from the squash and cut into thin slices. Coat with extra-virgin olive oil and grapeseed oil.

Add a sprinkle of salt and toss to coat well.

2. Arrange the squash slices onto three baking sheets and bake for 10 minutes until crispy.

Nutrition: Calories: 40 Carbs: 10 g Fat: 0 g Protein: 1 g

196. Dried Fig Tapenade
Preparation Time: 5 minutes
Cooking Time: 0 minutes
Servings: 1
Ingredients:

- 1 cup dried figs
- 1 cup Kalamata olives
- ½ cup water
- 1 tablespoon chopped fresh thyme
- 1 tablespoon extra-virgin olive oil
- ½ teaspoon balsamic vinegar

Directions:

1. Prepare figs in a food processor until well chopped, add water, and continue processing to form a paste.
2. Add olives and pulse until well blended. Add thyme, vinegar, and extra-virgin olive oil and pulse until very smooth. Best served with crackers of your choice.

Nutrition: Calories: 249 Carbs: 64 g Fat: 1 g Protein: 3 g

197. Chickpea Patties in Pitas
Preparation Time: 10 minutes
Cooking Time: 15 minutes
Servings: 2
Ingredients:

- 1 (15-oz.) can chickpeas, drained and rinsed
- ½ cup Lemony Garlic Hummus or ½ cup prepared hummus
- ½ cup whole-wheat panko bread crumbs
- 1 large egg
- 2 teaspoons dried oregano
- ¼ teaspoon freshly ground black pepper
- 1 tablespoon extra-virgin olive oil

- 1 cucumber, unpeeled (or peeled if desired), cut in half lengthwise
- 1 (6-oz.) container 2% plain Greek yogurt
- 1 garlic clove, minced (about ½ teaspoon)
- 2 whole-wheat pita bread, cut in half
- 1 medium tomato, cut into 4 thick slices

Directions:

1. In a large bowl, mash the chickpeas with a potato masher or fork until coarsely mashed (they should still be somewhat chunky). Add the hummus, bread crumbs, egg, oregano, and pepper. Stir well to combine.
2. With your hands, form the mixture into 4 (½-cup-size) patties. Press each patty flat to about ¾ inch thick and put on a plate.
3. In a large skillet over medium-high heat, heat the oil until very hot, about 3 minutes.
4. Cook the patties for 5 minutes, then flip with a spatula. Cook for an additional 5 minutes.
5. While the patties are cooking, shred half of the cucumber with a box grater or finely chop with a knife. In a small bowl, stir together the shredded cucumber, yogurt, and garlic to make the tzatziki sauce.
6. Slice the remaining half of the cucumber into ¼-inch-thick slices and set aside.
7. Toast the pita bread. To assemble the sandwiches, lay the pita halves on a work surface. Into each pita, place a few slices of cucumber, a chickpea patty, and a tomato slice, then drizzle the sandwich with the tzatziki sauce and serve.

Nutrition: Calories: 375; Total Fat: 12g; Saturated Fat: 2g; Cholesterol: 49mg; Sodium: 632mg; Total

Carbohydrates: 53g; Fiber: 10g; Protein: 17g

198. Roast Asparagus

Preparation Time: 15 minutes
Cooking Time: 5 minutes
Servings: 4
Ingredients:

- 1 tablespoon Extra-virgin olive oil
- 1 medium lemon
- ½ teaspoon Freshly grated nutmeg
- ½ teaspoon black pepper
- ½ teaspoon Kosher salt

Directions:

1. Warm the oven to 500°F. Put the asparagus on an aluminum foil and drizzle with extra-virgin olive oil, and toss until well coated.
2. Roast the asparagus in the oven for about five minutes; toss and continue roasting until browned. Sprinkle the roasted asparagus with nutmeg, salt, zest, and pepper.

Nutrition: Calories: 123 Carbs: 5 g Fat: 11 g Protein: 3 g

199. Za'atar Fries

Preparation Time: 10 minutes
Cooking Time: 35 minutes
Servings: 5
Ingredients:

- 1 teaspoon Za'atar spices
- 3 sweet potatoes
- 1 tablespoon dried dill
- 1 teaspoon salt
- 3 teaspoons sunflower oil
- ½ teaspoon paprika

Directions:

1. Pour water into the crockpot. Cut the sweet potatoes into fries.
2. Line the baking tray with parchment. Place the layer of the sweet potato in the tray.
3. Sprinkle the vegetables with dried dill, salt, and paprika. Then sprinkle sweet potatoes with Zaatar and mix up well with the help of the fingertips.
4. Sprinkle the sweet potato fries with sunflower oil— Preheat the oven to 375°F.

5. Bake the sweet potato fries within 35 minutes. Stir the fries every 10 minutes.

Nutrition: Calories 28 Fat 2.9 Fiber 0.2 Carbs 0.6 Protein 0.2

200. Summertime Vegetable Chicken Wraps

Preparation Time: 15 minutes
Cooking Time: 0 minutes
Servings: 4
Ingredients:

- 2 cups cooked chicken, chopped
- ½ English cucumbers, diced
- ½ red bell pepper, diced
- ½ cup carrot, shredded
- 1 scallion, white and green parts, chopped
- ¼ cup plain Greek yogurt
- 1 tablespoon freshly squeezed lemon juice
- ½ teaspoon fresh thyme, chopped
- Pinch of salt
- Pinch of ground black pepper
- 4 multigrain tortillas

Directions:

1. Take a medium bowl and mix in chicken, red bell pepper, cucumber, carrot, yogurt, scallion, lemon juice, thyme, sea salt and pepper.
2. Mix well.
3. Spoon one-quarter of the chicken mix into the middle of the tortilla and fold the opposite ends of the tortilla over the filling.
4. Roll the tortilla from the side to create a snug pocket.
5. Repeat with the remaining ingredients and serve.
6. Enjoy!

Nutrition: Calories: 278 Fat: 4 g Carbohydrates: 28 g Protein: 27 g

201. Speedy Sweet Potato Chips

Preparation Time: 15 minutes
Cooking Time: 0 minutes
Servings: 4
Ingredients:

- 1 large Sweet potato
- 1 tablespoon Extra-virgin olive oil
- Salt

Directions:

1. 300°F preheated oven. Slice your potato into nice, thin slices that resemble fries.
2. Toss the potato slices with salt and extra-virgin olive oil in a bowl. Bake for about one hour, flipping every 15 minutes until crispy and browned.

Nutrition: Calories: 150 Carbs: 16 g Fat: 9 g Protein: 1 g

202. Nachos with Hummus (Mediterranean Inspired)

Preparation Time: 15 minutes
Cooking Time: 20 minutes
Servings: 4
Ingredients:

- 4 cups salted pita chips
- 1 (8-oz.) red pepper (roasted)
- Hummus
- 1 teaspoon Finely shredded lemon peel
- ¼ cup Chopped pitted Kalamata olives
- ¼ cup crumbled feta cheese
- 1 plum (Roma) tomato, seeded, chopped
- ½ cup chopped cucumber
- 1 teaspoon Chopped fresh oregano leaves

Directions:

1. 400°F preheated oven. Arrange the pita chips on a heatproof platter and drizzle with hummus.
2. Top with olives, tomato, cucumber, and cheese and bake until warmed through. Sprinkle lemon zest and oregano and enjoy while it's hot.

Nutrition: Calories: 130 Carbs: 18 g Fat: 5 g Protein: 4 g

203. Hummus and Olive Pita Bread

Preparation Time: 5 minutes
Cooking Time: 0 minutes
Servings: 3
Ingredients:

- 7 pita bread cut into 6 wedges each
- 1 (7-oz.) container plain hummus
- 1 tablespoon Greek vinaigrette

- ½ cup Chopped pitted Kalamata olives

Directions:

1. Spread the hummus on a serving plate—Mix vinaigrette and olives in a bowl and spoon over the hummus. Enjoy with wedges of pita bread.

Nutrition: Calories: 225 Carbs: 40 g Fat: 5 g Protein: 9 g

204. Margherita Open-Face Sandwiches

Preparation Time: 10 minutes
Cooking Time: 5 minutes
Servings: 2
Ingredients:

- 2 (6- to 7-inch) whole-wheat submarine or hoagie rolls, sliced open horizontally
- 1 tablespoon extra-virgin olive oil
- 1 garlic clove, halved
- 1 large ripe tomato, cut into 8 slices
- ¼ teaspoon dried oregano
- 1 cup fresh mozzarella (about 4-oz.), patted dry and sliced
- ¼ cup lightly packed fresh basil leaves, torn into small pieces
- ¼ teaspoon freshly ground black pepper

Directions:

1. Preheat the broiler to high with the rack 4 inches under the heating element.
2. Place the sliced bread on a large, rimmed baking sheet. Place under the broiler for 1 minute, until the bread is just lightly toasted. Remove from the oven.
3. Brush each piece of the toasted bread with the oil, and rub garlic half over each piece.
4. Place the toasted bread back on the baking sheet. Evenly distribute the tomato slices on each piece, sprinkle with the oregano, and layer the cheese on top.
5. Place the baking sheet under the broiler. Set the timer for

1½ minutes, but check after 1 minute.

6. When the cheese is melted and the edges are just starting to get dark brown, remove the sandwiches from the oven (this can take anywhere from 1½ to 2 minutes).
7. Top each sandwich with fresh basil and pepper.

Nutrition: Calories 297; Total Fat: 11g; Saturated Fat: 5g; Cholesterol: 22mg; Sodium: 450mg; Total Carbohydrates: 38g; Fiber: 4g; Protein: 12g

205. Roasted Veggie Panini

Preparation Time: 10 minutes
Cooking Time: 15 minutes
Servings: 2
Ingredients:

- 2 tablespoons extra-virgin olive oil, divided
- 1½ cups diced broccoli (about 1 large stalk)
- 1 cup diced zucchini (about ½ large zucchini)
- ¼ cup diced onion (about ⅛ onion)
- ¼ teaspoon dried oregano
- ⅛ teaspoon freshly ground black pepper
- ⅛ teaspoon kosher or sea salt
- Nonstick cooking spray
- 1 (12-oz.) jar roasted red peppers, drained and finely chopped
- 2 tablespoons grated Parmesan or Asiago cheese
- 1 cup fresh mozzarella (about 4 ounces), sliced
- 1 (2-foot-long) whole-grain Italian loaf, cut into 4 equal lengths

Directions:

1. Place a large, rimmed baking sheet in the oven. Preheat the oven to 450°F with the pan inside.
2. In a large bowl, mix together 1 tablespoon of oil with broccoli, zucchini, onion, oregano, pepper, and salt.
3. Remove the baking sheet from the oven, and carefully

coat the pan with nonstick cooking spray.

4. Spread the vegetable mixture on the pan and roast for 5 minutes, stirring once halfway through cooking.
5. Remove the pan from the oven. Add the red peppers and Parmesan cheese to the vegetables on the baking sheet and mix together
6. In your panini maker, grill pan, or large skillet over medium-high heat, heat the remaining tablespoon of oil.
7. Cut open each section of bread horizontally, but don't cut all the way through. Fill each with the vegetable mix (about ½ cup), and layer 1 ounce of sliced mozzarella cheese on top.
8. Close the sandwiches, and place two of them on the panini press, pan, or skillet. If you're using a panini press, close it and grill for 3 to 5 minutes, or until the crust is golden and the cheese has melted.
9. For a pan or skillet, place a heavy object on top (see tip), and grill for 2½ minutes. Flip the sandwiches and grill for another 2½ minutes.
10. Repeat the grilling process with the remaining two sandwiches.

Nutrition: Calories: 352; Total Fat: 15g; Saturated Fat: 5g; Cholesterol: 12mg; Sodium: 658mg; Total Carbohydrates: 45g; Fiber: 2g; Protein: 16g

206. Premium Roasted Baby Potatoes

Preparation Time: 10 Minutes
Cooking Time: 35 Minutes
Servings: 4
Ingredients:

- 2 pounds new yellow potatoes, scrubbed and cut into wedges
- 2 tablespoons extra-virgin olive oil
- 2 teaspoons fresh rosemary, chopped

- 1 teaspoon garlic powder
- 1 teaspoon sweet paprika
- ½ teaspoon sea salt
- ½ teaspoon freshly ground black pepper

Directions:

1. Preheat your oven to 400°F.
2. Take a large bowl and add potatoes, olive oil, garlic, rosemary, paprika, sea salt and pepper.
3. Spread potatoes in a single layer on a baking sheet and bake for 35 minutes.
4. Serve and enjoy!

Nutrition: Calories: 225 Fat: 7 g Carbohydrates: 37 g Protein: 5 g

207. Fig with Yogurt and Honey

Preparation Time: 5 minutes
Cooking Time: 0 minutes
Servings: 2
Ingredients:

- 6 dried figs, sliced
- 4 teaspoons honey
- 1⅓ cups low-fat plain Greek-style yogurt

Directions:

1. Divide the figs into 2 bowls. Add honey and yogurt into a bowl and stir. Pour over the figs and serve.

Nutrition: Calories 208 Fat 3 g Carbohydrate 39 g Protein 9 g

208. Greek Shrimp Saganaki

Preparation Time: 5 minutes
Cooking Time: 35 minutes
Servings: 4
Ingredients:

- 2 pounds medium-sized shrimps, peeled, deveined, with tails
- ½ cup olive oil
- 2 cups chopped onion
- 2 teaspoons crushed red pepper flakes
- 8 cloves garlic, chopped
- 4 cups chopped tomatoes
- 4 ounces proof (40% alcohol)
- 2 teaspoons chopped oregano leaves
- 4 cups, crumbled Greek feta cheese
- 8 sprigs parsley

Directions:

1. Place shrimp in a bowl. Season with salt. Add half the lemon juice. Toss. Place a large saganaki (It is a skillet with 2 handles that is available in Greece) over medium heat.
2. Add oil. When oil is heated, add onion. Sauté for about 3 minutes or until light brown. Stir in garlic and red pepper flakes and sauté until aromatic.
3. Stir in tomatoes, proof and oregano and sauté until thick and the tomatoes are softened.
4. Mix well. Lay shrimp on top, over the scallion mixture, all over the saganaki. Cover and cook until shrimp is pink and tender.
5. When done, remove from heat. Transfer shrimp to a serving platter. Sprinkle feta cheese on top and serve.

Nutrition: Calories 976 Fat 62 g Carbohydrate 37 g Protein 55 g

209. Greek Fava

Preparation Time: 10 minutes
Cooking Time: 30 minutes
Servings: 4
Ingredients:

- 2 cups Santorini fava (yellow split peas), rinsed
- 2 medium onions, chopped
- 2½ cups water
- 2 cups +2 tablespoons vegetable broth
- 1 teaspoon salt or Himalayan pink salt

To garnish:

- Lemon juice as required
- Chopped parsley

Directions:

1. Place fava in a large pot. Add onions, broth, water and salt and stir. Place over medium heat. When it begins to boil, reduce the heat and cook until fava is tender.
2. Remove from heat and cool. Blend until creamy. Ladle into small plates. Add

lemon juice and stir. Garnish with parsley and serve.

Nutrition: Calories 405 Fat 1 g Carbohydrate 75 g Protein 25 g

210. Hummus, Feta & Bell Pepper Crackers

Preparation Time: 10 minutes
Cooking Time: 0 minutes
Servings: 2
Ingredients:

- 4 tablespoons hummus
- 2 large whole grain crispbread
- 4 tablespoons crumbled feta
- 1 small bell pepper, diced

Directions:

1. Top the pieces of crispbread with hummus. Sprinkle feta cheese and bell peppers and serve.

Nutrition: Calories 136 Fat 7 g Carbohydrate 13 g Protein 6 g

211. Tomato & Basil Bruschetta

Preparation Time: 10 minutes
Cooking Time: 10 minutes
Servings: 3
Ingredients:

- 3 tomatoes, finely chopped
- 1 clove garlic, minced
- ¼ teaspoon garlic powder (optional)
- A handful basil leaves, coarsely chopped
- Salt to taste
- Pepper to taste
- ½ teaspoon olive oil
- ½ tablespoon balsamic vinegar
- ½ tablespoon butter
- ½ baguette French bread or Italian bread, cut into ½ inch thick slices

Directions:

1. Add tomatoes, garlic and basil in a bowl and toss well. Add salt and pepper. Drizzle oil and vinegar and toss well. Set aside for an hour.
2. Melt the butter and brush it over the baguette slices. Place in an oven and toast the slices. Sprinkle the

tomato mixture on top and serve right away.

Nutrition: Calories 162 Fat 4 g Carbohydrate 29 g Protein 4 g

212. Lemon-Pepper Cucumbers

Preparation Time: 5 minutes
Cooking Time: 0 minutes
Servings: 2
Ingredients:

- 1 large cucumber, sliced
- Lemon juice, to taste
- Freshly ground pepper to taste

Directions:

1. Place cucumber slices on a serving platter. Trickle lemon juice over it. Garnish with pepper and serve.

Nutrition: Calories 24 Fat 0 g Carbohydrate 6 g Protein 1 g

213. Falafel

Preparation Time: 30 minutes
Cooking Time: 15 minutes
Servings: 2
Ingredients:

- 1 cup dried chickpeas (do not use cooked or canned)
- ½ cup fresh parsley leaves, discard stems
- ¼ cup fresh dill leaves, discard stems
- ½ cup fresh cilantro leaves
- 4 cloves garlic, peeled
- ½ tablespoon ground black pepper
- ½ tablespoon ground coriander
- ½ tablespoon ground cumin
- ½ teaspoon cayenne pepper (optional)
- ½ teaspoon baking powder
- ¼ teaspoon baking soda
- Salt to taste
- 1 tablespoon toasted sesame seeds
- Oil, as required

Directions:

1. Rinse chickpeas and soak in water overnight. Cover with at least 3 inches of water. Drain and dry by patting with a kitchen towel.
2. Add all the fresh herbs into a food processor. Process

until finely chopped. Add chickpeas, spices and garlic and pulse for not more than 40 seconds each time until smooth.

3. Transfer into a container. Cover and chill for at least 1 hour or until use. Divide the mixture into 12 equal portions and shape into patties.
4. Place a deep pan over medium heat. Pour enough oil to cover at least 3 inches from the bottom of the pan.
5. When the oil is well heated, but not smoking, drop falafel, a few at a time and fry until medium brown.
6. Remove with a spoon and place on a plate lined with paper towels. Serve with a dip of your choice.

Nutrition: Calories 93 Fat 3.8 g Carbohydrate 1.3 g Protein 3.9 g

214. Walnut-Feta Yogurt Dip

Preparation Time: 15 minutes + chilling
Cooking Time: 0 minutes
Servings: 8 (2 tablespoons dip without vegetable sticks)
Ingredients:

- 2 cups plain low-fat yogurt
- ¼ cup crumbled feta cheese
- 3 tablespoons chopped walnuts or pine nuts
- 1 teaspoon chopped fresh oregano or marjoram or ½ teaspoon dried oregano or marjoram, crushed
- Freshly ground pepper to taste
- Salt to taste
- 1 tablespoon snipped dried tomatoes (not oil packed)
- Salt to taste
- Walnut halves to garnish
- Assorted vegetable sticks to serve

Directions:

1. For yogurt dip, place 3 layers of cotton cheesecloth over a strainer. Place strainer over a bowl. Add yogurt into the strainer. Cover the strainer with cling

wrap. Refrigerate for 24-48 hours.

2. Discard the strained liquid and add yogurt into a bowl. Add feta cheese, walnuts, seasoning, and herbs and mix well. Cover and chill for an hour.
3. Garnish with walnut halves. Serve with vegetable sticks.

Nutrition: Calories 68 Fat 4 g Carbohydrate 5 g Protein 4 g

215. Date Wraps

Preparation Time: 10 minutes
Cooking Time: 0 minutes
Servings: 8
Ingredients:

- 8 whole dates, pitted
- 8 thin slices prosciutto
- Freshly ground pepper to taste

Directions:

1. Take the one date and one slice prosciutto. Wrap the prosciutto around the dates and place on a serving platter. Garnish with pepper and serve.

Nutrition: Calories 35 Fat 1 g Carbohydrate 6 g Protein 2 g

216. Clementine & Pistachio Ricotta

Preparation Time: 5 minutes
Cooking Time: 0 minutes
Servings: 2
Ingredients:

- 2/3 cup part-skim ricotta
- 2 clementine's, peeled, separated into segments, deseeded
- 4 teaspoons chopped pistachio nuts

Directions:

1. Place ⅓ cup ricotta in each of the 2 bowls. Divide the clementine segments equally and place over the ricotta. Sprinkle pistachio nuts on top and serve.

Nutrition: Calories 178 Fat 9 g Carbohydrate 15 g Protein 11 g

217. Serrano-Wrapped Plums

Preparation Time: 10 minutes
Cooking Time: 0 minutes

Servings: 4
Ingredients:

- 2 firm-ripe plums or peaches or nectarines, quartered
- 1 ounce thinly sliced Serrano ham or prosciutto or Jamón Ibérico, cut into 8 pieces

Directions:

1. Take one piece of ham and one piece of fruit. Wrap the ham around the fruit and place on a serving platter. Serve.

Nutrition: Calories 30 Fat 1 g Carbohydrate 4 g Protein 2 g

218. Classic Apple Oats

Preparation Time: 10 minutes
Cooking Time: 15 minutes
Servings: 2
Ingredients:

- ½ teaspoon cinnamon
- ¼ teaspoon ginger
- 2 apples make half-inch chunks
- ½ cup oats, steel cut
- 1½ cups water
- Maple syrup
- ¼ teaspoon salt
- Clove
- ¼ teaspoon nutmeg

Directions:

1. Take Instant Pot and carefully arrange it over a clean, dry kitchen platform.
2. Turn on the appliance.
3. In the cooking pot area, add the water, oats, cinnamon, ginger, clove, nutmeg, apple, and salt. Stir the ingredients gently.
4. Close the pot lid and seal the valve to avoid any leakage. Find and press the "Manual" cooking setting and set the cooking time to 5 minutes.
5. Allow the recipe ingredients to cook for the set time, and after that, the timer reads "zero."
6. Press "Cancel" and press the "NPR" setting for natural pressure release. It takes 8-10 times for all inside pressure to release.

7. Open the pot and arrange the cooked recipe on serving plates.
8. Sweeten as needed with maple or agave syrup and serve immediately.
9. Top with some chopped nuts, optional.

Nutrition: Calories: 232, Fat: 5.7 g, Carbs: 48.1 g, Protein: 5.2 g

219. Peach & Chia Seed

Preparation Time: 10 minutes
Cooking Time: 10 minutes
Servings: 2
Ingredients:

- ½ ounce chia seeds
- 1 tablespoon pure maple syrup
- 1 cup coconut milk
- 1 teaspoon ground cinnamon
- 3 diced peaches
- 2/3 cup granola

Directions:

1. Find a small bowl and add the chia seeds, maple syrup, and coconut milk.
2. Stir well, then cover and pop into the fridge for at least one hour.
3. Find another bowl, add the peaches and sprinkle with the cinnamon. Pop to one side
4. When it's time to serve, take two glasses, and pour the chia mixture between the two.
5. Sprinkle the granola over the top, keeping a tiny amount to one side to use to decorate later.
6. Top with the peaches and top with the reserved granola and serve.

Nutrition: Calories: 415, Protein: 13.9 g, Carbs: 54.4 g, Fat: 16.9 g

220. Almond Butter and Blueberry Smoothie

Preparation Time: 10 minutes
Cooking Time: 1 minute
Servings: 2
Ingredients:

- 1 cup almond milk
- 1 cup blueberries
- 4 ice cubes
- 1 scoop vanilla protein powder

- 1 tablespoon almond butter
- 1 tablespoon chia seeds

Directions:

1. Use a blender to mix the almond butter, vanilla protein powder, chia seeds, almond milk, ice cubes and blueberries together until the consistency is smooth.

Nutrition: Calories: 230, Carbs: 20 g, Fat: 8.1 g, Protein: 21.6 g

221. Salmon and Egg Muffins

Preparation Time: 10 minutes
Cooking Time: 15 minutes
Servings: 2
Ingredients:

- 4 eggs
- ⅓ cup milk
- Salt and pepper
- 1½ ounces smoked salmon
- 1 tablespoon chopped chives
- Green onions, optional

Directions:

1. Preheat the oven to 356°F and grease 6 muffin tin holes with a small amount of olive oil.
2. Place the eggs, milk, and a pinch of salt and pepper into a small bowl and lightly beat to combine.
3. Divide the egg mixture between the 6 muffin holes, then divide the salmon between the muffins and place into each hole, gently pressing down to submerge in the egg mixture, chopped
4. Sprinkle each muffin with chopped chives and place in the oven for about 8-10 minutes or until just set.
5. Leave to cool for about 5 minutes before turning out and storing in an airtight container in the fridge.

Nutrition: Calories: 93, Fat: 6 g, Protein: 8 g, Carbs: 1 g

222. Nachos

Preparation Time: 5 minutes

Cooking Time: 10 minutes
Servings: 4
Ingredients:

- 4 ounces restaurant-style corn tortilla chips
- 1 medium green onion, thinly sliced (about 1 tablespoon)
- 1 (4-oz.) package finely crumbled feta cheese
- 1 finely chopped and drained plum tomato
- 2 tablespoons sun-dried tomatoes in oil, finely chopped
- 2 tablespoons Kalamata olives

Directions:

1. Mix an onion, plum tomato, oil, sun-dried tomatoes, and olives in a small bowl.
2. Arrange the tortillas chips on a microwavable plate in a single layer topped evenly with cheese—microwave on high for one minute.
3. Rotate the plate half turn and continue microwaving until the cheese is bubbly. Spread the tomato mixture over the chips and cheese and enjoy.

Nutrition: Calories: 140 Carbs: 19 g Fat: 7 g Protein: 2 g

223. Tomato Cream Cheese Spread

Preparation Time: 15 minutes
Cooking Time: 0 minutes
Servings: 6
Ingredients:

- 12 ounces cream cheese, soft
- 1 big tomato, cubed
- ¼ cup homemade mayonnaise
- 2 garlic cloves, minced
- 2 tablespoons red onion, chopped
- 2 tablespoons lime juice
- Salt and black pepper to the taste

Directions:

1. In your blender, mix the cream cheese with the tomato and the rest of the ingredients, pulse well, divide into small cups and serve cold.

Nutrition: Calories 204 Fat 6.7 g Carbs 7.3 g Protein 4.5 g

224. Italian Fries

Preparation Time: 15 minutes
Cooking Time: 40 minutes
Servings: 4
Ingredients:

- ⅓ cup baby red potatoes
- 1 tablespoon Italian seasoning
- 3 tablespoons canola oil
- 1 teaspoon turmeric
- ½ teaspoon of sea salt
- ½ teaspoon dried rosemary
- 1 tablespoon dried dill

Directions:

1. Cut the red potatoes into wedges and transfer to the big bowl. After this, sprinkle the vegetables with Italian seasoning, canola oil, turmeric, sea salt, dried rosemary, and dried dill.
2. Shake the potato wedges carefully. Line the baking tray with baking paper. Place the potatoes wedges in the tray. Flatten it well to make one layer. Preheat the oven to 375F.
3. Place the tray with potatoes in the oven and bake for 40 minutes. Stir the potatoes with the help of the spatula from time to time. The potato fries are cooked when they have crunchy edges.

Nutrition: Calories 122 Fat 11.6 g Carbs 4.5 g Protein 0.6 g

225. Tempeh Snack

Preparation Time: 15 minutes
Cooking Time: 8 minutes
Servings: 6
Ingredients:

- 11 ounces soy tempeh
- 1 teaspoon olive oil
- ½ teaspoon ground black pepper
- ¼ teaspoon garlic powder

Directions:

1. Cut soy tempeh into the sticks. Sprinkle every tempeh stick with ground black pepper, garlic powder, and olive oil. Preheat the grill to 375°F.

2. Place the tempeh sticks in the grill and cook them for 4 minutes from each side. The time of cooking depends on the tempeh sticks' size. The cooked tempeh sticks will have a light brown color.

Nutrition: Calories 88 Fat 2.5 g Carbs 10.2 g Protein 6.5 g

226. Avocado Dip

Preparation Time: 15 minutes
Cooking Time: 0 minutes
Servings: 8
Ingredients:

- ½ cup heavy cream
- 1 green chili pepper, chopped
- Salt and pepper to the taste
- 4 avocados, pitted, peeled and chopped
- 1 cup cilantro, chopped
- ¼ cup lime juice

Directions:

1. In a blender, combine the cream with the avocados and the rest of the ingredients and pulse well. Divide the mix into bowls and serve cold as a party dip.

Nutrition: Calories 200 Fat 14.5 g Carbs 8.1 g Protein 7.6 g

227. Feta and Roasted Red Pepper Bruschetta

Preparation Time: 15 minutes
Cooking Time: 15 minutes
Servings: 24
Ingredients:

- 6 Kalamata olives, pitted, chopped
- 2 tablespoons green onion, minced
- ¼ cup Parmesan cheese, grated, divided
- ¼ cup extra-virgin olive oil brushing, or as needed
- ¼ cup cherry tomatoes, thinly sliced
- 1 teaspoon lemon juice
- 1 tablespoon extra-virgin olive oil
- 1 tablespoon basil pesto
- 1 red bell pepper, halved, seeded
- 1 piece (12-inch) whole-wheat baguette, cut into ½-inch-thick slices

- 1 package (4-oz.) feta cheese with basil and sun-dried tomatoes, crumbled
- 1 clove garlic, minced

Directions:

1. Preheat the oven broiler. Place the oven rack 6 inches from the source of heat. Brush both sides of the baguette slices, with the ¼ cup olive oil.
2. Arrange the bread slices on a baking sheet; toast for about 1 minute on each side, carefully watching to avoid burning. Remove the toasted slices, transferring into another baking sheet.
3. With the cut sides down, place the red peppers in a baking sheet; broil for about 8 to 10 minutes or until the skin is charred and blistered.
4. Transfer the roasted peppers into a bowl; cover with plastic wrap. Let cool, remove the charred skin. Discard skin and chop the roasted peppers.
5. In a bowl, mix the roasted red peppers, cherry tomatoes, feta cheese, green onion, olives, pesto, 1 tablespoon olive oil, garlic, and lemon juice.
6. Top each bread with 1 tablespoon of the roasted pepper mix, sprinkle lightly with the Parmesan cheese.
7. Return the baking sheet with the topped bruschetta; broil for about 1-2 minutes or until the topping is lightly browned.

Nutrition: Cal 73 Fat 4.8 g Carbs 5.3 g Protein 2.1 g

228. Meat-Filled Phyllo (Samboosek)

Preparation Time: 15 minutes
Cooking Time: 10 minutes
Servings: 1 Phyllo Pie
Ingredients:

- 1 pound ground beef or lamb
- 1 medium yellow onion, finely chopped
- 1 tablespoon seven spices
- 1 teaspoon salt

- 1 pkg. frozen phyllo dough (12 sheets)
- 2/3 cup butter, melted

Directions:

1. In a medium skillet over medium heat, brown beef for 3 minutes, breaking up chunks with a wooden spoon.
2. Add yellow onion, seven spices, and salt, and cook for 5 to 7 minutes or until beef is browned and onions are translucent. Set aside, and let cool.
3. Place the first sheet of phyllo on your work surface, brush with melted butter, lay the second sheet of phyllo on top, and brush with melted butter. Cut sheets into 3-inch-wide strips.
4. Spoon 2 tablespoons of meat filling at end of each strip, and fold the end strip to cover the meat and form a triangle.
5. Fold pointed end up and over to the opposite end, and you should see a triangle forming. Continue to fold up and then over until you come to the end of the strip.
6. Place phyllo pies on a baking sheet, seal side down, and brush tops with butter. Repeat with remaining phyllo and filling. Bake for 10 minutes or until golden brown.
7. Remove from the oven and set aside for 5 minutes before serving warm or at room temperature.

Nutrition: Calories: 299 Carbs: 53 g Fat: 6 g Protein: 7 g

229. Tasty Black Bean Dip

Preparation Time: 15 minutes
Cooking Time: 18 minutes
Servings: 6
Ingredients:

- 2 cups dry black beans, soaked overnight and drained
- 1½ cups cheese, shredded
- 1 teaspoon dried oregano

- 1½ teaspoon chili powder
- 2 cups tomatoes, chopped
- 2 tablespoons olive oil
- 1½ tablespoons garlic, minced
- 1 medium onion, sliced
- 4 cups vegetable stock
- Pepper
- Salt

Directions:

1. Add all ingredients except cheese into the instant pot. Seal pot with lid and cook on high for 18 minutes. Once done, allow to release pressure naturally. Remove lid. Drain excess water.
2. Add cheese and stir until cheese is melted. Blend bean mixture using an immersion blender until smooth. Serve and enjoy.

Nutrition: Calories 402 Fat 15.3 g Carbohydrates 46.6 g Protein 22.2 g

230. Zucchini Cakes

Preparation Time: 15 minutes
Cooking Time: 10 minutes
Servings: 4
Ingredients:

- 1 zucchini, grated
- ¼ carrot, grated
- ¼ onion, minced
- 1 teaspoon minced garlic
- 3 tablespoons coconut flour
- 1 teaspoon Italian seasonings
- 1 egg, beaten
- 1 teaspoon coconut oil

Directions:

1. In the mixing bowl combine together grated zucchini, carrot, minced onion, and garlic. Add coconut flour, Italian seasoning, and egg. Stir the mass until homogenous.
2. Heat up coconut oil in the skillet. Place the small zucchini fritters in the hot oil. Make them with the help of the spoon. Roast the zucchini fritters for 4 minutes from each side.

Nutrition: Calories 65 Fat 3.3 g Carbs 6.3 g Protein 3.3 g

231. Parsley Nachos

Preparation Time: 15 minutes
Cooking Time: 0 minutes

Servings: 3

Ingredients:

- 3 ounces tortilla chips
- ¼ cup Greek yogurt
- 1 tablespoon fresh parsley, chopped
- ¼ teaspoon minced garlic
- 2 kalamata olives, chopped
- 1 teaspoon paprika
- ¼ teaspoon ground thyme

Directions:

1. In the mixing bowl mix up together Greek yogurt, parsley, minced garlic, olives, paprika, and thyme. Then add tortilla chips and mix up gently. The snack should be served immediately.

Nutrition: Calories 81 Fat 1.6 g Carbs 14.1 g Protein 3.5 g

232. Plum Wraps

Preparation Time: 15 minutes

Cooking Time: 10 minutes

Servings: 4

Ingredients:

- 4 plums
- 4 prosciutto slices
- ¼ teaspoon olive oil

Directions:

1. Preheat the oven to 375°F. Wrap every plum in prosciutto slice and secure with a toothpick (if needed). Place the wrapped plums in the oven and bake for 10 minutes.

Nutrition: Calories 62 Fat 2.2 g Carbs 8 g Protein 4.3 g

233. Parmesan Chips

Preparation Time: 15 minutes

Cooking Time: 20 minutes

Servings: 4

Ingredients:

- 1 zucchini
- 2 ounces Parmesan, grated
- ½ teaspoon paprika
- 1 teaspoon olive oil

Directions:

1. Trim zucchini and slice it into the chips with the help of the vegetable slices. Then mix up together Parmesan and paprika. Sprinkle the zucchini chips with olive oil.

2. After this, dip every zucchini slice in the cheese mixture. Place the zucchini chips in the lined baking tray and bake for 20 minutes at 375°F.

3. Flip the zucchini sliced onto another side after 10 minutes of cooking. Chill the cooked chips well.

Nutrition: Calories 64 Fat 4.3 g Carbs 2.3 g Protein 5.2 g

234. Chicken Bites

Preparation Time: 15 minutes

Cooking Time: 5 minutes

Servings: 6

Ingredients:

- ½ cup coconut flakes
- 8 ounces chicken fillet
- ¼ cup Greek yogurt
- 1 teaspoon dried dill
- 1 teaspoon salt
- 1 teaspoon ground black pepper
- 1 tablespoon tomato sauce
- 1 teaspoon honey
- 4 tablespoons sunflower oil

Directions:

1. Chop the chicken fillet on the small cubes (popcorn cubes). Sprinkle them with dried dill, salt, and ground black pepper.

2. Then add Greek yogurt and stir carefully. After this, pour sunflower oil into the skillet and heat it up.

3. Coat chicken cubes in the coconut flakes and roast in the hot oil for 3-4 minutes or until the popcorn cubes are golden brown.

4. Dry the popcorn chicken with the help of a paper towel. Make the sweet sauce: whisk together honey and tomato sauce. Serve the popcorn chicken hot or warm with sweet sauce.

Nutrition: Calories 107 Fat 5.2 g Carbs 2.8 g Protein 12.1 g

235. Chicken Kale Wraps

Preparation Time: 15 minutes

Cooking Time: 10 minutes

Servings: 4

Ingredients:

- 4 kale leaves
- 4 ounces chicken fillet
- ½ apple
- 1 tablespoon butter
- ¼ teaspoon chili pepper
- ¾ teaspoon salt
- 1 tablespoon lemon juice
- ¾ teaspoon dried thyme

Directions:

1. Chop the chicken fillet into small cubes. Then mix up together chicken with chili pepper and salt. Heat up butter in the skillet. Add chicken cubes. Roast them for 4 minutes.

2. Meanwhile, chop the apple into small cubes and add it to the chicken. Mix up well. Sprinkle the ingredients with lemon juice and dried thyme.

3. Cook them for 5 minutes over medium-high heat. Fill the kale leaves with the hot chicken mixture and wrap.

Nutrition: Calories 106 Fat 5.1 g Carbs 6.3 g Protein 9 g

236. Savory Pita Chips

Preparation Time: 15 minutes

Cooking Time: 10 minutes

Servings: 1 cup

Ingredients:

- 3 pitas
- ¼ cup extra-virgin olive oil
- ¼ cup za'atar

Directions:

1. Preheat the oven to 450°F. Cut pitas into 2-inch pieces, and place in a large bowl. Drizzle pitas with extra-virgin olive oil, sprinkle with za'atar and toss to coat.

2. Spread out pitas on a baking sheet, and bake for 8 to 10 minutes or until lightly browned and crunchy.

3. Let pita chips cool before removing from the baking sheet. Store in an airtight container for up to 1 month.

Nutrition: Calories: 108 Carbs: 18 g
Fat: 2 g Protein: 5 g

237. Artichoke Skewers
Preparation Time: 15 minutes
Cooking Time: 0 minutes
Servings: 4
Ingredients:
- 4 prosciutto slices
- 4 artichoke hearts, canned
- 4 kalamata olives
- 4 cherry tomatoes
- ¼ teaspoon cayenne pepper
- ¼ teaspoon sunflower oil

Directions:
1. Skewer prosciutto slices, artichoke hearts, kalamata olives, and cherry tomatoes on the wooden skewers. Sprinkle antipasto skewers with sunflower oil and cayenne pepper.

Nutrition: Calories 152 Fat 3.7 g Carbs 23.2 g Protein 11.1 g

238. Kidney Bean Spread
Preparation Time: 15 minutes
Cooking Time: 18 minutes
Servings: 4
Ingredients:
- 1 pound dry kidney beans, soaked overnight and drained
- 1 teaspoon garlic, minced
- 2 tablespoons olive oil
- 1 tablespoon fresh lemon juice
- 1 tablespoon paprika
- 4 cups vegetable stock
- ½ cup onion, chopped
- Pepper
- Salt

Directions:
1. Add beans and stock into the instant pot. Seal pot with lid and cook on high for 18 minutes. Once done, allow to release pressure naturally. Remove lid.
2. Drain beans well and reserve ½ cup stock. Transfer beans, reserve stock, and remaining ingredients into the food processor and process until smooth. Serve and enjoy.

Nutrition: Calories 461 Fat 8.6 g Carbohydrates 73 g Protein 26.4 g

239. Mediterranean Polenta Cups
Preparation Time: 15 minutes
Cooking Time: 5 minutes
Servings: 24
Ingredients:
- 1 cup yellow cornmeal
- 1 garlic clove, minced
- ½ teaspoon fresh thyme, minced or ¼ teaspoon dried thyme
- ½ teaspoon salt
- ¼ cup feta cheese, crumbled
- ¼ teaspoon pepper
- 2 tablespoons fresh basil, chopped
- 4 cups water
- 4 plum tomatoes, finely chopped

Directions:
1. In a heavy, large saucepan, bring the water and the salt to a boil; reduce the heat to a gentle boil.
2. Slowly whisk in the cornmeal; cook, stirring with a wooden spoon for about 15 to 20 minutes, or until the polenta is thick and pulls away cleanly from the sides of the pan.
3. Remove from the heat; stir in the pepper and the thyme. Grease miniature muffin cups with cooking spray. Spoon a heaping tablespoon of the polenta mixture into each muffin cup.
4. With the back of a spoon, make an indentation in the center of each; cover and chill until the mixture is set.
5. Meanwhile, combine the feta cheese, tomatoes, garlic, and basil in a small-sized bowl. Unmold the chilled polenta cups; place them on an ungreased baking sheet.
6. Tops each indentation with 1 heaping tablespoon of the feta mixture. Broil the cups 4 inches from the heat source for about 5 to 7 minutes, or until heated through.

Nutrition: Calories: 70 Carbs: 15 g Fat: 0 g Protein: 2 g

240. Tomato Triangles
Preparation Time: 15 minutes
Cooking Time: 0 minutes
Servings: 6
Ingredients:
- 6 corn tortillas
- 1 tablespoon cream cheese
- 1 tablespoon ricotta cheese
- ½ teaspoon minced garlic
- 1 tablespoon fresh dill, chopped
- 2 tomatoes, sliced

Directions:
1. Cut every tortilla into 2 triangles. Then mix up together cream cheese, ricotta cheese, minced garlic, and dill.
2. Spread 6 triangles with cream cheese mixture. Then place sliced tomato on them and cover with remaining tortilla triangles.

Nutrition: Calories 71 Fat 1.6 g Carbs 12.8 g Protein 2.3 g

241. Chili Mango and Watermelon Salsa
Preparation Time: 15 minutes
Cooking Time: 0 minutes
Servings: 12
Ingredients:
- 1 red tomato, chopped
- Salt and black pepper to the taste
- 1 cup watermelon, seedless, peeled and cubed
- 1 red onion, chopped
- 2 mangos, peeled and chopped
- 2 chili peppers, chopped
- ¼ cup cilantro, chopped
- 3 tablespoons lime juice
- Pita chips for serving

Directions:
1. In a bowl, mix the tomato with the watermelon, the onion and the rest of the ingredients except the pita chips and toss well. Divide the mix into small cups and serve with pita chips on the side.

Nutrition: Calories 62 Fat 4.7 g Carbs 3.9 g Protein 2.3 g

242. Blueberry Fat Bombs

Preparation Time: 10 minutes
Cooking Time: 0 minutes
Servings: 12
Ingredients:

- ½ cup blueberries, mashed
- ½ cup coconut oil, at room temperature
- ½ cup cream cheese, at room temperature
- 1 pinch nutmeg
- 6 drops liquid stevia

Directions:

1. Line the 12-cup muffin tin with 12 paper liners.
2. Put all the ingredients and process until it has a thick and mousse-like consistency.
3. Pour the mixture into the 12 cups of the muffin tin. Put the muffin tin into the refrigerate to chill for 1 to 3 hours.

Nutrition: Calories: 120 Fat: 12.5 g Fiber: 1.4 g Carbohydrates: 2.1 g Protein: 3.1 g

243. Cheesy Zucchini Triangles with Garlic Mayo Dip

Preparation Time: 20 minutes
Cooking Time: 30 minutes
Servings: 4
Ingredients:
Garlic Mayo Dip:

- cup crème Fraiche
- ⅓ cup mayonnaise
- ¼ teaspoon sugar-free maple syrup
- 1 garlic clove, pressed
- ½ teaspoon vinegar
- Salt and black pepper to taste

Cheesy Zucchini Triangles:

- 2 large zucchinis, grated
- 1 egg
- ¼ cup almond flour
- ¼ teaspoon paprika powder
- ¾ teaspoon dried mixed herbs
- ¼ teaspoon swerve sugar
- ½ cup grated mozzarella cheese

Directions:

1. Start by making the dip; in a medium bowl, mix the crème Fraiche, mayonnaise, maple syrup, garlic, vinegar, salt, and black pepper.
2. Cover the bowl with a plastic wrap and refrigerate while you make the zucchinis.
3. Let the oven preheat at 400°F. And line a baking tray with greaseproof paper. Set aside.
4. Put the zucchinis in a cheesecloth and press out as much liquid as possible.
5. Pour the zucchinis into a bowl.
6. Add the egg, almond flour, paprika, dried mixed herbs, and swerve sugar.
7. Mix well and spread the mixture on the baking tray into a round pizza-like piece with 1-inch thickness.
8. Let it bake for 25 minutes.
9. Reduce the oven's heat to 350°F/175°C, take out the tray, and sprinkle the zucchini with the mozzarella cheese.
10. Let it melt in the oven.
11. Remove afterward, set aside to cool for 5 minutes, and then slice the snacks into triangles.
12. Serve immediately with the garlic mayo dip.

Nutrition: Calories: 286 Fat: 11.4 g Fiber: 8.4 g Carbohydrates: 4.3 g Protein: 10.1 g

244. Herbed Cheese Chips

Preparation Time: 15 minutes
Cooking Time: 15 minutes
Servings: 8
Ingredients:

- 3 tablespoons coconut flour
- ½ cup strong cheddar cheese, grated and divided
- ¼ cup Parmesan cheese, grated
- 2 tablespoons butter, melted
- 1 organic egg
- 1 teaspoon fresh thyme leaves, minced

Directions:

1. Preheat the oven to 3500°F. Line a large baking sheet with parchment paper.
2. In a bowl, place the coconut flour, ¼ cup of grated cheddar, Parmesan, butter, and egg and mix until well combined.
3. Make eight equal-sized balls from the mixture.
4. Arrange the balls onto a prepared baking sheet in a single layer about 2-inch apart.
5. Form into flat discs.
6. Sprinkle each disc with the remaining cheddar, followed by thyme.
7. Bake for around 15 minutes.

Nutrition: Calories: 101 Fat: 6.5 g Fiber: 1.4 g Carbohydrates: 1.2 g Protein: 3.1 g

245. Cauliflower Poppers

Preparation Time: 20 minutes
Cooking Time: 30 minutes
Servings: 4
Ingredients:

- 4 cups cauliflower florets
- 2 teaspoons olive oil
- ¼ teaspoon chili powder
- Pepper and salt

Directions:

1. Preheat the oven to 4500°F. Grease a roasting pan.
2. In a bowl, add all ingredients and toss to coat well.
3. Transfer the cauliflower mixture into a prepared roasting pan and spread in an even layer.
4. Roast for about 25-30 minutes.
5. Serve warm.

Nutrition: Calories: 102 Fat: 8.5 g Fiber: 4.7 g Carbohydrates: 2.1 g Protein: 4.2 g

246. Crispy Parmesan Chips

Preparation Time: 10 minutes
Cooking Time: 5 minutes
Servings: 8
Ingredients:

- teaspoon butter
- 8 ounces full-fat Parmesan cheese, shredded or freshly grated

Directions:

1. Preheat the oven to 400°F.

2   The Parmesan cheese must be spooned onto the baking sheet in mounds, spread evenly apart.

3   Spread out the mounds with the back of a spoon until they are flat.

4   Bake the crackers until the edges are browned, and the centers are still pale for about 5 minutes.

Nutrition: Calories: 101 Fat: 9.4 g Fiber: 3.1 g Carbohydrates: 2.5 g Protein: 1.2 g

247. Tex-Mex Queso Dip

Preparation Time: 5 minutes
Cooking Time: 10 minutes
Servings: 6
Ingredients:

- ½ cup of coconut milk
- ½ jalapeño pepper, seeded and diced
- 1 teaspoon minced garlic
- ½ teaspoon onion powder
- 1-ounce goat cheese
- 6 ounces sharp cheddar cheese, shredded
- ¼ teaspoon cayenne pepper

Directions:

1. Preheat a pot then add the coconut milk, jalapeño, garlic, and onion powder.
2. Simmer then whisk in the goat cheese until smooth.
3. Add the Cheddar cheese and cayenne and whisk until the dip is thick, 30 seconds to 1 minute.

Nutrition: Calories: 149 Fat: 12.1 g Fiber: 3.1 g Carbohydrates: 5.1 g Protein: 4.2 g

248. Sweet Onion Dip

Preparation Time: 15 minutes
Cooking Time: 25-30 minutes
Servings: 4
Ingredients:

- 3 cup sweet onion chopped
- teaspoon pepper sauce
- cups Swiss cheese shredded
- Ground black pepper
- cups mayonnaise
- ¼ cup horseradish

Directions:

1. Take a bowl, add sweet onion, horseradish, pepper sauce, mayonnaise, and

Swiss cheese, mix them well and transfer into the pie plate.

2. Preheat oven at 375°F.
3. Now put the plate into the oven and bake for 25 to 30 minutes until edges turn golden brown.
4. Sprinkle pepper to taste and serve with crackers.

Nutrition: Calories: 278 Fat: 11.4 g Fiber: 4.1 g Carbohydrates: 2.9 g Protein: 6.9 g

249. Trail Mix

Preparation Time: 5 minutes
Cooking Time: 0 minutes
Servings: 3
Ingredients:

- ½ cup salted pumpkin seeds
- ½ cup slivered almonds
- ¾ cup roasted pecan halves
- ¾ cup unsweetened cranberries
- 1 cup toasted coconut flakes

Directions:

1. In a skillet, place almonds and pecans. Heat for 2-3 minutes and let cool.
2. Once cooled, in a large resealable plastic bag, combine all ingredients.
3. Seal and shake vigorously to mix.
4. Evenly divide into suggested servings and store in airtight meal prep containers.

Nutrition: Calories: 98 Fat: 1.2 g Fiber: 4.1 g Carbohydrates: 1.1 g Protein: 3.2 g

250. Cold Cuts and Cheese Pinwheels

Preparation Time: 20 minutes
Cooking Time: 0 minutes
Servings: 2
Ingredients:

- 8 ounces cream cheese, at room temperature
- ¼ pound salami, thinly sliced
- 2 tablespoons sliced pepperoncini

Directions:

1. Layout a sheet of plastic wrap on a large cutting board or counter.

2. Place the cream cheese in the center of the plastic wrap, and then add another layer of plastic wrap on top.
3. Using a rolling pin, roll the cream cheese until it is even and about ¼ inch thick.
4. Try to make the shape somewhat resemble a rectangle.
5. Pull off the top layer of plastic wrap.
6. Place the salami slices so they overlap to cover the cream-cheese layer completely.
7. Place a new piece of plastic wrap on top of the salami layer to flip over your cream cheese–salami rectangle. Flip the layer, so the cream cheese side is up.
8. Remove the plastic wrap and add the sliced pepperoncini to a layer on top.
9. Roll the layered ingredients into a tight log, pressing the meat and cream cheese together. (You want it as tight as possible.)
10. Then wrap the roll with plastic wrap and refrigerate for at least 6 hours so it will set.
11. Slice and serve.

Nutrition: Calories: 141 Fat: 4.9 g Fiber: 2.1 g Carbohydrates: 0.3 g Protein: 8.5 g

251. Zucchini Balls with Capers and Bacon

Preparation Time: 3 hours
Cooking Time: 20 minutes
Servings: 10
Ingredients:

- 2 zucchinis, shredded
- 2 bacon slices, chopped
- ½ cup cream cheese, at room temperature
- 1 cup fontina cheese
- ¼ cup capers & 1 clove garlic, crushed
- ½ cup grated Parmesan cheese
- ½ teaspoon poppy seeds
- ¼ teaspoon dried dill weed
- ½ teaspoon onion powder

- Salt and black pepper, to taste
- 1 cup crushed pork rinds

Directions:
1. Preheat oven to 360°F.
2. Thoroughly mix zucchinis, capers, ½ of Parmesan cheese, garlic, cream cheese, bacon, and fontina cheese until well combined.
3. Shape the mixture into balls.
4. Refrigerate for 3 hours.
5. In a mixing bowl, mix the remaining Parmesan cheese, crushed pork rinds, dill, black pepper, onion powder, poppy seeds, and salt.
6. Roll cheese ball in Parmesan mixture to coat.
7. Arrange in a greased baking dish in a single layer and bake in the oven for 15-20 minutes, shaking once.

Nutrition: Calories: 227 Fat: 12.5 g Fiber: 9.4 g Carbohydrates: 4.3 g Protein: 14.5 g

252. Strawberry Fat Bombs
Preparation Time: 30 minutes
Cooking Time: 0 minutes
Servings: 6
Ingredients:
- 100 g strawberries
- 100 g cream cheese
- 50 g butter
- 2 tablespoons erythritol powder
- ½ teaspoon vanilla extract

Directions:
1. Put the cream cheese and butter (cut into small pieces) in a mixing bowl.
2. Let rest for 30 to 60 minutes at room temperature.
3. In the meantime, wash the strawberries and remove the green parts.
4. Pour into a bowl and process into a puree with a serving of oil or a mixer.
5. Add erythritol powder and vanilla extract and mix well.
6. Mix the strawberries with the other ingredients and

make sure that they have reached room temperature.
7. Put the cream cheese and butter into a container.
8. Mix with a hand mixer or a food processor to a homogeneous mass.
9. Pour the mixture into small silicone muffin molds. Freeze.

Nutrition: Calories: 95 Fat: 9.1 g Fiber: 4.1 g Carbohydrates: 0.9 g Protein: 2.1 g

253. Kale Chips
Preparation Time: 5 minutes
Cooking Time: 25 minutes
Servings: 6
Ingredients:
- 400 g of kale
- to 2 teaspoons of salt
- tablespoons butter
- 50 g bacon fat

Directions:
1. Remove the stems and coarse ribs from the kale and tear the leaves into 5 cm pieces.
2. Wash the kale leaves thoroughly and dry them in a salad spinner.
3. Put the butter in a pan with the bacon fat and warm it up over low heat. Add salt and stir well.
4. Set aside and let cool.
5. Pack the kale in a zippered bag and pour the cooled, liquid mixture of bacon fat and butter into it.
6. Close the zippered bag and gently shake the kale leaves with the butter mixture. The leaves should take on a glossy color due to an even film of fat.
7. Place the kale leaves on a baking sheet and sprinkle with salt as desired.
8. Bake it for 25 minutes or until the leaves turn brown and crispy.
9. Let cool, divide into the recommended portions, and store in an airtight container.

Nutrition: Calories: 59 Fat: 2.1 g Fiber: 4.5 g Carbohydrates: 0.9 g Protein: 0.4 g

254. Plantains with Tapioca Pearls
Preparation Time: 15 minutes
Cooking Time: 3 mours
Servings: 6
Ingredients:
- 5 ripe plantains, sliced into thick disks
- 1 can thick coconut cream
- 1 teaspoon coconut oil
- ¼ cup tiny tapioca pearls, dried
- 1 cup white sugar
- 2 cups water
- Pinch of salt

Directions:
1. Grease the Instant Pot Pressure Cooker with coconut oil.
2. Place ripe plantains. Top this with tapioca pearls, coconut oil, white sugar, and salt. Pour just the right amount of water into the Instant Pot.
3. Lock the lid in place. Press the high pressure and cook for 5 minutes.
4. When the beep sounds, Choose the Quick Pressure Release. This will depressurize for 7 minutes. Remove the lid.
5. Tip in coconut cream. Allow residual heat to cook the last ingredient.
6. To serve, ladle just the right amount of plantains into dessert bowls.

Nutrition: Calories 345 Fat 8 Fiber 4.5 Carbs 3.5 Protein 20

255. Brown Rice Pudding with Pumpkin Spice
Preparation Time: 15 minutes
Cooking Time: 1 hour
Servings: 4
Ingredients:
For the Pumpkin pie spice mix:
- 1 teaspoon allspice powder
- 4 teaspoon ginger powder
- 1 teaspoon mace powder
- 1 teaspoon nutmeg powder
- ½ teaspoon clove powder
- 2 tablespoons cinnamon powder

For the Pudding:
- ½ cup pumpkin puree
- ½ cup brown sticky rice
- ¼ cup water
- 1 cinnamon stick
- 1½ cups coconut milk
- ¼ cup dried pitted dates, minced
- ½ teaspoon pumpkin pie spice mix
- ¼ cup pure maple syrup
- 1 vanilla pod, halved lengthwise
- Pinch of salt

For the Whipped cream:
- 1/16 teaspoon maple syrup
- ¼ cup thick coconut cream
- 1 tablespoon lemon juice, freshly squeezed

Directions:
1. Sieve allspice powder, clove powder, cinnamon powder, pumpkin pie mix, nutmeg powder, mace powder, and ginger powder. Mix well. Set aside.
2. To make the whipped cream, combine lemon juice, coconut cream, and maple syrup. Whisk well until it thickens. Place inside the fridge for 1 -2 hours to chill or until ready to use.
3. To make the pudding, put together coconut milk, brown sticky rice, date, pumpkin pie spice mix, cinnamon stick, pumpkin puree, vanilla pod maple syrup, water, and salt into the Instant Pot Pressure Cooker. Stir well.
4. Lock the lid in place. Press the high pressure and cook for 28 minutes.
5. When the beep sounds, Choose Natural Pressure Release. Depressurizing would take 20 minutes. Remove the lid. Discard cinnamon stick and vanilla pod.
6. To serve, ladle an equal amount of pudding into dessert bowls. Sprinkle pumpkin spice mix. Top with whipped cream.

Nutrition: Calories 321 Fat 18 Fiber 4.5 Carbs 1.5 Protein 20

256. Mango Cashew Cake

Preparation Time: 15 minutes
Cooking Time: 1 hour
Servings: 8
Ingredients:
- ¼ teaspoon coconut oil, for greasing
- 1 teaspoon baking powder
- ½ teaspoon baking soda
- ¼ cup coconut butter
- 1 tablespoon flour & ½ cup all-purpose flour
- ¼ cup mango jam
- ½ cup cashew milk
- ¼ cup ground cashew nuts
- 1 teaspoon vanilla essence
- ½ cup powdered sugar
- 2½ cups water

Directions:
1. Lightly grease the Instant Pot Pressure Cooker with coconut oil. Dust with flour. Set aside.
2. Meanwhile, combine all-purpose flour, coconut butter, baking powder, cashew milk, baking soda, vanilla essence, mango jam, and cashew nuts in a large mixing bowl. Stir until all ingredients come together. Pour batter on a Bundt pan.
3. Place trivet on the pressure cooker. Pour 2½ cups of water.
4. Lock the lid in place. Press the high pressure and cook for 35 minutes.
5. When the beep sounds, Choose Natural Pressure Release. Depressurizing would take 20 minutes. Remove the lid.
6. Take out Bundt cake. Transfer to a cake rack. Let cool for 10 minutes at room temperature.
7. Turn cake over on a serving dish. Sprinkle powdered sugar. Slice and serve.

Nutrition: Calories 213 Fat 21 Fiber 5 Carbs 1.9 Protein 21

257. Sweet Orange and Lemon Barley Risotto

Preparation Time: 5 minutes
Cooking Time: 45 minutes
Servings: 4
Ingredients:
- 1½ cups barley pearls
- ¼ cup raisins
- 1 cup sweet orange, chopped, reserve juice
- 4 cups water
- 4 strips lemon peels
- ¼ cup white sugar, add more if needed

Directions:
1. Combine barley pearls, lemon peels, raisins, water, and white sugar into the Instant Pot Pressure Cooker.
2. Lock the lid in place. Press the high pressure and cook for 10 minutes.
3. When the beep sounds, Choose the Quick Pressure Release. This will depressurize for 7 minutes. Remove the lid. Discard lemon peels.
4. Add in sweet orange and juices. Pour coconut cream. Allow residual heat to cook the coconut cream. Adjust seasoning according to your preferred taste.
5. To serve, ladle equal amounts into dessert bowls. Cool slightly before serving.

Nutrition: Calories 124 Fat 11 Fiber 15 Carbs 3.9 Protein 28

258. Homemade Applesauce

Preparation Time: 5 minutes
Cooking Time: 45 minutes
Servings: 8
Ingredients:
- 10 soft-fleshed apples, quartered
- ¼ teaspoon nutmeg powder
- 1 teaspoon cinnamon powder
- ¼ cup sugar
- ¼ cup water

Directions:
1. Put together apples, nutmeg powder, cinnamon powder,

sugar, and water into the Instant Pot Pressure Cooker.

2. Lock the lid in place. Press the high pressure and cook for 15 minutes.

3. When the beep sounds, Choose the Quick Pressure Release. This will depressurize for 7 minutes. Remove the lid.

4. Mash apples until the desired consistency is achieved. Adjust seasoning according to your preferred taste.

5. Spoon applesauce into bowls. Store leftovers in the fridge. This is best served cold.

Nutrition: Calories 345 Fat 12 Fiber 5 Carbs 3.4 Protein 28

259. Boiled Peanuts

Preparation Time: 5 minutes
Cooking Time: 45 minutes
Servings: 4-6
Ingredients:

- 2½ pounds raw, unshelled peanuts
- 1 cup salt
- 4 cups water

Directions:

1. Place unshelled peanuts, salt, and water into the Instant Pot Pressure Cooker.

2. Lock the lid in place. Press the high pressure and cook for 10 minutes.

3. When the beep sounds, Choose Natural Pressure Release. Depressurizing would take 20 minutes. Remove the lid.

4. Cool before pouring to a colander. Rinse well to remove most of the salt. Drain.

5. To serve, scoop just the right number of peanuts into bowls. Shell peanuts as you eat.

Nutrition: Calories 132 Fat 11 Fiber 8 Carbs 1.4 Protein 13

260. Homemade Beet Hummus

Preparation Time: 5 minutes
Cooking Time: 45 minutes
Servings: 8
Ingredients:

- 5 pieces cucumbers, thickly sliced
- 6 cups water
- 2 pounds red beets, peeled
- 1 garlic clove, peeled
- 3 tablespoons tahini
- 3 tablespoons cumin powder
- 2 tablespoons Spanish paprika
- 3 tablespoons lemon juice, freshly squeezed
- ¼ teaspoon salt
- 1 tablespoon olive oil
- 1 teaspoon white sesame seeds, toasted
- ¼ cup fresh cilantro, chopped

Directions:

1. Place water, red beets, and garlic clove into the Instant Pot Pressure Cooker.

2. Lock the lid in place. Press the high pressure and cook for 1 minute.

3. When the beep sounds, Choose the Quick Pressure Release. This will depressurize for 7 minutes. Remove the lid. Cool slightly before proceeding.

4. Discard solids but keep 1 cup of the cooking liquid.

5. Transfer beets to an immersion blender, along with the cooking liquid. Season with tahini, cumin powder, Spanish paprika, lemon juice, and salt. Process until smooth. Adjust seasoning according to your preferred taste.

6. Pour beet hummus into a bowl. Garnish with sesame seeds, cilantro, and olive oil. Serve with sliced cucumbers or crackers.

7. Store leftovers in the fridge. Use as needed.

Nutrition: Calories 154 Fat 12 Fiber 8 Carbs 1.9 Protein 11

261. Coconut Pudding with Tropical Fruit

Preparation Time: 15 minutes
Cooking Time: 10 minutes
Servings: 4
Ingredients:

- ¼ pound sticky rice balls
- 2 cups ripe plantains, sliced into thick disks
- 2 cans thick coconut cream, divided
- 1 cup taro, diced
- ½ cup tapioca pearls
- 1 cup sweet potato, diced
- 4 cups water
- 1 cup sugar
- Pinch of salt

Directions:

1. Combine sticky rice balls, taro, ripe plantains, tapioca pearls, water, white sugar, sweet potato, 1 can of coconut cream, and salt into the Instant Pot Pressure Cooker.

2. Lock the lid in place. Press the high pressure and cook for 10 minutes.

3. When the beep sounds, Choose the Quick Pressure Release. This will depressurize for 7 minutes. Remove the lid.

4. Tip in the remaining can of coconut cream. Allow residual heat to cook the coconut cream.

5. To serve, ladle equal amounts into dessert bowls.

Nutrition: Calories 213 Fat 11 Fiber 18 Carbs 2.7 Protein 21

262. Sweet Coconut Cassava

Preparation Time: 15 minutes
Cooking Time: 10 minutes
Servings: 4
Ingredients:

- 2 pounds yellow cassava, chopped into large chunks
- 1 cup white sugar
- 1 can thick coconut cream
- ¼ teaspoon coconut oil
- 4 cups water
- ⅛ teaspoon vanilla extract
- Pinch of salt

Directions:

1. Lightly grease the insides of the Instant Pot Pressure Cooker with coconut oil.
2. Pour water. Add in yellow cassava, sugar, and salt.
3. Lock the lid in place. Press the high pressure and cook for 7 minutes.
4. When the beep sounds, Choose the Quick Pressure Release. This will depressurize for 7 minutes. Remove the lid.
5. Tip in coconut cream and vanilla extract. Allow residual heat to cook the last two ingredients. Adjust seasoning according to your preferred taste.
6. To serve, ladle equal amounts into dessert bowls.

Nutrition: Calories 345 Fat 12 Fiber 9 Carbs 2.9 Protein 29

263. Tofu with Salted Caramel Pearls

Preparation Time: 5 minutes
Cooking Time: 1 hour
Servings: 4
Ingredients:

- 1 cup tapioca pearls, no need to soak
- 2 packs (12-oz.) soft silken tofu
- 5 cups water, divided
- 1 cup brown sugar
- 1/16 teaspoon salt

Directions:

1. Pour tapioca pearls and water into the Instant Pot Pressure Cooker crockpot.
2. Lock the lid in place. Press the high pressure and cook for 10 minutes.
3. When the beep sounds, Choose Natural Pressure Release. Depressurizing would take 20 minutes. Remove the lid.
4. Reposition the lid and cook for another 5 minutes on high.
5. When the beep sounds, Choose Natural Pressure Release. Depressurizing would take 20 minutes. Remove the lid. Pour out

contents of the pressure cooker over a colander to drain.
6. Press the "sauté" button. Put back tapioca pearls to the crockpot. Add silken tofu, brown sugar, and salt.
7. Cook for 10 minutes or until the caramel thickens. Turn off the machine.
8. Meanwhile, scoop silken tofu into heat-resistant cups. Pour tapioca pearls and caramel on top. Serve.

Nutrition: Calories 125 Fat 18 Fiber 19 Carbs 1 Protein 13

264. Homemade Hummus

Preparation Time: 5 minutes
Cooking Time: 1 hour
Servings: 4
Ingredients:

- 6 cups water
- 1 cup dry chickpeas
- 2 fresh bay leaves
- 4 garlic cloves, peeled
- 5 pieces crackers per person as the base
- 3 tablespoons tahini
- ¼ teaspoon cumin powder
- ½ cup lemon juice, freshly squeezed
- ¼ teaspoon salt
- 1/16 teaspoon toasted black sesame seeds
- 1/16 teaspoon toasted white sesame seeds
- 1/16 teaspoon red pepper flakes
- 2 tablespoons extra-virgin olive oil
- 1 sprig of basil

Directions:

1. Place chickpeas, bay leaves, garlic cloves, and water into the Instant Pot Pressure Cooker.
2. Lock the lid in place. Press the high pressure and cook for 20 minutes.
3. When the beep sounds, Choose Natural Pressure Release. Depressurizing would take 20 minutes. Remove the lid. Reserve 1 cup of cooking liquid. Discard the rest.

4. Transfer chickpeas to an immersion blender, along with the cooking liquid. Season with tahini, cumin powder, lemon juice, and salt. Process until smooth. Adjust seasoning according to your preferred taste.
5. Pour chickpeas into a bowl. Garnish with toasted black and white sesame seeds, red pepper flakes, basil, and olive oil. Serve with crackers.
6. Store leftovers in the fridge. Use as needed.

Nutrition: Calories 122 Fat 11 Fiber 21 Carbs 1.3 Protein 13

265. Corn Coconut Pudding

Preparation Time: 5 minutes
Cooking Time: 45 minutes
Servings: 3
Ingredients:

- 3 cups water
- 1 cup corn kernels
- ½ cup sticky rice
- ¼ cup ripe jackfruit, shredded,
- ¼ teaspoon vanilla extract
- ½ cup sugar
- ⅛ teaspoon nutmeg powder
- 1/16 teaspoon salt
- 2 cans thick coconut cream, divided

Directions:

1. Pour water, sticky rice, jackfruit, corn kernels, 1 can of coconut cream, nutmeg powder, vanilla extract, white sugar, and salt in the Instant Pot Pressure Cooker.
2. Lock the lid in place. Press the high pressure and cook for 7 minutes.
3. When the beep sounds, Choose the Quick Pressure Release. This will depressurize for 7 minutes. Remove the lid.
4. Tip in the remaining can of coconut cream. Allow residual heat to cook the coconut cream. Adjust seasoning according to your preferred taste.

5. To serve, ladle equal amounts into dessert bowls.

Nutrition: Calories 213 Fat 12 Fiber 21 Carbs 2 Protein 13

266. Raspberry Chocolate Parfait

Preparation Time: 5 minutes
Cooking Time: 45 minutes
Servings: 3
Ingredients:

- Raspberry chia seeds
- 3 tablespoons chia seeds
- 1 cup frozen raspberries, reserve some for garnish
- ⅛ teaspoon lemon juice, freshly squeezed
- ½ cup unsweetened almond milk
- ¼ teaspoon sugar
- ⅛ cup seed tapioca
- ½ tablespoon cocoa powder
- 1 bar dark chocolate, chopped, reserve some for garnish
- 1 cup unsweetened almond milk
- 1 cup water

Directions:

1. For the raspberry chia seeds, combine chia seeds, raspberries, almond milk, lemon juice, and white sugar. Mash berries. Mix ingredients well. Cover with saran wrap and place inside the fridge for 1 hour or until ready to use.
2. To make chocolate tapioca, combine dark chocolate, tapioca, cocoa powder, almond milk, and water.
3. Lock the lid in place. Press the high pressure and cook for 10 minutes.
4. When the beep sounds, Choose Natural Pressure Release. Depressurizing would take 20 minutes. Remove the lid.
5. To serve, spoon just the right amount of chocolate tapioca in glasses. Top with raspberry-chia mixture. Garnish with chopped chocolate and fresh raspberries.

Nutrition: Calories 213 Fat 12 Fiber 21 Carbs 2 Protein 13

267. Berry Jam with Chia Seeds

Preparation Time: 5 minutes
Cooking Time: 45 minutes
Servings: 3
Ingredients:

- 2 cups fresh blueberries, stemmed
- 1½ cups water
- 1 cup fresh raspberries, stemmed
- 1 cup sugar
- 1/16 teaspoon salt
- ½ cup chia seeds
- ¼ tablespoons lemon juice, freshly squeezed

Directions:

1. Place raspberries, blueberries, water, sugar, and salt into the Instant Pot Pressure Cooker. Stir.
2. Lock the lid in place. Press the high pressure and cook for 3 minutes.
3. When the beep sounds, Choose the Quick Pressure Release. This will depressurize for 7 minutes. Remove the lid.
4. Add in chia seeds and lemon juice.
5. Process jam into desired consistency using a potato masher. You may choose to have your jam smooth or chunky. Allow to cool before storing jam into an airtight container. Use as needed.

Nutrition: Calories 128 Fat 11 Fiber 13 Carbs 4.8 Protein 12

268. Apple Risotto

Preparation Time: 5 minutes
Cooking Time: 45 minutes
Servings: 3
Ingredients:

- ½ cup apples, sliced into thick disks
- 1½ cups barley pearls
- ¼ teaspoon cinnamon powder
- 2 cups water
- 1 cup apple juice
- 1 cup cashew milk

- ¼ cup cashew nuts, chopped
- ⅛ teaspoon nutmeg powder
- ¼ cup sugar

Directions:

1. Place apples, apple juice, barley pearls, water, cinnamon powder, cashew nuts, cashew milk, nutmeg powder, and sugar inside the Instant Pot Pressure Cooker.
2. Lock the lid in place. Press the high pressure and cook for 7 minutes.
3. When the beep sounds, Choose the Quick Pressure Release. This will depressurize for 7 minutes. Remove the lid. Adjust seasoning according to your preferred taste.
4. To serve, ladle equal amounts into dessert bowls.

Nutrition: Calories 128 Fat 11 Fiber 13 Carbs 4.8 Protein 12

269. Nectarines with Dried Cloves

Preparation Time: 5 minutes
Cooking Time: 50 minutes
Servings: 4
Ingredients:

- 4 dried cloves, whole
- 2 pounds nectarine, cubed
- ¼ cup agave sugar, reserve for garnish
- 1/16 teaspoon cinnamon powder
- 2 cups water

Directions:

1. Combine dried cloves, nectarine, water, cinnamon powder, and agave sugar into the Instant Pot Pressure Cooker.
2. Lock the lid in place. Press the high pressure and cook for 5 minutes.
3. When the beep sounds, Choose the Quick Pressure Release. This will depressurize for 7 minutes. Remove the lid. Discard dried cloves.
4. To serve, ladle just the right amount into dessert bowls. Sprinkle agave sugar.

Nutrition: Calories 267 Fat 23 Fiber 19 Carbs 5 Protein 21

270. Chocolate Raspberry Parfait

Preparation Time: 5 minutes
Cooking Time: 50 minutes
Servings: 2
Ingredients:

- Raspberry chia seeds
- 3 tablespoons chia seeds
- ½ cup almond milk, unsweetened
- ¼ teaspoon sugar
- 1 cup frozen raspberries, reserve some for garnish
- ⅛ teaspoon lemon juice, freshly squeezed
- Chocolate tapioca
- ½ tablespoon Dutch cocoa powder
- ⅛ cup seed tapioca, picked over
- 1 cup almond milk, unsweetened
- 1 cup water
- 4 squares dark chocolate, chopped, reserve some for garnish

Directions:

1. For the raspberry chia seeds, combine chia seeds, almond milk, sugar, raspberries, and lemon juice in a bowl. Mix well. Mash berries. Seal with saran wrap. Place inside the fridge until ready to use.
2. For the chocolate tapioca, put together cocoa powder, tapioca, almond milk, water, and dark chocolate into the crockpot. Stir.
3. Lock the lid in place. Press the high pressure and cook for 8 minutes.
4. When the beep sounds, Choose Natural Pressure Release. Depressurizing would take 20 minutes. Remove the lid.
5. To serve, spoon in half portions of chocolate tapioca in the heat-proof glass. Put just the right amount of raspberry-chia mixture on top. Garnish with whole raspberries and chopped chocolate.

Nutrition: Calories 321 Fat 22 Fiber 11 Carbs 4 Protein 26

271. Patbingsu – In Moderation

Preparation Time: 5 minutes
Cooking Time: 55 minutes
Servings: 6
Ingredients:

- ¼ cup dried red kidney beans, picked over
- 1 cup dried Adzuki beans, picked over
- ¼ cup dried pinto beans, picked over
- 6 cups water
- ½ tablespoon coconut oil
- 1 cup brown sugar
- 1/16 teaspoon green tea powder
- ½ cup loosely packed shaved ice, per person, prepare this only when about to serve
- ¼ cup almond milk, chilled

Directions:

1. For the bean base, place red kidney beans, adzuki beans, pinto beans, water, and coconut oil into the Instant Pot Pressure Cooker. Stir well.
2. Lock the lid in place. Press the high pressure and cook for 30 minutes.
3. When the beep sounds, Choose Natural Pressure Release. Depressurizing would take 20 minutes. Remove the lid.
4. Drain beans and reserve at least half of the cooking liquid. Put back into the crockpot.
5. Press the "Sauté" button. Stir in brown sugar. Turn off the machine immediately. Let it for 15 minutes or until it thickens.
6. To serve, place shaved ice into bowls. Spoon just the right amount of bean base. Garnish with green tea powder. Drizzle in almond milk. Serve.

Nutrition: Calories 216 Fat 32 Fiber 11 Carbs 4.9 Protein 26

272. Coconut Brown Rice Cake

Preparation Time: 5 minutes
Cooking Time: 55 minutes
Servings: 6
Ingredients:

- 1 cup brown rice
- ½ cup coconut flakes, for garnish
- ¼ cup raisins
- 2 cans thick coconut cream, reserve 3 teaspoon for garnish
- ⅛ teaspoon coconut oil, for greasing
- ½ cup water
- ¼ cup brown sugar

Directions:

1. Pour coconut flakes into the Instant Pot Pressure Cooker. Press the "sauté" button. Toast flakes until lightly brown. Set aside.
2. Meanwhile, lightly grease the sides and bottom of the pressure cooker.
3. Add in brown rice, 1 can of coconut cream, water brown sugar, and raisins.
4. Lock the lid in place. Press the high pressure and cook for 30 minutes.
5. When the beep sounds, Choose Natural Pressure Release. Depressurizing would take 20 minutes. Remove the lid.
6. To serve, place just the right amount of rice cake on a dessert plate. Put coconut flakes on top. Spoon coconut cream.

Nutrition: Calories 216 Fat 32 Fiber 11 Carbs 4.9 Protein 26

273. Rice Dumplings in Coconut Sauce

Preparation Time: 5 minutes
Cooking Time: 45 minutes
Servings: 4
Ingredients:

- ½ cup glutinous rice flour
- ¼ cup water
- 2 tablespoons heaping tapioca pearls, uncooked, picked over

- 2 cans (15-oz.) each thick coconut cream, divided
- ¼ cup sugar & 1/16 teaspoon salt
- 2 cups water
- ½ cup fresh ripe jackfruits, shredded, reserved half for garnish

Directions:

1. For the dumplings, put together glutinous rice flour and water in a bowl. Massage until dough forms into a soft ball. Seal bowl with saran wrap. Let the dough rest for 5 minutes.
2. Roll dough in the palm of your hands. Place on a baking sheet lined with parchment paper. Repeat the same procedure for the rest of the dumplings. Set aside.
3. For the coconut sauce, pour tapioca pearls, 1 can of coconut cream, sugar, salt, water, and ripe jackfruit into the Instant Pot Pressure Cooker
4. Lock the lid in place. Press the high pressure and cook for 7 minutes.
5. When the beep sounds, Choose the Quick Pressure Release. This will depressurize for 7 minutes. Remove the lid.
6. Press the "Sauté" button once again. Bring coconut sauce to a boil.
7. Drop dumplings or until they rise to the top of the cooking liquid. Do not stir.
8. Turn off the machine. Stir in the remaining can of coconut cream. Adjust seasoning according to your preferred taste.
9. To serve, ladle equal amounts into dessert bowls. Garnish with shredded jackfruits.

Nutrition: Calories 149 Fat 33 Fiber 13 Carbs 3.9 Protein 23

274. Roasted Cauliflower with Prosciutto, Capers, and Almonds

Preparation Time: 5 minutes
Cooking Time: 23 minutes
Servings: 4
Ingredients:

- 12 ounces cauliflower florets (I get precut florets at Trader Joe's)
- 2 tablespoons leftover bacon grease, or olive oil
- Pink Himalayan salt
- Freshly ground black pepper
- 2 ounces sliced prosciutto, torn into small pieces
- ¼ cup slivered almonds
- 2 tablespoons capers
- 2 tablespoons grated Parmesan cheese

Directions:

- Preheat the oven to 400°F. Line a baking pan with a silicone baking mat or parchment paper.
- Put the cauliflower florets in the prepared baking pan with the bacon grease, and season with pink Himalayan salt and pepper. Or if you are using olive oil instead, drizzle the cauliflower with olive oil and season with pink Himalayan salt and pepper.
- Roast the cauliflower for 15 minutes.
- Stir the cauliflower so all sides are coated with the bacon grease.
- Distribute the prosciutto pieces in the pan. Then add the slivered almonds and capers. Stir to combine. Sprinkle the Parmesan cheese on top, and roast for 10 minutes more.
- Divide between two plates, using a slotted spoon so you don't get excess grease in the plates, and serve.

Nutrition: Calories: 576; Total Fat: 48 g; Carbs: 1.4 g; Fiber: 6 g; Protein: 28 g

275. Buttery Slow-Cooker Mushrooms

Preparation Time: 5 minutes
Cooking Time: 4 hours
Servings: 4
Ingredients:

- 6 tablespoons butter
- 1 tablespoon packaged dry ranch-dressing mix
- 8 ounces fresh cremini mushrooms
- ½ tablespoons grated Parmesan cheese
- 1 tablespoon chopped fresh flat-leaf Italian parsley

Directions:

1. With the crock insert in place, preheat the slow cooker to low.
2. Put the butter and the dry ranch dressing in the bottom of the slow cooker, and allow the butter to melt. Stir to blend the dressing mix and butter.
3. Add the mushrooms to the slow cooker, and stir to coat with the butter-dressing mixture. Sprinkle the top with Parmesan cheese.
4. Cover and cook on low for 4 hours.
5. Use a slotted spoon to transfer the mushrooms to a serving dish. Top with the chopped parsley and serve.

Nutrition: Calories: 701; Total Fat: 72 g; Carbs: 3; Fiber: 2 g Protein: 11 g

276. Roasted Radishes with Brown Butter Sauce

Preparation Time: 10 minutes
Cooking Time: 15 minutes
Servings: 2
Ingredients:

- 2 cups halved radishes
- 1 tablespoon olive oil
- Pink Himalayan salt
- Freshly ground black pepper
- ½ tablespoons butter
- 1 tablespoon chopped fresh flat-leaf Italian parsley

Directions:

1. Preheat the oven to 450°F.
2. In a medium bowl, toss the radishes in olive oil and season with pink Himalayan salt and pepper.

3. Spread the radishes on a baking sheet in a single layer. Roast for 15 minutes, stirring halfway through.
4. Meanwhile, when the radishes have been roasting for about 10 minutes, in a small, light-colored saucepan over medium heat, melt the butter completely, stirring frequently, and season with pink Himalayan salt. When the butter begins to bubble and foam, continue stirring. When the bubbling diminishes a bit, the butter should be a nice nutty brown. The browning process should take about 3 minutes total. Transfer the browned butter to a heat-safe container (I use a mug).
5. Remove the radishes from the oven, and divide them between two plates. Spoon the brown butter over the radishes, top with the chopped parsley, and serve.

Nutrition: Calories: 361; Total Fat: 37 g; Carbs: 3.8 g; Fiber: 4 g; Protein: 2 g

277. Parmesan and Pork Rind Green Beans

Preparation Time: 5 minutes
Cooking Time: 15 minutes
Servings: 4
Ingredients:

- ½ pound fresh green beans
- 2 tablespoons crushed pork rinds
- 2 tablespoons olive oil
- 1 tablespoon grated Parmesan cheese
- Pink Himalayan salt
- Freshly ground black pepper

Directions:

1. Preheat the oven to 400°F.
2. In a medium bowl, combine the green beans, pork rinds, olive oil, and Parmesan cheese. Season with pink Himalayan salt and pepper, and toss until the beans are thoroughly coated.
3. Spread the bean mixture on a baking sheet in a single layer, and roast for about 15

minutes. At the halfway point, give the pan a little shake to move the beans around, or just give them a stir.
4. Divide the beans between two plates and serve.

Nutrition: Calories: 350; Total Fat: 30 g; Carbs: 1.6 g; Fiber: 6 g; Protein: 8 g

278. Pesto Cauliflower Steaks

Preparation Time: 5 minutes
Cooking Time: 20 minutes
Servings: 4
Ingredients:

- 2 tablespoons olive oil, plus more for brushing
- ½ head cauliflower
- Pink Himalayan salt & Freshly ground black pepper
- 2 cups fresh basil leaves
- ½ cup grated Parmesan cheese
- ¼ cup almonds
- ½ cup shredded mozzarella cheese

Directions:

1. Preheat the oven to 425°F. Brush a baking sheet with olive oil or line with a silicone baking mat.
2. To prep, the cauliflower steaks, remove and discard the leaves and cut the cauliflower into 1-inch-thick slices. You can roast the extra floret crumbles that fall off with the steaks.
3. Place the cauliflower steaks on the prepared baking sheet, and brush them with olive oil. You want the surface just lightly coated so it gets caramelized. Season with pink Himalayan salt and pepper.
4. Roast the cauliflower steaks for 20 minutes.
5. Meanwhile, put the basil, Parmesan cheese, almonds, and 2 tablespoons of olive oil in a food processor (or blender), and season with pink Himalayan salt and pepper. Mix until combined.

6. Spread some pesto on top of each cauliflower steak, and top with the mozzarella cheese. Return to the oven and bake until the cheese melts, about 2 minutes.
7. Place the cauliflower steaks on two plates, and serve hot.

Nutrition: Calories: 895; Total Fat: 68 g; Carbs: 3.4 g; Net Carbs: 20 g; Fiber: 14 g; Protein: 47 g

279. Tomato, Avocado, and Cucumber Salad

Preparation Time: 5 minutes
Cooking Time: 5 minutes
Servings: 2
Ingredients:

- ½ cup grape tomatoes, halved
- 4 small Persian cucumbers or 1 English cucumber, peeled and finely chopped
- 1 avocado, finely chopped
- ¼ cup crumbled feta cheese
- 1 tablespoon vinaigrette salad dressing (I use Primal Kitchen Greek Vinaigrette)
- Pink Himalayan salt
- Freshly ground black pepper

Directions:

1. In a large bowl, combine the tomatoes, cucumbers, avocado, and feta cheese.
2. Add the vinaigrette, and season with pink Himalayan salt and pepper. Toss to thoroughly combine.
3. Divide the salad between two plates and serve.

Nutrition: Calories: 516; Total Fat: 45 g; Carbs: 2.3 g; Net Carbs: 11 g; Fiber: 12 g; Protein: 10 g

280. Crunchy Pork Rind Zucchini Sticks

Preparation Time: 5 minutes
Cooking Time: 25 minutes
Servings: 4
Ingredients:

- 2 medium zucchini, halved lengthwise and seeded
- ¼ cup crushed pork rinds
- ¼ cup grated Parmesan cheese
- 2 garlic cloves, minced
- 2 tablespoons melted butter
- Pink Himalayan salt

- Freshly ground black pepper
- Olive oil, for drizzling

Directions:

1. Preheat the oven to 400°F. Line a baking sheet with aluminum foil or a silicone baking mat.
2. Place the zucchini halves cut-side up on the prepared baking sheet.
3. In a medium bowl, combine the pork rinds, Parmesan cheese, garlic, and melted butter, and season with pink Himalayan salt and pepper. Mix until well combined.
4. Spoon the pork-rind mixture onto each zucchini stick, and drizzle each with a little olive oil.
5. Bake for about 20 minutes, or until the topping is golden brown.
6. Turn on the broiler to finish browning the zucchini sticks, 3 to 5 minutes, and serve.

Nutrition: Calories: 461 Total Fat: 39 g; Carbs: 1.5 g; Fiber: 4 g; Protein: 17 g

281. Cheese Chips and Guacamole

Preparation Time: 10 minutes
Cooking Time: 10 minutes
Servings: 4
Ingredients:

- 1 cup shredded cheese (I use Mexican blend)

For the Guacamole:

- 1 avocado, mashed
- Juice of ½ lime
- 1 teaspoon diced jalapeño
- 1 tablespoon chopped fresh cilantro leaves
- Pink Himalayan salt
- Freshly ground black pepper

Directions:

1. Preheat the oven to 350°F. Line a baking sheet with parchment paper or a silicone baking mat.
2. Add ¼-cup mounds of shredded cheese to the pan, leaving plenty of space between them, and bake

until the edges are brown and the middles have fully melted, about 7 minutes.

3. Set the pan on a cooling rack, and let the cheese chips cool for 5 minutes. The chips will be floppy when they first come out of the oven but will crisp as they cool.
4. In a medium bowl, mix together the avocado, lime juice, jalapeño, and cilantro, and season with pink Himalayan salt and pepper.
5. Top the cheese chips with the guacamole, and serve.

Nutrition: Calories: 646; Total Fat: 54 g; Carbs: 1.6 g; Fiber: 10 g; Protein: 30 g

282. Cauliflower "Potato" Salad

Preparation Time: 5 minutes
Cooking Time: 45 minutes
Servings: 4
Ingredients:

- ½ head cauliflower
- 1 tablespoon olive oil
- Pink Himalayan salt
- Freshly ground black pepper
- ⅓ cup mayonnaise
- 1 tablespoon mustard
- ¼ cup diced dill pickles
- 1 teaspoon paprika

Directions:

1. Preheat the oven to 400°F. Line a baking sheet with aluminum foil or a silicone baking mat.
2. Cut the cauliflower into 1-inch pieces.
3. Put the cauliflower in a large bowl, add the olive oil, season with the pink Himalayan salt and pepper, and toss to combine.
4. Spread the cauliflower out on the prepared baking sheet and bake for 25 minutes, or just until the cauliflower begins to brown. Halfway through the cooking time, give the pan a couple of shakes or stir so all sides of the cauliflower cook.

5. In a large bowl, mix the cauliflower together with the mayonnaise, mustard, and pickles. Sprinkle the paprika on top, and chill in the refrigerator for 3 hours before serving.

Nutrition: Calories: 772; Total Fat: 74 g; Carbs: 2.6 g; Fiber: 10 g; Protein: 10 g

283. Loaded Cauliflower Mashed "Potatoes"

Preparation Time: 10 minutes
Cooking Time: 10 minutes
Servings: 4
Ingredients:

- 1 head fresh cauliflower, cut into cubes
- 2 garlic cloves, minced
- 6 tablespoons butter
- ½ tablespoons sour cream
- Pink Himalayan salt
- Freshly ground black pepper
- 1 cup shredded cheese (I use Colb. y Jack)
- 6 bacon slices, cooked and crumbled

Directions:

1. Boil a large pot of water over high heat. Add the cauliflower. Reduce the heat to medium-low and simmer for 8 to 10 minutes, until fork-tender. (You can also steam the cauliflower if you have a steamer basket.)
2. Drain the cauliflower in a colander, and turn it out onto a paper towel-lined plate to soak up the water. Blot to remove any remaining water from the cauliflower pieces. This step is important; you want to get out as much water as possible so the mash won't be runny.
3. Add the cauliflower to the food processor (or blender) with the garlic, butter, and sour cream, and season with pink Himalayan salt and pepper.
4. Mix for about 1 minute, stopping to scrape down the sides of the bowl every 30 seconds.

5. Divide the cauliflower mix evenly among four small serving dishes, and top each with the cheese and bacon crumbles. (The cheese should melt from the hot cauliflower. But if you want to reheat it, you can put the cauliflower in oven-safe serving dishes and pop them under the broiler for 1 minute to heat up the cauliflower and melt the cheese.)

Nutrition: Calories: 131; Total Fat: 132 g; Carbs: 3.4 g; Fiber: 12 g; Protein: 58 g

284. Almond Bread

Preparation Time: 5 minutes
Cooking Time: 25 minutes
Servings: 4
Ingredients:

- 5 tablespoons butter, at room temperature, divided
- 6 large eggs, lightly beaten
- 1½ cups almond flour
- 3 teaspoons baking powder
- Pinch pink Himalayan salt

Directions:

1. Preheat the oven to 390°F. Coat a 9-by-5-inch loaf pan with 1 tablespoon of butter.
2. In a large bowl, use a hand mixer to mix the eggs, almond flour, remaining 4 tablespoons of butter, baking powder, MCT oil powder (if using), and pink Himalayan salt until thoroughly blended. Pour into the prepared pan.
3. Bake for 25 minutes, or until a toothpick inserted in the center comes out clean.
4. Slice and serve.

Nutrition: Calories: 165 TotalFat: 178 g; Carbs: 4.6 g; Net Carbs: 27 g; Fiber: 19 g; Protein: 74 g

285. Cheese Stuffed Mushrooms

Preparation Time: 10 minutes
Cooking Time: 15 minutes
Servings: 12
Ingredients:

- 12 large mushrooms, clean, remove stems and chopped stems finely
- 1½ tablespoons fresh parsley, chopped

- 4 garlic cloves, minced
- ½ cup parmesan cheese, grated
- ¼ cup Swiss cheese, grated
- 3.5 ounces cream cheese
- 1 tablespoon olive oil Salt

Directions:

1. Preheat the oven to 375°F.
2. Toss mushrooms with vegetable oil and place onto a baking tray.
3. In a bowl, combine cheese, chopped mushrooms stems, parsley, garlic, parmesan cheese, Swiss cheese, and salt.
4. Stuff cheese mixture into the mushroom caps and arrange mushrooms on the baking tray.
5. Bake in a preheated oven for 10-15 minutes.
6. Serve and luxuriate in.

Nutrition: Calories 79 Fat 6.3 g Carbohydrates 1.5 g Sugar 0.5 g Protein 4 g Cholesterol 16 mg

286. Delicious Chicken Alfredo Dip

Preparation Time: 10 minutes
Cooking Time: 20 minutes
Servings: 8
Ingredients:

- 2 cups chicken, cooked and chopped into small pieces
- 1½ tablespoons fresh parsley, chopped
- 1 tomato, diced
- 2 bacon slices, cooked and crumbled
- 1½ cups mozzarella cheese, shredded
- 1 teaspoon Italian seasoning
- ½ cup parmesan cheese, grated
- 8 ounces cream cheese, softened
- 1½ cups Alfredo sauce, homemade & low-carb

Directions:

1. Preheat the oven to 375°F.
2. Spray a baking dish with cooking spray and put aside.
3. Add chicken, ½ cup mozzarella cheese, Italian seasoning, parmesan cheese,

cheese, and Alfredo sauce to the bowl and mix.
4. Spread chicken mixture into the prepared baking dish and top with remaining mozzarella cheese.
5. Bake in a preheated oven for 20 minutes. Top with parsley, tomatoes, and bacon.
6. Serve and luxuriate in.

Nutrition: Calories 144 Fat 0.5 g Carbohydrates 7.4 g Sugar 1.3 g Protein 29.3 g Cholesterol 216 mg

287. Perfect Cucumber Salsa

Preparation Time: 5 minutes
Cooking Time: 5 minutes
Servings: 10
Ingredients:

- 2½ cups cucumbers, peeled, seeded, and chopped
- 2 teaspoons fresh cilantro, chopped
- 2 teaspoons fresh parsley, chopped
- 1½ tablespoons fresh lemon juice
- 1 garlic clove, minced
- 1 small onion, chopped
- 2 large jalapeno peppers, chopped
- 1½ cups tomatoes, chopped
- ½ teaspoon salt

Directions:

1. Add all ingredients into the massive bowl and blend until well combined.
2. Serve and luxuriate in.

Nutrition: Calories 14 Fat 0.2 g Carbohydrates 3 g Sugar 1.6 g Protein 0.6 g Cholesterol 0 mg

288. Creamy Avocado Sauce

Preparation Time: 5 minutes
Cooking Time: 5 minutes
Servings: 8
Ingredients:

- 1 avocado, halved, seeded, and peeled
- 1 tablespoon fresh lemon juice
- 2 garlic cloves
- 2 tablespoons olive oil
- 3 tablespoons fresh parsley, chopped

- Pepper Salt

Directions:
1. Add all ingredients into the food processor and process until smooth.
2. Serve and enjoy.

Nutrition: Calories 83 Fat 8.4 g Carbohydrates 2.6 g Sugar 0.2 g Protein 0.6 g Cholesterol 0 mg

289. Zucchini Tots

Preparation Time: 10 minutes
Cooking Time: 20 minutes
Servings: 4
Ingredients:

- 5 cups zucchini, grated and squeeze out all liquid
- ½ teaspoon garlic powder ½ teaspoon dried oregano
- ½ cup parmesan cheese, grated
- ½ cup cheddar cheese, shredded
- 2 eggs, lightly beaten
- Pepper Salt

Directions:
1. Preheat the oven to 400°F.
2. Spray a baking tray with cooking spray and put aside.
3. Add all ingredients into the bowl and blend until well combined.
4. Make small tots from the zucchini mixture and place onto the prepared baking tray.
5. Bake in a preheated oven for 15-20 minutes.
6. Serve and luxuriate in.

Nutrition: Calories 353 Fat 23.1 g Carbohydrates 9.5 g Sugar 2.8 g Protein 32.1g Cholesterol 157mg

290. Avocado Yogurt Dip

Preparation Time: 5 minutes
Cooking Time: 5 minutes
Servings: 4
Ingredients:

- 2 avocados
- 1 lime juice
- 3 garlic cloves, minced
- ½ cup Greek yogurt
- Pepper Salt

Directions:
1. Scoop out avocado flesh using the spoon and place it during a bowl.
2. Mash avocado flesh using the fork.

3. Add remaining ingredients and stir to mix.
4. Serve and luxuriate in.

Nutrition: Calories 139 Fat 11 g Carbohydrates 9 g Protein 4 g Sugar 2 g Cholesterol 15 mg

291. Macadamia Hummus

Preparation Time: 10 minutes
Cooking Time: 5 minutes
Servings: 8
Ingredients:

- 1 cup macadamia nuts, soaked in water overnight, drained and rinsed
- 1½ tablespoons tahini
- 2 tablespoons water
- 2 tablespoons fresh lime juice
- 2 garlic cloves
- ⅛ teaspoon cayenne pepper
- Pepper Salt

Directions:
1. Add all ingredients into the food processor and process until smooth.
2. Serve and enjoy.

Nutrition: Calories 138 Fat 14.2 g Carbohydrates 3.2 g Protein 1.9 g Sugar 1.9 g Cholesterol 0 mg

292. Easy & Perfect Meatballs

Preparation Time: 10 minutes
Cooking Time: 20 minutes
Servings: 8
Ingredients:

- 1 egg, lightly beaten
- 3 garlic cloves, minced
- ½ cup mozzarella cheese, shredded
- ½ cup parmesan cheese, grated
- 1 pound ground beef
- Pepper Salt

Directions:
1. Preheat the oven to 400°F.
2. Line baking tray with parchment paper and put aside.
3. Add all ingredients into the blending bowl and blend until well combined.
4. Make small balls from the meat mixture and place on a prepared baking tray.
5. Bake in a preheated oven for 20 minutes.
6. Serve and luxuriate in.

Nutrition: Calories 157 Fat 6.7 g Carbohydrates 0.5 g Protein 21.5 g Sugar 0.1 g Cholesterol 80 mg

293. Eggplant Chips

Preparation Time: 10 minutes
Cooking Time: 20 minutes
Servings: 15
Ingredients:

- 1 large eggplant, thinly sliced
- ¼ cup parmesan cheese, grated
- 1 teaspoon dried oregano
- ¼ tsp dried basil
- ½ teaspoon garlic powder
- ¼ cup olive oil
- ¼ tsp pepper
- ½ teaspoon salt

Directions:
1. Preheat the oven to 325°F.
2. Using a small bowl, mix oil, and dried spices.
3. Coat eggplant with oil and spice mixture and arrange eggplant slices on a baking tray.
4. Bake in a preheated oven for 15-20 minutes. Turn halfway through.
5. Remove from oven and sprinkle with cheese.
6. Serve and luxuriate in.

Nutrition: Calories 77 Fat 5.8 g Carbohydrates 2 g Protein 3.5 g Sugar 0.9 g Cholesterol 8 mg

294. Creamy Crab Dip

Preparation Time: 5 minutes
Cooking Time: 5 minutes
Servings: 16
Ingredients:

- 8 ounces crab meat
- ¼ teaspoon garlic powder
- 2 tablespoons green onion, chopped
- 1 teaspoon Cajun seasoning
- 1 tablespoon lime juice
- ¼ cup mayonnaise
- 3.5 ounces cream cheese
- ¼ teaspoon pepper
- ½ teaspoon salt

Directions:
1. Add all ingredients into the mixing bowl and whisk until well combined.
2. Serve and enjoy.

Nutrition: Calories 49 Fat 3.6 g Carbohydrates 1.4 g Protein 2.3 g Sugar 0.3 g Cholesterol 15 mg

295. Healthy Chicken Fritters

Preparation Time: 10 minutes
Cooking Time: 20 minutes
Servings: 4
Ingredients:

- 1½ pounds chicken breast, skinless, boneless, and chopped into small pieces
- 1 tablespoon olive oil
- ½ teaspoon garlic powder
- 2 tablespoons fresh parsley, chopped1½ tablespoons chives, chopped
- 1½ tablespoons fresh basil, chopped
- 1 cup mozzarella cheese, shredded
- ⅓ cup almond flour
- 2 eggs, lightly beaten
- Pepper Salt

Directions:

1. Add all ingredients except oil into the massive bowl and blend until well combined.
2. Heat oil during a pan over medium heat.
3. Scoop fritter mixture employing a large spoon and transfer it to the pan and cook for 6-8 minutes or until golden brown on each side.
4. Serve and luxuriate in.

Nutrition: Calories 331 Fat 15.9 g Carbohydrates 2.9 g Protein 43 g Sugar 0.6 g Cholesterol 194 mg

296. Creamy Mushrooms with Garlic and Thyme

Preparation Time: 5 minutes
Cooking Time: 15 minutes
Servings: 4
Ingredients:

- 4 tablespoons unsalted butter
- ½ cup onion, chopped
- 1-pound button mushrooms
- 2 teaspoons garlic, diced
- 1 tablespoon fresh thyme
- 1 tablespoon parsley, chopped
- ½ teaspoon salt
- ¼ teaspoon black pepper

Directions:

1. Melt the butter during a pan. Place the mushrooms into the pan. Add salt and pepper. Cook the mushroom mix for about 5 minutes until they're browned on each side.
2. Add the garlic and thyme. Additionally, sauté the mushrooms for 1-2 minutes. Top them with parsley.

Nutrition: Carbohydrates: 45 g Fat: 8 g Protein: 3 g Calories: 99

297. Easy Roasted Broccoli

Preparation Time: 2 minutes
Cooking Time: 19 minutes
Servings: 4
Ingredients:

- 1-pound frozen broccoli, cut into florets
- 3 teaspoons olive oil
- Sea salt, to taste

Directions:

1. Place broccoli florets on a baking sheet greased with oil and put in the oven (preheated to 400°F).
2. Sprinkle the olive oil over the florets.
3. Cook for 12 minutes. Whisk well and bake for an additional 7 minutes.

Nutrition: Carbohydrates: 8 g Fat: 3 g Protein: 3 g Calories: 58

298. Zucchini Strips with Marinara Dip

Preparation Time: 1 hour and 10 minutes
Cooking Time: 30 minutes
Servings: 8
Ingredients:

- 2 zucchinis, sliced into strips
- Salt to taste
- 1½ cups all-purpose flour
- 2 eggs, beaten
- 2 cups bread crumbs
- 2 teaspoons onion powder
- 1 tablespoon garlic powder
- ¼ cup Parmesan cheese, grated
- ½ cup marinara sauce

Directions:

1. Season zucchini with salt.
2. Let sit for 15 minutes.
3. Pat dry with paper towels.
4. Add flour to a bowl.
5. Add eggs to another bowl.
6. Mix remaining ingredients except marinara sauce in a third bowl.
7. Dip zucchini strips in the first, second and third bowls.
8. Cover with foil and freeze for 45 minutes.
9. Add crisper plate to the Air Fryer basket inside the Power XL Grill.
10. Select the Air Fry function.
11. Preheat to 360°F for 3 minutes.
12. Add zucchini strips to the crisper plate.
13. Air Fry for 20 minutes.
14. Flip and cook for another 10 minutes.
15. Serve with marinara dip.

Nutrition: Calories: 364 Fat: 35 g Saturated Fat: 17 g Trans Fat: 0 g Carbohydrates: 8 g Fiber: 1.5 g Sodium: 291 mg Protein: 8 g

299. Roasted Garlic Dip

Preparation Time: 10 minutes
Cooking Time: 20 minutes
Servings: 6
Ingredients:

- 1 head garlic
- ½ tablespoon olive oil

Directions:

1. Slice the top off the garlic.
2. Drizzle with olive oil.
3. Add to the Air Fryer.
4. Set it to roast.
5. Cook at 390°F for 20 minutes.
6. Peel the garlic.
7. Transfer to a food processor.
8. Pulse until smooth.

Nutrition: Calories: 207cal, Carbs: 17 g, Protein: 9 g, Fat: 12 g.

300. Kohlrabi Chips

Preparation Time: 10 minutes
Cooking Time: 20 minutes
Servings: 10
Ingredients:

- 1 pound kohlrabi, peel and slice thinly
- 1 teaspoon paprika
- 1 tablespoon olive oil
- 1 teaspoon salt

Directions:

1. Preheat the Air Fryer to 320°F.
2. Add all ingredients into the bowl and toss to coat.
3. Transfer kohlrabi into the Air Fryer basket and cook for 20 minutes. Toss halfway through.
4. Serve and enjoy.

Nutrition: Calories 108 Fat 1.4 g Carbohydrates 17.4 g Sugar 2.4 g Protein 7.3 g Cholesterol 0 mg

301. Daikon Chips

Preparation Time: 10 minutes
Cooking Time: 16 minutes
Servings: 6
Ingredients:

- 15 ounces Daikon, slice into chips
- 1 tablespoon olive oil
- 1 teaspoon chili powder
- ½ teaspoon pepper
- 1 teaspoon salt

Directions:

1. Preheat the Air Fryer to 375°F.
2. Add all ingredients into the bowl and toss to coat.
3. Transfer sliced the daikon into the Air Fryer basket and cook for 16 minutes. Toss halfway through.
4. Serve and enjoy.

Nutrition:
Calories: 207cal, Carbs: 17 g, Protein: 9 g, Fat: 12 g.

302. Kale Dip

Preparation Time: 10 minutes
Cooking Time: 12 minutes
Servings: 6
Ingredients:

- 1 pound kale, wash and chopped
- 1 cup heavy cream
- 1 onion, diced
- 1 teaspoon butter
- oz parmesan cheese, shredded
- ¼ teaspoon pepper
- 1 teaspoon salt

Directions:

1. Add all ingredients into the Air Fryer baking dish and stir well.
2. Preheat the Air Fryer to 250°F.

3. Place dish in the Air Fryer and cook for 12 minutes.
4. Serve and enjoy.

Nutrition: Calories: 117 cal, Carbs: 27 g, Protein:11 g, Fat: 12 g.

303. Jalapeno Cheese Dip

Preparation Time: 10 minutes
Cooking Time: 16 minutes
Servings: 6
Ingredients:

- 1½ cup Monterey jack cheese, shredded
- ½ cup cheddar cheese, shredded
- jalapeno pepper, minced
- 1 teaspoon garlic powder
- ⅓ cup sour cream
- ⅓ cup mayonnaise
- ounce cream cheese, softened
- bacon slices, cooked and crumbled
- Pepper Salt

Directions:

1. Preheat the Air Fryer to 325°F.
2. Add all ingredients into the bowl and mix until combined.
3. Transfer bowl mixture into the Air Fryer baking dish and place in the Air Fryer and cook for 16 minutes.
4. Serve and enjoy.

Nutrition: Calories: 227cal, Carbs: 27 g, Protein: 9 g, Fat: 10 g.

304. Spicy Dip

Preparation Time: 5 minutes
Cooking Time: 5 minutes
Servings: 6
Ingredients:

- 12 ounces hot peppers, chopped
- 1½ cups apple cider vinegar
- Pepper Salt

Directions:

1. Add all ingredients into the Air Fryer baking dish and stir well.
2. Place dish in the Air Fryer and cook at 380°F for 5 minutes.
3. Transfer pepper mixture into the blender and blend until smooth.
4. Serve and enjoy.

Nutrition: Calories: 207cal, Carbs: 17 g, Protein: 9 g, Fat: 12 g.

305. Onion Dip

Preparation Time: 10 minutes
Cooking Time: 25 minutes
Servings: 8
Ingredients:

- 2 pounds onion, chopped
- ½ teaspoon baking soda
- tablespoon butter, softened
- Pepper Salt

Directions:

1. Melt butter in a pan over medium heat.
2. Add onion and baking soda and sauté for 5 minutes.
3. Transfer the onion mixture into the Air Fryer baking dish.
4. Place in the Air Fryer and cook at 370°F for 25 minutes.
5. Serve and enjoy.

Nutrition: Calories 143 Fat 9 g Carbohydrates 8.1 g Sugar 5.7 g Protein 9 g Cholesterol 175 mg

306. Easy Carrot Dip

Preparation Time: 10 minutes
Cooking Time: 15 minutes
Servings: 6
Ingredients:

- 2 cups carrots, grated
- ¼ teaspoon cayenne pepper
- 1 tablespoon butter, melted
- 1 tablespoon chives, chopped
- Pepper Salt

Directions:

1. Add all ingredients into the Air Fryer baking dish and stir until well combined.
2. Place dish in the Air Fryer and cook at 380°F for 15 minutes.
3. Transfer cook carrot mixture into the blender and blend until smooth.
4. Serve and enjoy.

Nutrition: Calories 211 Fat 9 g Carbohydrates 7.2 g Sugar 3.4 g Protein 9 g Cholesterol 155 mg

307. Panko Tofu with Mayo Sauce

Preparation Time: 10 minutes
Cooking Time: 20 minutes
Servings: 4
Ingredients:

- 8 tofu cutlets

For the Marinade:
- 1 tablespoon toasted sesame oil
- ¼ cup soy sauce
- 1 teaspoon rice vinegar
- ½ teaspoon garlic powder
- 1 teaspoon ground ginger

Make the Tofu:
- ½ cup vegan mayo
- 1 cup panko breadcrumbs
- 1 teaspoon of sea salt

Directions:
1. Whisk the marinade ingredients in a bowl and add tofu cutlets. Mix well to coat the cutlets. Cover and marinate for 1 hour.
2. Meanwhile, whisk crumbs with salt and mayo in a bowl. Coat the cutlets with crumbs mixture. Place the tofu cutlets in the Air Fryer basket. Set the basket inside the Air Fryer toaster oven and close the lid.
3. Select the Air Fry mode at 370°F temperature for 20 minutes. Flip the cutlets after 10 minutes then resume cooking. Serve warm.

Nutrition: Calories: 151 Cal Protein: 1.9 g Carbs: 6.9 g Fat: 8.6 g

308. Lemon Avocado Salad Dressing
Preparation Time: 5 minutes
Cooking Time: 5 minutes
Servings: 2-3
Ingredients:
- 2 tablespoons olive oil
- 1 garlic clove, minced
- ½ teaspoon seasoned salt
- 1 medium ripe avocado, peeled and mashed
- ¼ cup water
- 2 tablespoons sour cream
- 2 tablespoons lemon juice
- 1 tablespoon minced fresh dill or 1 teaspoon dill weed
- ½ teaspoon honey
- Salad greens, cherry tomatoes, sliced cucumbers, and sweet red and yellow pepper strips

Directions:
1. In a blender, combine the first nine ingredients; cover and process until blended.
2. Serve with salad greens, tomatoes, cucumbers, and peppers. Store in the refrigerator.

Nutrition: Calories: 38.2 Fat: 2.6g Cholesterol: 1.2mg Carbohydrates: 3.6 g Fiber: 1.0 g Protein: 0.8g

309. Creamy Avocado Cilantro Lime Dressing
Preparation Time: 20 minutes
Cooking Time: 10 minutes
Servings: 6-8
Ingredients:
- ¼ cup olive oil
- ¼ teaspoon of sea salt
- ½ cup cilantro, chopped
- ¼ cup plain goat yogurt
- Juice of ½ lime
- 1 teaspoon lime zest
- 1 avocado
- 1 clove garlic, peeled
- ½ jalapeno, chopped
- ¼ teaspoon pepper
- ½ teaspoon cumin

Directions:
1. Place/put all the ingredients in a food processor or mixer and mix it until well balanced.

Nutrition: Calories: 123 Protein: 1 g Fat: 12 g Carbohydrates: 3.6 g

310. Creamy Avocado Dressing
Preparation Time: 5 minutes
Cooking Time: 5 minutes
Servings: 4
Ingredients:
- ¼ teaspoon ground black pepper
- Water, as needed
- 1 whole large avocado
- 1 clove garlic, peeled
- ½ tablespoon fresh lime or lemon juice
- 3 tablespoons olive oil or avocado oil
- ¼ teaspoon kosher salt

Directions:
1. Put the peeled clove of garlic, lime or lemon juice, avocado, olive oil, salt, and pepper into a mini food processor.
2. Process till smooth, stopping a few times to scrape the sides down. Thin the salad dressing out with some water (¼ cup to ½ cup) before a perfect consistency is achieved.
3. Maintain/keep at least a week in an airtight container, but 3 to 4 days is best.

Nutrition: Calories: 38.2 Fat: 2.6 g Cholesterol: 1.2 mg Carbohydrates: 3.6 g Fiber: 1.0 g

311. Southwestern Avocado Salad Dressing
Preparation Time: 5 minutes
Cooking Time: 1 hour
Servings: 8
Ingredients:
- 1 ripe avocado
- 1 cup buttermilk
- ½ teaspoon garlic powder
- ½ teaspoon chipotle chili powder
- ½ teaspoon salt
- ¼ cup cilantro
- Juice of ½ lime
- 1 teaspoon ranch seasoning powder homemade or store-bought

Directions:
1. Break the avocado in half, extract the pit from the flesh and scoop the skin.
2. Attach all the other ingredients together to a mixer.
3. Blend in until creamy and smooth.
4. Prior to serving, refrigerate for one hour.
5. Keeps in the refrigerator for 3 days.

Nutrition: Calories: 61 Fat: 4 g Cholesterol: 3 mg Carbohydrates: 4 g Fiber: 1 g Protein: 1 g

312. Mango Salsa
Preparation Time: 15 minutes
Cooking Time: 15 minutes
Servings: 6
Ingredients:
- 1 avocado; peeled, pitted, and cubed
- 2 tablespoons fresh key lime juice
- 1 mango; peeled, pitted, and cubed
- 1 cup cherry tomatoes, quartered

- 1 tablespoon fresh cilantro, chopped
- Sea salt, as needed

Directions:
1. In a bowl, add avocado cubes and lime juice and mix well.
2. In the bowl, add remaining ingredients and stir to combine.
3. Serve immediately.

Nutrition: Calories 108 Fats 1.4 g Cholesterol 0 mg Carbohydrates 12.5 g Fiber 3.5 g Protein 1.4 g

313. Roasted Tomato Sauce

Preparation Time: 15 minutes
Cooking Time: 40 minutes
Servings: 6
Ingredients:
- 18 Roma tomatoes
- ½ red bell pepper
- ½ sweet onion
- ½ red onion
- 1 medium shallot
- ⅛ cup grapeseed oil
- 1 tablespoon agave
- 3 teaspoons sea salt
- 3 teaspoons basil
- 2 teaspoons oregano
- 2 teaspoons onion powder
- ⅛ teaspoon cayenne powder

Equipment:
- Blender
- Cookie sheet
- Parchment paper
- Pot—at least 4 quart

Directions:
1. Preheat your oven to 400°F.
2. Chop the vegetables in half and place them in a bowl.
3. Sprinkle grapeseed oil and a teaspoon of both basil and sea salt.
4. Sprinkle the chopped vegetables in the mixture until it is fully coated.
5. Place all the vegetables on a cookie sheet.
6. Bake in the oven for 30 minutes.
7. Toss the roasted vegetables into a blender and blend at high speed.
8. Pour the pasta and the remaining ingredients into a pot. Allow it to cook for 20 minutes.

Nutrition: Calories: 25 Fat: 2 g Sodium: 80 mg Carbohydrates: 2 g

Chapter 5. Pasta/Main Course

314. Creamy Chicken Breast

Preparation Time: 10 minutes
Cooking Time: 20 minutes
Servings: 4
Ingredients:

- 1 tablespoon olive oil
- A pinch of black pepper
- 2 pounds chicken breasts, skinless, boneless, and cubed
- 4 garlic cloves, minced
- 2½ cups low-sodium chicken stock
- 2 cups coconut cream
- ½ cup low-fat parmesan, grated
- 1 tablespoon basil, chopped

Directions:

1 Heat up a pan with the oil over medium-high heat, add chicken cubes, and brown them for 3 minutes on each side. Add garlic, black pepper, stock, and cream, toss, cover the pan and cook everything for 10 minutes more. Add cheese and basil, toss, divide between plates and serve for lunch. Enjoy!

Nutrition: Calories 221 Fat 6 g Fiber 9 g Carbs 14 g Protein 7 g Sodium 197 mg

315. Indian Chicken Stew

Preparation Time: 1 hour
Cooking Time: 20 minutes
Servings: 4
Ingredients:

- 1-pound chicken breasts, skinless, boneless, and cubed
- 1 tablespoon garam masala
- 1 cup fat-free yogurt
- 1 tablespoon lemon juice
- A pinch of black pepper
- ¼ teaspoon ginger, ground
- 15 ounces tomato sauce, no-salt-added
- 5 garlic cloves, minced
- ½ teaspoon sweet paprika

Directions:

1. In a bowl, mix the chicken with garam masala, yogurt, lemon juice, black pepper, ginger, and fridge for 1 hour. Heat up a pan over medium heat, add chicken mix, toss and cook for 5-6 minutes.
2. Add tomato sauce, garlic and paprika, toss, cook for 15 minutes, divide between plates and serve for lunch. Enjoy!

Nutrition: Calories 221 Fat 6 g Fiber 9 g Carbs 14 g Protein 16 g Sodium 4 mg

316. Chicken, Bamboo, and Chestnuts Mix

Preparation Time: 10 minutes
Cooking Time: 20 minutes
Servings: 4
Ingredients:

- 1-pound chicken thighs, boneless, skinless, and cut into medium chunks
- 1 cup low-sodium chicken stock
- 1 tablespoon olive oil
- 2 tablespoons coconut aminos
- 1-inch ginger, grated
- 1 carrot, sliced
- 2 garlic cloves, minced
- 8 ounces canned bamboo shoots, no-salt-added and drained
- 8 ounces water chestnuts

Directions:

1. Heat up a pan with the oil over medium-high heat, add chicken, stir, and brown for 4 minutes on each side. Add the stock, aminos, ginger, carrot, garlic, bamboo, and chestnuts, toss, cover the pan, and cook everything over medium heat for 12 minutes. Divide everything between plates and serve. Enjoy!

Nutrition: Calories 281 Fat 7 g Fiber 9 g Carbs 14 g Protein 14 g Sodium 125 mg

317. Salsa Chicken

Preparation Time: 10 minutes
Cooking Time: 25 minutes
Servings: 4
Ingredients:

- 1 cup mild salsa, no-salt-added
- ½ teaspoon cumin, ground
- Black pepper to the taste
- 1 tablespoon chipotle paste
- 1-pound chicken thighs, skinless and boneless
- 2 cups corn
- Juice of 1 lime
- ½ tablespoon olive oil
- 2 tablespoons cilantro, chopped
- 1 cup cherry tomatoes, halved
- 1 small avocado, pitted, peeled, and cubed

Directions:

1. In a pot, combine the salsa with the cumin, black pepper, chipotle paste, chicken thighs, and corn, toss, bring to a simmer and cook over medium heat for 25 minutes. Add lime juice, oil, cherry tomatoes, and avocado, toss, divide into bowls and serve for lunch. Enjoy!

Nutrition: Calories 269 Fat 6 g Fiber 9 g Carbs 18 g Protein 7 g Sodium 500 mg

318. Quinoa Chicken Salad

Preparation Time: 15 minutes
Cooking Time: 20 minutes
Servings: 8
Ingredients:

- 2 cups water & 2 cubes chicken bouillon
- 1 smashed garlic clove
- 1 cup uncooked quinoa
- 2 large-sized chicken breasts cut up into bite-sized portions and cooked
- 1 large-sized diced red onion
- 1 large-sized green bell pepper

- ½ cup Kalamata olives
- ½ cup crumbled feta cheese
- ¼ cup chopped up parsley
- ¼ cup chopped up fresh chives
- ½ teaspoon salt & 1 tablespoon balsamic vinegar
- ¼ cup olive oil

Directions:

1. Take a saucepan and bring your water, garlic and bouillon cubes to a boil. Stir in quinoa and reduce the heat to medium-low.
2. Simmer for about 15-20 minutes until the quinoa has absorbed all the water and is tender. Discard your garlic cloves and scrape the quinoa into a large-sized bowl.
3. Gently stir in the cooked chicken breast, bell pepper, onion, feta cheese, chives, salt and parsley into your quinoa.
4. Drizzle some lemon juice, olive oil and balsamic vinegar. Stir everything until mixed well. Serve warm and enjoy!

Nutrition: Calories: 99 Fat: 7 g Carbohydrates: 7 g Protein: 3.4 g

319. Rice with Chicken
Preparation Time: 10 minutes
Cooking Time: 30 minutes
Servings: 4
Ingredients:

- ½ cup coconut aminos
- ⅓ cup rice wine vinegar
- 2 tablespoons olive oil
- 1 chicken breast, skinless, boneless, and cubed
- ½ cup red bell pepper, chopped
- A pinch of black pepper
- 2 garlic cloves, minced
- ½ teaspoon ginger, grated
- ½ cup carrots, grated
- 1 cup white rice
- 2 cups of water

Directions:

1 Heat up a pan with the oil over medium-high heat, add the chicken, stir and brown

for 4 minutes on each side. Add aminos, vinegar, bell pepper, black pepper, garlic, ginger, carrots, rice and stock, stock, cover the pan and cook over medium heat for 20 minutes. Divide everything into bowls and serve for lunch. Enjoy!

Nutrition: Calories: 70 Carbs: 13 g Fat: 2 g Protein: 2 g Sodium 5 mg

320. Tomato Soup
Preparation Time: 10 minutes
Cooking Time: 20 minutes
Servings: 4
Ingredients:

- 3 garlic cloves, minced
- 1 yellow onion, chopped
- 3 carrots, chopped
- 15 ounces tomato sauce, no-salt-added
- 1 tablespoon olive oil
- 15 ounces roasted tomatoes, no-salt-added
- 1 cup low-sodium veggie stock
- 1 tablespoon tomato paste, no-salt-added
- 1 tablespoon basil, dried
- ¼ teaspoon oregano, dried
- 3 ounces coconut cream
- A pinch of black pepper

Directions:

1. Heat up a pot with the oil over medium heat, add garlic and onion, stir and cook for 5 minutes. Add carrots, tomato sauce, tomatoes, stock, tomato paste, basil, oregano, and black pepper, stir, bring to a simmer, cook for 15 minutes, add cream, blend the soup using an immersion blender, divide into bowls and serve for lunch. Enjoy!

Nutrition: Calories: 90 Carbs: 20 g Fat: 0 g Protein: 2 g Sodium: 480 mg

321. Cod Soup
Preparation Time: 10 minutes
Cooking Time: 25 minutes
Servings: 4
Ingredients:

- 1 yellow onion, chopped
- 12 cups low-sodium fish stock
- 1-pound carrots, sliced

- 1 tablespoon olive oil
- Black pepper to the taste
- 2 tablespoons ginger, minced
- 1 cup of water
- 1-pound cod, skinless, boneless, and cut into medium chunks

Directions:

1. Heat up a pot with the oil over medium-high heat, add onion, stir and cook for 4 minutes. Add water, stock, ginger, and carrots, stir and cook for 10 minutes more.
2. Blend soup using an immersion blender, add the fish and pepper, stir, cook for 10 minutes more, ladle into bowls and serve. Enjoy!

Nutrition: Calories: 344 Carbs: 35 g Fat: 4 g Protein: 46 g Sodium 334 mg

322. Tuna Croquettes
Preparation Time: 40 minutes
Cooking Time: 25 minutes
Servings: 36
Ingredients:

- 6 tablespoons extra-virgin olive oil, plus 1 to 2 cups
- 5 tablespoons almond flour, plus 1 cup, divided
- 1¼ cups heavy cream
- 1 (4-oz.) can olive oil-packed yellowfin tuna
- 1 tablespoon chopped red onion
- 2 teaspoons minced capers
- ½ teaspoon dried dill
- ¼ teaspoon freshly ground black pepper
- 2 large eggs
- 1 cup panko breadcrumbs (or a gluten-free version)

Directions:

1. In a large skillet, warm up 6 tablespoons olive oil over medium-low heat. Add 5 tablespoons almond flour and cook, stirring constantly, until a smooth paste forms and the flour browns slightly, 2 to 3 minutes.
2. Select the heat to medium-high and gradually mix in the heavy cream, whisking

constantly until completely smooth and thickened, another 4 to 5 minutes. Remove and add in the tuna, red onion, capers, dill, and pepper.

3. Transfer the mixture to an 8-inch square baking dish that is well coated with olive oil and set aside at room temperature.

4. Wrap and cool for 4 hours or up to overnight. To form the croquettes, set out three bowls. In one, beat together the eggs.

5. In another, add the remaining almond flour. In the third, add the panko. Line a baking sheet with parchment paper.

6. Scoop about a tablespoon of cold prepared dough into the flour mixture and roll to coat. Shake off excess and, using your hands, roll into an oval.

7. Dip the croquette into the beaten egg, then lightly coat in panko. Set on a lined baking sheet and repeat with the remaining dough.

8. In a small saucepan, warm up the remaining 1 to 2 cups of olive oil, over medium-high heat.

9. Once the oil is heated, fry the croquettes 3 or 4 at a time, depending on the size of your pan, removing with a slotted spoon when golden brown.

10. You will need to adjust the temperature of the oil occasionally to prevent burning. If the croquettes get dark brown very quickly, lower the temperature.

Nutrition: Calories 245 Fat 22 g Carbohydrates 1 g Protein 6 g

323. Sweet Potatoes and Zucchini Soup

Preparation Time: 10 minutes
Cooking Time: 20 minutes
Servings: 8
Ingredients:

- 4 cups veggie stock
- 2 tablespoons olive oil
- 2 sweet potatoes, peeled and cubed
- 8 zucchinis, chopped
- 2 yellow onions, chopped
- 1 cup of coconut milk
- A pinch of black pepper
- 1 tablespoon coconut aminos
- 4 tablespoons dill, chopped
- ½ teaspoon basil, chopped

Directions:

1 Heat up a pot with the oil over medium heat, add onion, stir and cook for 5 minutes. Add zucchinis, stock, basil, potato, and pepper, stir and cook for 15 minutes more. Add milk, aminos, and dill, pulse using an immersion blender, ladle into bowls and serve for lunch.

Nutrition: Calories: 270 Carbs: 50 g Fat: 4 g Protein: 11 g Sodium 416 mg

324. Lemongrass and Chicken Soup

Preparation Time: 10 minutes
Cooking Time: 25 minutes
Servings: 4
Ingredients:

- 4 lime leaves, torn
- 4 cups veggie stock, low-sodium
- 1 lemongrass stalk, chopped
- 1 tablespoon ginger, grated
- 1-pound chicken breast, skinless, boneless, and cubed
- 8 ounces mushrooms, chopped
- 4 Thai chilies, chopped
- 13 ounces of coconut milk
- ¼ cup lime juice
- ¼ cup cilantro, chopped
- A pinch of black pepper

Directions:

1. Put the stock into a pot, bring to a simmer over medium heat, add lemongrass, ginger, and lime leaves, stir, cook for 10 minutes, strain into another pot, and heat up over medium heat again.

2. Add chicken, mushrooms, milk, cilantro, black pepper, chilies, and lime juice, stir, simmer for 15 minutes, ladle into bowls and serve.

Nutrition: Calories: 105 Carbs: 1 g Fat: 2 g Protein: 15 g Sodium 200 mg

325. Easy Lunch Salmon Steaks

Preparation Time: 10 minutes
Cooking Time: 20 minutes
Servings: 4
Ingredients:

- 1 big salmon fillet, cut into 4 steaks
- 3 garlic cloves, minced
- 1 yellow onion, chopped
- Black pepper to the taste
- 2 tablespoons olive oil
- ¼ cup parsley, chopped
- Juice of 1 lemon
- 1 tablespoon thyme, chopped
- 4 cups of water

Directions:

1. Heat a pan with the oil on medium-high heat, cook onion and garlic within 3 minutes.

2. Add black pepper, parsley, thyme, water, and lemon juice, stir, bring to a gentle boil, add salmon steaks, cook them for 15 minutes, drain, divide between plates and serve with a side salad for lunch.

Nutrition: Calories: 110 Carbs: 3 g Fat: 4 g Protein: 15 g Sodium 330 mg

326. Light Balsamic Salad

Preparation Time: 10 minutes
Cooking Time: 0 minutes
Servings: 3
Ingredients:

- 1 orange, cut into segments
- 2 green onions, chopped
- 1 romaine lettuce head, torn
- 1 avocado, pitted, peeled, and cubed
- ¼ cup almonds, sliced

For the salad dressing:

- 1 teaspoon mustard
- ¼ cup olive oil
- 2 tablespoons balsamic vinegar

- Juice of ½ orange
- Salt and black pepper

Directions:

1. In a salad bowl, mix oranges with avocado, lettuce, almonds, and green onions. In another bowl, mix olive oil with vinegar, mustard, orange juice, salt, and pepper, whisk well, add this to your salad, toss and serve.

Nutrition: Calories: 35 Carbs: 5 g Fat: 2 g Protein: 0 g Sodium 400 mg

327. Purple Potato Soup

Preparation Time: 10 minutes
Cooking Time: 1 hour and 15 minutes
Servings: 6
Ingredients:

- 6 purple potatoes, chopped
- 1 cauliflower head, florets separated
- Black pepper to the taste
- 4 garlic cloves, minced
- 1 yellow onion, chopped
- 3 tablespoons olive oil
- 1 tablespoon thyme, chopped
- 1 leek, chopped
- 2 shallots, chopped
- 4 cups chicken stock, low-sodium

Directions:

1. In a baking dish, mix potatoes with onion, cauliflower, garlic, pepper, thyme, and half of the oil, toss to coat, introduce in the oven and bake for 45 minutes at 400°F.
2. Heat a pot with the rest of the oil over medium-high heat, add leeks and shallots, stir and cook for 10 minutes.
3. Add roasted veggies and stock, stir, bring to a boil, cook for 20 minutes, transfer soup to your food processor, blend well, divide into bowls, and serve.

Nutrition: Calories: 70 Carbs: 15 g Fat: 0 g Protein: 2 g Sodium 6 mg

328. CURRY

Preparation Time: 10 minutes
Cooking Time: 1 hour and 15 minutes
Servings: 6
Ingredients:

- 2 gold potatoes, chopped
- 1 cup cauliflower florets
- Black pepper to the taste
- 5 leeks, chopped
- 4 garlic cloves, minced
- 1 yellow onion, chopped
- 3 tablespoons olive oil
- Handful parsley, chopped
- 4 cups low-sodium chicken stock

Directions:

1. Heat up a pot with the oil over medium-high heat, add onion and garlic, stir and cook for 5 minutes.
2. Add potatoes, cauliflower, black pepper, leeks, and stock, stir, bring to a simmer, cook over medium heat for 30 minutes, blend using an immersion blender, add parsley, stir, ladle into bowls and serve.

Nutrition: Calories: 125 Carbs: 29 g Fat: 1 g Protein: 4 g Sodium 52 mg

329. Cauliflower Lunch Salad

Preparation Time: 2 hours
Cooking Time: 10 minutes
Servings: 4
Ingredients:

- ⅓ cup low-sodium veggie stock
- 2 tablespoons olive oil
- 6 cups cauliflower florets, grated
- Black pepper to the taste
- ¼ cup red onion, chopped
- 1 red bell pepper, chopped
- Juice of ½ lemon
- ½ cup kalamata olives halved
- 1 teaspoon mint, chopped
- 1 tablespoon cilantro, chopped

Directions:

1. Heat up a pan with the oil over medium-high heat, add cauliflower, pepper and stock, stir, cook within 10 minutes, transfer to a bowl,

and keep in the fridge for 2 hours. Mix cauliflower with olives, onion, bell pepper, black pepper, mint, cilantro, and lemon juice, toss to coat and serve.

Nutrition: Calories: 102 Carbs: 3 g Fat: 10 g Protein: 0 g Sodium 97 mg

330. Shrimp Cocktail

Preparation Time: 10 minutes
Cooking Time: 5 minutes
Servings: 8
Ingredients:

- 2 pounds big shrimp, deveined
- 4 cups of water
- 2 bay leaves
- 1 small lemon, halved
- Ice for cooling the shrimp
- Ice for serving
- 1 medium lemon sliced for serving
- ¾ cup tomato passata
- 2½ tablespoons horseradish, prepared
- ¼ teaspoon chili powder
- 2 tablespoons lemon juice

Directions:

1. Pour the 4 cups water into a large pot, add lemon and bay leaves. Boil over medium-high heat, reduce temperature and boil for 10 minutes. Put shrimp, stir and cook within 2 minutes. Move the shrimp to a bowl filled with ice and leave aside for 5 minutes.
2. In a bowl, mix tomato passata with horseradish, chili powder, and lemon juice and stir well. Place shrimp in a serving bowl filled with ice, with lemon slices, and serve with the cocktail sauce you've prepared.

Nutrition: Calories: 276 Carbs: 0 g Fat: 8 g Protein: 25 g Sodium: 182 mg

331. Quinoa and Scallops Salad

Preparation Time: 10 minutes
Cooking Time: 35 minutes
Servings: 6
Ingredients:

- 12 ounces dry sea scallops
- 4 tablespoons canola oil
- 2 teaspoons canola oil

- 4 teaspoons low sodium soy sauce
- 1½ cup quinoa, rinsed
- 2 teaspoons garlic, minced
- 3 cups of water
- 1 cup snow peas, sliced diagonally
- 1 teaspoon sesame oil
- ⅓ cup rice vinegar
- 1 cup scallions, sliced
- ⅓ cup red bell pepper, chopped
- ¼ cup cilantro, chopped

Directions:
1. In a bowl, mix scallops with 2 teaspoons soy sauce, stir gently, and leave aside for now. Heat a pan with 1 tablespoon canola oil over medium-high heat, add the quinoa, stir and cook for 8 minutes. Put garlic, stir and cook within 1 more minute.
2. Put the water, boil over medium heat, stir, cover, and cook for 15 minutes. Remove from heat and leave aside covered for 5 minutes. Add snow peas, cover again and leave for 5 more minutes.
3. Meanwhile, in a bowl, mix 3 tablespoons canola oil with 2 teaspoons soy sauce, vinegar, and sesame oil and stir well. Add quinoa and snow peas to this mixture and stir again. Add scallions, bell pepper, and stir again.
4. Pat dry the scallops and discard the marinade. Heat another pan with 2 teaspoons canola oil over high heat, add scallops, and cook for 1 minute on each side. Add them to the quinoa salad, stir gently, and serve with chopped cilantro.

Nutrition: Calories: 181 Carbs: 12 g Fat: 6 g Protein: 13 g Sodium: 153 mg

332. Squid and Shrimp Salad

Preparation Time: 10 minutes
Cooking Time: 15 minutes
Servings: 4
Ingredients:
- 8 ounces squid, cut into medium pieces

- 8 ounces shrimp, peeled and deveined
- 1 red onion, sliced
- 1 cucumber, chopped
- 2 tomatoes, cut into medium wedges
- 2 tablespoons cilantro, chopped
- 1 hot jalapeno pepper, cut in rounds
- 3 tablespoons rice vinegar
- 3 tablespoons dark sesame oil
- Black pepper to the taste

Directions:
1. In a bowl, mix the onion with cucumber, tomatoes, pepper, cilantro, shrimp, and squid and stir well. Cut a big parchment paper in half, fold it in half heart shape and open. Place the seafood mixture in this parchment piece, fold over, seal edges, place on a baking sheet, and introduce in the oven at 400°F for 15 minutes.
2. Meanwhile, in a small bowl, mix sesame oil with rice vinegar and black pepper and stir very well. Take the salad out of the oven, leave to cool down for a few minutes, and transfer to a serving plate. Put the dressing over the salad and serve right away.

Nutrition: Calories: 235 Carbs: 9 g Fat: 8 g Protein: 30 g Sodium: 165 mg

333. Parsley Seafood Cocktail

Preparation Time: 2 hours and 10 minutes
Cooking Time: 1 hour and 30 minutes
Servings: 4
Ingredients:
- 1 big octopus, cleaned
- 1-pound mussels
- 2 pounds clams
- 1 big squid cut in rings
- 3 garlic cloves, chopped
- 1 celery rib, cut crosswise into thirds
- ½ cup celery rib, sliced
- 1 carrot, cut crosswise into 3 pieces

- 1 small white onion, chopped
- 1 bay leaf
- ¾ cup white wine
- 2 cups radicchio, sliced
- 1 red onion, sliced
- 1 cup parsley, chopped
- 1 cup olive oil
- 1 cup red wine vinegar
- Black pepper to the taste

Directions:
1. Put the octopus in a pot with celery rib cut in thirds, garlic, carrot, bay leaf, white onion, and white wine. Add water to cover the octopus, cover with a lid, bring to a boil over high heat, reduce to low, and simmer within 1½ hours.
2. Drain octopus, reserve boiling liquid, and leave aside to cool down. Put ¼ cup octopus cooking liquid in another pot, add mussels, heat up over medium-high heat, cook until they open, transfer to a bowl, and leave aside.
3. Add clams to the pan, cover, cook over medium-high heat until they open, transfer to the bowl with mussels, and leave aside. Add squid to the pan, cover and cook over medium-high heat for 3 minutes, transfer to the bowl with mussels and clams.
4. Meanwhile, slice octopus into small pieces and mix with the rest of the seafood. Add sliced celery, radicchio, red onion, vinegar, olive oil, parsley, salt, and pepper, stir gently and leave aside in the fridge within 2 hours before serving.

Nutrition: Calories: 102 Carbs: 7 g Fat: 1 g Protein: 16 g Sodium: 0 mg

334. Shrimp and Onion Ginger Dressing

Preparation Time: 10 minutes
Cooking Time: 5 minutes
Servings: 2
Ingredients:
- 8 medium shrimp, peeled and deveined

- 12 ounces package mixed salad leaves
- 10 cherry tomatoes, halved
- 2 green onions, sliced
- 2 medium mushrooms, sliced
- ⅓ cup rice vinegar
- ¼ cup sesame seeds, toasted
- 1 tablespoon low-sodium soy sauce
- 2 teaspoons ginger, grated
- 2 teaspoons garlic, minced
- 2/3 cup canola oil
- ⅓ cup sesame oil

Directions:
1. In a bowl, mix rice vinegar with sesame seeds, soy sauce, garlic, ginger, and stir well. Pour this into your kitchen blender, add canola oil and sesame oil, pulse very well, and leave aside. Brush shrimp with 3 tablespoons of the ginger dressing you've prepared.
2. Heat your kitchen grill over high heat, add shrimp and cook for 3 minutes, flipping once. In a salad bowl, mix salad leaves with grilled shrimp, mushrooms, green onions, and tomatoes. Drizzle ginger dressing on top and serve right away!

Nutrition: Calories: 360 Carbs: 14 g Fat: 11 g Protein: 49 g Sodium: 469 mg

335. Fruit Shrimp Soup

Preparation Time: 10 minutes
Cooking Time: 25 minutes
Servings: 6
Ingredients:
- 8 ounces shrimp, peeled and deveined
- 1 stalk lemongrass, smashed
- 2 small ginger pieces, grated
- 6 cup chicken stock
- 2 jalapenos, chopped
- 4 lime leaves
- 1½ cups pineapple, chopped
- 1 cup shiitake mushroom caps, chopped
- 1 tomato, chopped
- ½ bell pepper, cubed
- 2 tablespoons fish sauce

- 1 teaspoon sugar
- ¼ cup lime juice
- ⅓ cup cilantro, chopped
- 2 scallions, sliced

Directions:
1. In a pot, mix ginger with lemongrass, stock, jalapenos, and lime leaves, stir, boil over medium heat, cook within 15 minutes. Strain liquid in a bowl and discard solids.
2. Return soup to the pot again, add pineapple, tomato, mushrooms, bell pepper, sugar, and fish sauce, stir, boil over medium heat, cook for 5 minutes, add shrimp and cook for 3 more minutes. Remove from heat, add lime juice, cilantro, and scallions, stir, ladle into soup bowls and serve.

Nutrition: Calories: 290 Carbs: 39 g Fat: 12 g Protein: 7 g Sodium: 21 mg

336. Mussels and Chickpea Soup

Preparation Time: 10 minutes
Cooking Time: 10 minutes
Servings: 6
Ingredients:
- 3 garlic cloves, minced
- 2 tablespoons olive oil
- A pinch of chili flakes
- 1½ tablespoons fresh mussels, scrubbed
- 1 cup white wine
- 1 cup chickpeas, rinsed
- 1 small fennel bulb, sliced
- Black pepper to the taste
- Juice of 1 lemon
- 3 tablespoons parsley, chopped

Directions:
1. Heat a big saucepan with the olive oil over medium-high heat, add garlic and chili flakes, stir and cook within a couple of minutes. Add white wine and mussels, stir, cover, and cook for 3-4 minutes until mussels open.
2. Transfer mussels to a baking dish, add some of the

cooking liquid over them and fridge until they are cold enough. Take mussels out of the fridge and discard shells.
3. Heat another pan over medium-high heat, add mussels, reserved cooking liquid, chickpeas, and fennel, stir well, and heat them. Add black pepper to the taste, lemon juice, and parsley, stir again, divide between plates and serve.

Nutrition: Calories: 286 Carbs: 49 g Fat: 4 g Protein: 14 g Sodium: 145 mg

337. Lemon and Garlic Fettucine

Preparation Time: 5 minutes
Cooking Time: 15 minutes
Servings: 5
Ingredients:
- 8 ounces of whole-wheat fettuccine
- 4 tablespoons of extra-virgin olive oil
- 4 cloves of minced garlic
- 1 cup of fresh breadcrumbs
- ¼ cup of lemon juice
- 1 teaspoon of freshly ground pepper
- ½ teaspoon of salt
- 2 cans of 4 ounce boneless and skinless sardines (dipped in tomato sauce)
- ½ cup of chopped up fresh parsley
- ¼ cup of finely shredded Parmesan cheese

Directions:
1. Take a large-sized pot and bring water to a boil.
2. Cook pasta for 10 minutes until Al Dente.
3. Take a small-sized skillet and place it over medium heat.
4. Add 2 tablespoons of oil and allow it to heat up.
5. Add garlic and cook for 20 seconds.
6. Transfer the garlic to a medium-sized bowl
7. Add breadcrumbs to the hot skillet and cook for 5-6 minutes until golden
8. Whisk in lemon juice, pepper and salt into the garlic bowl

9. Add pasta to the bowl (with garlic) and sardines, parsley and Parmesan
10. Stir well and sprinkle bread crumbs
11. Enjoy!

Nutrition: Calories: 480 Fat: 21 g Carbohydrates: 53 g Protein: 23 g

338. Shrimp and Broccoli Soup

Preparation Time: 5 minutes
Cooking Time: 25 minutes
Servings: 4
Ingredients:

- 2 tablespoons olive oil
- 1 yellow onion, chopped
- 4 cups chicken stock
- Juice of 1 lime
- 1-pound shrimp, peeled and deveined
- ½ cup coconut cream
- ½ pound broccoli florets
- 1 tablespoon parsley, chopped

Directions:

1. Heat a pot with the oil over medium heat, add the onion and sauté for 5 minutes. Add the shrimp and the other ingredients, simmer over medium heat for 20 minutes more. Ladle the soup into bowls and serve.

Nutrition: Calories: 220 Carbs: 12 g Fat: 7 g Protein: 26 g Sodium: 577 mg

339. Coconut Turkey Mix

Preparation Time: 10 minutes
Cooking Time: 30 minutes
Servings: 4
Ingredients:

- 1 yellow onion, chopped
- 1-pound turkey breast, skinless, boneless, and cubed
- 2 tablespoons olive oil
- 2 garlic cloves, minced
- 1 zucchini, sliced
- 1 cup coconut cream
- A pinch of sea salt
- Black pepper

Directions:

1. Bring the pan to medium heat, add the onion and the garlic and sauté for 5 minutes. Put the meat and brown within 5 minutes more. Add the rest of the ingredients, toss, bring to a

simmer and cook over medium heat for 20 minutes more. Serve for lunch.

Nutrition: Calories 200 Fat 4 g Fiber 2 g Carbs 14 g Protein 7 g Sodium 111 mg

340. Lime Shrimp and Kale

Preparation Time: 10 minutes
Cooking Time: 20 minutes
Servings: 4
Ingredients:

- 1-pound shrimp, peeled and deveined
- 4 scallions, chopped
- 1 teaspoon sweet paprika
- 1 tablespoon olive oil
- Juice of 1 lime
- Zest of 1 lime, grated
- A pinch of salt and black pepper
- 2 tablespoons parsley, chopped

Directions:

1. Bring the pan to medium heat, add the scallions and sauté for 5 minutes. Add the shrimp and the other ingredients, toss, cook over medium heat for 15 minutes more, divide into bowls and serve.

Nutrition: Calories: 149 Carbs: 12 g Fat: 4 g Protein: 21 g Sodium: 250 mg

341. Parsley Cod Mix

Preparation Time: 10 minutes
Cooking Time: 20 minutes
Servings: 4
Ingredients:

- 1 tablespoon olive oil
- 2 shallots, chopped
- 4 cod fillets, boneless and skinless
- 2 garlic cloves, minced
- 2 tablespoons lemon juice
- 1 cup chicken stock
- A pinch of salt and black pepper

Directions:

1. Bring the pan to medium heat -high heat, add the shallots and the garlic and sauté for 5 minutes. Add the cod and the other ingredients, cook everything for 15 minutes more, divide

between plates and serve for lunch.

Nutrition: Calories: 216 Carbs: 7 g Fat: 5 g Protein: 34 g Sodium: 380 mg

342. Salmon and Cabbage Mix

Preparation Time: 5 minutes
Cooking Time: 25 minutes
Servings: 4
Ingredients:

- 4 salmon fillets, boneless
- 1 yellow onion, chopped
- 2 tablespoons olive oil
- 1 cup red cabbage, shredded
- 1 red bell pepper, chopped
- 1 tablespoon rosemary, chopped
- 1 tablespoon coriander, ground
- 1 cup tomato sauce
- A pinch of sea salt
- Black pepper

Directions:

1. Bring the pan to medium heat, add the onion and sauté for 5 minutes. Put the fish and sear it within 2 minutes on each side. Add the cabbage and the remaining ingredients, toss, cook over medium heat for 20 minutes more, divide between plates and serve.

Nutrition: Calories: 130 Carbs: 8 g Fat: 6 g Protein: 12 g Sodium: 345 mg

343. Tofu & Green Bean Stir-Fry

Preparation Time: 15 minutes
Cooking Time: 20 minutes
Servings: 4
Ingredients:

- 1 (14-oz.) package extra-firm tofu
- 2 tablespoons canola oil
- 1-pound green beans, chopped
- 2 carrots, peeled and thinly sliced
- ½ cup Stir-Fry Sauce or store-bought lower-sodium stir-fry sauce
- 2 cups Fluffy Brown Rice
- 2 scallions, thinly sliced
- 2 tablespoons sesame seeds

Directions:

1. Put the tofu on your plate lined with a kitchen towel, put a separate kitchen towel over the tofu, and place a heavy pot on top, changing towels every time they become soaked. Let sit within 15 minutes to remove the moisture. Cut the tofu into 1-inch cubes.
2. Heat the canola oil in a large wok or skillet to medium-high heat. Add the tofu cubes and cook, flipping every 1 to 2 minutes, so all sides become browned. Remove from the skillet and place the green beans and carrots in the hot oil. Stir-fry for 4 to 5 minutes, occasionally tossing, until crisp and slightly tender.
3. While the vegetables are cooking, prepare the Stir-Fry Sauce (if using homemade). Place the tofu back in the skillet. Put the sauce over the tofu and vegetables and let simmer for 2 to 3 minutes. Serve over rice, then top with scallions and sesame seeds.

Nutrition:
Calories: 380 Fat: 15 g Sodium: 440 mg Potassium: 454 mg Carbohydrate: 45 g Protein: 16 g

344. Peanut Vegetable Pad Thai

Preparation Time: 15 minutes
Cooking Time: 20 minutes
Servings: 6
Ingredients:

- 8 ounces brown rice noodles
- ⅓ cup natural peanut butter
- 3 tablespoons unsalted vegetable broth
- 1 tablespoon low-sodium soy sauce
- 2 tablespoons of rice wine vinegar
- 1 tablespoon honey
- 2 teaspoons sesame oil
- 1 teaspoon sriracha (optional)
- 1 tablespoon canola oil

- 1 red bell pepper, thinly sliced
- 1 zucchini, cut into matchsticks
- 2 large carrots, cut into matchsticks
- 3 large eggs, beaten
- ¾ teaspoon kosher or sea salt
- ½ cup unsalted peanuts, chopped
- ½ cup cilantro leaves, chopped

Directions:

1. Boil a large pot of water. Cook the rice noodles as stated in package directions. Mix the peanut butter, vegetable broth, soy sauce, rice wine vinegar, honey, sesame oil, and sriracha in a bowl. Set aside.
2. Warm-up canola oil over medium heat in a large nonstick skillet. Add the red bell pepper, zucchini, and carrots, and sauté for 2 to 3 minutes, until slightly soft. Stir in the eggs and fold with a spatula until scrambled. Add the cooked rice noodles, sauce, and salt. Toss to combine. Spoon into bowls and evenly top with the peanuts and cilantro.

Nutrition: Calories: 393 Fat: 19 g Sodium: 561 mg Carbohydrate: 45 g Protein: 13 g

345. Spicy Tofu Burrito Bowls with Cilantro Avocado Sauce

Preparation Time: 15 minutes
Cooking Time: 15 minutes
Servings: 4
Ingredients:
For the sauce:

- ¼ cup plain nonfat Greek yogurt
- ½ cup fresh cilantro leaves
- ½ ripe avocado, peeled
- Zest and juice of 1 lime
- 2 garlic cloves, peeled
- ¼ teaspoon kosher or sea salt
- 2 tablespoons water

For the burrito bowls:

- 1 (14-oz.) package extra-firm tofu
- 1 tablespoon canola oil
- 1 yellow or orange bell pepper, diced
- 2 tablespoons Taco Seasoning
- ¼ teaspoon kosher or sea salt
- 2 cups Fluffy Brown Rice
- 1 (15-oz.) can black beans, drained

Directions:

1. Place all the sauce ingredients in the bowl of a food processor or blender and purée until smooth. Taste and adjust the seasoning, if necessary. Refrigerate until ready for use.
2. Put the tofu on your plate lined with a kitchen towel. Put another kitchen towel over the tofu and place a heavy pot on top, changing towels if they become soaked. Let it stand within 15 minutes to remove the moisture. Cut the tofu into 1-inch cubes.
3. Warm-up canola oil in a large skillet over medium heat. Add the tofu and bell pepper and sauté, breaking up the tofu into smaller pieces for 4 to 5 minutes. Stir in the taco seasoning, salt, and ¼ cup of water. Evenly divide the rice and black beans among 4 bowls. Top with the tofu/bell pepper mixture and top with the cilantro avocado sauce.

Nutrition: Calories: 383 Fat: 13 g Sodium: 438 mg Carbohydrate: 48 g Protein: 21 g

346. Sweet Potato Cakes with Classic Guacamole

Preparation Time: 15 minutes
Cooking Time: 20 minutes
Servings: 4
Ingredients:
For the guacamole:

- 2 ripe avocados, peeled and pitted

- ½ jalapeño, seeded and finely minced
- ¼ red onion, peeled and finely diced
- ¼ cup fresh cilantro leaves, chopped
- Zest and juice of 1 lime
- ¼ teaspoon kosher or sea salt

For the cakes:
- 3 sweet potatoes, cooked and peeled
- ½ cup cooked black beans
- 1 large egg
- ½ cup panko bread crumbs
- 1 teaspoon ground cumin
- 1 teaspoon chili powder
- ½ teaspoon kosher or sea salt
- ¼ teaspoon ground black pepper
- 2 tablespoons canola oil

Directions:
1. Mash the avocado, then stir in the jalapeño, red onion, cilantro, lime zest and juice, and salt in a bowl. Taste and adjust the seasoning, if necessary.
2. Put the cooked sweet potatoes plus black beans in a bowl and mash until a paste form. Stir in the egg, bread crumbs, cumin, chili powder, salt, and black pepper until combined.
3. Warm-up canola oil in a large skillet at medium heat. Form the sweet potato mixture into 4 patties, place them in the hot skillet, and cook within 3 to 4 minutes per side, until browned and crispy. Serve the sweet potato cakes with guacamole on top.

Nutrition: Calories: 369 Fat: 22 g Sodium: 521 mg Carbohydrate: 38 g Protein: 8 g

347. Chickpea Cauliflower Tikka Masala

Preparation Time: 15 minutes
Cooking Time: 40 minutes
Servings: 6
Ingredients:
- 2 tablespoons olive oil
- 1 yellow onion, peeled and diced

- 4 garlic cloves, peeled and minced
- 1-inch piece fresh ginger, peeled and minced
- 2 tablespoons Garam Masala
- 1 teaspoon kosher or sea salt
- ½ teaspoon ground black pepper
- ¼ teaspoon ground cayenne pepper
- ½ small head cauliflower, small florets
- 2 (15-oz.) cans no-salt-added chickpeas, rinsed and drained
- 1 (15-oz.) can no-salt-added petite diced tomatoes, drained
- 1½ cups unsalted vegetable broth
- ½ (15-oz.) can coconut milk
- Zest and juice of 1 lime
- ½ cup fresh cilantro leaves, chopped, divided
- 1½ cups cooked Fluffy Brown Rice, divided

Directions:
1. Warm up olive oil over medium heat, then put the onion and sauté within 4 to 5 minutes in a large Dutch oven or stockpot. Stir in the garlic, ginger, garam masala, salt, black pepper, and cayenne pepper and toast for 30 to 60 seconds, until fragrant.
2. Stir in the cauliflower florets, chickpeas, diced tomatoes, and vegetable broth and increase to medium-high. Simmer within 15 minutes, until the cauliflower is fork-tender.
3. Remove, then stir in the coconut milk, lime juice, lime zest, and half of the cilantro. Taste and adjust the seasoning, if necessary. Serve over the rice and the remaining chopped cilantro.

Nutrition: Calories: 323 Fat: 12 g Sodium: 444 mg Carbohydrate: 44 g Protein: 11 g

348. Eggplant Parmesan Stacks

Preparation Time: 15 minutes
Cooking Time: 20 minutes
Servings: 4
Ingredients:
- 1 large eggplant, cut into thick slices
- 2 tablespoons olive oil, divided
- ¼ teaspoon kosher or sea salt
- ¼ teaspoon ground black pepper
- 1 cup panko bread crumbs
- ¼ cup freshly grated Parmesan cheese
- 5 to 6 garlic cloves, minced
- ½ pound fresh mozzarella, sliced
- 1½ cups lower-sodium marinara
- ½ cup fresh basil leaves, torn

Directions:
1. Preheat the oven to 425°F. Coat the eggplant slices in 1 tablespoon olive oil and sprinkle with salt and black pepper. Put on a large baking sheet, then roast for 10 to 12 minutes, until soft with crispy edges. Remove the eggplant and set the oven to a low boil.
2. In a bowl, stir the remaining tablespoon of olive oil, bread crumbs, Parmesan cheese, and garlic. Remove the cooled eggplant from the baking sheet and clean it.
3. Create layers on the same baking sheet by stacking a roasted eggplant slice with a slice of mozzarella, a tablespoon of marinara, and a tablespoon of the bread crumb mixture, repeating with 2 layers of each ingredient. Cook under the broiler within 3 to 4 minutes until the cheese is melted and bubbly.

Nutrition: Calories: 377 Fat: 22 g Sodium: 509 mg Carbohydrate: 29 g Protein: 16 g

349. Roasted Vegetable Enchiladas

Preparation Time: 15 minutes
Cooking Time: 45 minutes
Servings: 8
Ingredients:

- 2 zucchinis, diced
- 1 red bell pepper, seeded and sliced
- 1 red onion, peeled and sliced
- 2 ears corn
- 2 tablespoons canola oil
- 1 can no-salt-added black beans, drained
- 1½ tablespoons chili powder
- 2 teaspoon ground cumin
- ⅛ teaspoon kosher or sea salt
- ½ teaspoon ground black pepper
- 8 (8-inch) whole-wheat tortillas
- 1 cup Enchilada Sauce or store-bought enchilada sauce
- ½ cup shredded Mexican-style cheese
- ½ cup plain nonfat Greek yogurt
- ½ cup cilantro leaves, chopped

Directions:

1. Preheat oven to 400°F. Place the zucchini, red bell pepper, and red onion on a baking sheet. Place the ears of corn separately on the same baking sheet. Drizzle all with the canola oil and toss to coat. Roast for 10 to 12 minutes, until the vegetables are tender. Remove and reduce the temperature to 375°F.
2. Cut the corn from the cob. Transfer the corn kernels, zucchini, red bell pepper, and onion to a bowl and stir in the black beans, chili powder, cumin, salt, and black pepper until combined.
3. Oiled a 9-by-13-inch baking dish with cooking spray.

Line up the tortillas in the greased baking dish. Evenly distribute the vegetable bean filling into each tortilla. Pour half of the enchilada sauce and sprinkle half of the shredded cheese on top of the filling.
4. Roll each tortilla into an enchilada shape and place them seam-side down. Pour the remaining enchilada sauce and sprinkle the remaining cheese over the enchiladas. Bake for 25 minutes until the cheese is melted and bubbly. Serve the enchiladas with Greek yogurt and chopped cilantro.

Nutrition: Calories: 335 Fat: 15 g Sodium: 557 mg Carbohydrate: 42 g Protein: 13 g

350. Lentil Avocado Tacos

Preparation Time: 15 minutes
Cooking Time: 35 minutes
Servings: 6
Ingredients:

- 1 tablespoon canola oil
- ½ yellow onion, peeled and diced
- 2-3 garlic cloves, minced
- 1½ cups dried lentils
- ½ teaspoon kosher or sea salt
- 3 to 3½ cups unsalted vegetable or chicken stock
- 2½ tablespoons Taco Seasoning or store-bought low-sodium taco seasoning
- 16 (6-inch) corn tortillas, toasted
- 2 ripe avocados, peeled and sliced

Directions:

1. Heat up the canola oil in a large skillet or Dutch oven over medium heat. Cook the onion within 4 to 5 minutes, until soft. Mix in the garlic and cook within 30 seconds until fragrant. Then add the lentils, salt, and stock. Bring to a simmer for 25 to 35 minutes, adding additional stock if needed.

2. When there's only a small amount of liquid left in the pan, and the lentils are al dente, stir in the taco seasoning and let simmer for 1 to 2 minutes. Taste and adjust the seasoning, if necessary. Spoon the lentil mixture into tortillas and serve with the avocado slices.

Nutrition: Calories: 400 Fat: 14 g Sodium: 336 mg Carbohydrate: 64 g Fiber: 15 g Protein: 16 g

351. Tomato & Olive Orecchiette with Basil Pesto

Preparation Time: 15 minutes
Cooking Time: 25 minutes
Servings: 6
Ingredients:

- 12 ounces orecchiette pasta
- 2 tablespoons olive oil
- 1-pint cherry tomatoes, quartered
- ½ cup Basil Pesto or store-bought pesto
- ¼ cup kalamata olives, sliced
- 1 tablespoon dried oregano leaves
- ¼ teaspoon kosher or sea salt
- ½ teaspoon freshly cracked black pepper
- ¼ teaspoon crushed red pepper flakes
- 2 tablespoons freshly grated Parmesan cheese

Directions:

1. Boil a large pot of water. Cook the orecchiette, drain and transfer the pasta to a large nonstick skillet.
2. Put the skillet over medium-low heat, then heat the olive oil. Stir in the cherry tomatoes, pesto, olives, oregano, salt, black pepper, and crushed red pepper flakes. Cook within 8 to 10 minutes, until heated throughout. Serve the pasta with the freshly grated Parmesan cheese.

Nutrition: Calories: 332 Fat: 13 g Sodium: 389 mg Carbohydrate: 44 g Protein: 9 g

352. Italian Stuffed Portobello Mushroom Burgers

Preparation Time: 15 minutes
Cooking Time: 25 minutes
Servings: 4
Ingredients:

- 1 tablespoon olive oil
- 4 large portobello mushrooms, washed and dried
- ½ yellow onion, peeled and diced
- 4 garlic cloves, peeled and minced
- 1 can cannellini beans, drained
- ½ cup fresh basil leaves, torn
- ½ cup panko bread crumbs
- ⅛ teaspoon kosher or sea salt
- ¼ teaspoon ground black pepper
- 1 cup lower-sodium marinara, divided
- ½ cup shredded mozzarella cheese
- 4 whole-wheat buns, toasted
- 1 cup fresh arugula

Directions:

1. Heat up the olive oil in a large skillet to medium-high heat. Sear the mushrooms for 4 to 5 minutes per side, until slightly soft. Place on a baking sheet. Preheat the oven to a low boil.
2. Put the onion in the skillet and cook for 4 to 5 minutes, until slightly soft. Mix in the garlic then cooks within 30 to 60 seconds. Move the onions plus garlic to a bowl. Add the cannellini beans and smash with the back of a fork to form a chunky paste. Stir in the basil, bread crumbs, salt, and black pepper and half of the marinara. Cook for 5 minutes.
3. Remove the bean mixture from the stove and divide among the mushroom caps. Spoon the remaining marinara over the stuffed mushrooms and top each with mozzarella cheese. Broil within 3 to 4 minutes, until the cheese is melted and bubbly. Transfer the burgers to the toasted whole-wheat buns and top with the arugula.

Nutrition: Calories: 407 Fat: 9 g Sodium: 575 mg Carbohydrate: 63 g Protein: 25 g

353. Gnocchi with Tomato Basil Sauce

Preparation Time: 15 minutes
Cooking Time: 25 minutes
Servings: 6
Ingredients:

- 2 tablespoons olive oil
- ½ yellow onion, peeled and diced
- 3 cloves garlic, peeled and minced
- 1 (32-oz.) can no-salt-added crushed San Marzano tomatoes
- ¼ cup fresh basil leaves
- 2 teaspoons Italian seasoning
- ½ teaspoon kosher or sea salt
- 1 teaspoon granulated sugar
- ½ teaspoon ground black pepper
- ⅛ teaspoon crushed red pepper flakes
- 1 tablespoon heavy cream (optional)
- 12 ounces gnocchi
- ¼ cup freshly grated Parmesan cheese

Directions:

1. Heat up the olive oil in a Dutch oven or stockpot over medium heat. Add the onion and sauté for 5 to 6 minutes, until soft. Stir in the garlic and stir until fragrant, 30 to 60 seconds. Then stir in the tomatoes, basil, Italian seasoning, salt, sugar, black pepper, and crushed red pepper flakes.
2. Bring to a simmer for 15 minutes. Stir in the heavy cream, if desired. For a smooth, puréed sauce, use an immersion blender or transfer sauce to a blender and purée until smooth. Taste and adjust the seasoning, if necessary.
3. While the sauce simmers, cook the gnocchi according to the package instructions, remove with a slotted spoon, and transfer to 6 bowls. Pour the sauce over the gnocchi and top with the Parmesan cheese.

Nutrition: Calories: 287 Fat: 7 g Sodium: 527 mg Carbohydrate: 41 g Protein: 10 g

354. Creamy Pumpkin Pasta

Preparation Time: 15 minutes
Cooking Time: 30 minutes
Servings: 6
Ingredients:

- 1-pound whole-grain linguine
- 1 tablespoon olive oil
- 3 garlic cloves, peeled and minced
- 2 tablespoons chopped fresh sage
- 1½ cups pumpkin purée
- 1 cup unsalted vegetable stock
- ½ cup low-fat evaporated milk
- ¾ teaspoon kosher or sea salt
- ½ teaspoon ground black pepper
- ½ teaspoon ground nutmeg
- ¼ teaspoon ground cayenne pepper
- ½ cup freshly grated Parmesan cheese, divided

Directions:

1. Cook the whole-grain linguine in a large pot of boiled water. Reserve ½ cup of pasta water and drain the rest. Set the pasta aside.
2. Warm-up olive oil over medium heat in a large skillet. Add the garlic and sage and sauté for 1 to 2 minutes, until soft and fragrant. Whisk in the pumpkin purée, stock, milk,

and reserved pasta water and simmer for 4 to 5 minutes, until thickened.

3. Whisk in the salt, black pepper, nutmeg, and cayenne pepper and half of the Parmesan cheese. Stir in the cooked whole-grain linguine. Evenly divide the pasta among 6 bowls and top with the remaining Parmesan cheese.

Nutrition: Calories: 381 Fat: 8 g Sodium: 175 mg Carbohydrate: 63 g Protein: 15 g

355. Mexican-Style Potato Casserole

Preparation Time: 15 minutes
Cooking Time: 60 minutes
Servings: 8
Ingredients:

- Cooking spray
- 2 tablespoons canola oil
- ½ yellow onion, peeled and diced
- 4 garlic cloves, peeled and minced
- 2 tablespoons all-purpose flour
- 1¼ cups milk
- 1 tablespoon chili powder
- ½ tablespoon ground cumin
- 1 teaspoon kosher salt or sea salt
- ½ teaspoon ground black pepper
- ¼ teaspoon ground cayenne pepper
- 1½ cups shredded Mexican-style cheese, divided
- 1 (4-oz.) can green chilis, drained
- 1½ pounds baby Yukon Gold or red potatoes, thinly sliced
- 1 red bell pepper, thinly sliced

Directions:

1. Preheat the oven to 400°F. Oiled a 9-by-13-inch baking dish with cooking spray. In a large saucepan, warm canola oil on medium heat. Add the onion and sauté for 4 to 5 minutes, until soft. Mix in the garlic, then cook

until fragrant, 30 to 60 seconds.

2. Mix in the flour, then put in the milk while whisking. Slow simmer for about 5 minutes, until thickened. Whisk in the chili powder, cumin, salt, black pepper, and cayenne pepper.

3. Remove from the heat and whisk in half of the shredded cheese and the green chilis. Taste and adjust the seasoning, if necessary. Line up one-third of the sliced potatoes and sliced bell pepper in the baking dish and top with a quarter of the remaining shredded cheese.

4. Repeat with 2 more layers. Pour the cheese sauce over the top and sprinkle with the remaining shredded cheese. Cover it with aluminum foil and bake within 45 to 50 minutes, until the potatoes are tender.

5. Remove the foil and bake again within 5 to 10 minutes, until the topping is slightly browned. Let cool within 20 minutes before slicing into 8 pieces. Serve.

Nutrition: Calories: 195 Fat: 10 g Sodium: 487 mg Carbohydrate: 19 g Protein: 8 g

356. Black Bean Stew with Cornbread

Preparation Time: 15 minutes
Cooking Time: 55 minutes
Servings: 6
Ingredients:
For the black bean stew:

- 2 tablespoons canola oil
- 1 yellow onion, peeled and diced
- 4 garlic cloves, peeled and minced
- 1 tablespoon chili powder
- 1 tablespoon ground cumin
- ¼ teaspoon kosher or sea salt
- ½ teaspoon ground black pepper

- 2 cans no-salt-added black beans, drained
- 1 (10-oz.) can fire-roasted diced tomatoes
- ½ cup fresh cilantro leaves, chopped

For the cornbread topping:

- 1¼ cups cornmeal
- ½ cup all-purpose flour
- ½ teaspoon baking powder
- ¼ teaspoon baking soda
- ⅛ teaspoon kosher or sea salt
- 1 cup low-fat buttermilk
- 2 tablespoons honey
- 1 large egg

Directions:

1. Warm-up canola oil over medium heat in a large Dutch oven or stockpot. Add the onion and sauté for 4 to 6 minutes, until the onion is soft. Stir in the garlic, chili powder, cumin, salt, and black pepper.

2. Cook within 1 to 2 minutes, until fragrant. Add the black beans and diced tomatoes. Bring to a simmer and cook for 15 minutes. Remove, then stir in the fresh cilantro. Taste and adjust the seasoning, if necessary.

3. Preheat the oven to 375°F. While the stew simmers, prepare the cornbread topping. Mix the cornmeal, baking soda, flour, baking powder, plus salt in a bowl. In a measuring cup, whisk the buttermilk, honey, and egg until combined. Put the batter into the dry fixing until just combined.

4. In oven-safe bowls or dishes, spoon out the black bean soup. Distribute dollops of the cornbread batter on top and then spread it out evenly with a spatula. Bake within 30 minutes, until the cornbread is just set.

Nutrition: Calories: 359 Fat: 7 g Sodium: 409 mg Carbohydrate: 61 g Protein: 14 g

357. Mushroom Florentine

Preparation Time: 15 minutes
Cooking Time: 20 minutes
Servings: 4
Ingredients:

- 5 ounces whole-grain pasta
- ¼ cup low-sodium vegetable broth
- 1 cup mushrooms, sliced
- ¼ cup of soy milk
- 1 teaspoon olive oil
- ½ teaspoon Italian seasonings

Directions:

1. Cook the pasta according to the direction of the manufacturer. Then pour olive oil into the saucepan and heat it. Add mushrooms and Italian seasonings. Stir the mushrooms well and cook for 10 minutes.
2. Then add soy milk and vegetable broth. Add cooked pasta and mix up the mixture well. Cook it for 5 minutes on low heat.

Nutrition: Calories 287 Protein 12.4 g Carbohydrates 50.4 g Fat 4.2 g Sodium 26 mg

358. Hasselback Eggplant

Preparation Time: 15 minutes
Cooking Time: 25 minutes
Servings: 2
Ingredients:

- 2 eggplants, trimmed
- 2 tomatoes, sliced
- 1 tablespoon low-fat yogurt
- 1 teaspoon curry powder
- 1 teaspoon olive oil

Directions:

1. Make the cuts in the eggplants in the shape of the Hasselback. Then rub the vegetables with curry powder and fill with sliced tomatoes. Sprinkle the eggplants with olive oil and yogurt and wrap in the foil (each Hasselback eggplant wrap separately). Bake the vegetables at 375F for 25 minutes.

Nutrition: Calories 188 Protein 7 g Carbohydrates 38.1 g Fat 3 g Sodium 23 mg

359. Vegetarian Kebabs

Preparation Time: 15 minutes
Cooking Time: 6 minutes
Servings: 4
Ingredients:

- 2 tablespoons balsamic vinegar
- 1 tablespoon olive oil
- 1 teaspoon dried parsley
- 2 tablespoons water
- 2 sweet peppers
- 2 red onions, peeled
- 2 zucchinis, trimmed

Directions:

1. Cut the sweet peppers and onions into medium size squares. Then slice the zucchini. String all vegetables into the skewers. After this, in the shallow bowl, mix up olive oil, dried parsley, water, and balsamic vinegar.
2. Sprinkle the vegetable skewers with olive oil mixture and transfer to the preheated to 390°F grill. Cook the kebabs within 3 minutes per side or until the vegetables are light brown.

Nutrition: Calories 88 Protein 2.4 g Carbohydrates 13 g Fat 3.9 g Sodium 14 mg

360. White Beans Stew

Preparation Time: 15 minutes
Cooking Time: 55 minutes
Servings: 4
Ingredients:

- 1 cup white beans, soaked
- 1 cup low-sodium vegetable broth
- 1 cup zucchini, chopped
- 1 teaspoon tomato paste
- 1 tablespoon avocado oil
- 4 cups of water
- ½ teaspoon peppercorns
- ½ teaspoon ground black pepper
- ¼ teaspoon ground nutmeg

Directions:

1. Heat avocado oil in the saucepan, add zucchinis and roast them for 5 minutes. After this, add white beans, vegetable broth, tomato paste, water, peppercorns, ground black pepper, and ground nutmeg. Simmer the stew within 50 minutes on low heat.

Nutrition: Calories 184 Protein 12.3 g Carbohydrates 32.6 g Fat 1 g Sodium 55 mg

361. Vegetarian Lasagna

Preparation Time: 15 minutes
Cooking Time: 30 minutes
Servings: 6
Ingredients:

- 1 cup carrot, diced
- ½ cup bell pepper, diced
- 1 cup spinach, chopped
- 1 tablespoon olive oil
- 1 teaspoon chili powder
- 1 cup tomatoes, chopped
- 4 ounces low-fat cottage cheese
- 1 eggplant, sliced
- 1 cup low-sodium vegetable broth

Directions:

- Put carrot, bell pepper, and spinach in the saucepan. Add olive oil and chili powder and stir the vegetables well. Cook them for 5 minutes.
- Make the sliced eggplant layer in the casserole mold and top it with a vegetable mixture. Add tomatoes, vegetable stock, and cottage cheese. Bake the lasagna for 30 minutes at 375°F.

Nutrition: Calories 77 Protein 4.1 g Carbohydrates 9.7 g Fat 3 g Sodium 124 mg

362. Carrot Cakes

Preparation Time: 15 minutes
Cooking Time: 10 minutes
Servings: 4
Ingredients:

- 1 cup carrot, grated
- 1 tablespoon semolina
- 1 egg, beaten
- 1 teaspoon Italian seasonings
- 1 tablespoon sesame oil

Directions:

1. In the mixing bowl, mix up grated carrot, semolina, egg,

and Italian seasonings. Heat sesame oil in the skillet. Make the carrot cakes with the help of 2 spoons and put in the skillet. Roast the cakes for 4 minutes per side.

Nutrition: Calories 70 Protein 1.9 g Carbohydrates 4.8 g Fat 4.9 g Sodium 35 mg

363. Vegan Chili

Preparation Time: 15 minutes
Cooking Time: 25 minutes
Servings: 4
Ingredients:

- ½ cup bulgur
- 1 cup tomatoes, chopped
- 1 chili pepper, chopped
- 1 cup red kidney beans, cooked
- 2 cups low-sodium vegetable broth
- 1 teaspoon tomato paste
- ½ cup celery stalk, chopped

Directions:

1. Put all ingredients in the big saucepan and stir well. Close the lid and simmer the chili for 25 minutes over medium-low heat.

Nutrition: Calories 234 Protein 13.1 g Carbohydrates 44.9 g Fat 0.9 g Sodium 92 mg

364. Aromatic Whole Grain Spaghetti

Preparation Time: 15 minutes
Cooking Time: 10 minutes
Servings: 2
Ingredients:

- 1 teaspoon dried basil
- ¼ cup of soy milk
- 6 ounces whole grain spaghetti
- 2 cups of water
- 1 teaspoon ground nutmeg

Directions:

1. Bring the water to boil, add spaghetti, and cook them for 8-10 minutes. Meanwhile, bring the soy milk to boil. Drain the cooked spaghetti and mix them up with soy milk, ground nutmeg, and dried basil. Stir the meal well.

Nutrition: Calories 128 Protein 5.6 g Carbohydrates 25 g Fat 1.4 g Sodium 25 mg

365. Baked Falafel

Preparation Time: 15 minutes
Cooking Time: 25 minutes
Servings: 6
Ingredients:

- 2 cups chickpeas, cooked
- 1 yellow onion, diced
- 3 tablespoons olive oil
- 1 cup fresh parsley, chopped
- 1 teaspoon ground cumin
- ½ teaspoon coriander
- 2 garlic cloves, diced

Directions:

1. Blend all fixing in the food processor. Preheat the oven to 375°F. Then line the baking tray with the baking paper. Make the balls from the chickpeas mixture and press them gently in the shape of the falafel. Put the falafel in the tray and bake in the oven for 25 minutes.

Nutrition: Calories 316 Protein 13.5 g Carbohydrates 43.3 g Fat 11.2 g Fiber 12.4 g Sodium 23 mg

366. Paella

Preparation Time: 15 minutes
Cooking Time: 25 minutes
Servings: 6
Ingredients:

- 1 teaspoon dried saffron
- 1 cup short-grain rice
- 1 tablespoon olive oil
- 2 cups of water
- 1 teaspoon chili flakes
- 6 ounces artichoke hearts, chopped
- ½ cup green peas
- 1 onion, sliced
- 1 cup bell pepper, sliced

Directions:

1. Pour water into the saucepan. Add rice and cook it for 15 minutes. Meanwhile, heat olive oil in the skillet. Add dried saffron, chili flakes, onion, and bell pepper. Roast the vegetables for 5 minutes.

2. Add them to the cooked rice. Then add artichoke hearts and green peas. Stir the paella well and cook it for 10 minutes over low heat.

Nutrition: Calories 170 Protein 4.2 g Carbohydrates 32.7 g Fat 2.7 g Sodium 33 mg

367. Chunky Tomatoes

Preparation Time: 15 minutes
Cooking Time: 15 minutes
Servings: 3
Ingredients:

- 2 cups plum tomatoes, roughly chopped
- ½ cup onion, diced
- ½ teaspoon garlic, diced
- 1 teaspoon Italian seasonings
- 1 teaspoon canola oil
- 1 chili pepper, chopped

Directions:

1. Heat canola oil in the saucepan. Add chili pepper and onion. Cook the vegetables for 5 minutes. Stir them from time to time. After this, add tomatoes, garlic, and Italian seasonings. Close the lid and sauté the dish for 10 minutes.

Nutrition: Calories 550 Protein 1.7 g Carbohydrates 8.4 g Fat 2.3 g Sodium 17 mg

368. Mushroom Cakes

Preparation Time: 15 minutes
Cooking Time: 10 minutes
Servings: 4
Ingredients:

- 2 cups mushrooms, chopped
- 3 garlic cloves, chopped
- 1 tablespoon dried dill
- 1 egg, beaten
- ¼ cup of rice, cooked
- 1 tablespoon sesame oil
- 1 teaspoon chili powder

Directions:

1. Grind the mushrooms in the food processor. Add garlic, dill, egg, rice, and chili powder. Blend the mixture for 10 seconds.

After this, heat sesame oil for 1 minute.

2. Make the medium size mushroom cakes and put in the hot sesame oil. Cook the mushroom cakes for 5 minutes per side on medium heat.

Nutrition: Calories 103 Protein 3.7 g Carbohydrates 12 g Fat 4.8 g Sodium 27 mg

369. Glazed Eggplant Rings
Preparation Time: 15 minutes
Cooking Time: 10 minutes
Servings: 4
Ingredients:
- 3 eggplants, sliced
- 1 tablespoon liquid honey
- 1 teaspoon minced ginger
- 2 tablespoons lemon juice
- 3 tablespoons avocado oil
- ½ teaspoon ground coriander
- 3 tablespoons water

Directions:
1. Rub the eggplants with ground coriander. Then heat the avocado oil in the skillet for 1 minute. When the oil is hot, add the sliced eggplant and arrange it in one layer.
2. Cook the vegetables for 1 minute per side. Transfer the eggplant to the bowl. Then add minced ginger, liquid honey, lemon juice, and water in the skillet. Bring it to boil and add cooked eggplants. Coat the vegetables in the sweet liquid well and cook for 2 minutes more.

Nutrition: Calories 136 Protein 4.3 g Carbohydrates 29.6 g Fat 2.2 g Sodium 11 mg

370. Sweet Potato Balls
Preparation Time: 15 minutes
Cooking Time: 10 minutes
Servings: 4
Ingredients:
- 1 cup sweet potato, mashed, cooked
- 1 tablespoon fresh cilantro, chopped
- 1 egg, beaten

- 3 tablespoons ground oatmeal
- 1 teaspoon ground paprika
- ½ teaspoon ground turmeric
- 2 tablespoons coconut oil

Directions:
1. Mix mashed sweet potato, fresh cilantro, egg, ground oatmeal, paprika, and turmeric in a bowl. Stir the mixture until smooth and make the small balls. Heat the coconut oil in the saucepan. Put the sweet potato balls, then cook them until golden brown.

Nutrition: Calories 133 Protein 2.8 g Carbohydrates 13.1 g Fat 8.2 g Sodium 44mg

371. Chickpea Curry
Preparation Time: 15 minutes
Cooking Time: 10 minutes
Servings: 4
Ingredients:
- 1½ cup chickpeas, boiled
- 1 teaspoon curry powder
- ½ teaspoon garam masala
- 1 cup spinach, chopped
- 1 teaspoon coconut oil
- ¼ cup of soy milk
- 1 tablespoon tomato paste
- ½ cup of water

Directions:
1. Heat coconut oil in the saucepan. Add curry powder, garam masala, tomato paste, and soy milk. Whisk the mixture until smooth and bring it to boil.
2. Add water, spinach, and chickpeas. Stir the meal and close the lid. Cook it within 5 minutes over medium heat.

Nutrition: Calories 298 Protein 15.4 g Carbohydrates 47.8 g Fat 6.1 g Sodium 37 mg

372. Pan-Fried Salmon with Salad
Preparation Time: 15 minutes
Cooking Time: 20 minutes
Servings: 4
Ingredients:
- Pinch of salt and pepper

- 1 tablespoon extra-virgin olive oil
- 2 tablespoon unsalted butter
- ½ teaspoon fresh dill
- 1 tablespoon fresh lemon juice
- 100 g salad leaves, or bag of mixed leaves

Salad Dressing:
- 3 tablespoons olive oil
- 2 tablespoons balsamic vinaigrette
- ½ teaspoon maple syrup (honey)

Directions:
1. Pat-dry the salmon fillets with a paper towel and season with a pinch of salt and pepper. In a skillet, warm up oil over medium-high heat and add fillets. Cook each side within 5 to 7 minutes until golden brown.
2. Dissolve butter, dill, and lemon juice in a small saucepan. Put the butter mixture onto the cooked salmon. Lastly, combine all the salad dressing ingredients and drizzle to mixed salad leaves in a large bowl. Toss to coat. Serve with fresh salads on the side. Enjoy!

Nutrition: Calories 307 Fat 22 g Protein 34.6 g Sodium 80 mg Carbohydrate 1.7 g

373. Veggie Variety
Preparation Time: 15 minutes
Cooking Time: 15 minutes
Servings: 2
Ingredients:
- ½ onion, diced
- 1 teaspoon vegetable oil (corn or sunflower oil)
- 200 g Tofu/ bean curd
- 4 cherry tomatoes, halved
- 30 ml vegetable milk (soy or oat milk)
- ½ teaspoon curry powder
- ¼ teaspoon paprika
- Pinch of Salt & Pepper
- 2 slices Vegan protein bread/ Whole grain bread
- Chives for garnish

Directions:

1. Dice the onion and fry in a frying pan with the oil. Break the tofu by hand into small pieces and put them in the pan. Sauté 7-8 min. Season with curry, paprika, salt, and pepper. The cherry tomatoes and milk and cook it all over roast for a few minutes. Serve with bread as desired and sprinkle with chopped chives.

Nutrition: Calories 216 Fat 8.4 g Protein 14.1 g Sodium 140 mg Carbohydrate 24.8 g

374. Vegetable Pasta

Preparation Time: 15 minutes
Cooking Time: 15 minutes
Servings: 4
Ingredients:

- 1 kg thin zucchini
- 20 g fresh ginger
- 350 g smoked tofu
- 1 lime
- 2 cloves garlic
- 2 tablespoons sunflower oil
- 2 tablespoons sesame seeds
- Pinch of salt and pepper
- 4 tablespoons fried onions

Directions:

1. Wash and clean the zucchini and, using a julienne cutter, cut the pulp around the kernel into long thin strips (noodles). Ginger peel and finely chop. Crumble tofu. Halve lime, squeeze juice. Peel and chop garlic.
2. Warm up 1 tablespoon of oil in a large pan and fry the tofu for about 5 minutes. After about 3 minutes, add ginger, garlic, and sesame. Season with soy sauce. Remove from the pan and keep warm.
3. Wipe out the pan, then warm 2 tablespoons of oil in it. Stir fry zucchini strips for about 4 minutes while turning. Season with salt, pepper, and lime juice. Arrange pasta and tofu. Sprinkle with fried onions.

Nutrition: Calories 262 Fat 17.7 g Protein 15.4 g Sodium 62 mg Carbohydrate 17.1 g

375. Vegetable Noodles with Bolognese

Preparation Time: 15 minutes
Cooking Time: 15 minutes
Servings: 4
Ingredients:

- 1½ kg small zucchini (e.g., green and yellow)
- 600 g carrots
- 1 onion
- 1 tablespoon olive oil
- 250 g beef steak
- Pinch of salt and pepper
- 2 tablespoons tomato paste
- 1 tablespoon flour
- 1 teaspoon vegetable broth (instant)
- 40 g pecorino or parmesan
- 1 small potty of basil

Directions:

1. Clean and peel zucchini and carrots and wash. Using a sharp, long knife, cut first into thin slices, then into long, fine strips. Clean or peel the soup greens, wash and cut into tiny cubes. Peel the onion and chop finely. Heat the Bolognese oil in a large pan. Fry hack in it crumbly. Season with salt and pepper.
2. Briefly sauté the prepared vegetable and onion cubes. Stir in tomato paste. Dust the flour, sweat briefly. Pour in 400 ml of water and stir in the vegetable stock. Boil everything, simmer for 7-8 minutes.
3. Meanwhile, cook the vegetable strips in plenty of salted water for 3-5 minutes. Drain, collecting some cooking water. Add the vegetable strips to the pan and mix well. If the sauce is not liquid enough, stir in some vegetable cooking water and season everything again.
4. Slicing cheese into fine shavings. Wash the basil, shake dry, peel off the leaves, and cut roughly. Arrange vegetable noodles, sprinkle with parmesan and basil

Nutrition: Calories 269 Fat 9.7 g Protein 25.6 g Sodium 253 mg Carbohydrate 21.7 g

376. Harissa Bolognese with Vegetable Noodles

Preparation Time: 15 minutes
Cooking Time: 30 minutes
Servings: 4
Ingredients:

- 2 onions
- 1 clove garlic
- 3-4 tablespoons oil
- 400 g ground beef
- Pinch of salt, pepper, cinnamon
- 1 teaspoon Harissa (Arabic seasoning paste, tube)
- 1 tablespoon tomato paste
- 2 sweet potatoes
- 2 medium Zucchini
- 3 stems/basil
- 100 g of feta

Directions:

1. Peel onions and garlic, finely dice. Warm up 1 tablespoon of oil in a wide saucepan. Fry hack in it crumbly. Fry onions and garlic for a short time. Season with salt, pepper, and ½ teaspoon cinnamon. Stir in harissa and tomato paste.
2. Add tomatoes and 200 ml of water, bring to the boil and simmer for about 15 minutes with occasional stirring. Peel sweet potatoes and zucchini or clean and wash. Cut vegetables into spaghetti with a spiral cutter.
3. Warm up 2-3 tablespoons of oil in a large pan. Braise sweet potato spaghetti in it for about 3 minutes. Add the zucchini spaghetti and continue to simmer for 3-4 minutes while turning.
4. Season with salt and pepper. Wash the basil, shake dry and peel off the leaves. Garnish vegetable spaghetti and Bolognese on plates.

Feta crumbles over. Sprinkle with basil.

Nutrition: Calories 452 Fat 22.3 g Protein 37.1 g Sodium 253 mg Carbohydrate 27.6 g

377. Curry Vegetable Noodles with Chicken

Preparation Time: 15 minutes
Cooking Time: 15 minutes
Servings: 2
Ingredients:

- 600 g zucchini
- 500 g chicken fillet
- Pinch of salt and pepper
- 2 tablespoons oil
- 150 g red and yellow cherry tomatoes
- 1 teaspoon curry powder
- 150g fat-free cheese
- 200 ml vegetable broth
- 4 stalk (s) of fresh basil

Directions:

1. Wash the zucchini, clean, and cut into long thin strips with a spiral cutter. Wash meat, pat dry, and season with salt. Heat 1 tablespoon oil in a pan. Roast chicken in it for about 10 minutes until golden brown.
2. Wash cherry tomatoes and cut in half. Approximately 3 minutes before the end of the cooking time to the chicken in the pan. Heat 1 tablespoon oil in another pan. Sweat curry powder into it then stirs in cream cheese and broth. Flavor the sauce with salt plus pepper and simmer for about 4 minutes.
3. Wash the basil, shake it dry and pluck the leaves from the stems. Cut small leaves of 3 stems. Remove meat from the pan and cut it into strips. Add tomatoes, basil, and zucchini to the sauce and heat for 2-3 minutes. Serve vegetable noodles and meat on plates and garnish with basil.

Nutrition:
Calories 376 Fat 17.2 g Protein 44.9 g Sodium 352 mg Carbohydrate 9.5 Cholesterol 53 mg

378. Sweet and Sour Vegetable Noodles

Preparation Time: 15 minutes
Cooking Time: 30 minutes
Servings: 4
Ingredients:

- 4 chicken fillets (75 g each)
- 300 g whole-wheat spaghetti
- 750 g carrots
- ½ liter clear chicken broth (instant)
- 1 tablespoon sugar
- 1 tablespoon green peppercorns
- 2-3 tablespoons balsamic vinegar
- Capuchin flowers
- Pinch of salt

Directions:

1. Cook spaghetti in boiling water for about 8 minutes. Then drain. In the meantime, peel and wash carrots. Cut into long strips (best with a special grater). Blanch within 2 minutes in boiling salted water, drain. Wash chicken fillets. Add to the boiling chicken soup and cook for about 15 minutes.
2. Melt the sugar until golden brown. Measure ¼ liter of chicken stock and deglaze the sugar with it. Add peppercorns, cook for 2 minutes. Season with salt and vinegar. Add the fillets, then cut into thin slices. Then turn the pasta and carrots in the sauce and serve garnished with capuchin blossoms. Serve and enjoy.

Nutrition: Calories 374 Fat 21 g Protein 44 g Sodium 295 mg Carbohydrate 23.1

379. Farro Cucumber-Mint Salad

Preparation Time: 15 minutes
Cooking Time: 30 minutes
Servings: 4-6
Ingredients:

- 1 cup baby arugula
- 1 English cucumber, halved along the length, seeded, and cut into ¼-inch pieces
- 1½ cups whole farro
- 2 tablespoons lemon juice
- 2 tablespoons minced shallot
- 2 tablespoons plain Greek yogurt
- 3 tablespoons chopped fresh mint
- 3 tablespoons extra-virgin olive oil
- 6 ounces cherry tomatoes, halved
- Salt and pepper

Directions:

1. Bring 4 quarts of water to boil in a Dutch oven. Put in farro and 1 tablespoon salt, return to boil and cook until grains are soft with a slight chew, 15 to 30 minutes.
2. Drain farro, spread in rimmed baking sheet, and allow to cool completely, about fifteen minutes.
3. Beat oil, lemon juice, shallot, yogurt, ¼ teaspoon salt, and ¼ teaspoon pepper together in a big container.
4. Put in farro, cucumber, tomatoes, arugula, and mint and toss gently to combine. Sprinkle with salt and pepper to taste. Serve.

Nutrition: Calories: 97 Carbs: 15 g Fat: 4 g Protein: 2 g

380. Chorizo-Kidney Beans Quinoa Pilaf

Preparation Time: 15 minutes
Cooking Time: 37 minutes
Servings: 4
Ingredients:

- ¼ pound dried Spanish chorizo diced (about 2/3 cup)
- ¼ teaspoon red pepper flakes
- ¼ teaspoon smoked paprika
- ½ teaspoon cumin
- ½ teaspoon sea salt
- 1¾ cups water
- 1 cup quinoa
- 1 large clove garlic minced
- 1 small red bell pepper finely diced
- 1 small red onion finely diced
- 1 tablespoon tomato paste

- 1 (15-oz.) can kidney beans rinsed and drained

Directions:

1. Place a nonstick pot on medium-high fire and heat for 2 minutes. Add chorizo and sauté for 5 minutes until lightly browned. Stir in peppers and onion. Sauté for 5 minutes.
2. Add tomato paste, red pepper flakes, salt, paprika, cumin, and garlic. Sauté for 2 minutes. Stir in quinoa and mix well. Sauté for 2 minutes.
3. Add water and beans. Mix well. Cover and simmer for 20 minutes or until liquid is fully absorbed. Turn off fire and fluff quinoa. Let it sit for 5 minutes more while uncovered. Serve and enjoy.

Nutrition: Calories: 260 Protein: 9.6 g Carbs: 40.9 g Fat: 6.8 g

381. Goat Cheese 'N Red Beans Salad

Preparation Time: 15 minutes
Cooking Time: 0 minutes
Servings: 6
Ingredients:

- 2 cans of Red Kidney Beans, drained and rinsed well
- Water or vegetable broth to cover beans
- 1 bunch parsley, chopped
- 1½ cups red grape tomatoes, halved
- 3 cloves garlic, minced
- 3 tablespoons olive oil
- 3 tablespoons lemon juice
- ½ teaspoon salt
- ½ teaspoon white pepper
- 6 ounces goat cheese, crumbled

Directions:

1. In a large bowl, combine beans, parsley, tomatoes and garlic. Add olive oil, lemon juice, salt and pepper.
2. Mix well and refrigerate until ready to serve. Spoon into individual dishes topped with crumbled goat cheese.

Nutrition: Calories: 385 Protein: 22.5 g Carbs: 44.0 g Fat: 15.0 g

382. Greek Farro Salad

Preparation Time: 15 minutes
Cooking Time: 20 minutes
Servings: 4
Ingredients:
Farro:

- ½ teaspoon fine-grain sea salt
- 1 cup farro, rinsed
- 1 tablespoon olive oil
- 2 garlic cloves, pressed or minced

Salad:

- ½ small red onion, chopped and then rinsed under water to mellow the flavor
- 1 avocado, sliced into strips
- 1 cucumber, sliced into thin rounds
- 15 pitted Kalamata olives, sliced into rounds
- 1-pint cherry tomatoes, sliced into rounds
- 2 cups cooked chickpeas or 1 (14-oz.) can, rinsed and drained)
- 5 ounces mixed greens
- Lemon wedges
- Herbed Yogurt
- ⅛ teaspoon salt
- 1¼ cups plain Greek yogurt
- 1½ tablespoon lightly packed fresh dill, roughly chopped
- 1½ tablespoon lightly packed fresh mint, torn into pieces
- 1 tablespoon lemon juice (about ½ lemon)
- 1 tablespoon olive oil

Directions:

1. In a blender, blend and puree all herbed yogurt ingredients and set aside. Then cook the farro by placing in a pot filled halfway with water.
2. Bring to a boil, reduce fire to a simmer and cook for 15 minutes or until farro is tender. Drain well. Mix in salt, garlic, and olive oil and fluff to coat.
3. Evenly divide the cooled farro into 4 bowls. Evenly divide the salad ingredients on the 4 farro bowl. Top with ¼ of the yogurt dressing. Serve and enjoy.

Nutrition: Calories: 428 Protein: 17.7 g Carbs: 47.6 g Fat: 24.5 g

383. White Bean and Tuna Salad

Preparation Time: 15 minutes
Cooking Time: 8 minutes
Servings: 4
Ingredients:

- 1 (12-oz.) can solid white albacore tuna, drained
- 1 (16-oz.) can Great Northern beans, drained and rinsed
- 1 (2.25-oz.) can sliced black olives, drained
- 1 teaspoon dried oregano
- ½ teaspoon finely grated lemon zest
- ¼ medium red onion, thinly sliced
- 3 tablespoons lemon juice
- ¾-pound green beans, trimmed and snapped in half
- 4 large hard-cooked eggs, peeled and quartered
- 6 tablespoons extra-virgin olive oil
- Salt and ground black pepper, to taste

Directions:

1. Place a saucepan on the medium-high fire. Add a cup of water and the green beans. Cover and cook for 8 minutes. Drain immediately once tender.
2. In a salad bowl, whisk well oregano, olive oil, lemon juice, and lemon zest. Season generously with pepper and salt and mix until salt is dissolved.
3. Stir in drained green beans, tuna, beans, olives, and red onion. Mix thoroughly to coat. Adjust seasoning to taste. Spread eggs on top. Serve and enjoy.

Nutrition: Calories: 551 Protein: 36.3 g Carbs: 33.4 g Fat: 30.3 g

384. Spicy Sweet Red Hummus

Preparation Time: 15 minutes
Cooking Time: 0 minutes
Servings: 8
Ingredients:

- 1 (15-oz.) can garbanzo beans, drained
- 1 (4-oz.) jar roasted red peppers
- 1½ tablespoons tahini
- 1 clove garlic, minced
- 1 tablespoon chopped fresh parsley
- ½ teaspoon cayenne pepper
- ½ teaspoon ground cumin
- ¼ teaspoon salt
- 3 tablespoons lemon juice

Directions:

1. In a blender, add all ingredients and process until smooth and creamy. Adjust seasoning to taste if needed. Can be stored in an airtight container for up to 5 days.

Nutrition: Calories: 64 Protein: 2.5 g Carbs: 9.6 g Fat: 2.2 g

385. Black Bean Chili with Mangoes

Preparation Time: 15 minutes
Cooking Time: 10 minutes
Servings: 4
Ingredients:

- 2 tablespoons coconut oil
- 1 onion, chopped
- 2 (15-oz. / 425-g.) cans black beans, drained and rinsed
- 1 tablespoon chili powder
- 1 teaspoon sea salt
- ¼ teaspoon freshly ground black pepper
- 1 cup water
- 2 ripe mangoes, sliced thinly
- ¼ cup chopped fresh cilantro, divided
- ¼ cup sliced scallions, divided

Directions:

1. Heat the coconut oil in a pot over high heat until melted. Put the onion in the pot and sauté for 5 minutes or until translucent.

2. Add the black beans to the pot. Sprinkle with chili powder, salt, and ground black pepper. Pour in the water. Stir to mix well.

3. Bring to a boil. Reduce the heat to low, then simmering for 5 minutes or until the beans are tender. Turn off the heat and mix in the mangoes, then garnish with scallions and cilantro before serving.

Nutrition: Calories: 430 Fat: 9.1 g Protein: 20.2 g Carbs: 71.9 g

386. Israeli Style Eggplant and Chickpea Salad

Preparation Time: 5 minutes
Cooking Time: 20 minutes
Servings: 6
Ingredients:

- 2 tablespoons balsamic vinegar
- 2 tablespoons freshly squeezed lemon juice
- 1 teaspoon ground cumin
- ¼ teaspoon sea salt
- 2 tablespoons olive oil, divided
- 1 (1-lb. / 454-g.) medium globe eggplant, stem removed, cut into flat cubes (about ½ inch thick)
- 1 (15-oz. / 425-g.) can chickpeas, drained and rinsed
- ¼ cup chopped mint leaves
- 1 cup sliced sweet onion
- 1 garlic clove, finely minced
- 1 tablespoon sesame seeds, toasted

Directions:

1. Preheat the oven to 550°F (288°C) or the highest level of your oven or broiler. Grease a baking sheet with 1 tablespoon of olive oil.

2. Combine the balsamic vinegar, lemon juice, cumin, salt, and 1 tablespoon of olive oil in a small bowl. Stir to mix well.

3. Arrange the eggplant cubes on the baking sheet, then brush with 2 tablespoons of the balsamic vinegar mixture on both sides.

4. Broil in the preheated oven for 8 minutes or until lightly browned. Flip the cubes halfway through the cooking time.

5. Meanwhile, combine the chickpeas, mint, onion, garlic, and sesame seeds in a large serving bowl. Drizzle with the remaining balsamic vinegar mixture. Stir to mix well.

6. Remove the eggplant from the oven. Allow to cool for 5 minutes, then slice them into ½-inch strips on a clean work surface.

7. Add the eggplant strips to the serving bowl, then toss to combine well before serving.

Nutrition: Calories: 125 Fat: 2.9g Protein: 5.2 g Carbs: 20.9 g

387. Italian Sautéed Cannellini Beans

Preparation Time: 15 minutes
Cooking Time: 15 minutes
Servings: 6
Ingredients:

- 2 teaspoons extra-virgin olive oil
- ½ cup minced onion
- ¼ cup red wine vinegar
- 1 (12-oz. / 340-g.) can no-salt-added tomato paste
- 2 tablespoons raw honey
- ½ cup water
- ¼ teaspoon ground cinnamon
- 2 (15-oz. / 425-g.) cans cannellini beans

Directions:

1. Heat the olive oil in a saucepan over medium heat until shimmering. Add the onion and sauté for 5 minutes or until translucent.

2. Pour in the red wine vinegar, tomato paste, honey, and water. Sprinkle with cinnamon. Stir to mix well.

3. Reduce the heat to low, then pour all the beans into the saucepan. Cook for 10 more minutes. Stir constantly. Serve immediately.

Nutrition: Calories: 435 Fat: 2.1 g Protein: 26.2 g Carbs: 80.3 g

388. Lentil and Vegetable Curry Stew

Preparation Time: 15 minutes
Cooking Time: 4 hours & 7 minutes
Servings: 8
Ingredients:

- 1 tablespoon coconut oil
- 1 yellow onion, diced
- ¼ cup yellow Thai curry paste
- 2 cups unsweetened coconut milk
- 2 cups dry red lentils, rinsed well and drained
- 3 cups bite-sized cauliflower florets
- 2 golden potatoes, cut into chunks
- 2 carrots, peeled and diced
- 8 cups low-sodium vegetable soup, divided
- 1 bunch kale, stems removed and roughly chopped
- Sea salt, to taste
- ½ cup fresh cilantro, chopped
- Pinch crushed red pepper flakes

Directions:

1. Heat the coconut oil in a nonstick skillet over medium-high heat until melted. Add the onion and sauté for 5 minutes or until translucent.
2. Pour in the curry paste and sauté for another 2 minutes, then fold in the coconut milk and stir to combine well. Bring to a simmer and turn off the heat.
3. Put the lentils, cauliflower, potatoes, and carrot in the slow cooker. Pour in 6 cups of vegetable soup and the curry mixture. Stir to combine well.
4. Cover and cook on high for 4 hours or until the lentils and vegetables are soft. Stir periodically.
5. During the last 30 minutes, fold the kale in the slow cooker and pour in the remaining vegetable soup. Sprinkle with salt.
6. Pour the stew in a large serving bowl and spread the cilantro and red pepper flakes on top before serving hot.

Nutrition: Calories: 530 Fat: 19.2 g Protein: 20.3 g Carbs: 75.2 g

389. Lush Moroccan Chickpea, Vegetable, and Fruit Stew

Preparation Time: 15 minutes
Cooking Time: 6 hours & 4 minutes
Servings: 6
Ingredients:

- 1 large bell pepper, any color, chopped
- 6 ounces (170-g.) green beans, trimmed and cut into bite-size pieces
- 3 cups canned chickpeas, rinsed and drained
- 1 (15-oz. / 425-g.) can diced tomatoes, with the juice
- 1 large carrot, cut in to ¼-inch rounds
- 2 large potatoes, peeled and cubed
- 1 large yellow onion, chopped
- 1 teaspoon grated fresh ginger
- 2 garlic cloves, minced
- 1¾ cups low-sodium vegetable soup
- 1 teaspoon ground cumin
- 1 tablespoon ground coriander
- ¼ teaspoon ground red pepper flakes
- Sea salt and ground black pepper, to taste
- 8 ounces (227-g.) fresh baby spinach
- ¼ cup diced dried figs
- ¼ cup diced dried apricots
- 1 cup plain Greek yogurt

Directions:

1. Place the bell peppers, green beans, chicken peas, tomatoes and juice, carrot, potatoes, onion, ginger, and garlic in the slow cooker.
2. Pour in the vegetable soup and sprinkle with cumin, coriander, red pepper flakes, salt, and ground black pepper. Stir to mix well.
3. Put the slow cooker lid on and cook on high for 6 hours or until the vegetables are soft. Stir periodically. Open the lid and fold in the spinach, figs, apricots, and yogurt. Stir to mix well.
4. Cook for 4 minutes or until the spinach is wilted. Pour them in a large serving bowl. Allow to cool for at least 20 minutes, then serve warm.

Nutrition: Calories: 611 Fat: 9.0 g Protein: 30.7 g Carbs: 107.4 g

390. Simple Pork Stir Fry

Preparation Time: 10 minutes
Cooking Time: 15 minutes
Servings: 4
Ingredients:

- 4 ounces bacon, chopped
- 4 ounces snow peas
- 2 tablespoons butter
- 1-pound pork loin, cut into thin strips
- 2 cups mushrooms, sliced
- ¾ cup white wine
- ½ cup yellow onion, chopped
- 3 tablespoons sour cream
- Salt and white pepper to taste

Directions:

1. Put snow peas in a saucepan, add water to cover, add a pinch of salt, bring to a boil over medium heat, cook until they are soft, drain and leave aside.
2. Heat a pan over medium-high heat, add bacon, cook for a few minutes, drain grease, transfer to a bowl and leave aside.
3. Heat a pan with 1 tablespoon butter over medium heat, add pork strips, salt and pepper to taste, brown for a few minutes, and transfer to a plate as well.

4. Return pan to medium heat, add remaining butter, and melt it. Add onions and mushrooms, stir and cook for 4 minutes.
5. Add wine, and simmer until it's reduced. Add cream, peas, pork, salt and pepper to taste, stir, heat up, divide between plates, top with bacon and serve.

Nutrition: Calories 343 Fat 31 g Carbs 21 g Protein 23g

391. Pork and Lentil Soup

Preparation Time: 10 minutes
Cooking Time: 1 hour
Servings: 6
Ingredients:

- 1 small yellow onion, chopped
- 1 tablespoon olive oil
- 1½ teaspoons basil, chopped
- 1½ teaspoons ginger, grated
- 3 garlic cloves, chopped
- Salt and black pepper to taste
- ½ teaspoon cumin, ground
- 1 carrot, chopped
- 1-pound pork chops, bone-in 3 ounces brown lentils, rinsed
- 3 cups chicken stock
- 2 tablespoons tomato paste
- 2 tablespoons lime juice
- 1 teaspoon red chili flakes, crushed

Directions:

1. Heat a saucepan with the oil over medium heat, add garlic, onion, basil, ginger, salt, pepper and cumin, stir well and cook for 6 minutes.
2. Add carrots, stir and cook for 5 more minutes. Add pork and brown for a few minutes. Add lentils, tomato paste and stock, stir, bring to a boil, cover pan and simmer for 50 minutes.
3. Transfer pork to a plate, discard bones, shred it and return to pan. Add chili flakes and lime juice, stir, ladle into bowls and serve.

Nutrition: Calories 343 Fat 31 g Carbs 21 g Protein 23 g

392. Simple Braised Pork

Preparation Time: 40 minutes
Cooking Time: 1 hour
Servings: 4
Ingredients:

- 2 pounds pork loin roast, boneless and cubed
- 5 tablespoons butter
- Salt and black pepper to taste
- 2 cups chicken stock
- ½ cup dry white wine
- 2 garlic cloves, minced
- 1 teaspoon thyme, chopped
- 1 thyme spring
- 1 bay leaf
- ½ yellow onion, chopped
- 2 tablespoons white flour
- ¾ pound pearl onions
- ½ pound red grapes

Directions:

1. Heat a pan with 2 tablespoons butter over high heat, add pork loin, some salt and pepper, stir, brown for 10 minutes, and transfer to a plate.
2. Add wine to the pan, bring to a boil over high heat and cook for 3 minutes.
3. Add stock, garlic, thyme spring, bay leaf, yellow onion and return meat to the pan, bring to a boil, cover, reduce heat to low, cook for 1 hour, strain liquid into another saucepan, and transfer pork to a plate.
4. Put pearl onions in a small saucepan, add water to cover, bring to a boil over medium-high heat, boil them for 5 minutes, drain, peel them and leave aside for now.
5. In a bowl, mix 2 tablespoons butter with flour and stir well. Add ½ cup of the strained cooking liquid and whisk well.
6. Pour this into cooking liquid, bring to a simmer over medium heat and cook for 5 minutes. Add salt and pepper, chopped thyme,

pork and pearl onions, cover and simmer for a few minutes.

7. Meanwhile, heat a pan with 1 tablespoon butter, add grapes, stir and cook them for 1-2 minutes. Divide pork meat on plates, drizzle the sauce all over, and serve with onions and grapes on the side.

Nutrition: Calories 320 Fat 31 g Carbs 21 g Protein 23 g

393. Pork and Chickpea Stew

Preparation Time: 20 minutes
Cooking Time: 8 hours
Servings: 4
Ingredients:

- 2 tablespoons white flour
- ½ cup chicken stock
- 1 tablespoon ginger, grated
- 1 teaspoon coriander, ground
- 2 teaspoons cumin, ground
- Salt and black pepper to taste
- 2½ pounds pork butt, cubed
- 28 ounces canned tomatoes, drained and chopped
- 4 ounces carrots, chopped
- 1 red onion cut in wedges
- 4 garlic cloves, minced
- ½ cup apricots, cut in quarters
- 1 cup couscous, cooked
- 15 ounces canned chickpeas, drained
- Cilantro, chopped for serving

Directions:

1. Put stock in your slow cooker. Add flour, cumin, ginger, coriander, salt and pepper, and stir. Add tomatoes, pork, carrots, garlic, onion and apricots, cover the cooker and cook on Low for 7 hours and 50 minutes.
2. Add chickpeas and couscous, cover and cook for 10 more minutes. Divide on plates, sprinkle cilantro, and serve right away.

Nutrition: Calories 216 Fat 31 g Carbs 21 g Protein 23 g

394. Pork and Greens Salad

Preparation Time: 10 minutes
Cooking Time: 15 minutes
Servings: 4
Ingredients:

- 1-pound pork chops, boneless and cut into strips
- 8 ounces white mushrooms, sliced
- ½ cup Italian dressing
- 6 cups mixed salad greens
- 6 ounces jarred artichoke hearts, drained
- Salt and black pepper to the taste
- ½ cup basil, chopped
- 1 tablespoon olive oil

Directions:

1. Heat a pan with the oil over medium-high heat, add the pork and brown for 5 minutes. Add the mushrooms, stir and sauté for 5 minutes more.
2. Add the dressing, artichokes, salad greens, salt, pepper and basil, cook for 4-5 minutes, divide everything into bowls and serve.

Nutrition: Calories 320 Fat 31 g Carbs 21 g Protein 23 g

395. Pork Strips and Rice

Preparation Time: 10 minutes
Cooking Time: 25 minutes
Servings: 4
Ingredients:

- ½ pound pork loin, cut into strips
- Salt and black pepper to taste
- 2 tablespoons olive oil
- 2 carrots, chopped
- 1 red bell pepper, chopped
- 3 garlic cloves, minced
- 2 cups veggie stock
- 1 cup basmati rice
- ½ cup garbanzo beans
- 10 black olives, pitted and sliced
- 1 tablespoon parsley, chopped

Directions:

1. Heat a pan with the oil over medium-high heat. Add the pork fillets, stir, cook for 5 minutes and transfer them to a plate.
2. Add the carrots, bell pepper and garlic, stir and cook for 5 more minutes.
3. Add the rice, the stock, beans and the olives, stir, cook for 14 minutes, divide between plates, sprinkle the parsley on top and serve.

Nutrition: Calories 220 Fat 31 g Carbs 21 g Protein 23 g

396. Pork and Bean Stew

Preparation Time: 20 minutes
Cooking Time: 4 hours
Servings: 4
Ingredients:

- 2 pounds pork neck
- 1 tablespoon white flour
- 1½ tablespoons olive oil
- 2 eggplants, chopped
- 1 brown onion, chopped & 1 red bell pepper, chopped
- 3 garlic cloves, minced
- 1 tablespoon thyme, dried
- 2 teaspoons sage, dried
- 4 ounces canned white beans, drained
- 1 cup chicken stock
- 12 ounces zucchinis, chopped
- Salt and pepper to taste
- 2 tablespoons tomato paste

Directions:

1. In a bowl, mix flour with salt, pepper, pork neck and toss. Heat a pan with 2 teaspoons oil over medium-high heat, add pork and cook for 3 minutes on each side.
2. Transfer pork to a slow cooker and leave aside. Heat the remaining oil in the same pan over medium heat, add eggplant, onion, bell pepper, thyme, sage and garlic, stir and cook for 5 minutes.
3. Add reserved flour, stir and cook for 1 more minute. Add to pork, then add beans, stock, tomato paste and zucchinis. Cover and cook on high for 4 hours. Uncover, transfer to plates and serve.

Nutrition: Calories: 310 fat 31 g carbs 21 g protein 23 g

397. Pork with Couscous

Preparation Time: 10 minutes
Cooking Time: 7 hours
Servings: 6
Ingredients:

- 2½ pounds pork loin boneless and trimmed
- ¾ cup chicken stock
- 2 tablespoons olive oil
- ½ tablespoon sweet paprika
- 2¼ teaspoons sage, dried
- ½ tablespoon garlic powder
- ¼ teaspoon rosemary, dried
- ¼ teaspoon marjoram, dried
- 1 teaspoon basil, dried
- 1 teaspoon oregano, dried
- Salt and black pepper to taste
- 2 cups couscous, cooked

Directions:

1. In a bowl, mix oil with stock, paprika, garlic powder, sage, rosemary, thyme, marjoram, oregano, salt and pepper to taste and whisk well. Put pork loin in your crockpot.
2. Add stock and spice mix, stir, cover, and cook on Low for 7 hours. Slice pork return to pot and toss with cooking juices. Divide between plates and serve with couscous on the side.

Nutrition: Calories 320 Fat 31 g Carbs 21 g Protein 23 g

398. Grilled Steak, Mushroom, and Onion Kebabs

Preparation Time: 10 minutes
Cooking Time: 10 minutes
Servings: 2
Ingredients:

- 1-pound boneless top sirloin steak
- 8 ounces white button mushrooms
- 1 medium red onion
- 4 peeled garlic cloves
- 2 Rosemary sprigs
- 2 tablespoons extra-virgin olive oil
- ¼ teaspoon black pepper
- 2 tablespoons red wine vinegar

- ¼ teaspoon sea salt

Directions:

1. Soak 12 (10-inch) wooden skewers in water. Spray the cold grill with nonstick cooking spray, and heat the grill to medium-high.
2. Cut a piece of aluminum foil into a 10-inch square. Place the garlic and rosemary sprigs in the center, drizzle with 1 tablespoon of oil, and wrap tightly to form a foil packet.
3. Arrange it on the grill, and seal the grill cover.
4. Cut the steak into 1-inch cubes. Thread the beef onto the wet skewers, alternating with whole mushrooms and onion wedges. Spray the kebabs thoroughly with nonstick cooking spray, and sprinkle with pepper.
5. Cook the kebabs on the covered grill for 5 minutes.
6. Flip and grill for 5 more minutes while covered.
7. Unwrap foil packets with garlic and rosemary sprigs and put them into a small bowl.
8. Carefully strip the rosemary sprigs of their leaves into the bowl and pour in any accumulated juices and oil from the foil packet.
9. Mix in the remaining 1 tablespoon of oil and the vinegar and salt.
10. Mash the garlic with a fork, and mix all ingredients in the bowl together. Pour over the finished steak kebabs and serve.

Nutrition: Calories: 410, Protein: 36 g, Carbohydrates: 12 g, Fat: 14 g

399. Kale Sprouts & Lamb

Preparation Time: 10 minutes
Cooking Time: 30 minutes
Servings: 2
Ingredients:

- 2 pounds lamb, cut into chunks
- 1 tablespoon Parsley, chopped
- 2 tablespoons Olive oil
- 1 cup kale, chopped
- 1 cup Brussels sprouts, halved
- 1 cup beef stock
- Pepper
- Salt

Directions:

1. Add all ingredients into the inner pot of the instant pot and stir well.
2. Seal pot with lid and cook on high for 30 minutes.
3. Once done, allow to release pressure naturally. Remove lid.
4. Serve and enjoy.

Nutrition:

Calories 504, Fat 23.8 g, Carbohydrates 3.9 g, Sugar 0.5 g, Protein 65.7 g, Cholesterol 204 mg

400. Shrimp with Garlic and Mushrooms

Preparation Time: 15 minutes
Cooking Time: 15 minutes
Servings: 4
Ingredients:

- 1 pound (454-g.) peeled and deveined fresh shrimp
- 1 teaspoon salt
- 1 cup extra-virgin olive oil
- 8 large garlic cloves, thinly sliced
- 4 ounces (113-g.) sliced mushrooms (shiitake, baby bella, or button)
- ½ teaspoon red pepper flakes
- ¼ cup chopped fresh flat-leaf Italian parsley
- Zucchini noodles or riced cauliflower, for serving

Directions:

1. Rinse the shrimp and pat dry. Place in a small bowl and sprinkle with salt. In a large rimmed, thick skillet, heat the olive oil over medium-low heat.
2. Add the garlic and heat until very fragrant, 3 to 4 minutes, reducing the heat if the garlic starts to burn.
3. Add the mushrooms and sauté for 5 minutes, until softened. Add the shrimp and red pepper flakes and sauté until the shrimp

begins to turn pink, another 3 to 4 minutes.

4. Remove from the heat and stir in the parsley. Serve over zucchini noodles or riced cauliflower.

Nutrition: Calories: 620 Fat: 56 g Protein: 24 g Carbs: 4 g

401. Pistachio-Crusted Whitefish

Preparation Time: 10 minutes
Cooking Time: 20 minutes
Servings: 2
Ingredients:

- ¼ cup shelled pistachios
- 1 tablespoon fresh parsley
- 1 tablespoon grated Parmesan cheese
- 1 tablespoon panko bread crumbs
- 2 tablespoons olive oil
- ¼ teaspoon salt
- 10 ounces skinless whitefish (1 large piece or 2 smaller ones)

Directions:

1. Preheat the oven to 350°F and set the rack to the middle position. Line a sheet pan with foil or parchment paper.
2. Combine all of the ingredients except the fish in a mini food processor, and pulse until the nuts are finely ground.
3. Alternatively, you can mince the nuts with a chef's knife and combine the ingredients by hand in a small bowl.
4. Place the fish on the sheet pan. Spread the nut mixture evenly over the fish and pat it down lightly.
5. Bake the fish for 20 to 30 minutes, depending on the thickness, until it flakes easily with a fork.
6. Keep in mind that a thicker cut of fish takes a bit longer to bake. You'll know it's done when it's opaque, flakes apart easily with a fork, or reaches an internal temperature of 145°F.

Nutrition: Calories 185, Carbs 23.8 g, Protein 10.1 g, Fat 5.2 g

402. Crispy Homemade Fish Sticks Recipe

Preparation Time: 10 minutes
Cooking Time: 15 minutes
Servings: 2
Ingredients:

- ½ cup of flour
- 1 beaten egg
- 1 cup of flour
- ½ cup parmesan cheese
- ½ cup bread crumbs.
- Zest of 1 lemon juice
- Parsley
- Salt
- 1 teaspoon black pepper
- 1 tablespoon sweet paprika
- 1 teaspoon oregano
- 1½ pounds salmon
- Extra-virgin olive oil

Directions:

1. Preheat your oven to about 450°F. Get a bowl, dry your salmon, and season its two sides with salt.
2. Then chop into small sizes of 1½ inch length each. Get a bowl and mix black pepper with oregano.
3. Add paprika to the mixture and blend it. Then spice the fish stick with the mixture you have just made. Get another dish and pour your flours.
4. You will need a different bowl again to pour your egg wash into. Pick yet the fourth dish, mix your breadcrumb with your parmesan and add lemon zest to the mixture.
5. Return to the fish sticks and dip each fish into flour such that both sides are coated with flour. As you dip each fish into flour, take it out and dip it into the egg wash and lastly, dip it in the breadcrumb mixture.
6. Do this for all fish sticks and arrange on a baking sheet. Ensure you oil the baking sheet before arranging the stick thereon and drizzle the top of the fish sticks with extra-virgin olive oil.
7. Caution: allow excess flours to fall off a fish before dipping it into other ingredients.
8. Also, ensure that you do not let the coating peel while you add extra-virgin olive oil on top of the fish.
9. Fix the baking sheet in the middle of the oven and allow it to cook for 13 min. By then, the fishes should be golden brown and you can collect them from the oven, and you can serve immediately.
10. Top it with your lemon zest, parsley and fresh lemon juice.

Nutrition: 119 Cal, 3.4 g of fat, 293.1 mg of sodium, 9.3 g of carbs, 13.5 g of protein.

403. Sauced Shellfish in White Wine

Preparation Time: 10 minutes
Cooking Time: 10 minutes
Servings: 2
Ingredients:

- 2 pounds fresh cuttlefish
- ½-cup olive oil
- 1-pc large onion, finely chopped
- 1-cup of Robiola white wine
- ¼-cup lukewarm water
- 1-pc bay leaf & ½-bunch parsley, chopped
- 4-pcs tomatoes, grated
- Salt and pepper

Directions:

1. Take out the hard centerpiece of cartilage (cuttlebone), the bag of ink, and the intestines from the cuttlefish.
2. Wash the cleaned cuttlefish with running water. Slice it into small pieces, and drain excess water.
3. Heat the oil in a saucepan placed over medium-high heat and sauté the onion for 3 minutes until tender.
4. Add the sliced cuttlefish and pour in the white wine. Cook for 5 minutes until it simmers.
5. Pour in the water, and add the tomatoes, bay leaf, parsley, tomatoes, salt, and pepper. Simmer the mixture over low heat until the cuttlefish slices are tender and left with their thick sauce. Serve them warm with rice.
6. Be careful not to overcook the cuttlefish as its texture becomes very hard. A safe rule of thumb is grilling the cuttlefish over a ragingly hot fire for 3 minutes before using it in any recipe.

Nutrition: Calories: 308, Fats: 18.1 g, Dietary Fiber: 1.5 g, Carbohydrates: 8 g, Protein: 25.6 g

404. Pistachio Sole Fish

Preparation Time: 5 minutes
Cooking Time: 10 minutes
Servings: 2
Ingredients:

- 4 (5-oz.) boneless sole fillets
- ½ cup pistachios, finely chopped
- Juice of 1 lemon
- Teaspoon extra-virgin olive oil

Directions:

1. Preheat your oven to 350°F
2. Wrap baking sheet using parchment paper and keep it on the side
3. Pat fish dry with kitchen towels and lightly season with salt and pepper
4. Take a small bowl and stir in pistachios
5. Place sol on the prepped sheet and press 2 tablespoons of pistachio mixture on top of each fillet
6. Rub the fish with lemon juice and olive oil
7. Bake for 10 minutes until the top is golden and fish flakes with a fork

Nutrition: 166 Calories 6 g Fat 2 g Carbohydrates

405. Speedy Tilapia with Red Onion and Avocado

Preparation Time: 10 minutes
Cooking Time: 5 minutes
Servings: 2
Ingredients:

- 1 tablespoon extra-virgin olive oil
- 1 tablespoon freshly squeezed orange juice

- ¼ teaspoon kosher or sea salt
- 4 (4-oz.) tilapia fillets, more oblong than square, skin-on or skinned
- ¼ cup chopped red onion (about ⅛ onion)
- 1 avocado, pitted, skinned, and sliced

Directions:

1. In a 9-inch glass pie dish, use a fork to mix together the oil, orange juice, and salt. Working with one fillet at a time, place each in the pie dish and turn to coat on all sides.
2. Arrange the fillets in a wagon-wheel formation, so that one end of each fillet is in the center of the dish and the other end is temporarily draped over the edge of the dish.
3. Top each fillet with 1 tablespoon of onion, then fold the end of the fillet that's hanging over the edge in half over the onion.
4. When finished, you should have 4 folded-over fillets with the fold against the outer edge of the dish and the ends all in the center.
5. Cover the dish with plastic wrap, leaving a small part open at the edge to vent the steam. Microwave on high for about 3 minutes.
6. The fish is done when it just begins to separate into flakes (chunks) when pressed gently with a fork. Top the fillets with the avocado and serve.

Nutrition: 4 g carbohydrates, 3 g fiber, 22 g protein

406. Steamed Mussels in White Wine Sauce

Preparation Time: 5 minutes
Cooking Time: 10 minutes
Servings: 2
Ingredients:

- 2 pounds small mussels
- 1 tablespoon extra-virgin olive oil
- 1 cup thinly sliced red onion & 3 garlic cloves, sliced
- 1 cup dry white wine

- 2 (¼-inch-thick) lemon slices
- ¼ teaspoon freshly ground black pepper
- ¼ teaspoon kosher or sea salt
- Fresh lemon wedges, for serving (optional)

Directions:

1. In a large colander in the sink, run cold water over the mussels (but don't let the mussels sit in standing water).
2. All the shells should be closed tight; discard any shells that are a little bit open or any shells that are cracked. Leave the mussels in the colander until you're ready to use them.
3. In a large skillet over medium-high heat, heat the oil. Add the onion and cook for 4 minutes, stirring occasionally.
4. Add the garlic and cook for 1 minute, stirring constantly. Add the wine, lemon slices, pepper, and salt, and bring to a simmer. Cook for 2 minutes.
5. Add the mussels and cover. Cook for 3 minutes, or until the mussels open their shells. Gently shake the pan two or three times while they are cooking.
6. All the shells should now be wide open. Using a slotted spoon, discard any mussels that are still closed. Spoon the opened mussels into a shallow serving bowl, and pour the broth over the top. Serve with additional fresh lemon slices, if desired.

Nutrition: Calories 22, 7 g total fat, 1 g fiber, 18 g protein

407. Orange and Garlic Shrimp

Preparation Time: 20 minutes
Cooking Time: 10 minutes
Servings: 2
Ingredients:

- 1 large orange
- 3 tablespoons extra-virgin olive oil, divided

- 1 tablespoon chopped fresh Rosemary
- 1 tablespoon chopped fresh thyme
- 3 garlic cloves, minced (about 1½ teaspoons)
- ¼ teaspoon freshly ground black pepper
- ¼ teaspoon kosher or sea salt
- 1½ pounds fresh raw shrimp, shells, and tails removed

Directions:

1. Zest the entire orange using a citrus grater. In a large zip-top plastic bag, combine the orange zest and 2 tablespoons of oil with the Rosemary, thyme, garlic, pepper, and salt.
2. Add the shrimp, seal the bag, and gently massage the shrimp until all the ingredients are combined and the shrimp is completely covered with the seasonings. Set aside.
3. Heat a grill, grill pan, or a large skillet over medium heat. Brush on or swirl in the remaining 1 tablespoon of oil.
4. Add half the shrimp, and cook for 4 to 6 minutes, or until the shrimp turn pink and white, flipping halfway through if on the grill or stirring every minute if in a pan. Transfer the shrimp to a large serving bowl.
5. Repeat with the remaining shrimp, and add them to the bowl.
6. While the shrimp cook, peel the orange and cut the flesh into bite-size pieces. Add to the serving bowl, and toss with the cooked shrimp. Serve immediately or refrigerate and serve cold.

Nutrition: Calories 190, 8 g total fat, 1 g fiber, 24 g protein

408. Roasted Shrimp-Gnocchi Bake

Preparation Time: 10 minutes
Cooking Time: 20 minutes
Servings: 2
Ingredients:

- 1 cup chopped fresh tomato
- 2 tablespoons extra-virgin olive oil

- 2 garlic cloves, minced
- ½ teaspoon freshly ground black pepper
- ¼ teaspoon crushed red pepper
- 1 (12-oz.) jar roasted red peppers
- 1-pound fresh raw shrimp, shells and tails removed
- 1-pound frozen gnocchi (not thawed)
- ½ cup cubed feta cheese
- ⅓ cup fresh torn basil leaves

Directions:

1. Preheat the oven to 425°F. In a baking dish, mix the tomatoes, oil, garlic, black pepper, and crushed red pepper. Roast in the oven for 10 minutes.
2. Stir in the roasted peppers and shrimp. Roast for 10 more minutes, until the shrimp turn pink and white.
3. While the shrimp cooks, cook the gnocchi on the stovetop according to the package directions.
4. Drain in a colander and keep warm. Remove the dish from the oven. Mix in the cooked gnocchi, feta, and basil, and serve.

Nutrition: Calories 227, 7 g total fat, 1 g fiber, 20 g protein

409. Tuna Sandwich

Preparation Time: 15 minutes
Cooking Time: 0 minutes
Servings: 1
Ingredients:

- 2 slices whole-grain bread
- 1 (6-oz.) can low sodium tuna in water, in its juice
- 2 teaspoons Yogurt (1.5% fat) or low-fat mayonnaise
- 1 medium tomato, diced
- ½ small sweet onion, finely diced
- Lettuce leaves

Directions:

1. Toast whole grain bread slices. Mix tuna, yogurt, or mayonnaise, diced tomato, and onion. Cover a toasted bread with lettuce leaves and spread the tuna mixture on the sandwich. Spread

tuna mixed on toasted bread with lettuce leaves. Place another disc as a cover on top. Enjoy the sandwich.

Nutrition: Calories 235 Fat 3 g Protein 27.8 g Sodium 350 mg Carbohydrate 25.9

410. Fruited Quinoa Salad

Preparation Time: 15 minutes
Cooking Time: 0 minutes
Servings: 2
Ingredients:

- 2 cups cooked quinoa
- 1 mango, sliced and peeled
- 1 cup strawberry, quartered
- ½ cup blueberries
- 2 tablespoon pine nuts
- Chopped mint leave for garnish
- Lemon vinaigrette:
- ¼ cup olive oil
- ¼ cup apple cider vinegar
- Zest of lemon
- 3 tablespoon lemon juice
- 1 teaspoon sugar

Directions:

1. For the Lemon Vinaigrette, whisk olive oil, apple cider vinegar, lemon zest and juice, and sugar to a bowl; set aside. Combine quinoa, mango strawberries, blueberries, and pine nuts in a large bowl. Stir the lemon vinaigrette and garnish with mint. Serve and enjoy!

Nutrition: Calories 425 Carbohydrates 76.1 g Proteins 11.3 g Fat 10.9 Sodium 16mg

411. Turkey Wrap

Preparation Time: 15 minutes
Cooking Time: 0 minutes
Servings: 2
Ingredients:

- 2 slices of low-fat Turkey breast (deli-style)
- 4 tablespoon non-fat cream cheese
- ½ cup lettuce leaves
- ½ cup carrots, slice into a stick
- 2 Homemade wraps or store-bought whole-wheat tortilla wrap

Directions:

1. Prepare all the ingredients. Spread 2 tablespoons of non-fat cream cheese on each wrap. Arrange lettuce leaves, then add a slice of turkey breast; a slice of carrots stick on top. Roll and cut into half. Serve and enjoy!

Nutrition: Calories 224 Carbohydrates 35 g Protein 10.3 g Fat 3.8 g Sodium 293 mg

412. Chicken Wrap

Preparation Time: 15 minutes
Cooking Time: 15 minutes
Servings: 2
Ingredients:

- 1 tablespoon extra-virgin olive oil
- Lemon juice, divided into 3 parts
- 2 cloves garlic, minced
- 1 pound boneless skinless chicken breasts
- ½ cup non-fat plain Greek yogurt
- ½ teaspoon paprika
- Pinch of salt and pepper
- Hot sauce to taste
- Pita bread
- Tomato slice

Directions:

1. For the marinade, whisk 1 tablespoon olive oil, juice of 2 lemons, garlic, salt, and pepper in a bowl. Add chicken breasts to the marinade and place it into a large Ziploc. Let marinate for 30 mins. to 4 hours.
2. For the yogurt sauce, mix yogurt, hot sauce, and the remaining lemon juice season with paprika and a pinch of salt and pepper.
3. Warm skillet over medium heat and coat it with oil. Add chicken breast and cook until golden brown and cook about 8 minutes per side. Remove from pan and rest for few minutes, then slice.
4. To a piece of pita bread, add lettuce, tomato, and chicken slices. Drizzle with the

prepared spicy yogurt sauce. Serve and enjoy!

Nutrition: Calories 348 Carbohydrates 8.7 g Proteins 56 g Fat 10.2 g Sodium 198 mg

413. Veggie Wrap

Preparation Time: 15 minutes
Cooking Time: 0 minutes
Servings: 2
Ingredients:

- 2 Homemade wraps or any flour tortillas
- ½ cup spinach
- ½ cup alfalfa sprouts
- ½ cup avocado, sliced thinly
- 1 medium tomato, sliced thinly
- ½ cup cucumber, sliced thinly
- Pinch of salt and pepper

Directions:

1. Put 2 tablespoons of cream cheese on each tortilla. Layer each veggie according to your liking. Pinch of salt and pepper. Roll and cut into half. Serve and Enjoy!

Nutrition: Calories 249 Carbohydrates 12.3 g Protein 5.7 g Fat 21.5 g Sodium 169 mg

414. Salmon Wrap

Preparation Time: 15 minutes
Cooking Time: 0 minutes
Servings: 1
Ingredients:

- 2 ounces Smoke Salmon
- 2 teaspoon low-fat cream cheese
- ½ medium-size red onion, finely sliced
- ½ teaspoon fresh basil or dried basil
- Pinch of pepper
- Arugula leaves
- 1 Homemade wrap or any whole-meal tortilla

Directions:

1. Warm wraps or tortillas into a heated pan or oven. Combine cream cheese, basil, pepper, and spread into the tortilla. Top with salmon, arugula, and sliced onion. Roll up and slice. Serve and Enjoy!

Nutrition: Calories 151 Carbohydrates 19.2 g Protein 10.4 g Fat 3.4 g Sodium 316 mg

415. Dill Chicken Salad

Preparation Time: 15 minutes
Cooking Time: 15 minutes
Servings: 3
Ingredients:

- 1 tablespoon unsalted butter
- 1 small onion, diced
- 2 cloves garlic, minced
- 500 g boneless skinless chicken breasts

Salad:

- 2/3 cup Fat-free yogurt
- ¼ cup mayonnaise light
- 2 large shallots, minced
- ½ cup fresh dill, finely chopped

Directions:

1. Dissolve the butter over medium heat in a wide pan. Sauté onion and garlic in the butter and chicken breasts. Put water to cover the chicken breasts by 1 inch. Bring to boil. Cover and reduce the heat to a bare simmer.
2. Cook within 8 to 10 minutes or until the chicken is cooked through. Cool thoroughly. The shred chicken finely using 2 forks. Set aside. Whisk yogurt and mayonnaise. Then toss with the chicken. Add shallots and dill. Mix again all. Serve and Enjoy!

Nutrition: Calories 253 Carbohydrates 9 g Protein 33.1 g Fat 9.5 g Sodium 236 mg

416. Dill Chutney Salmon

Preparation Time: 5 minutes
Cooking Time: 3 minutes
Servings: 2
Ingredients:
Chutney:

- ¼ cup fresh dill
- ¼ cup extra-virgin olive oil
- Juice from ½ lemon
- Sea salt, to taste

Fish:

- 2 cups water
- 2 salmon fillets

- Juice from ½ lemon
- ¼ teaspoon paprika
- Salt and freshly ground pepper to taste

Directions:

1. Pulse all the chutney ingredients in a food processor until creamy. Set aside.
2. Add the water and steamer basket to the Instant Pot. Place salmon fillets, skin-side down, on the steamer basket. Drizzle the lemon juice over salmon and sprinkle with the paprika.
3. Secure the lid. Select the Manual mode and set the cooking time for 3 minutes at High Pressure.
4. Once cooking is complete, do a quick pressure release. Carefully open the lid.
5. Season the fillets with pepper and salt to taste. Serve topped with the dill chutney.

Nutrition: Calories 636, 41 g fat, 65 g protein

Chapter 6. Dressings, Sauces and Seasonings

417. Pasta with Chickpea Sauce

Preparation Time: 10 minutes
Cooking Time: 10 minutes
Ingredients:

- ½ cup cooked chickpeas
- 2 cups cooked spelled pasta, hot
- ½ cup chopped onion
- 2 tablespoons chopped basil

Extra:

- 1½ tablespoon olive oil
- ⅓ cup spring water
- ½ teaspoon salt
- ¼ teaspoon cayenne pepper

Directions:

1. Take a medium skillet pan, place it over medium heat, add oil and when hot, add onion and cook for 5 to 8 minutes until golden brown.
2. Spoon the onion mixture into a food processor, add chickpeas, salt, cayenne pepper, and water and then pulse until smooth.
3. Place pasta into a large bowl, add blended chickpea sauce, toss until mixed, and then garnish with basil.

Nutrition: 197 Calories; 6.1 g Fats; 6 g Protein; 30.5 g Carbohydrates; 5 g Fiber;

418. Zoodles with Basil & Avocado Sauce

Preparation Time: 10 minutes
Cooking Time: 0 minutes
Ingredients:

- 2 zucchinis, spiralized into noodles
- 2 avocados, peeled, pitted
- ½ cup walnuts
- 2 cups basil leaves
- 24 cherry tomatoes, sliced

Extra:

- ⅓ teaspoon salt
- 4 tablespoons key lime juice
- ½ cup spring water

Directions:

1. Prepare the sauce and for this, place all the ingredients except for zucchini noodles and tomatoes in a food processor and then pulse until smooth.

2. Take a large bowl, place zucchini noodles in it, add tomato slices, pour in the prepared sauce and then toss until coated.

Nutrition: 330 Calories; 20.7 g Fats; 7.1 g Protein; 35.3 g Carbohydrates; 7.8 g Fiber;

419. Mango & Apple Sauce

Preparation Time: 10 minutes
Cooking Time: 10 minutes
Servings: 6
Ingredients:

- 1 cup mango; peeled, pitted, and chopped
- 2 large apples; peeled, cored, and chopped
- 3–4 tablespoons fresh key lime juice
- 2 tablespoons agave nectar
- ½ cup fresh orange juice

Directions:

1. Add all the sauce ingredients to a high-powered blender and pulse at high speed until smooth.
2. Serve immediately.

Nutrition: Calories 85, Fats 0 g, Cholesterol 0 mg, Carbohydrates 22 g, Fiber 2.6 g, Protein 0.6 g

420. Cottage Cheese Salad Dressing

Preparation Time: 5 minutes
Cooking Time: 3 minutes
Servings: 2
Ingredients:

- ½ cup cottage cheese
- ½ cup plain Greek yogurt
- ½ tablespoon Worcestershire sauce
- 1 tablespoon white wine vinegar
- ¼ cup parmesan cheese
- 2 cloves crushed garlic
- ¼ teaspoon salt
- ¼ teaspoon pepper

Directions:

1. Put all the ingredients into a food processor.
2. Blend them until it becomes smooth.
3. Transfer it to a bowl.
4. Cover it tightly, refrigerate.
5. Use it along with different salads.

Nutrition: Calories 214, Fat 2, Carbs 18, Protein 6, Sodium 276

421. Simple Spinach Dip

Preparation Time: 10 minutes + 2 hours to chill
Cooking Time: 0 minutes
Servings: 12
Ingredients:

- 1 cup plain nonfat Greek yogurt
- 4 ounces Neufchâtel cheese
- ½ cup olive oil-based mayonnaise
- 2 teaspoons minced garlic
- 1½ teaspoons onion powder
- 1 teaspoon smoked paprika
- ¾ teaspoon freshly ground black pepper
- ¼ teaspoon red pepper flakes
- 2 teaspoons Worcestershire sauce
- 1 (8-oz.) can water chestnuts, drained and finely chopped
- ½ cup chopped scallions
- 1 (10-oz.) package frozen chopped spinach, thawed and squeezed of excess moisture

Directions:

1. In a large bowl, use a hand mixer on low speed to mix the yogurt, Neufchâtel cheese, mayonnaise, garlic, onion powder, paprika, black pepper, red pepper flakes, and Worcestershire sauce.
2. Add the water chestnuts, scallions, and spinach and stir by hand until well combined.
3. Cover and refrigerate for at least 2 hours prior to serving, or overnight.
4. Serve with raw vegetables or whole-grain crackers.

Nutrition: Calories: 71; Total fat: 4 g; Protein: 3 g; Carbs: 5 g; Fiber: 1 g; Sugar: 2 g; Sodium: 131 mg

422. Avocado Mayo

Preparation Time: 10 minutes
Cooking Time: 10 minutes
Servings: 1 cup
Ingredients:

- Juice from half of a lime
- 1 avocado
- ¼ cup cilantro
- ½ tablespoon Sea salt
- ½ tablespoon Onion powder
- 2-4 tablespoon Olive oil
- Pinch of cayenne powder
- Blender or hand mixer

Directions:

1. Remove the pit of the avocado and scoop the insides into a blender.
2. Add the rest of the ingredients and blend at a high speed.
3. For hand mixers, add all other ingredients except the oil which should be added slowly until the desired consistency is reached.

Nutrition: Calories: 45 Fat: 4.5 g Sodium: 100 mg Carbohydrates: 0.5 g

423. Applesauce

Preparation Time: 5 minutes
Cooking Time: 10 minutes
Servings: 2
Ingredients:

- 3 tablespoons agave
- ⅛ teaspoon cloves
- 3 cups apples peeled, chopped
- 1 teaspoon of Seamoss gel
- 1 teaspoon lime juice
- ½ cup of strawberries
- ⅛ teaspoon sea salt
- Spring water

Equipment:

- Blender

Directions:

1. In addition to cloves, salt, lime juice, & agave, apply sliced apples to the blender.
2. Pulse to obtain the optimal quality using the blender.
3. Pulse through the strawberries just until combined.
4. If it doesn't mix well, apply 1 tablespoon of spring water.

5. Serving and relax! Preserve the leftover food in the freezer.

Nutrition: Calories 294, Fat 12 g, Fiber 2 g, Carbohydrates 8 g, Protein 45 g

424. Beef Roasted Wine Sauce

Preparation Time: 10 minutes
Cooking Time: 45 minutes
Servings: 6
Ingredients:

- 3 pounds beef roast
- 1 carrot (chopped)
- 3 ounces red wine
- ½ teaspoon smoked paprika
- 5 potatoes chopped
- ½ teaspoon salt
- 1 yellow onion (chopped)
- 4 garlic cloves (pressed)
- 17 ounces beef stock
- ½ teaspoon chicken salt

Directions:

1. Preheat the Air Fryer to 3600°F.
2. In a bowl, add salt, paprika, and chicken salt, stir. Rub the beef with the mixture and transfer to a plan that will fit into the air dryer.
3. Add the remaining ingredients and cook for 45 minutes.
4. Enjoy and serve.

Nutrition: Calories: 304 kcal, Fat: 20 g, Carb: 18 g, Proteins: 32 g

425. Beet Salad Dressing

Preparation Time: 15 minutes
Cooking Time: 15 minutes
Servings: 4
Ingredients:

- Black pepper and salt
- 1 clove of garlic
- 2 tablespoons of balsamic vinegar
- 4 beets
- 2 tablespoons of capers
- 1 bunch of chopped parsley
- 1 tablespoon of olive oil

Directions:

1. Place bets on the Power XL Air Fryer Grill pan.
2. Set the Power XL Air Fryer Grill to the Air Fry function.
3. Set Timer and temperature to 15 minutes and 3600°F.

4. In another bowl, mix pepper, garlic, capers, salt, and olive oil. Mix well
5. Remove the beets from the Power XL Air Fryer Grill and place it on a flat surface.
6. Peel and put it in the salad bowl
7. Serve with vinegar.

Serving Suggestions: Dress with parsley mixture.
Directions & Cooking Tips: rinse beets before cooking.
Nutrition: Calories: 185 kcal, Fat: 16 g, Carb: 11 g, Proteins: 8 g

426. Short Ribs and Beer Sauce

Preparation Time: 15 minutes
Cooking Time: 43 minutes
Servings: 6
Ingredients:

- 4 pounds short ribs (cut into small pieces)
- 1 dried Portobello mushroom
- 1 yellow onion (chopped)
- 1 cup chicken stock
- 6 thyme sprigs (chopped)
- ¼ cup tomato paste
- 1 bay leaf
- 1 cup dark beer
- Salt and pepper to taste

Directions:

1. Preheat the Air Fryer to 3500°F.
2. In a pan that fits into your Air Fryer, heat oil over medium heat, add onion, stock, tomato paste, beer, mushroom, bay leaf, and thyme. Simmer for 3-5minutes.
3. Add the rib and transfer to the Air Fryer, cook for 40 minutes.
4. Bon appetite!

Nutrition: Calories: 300 kcal, Fat: 7 g, Carb: 18 g, Proteins: 23 g

427. Short Ribs and Special Sauce

Preparation Time: 10 minutes
Cooking Time: 46 minutes
Servings: 4
Ingredients:

- 4 pounds short ribs
- ½ cup of soy sauce

- 3 cloves garlic (pressed)
- ½ cup of water
- 2 tablespoons sesame oil
- ¼ cup of rice wine
- 3 ginger slices
- ¼ cup pear juice
- 1 teaspoon vegetable oil
- 2 green onions chopped

Directions:
1. Preheat the Air Fryer to 3500°F.
2. Heat oil in a pan, then put green onions, garlic, and ginger, stir and cook for 1 minute.
3. Add the rib and the remaining ingredients transfer to the Air Fryer and cook for 35 minutes.
4. Serve and enjoy.

Nutrition: Calories: 321 kcal, Fat: 12 g, Carb: 20 g, Proteins: 14 g

428. Beef Patty in Mushroom Sauce

Preparation Time: 15 minutes
Cooking Time: 22 minutes
Servings: 6
Ingredients:
- 2 pounds ground beef
- ¾ cup flour
- 1 tablespoon onion flakes
- ½ teaspoon garlic powder
- ¼ cup beef stock
- 1 tablespoon chopped parsley
- 1 tablespoon soy sauce
- Salt and pepper to taste
- ½ cup beef stock
- ½ teaspoon soy sauce
- 2 cups mushroom, sliced
- 2 tablespoons butter
- 1 cup yellow onion, chopped
- 2 tablespoons bacon fat
- ¼ cup sour cream
- Salt and black pepper to taste

Directions:
1. Preheat the Air Fryer to 3500°F.
2. In a bowl, mix beef, pepper, salt, garlic powder, 1 tablespoon soy sauce, ¼ cup beef stock, parsley,

onions flakes, and flour. Stir and shape six patties. Move it into the Air Fryer and cook for 14 minutes.
3. While the patties are still cooking, heat butter in a pan on medium heat, add the mushroom, and cook for 4 minutes with constant stirring. Add onions and cook for another 4 minutes, add the soy sauce, sour cream, and simmer. Remove from heat.
4. Serve patties with mushroom sauce.

Nutrition: Calories: 235 kcal, Fat: 23 g, Carb: 6 g, Proteins: 32 g

429. Beef Brisket and Onion Sauce

Preparation Time: 10 minutes
Cooking Time: 2 hours
Servings: 6
Ingredients:
- 4 pounds beef brisket
- 1 pound yellow onion (chopped)
- ½ pound chopped celery
- 1 pound chopped carrot
- 4 cups of water
- 8 earl gray tea bags
- Salt and black pepper to taste
- 4 pounds beef brisket
- 1 pound yellow onion (chopped)
- ½ pound chopped celery
- 1 pound chopped carrot
- 4 cups of water
- 8 earl gray tea bags
- Salt and black pepper to taste

Directions:
1. Preheat the Air Fryer to 3000°F.
2. Put water in a pan that fits into the Air Fryer. Add the onions, celery, carrots, salt, and pepper. Stir and allow to simmer over medium-high heat.
3. Add the beef brisket, 8 earl grey tea bags, and stir. Put it into the Air Fryer then cook for 1 hour 30 minutes.
4. Meanwhile, place a pan over medium-high heat, add vegetable oil, and heat until

shimmering. Add the sweet onion and sauté for 10 minutes. Add the remaining sauce ingredients and cook for 10 minutes. Remove and discard the teabags.
5. Cut and serve the beef brisket with the onion sauce.

Nutrition: Calories: 400 kcal, Fat: 12 g, Carb: 26 g, Proteins: 34 g

430. Turkey Wraps with Sauce

Preparation Time: 10 minutes
Cooking Time: 16 minutes
Servings: 6
Ingredients:
Wraps:
- 4 large collard leaves, stems removed
- 1 medium avocado, sliced
- ½ cucumber, thinly sliced
- 1 cup diced mango
- 6 large strawberries, thinly sliced
- 6 (200-g.) grilled turkey breasts, diced
- 24 mint leaves

Dipping Sauce:
- 2 tablespoons almond butter
- 2 tablespoons coconut cream
- 1 bird eye chili, finely chopped
- 2 tablespoons unsweetened applesauce
- ¼ cup fresh lime juice
- 1 teaspoon sesame oil
- 1 tablespoon apple cider vinegar
- 1 tablespoon tahini
- 1 clove garlic, crushed
- 1 tablespoon grated fresh ginger
- ⅛ teaspoon sea salt

Directions:
For the chicken breasts:
1. Start by setting your Air Fryer toast oven to 350°F.
2. Lightly coat the basket of the Air Fryer toast oven with oil.
3. Season the turkey with salt and pepper and arrange on the directions red basket and Air Fry for 8 minutes on each side.

4. Once done, remove from Air Fryer toast oven and set on a platter to cool slightly then dice them up.

For the wraps:

1. Divide the veggies and diced turkey breasts equally among the four large collard leaves; fold bottom edges over the filling, and then both sides and roll very tightly up to the end of the leaves; secure with toothpicks and cut each in half.
2. Make the sauce:
3. Combine all the sauce ingredients in a blender and blend until very smooth. Divide between bowls and serve with the wraps.

Nutrition: Calories: 389 kcal, Carbs: 11.7 g, Fat: 38.2 g, Protein: 26 g.

431. Cod Steaks and Plum Sauce

Preparation time: 10 minutes
Cooking Time: 30 minutes
Servings: 3
Ingredients:

- 1 tablespoon of plum sauce
- ½ teaspoon of garlic powder
- 3 large cod steaks
- Cooking spray
- ½ teaspoon of ginger powder
- Black pepper and salt
- ¼ teaspoon of turmeric powder

Directions:

1. Drizzle the cod steaks with cooking spray.
2. Add pepper, ginger powder, salt, turmeric powder, and garlic powder.
3. Place the coated cod steaks in the Power XL Air Fryer Grill.
4. Set the function to Air Fryer/Grill.
5. Grill for about 20 minutes at 3600°F.
6. Flip while cooking for uniformity.
7. Heat plum sauce over medium heat for 2 minutes at reheat function.

8. Divide the cod steaks and serve immediately

Serving Suggestions: Serve with plum sauce

Directions & Cooking Tips: Allow the coated shrimps to rest for some minutes before grilling.

Nutrition: Calories: 330 kcal, Fat: 3 g, Carb: 25 g, Proteins: 30 g

432. Steamed Salmon and Sauce

Preparation Time: 5 minutes
Cooking Time: 10 minutes
Servings: 2
Ingredients:

- 1 cup water
- x (6-oz.) fresh salmon
- teaspoon vegetable oil
- A pinch of salt for each fish
- ½ cup plain Greek yogurt
- ½ cup sour cream
- tablespoon finely chopped dill (keep a bit for garnishing)
- A pinch of salt to taste

Directions:

1. Pour the water into the tray of the Air Fryer oven and start heating to 285°F.
2. Drizzle oil over the fish and spread it. Salt the fish to taste.
3. Now pop it into the Air Fryer oven for 10 minutes.
4. In the meantime, mix the yogurt, cream, dill and a bit of salt to make the sauce. When the fish is done, serve with the sauce and garnish with sprigs of dill.

Nutrition: Calories 185 Fat 11 g Protein 21 g Sugar 0 g

433. Salmon and Coconut Sauce

Preparation Time: 25 minutes
Cooking Time: 10 minutes
Servings: 4
Ingredients:

- Salmon fillets; boneless
- ⅓ cup heavy cream
- ¼ cup lime juice
- ½ cup coconut; shredded
- ¼ cup coconut cream
- 1 teaspoon lime zest; grated

- A pinch of salt and black pepper

Directions:

1. Take a bowl and mix all the ingredients except the salmon and whisk.
2. Arrange the fish in a pan that fits your Air Fryer, drizzle the coconut sauce all over, put the pan in the machine, and cook at 360°F for 20 minutes Divide between plates and serve.

Nutrition: Calories: 227 Total Fat: 12 g Saturated Fat: 0 g Cholesterol: 0 mg Sodium: 0 mg Total Carbs: 4 g Fiber: 2 g Sugar: 0 g Protein: 9 g

434. Salmon and Sauce

Preparation Time: 10 minutes
Cooking Time: 25 minutes
Servings: 4
Ingredients:

- Salmon fillets; boneless
- Garlic cloves; minced
- ¼ cup ghee; melted
- ½ cup heavy cream
- 1 tablespoon chives; chopped.
- 1 teaspoon lemon juice
- 1 teaspoon dill; chopped.
- A pinch of salt and black pepper

Directions:

1. Take a bowl and mix all the ingredients except the salmon and whisk well.
2. Arrange the salmon in a pan that fits the Air Fryer, drizzle the sauce all over, introduce the pan in the machine and cook at 360°F for 20 minutes. Divide everything between plates and serve

Nutrition: Calories: 220 Total Fat: 14 g Saturated Fat: 0 g Cholesterol: 0 mg Sodium: 0 mg Total Carbs: 5 g Fiber: 2 g Sugar: 0 g Protein: 12 g

435. Lobster Tails with White Wine Sauce

Preparation Time: 10 minutes
Cooking Time: 14 minutes
Servings: 4
Ingredients:

- 4 lobster tails, shell cut from the top
- ½ onion, quartered
- ½ cup butter

- ⅓ cup wine
- ¼ cup honey
- 6 garlic cloves crushed
- 1 tablespoon lemon juice
- 1 teaspoon salt or to taste
- Cracked pepper to taste
- Lemon slices to serve
- 2 tablespoons fresh chopped parsley

Directions:

1. Place the lobster tails in the oven's baking tray.
2. Whisk the rest of the ingredients in a bowl and pour over the lobster tails.
3. Press the "power button" of the Air Fry oven and turn the dial to select the "broil" mode.
4. Press the Time button and again turn the dial to set the cooking time to 14 minutes.
5. Now push the temp button and rotate the dial to set the temperature at 350°F.
6. Once preheated, place the lobster's baking tray in the oven and close its lid.
7. Serve warm.

Nutrition: Calories 340 Fat: 23.1 g carbohydrate 20.4 g protein 0.7 g

436. Beet Salad with Parsley Dressing

Preparation Time: 15 minutes
Cooking Time: 15 minutes
Servings: 4
Ingredients:

- Black pepper and salt
- 1 clove of garlic
- 2 tablespoons of balsamic vinegar
- 4 beets
- 2 tablespoons of capers
- 1 bunch of chopped parsley
- 1 tablespoon of olive oil

Directions:

1. Place bets on the Power XL Air Fryer Grill pan.
2. Set the Power XL Air Fryer Grill to the Air Fry function.
3. Set Timer and temperature to 15 minutes and 3600F.
4. In another bowl, mix pepper, garlic, capers, salt, and olive oil. Mix well

5. Remove the beets from the Power XL Air Fryer Grill and place it on a flat surface.
6. Peel and put it in the salad bowl
7. Serve with vinegar.

Serving Suggestions: Dress with parsley mixture.
Directions & Cooking Tips: rinse beets before cooking.
Nutrition: Calories: 185 kcal, Fat: 16 g, Carb: 11 g, Proteins: 8 g

437. Chicken Wings with Alfredo Sauce

Preparation Time: 5 minutes
Cooking Time: 20 minutes
Servings: 4
Ingredients:

- 1½ pounds chicken wings, pat-dried
- Salt to taste
- ½ cup Alfredo sauce

Directions:

1. Season the wings with salt. Arrange them in the greased Air Fryer basket, without touching and Air Fry for 12 minutes until no longer pink in the center. Work in batches if needed. Flip them, increase the heat to 390°F and cook for 5 more minutes. Plate the wings and drizzle with Alfredo sauce to serve.

Nutrition: Calories: 150 Carbs: 7 g Fat: 5 g Protein: 14 g

438. Small Pasta and Beans Pot

Preparation Time: 15 minutes
Cooking Time: 15 minutes
Servings: 2-4
Ingredients:

- 1 pound (454-g.) small whole wheat pasta
- 1 (14.5-oz. / 411-g.) can diced tomatoes, juice reserved
- 1 (15-oz. / 425-g.) can cannellini beans, drained and rinsed
- 2 tablespoons no-salt-added tomato paste
- 1 red or yellow bell pepper, chopped
- 1 yellow onion, chopped

- 1 tablespoon Italian seasoning mix
- 3 garlic cloves, minced
- ¼ teaspoon crushed red pepper flakes, optional
- 1 tablespoon extra-virgin olive oil
- 5 cups water
- 1 bunch kale, stemmed and chopped
- ½ cup pitted Kalamata olives, chopped
- 1 cup sliced basil

Directions:

1. Except for the kale, olives, and basil, combine all the ingredients in a pot. Stir to mix well. Bring to a boil over high heat. Stir constantly.
2. Reduce the heat to medium-high and add the kale. Cook for 10 minutes or until the pasta is al dente. Stir constantly. Transfer all of them on a large plate and serve with olives and basil on top.

Nutrition: Calories: 357 Fat: 7.6 g Protein: 18.2 g Carbs: 64.5 g

439. Wild Rice, Celery, and Cauliflower Pilaf

Preparation Time: 15 minutes
Cooking Time: 45 minutes
Servings: 4
Ingredients:

- 1 tablespoon olive oil, plus more for greasing the baking dish
- 1 cup wild rice
- 2 cups low-sodium chicken broth
- 1 sweet onion, chopped
- 2 stalks celery, chopped
- 1 teaspoon minced garlic
- 2 carrots, peeled, halved lengthwise, and sliced
- ½ cauliflower head, cut into small florets
- 1 teaspoon chopped fresh thyme
- Sea salt, to taste

Directions:

1. Preheat the oven to 350°F (180°C). Line a baking sheet

with parchment paper and grease with olive oil.

2. Put the wild rice in a saucepan, then pour in the chicken broth. Bring to a boil. Reduce the heat to low and simmer for 30 minutes or until the rice is plump.

3. Meanwhile, heat the remaining olive oil in an oven-proof skillet over medium-high heat until shimmering.

4. Add the onion, celery, and garlic to the skillet and sauté for 3 minutes or until the onion is translucent.

5. Add the carrots and cauliflower to the skillet and sauté for 5 minutes. Turn off the heat and set aside.

6. Pour the cooked rice into the skillet with the vegetables. Sprinkle with thyme and salt. Set the skillet in the preheated oven and bake for 15 minutes or until the vegetables are soft. Serve immediately.

Nutrition: Calories: 214 Fat: 3.9 g Protein: 7.2 g Carbs: 37.9 g

Chapter 7. Fish and Seafood Recipes

440. Baked Cod Fillets with Ghee Sauce

Preparation Time: 10 minutes
Cooking Time: 15 minutes
Servings: 2
Ingredients:

- Pepper and salt to taste
- 2 tablespoons minced parsley
- 1 lemon, sliced into ¼-inch thick circles
- 1 lemon, juiced and zested
- 4 garlic cloves, crushed, peeled, and minced
- ¼ cup melted ghee
- 4 Cod fillets

Directions:

1. Bring oven to 4250°F.
2. Mix parsley, lemon juice, lemon zest, garlic, and melted ghee in a small bowl. Mix well and then season with pepper and salt to taste.
3. Prepare a large baking dish by greasing it with cooking spray.
4. Evenly lay the cod fillets on the greased dish. Season generously with pepper and salt.
5. Pour the bowl of garlic-ghee sauce from step 2 on top of cod fillets. Top the cod fillets with the thinly sliced lemon.
6. Pop in the preheated oven and bake until flaky, around 13 to 15 minutes. Remove from oven, transfer to dishes, serve, and enjoy.

Nutrition: Calories: 200; Fat: 12 g; Protein: 21 g; Carbs: 2 g

441. Avocado Peach Salsa on Grilled Swordfish

Preparation Time: 15 minutes
Cooking Time: 12 minutes
Servings: 2
Ingredients:

- 1 garlic clove, minced
- 1 lemon juice
- 1 tablespoon apple cider vinegar
- 1 tablespoon coconut oil
- 1 teaspoon honey
- 2 swordfish fillets (around 4-oz. each)
- Pinch cayenne pepper
- Pinch of pepper and salt

Salsa:

- ¼ red onion, finely chopped
- ½ cup cilantro, finely chopped
- 1 avocado, halved and diced
- 1 garlic clove, minced
- 2 peaches, seeded and diced
- Juice of 1 lime
- Salt to taste

Directions:

1. In a shallow dish, mix all swordfish marinade ingredients except fillet. Mix well then add fillets to marinate. Place in refrigerator for at least an hour.
2. Meanwhile, create salsa by mixing all salsa ingredients in a medium bowl. Put in the refrigerator to cool.
3. Preheat grill and grill fish on medium fire after marinating until cooked around 4 minutes per side.
4. Place each cooked fillet on one serving plate, top with half of the salsa, serve and enjoy.

Nutrition: Calories: 416; Carbs: 21 g; Protein: 30 g; Fat: 23.5 g

442. Breaded and Spiced Halibut

Preparation Time: 10 minutes
Cooking Time: 15 minutes
Servings: 4
Ingredients:

- ¼ cup chopped fresh chives
- ¼ cup chopped fresh dill
- ¼ teaspoon ground black pepper
- ¾ cup panko breadcrumbs
- 1 tablespoon extra-virgin olive oil
- 1 teaspoon finely grated lemon zest
- 1 teaspoon sea salt
- ⅓ cup chopped fresh parsley
- 4 pieces of (6-oz.) halibut fillets

Directions:

1. Line a baking sheet with foil, grease with cooking spray, and preheat the oven to 400°F.
2. In a small bowl, mix black pepper, sea salt, lemon zest, olive oil, chives, dill, parsley and breadcrumbs. If needed add more salt to taste. Set aside.
3. Meanwhile, wash halibut fillets on cold tap water. Dry with paper towels and place on prepared baking sheet.
4. Generously spoon crumb mixture onto halibut fillets. Ensure that fillets are covered with crumb mixture. Press down on crumb mixture onto each fillet.
5. Pop into the oven and bake for 10-15 minutes or until fish is flaky and crumb topping are already lightly browned.

Nutrition: Calories: 336.4; Protein: 25.3 g; Fat: 25.3 g; Carbs: 4.1 g

443. Berries and Grilled Calamari

Preparation Time: 10 minutes
Cooking Time: 5 minutes
Servings: 4
Ingredients:

- ¼ cup dried cranberries
- ¼ cup extra-virgin olive oil
- ¼ cup olive oil
- ¼ cup sliced almonds
- ½ lemon, juiced
- ¾ cup blueberries
- 1½ pounds calamari tube, cleaned
- 1 granny smith apple, sliced thinly
- 1 tablespoon fresh lemon juice

- 2 tablespoons apple cider vinegar
- 6 cups fresh spinach
- Freshly grated pepper to taste
- Sea salt to taste

Directions:

1. In a small bowl, make the vinaigrette by mixing well the tablespoons of lemon juice, apple cider vinegar, and extra-virgin olive oil. Season with pepper and salt to taste. Set aside.
2. Turn on the grill to medium fire and let the grates heat up for a minute or two.
3. In a large bowl, add olive oil and the calamari tube. Season calamari generously with pepper and salt.
4. Place seasoned and oiled calamari onto heated grate and grill until cooked or opaque. This is around two minutes per side.
5. As you wait for the calamari to cook, you can combine almonds, cranberries, blueberries, spinach, and the thinly sliced apple in a large salad bowl. Toss to mix.
6. Remove cooked calamari from the grill and transfer on a chopping board. Cut into ¼-inch thick rings and throw into the salad bowl.
7. Drizzle with vinaigrette and toss well to coat the salad.
8. Serve and enjoy!

Nutrition: Calories: 567; Fat: 24.5 g; Protein: 54.8 g; Carbs: 30.6 g

444. Coconut Salsa on Chipotle Fish Tacos

Preparation Time: 10 minutes
Cooking Time: 10 minutes
Servings: 4
Ingredients:

- ¼ cup chopped fresh cilantro
- ½ cup seeded and finely chopped plum tomato
- 1 cup peeled and finely chopped mango
- 1 lime cut into wedges
- 1 tablespoon chipotle Chile powder

- 1 tablespoon safflower oil
- ⅓ cup finely chopped red onion
- 10 tablespoons fresh lime juice, divided
- 4 (6-oz.) boneless, skinless cod fillets
- 5 tablespoons dried unsweetened shredded coconut
- 8 pcs of 6-inch tortillas, heated

Directions:

1. Whisk well Chile powder, oil, and 4 tablespoons lime juice in a glass baking dish. Add cod and marinate for 12 – 15 minutes. Turning once halfway through the marinating time.
2. Make the salsa by mixing coconut, 6 tablespoons lime juice, cilantro, onions, tomatoes and mangoes in a medium bowl. Set aside.
3. On high, heat a grill pan. Place cod and grill for four minutes per side turning only once.
4. Once cooked, slice cod into large flakes and evenly divide onto tortilla.
5. Evenly divide salsa on top of cod and serve with a side of lime wedges.

Nutrition: Calories: 477; Protein: 35.0 g; Fat: 12.4 g; Carbs: 57.4 g

445. Baked Cod Crusted with Herbs

Preparation Time: 5 minutes
Cooking Time: 10 minutes
Servings: 4
Ingredients:

- ¼ cup honey
- ¼ teaspoon salt
- ½ cup panko
- ½ teaspoon pepper
- 1 tablespoon extra-virgin olive oil
- 1 tablespoon lemon juice
- 1 teaspoon dried basil
- 1 teaspoon dried parsley
- 1 teaspoon rosemary
- 4 pieces of (4-oz.) cod fillets

Directions:

1. With olive oil, grease a 9 x 13-inch baking pan and preheat the oven to 375°F.
2. In a zip-top bag mix panko, rosemary, salt, pepper, parsley and basil.
3. Evenly spread cod fillets in prepped dish and drizzle with lemon juice.
4. Then brush the fillets with honey on all sides. Discard remaining honey if any.
5. Then evenly divide the panko mixture on top of cod fillets.
6. Pop in the oven and bake for ten minutes or until fish is cooked.
7. Serve and enjoy.

Nutrition: Calories: 137; Protein: 5 g; Fat: 2 g; Carbs: 21 g

446. Cajun Garlic Shrimp Noodle Bowl

Preparation Time: 10 minutes
Cooking Time: 15 minutes
Servings: 2
Ingredients:

- ½ teaspoon salt
- 1 onion, sliced
- 1 red pepper, sliced
- 1 tablespoon butter
- 1 teaspoon garlic granules
- 1 teaspoon onion powder
- 1 teaspoon paprika
- 2 large zucchinis, cut into noodle strips
- 20 jumbo shrimps, shells removed and deveined
- 3 cloves garlic, minced
- 3 tablespoons ghee
- A dash of cayenne pepper
- A dash of red pepper flakes

Directions:

1. Prepare the Cajun seasoning by mixing the onion powder, garlic granules, pepper flakes, cayenne pepper, paprika and salt. Toss in the shrimp to coat in the seasoning.
2. In a skillet, heat the ghee and sauté the garlic. Add in the red pepper and onions and continue sautéing for 4 minutes.

3. Add the Cajun shrimp and cook until opaque. Set aside.
4. In another pan, heat the butter and sauté the zucchini noodles for three minutes.
5. Assemble by placing the Cajun shrimps on top of the zucchini noodles.

Nutrition: Calories: 712; Fat: 30.0 g; Protein: 97.8 g; Carbs: 20.2 g

447. Crazy Saganaki Shrimp

Preparation Time: 10 minutes
Cooking Time: 10 minutes
Servings: 4
Ingredients:

- ¼ teaspoon salt
- ½ cup Chardonnay
- ½ cup crumbled Greek feta cheese
- 1 medium bulb. fennel, cored and finely chopped
- 1 small Chile pepper, seeded and minced
- 1 tablespoon extra-virgin olive oil
- 12 jumbo shrimps, peeled and deveined with tails left on
- 2 tablespoons lemon juice, divided
- 5 scallions sliced thinly
- Pepper to Taste

Directions:

1. In a medium bowl, mix salt, lemon juice and shrimp.
2. On medium fire, place a saganaki pan (or large nonstick saucepan) and heat oil.
3. Sauté Chile pepper, scallions, and fennel for 4 minutes or until starting to brown and is already soft.
4. Add wine and sauté for another minute.
5. Place shrimps on top of the fennel, cover and cook for 4 minutes or until shrimps are pink.
6. Remove just the shrimp and transfer to a plate.
7. Add pepper, feta and 1 tablespoon lemon juice to pan and cook for a minute or until cheese begins to melt.

8. To serve, place cheese and fennel mixture on a serving plate and top with shrimps.

Nutrition: Calories: 310; Protein: 49.7 g; Fat: 6.8 g; Carbs: 8.4 g

448. Creamy Bacon-Fish Chowder

Preparation Time: 10 minutes
Cooking Time: 30 minutes
Servings: 8
Ingredients:

- 1½ pounds cod
- 1½ teaspoon dried thyme
- 1 large onion, chopped
- 1 medium carrot, coarsely chopped
- 1 tablespoon butter, cut into small pieces
- 1 teaspoon salt, divided
- 3½ cups baking potato, peeled and cubed
- 3 slices uncooked bacon
- ¾ teaspoon freshly ground black pepper, divided
- 4½ cups water
- 4 bay leaves
- 4 cups 2% reduced-fat milk

Directions:

1. In a large skillet, add the water and bay leaves and let it simmer. Add the fish. Cover and let it simmer some more until the flesh flakes easily with a fork. Remove the fish from the skillet and cut into large pieces. Set aside the cooking liquid.
2. Place Dutch oven on medium heat and cook the bacon until crisp. Remove the bacon and reserve the bacon drippings. Crush the bacon and set aside.
3. Stir potato, onion and carrot in the pan with the bacon drippings, cook over medium heat for 10 minutes. Add the cooking liquid, bay leaves, ½ teaspoon salt, ¼ teaspoon pepper and thyme, let it boil. Lower the heat and let simmer for 10 minutes. Add the milk and butter, simmer until the potatoes become tender, but do not boil. Add

the fish, ½ teaspoon salt, ½ teaspoon pepper. Remove the bay leaves.
4. Serve sprinkled with the crushed bacon.

Nutrition: Calories: 400; Carbs: 34.5 g; Protein: 20.8 g; Fat: 19.7 g

449. Trout and Peppers Mix

Preparation Time: 10 minutes
Cooking Time: 20 minutes
Servings: 4
Ingredients:

- 4 trout fillets, boneless
- 2 tablespoons kalamata olives, pitted and chopped
- 1 tablespoon capers, drained
- 2 tablespoons olive oil
- A pinch of salt and black pepper
- 1½ teaspoon chili powder
- 1 yellow bell pepper, chopped
- 1 red bell pepper, chopped
- 1 green bell pepper, chopped

Directions:

1. Heat up a pan with the oil over medium-high heat, add the trout, salt and pepper and cook for 10 minutes.
2. Flip the fish, add the peppers and the rest of the ingredients, cook for 10 minutes more, divide the whole mix between plates and serve.

Nutrition: Calories 572, Fat 17.4 g, Fiber 6 g, Carbs 71 g, Protein 33.7 g

450. Crisped Coco-Shrimp with Mango Dip

Preparation Time: 10 minutes
Cooking Time: 20 minutes
Servings: 4
Ingredients:

- 1 cup shredded coconut
- 1 pound raw shrimp, peeled and deveined
- 2 egg whites & 4 tablespoons tapioca starch
- Pepper and salt to taste

Mango Dip:

- 1 cup mango, chopped
- 1 jalapeño, thinly minced
- 1 teaspoon lime juice & ⅓ cup coconut milk
- 3 teaspoons raw honey

Directions:

1. Preheat oven to 400°F.
2. Ready a pan with a wire rack on top.
3. In a medium bowl, add tapioca starch and season with pepper and salt.
4. In a second medium bowl, add egg whites and whisk.
5. In a third medium bowl, add coconut.
6. To ready shrimps, dip first in tapioca starch, then egg whites, and then coconut. Place dredged shrimp on a wire rack. Repeat until all shrimps are covered.
7. Pop shrimp in the oven and roast for 10 minutes per side.
8. Meanwhile, make the dip by adding all ingredients to a blender. Puree until smooth and creamy. Transfer to a dipping bowl.
9. Once shrimps are golden brown, serve with mango dip.

Nutrition: Calories: 294.2; Protein: 26.6 g; Fat: 7 g; Carbs: 31.2 g

451. Cucumber-Basil Salsa on Halibut Pouches

Preparation Time: 10 minutes
Cooking Time: 17 minutes
Servings: 4
Ingredients:

- 1 lime, thinly sliced into 8 pieces
- 2 cups mustard greens, stems removed
- 2 teaspoons olive oil
- 4 – 5 radishes trimmed and quartered
- 4 (4-oz.) skinless halibut fillets
- 4 large fresh basil leaves
- Cayenne pepper to taste – optional
- Pepper and salt to taste

Salsa:

- 1½ cups diced cucumber
- 1½ finely chopped fresh basil leaves
- 2 teaspoons fresh lime juice
- Pepper and salt to taste

Directions:

1. Preheat oven to 400°F.
2. Prepare parchment papers by making 4 pieces of 15 x 12-inch rectangles. Lengthwise, fold in half and unfold pieces on the table.
3. Season halibut fillets with pepper, salt and cayenne—if using cayenne.
4. Just to the right of the fold going lengthwise, place ½ cup of mustard greens. Add a basil leaf to the center of mustard greens and topped with 1 lime slice. Around the greens, layer ¼ of the radishes. Drizzle with ½ teaspoon of oil, season with pepper and salt. Top it with a slice of halibut fillet.
5. Just as you would make a calzone, fold the parchment paper over your filling and crimp the edges of the parchment paper beginning from one end to the other end. To seal the end of the crimped parchment paper, pinch it.
6. Repeat the process to the remaining ingredients until you have 4 pieces of parchment paper filled with halibut and greens.
7. Place pouches in a baking pan and bake in the oven until halibut is flaky, around 15 to 17 minutes.
8. While waiting for halibut pouches to cook, make your salsa by mixing all salsa ingredients in a medium bowl.
9. Once halibut is cooked, remove from the oven and make a tear on top. Be careful of the steam as it is very hot. Equally, divide salsa and spoon ¼ of salsa on top of halibut through the slit you have created.

Nutrition: Calories: 335.4; Protein: 20.2 g; Fat: 16.3 g; Carbs: 22.1 g

452. Curry Salmon with Mustard

Preparation Time: 10 minutes
Cooking Time: 8 minutes
Servings: 4
Ingredients:

- ¼ teaspoon ground red pepper or chili powder
- ¼ teaspoon ground turmeric
- ¼ teaspoon salt
- 1 teaspoon honey
- ⅛ teaspoon garlic powder or 1 clove garlic minced
- 2 teaspoons whole grain mustard
- 4 pcs (6-oz.) salmon fillets

Directions:

1. In a small bowl mix well salt, garlic powder, red pepper, turmeric, honey and mustard.
2. Preheat the oven to broil and grease a baking dish with cooking spray.
3. Place salmon on a baking dish with skin side down and spread evenly the mustard mixture on top of salmon.
4. Pop in the oven and broil until flaky around 8 minutes.

Nutrition: Calories: 324; Fat: 18.9 g; Protein: 34 g; Carbs: 2.9 g

453. Dijon Mustard and Lime Marinated Shrimp

Preparation Time: 10 minutes
Cooking Time: 10 minutes
Servings: 8
Ingredients:

- ½ cup fresh lime juice, plus lime zest as garnish
- ½ cup rice vinegar
- ½ teaspoon hot sauce
- 1 bay leaf
- 1 cup water
- 1 pound uncooked shrimp, peeled and deveined
- 1 medium red onion, chopped
- 2 tablespoons capers
- 2 tablespoons Dijon mustard
- 3 whole cloves

Directions:

1. Mix hot sauce, mustard, capers, lime juice and onion in a shallow baking dish and set aside.
2. Bring to a boil in a large saucepan bay leaf, cloves, vinegar and water.

3. Once boiling, add shrimps and cook for a minute while stirring continuously.
4. Drain shrimps and pour shrimps into the onion mixture.
5. For an hour, refrigerate while covered the shrimps.
6. Then serve shrimps cold and garnished with lime zest.

Nutrition: Calories: 232.2; Protein: 17.8 g; Fat: 3 g; Carbs: 15 g

454. Dill Relish on White Sea Bass

Preparation Time: 10 minutes
Cooking Time: 12 minutes
Servings: 4
Ingredients:

- 1½ tablespoons chopped white onion
- 1½ teaspoons chopped fresh dill
- 1 lemon, quartered
- 1 teaspoon Dijon mustard
- 1 teaspoon lemon juice
- 1 teaspoon pickled baby capers, drained
- 4 pieces of (4-oz.) white sea bass fillets

Directions:

1. Preheat oven to 375°F.
2. Mix lemon juice, mustard, dill, capers and onions in a small bowl.
3. Prepare four aluminum foil squares and place 1 fillet per foil.
4. Squeeze a lemon wedge per fish.
5. Evenly divide into 4 the dill spread and drizzle over the fillet.
6. Close the foil over the fish securely and pop in the oven.
7. Bake for 10 to 12 minutes or until fish is cooked through.
8. Remove from foil and transfer to a serving platter, serve and enjoy.

Nutrition: Calories: 115; Protein: 7 g; Fat: 1 g; Carbs: 12 g

455. Garlic Roasted Shrimp with Zucchini Pasta

Preparation Time: 10 minutes
Cooking Time: 10 minutes
Servings: 2
Ingredients:

- 2 medium-sized zucchinis, cut into thin strips or spaghetti noodles
- Salt and pepper to taste
- 1 lemon, zested and juiced
- 2 garlic cloves, minced
- 2 tablespoons ghee, melted
- 2 tablespoons olive oil
- 8 ounces shrimps, cleaned and deveined

Directions:

1. Preheat the oven to 400°F.
2. In a mixing bowl, mix all ingredients except the zucchini noodles. Toss to coat the shrimp.
3. Bake for 10 minutes until the shrimps turn pink.
4. Add the zucchini pasta then toss.

Nutrition: Calories: 299; Fat: 23.2 g; Protein: 14.3 g; Carbs: 10.9 g

456. Easy Seafood French Stew

Preparation Time: 10 minutes
Cooking Time: 45 minutes
Servings: 12
Ingredients:

- Pepper and Salt
- ½ pound littleneck clams
- ½ pound mussels
- 1 pound shrimp, peeled and deveined
- 1 large lobster
- 2 pounds assorted small whole fresh fish, scaled and cleaned
- 2 tablespoons parsley, finely chopped
- 2 tablespoons garlic, chopped
- 1 cup fennel, julienned
- Juice and zest of one orange
- 3 cups tomatoes, peeled, seeded, and chopped
- 1 cup leeks, julienned
- Pinch of Saffron

Stew:

- 1 cup white wine
- Water
- 1 pound fish bones
- 2 sprigs thyme
- 8 peppercorns
- 1 bay leaf
- 3 cloves garlic
- Salt and pepper
- ½ cup chopped celery
- ½ cup chopped onion
- 2 tablespoons olive oil

Directions:

1. Do the stew: Heat oil in a large saucepan. Sauté the celery and onions for 3 minutes. Season with pepper and salt. Stir in the garlic and cook for about a minute. Add the thyme, peppercorns, and bay leaves. Stir in the wine, water and fish bones. Let it boil then before reducing to a simmer. Take the pan off the fire and strain the broth into another container.
2. For the Bouillabaisse: Bring the strained broth to a simmer and stir in the parsley, leeks, orange juice, orange zest, garlic, fennel, tomatoes and saffron. Sprinkle with pepper and salt. Stir in the lobsters and fish. Let it simmer for eight minutes before stirring in the clams, mussels and shrimps. For six minutes, allow to cook while covered before seasoning again with pepper and salt.
3. Assemble in a shallow dish all the seafood and pour the broth over it.

Nutrition: Calories: 348; Carbs: 20.0 g; Protein: 31.8 g; Fat: 15.2 g

457. Fresh and No-Cook Oysters

Preparation Time: 10 minutes
Cooking Time: 5 minutes
Servings: 4
Ingredients:

- 2 lemons
- 24 medium oysters
- Tabasco sauce

Directions:

1. If you are a newbie when it comes to eating oysters, then I suggest that you blanch the oysters before eating.
2. For some, eating oysters raw is a great way to enjoy this dish because of the consistency and juiciness of raw oysters. Plus, adding lemon juice prior to eating the raw oysters cooks it a bit.
3. So, to blanch oysters, bring a big pot of water to a rolling boil. Add oysters in batches of 6-10 pieces. Leave on the boiling pot of water for between 3-5 minutes and remove oysters right away. To eat oysters, squeeze lemon juice on the oyster on the shell, add tabasco as desired and eat.

Nutrition: Calories: 247; Protein: 29 g; Fat: 7 g; Carbs: 17 g

458. Easy Broiled Lobster Tails

Preparation Time: 10 minutes
Cooking Time: 10 minutes
Servings: 2
Ingredients:

- 1 (6-oz.) frozen lobster tails
- 1 tablespoon olive oil
- 1 teaspoon lemon pepper seasoning

Directions:

1. Preheat the oven broiler.
2. With kitchen scissors, cut thawed lobster tails in half lengthwise.
3. Brush with oil the exposed lobster meat. Season with lemon pepper.
4. Place lobster tails on a baking sheet with exposed meat facing up.
5. Place on top broiler rack and broil for 10 minutes until lobster meat is lightly browned on the sides and center meat is opaque. Serve and enjoy.

Nutrition: Calories: 175.6; Protein: 23 g; Fat: 10 g; Carbs: 18.4 g

459. Ginger Scallion Sauce Over Seared Ahi

Preparation Time: 10 minutes
Cooking Time: 6 minutes
Servings: 4
Ingredients:

- 1 Bunch scallions, bottoms removed, finely chopped
- 1 tablespoon rice wine vinegar
- 1 tablespoon Bragg's liquid amino
- 16-oz. ahi tuna steaks
- 2 tablespoons fresh ginger, peeled and grated
- 3 tablespoons coconut oil, melted
- Pepper and salt to taste

Directions:

1. In a small bowl mix together vinegar, 2 tablespoons oil, soy sauce, ginger and scallions. Put aside.
2. On medium fire, place a large saucepan and heat the remaining oil. Once the oil is hot and starts to smoke, sear tuna until deeply browned or for two minutes per side.
3. Place seared tuna on a serving platter and let it stand for 5 minutes before slicing into 1-inch-thick strips.
4. Drizzle ginger-scallion mixture over seared tuna, serve and enjoy.

Nutrition: Calories: 247; Protein: 29 g; Fat: 1 g; Carbs: 8 g

460. Healthy Poached Trout

Preparation Time: 10 minutes
Cooking Time: 10 minutes
Servings: 2
Ingredients:

- 1 (8-oz.) boneless, skin-on trout fillet
- 2 cups chicken broth or water
- 2 leeks, halved
- 6-8 slices lemon
- Salt and pepper to taste

Directions:

1. On medium fire, place a large nonstick skillet and arrange leeks and lemons on a pan in a layer. Cover with soup stock or water and bring to a simmer.
2. Meanwhile, season trout on both sides with pepper and salt. Place trout on a simmering pan of water. Cover and cook until trout is flaky, around 8 minutes.
3. In a serving platter, spoon leek and lemons on the bottom of the plate, top with trout and spoon sauce into the plate. Serve and enjoy.

Nutrition: Calories: 360.2; Protein: 13.8 g; Fat: 7.5 g; Carbs: 51.5 g

461. Leftover Salmon Salad Power Bowls

Preparation Time: 10 minutes
Cooking Time: 10 minutes
Servings: 1
Ingredients:

- ½ cup raspberries
- ½ cup zucchini, sliced
- 1 lemon, juice squeezed
- 1 tablespoon balsamic glaze
- 2 sprigs of thyme, chopped
- 2 tablespoons olive oil
- 4 cups seasonal greens
- 4 ounces leftover grilled salmon
- Salt and pepper to taste

Directions:

1. Heat oil in a skillet over medium flame and sauté the zucchini. Season with salt and pepper to taste.
2. In a mixing bowl, mix all ingredients together.
3. Toss to combine everything.
4. Sprinkle with nut cheese.

Nutrition: Calories: 450.3; Fat: 35.5 g; Protein: 23.4 g; Carbs: 9.3 g

462. Lemon-Garlic Baked Halibut

Preparation Time: 10 minutes
Cooking Time: 15 minutes
Servings: 2
Ingredients:

- 1 large garlic clove, minced
- 1 tablespoon chopped flat leaf parsley
- 1 teaspoon olive oil

- 2 (5-oz.) boneless, skin-on halibut fillets
- 2 teaspoons lemon zest
- Juice of ½ lemon, divided
- Salt and pepper to taste

Directions:

1. Grease a baking dish with cooking spray and preheat the oven to 400°F.
2. Place halibut with skin touching the dish and drizzle with olive oil.
3. Season with pepper and salt.
4. Pop into the oven and bake until flaky around 12-15 minutes.
5. Remove from oven and drizzle with remaining lemon juice, serve and enjoy with a side of salad greens.

Nutrition: Calories: 315.3; Protein: 14.1 g; Fat: 10.5 g; Carbs: 36.6 g

463. Minty-Cucumber Yogurt Topped Grilled Fish

Preparation Time: 10 minutes
Cooking Time: 2 minutes
Servings: 4
Ingredients:

- ¼ cup 2% plain Greek yogurt
- ¼ teaspoon + ⅛ teaspoon salt
- ¼ teaspoon black pepper
- ½ green onion, finely chopped
- ½ teaspoon dried oregano
- 1 tablespoon finely chopped fresh mint leaves
- 3 tablespoons finely chopped English cucumber
- 4 (5-oz.) cod fillets
- Cooking oil as needed

Directions:

1. Brush grill grate with oil and preheat grill to high.
2. Season cod fillets on both sides with pepper, ¼ teaspoon salt and oregano.
3. Grill cod for 3 minutes per side or until cooked to desired doneness.
4. Mix thoroughly ⅛ teaspoon salt, onion, mint, cucumber and yogurt in a small bowl. Serve cod with a dollop of

the dressing. This dish can be paired with salad greens or brown rice.

Nutrition: Calories: 253.5; Protein: 25.5 g; Fat: 1 g; Carbs: 5 g

464. One-Pot Seafood Chowder

Preparation Time: 10 minutes
Cooking Time: 10 minutes
Servings: 3
Ingredients:

- 3 cans coconut milk
- 1 tablespoon garlic, minced
- Salt and pepper to taste
- 3 cans clams, chopped
- 2 cans shrimps, canned
- 1 package fresh shrimps, shelled and deveined
- 1 can corn, drained
- 4 large potatoes, diced
- 2 carrots, peeled and chopped
- 2 celery stalks, chopped

Directions:

1. Place all ingredients in a pot and give a good stir to mix everything.
2. Close the lid and turn on the heat to medium.
3. Bring to a boil and allow to simmer for 10 minutes.
4. Place in individual containers.
5. Put a label and store in the fridge.
6. Allow to warm at room temperature before heating in the microwave oven.

Nutrition: Calories: 532; Carbs: 92.5 g; Protein: 25.3 g; Fat: 6.7 g

465. Orange Rosemary Seared Salmon

Preparation Time: 10 minutes
Cooking Time: 10 minutes
Servings: 4
Ingredients:

- ½ cup chicken stock
- 1 cup fresh orange juice
- 1 tablespoon coconut oil
- 1 tablespoon tapioca starch
- 2 garlic cloves, minced
- 2 tablespoons fresh lemon juice

- 2 teaspoons fresh rosemary, minced
- 2 teaspoons orange zest
- 4 salmon fillets, skins removed
- Salt and pepper to taste

Directions:

1. Season the salmon fillet on both sides.
2. In a skillet, heat coconut oil over medium-high heat. Cook the salmon fillets for 5 minutes on each side. Set aside.
3. In a mixing bowl, combine the orange juice, chicken stock, lemon juice and orange zest.
4. In the skillet, sauté the garlic and rosemary for 2 minutes and pour the orange juice mixture. Bring to a boil. Lower the heat to medium-low and simmer. Season with salt and pepper to taste.
5. Pour the sauce all over the salmon fillet then serve.

Nutrition: Calories: 493; Fat: 17.9 g; Protein: 66.7 g; Carbs: 12.8 g

466. Orange Herbed Sauced White Bass

Preparation Time: 10 minutes
Cooking Time: 33 minutes
Servings: 6
Ingredients:

- ¼ cup thinly sliced green onions
- ½ cup orange juice
- 1½ tablespoons fresh lemon juice
- 1½ tablespoons olive oil
- 1 large onion, halved, thinly sliced
- 1 large orange, unpeeled, sliced
- 3 tablespoons chopped fresh dill
- 6 (3-oz.) skinless white bass fillets
- Additional unpeeled orange slices

Directions:

1. Grease a 13 x 9-inch glass baking dish and preheat the oven to 400°F.

2. Arrange orange slices in a single layer on a baking dish, top with onion slices, seasoned with pepper and salt plus drizzled with oil.
3. Pop in the oven and roast for 25 minutes or until onions are tender and browned.
4. Remove from oven and increased oven temperature to 450°F.
5. Push onion and orange slices on the sides of the dish and place bass fillets in the middle of the dish. Season with 1½ tablespoons dill, pepper and salt. Arrange onions and orange slices on top of fish and pop into the oven.
6. Roast for 8 minutes or until salmon is opaque and flaky.
7. In a small bowl, mix 1½ tablespoons dill, lemon juice, green onions and orange juice.
8. Transfer salmon to a serving plate, discard roasted onions, drizzle with the newly made orange sauce, and garnish with fresh orange slices. Serve and enjoy.

Nutrition: Calories: 312.42; Protein: 84.22; Fat: 23.14; Carbs: 33.91 g

467. Pan Fried Tuna with Herbs and Nut

Preparation Time: 10 minutes
Cooking Time: 5 minutes
Servings: 4
Ingredients:

- ¼ cup almonds, chopped finely
- ¼ cup fresh tangerine juice
- ½ teaspoon fennel seeds, chopped finely
- ½ teaspoon ground pepper, divided
- ½ teaspoon sea salt, divided
- 1 tablespoon olive oil
- 2 tablespoons fresh mint, chopped finely
- 2 tablespoons red onion, chopped finely
- 4 pieces of (6-oz.) Tuna steak cut in half

Directions:

1 Mix fennel seeds, olive oil, mint, onion, tangerine juice and almonds in a small bowl. Season with ¼ each of pepper and salt.
2 Season fish with the remaining pepper and salt.
3 On medium-high fire, place a large nonstick fry pan and grease with cooking spray.
4 Pan fry tuna until the desired doneness is reached or for one minute per side.
5 Transfer cooked tuna to the serving plate, drizzle with dressing and serve.

Nutrition: Calories: 272; Fat: 9.7 g; Protein: 42 g; Carbs: 4.2 g

468. Paprika Salmon and Green Beans

Preparation Time: 10 minutes
Cooking Time: 20 minutes
Servings: 3
Ingredients:

- ¼ cup olive oil
- ½ tablespoons onion powder
- ½ teaspoon bouillon powder
- ½ teaspoon cayenne pepper
- 1 tablespoon smoked paprika
- 1 pound green beans
- 2 teaspoons minced garlic
- 3 tablespoons fresh herbs
- 6 ounces of salmon steak
- Salt and pepper to taste

Directions:

1. Preheat the oven to 400°F.
2. Grease a baking sheet and set aside.
3. Heat a skillet over medium-low heat and add the olive oil. Sauté the garlic, smoked paprika, fresh herbs, cayenne pepper and onion powder. Stir for a minute then let the mixture sit for 5 minutes. Set aside.
4. Put the salmon steaks in a bowl and add salt and the paprika spice mixture. Rub to coat the salmon well.

5. Place the salmon on the baking sheet and cook for 18 minutes.
6. Meanwhile, blanch the green beans in boiling water with salt.
7. Serve the beans with the salmon.

Nutrition: Calories: 945.8; Fat: 66.6 g; Protein: 43.5 g; Carbs: 43.1 g

469. Pecan Crusted Trout

Preparation Time: 10 minutes
Cooking Time: 12 minutes
Servings: 4
Ingredients:

- ½ cup crushed pecans
- ½ teaspoon grated fresh ginger
- 1 egg, beaten
- 1 teaspoon crush dried rosemary
- 1 teaspoon salt
- 4 (4-oz.) trout fillets
- Black pepper to taste
- Cooking spray
- Whole wheat flour, as needed

Directions:

1. Grease baking sheet lightly with cooking spray and preheat oven to 400oF.
2. In a shallow bowl, combine black pepper, salt, rosemary and pecans. In another shallow bowl, add whole wheat flour. In a third bowl, add beaten egg.
3. To prepare fish, dip in flour until covered well. Shake off excess flour. Then dip into beaten egg until coated well. Let excess egg drip off before dipping trout fillet into pecan crumbs. Press the trout lightly onto pecan crumbs to make it stick to the fish.
4. Place breaded fish onto prepared pan. Repeat process for remaining fillets.
5. Pop into the oven and bake for 10 to 12 minutes or until the fish is flaky.

Nutrition: Calories: 329; Fat: 19 g; Protein: 26.95 g; Carbs: 3 g

470. Pesto and Lemon Halibut

Preparation Time: 10 minutes
Cooking Time: 10 minutes
Servings: 4
Ingredients:

- 1 tablespoon fresh lemon juice
- 1 tablespoon lemon rind, grated
- 2 garlic cloves, peeled
- 2 tablespoons olive oil
- ¼ cup Parmesan Cheese, freshly grated
- 2/3 cups firmly packed basil leaves
- ⅛ teaspoon freshly ground black pepper
- ¼ teaspoon salt, divided
- 4 pcs (6-oz.) halibut fillets

Directions:

1. Preheat grill to medium fire and grease grate with cooking spray.
2. Season fillets with pepper and ⅛ teaspoon salt. Place on grill and cook until halibut is flaky around 4 minutes per side.
3. Meanwhile, make your lemon pesto by combining lemon juice, lemon rind, garlic, olive oil, Parmesan cheese, basil leaves and remaining salt in a blender. Pulse mixture until finely minced but not pureed.
4. Once fish is done cooking, transfer to a serving platter, pour over the lemon pesto sauce, serve and enjoy.

Nutrition: Calories: 277.4; Fat: 13 g; Protein: 38.7 g; Carbs: 1.4 g

471. Red Peppers & Pineapple Topped Mahi-Mahi

Preparation Time: 10 minutes
Cooking Time: 30 minutes
Servings: 4
Ingredients:

- ¼ teaspoon black pepper
- ¼ teaspoon salt
- 1 cup whole wheat couscous
- 1 red bell pepper, diced

- 2⅓ cups low sodium chicken broth
- 2 cups chopped fresh pineapple
- 2 tablespoons chopped fresh chives
- 2 teaspoons olive oil
- 4 pieces of skinless, boneless Mahi midsolo (dolphin fish) fillets (around 4-oz each)

Directions:

1. On high fire, add 1⅓ cups of broth to a small saucepan and heat until boiling. Once boiling, add couscous. Turn off fire, cover, and set aside to allow liquid to be fully absorbed for around 5 minutes.
2. On medium-high fire, place a large nonstick saucepan and heat oil.
3. Season fish on both sides with pepper and salt. Add Mahi midsolo to a hot pan and pan fry until golden around one minute on each side. Once cooked, transfer to plate.
4. On the same pan, sauté bell pepper and pineapples until soft, around 2 minutes on medium-high fire.
5. Add couscous to the pan along with chives, and remaining broth.
6. On top of the mixture in the pan, place fish. With foil, cover the pan and continue cooking until fish is steaming and tender underneath the foil, around 3-5 minutes.

Nutrition: Calories: 302; Protein: 43.1 g; Fat: 4.8 g; Carbs: 22.0 g

472. Roasted Halibut with Banana Relish

Preparation Time: 10 minutes
Cooking Time: 12 minutes
Servings: 4
Ingredients:

- ¼ cup cilantro
- ½ teaspoon freshly grated orange zest
- ½ teaspoon kosher salt, divided

- 1 pound halibut or any deep-water fish
- 1 teaspoon ground coriander, divided into half
- 2 oranges (peeled, segmented and chopped)
- 2 ripe bananas, diced
- 2 tablespoons lime juice

Directions:

1. In a pan, prepare the fish by rubbing ½ teaspoon coriander and ¼ teaspoon kosher salt.
2. Place in a baking sheet with cooking spray and bake for 8 to 12 minutes inside a 450°F preheated oven.
3. Prepare the relish by stirring the orange zest, bananas, chopped oranges, lime juice, cilantro and the rest of the salt and coriander in a medium bowl.
4. Spoon the relish over the roasted fish.
5. Serve and enjoy.

Nutrition: Calories: 245.7; Protein: 15.3 g; Fat: 6 g; Carbs: 21 g

473. Roasted Pollock Fillet with Bacon and Leeks

Preparation Time: 10 minutes
Cooking Time: 30 minutes
Servings: 2
Ingredients:

- ¼ cup olive oil
- ½ cup white wine
- 1½ pounds Pollock fillets
- 1 sprig of fresh thyme
- 1 tablespoon chopped fresh thyme
- 2 tablespoons olive oil
- 4 leeks, sliced

Directions:

1. Grease a 9x13 baking dish and preheat the oven to 400°F.
2. In the baking pan add olive oil and leeks. Toss to combine.
3. Pop into the oven and roast for 10 minutes.
4. Remove from oven; add white wine and 1 tablespoon chopped thyme. Return to oven and roast for another 10 minutes.

5. Remove pan from oven and add fish on top. With a spoon, spoon olive oil mixture onto fish until coated fully. Return to oven and roast for another ten minutes.

6. Remove from oven, garnish with a sprig of thyme and serve.

Nutrition: Calories: 442; Carbs: 13.6 g; Protein: 42.9 g; Fat: 24 g

474. Scallops in Wine 'n Olive Oil

Preparation Time: 10 minutes
Cooking Time: 8 minutes
Servings: 4
Ingredients:

- ¼ teaspoon salt
- ½ cup dry white wine
- 1½ pounds large sea scallops
- 1½ teaspoons chopped fresh tarragon
- 2 tablespoons olive oil
- Black pepper – optional

Directions:

1. On medium-high fire, place a large nonstick fry pan and heat oil.
2. Add scallops and fry for 3 minutes per side or until edges are lightly browned. Transfer to a serving plate.
3. On the same pan, add salt, tarragon and wine while scraping the pan to loosen browned bits.
4. Turn off the fire.
5. Pour sauce over scallops and serve.

Nutrition: Calories: 205.2; Fat: 8 g; Protein: 28.6 g; Carbs: 4.7 g

475. Seafood Stew Cioppino

Preparation Time: 10 minutes
Cooking Time: 40 minutes
Servings: 6
Ingredients:

- ¼ cup Italian parsley, chopped
- ¼ teaspoon dried basil
- ¼ teaspoon dried thyme
- ½ cup dry white wine like pinot grigio
- ½ pound King crab legs, cut at each joint

- ½ onion, chopped
- ½ teaspoon red pepper flakes (adjust to the desired spiciness)
- 1 28-oz can crush tomatoes
- 1 pound Mahi midsolo, cut into ½-inch cubes
- 1 pound raw shrimp
- 1 tablespoon olive oil
- 2 bay leaves
- 2 cups clam juice
- 50 live clams, washed
- 6 cloves garlic, minced
- Pepper and salt to taste

Directions:

1. On medium fire, place a stockpot and heat oil.
2. Add onion and for 4 minutes sauté until soft.
3. Add bay leaves, thyme, basil, red pepper flakes and garlic. Cook for a minute while stirring a bit.
4. Add clam juice and tomatoes. Once simmering, place fire to medium-low and cook for 20 minutes uncovered.
5. Add white wine and clams. Cover and cook for 5 minutes or until clams have slightly opened.
6. Stir pot then add fish pieces, crab legs and shrimps. Do not stir the soup to maintain the fish's shape. Cook, while covered for 4 minutes or until clams, are fully opened; fish and shrimps are opaque and cooked.
7. Season with pepper and salt to taste.
8. Transfer Cioppino to serving bowls and garnish with parsley before serving.

Nutrition: Calories: 371; Carbs: 15.5 g; Protein: 62 g; Fat: 6.8 g

476. Simple Cod Piccata

Preparation Time: 10 minutes
Cooking Time: 15 minutes
Servings: 3
Ingredients:

- ¼ cup capers, drained
- ½ teaspoon salt
- ¾ cup chicken stock
- ⅓ cup almond flour

- 1-pound cod fillets, patted dry
- 2 tablespoons fresh parsley, chopped
- 2 tablespoons grapeseed oil
- 3 tablespoons extra-virgin oil
- 3 tablespoons lemon juice

Directions:

1. In a bowl, combine the almond flour and salt.
2. Dredge the fish in the almond flour to coat. Set aside.
3. Heat a little bit of olive oil to coat a large skillet. Heat the skillet over medium-high heat. Add grapeseed oil. Cook the cod for 3 minutes on each side to brown. Remove from the plate and place on a paper towel-lined plate.
4. In a saucepan, mix together the chicken stock, capers and lemon juice. Simmer to reduce the sauce to half. Add the remaining grapeseed oil.
5. Drizzle the fried cod with the sauce and sprinkle with parsley.

Nutrition: Calories: 277.1; Fat: 28.3 g; Protein: 21.9 g; Carbs: 3.7 g

477. Smoked Trout Tartine

Preparation Time: 10 minutes
Cooking Time: 0 minutes
Servings: 4
Ingredients:

- ½ (15-oz.) can cannellini beans
- ½ cup diced roasted red peppers
- ¾ pound smoked trout, flaked into bite-sized pieces
- 1 stalk celery, finely chopped
- 1 tablespoon extra-virgin olive oil
- 1 teaspoon chopped fresh dill
- 1 teaspoon Dijon mustard
- 2 tablespoons capers, rinsed and drained
- 2 tablespoons freshly squeezed lemon juice

- 2 teaspoons minced onion
- 4 large whole grain bread, toasted
- Dill sprigs – for garnish
- Pinch of sugar

Directions:
1. Mix sugar, mustard, olive oil and lemon juice in a big bowl.
2. Add the rest of the ingredients except for toasted bread.
3. Toss to mix well.
4. Evenly divide fish mixture on top of bread slices and garnish with dill sprigs.
5. Serve and enjoy.

Nutrition: Calories: 348.1; Protein: 28.2 g; Fat: 10.1 g; Carbs: 36.1 g

478. Steamed Mussels Thai Style

Preparation Time: 10 minutes
Cooking Time: 15 minutes
Servings: 4
Ingredients:
- ¼ cup minced shallots
- ½ teaspoon Madras curry
- 1 cup dry white wine
- 1 small bay leaf
- 1 tablespoon chopped fresh basil
- 1 tablespoon chopped fresh cilantro
- 1 tablespoon chopped fresh mint
- 2 pounds mussel, cleaned and debearded
- 2 tablespoons butter
- 4 medium garlic cloves, minced

Directions:
1. In a large heavy-bottomed pot, on medium-high fire add to the pot the curry powder, bay leaf, wine plus minced garlic and shallots. Bring to a boil and simmer for 3 minutes.
2. Add the cleaned mussels, stir, cover, and cook for 3 minutes.
3. Stir mussels again, cover, and cook for another 2 or 3 minutes. Cooking is done when the majority of shells have opened.
4. With a slotted spoon, transfer cooked mussels to a large bowl. Discard any unopened mussels.
5. Continue heating the pot with sauce. Add butter and the chopped herbs.
6. Season with pepper and salt to taste.
7. Once good, pour over mussels, serve and enjoy.

Nutrition: Calories: 407.2; Protein: 43.4 g; Fat: 21.2 g; Carbs: 10.8 g

479. Tasty Tuna Scaloppine

Preparation Time: 10 minutes
Cooking Time: 10 minutes
Servings: 4
Ingredients:
- ¼ cup chopped almonds
- ¼ cup fresh tangerine juice
- ½ teaspoon fennel seeds
- ½ teaspoon ground black pepper, divided
- ½ teaspoon salt
- 1 tablespoon extra-virgin olive oil
- 2 tablespoons chopped fresh mint
- 2 tablespoons chopped red onion
- 4 (6-oz.) sushi-grade Yellowfin tuna steaks, each split in half horizontally
- Cooking spray

Directions:
1. In a small bowl mix fennel seeds, olive oil, mint, onion, tangerine juice, almonds, ¼ teaspoon pepper, and ¼ teaspoon salt. Combine thoroughly.
2. Season fish with remaining salt and pepper.
3. On medium-high fire, place a large nonstick pan and grease with cooking spray. Pan fry fish in two batches cooking each side for a minute.
4. Fish is best served with a side of salad greens or a half cup of cooked brown rice.

Nutrition: Calories: 405; Protein: 27.5 g; Fat: 11.9 g; Carbs: 27.5

480. Thyme and Lemon on Baked Salmon

Preparation Time: 10 minutes
Cooking Time: 25 minutes
Servings: 2
Ingredients:
- 1 (32-oz.) salmon fillet
- 1 lemon, sliced thinly
- 1 tablespoon capers
- 1 tablespoon fresh thyme
- Olive oil for drizzling
- Pepper and salt to taste

Directions:
1. In a foil line baking sheet, place parchment paper on top.
2. Place salmon with skin side down on parchment paper.
3. Season generously with pepper and salt.
4. Place capers on top of the fillet. Cover with thinly sliced lemon.
5. Garnish with thyme.
6. Pop in the cold oven and bake for 25 minutes at 400°F settings.
7. Serve right away and enjoy.

Nutrition: Calories: 684.4; Protein: 94.3 g; Fat: 32.7 g; Carbs: 4.3 g

481. Warm Caper Tapenade on Cod

Preparation Time: 10 minutes
Cooking Time: 30 minutes
Servings: 4
Ingredients:
- ¼ cup chopped cured olives
- ¼ teaspoon freshly ground pepper
- 1½ tcaspoon chopped fresh oregano
- 1 cup halved cherry tomatoes
- 1 pound cod fillet
- 1 tablespoon capers, rinsed and chopped
- 1 tablespoon minced shallot
- 1 teaspoon balsamic vinegar
- 3 teaspoons extra-virgin olive oil, divided

Directions:
1. Grease baking sheet with cooking spray and preheat oven to 450°F.
2. Place cod on a prepared baking sheet. Rub with 2 teaspoons oil and season with pepper.

3. Roast in for 15 to 20 minutes or until the cod is flaky.
4. While waiting for cod to cook, on medium fire, place a small fry pan and heat 1 teaspoon oil.
5. Sauté shallots for a minute.
6. Add tomatoes and cook for two minutes or until soft.
7. Add capers and olives. Sauté for another minute.
8. Add vinegar and oregano. Turn off fire and stir to mix well.
9. Evenly divide cod into 4 servings and place on a plate.
10. To serve, top cod with Caper-Olive-Tomato Tapenade and enjoy.

Nutrition: Calories: 107; Fat: 2. 9g; Protein: 17.6 g; Carbs: 2.0 g

482. Yummy Salmon Panzanella

Preparation Time: 10 minutes
Cooking Time: 10 minutes
Servings: 4
Ingredients:

- ¼ cup thinly sliced fresh basil
- ¼ cup thinly sliced red onion
- ¼ teaspoon freshly ground pepper, divided
- ½ teaspoon salt
- 1 pound center-cut salmon, skinned and cut into 4 equal portions
- 1 medium cucumber, peeled, seeded, and cut into 1-inch slices
- 1 tablespoon capers, rinsed and chopped
- 2 large tomatoes, cut into 1-inch pieces
- 2 thick slices day old whole grain bread, sliced into 1-inch cubes
- 3 tablespoons extra-virgin olive oil
- 3 tablespoons red wine vinegar
- 8 Kalamata olives, pitted and chopped

Directions:

1. Grease grill grate and preheat grill to high.
2. In a large bowl, whisk ⅛ teaspoon pepper, capers, vinegar, and olives. Add oil and whisk well.
3. Stir in basil, onion, cucumber, tomatoes, and bread.
4. Season both sides of salmon with remaining pepper and salt.
5. Grill on high for 4 minutes per side.
6. Into 4 plates, evenly divide salad, top with grilled salmon, and serve.

Nutrition: Calories: 383; Fat: 20.6 g; Protein: 34.8 g; Carbs: 13.6 g

483. Fish and Orzo

Preparation Time: 10 minutes
Cooking Time: 35 minutes
Servings: 4
Ingredients:

- 1 teaspoon garlic, minced
- 1 teaspoon red pepper, crushed
- 2 shallots, chopped
- 1 tablespoon olive oil
- 1 teaspoon anchovy paste
- 1 tablespoon oregano, chopped
- 2 tablespoons black olives, pitted and chopped
- 2 tablespoons capers, drained
- 15 ounces canned tomatoes, crushed
- A pinch of salt and black pepper
- 4 cod fillets, boneless
- 1-ounce feta cheese, crumbled
- 1 tablespoon parsley, chopped
- 3 cups chicken stock
- 1 cup orzo pasta
- Zest of 1 lemon, grated

Directions:

1. Heat up a pan with the oil over medium heat, add the garlic, red pepper and the shallots and sauté for 5 minutes.
2. Add the anchovy paste, oregano, black olives, capers, tomatoes, salt and

pepper, stir and cook for 5 minutes more.
3. Add the cod fillets, sprinkle the cheese and the parsley on top, introduce in the oven and bake at 375°F for 15 minutes more.
4. Meanwhile, put the stock in a pot, bring to a boil over medium heat, add the orzo and the lemon zest, bring to a simmer, cook for 10 minutes, fluff with a fork, and divide between plates.
5. Top each serving with the fish mix and serve.

Nutrition: Calories 402, Fat 21 g, Fiber 8 g, Carbs 21 g, Protein 31 g

484. Baked Sea Bass

Preparation Time: 10 minutes
Cooking Time: 12 minutes
Servings: 4
Ingredients:

- 4 sea bass fillets, boneless
- Sal and black pepper to the taste
- 2 cups potato chips, crushed
- 1 tablespoon mayonnaise

Directions:

1. Season the fish fillets with salt and pepper, brush with the mayonnaise and dredge each in the potato chips.
2. Arrange the fillets on a baking sheet lined with parchment paper and bake at 400°F for 12 minutes.
3. Divide the fish between plates and serve with a side salad.

Nutrition: Calories 228, Fat 8.6 g, Fiber 0.6 g, Carbs 9.3 g, Protein 25 g

485. Fish and Tomato Sauce

Preparation Time: 10 minutes
Cooking Time: 30 minutes
Servings: 4
Ingredients:

- 4 cod fillets, boneless
- 2 garlic cloves, minced
- 2 cups cherry tomatoes, halved
- 1 cup chicken stock
- A pinch of salt and black pepper
- ¼ cup basil, chopped

Directions:

1. Put the tomatoes, garlic, salt and pepper in a pan, heat up over medium heat, and cook for 5 minutes.
2. Add the fish and the rest of the ingredients, bring to a simmer, cover the pan and cook for 25 minutes.
3. Divide the mix between plates and serve.

Nutrition: Calories 180, Fat 1.9 g, Fiber 1.4 g, Carbs 5.3 g, Protein 33.8 g

486. Halibut and Quinoa Mix

Preparation Time: 10 minutes
Cooking Time: 12 minutes
Servings: 4
Ingredients:

- 4 halibut fillets, boneless
- 2 tablespoons olive oil
- 1 teaspoon Rosemary, dried
- 2 teaspoons cumin, ground
- 1 tablespoon coriander, ground
- 2 teaspoons cinnamon powder
- 2 teaspoons oregano, dried
- A pinch of salt and black pepper
- 2 cups quinoa, cooked
- 1 cup cherry tomatoes, halved
- 1 avocado, peeled, pitted and sliced
- 1 cucumber, cubed & Juice of 1 lemon
- ½ cup black olives, pitted and sliced

Directions:

1. In a bowl, combine the fish with the rosemary, cumin, coriander, cinnamon, oregano, salt and pepper and toss.
2. Heat up a pan with the oil over medium heat, add the fish, and sear for 2 minutes on each side.
3. Introduce the pan in the oven and bake the fish at 425°F for 7 minutes.
4. Meanwhile, in a bowl, mix the quinoa with the remaining ingredients, toss and divide between plates.

5. Add the fish next to the quinoa mix and serve right away.

Nutrition: Calories 364, Fat 15.4 g, Fiber 11.2 g, Carbs 56.4 g, Protein 24.5 g

487. Lemon and Dates Barramundi

Preparation Time: 10 minutes
Cooking Time: 12 minutes
Servings: 2
Ingredients:

- 2 barramundi fillets, boneless
- 1 shallot, sliced
- 4 lemon slices
- Juice of ½ lemon
- Zest of 1 lemon, grated
- 2 tablespoons olive oil
- 6 ounces baby spinach
- ¼ cup almonds, chopped
- 4 dates, pitted and chopped
- ¼ cup parsley, chopped
- Salt and black pepper to the taste

Directions:

1. Season the fish with salt and pepper and arrange on 2 parchment paper pieces.
2. Top the fish with the lemon slices, drizzle the lemon juice, and then top with the other ingredients except for the oil.
3. Drizzle 1 tablespoon oil over each fish mix, wrap the parchment paper around the fish shaping into packets, and arrange them on a baking sheet.
4. Bake at 400°F for 12 minutes, cool the mix a bit, unfold, divide everything between plates and serve.

Nutrition: Calories 232, Fat 16.5 g, Fiber 11.1 g, Carbs 24.8 g, Protein 6.5 g

488. Fish Cakes

Preparation Time: 10 minutes
Cooking Time: 10 minutes
Servings: 6
Ingredients:

- 20 ounces canned sardines, drained and mashed well
- 2 garlic cloves, minced
- 2 tablespoons dill, chopped
- 1 yellow onion, chopped
- 1 cup panko breadcrumbs

- 1 egg, whisked
- A pinch of salt and black pepper
- 2 tablespoons lemon juice
- 5 tablespoons olive oil

Directions:

1. In a bowl, combine the sardines with the garlic, dill and the rest of the ingredients except the oil, stir well and shape medium cakes out of this mix.
2. Heat up a pan with the oil over medium-high heat, add the fish cakes, cook for 5 minutes on each side.
3. Serve the cakes with a side salad.

Nutrition: Calories 288, Fat 12.8 g, Fiber 10.2 g, Carbs 22.2 g, Protein 6.8 g

489. Catfish Fillets and Rice

Preparation Time: 10 minutes
Cooking Time: 55 minutes
Servings: 2
Ingredients:

- 2 catfish fillets, boneless
- 2 tablespoons Italian seasoning
- 2 tablespoons olive oil

For the rice:

- 1 cup brown rice
- 2 tablespoons olive oil
- 1½ cups water
- ½ cup green bell pepper, chopped
- 2 garlic cloves, minced
- ½ cup white onion, chopped
- 2 teaspoons Cajun seasoning
- ½ teaspoon garlic powder
- Salt and black pepper to the taste

Directions:

1. Heat up a pot with 2 tablespoons of oil over medium heat, add the onion, garlic, garlic powder, salt and pepper and sauté for 5 minutes.
2. Add the rice, water, bell pepper and the seasoning, bring to a simmer, and cook over medium heat for 40 minutes.
3. Heat up a pan with 2 tablespoons oil over

medium heat, add the fish and the Italian seasoning, and cook for 5 minutes on each side.

4. Divide the rice between plates, add the fish on top and serve.

Nutrition: Calories 261, Fat 17.6 g, Fiber 12.2 g, Carbs 24.8 g, Protein 12.5 g

490. Halibut Pan

Preparation Time: 10 minutes
Cooking Time: 20 minutes
Servings: 4
Ingredients:

- 4 halibut fillets, boneless
- 1 red bell pepper, chopped
- 2 tablespoons olive oil
- 1 yellow onion, chopped
- 4 garlic cloves, minced
- ½ cup chicken stock
- 1 teaspoon basil, dried
- ½ cup cherry tomatoes, halved
- ⅓ cup kalamata olives, pitted and halved
- Salt and black pepper to the taste

Directions:

1. Heat up a pan with the oil over medium heat, add the fish, cook for 5 minutes on each side, and divide between plates.
2. Add the onion, bell pepper, garlic and tomatoes to the pan, stir and sauté for 3 minutes.
3. Add salt, pepper and the rest of the ingredients, toss, cook for 3 minutes more, divide next to the fish and serve.

Nutrition: Calories 253, Fat 8 g, Fiber 1 g, Carbs 5 g, Protein 28 g

491. Baked Shrimp Mix

Preparation Time: 10 minutes
Cooking Time: 32 minutes
Servings: 4
Ingredients:

- 4 gold potatoes, peeled and sliced
- 2 fennel bulbs, trimmed and cut into wedges
- 2 shallots, chopped
- 2 garlic cloves, minced
- 3 tablespoons olive oil

- ½ cup kalamata olives, pitted and halved
- 2 pounds shrimp, peeled and deveined
- 1 teaspoon lemon zest, grated
- 2 teaspoons oregano, dried
- 4 ounces feta cheese, crumbled
- 2 tablespoons parsley, chopped

Directions:

1. In a roasting pan, combine the potatoes with 2 tablespoons of oil, garlic and the rest of the ingredients except the shrimp, toss, introduce in the oven and bake at 450°F for 25 minutes.
2. Add the shrimp, toss, bake for 7 minutes more, divide between plates and serve.

Nutrition: Calories 341, Fat 19 g, Fiber 9 g, Carbs 34 g, Protein 10 g

492. Shrimp and Lemon Sauce

Preparation Time: 10 minutes
Cooking Time: 15 minutes
Servings: 4
Ingredients:

- 1 pound shrimp, peeled and deveined
- ⅓ cup lemon juice
- 4 egg yolks
- 2 tablespoons olive oil
- 1 cup chicken stock
- Salt and black pepper to the taste
- 1 cup black olives, pitted and halved
- 1 tablespoon thyme, chopped

Directions:

1. In a bowl, mix the lemon juice with the egg yolks and whisk well.
2. Heat up a pan with the oil over medium heat, add the shrimp and cook for 2 minutes on each side and transfer to a plate.
3. Heat up a pan with the stock over medium heat, add some of this over the egg yolks and lemon juice mix and whisk well.

4. Add this over the rest of the stock, also add salt and pepper, whisk well and simmer for 2 minutes.
5. Add the shrimp and the rest of the ingredients, toss and serve right away.

Nutrition: Calories 237, Fat 15.3 g, Fiber 4.6 g, Carbs 15.4 g, Protein 7.6 g

493. Shrimp and Beans Salad

Preparation Time: 10 minutes
Cooking Time: 4 minutes
Servings: 4
Ingredients:

- 1 pound shrimp, peeled and deveined
- 30 ounces canned cannellini beans, drained and rinsed
- 2 tablespoons olive oil
- 1 cup cherry tomatoes, halved
- 1 teaspoon lemon zest, grated
- ½ cup red onion, chopped
- 4 handfuls baby arugula
- A pinch of salt and black pepper

For the dressing:

- 3 tablespoons red wine vinegar
- 2 garlic cloves, minced
- ½ cup olive oil

Directions:

1. Heat up a pan with 2 tablespoons oil over medium-high heat, add the shrimp and cook for 2 minutes on each side.
2. In a salad bowl, combine the shrimp with the beans and the rest of the ingredients except the ones for the dressing and toss.
3. In a separate bowl, combine the vinegar with ½ cup oil and the garlic and whisk well.
4. Pour over the salad, toss and serve right away.

Nutrition: Calories 207, Fat 12.3 g, Fiber 6.6 g, Carbs 15.4 g, Protein 8.7 g

494. Pecan Salmon Fillets

Preparation Time: 10 minutes
Cooking Time: 15 minutes
Servings: 6
Ingredients:

- 3 tablespoons olive oil
- 3 tablespoons mustard
- 5 teaspoons honey
- 1 cup pecans, chopped
- 6 salmon fillets, boneless
- 1 tablespoon lemon juice
- 3 teaspoons parsley, chopped
- Salt and pepper to the taste

Directions:

1. In a bowl, mix the oil with the mustard and honey and whisk well.
2. Put the pecans and the parsley in another bowl.
3. Season the salmon fillets with salt and pepper, arrange them on a baking sheet lined with parchment paper, brush with the honey and mustard mix, and top with the pecans mix.
4. Introduce in the oven at 400°F, bake for 15 minutes, divide between plates, drizzle the lemon juice on top and serve.

Nutrition: Calories 282, Fat 15.5 g, Fiber 8.5 g, Carbs 20.9 g, Protein 16.8 g

495. Salmon and Broccoli

Preparation Time: 10 minutes
Cooking Time: 20 minutes
Servings: 4
Ingredients:

- 2 tablespoons balsamic vinegar
- 1 broccoli head, florets separated
- 4 pieces salmon fillets, skinless
- 1 big red onion, roughly chopped
- 1 tablespoon olive oil
- Sea salt and black pepper to the taste

Directions:

1. In a baking dish, combine the salmon with the broccoli and the rest of the ingredients, introduce in the oven and bake at 390°F for 20 minutes.

2. Divide the mix between plates and serve.

Nutrition: Calories 302, Fat 15.5 g, Fiber 8.5 g, Carbs 18.9 g, Protein 19.8 g

496. Salmon and Peach Pan

Preparation Time: 10 minutes
Cooking Time: 11 minutes
Servings: 4
Ingredients:

- 1 tablespoon balsamic vinegar
- 1 teaspoon thyme, chopped
- 1 tablespoon ginger, grated
- 2 tablespoons olive oil
- Sea salt and black pepper to the taste
- 3 peaches, cut into medium wedges
- 4 salmon fillets, boneless

Directions:

1. Heat up a pan with the oil over medium-high heat, add the salmon and cook for 3 minutes on each side.
2. Add the vinegar, the peaches and the rest of the ingredients, cook for 5 minutes more, divide everything between plates and serve.

Nutrition: Calories 293, Fat 17.1 g, Fiber 4.1 g, Carbs 26.4 g, Protein 24.5 g

497. Tarragon Cod Fillets

Preparation Time: 10 minutes
Cooking Time: 12 minutes
Servings: 4
Ingredients:

- 4 cod fillets, boneless
- ¼ cup capers, drained
- 1 tablespoon tarragon, chopped
- Sea salt and black pepper to the taste
- 2 tablespoons olive oil
- 2 tablespoons parsley, chopped
- 1 tablespoon olive oil
- 1 tablespoon lemon juice

Directions:

1. Heat up a pan with the oil over medium-high heat, add the fish and cook for 3 minutes on each side.
2. Add the rest of the ingredients, cook everything

for 7 minutes more, divide between plates and serve.

Nutrition: Calories 162, Fat 9.6 g, Fiber 4.3 g, Carbs 12.4 g, Protein 16.5 g

498. Salmon and Radish Mix

Preparation Time: 10 minutes
Cooking Time: 15 minutes
Servings: 4
Ingredients:

- 2 tablespoons olive oil
- 1 tablespoon balsamic vinegar
- 1½ cup chicken stock
- 4 salmon fillets, boneless
- 2 garlic cloves, minced
- 1 tablespoon ginger, grated
- 1 cup radishes, grated
- ¼ cup scallions, chopped

Directions:

1. Heat up a pan with the oil over medium-high heat, add the salmon, cook for 4 minutes on each side, and divide between plates
2. Add the vinegar and the rest of the ingredients to the pan, toss gently, cook for 10 minutes, add over the salmon and serve.

Nutrition: Calories 274, Fat 14.5 g, Fiber 3.5 g, Carbs 8.5 g, Protein 22.3 g

499. Smoked Salmon and Watercress Salad

Preparation Time: 5 minutes
Cooking Time: 0 minutes
Servings: 4
Ingredients:

- 2 bunches watercress
- 1 pound smoked salmon, skinless, boneless and flaked
- 2 teaspoons mustard
- ¼ cup lemon juice
- ½ cup Greek yogurt
- Salt and black pepper to the taste
- 1 big cucumber, sliced
- 2 tablespoons chives, chopped

Directions:

1. In a salad bowl, combine the salmon with the watercress and the rest of the ingredients toss and serve right away.

Nutrition: Calories 244, Fat 16.7 g, Fiber 4.5 g, Carbs 22.5 g, Protein 15.6 g

500. Salmon and Corn Salad
Preparation Time: 5 minutes
Cooking Time: 0 minutes
Servings: 4
Ingredients:

- ½ cup pecans, chopped
- 2 cups baby arugula
- 1 cup corn
- ¼ pound smoked salmon, skinless, boneless and cut into small chunks
- 2 tablespoons olive oil
- 2 tablespoons lemon juice
- Sea salt and black pepper to the taste

Directions:

1. In a salad bowl, combine the salmon with the corn and the rest of the ingredients, toss and serve right away.

Nutrition: Calories 284, Fat 18.4 g, Fiber 5.4 g, Carbs 22.6 g, Protein 17.4 g

501. Cod and Mushrooms Mix
Preparation Time: 10 minutes
Cooking Time: 25 minutes
Servings: 4
Ingredients:

- 2 cod fillets, boneless
- 4 tablespoons olive oil
- 4 ounces mushrooms, sliced
- Sea salt and black pepper to the taste
- 12 cherry tomatoes, halved
- 8 ounces lettuce leaves, torn
- 1 avocado, pitted, peeled and cubed
- 1 red chili pepper, chopped
- 1 tablespoon cilantro, chopped
- 2 tablespoons balsamic vinegar
- 1-ounce feta cheese, crumbled

Directions:

1. Put the fish in a roasting pan, brush it with 2 tablespoons oil, sprinkle salt and pepper all over and broil under medium-high heat for 15 minutes. Meanwhile, heat up a pan

with the rest of the oil over medium heat, add the mushrooms, stir and sauté for 5 minutes.
2. Add the rest of the ingredients, toss, cook for 5 minutes more, and divide between plates.
3. Top with the fish and serve right away.

Nutrition: Calories 257, Fat 10 g, Fiber 3.1 g, Carbs 24.3 g, Protein 19.4 g

502. Sesame Shrimp Mix
Preparation Time: 10 minutes
Cooking Time: 0 minutes
Servings: 4
Ingredients:

- 2 tablespoons lime juice
- 3 tablespoons teriyaki sauce
- 2 tablespoons olive oil
- 8 cups baby spinach
- 14 ounces shrimp, cooked, peeled and deveined
- 1 cup cucumber, sliced
- 1 cup radish, sliced
- ¼ cup cilantro, chopped
- 2 teaspoons sesame seeds, toasted

Directions:

1. In a bowl, mix the shrimp with the lime juice, spinach and the rest of the ingredients, toss and serve cold.

Nutrition: Calories 177, Fat 9 g, Fiber 7.1 g, Carbs 14.3 g, Protein 9.4 g

503. Creamy Curry Salmon
Preparation Time: 10 minutes
Cooking Time: 20 minutes
Servings: 2
Ingredients:

- 2 salmon fillets, boneless and cubed
- 1 tablespoon olive oil
- 1 tablespoon basil, chopped
- Sea salt and black pepper to the taste
- 1 cup Greek yogurt
- 2 teaspoons curry powder
- 1 garlic clove, minced
- ½ teaspoon mint, chopped

Directions:

1. Heat up a pan with the oil over medium-high heat, add the salmon and cook for 3 minutes.

2. Add the rest of the ingredients, toss, cook for 15 minutes more, divide between plates and serve.

Nutrition: Calories 284, Fat 14.1 g, Fiber 8.5 g, Carbs 26.7 g, Protein 31.4 g

504. Mahi midsolo and Pomegranate Sauce
Preparation Time: 10 minutes
Cooking Time: 10 minutes
Servings: 4
Ingredients:

- 1½ cups chicken stock
- 1 tablespoon olive oil
- 4 Mahi midsolo fillets, boneless
- 4 tablespoons tahini paste
- Juice of 1 lime
- Seeds from 1 pomegranate
- 1 tablespoon parsley, chopped

Directions:

1. Heat up a pan with the oil over medium-high heat, add the fish and cook for 3 minutes on each side.
2. Add the rest of the ingredients, flip the fish again, cook for 4 minutes more, divide everything between plates and serve.

Nutrition: Calories 224, Fat 11.1 g, Fiber 5.5 g, Carbs 16.7 g, Protein 11.4 g

505. Smoked Salmon and Veggies Mix
Preparation Time: 10 minutes
Cooking Time: 20 minutes
Servings: 4
Ingredients:

- 3 red onions, cut into wedges
- ¾ cup green olives, pitted and halved
- 3 red bell peppers, roughly chopped
- ½ teaspoon smoked paprika
- Salt and black pepper to the taste
- 3 tablespoons olive oil
- 4 salmon fillets, skinless and boneless
- 2 tablespoons chives, chopped

Directions:

1. In a roasting pan, combine the salmon with the onions

and the rest of the ingredients, introduce in the oven and bake at 390°F for 20 minutes.

2. Divide the mix between plates and serve.

Nutrition: Calories 301, Fat 5.9 g, Fiber 11.9 g, Carbs 26.4 g, Protein 22.4 g

506. Salmon and Mango Mix

Preparation Time: 10 minutes
Cooking Time: 25 minutes
Servings: 2
Ingredients:

- 2 salmon fillets, skinless and boneless
- Salt and pepper to the taste
- 2 tablespoons olive oil
- 2 garlic cloves, minced
- 2 mangos, peeled and cubed
- 1 red chili, chopped
- 1 small piece ginger, grated
- Juice of 1 lime
- 1 tablespoon cilantro, chopped

Directions:

1. In a roasting pan, combine the salmon with the oil, garlic and the rest of the ingredients except the cilantro, toss, introduce in the oven at 350°F and bake for 25 minutes.

2. Divide everything between plates and serve with the cilantro sprinkled on top.

Nutrition: Calories 251, Fat 15.9 g, Fiber 5.9 g, Carbs 26.4 g, Protein 12.4 g

507. Salmon and Creamy Endives

Preparation Time: 10 minutes
Cooking Time: 15 minutes
Servings: 4
Ingredients:

- 4 salmon fillets, boneless
- 2 endives, shredded
- Juice of 1 lime
- Salt and black pepper to the taste
- ¼ cup chicken stock
- 1 cup Greek yogurt
- ¼ cup green olives pitted and chopped

- ¼ cup fresh chives, chopped
- 3 tablespoons olive oil

Directions:

1. Heat up a pan with half of the oil over medium heat, add the endives and the rest of the ingredients except the chives and the salmon, toss, cook for 6 minutes, and divide between plates.

2. Heat up another pan with the rest of the oil, add the salmon, season with salt and pepper, cook for 4 minutes on each side, add next to the creamy endives mix, sprinkle the chives on top and serve.

Nutrition: Calories 266, Fat 13.9 g, Fiber 11.1 g, Carbs 23.8 g, Protein 17.5 g

508. Trout and Tzatziki Sauce

Preparation Time: 10 minutes
Cooking Time: 10 minutes
Servings: 4
Ingredients:

- Juice of ½ lime
- Salt and black pepper to the taste
- 1½ teaspoon coriander, ground
- 1 teaspoon garlic, minced
- 4 trout fillets, boneless
- 1 teaspoon sweet paprika
- 2 tablespoons avocado oil

For the sauce:

- 1 cucumber, chopped
- 4 garlic cloves, minced
- 1 tablespoon olive oil
- 1 teaspoon white vinegar
- 1½ cups Greek yogurt
- A pinch of salt and white pepper

Directions:

1. Heat up a pan with the avocado oil over medium-high heat, add the fish, salt, pepper, lime juice, 1 teaspoon garlic and the paprika, rub the fish gently and cook for 4 minutes on each side.

2. In a bowl, combine the cucumber with 4 garlic

cloves and the rest of the ingredients for the sauce and whisk well.

3. Divide the fish between plates, drizzle the sauce all over and serve with a side salad.

Nutrition: Calories 393, Fat 18.5 g, Fiber 6.5 g, Carbs 18.3 g, Protein 39.6 g

509. Parsley Trout and Capers

Preparation Time: 10 minutes
Cooking Time: 10 minutes
Servings: 4
Ingredients:

- 4 trout fillets, boneless
- 3 ounces tomato sauce
- Handful of parsley, chopped
- 2 tablespoons olive oil
- Salt and black pepper to the taste

Directions:

1. Heat up a pan with the oil over medium-high heat, add the fish, salt and pepper and cook for 3 minutes on each side.

2. Add the rest of the ingredients, cook everything for 4 minutes more.

3. Divide everything between plates and serve.

Nutrition: Calories 308, Fat 17 g, Fiber 1 g, Carbs 3 g, Protein 16 g

510. Baked Trout and Fennel

Preparation Time: 10 minutes
Cooking Time: 22 minutes
Servings: 4
Ingredients:

- 1 fennel bulb, sliced
- 2 tablespoons olive oil
- 1 yellow onion, sliced
- 3 teaspoons Italian seasoning
- 4 rainbow trout fillets, boneless
- ¼ cup panko breadcrumbs
- ½ cup kalamata olives, pitted and halved
- Juice of 1 lemon

Directions:

1. Spread the fennel the onion and the rest of the ingredients except the trout and the breadcrumbs on a baking sheet lined with

parchment paper, toss them and cook at 400°F for 10 minutes.

2. Add the fish dredged in breadcrumbs and seasoned with salt and pepper and cook it at 400°F for 6 minutes on each side.

3. Divide the mix between plates and serve.

Nutrition: Calories 306, Fat 8.9 g, Fiber 11.1 g, Carbs 23.8 g, Protein 14.5 g

511. Lemon Rainbow Trout

Preparation Time: 10 minutes
Cooking Time: 15 minutes
Servings: 2
Ingredients:

- 2 rainbow trout
- Juice of 1 lemon
- 3 tablespoons olive oil
- 4 garlic cloves, minced
- A pinch of salt and black pepper

Directions:

1. Line a baking sheet with parchment paper, add the fish and the rest of the ingredients and rub.

2. Bake at 400°F for 15 minutes, divide between plates, and serve with a side salad.

Nutrition: Calories 321, Fat 19 g, Fiber 5 g, Carbs 6 g, Protein 35 g

512. Favorite Greek Salmon

Preparation Time: 10 minutes
Cooking Time: 1-2 hours
Servings: 6
Ingredients:

- 1 cup homemade chicken broth
- 2 tablespoons fresh lemon juice
- ¼ cup fresh dill, chopped
- 6 (4-oz.) salmon fillets
- Salt and freshly ground black pepper, to taste

Directions:

1. In the pot of crockpot, mix together the 2 cups of water, broth, lemon juice and dill.

2. Arrange the salmon fillets on top, skin side down and sprinkle with cayenne pepper, salt black pepper.

3. Set the crockpot on "Low" and cook, covered for about 1-2 hours.

4. Uncover the crockpot and serve hot.

Nutrition: Calories: 164; Carbohydrates: 1.6 g; Protein: 23.3 g; Fat: 7.4 g; Sugar: 0 g;

513. Citrus Flavored Salmon

Preparation Time: 10 minutes
Cooking Time: 2-2½ hours
Servings: 6
Ingredients:

- ¾ cup fresh cilantro leaves, chopped
- 2 garlic cloves, chopped finely
- 2-3 tablespoons fresh lime juice
- Salt, to taste
- 1 pound salmon fillets

Directions:

1. In a medium bowl, add all the ingredients except for salmon fillets and mix well.

2. In the bottom of a greased crockpot, place the salmon fillets and top with garlic mixture.

3. Set the crockpot on "Low" and cook, covered for about 2-2½ hours.

4. Uncover the crockpot and serve.

Nutrition: Calories: 154; Carbohydrates: 0.7 g; Protein: 22.2 g; Fat: 7 g; Sugar: 0.1 g; Fiber: 0.1 g

514. Lively Flavored Salmon

Preparation Time: 10 minutes
Cooking Time: 1-2 hours
Servings: 8
Ingredients:

- 2 (4-oz.) salmon fillets
- ½ cup scallions, thinly sliced
- 1 cup fresh mushrooms, sliced
- Salt and freshly ground black pepper, to taste
- 3 cups homemade fish broth

Directions:

1. In the pot of crockpot, place the ingredients and stir to combine.

2. Set the crockpot on "Low" and cook, covered for about 1-2 hours.

3. Uncover the crockpot and serve hot.

Nutrition: Calories: 225; Carbohydrates: 1.5 g; Protein: 54.7 g; Fat: 10 g; Sugar: 1.2 g; Fiber: 1 g

515. Simply Delicious Tilapia

Preparation Time: 10 minutes
Cooking Time: 1½ hours
Servings: 6
Ingredients:

- 4 tilapia fillets
- Salt and freshly ground black pepper, to taste
- 2 tablespoons unsalted butter, cubed
- 1 lemon, cut into slices

Directions:

1. In the pot of crockpot, place the tilapia fillets and sprinkle with salt and black pepper.

2. Top with butter, followed by the lemon.

3. Set the crockpot on "Low" and cook, covered for about 1½ hours.

4. Uncover the crockpot and serve hot.

Nutrition: Calories: 169; Carbohydrates: 0.4 g; Protein: 26.5 g; Fat: 7.1 g; Sugar: 0.1 g; Fiber: 0.1 g

516. Aromatic Tilapia

Preparation Time: 10 minutes
Cooking Time: 1½ hours
Servings: 6
Ingredients:

- 6 (4-oz.) tilapia fillets
- Sea salt and freshly ground black pepper, to taste
- ½ cup onion, chopped
- ¼ cup fresh parsley, chopped
- 2 tablespoons unsalted butter, melted

Directions:

1. Grease a crockpot.

2. Sprinkle the tilapia fillets with salt and black pepper generously.

3. Place onion and parsley over fillets evenly.

4. Drizzle with melted butter.

5. Set the crockpot on "Low" and cook, covered for about 1½ hours.

6. Uncover the crockpot and serve hot.

Nutrition: Calories: 133; Carbohydrates: 1.3 g; Protein: 21.3 g; Fat: 5 g; Sugar: 0 g; Fiber: 0 g

517. Richly Delicious Tilapia

Preparation Time: 10 minutes
Cooking Time: 3-4 hours
Servings: 6
Ingredients:

- ½ cup Parmesan cheese, grated
- ¼ cup mayonnaise
- ¼ cup fresh lemon juice
- Salt and freshly ground black pepper, to taste
- 4 (4-oz.) tilapia fillets

Directions:

1. In a bowl, mix together all ingredients except tilapia fillets and cilantro.
2. Coat the fillets with the mayonnaise mixture evenly.
3. Place the filets over a large piece of foil.
4. Wrap the foil around fillets to seal them.
5. Arrange the foil packet in the bottom of the crockpot.
6. Set the crockpot on "Low" and cook, covered for about 3-4 hours.
7. Uncover the crockpot and transfer the foil parcel onto a platter.
8. Carefully, open the parcel and serve hot

Nutrition: Calories: 190; Carbohydrates: 3.9 g; Protein: 25.4 g; Fat: 8.5 g; Sugar: 1.3 g; Fiber: 0.1 g

518. No-Fuss Sardine

Preparation Time: 10 minutes
Cooking Time: 8 hours
Servings: 6
Ingredients:

- 2 pounds fresh sardines, cubed
- 4 plum tomatoes, chopped finely
- 1 large onion, sliced
- 1 cup sugar-free tomato puree
- Salt and freshly ground black pepper, to taste

Directions:

1. Grease the crockpot
2. In the prepared crockpot, place the sardine cubes and top with remaining all ingredients.
3. Set the crockpot on "Low" and cook, covered for about 8 hours.
4. Uncover the crockpot and serve hot.

Nutrition: Calories: 269; Carbohydrates: 0 g; Protein: 7.7 g; Fat: 13.2 g; Sugar: 4 g; Fiber: 1.7 g

519. Spanish Style Sardine

Preparation Time: 10 minutes
Cooking Time: 8 hours
Servings: 6
Ingredients:

- 3 large carrots peeled, cut into thin discs
- 2¼ pounds sardine, heads, tails, and gut removed
- 1 cup olive oil
- 1 cup homemade fish broth
- Salt and freshly ground black pepper, to taste

Directions:

1. In the pot of a crockpot, place the carrots and top with sardine.
2. Drizzle with oil and sprinkle with salt and black pepper.
3. Set the crockpot on "Low" and cook, covered for about 8 hours.
4. Uncover the crockpot and serve hot.

Nutrition: Calories: 425; Carbohydrates: 7 g; Protein: 29.4 g; Fat: 21.5 g; Sugar: 4.8 g Fiber: 1.7 g

520. Mouth Watering Tuna

Preparation Time: 10 minutes
Cooking Time: 4 hours & 15 minutes
Servings: 6
Ingredients:

- 2 tablespoons olive oil
- 4-5 garlic cloves, chopped finely
- 1 small jalapeño pepper, chopped finely
- Salt and freshly ground black pepper, to taste
- ¾ pound fresh tuna, cut into 1-inch cubes

Directions:

1. In the pot of crockpot, add all the ingredients except for tuna and stir to combine.
2. Set the crockpot on "Low" and cook, covered for about 4 hours.
3. Uncover the crockpot and stir in the tuna cubes.
4. Set the crockpot on "High" and cook, covered for about 15 minutes.
5. Uncover the crockpot and stir the mixture.
6. Serve hot.

Nutrition: Calories: 326; Carbohydrates: 2 g; Protein: 43.8 g; Fat: 15.4 g; Sugar: 0.1 g

521. Satisfying Halibut Meal

Preparation Time: 10 minutes
Cooking Time: 2 hours
Servings: 6
Ingredients:

- 1½ pounds halibut, cubed
- ¾ cup yellow onion, sliced thinly
- ½ cup homemade chicken broth
- Salt and ground black pepper, as required
- 1½ cup Kalamata olives, pitted and halved

Directions:

1. In the pot of crockpot, add all the ingredients except for olives and stir to combine.
2. Set the crockpot on "Low" and cook, covered for about 1½ hours.
3. Uncover the crockpot and stir in the olives.
4. Set the crockpot on "Low" and cook, covered for about 30 minutes.
5. Uncover the crockpot and serve hot.

Nutrition: Calories: 196; Carbohydrates: 3.5 g; Protein: 31.9 g; Fat: 6.4 g; Sugar: 0.7 g;

522. Bold Flavored Halibut

Preparation Time: 10 minutes
Cooking Time: 1½ - 2 hours
Servings: 6
Ingredients:

- 12 ounces halibut fillet
- Salt and freshly ground black pepper, to taste

- 1 tablespoon balsamic vinegar
- 1 tablespoon butter, melted
- 1½ teaspoon dried parsley

Directions:
1. Arrange a large 18-inch piece of greased piece foil onto a smooth surface.
2. Season the halibut fillet with salt and black pepper.
3. In a small bowl, add the lemon juice, oil and dill and mix well.
4. Place the halibut fillet in the center of foil and drizzle with the oil mixture.
5. Carefully bring up the edges of the foil and crimp them together, leaving plenty of air inside of the foil packet.
6. Place the foil packet in the bottom of a crockpot.
7. Set the crockpot on "High" and cook, covered for about 1½-2 hours.
8. Uncover the crockpot and remove the foil packet.
9. Carefully open the foil packet and serve.

Nutrition: Calories: 242; Carbohydrates: 0.1 g; Protein: 35.9 g; Fat: 9.8 g; Sugar: 0 g;

523. Midweek Dinner Halibut
Preparation Time: 10 minutes
Cooking Time: 3-4 hours
Servings: 8
Ingredients:
- 1 (15-oz.) can diced tomatoes
- 1 large green bell pepper, seeded and chopped
- 1 pound halibut fillets
- Salt and freshly ground black pepper, to taste
- ⅓ cup homemade chicken broth

Directions:
1. Grease the pot of crockpot.
2. In the pot of crockpot, place the tomatoes and bell pepper.
3. Place the fish fillets on top of the tomato mixture and sprinkle with salt and black pepper.

4. Place the broth on top evenly.
5. Set the crockpot on "High" and cook, covered for about 3-4 hours.
6. Uncover the crockpot and serve hot.

Nutrition: Calories: 156; Carbohydrates: 3 g; Protein: 25.6 g; Fat: 3 g; Sugar: 3.8 g;

524. Delicate Cod Dish
Preparation Time: 10 minutes
Cooking Time: 2 hours & 30 minutes
Servings: 6
Ingredients:
- 1 pound cod fillets, cubed
- 1 small onion, sliced
- ½ cup fish broth
- Salt and black pepper, to taste
- 2 large tomatoes, cut into quarters

Directions:
1. In the pot of a crockpot, add cod cubes, onion, garlic and broth and stir to combine.
2. Set the crockpot on "Low" and cook, covered for about 2 hours.
3. During the last 30 minutes of cooking, stir in the tomatoes.

Nutrition: Calories: 119; Carbohydrates: 5.2 g; Protein: 21.9 g; Fat: 1.5 g; Sugar: 3.1 g;

525. Versatile Cod
Preparation Time: 10 minutes
Cooking Time: 6 hours
Servings: 6
Ingredients:
- 1 pound cod fillets, cubed
- 1 medium onion, chopped
- 2 red bell peppers, seeded and cubed
- ½ cup homemade fish broth
- Salt and freshly ground black pepper, to taste

Directions:
1. In the pot of crockpot, add all the ingredients and stir to combine.
2. Set the crockpot on "Low" and cook, covered for about 6 hours.

3. Uncover the crockpot and serve hot.

Nutrition: Calories: 119; Carbohydrates: 5 g; Protein: 21.7 g; Fat: 1.4 g; Sugar: 2.6 g;

526. Fancy Braeside Shrimp
Preparation Time: 10 minutes
Cooking Time: 1½ hours
Servings: 6
Ingredients:
- 1 pound raw shrimp, peeled and deveined
- ¼ cup homemade chicken broth
- 3 tablespoons olive oil
- 1 tablespoon fresh lime juice
- Salt and freshly ground black pepper, to taste

Directions:
1. In a crockpot, place all the ingredients and stir to combine.
2. Set the crockpot on "High" and cook, covered for about 1½ hours.
3. Uncover the crockpot and stir the mixture.
4. Serve hot.

Nutrition: Calories: 227; Carbohydrates: 1.8 g; Protein: 26.1 g; Fat: 12.5 g; Sugar: 0 g;

527. Enjoyable Shrimp
Preparation Time: 10 minutes
Cooking Time: 3 hours.
Servings: 6
Ingredients:
- 3 cups green bell pepper, seeded and sliced
- 2 cups tomatoes, chopped finely
- 1 cup sugar-free tomato sauce
- Salt and freshly ground black pepper, to taste
- 1¾ pounds large shrimp, peeled and deveined

Directions:
1. In a crockpot, add all ingredients except shrimp and stir to combine.
2. Set the crockpot on "High" and cook, covered for about 2-3 hours.
3. Uncover the crockpot and stir in the shrimp.

4. Set the crockpot on "High" and cook, covered for about 30 minutes.
5. Uncover the crockpot and serve hot.

Nutrition: Calories: 118; Carbohydrates: 3 g; Protein: 22.5 g; Fat: 0.2 g; Sugar: 3.3 g;

528. Outstanding Shrimp Meal

Preparation Time: 10 minutes
Cooking Time: 7 hours & 15 minutes
Servings: 6
Ingredients:

- 1 (14-oz.) can sugar-free peeled tomatoes, chopped finely
- 4 ounces canned sugar-free tomato paste
- 2 tablespoons fresh parsley, chopped
- Salt and ground black pepper, as required
- 2 pounds cooked shrimp, peeled and deveined

Directions:

1. In the pot of crockpot, add all the ingredients except for shrimp and stir to combine.
2. Set the crockpot on "Low" and cook, covered for about 6-7 hours.
3. Uncover the crockpot and stir in the shrimp.
4. Set the crockpot on "High" and cook, covered for about 15 minutes.
5. Uncover the crockpot and serve hot.

Nutrition: Calories: 199; Carbohydrates: 2.5 g; Protein: 35.4 g; Fat: 2.7 g; Sugar: 2.7 g;

529. Buttered Shrimp

Preparation Time: 10 minutes
Cooking Time: 50 minutes.
Servings: 6
Ingredients:

- 8 garlic cloves, chopped
- ¼ cup fresh cilantro, chopped
- ⅓ cup unsalted butter
- Salt and freshly ground black pepper, to taste
- 2 pounds extra-large shrimp, peeled and deveined

Directions:

1. In a crockpot, add all ingredients except shrimp and stir to combine.
2. Set the crockpot on "High" and cook, covered for about 30 minutes.
3. Uncover the crockpot and stir in shrimp.
4. Set the crockpot on "High" and cook, covered for about 20 minutes.
5. Uncover the crockpot and serve hot.

Nutrition: Calories: 276; Carbohydrates: 0 g; Protein: 34.8 g; Fat: 12.8 g; Sugar: 0.1 g;

530. Flavorful Shrimp Curry

Preparation Time: 10 minutes
Cooking Time: 2 hours.
Servings: 6
Ingredients:

- 3 cups tomatoes, chopped finely
- 1½ cups small cauliflower florets
- 1 cup unsweetened coconut milk
- Salt and freshly ground black pepper, to taste
- 1½ pounds shrimp, peeled and deveined

Directions:

1. In the pot of crockpot, add all the ingredients except for shrimp and stir to combine.
2. Set the crockpot on "High" and cook, covered for about 80 minutes.
3. Uncover the crockpot and stir in shrimp.
4. Set the crockpot on "High" and cook, covered for about 40 minutes.
5. Uncover the crockpot and serve hot.

Nutrition: Calories: 165 Carbohydrates: 6.9 g; Protein: 27.1 g Fat: 2.8 g Sugar: 3 g;

531. Mahi Taco Wraps

Preparation Time: 5 minutes
Cooking Time: 2 hours
Servings: 6
Ingredients:

- 1 pound Mahi Mahi, wild-caught
- ½ cup cherry tomatoes
- 1 small green bell pepper, cored and sliced

- ¼ of a medium red onion, thinly sliced
- ½ teaspoon garlic powder
- 1 teaspoon sea salt
- ½ teaspoon ground black pepper
- 1 teaspoon chipotle pepper
- ½ teaspoon dried oregano
- 1 teaspoon cumin
- 1 tablespoon avocado oil
- ¼ cup chicken stock
- 1 medium avocado, diced
- 1 cup sour cream
- 6 large lettuce leaves

Directions:

1. Grease a 6-quarts slow cooker with oil, place fish in it and then pour in chicken stock.
2. Stir together garlic powder, salt, black pepper, chipotle pepper, oregano and cumin and then season fish with half of this mixture.
3. Layer fish with tomatoes, pepper and onion, season with remaining spice mixture and shut with lid.
4. Plug in the slow cooker and cook fish for 2 hours at a high heat setting or until cooked through.
5. When done, evenly spoon fish among lettuce, top with avocado and sour cream and serve.

Nutrition: Calories: 260 Fat: 15.1 g Protein: 27.8 g Carbs: 1.9 g Fiber: 2.2 g Sugar: 3

532. Salmon

Preparation Time: 5 minutes
Cooking Time: 5 minutes
Servings: 4
Ingredients:

- 3 lemons, sliced
- ¾ cup water
- 4 salmon fillets
- 1 bunch of dill weed, fresh
- 1 tablespoon butter, unsalted
- ¼ teaspoon salt
- ¼ teaspoon ground black pepper

Directions:

1. Switch on the instant pot, pour in water, stir in lemon juice, and insert a steel steamer rack.

2. Place salmon on the steamer rack, sprinkle with dill and then top with lemon slices.

3. Press the 'keep warm' button, shut the instant pot with its lid in the sealed position, then press the 'manual' button, press '+/-' to set the cooking time to 5 minutes, and cook at a high-pressure setting; when the pressure builds in the pot, the cooking timer will start.

4. When the instant pot buzzes, press the 'keep warm' button, do a quick pressure release and open the lid.

5. Remove and discard the lemon slices, transfer salmon to a dish, season with salt and black pepper, garnish with more dill and serve with lemon wedges and cauliflower rice.

Nutrition: Calories: 199.2; Fat: 8.1 g Protein: 29.2 g Carbs: 0.8 g Fiber: 0.1 g

533. Shrimp Tacos

Preparation Time: 5 minutes
Cooking Time: 3 hours
Servings: 6
Ingredients:

- 1 pound medium wild-caught shrimp, peeled and tails off
- 12-ounce fire-roasted tomatoes, diced
- 1 small green bell pepper, chopped
- ½ cup chopped white onion
- 1 teaspoon minced garlic
- ½ teaspoon sea salt
- ½ teaspoon ground black pepper
- ½ teaspoon red chili powder
- ½ teaspoon cumin
- ¼ teaspoon cayenne pepper
- 2 tablespoons avocado oil
- ½ cup salsa
- 4 tablespoons chopped cilantro
- 1½cup sour cream
- 2 medium avocado, diced

Directions:

1. Rinse shrimps, layer into a 6-quarts slow cooker and drizzle with oil.

2. Add tomatoes, stir until mixed, then add peppers and remaining ingredients except for sour cream and avocado and stir until combined.

3. Plug in the slow cooker, shut with lid, and cook for 2 to 3 hours at low heat setting or 1 hour and 30 minutes to 2 hours at high heat setting or until shrimps turn pink.

4. When done, serve shrimps with avocado and sour cream.

Nutrition: Calories: 324 Fat: 12 g Protein: 28 g Carbs: 4.2 g Fiber: 13 Sugar: 2 g

534. Fish Curry

Preparation Time: 5 minutes
Cooking Time: 4 hours
Servings: 6
Ingredients:

- 2.2 pounds wild-caught white fish fillet, cubed
- 18-ounce spinach leaves
- 4 tablespoons red curry paste, organic
- 14-ounce coconut cream, unsweetened and full-fat
- 14-ounce water

Directions:

1. Plug in a 6-quart slow cooker and let preheat at a high heat setting.

2. In the meantime, whisk together coconut cream and water until smooth.

3. Place fish into the slow cooker, spread with curry paste, and then pour in coconut cream mixture.

4. Shut with lid and cook for 2 hours at high heat setting or 4 hours at low heat setting until tender.

5. Then add spinach and continue cooking for 20 to 30 minutes or until spinach leaves wilt.

6. Serve straight away.

Nutrition: Calories: 129 Fat: 6 g Protein: 12 g Carbs: 4.8 g Fiber: 10 g Sugar: 6 g

535. Salmon with Creamy Lemon Sauce

Preparation Time: 5 minutes
Cooking Time: 2 hours
Servings: 6
Ingredients:
For the Salmon:

- 2 pounds wild-caught salmon fillet, skin-on
- 1 teaspoon garlic powder
- 1½ teaspoons salt
- 1 teaspoon ground black pepper
- ½ teaspoon red chili powder
- ½ teaspoon Italian Seasoning
- 1 lemon, sliced
- 1 lemon, juiced
- 2 tablespoons avocado oil
- 1 cup chicken broth

For the Creamy Lemon Sauce:

- Chopped parsley, for garnish
- ⅛ teaspoon lemon zest
- ¼ cup heavy cream
- ¼ cup grated parmesan cheese

Directions:

1. Line a 6-quart slow cooker with a parchment sheet, spread its bottom with lemon slices, then top with salmon and drizzle with oil.

2. Stir together garlic powder, salt, black pepper, red chili powder, Italian seasoning, and oil until combined, and rub this mixture all over salmon.

3. Pour lemon juice and broth around the fish and shut with lid.

4. Plug in the slow cooker and cook for 2 hours at a low heat setting.

5. In the meantime, set the oven at 400°F and let preheat.

6. When fish is done, lift out an inner pot of slow cooker, place into the oven and cook for 5 to 8 minutes or until the top is nicely browned.

7. Lift out fish using a parchment sheet and keep it warm.
8. Transfer juices from slow cooker to a medium skillet pan, place it over medium-high heat, then bring to boil and cook for 1 minute.
9. Turn heat to a low level, whisk the cream into the sauce along with lemon zest and parmesan cheese and cook for 2 to 3 minutes or until thickened.
10. Cut salmon in pieces, then top each piece with lemon sauce and serve.

Nutrition: Calories: 364 Fat: 19 g Protein: 12.9 g Carbs: 3.8 g Fiber: 7 g Sugar: 9 g

536. Salmon with Lemon-Caper Sauce

Preparation Time: 5 minutes
Cooking Time: 1 hour
Servings: 4
Ingredients:

- 1 pound wild-caught salmon fillet
- 2 teaspoons capers, rinsed and mashed
- 1 teaspoon minced garlic
- 1 teaspoon salt
- ½ teaspoon ground black pepper
- ½ teaspoon dried oregano
- 1 teaspoon lemon zest
- 2 tablespoons lemon juice
- 4 tablespoons unsalted butter

Directions:

1. Cut salmon into 4 pieces, then season with salt and black pepper and sprinkle lemon zest on top.
2. Line a 6-quart slow cooker with parchment paper, place seasoned salmon pieces on it, and shut with a lid.
3. Plug in the slow cooker and cook for 1 hour and 30 minutes or until salmon is cooked through.
4. When 10 minutes of cooking time is left, prepare lemon-caper sauce and for this, place a small saucepan

over low heat, add butter and let it melt.
5. Then add capers, garlic, lemon juice, stir until mixed and simmer for 1 minute.
6. Remove saucepan from heat and stir in oregano.
7. When salmon is cooked, spoon lemon-caper sauce on it and serve.

Nutrition: Calories: 421 Fat: 11 g Protein: 13.8 g Carbs: 2.4 g Fiber: 7 g Sugar: 8 g

537. Spicy Barbecue Shrimp

Preparation Time: 5 minutes
Cooking Time: 1 hour
Servings: 6
Ingredients:

- 1½ pounds large wild-caught shrimp, unpeeled
- 1 green onion, chopped
- 1 teaspoon minced garlic
- 1½ teaspoon salt
- ¾ teaspoon ground black pepper
- 1 teaspoon Cajun seasoning
- 1 tablespoon hot pepper sauce
- ¼ cup Worcestershire Sauce
- 1 lemon, juiced
- 2 tablespoons avocado oil
- ½ cup unsalted butter, chopped

Directions:

1. Place all the ingredients except for shrimps in a 6-quart slow cooker and whisk until mixed.
2. Plug in the slow cooker, then shut with lid and cook for 30 minutes at high heat setting.
3. Then take out ½ cup of this sauce and reserve.
4. Add shrimps to the slow cooker.

Nutrition: Calories: 313 Fat: 15 g Protein: 13.8 g Carbs: 2.6 g Fiber: 7 g Sugar: 7 g

538. Lemon Dill Halibut

Preparation Time: 5 minutes
Cooking Time: 2 hours
Servings: 6
Ingredients:

- 12-ounce wild-caught halibut fillet

- 1 teaspoon salt
- ½ teaspoon ground black pepper
- 1½ teaspoons dried dill
- 1 tablespoon fresh lemon juice
- 3 tablespoons avocado oil

Directions:

1. Cut an 18-inch piece of aluminum foil, place halibut fillet in the middle and then season with salt and black pepper.
2. Whisk together remaining ingredients, drizzle this mixture over halibut, then crimp the edges of foil and place it into a 6-quart slow cooker.
3. Plug in the slow cooker, shut with lid, and cook for 1 hour and 30 minutes or 2 hours at high heat setting or until cooked through.
4. When done, carefully open the crimped edges and check the fish, it should be tender and flaky.
5. Serve straight away.

Nutrition: Calories: 312 Fat: 15 g Protein: 13.8 g Carbs: 0 g Fiber: 7 g Sugar: 0 g

539. Coconut Cilantro Curry Shrimp

Preparation Time: 5 minutes
Cooking Time: 2 hours
Servings: 4
Ingredients:

- 1 pound wild-caught shrimp, peeled and deveined
- 2½ teaspoons lemon garlic seasoning
- 2 tablespoons red curry paste
- 4 tablespoons chopped cilantro
- 30 ounces coconut milk, unsweetened
- 16 ounces water

Directions:

1. Whisk together all the ingredients except for shrimps and 2 tablespoons cilantro and add to a 4-quart slow cooker.
2. Plug in the slow cooker, shut with lid, and cook for 2

hours at high heat setting or 4 hours at low heat setting.

3. Then add shrimps, toss until evenly coated and cook for 20 to 30 minutes at high heat settings or until shrimps are pink.

4. Garnish shrimps with remaining cilantro and serve.

Nutrition: Calories: 213 Fat: 12 g Protein: 15 g Carbs: 1.9 g Fiber: 7 g Sugar: 1.4 g

540. Shrimp in Marinara Sauce

Preparation Time: 5 minutes
Cooking Time: 5 hours
Servings: 5
Ingredients:

- 1 pound cooked wild-caught shrimps, peeled and deveined
- 14½ ounce crushed tomatoes
- ½ teaspoon minced garlic
- 1 teaspoon salt
- ½ teaspoon seasoned salt
- ¼ teaspoon ground black pepper
- ½ teaspoon crushed red pepper flakes
- ½ teaspoon dried basil
- ½ teaspoon dried oregano
- ½ tablespoon avocado oil
- 6-ounce chicken broth
- 2 tablespoons minced parsley
- ½ cup grated Parmesan cheese

Directions:

1. Place all the ingredients except for shrimps, parsley, and cheese in a 4-quart slow cooker and stir well.

2. Then plug in the slow cooker, shut with lid, and cook for 4 to 5 hours at low heat setting.

3. Then add shrimps and parsley, stir until mixed and cook for 10 minutes at high heat setting.

4. Garnish shrimps with cheese and serve.

Nutrition: Calories: 213 Fat: 12 g Protein: 15 g Carbs: 3.9 g Fiber: 7 g Sugar: 3.6 g

541. Garlic Shrimp

Preparation Time: 5 minutes
Cooking Time: 1 hour
Servings: 5
Ingredients:
For the Garlic Shrimp:

- 1½ pounds large wild-caught shrimp, peeled and deveined
- ¼ teaspoon ground black pepper
- ⅛ teaspoon ground cayenne pepper
- 2½ teaspoons minced garlic
- ¼ cup avocado oil
- 4 tablespoons unsalted butter

For the Seasoning:

- 1 teaspoon onion powder
- 1 tablespoon garlic powder
- 1 tablespoon salt
- 2 teaspoons ground black pepper
- 1 tablespoon paprika
- 1 teaspoon cayenne pepper
- 1 teaspoon dried oregano
- 1 teaspoon dried thyme

Directions:

1. Stir together all the ingredients for seasoning, garlic, oil, and butter and add to a 4-quart slow cooker.

2. Plug in the slow cooker, shut with lid, and cook for 25 to 30 minutes at high heat setting or until cooked.

3. Then add shrimps, toss until evenly coated, and continue cooking for 20 to 30 minutes at high heat setting or until shrimps are pink.

4. When done, transfer shrimps to a serving plate, top with sauce and serve.

Nutrition: Calories: 227 Fat: 13 g Protein: 21 g Carbs: 1.2 g Fiber: 7 g Sugar: 5 g

542. Poached Salmon

Preparation Time: 5 minutes
Cooking Time: 3 hours
Servings: 4
Ingredients:

- 4 steaks of wild-caught salmon

- 1 medium white onion, peeled and sliced
- 2 teaspoons minced garlic
- ½ teaspoon salt
- ⅛ teaspoon ground white pepper
- ½ teaspoon dried dill weed
- 2 tablespoons avocado oil
- 2 tablespoons unsalted butter
- 2 tablespoons lemon juice
- 1 cup water

Directions:

1. Place butter in a 4-quart slow cooker, then add salmon and drizzle with oil.

2. Place remaining ingredients in a medium saucepan, stir until mixed and bring the mixture to boil over high heat.

3. Then pour this mixture all over salmon and shut with a lid.

4. Plug in the slow cooker and cook salmon for 3 hours and 30 minutes at low heat setting or until salmon is tender.

5. Serve straight away.

Nutrition: Calories: 338 Fat: 11 g Protein: 13 g Carbs: 2.8 g Fiber: 7 g Sugar: 1.2 g

543. Lemon Pepper Tilapia

Preparation Time: 5 minutes
Cooking Time: 3 hours
Servings: 6
Ingredients:

- 6 wild-caught Tilapia fillets
- 4 teaspoons lemon-pepper seasoning, divided
- 6 tablespoons unsalted butter, divided
- ½ cup lemon juice, fresh

Directions:

1. Cut a large piece of aluminum foil for each fillet and then arrange them in a clean working space.

2. Place each fillet in the middle of the foil, then season with lemon-pepper seasoning, drizzle with lemon juice, and top with 1 tablespoon butter.

3. Gently crimp the edges of foil to form a packet and

place it into a 6-quart slow cooker.

4. Plug in the slow cooker, shut with lid and cook for 3 hours at high heat setting or until cooked through.

5. When done, carefully remove packets from the slow cooker and open the crimped edges and check the fish, it should be tender and flaky.

6. Serve straight away.

Nutrition: Calories: 321 Fat: 10 g Protein: 21 g Carbs: 1.2 g Fiber: 7 g Sugar: 1.8 g

544. Clam Chowder

Preparation Time: 5 minutes
Cooking Time: 6 hours
Servings: 6
Ingredients:

- 20-ounce wild-caught baby clams, with juice
- ½ cup chopped scallion
- ½ cup chopped celery
- 1 teaspoon salt
- 1 teaspoon ground black pepper
- 1 teaspoon dried thyme
- 1 tablespoon avocado oil
- 2 cups coconut cream, full-fat
- 2 cups chicken broth

Directions:

1. Grease a 6-quart slow cooker with oil, then add ingredients and stir until mixed.

2. Plug in the slow cooker, shut with lid and cook for 4 to 6 hours at low heat setting or until cooked through.

3. Serve straight away.

Nutrition: Calories: 190 Fat: 14 g Protein: 12 g Carbs: 4.1 g Fiber: 17 g Sugar: 3.9 g

545. Soy-Ginger Steamed Pompano

Preparation Time: 5 minutes
Cooking Time: 1 hour
Servings: 6
Ingredients:

- 1 wild-caught whole pompano, gutted and scaled
- 1 bunch scallion, diced
- 1 bunch cilantro, chopped
- 3 teaspoons minced garlic

- 1 tablespoon grated ginger
- 1 tablespoon swerve sweetener
- ¼ cup soy sauce
- ¼ cup white wine
- ¼ cup sesame oil

Directions:

1. Place scallions in a 6-quart slow cooker and top with fish.

2. Whisk together remaining ingredients, except for cilantro, and pour the mixture all over the fish.

3. Plug in the slow cooker, shut with lid and cook for 1 hour at high heat setting or until cooked through.

4. Garnish with cilantro and serve.

Nutrition: Calories: 129 Fat: 13 g Protein: 18 g Carbs: 4 g Fiber: 17 g Sugar: 3.1 g

546. Vietnamese Braised Catfish

Preparation Time: 5 minutes
Cooking Time: 6 hours
Servings: 3
Ingredients:

- 1 fillet of wild-caught catfish, cut into bite-size pieces
- 1 scallion, chopped
- 3 red chilies, chopped
- 1 tablespoon grated ginger
- ½ cup swerve sweetener
- 2 tablespoons avocado oil
- ¼ cup fish sauce, unsweetened

Directions:

1. Place a small saucepan over medium heat, add sweetener and cook until it melts.

2. Then add scallion, chilies, ginger and fish sauce and stir until mixed.

3. Transfer this mixture to a 4-quart slow cooker, add fish and toss until coated.

4. Plug in the slow cooker, shut with lid and cook for 6 hours at low heat setting until cooked.

5. Drizzle with avocado oil and serve straight away.

Nutrition: Calories: 156 Fat: 21 g Protein: 19 g Carbs: 0.2 g Fiber: 17 g Sugar: 0.1 g

547. Chili Prawns

Preparation Time: 5 minutes
Cooking Time: 1 hour
Servings: 6
Ingredients:

- 18-ounce wild-caught prawns, shell-on
- ½ cup sliced scallions
- 1 thumb-sized ginger, minced
- 1 bulb. of garlic, peeled and minced
- 1 tablespoon swerve sweetener
- 2 tablespoons apple cider vinegar
- 2 tablespoons Sambal Oelek
- 1 tablespoon fish sauce, unsweetened
- 4 tablespoons sesame oil
- ½ cup tomato ketchup, keto and unsweetened
- 1 egg, beaten

Directions:

1. Place all the ingredients, except for prawns, oil, and egg in a 6-quart slow cooker and stir until mixed.

2. Plug in the slow cooker, shut with lid, and cook for 1 hour at high heat setting.

3. Then add prawns and continue cooking for 15 minutes at a high heat setting or until prawns turn pink.

4. Stir in oil and egg and cook for 10 minutes.

5. Drizzle with more fish sauce and serve.

Nutrition: Calories: 154 Fat: 13 g Protein: 15 g Carbs: 3.6 g Fiber: 17 g Sugar: 1.7 g

548. Tuna Salpicao

Preparation Time: 5 minutes
Cooking Time: 3 hours
Servings: 2
Ingredients:

- 8 ounce cooked wild-caught tuna, cut into inch cubes
- 4 jalapeno peppers, chopped
- 5 red chili, chopped
- 1 bulb. of garlic, peeled and minced
- 1 teaspoon salt

- 1 teaspoon ground black pepper
- 1 cup avocado oil

Directions:

1. Place all the ingredients except for tuna in a 4-quart slow cooker and stir until mixed.
2. Plug in the slow cooker, shut with lid and cook for 4 hours at low heat setting.
3. Then add tuna and continue cooking for 10 minutes at a high heat setting.
4. Serve straight away.

Nutrition: Calories: 154 Fat: 13 g Protein: 15 g Carbs: 1.8 g Fiber: 17 g Sugar: 1.0 g

549. Soy-Ginger Braised Squid

Preparation Time: 5 minutes
Cooking Time: 8 hours
Servings: 6
Ingredients:

- 18-ounce wild-caught squid, cut into rings
- 2 scallions, chopped
- 2 bay leaves
- 1 tablespoon grated ginger
- 1 bulb. of garlic, peeled and minced
- ½ cup swerve sweetener
- ¼ cup soy sauce
- ¼ cup oyster sauce
- ¼ cup avocado oil
- ¼ cup white wine

Directions:

1. Plug in a 6-quart slow cooker, add all the ingredients and stir until mixed.
2. Shut with lid and cook for 8 hours at low heat setting or until cooked through.
3. Serve straight away.

Nutrition: Calories: 154 Fat: 13 g Protein: 15 g Carbs: 3.4 g Fiber: 17 g Sugar: 1.9 g

550. Sea Bass in Coconut Cream Sauce

Preparation Time: 5 minutes
Cooking Time: 1 hour
Servings: 3
Ingredients:

- 18-ounce wild-caught sea bass
- 5 jalapeno peppers
- 4 stalks of bock Choy

- 2 stalks of scallions, sliced
- 1 tablespoon grated ginger
- 1½ teaspoons salt
- 1 tablespoon fish sauce, unsweetened
- 2 cups coconut cream

Directions:

1. Stir together all the ingredients except for bok choy and fish in a bowl and add this mixture to a 6-quarts slow cooker.
2. Plug in the slow cooker, then add fish, top with bok choy, and shut with a lid.
3. Cook sea bass for 1 hour and 30 minutes or until cooked.
4. Serve straight away.

Nutrition: Calories: 315 Fat: 17 g Protein: 15 g Carbs: 2.4 g Fiber: 17 g Sugar: 3.2 g

551. Cod Chowder

Preparation Time: 20 minutes
Cooking Time: 3 hours
Servings: 6
Ingredients:

- 1 yellow onion
- 10 ounces cod
- 3 ounces bacon, sliced
- 1 teaspoon sage
- 5 ounces potatoes
- 1 carrot, grated
- 5 cups water
- 1 tablespoon almond milk
- 1 teaspoon ground coriander
- 1 teaspoon salt

Directions:

1. Peel the onion and chop it.
2. Put the chopped onion and grated carrot in the slow cooker bowl. Add the sage, almond milk, ground coriander, and water. After this, chop the cod into 6 pieces.
3. Add the fish to the slow cooker bowl too. Then chop the sliced bacon and peel the potatoes.
4. Cut the potatoes into cubes.
5. Add the ingredients to the slow cooker bowl and close the slow cooker lid.
6. Cook the chowder for 3 hours on HIGH. Ladle the

prepared cod chowder in the serving bowls.

7. Sprinkle the dish with the chopped parsley if desired. Enjoy!

Nutrition: Calories 108 Fat 4.5 Fiber 2, Carbs 3.02 Protein 10

552. Tuna in Potatoes

Preparation Time: 16 minutes
Cooking Time: 4 hours
Servings: 8
Ingredients:

- 4 large potatoes
- 8 ounces tuna, canned
- ½ cup cream cheese
- 4 ounces Cheddar cheese
- 1 garlic clove
- 1 teaspoon onion powder
- ½ teaspoon salt
- 1 teaspoon ground black pepper
- 1 teaspoon dried dill

Directions:

1. Wash the potatoes carefully and cut them into halves.
2. Wrap the potatoes in the foil and place in the slow cooker. Close the slow cooker lid and cook the potatoes on HIGH for 2 hours.
3. Meanwhile, peel the garlic clove and mince it. Combine the minced garlic clove with the cream cheese, tuna, salt, ground black pepper, onion powder, and dill.
4. Then shred Cheddar cheese and add it to the mixture.
5. Mix it carefully until homogenous.
6. When the time is over – remove the potatoes from the slow cooker and discard the foil only from the flat surface of the potatoes.
7. Then take the fork and mash the flesh of the potato halves gently. Add the tuna mixture in the potato halves and return them back to the slow cooker.
8. Cook the potatoes for 2 hours more on HIGH. Enjoy!

Nutrition: Calories 247, Fat 5.9, Fiber 4, Carbs 3.31, Protein 14

553. Shrimp Scampi

Preparation Time: 15 minutes
Cooking Time: 3 hours
Servings: 4
Ingredients:

- ¼ cup chicken bone broth
- ½ cup white cooking wine
- 2 tablespoons olive oil
- 2 tablespoons butter
- 1 tablespoon garlic, minced
- 2 tablespoons parsley, chopped
- 1 tablespoon lemon juice
- Salt and pepper to taste
- 1 pound shrimp, peeled and deveined

Directions:

1. Mix all the ingredients in your slow cooker.
2. Cover the pot.
3. Cook on low for 3 hours.

Nutrition: Calories 256 Fat 14.7 g Sodium 466 mg Carbohydrate 2.1 g Fiber 0.1 g Protein 23.3 g Sugars 2 g

554. Shrimp Boil

Preparation Time: 15 minutes
Cooking Time: 4 hours
Servings: 4
Ingredients:

- 1½ pounds potatoes, sliced into wedges
- 2 cloves garlic, peeled
- 2 ears corn
- 1 pound sausage, sliced
- ¼ cup Old Bay seasoning
- 1 tablespoon lemon juice
- 2 cups water
- 2 pounds shrimp, peeled

Directions:

1. Put the potatoes in your slow cooker. Add the garlic, corn and sausage in layers.
2. Season with the Old Bay seasoning.
3. Drizzle lemon juice on top.
4. Pour in the water.
5. Do not mix.
6. Cover the pot.
7. Cook on high for 4 hours.
8. Add the shrimp on top.
9. Cook for 15 minutes.

Nutrition: Calories 585 Fat 25.1 g Sodium 2242 mg Potassium 1166 mg Carbohydrate 3.7 g Fiber 4.9 g Protein 53.8 g Sugars 3.9 g

555. Shrimp & Sausage Gumbo

Preparation Time: 15 minutes
Cooking Time: 1 hour and 15 minutes
Servings: 4
Ingredients:

- 2 tablespoons olive oil
- 2 pounds chicken thigh fillet, sliced into cubes
- 2 cloves garlic, crushed and minced
- 1 onion, sliced
- 2 stalks celery, chopped
- 1 green bell pepper, chopped
- 1 teaspoon Cajun seasoning
- Salt to taste
- 2 cups beef broth
- 28 ounces canned crushed tomatoes
- 4 ounces sausage
- 2 tablespoons butter
- 1 pounds shrimp, peeled and deveined

Directions:

1. Pour the olive oil into a pan over medium heat.
2. Cook the garlic and chicken for 5 minutes.
3. Add the onion, celery and bell pepper.
4. Cook until tender.
5. Season with the Cajun seasoning and salt.
6. Cook for 2 minutes.
7. Stir in the sausage, broth and tomatoes.
8. Cover and cook on low for 1 hour.
9. Add the butter and shrimp to the last 10 minutes of cooking.

Nutrition: Calories 467 Fat 33 g Sodium 1274 mg Potassium 658 mg Carbohydrate 5 g Fiber 2 g Protein 33 g Sugars 5 g

556. Fish Stew

Preparation Time: 15 minutes
Cooking Time: 1 hour and 24 minutes
Servings: 2
Ingredients:

- 1 pound white fish
- 1 tablespoon lime juice
- 1 onion, sliced
- 2 cloves garlic, sliced

- 1 red pepper, sliced
- 1 jalapeno pepper, sliced
- 1 teaspoon paprika
- 2 cups chicken broth
- 2 cups tomatoes, chopped
- Salt and pepper to taste
- 2 ounces coconut milk

Directions:

1. Marinate the fish in lime juice for 10 minutes.
2. Pour the olive oil into a pan over medium heat.
3. Add the onion, garlic and peppers.
4. Cook for 4 minutes.
5. Add the rest of the ingredients except the coconut milk.
6. Cover the pot.
7. Cook on low for 1 hour.
8. Stir in the coconut milk and simmer for 10 minutes

Nutrition: Calories 323 Fat 28.6 g Sodium 490 mg Carbohydrate 1.1 g Protein 9.3 g Fiber 3.2 g Sugars 6.2 g

557. Salmon with Lemon & Dill

Preparation Time: 15 minutes
Cooking Time: 2 hours
Servings: 4
Ingredients:

- Cooking spray
- 1 teaspoon olive oil
- 2 pounds salmon
- 1 tablespoon fresh dill, chopped
- Salt and pepper to taste
- 1 clove garlic, minced
- 1 lemon, sliced

Directions:

1. Spray your slow cooker with oil.
2. Brush both sides of salmon with olive oil.
3. Season the salmon with salt, pepper, dill and garlic
4. Add to the slow cooker.
5. Put the lemon slices on top.
6. Cover the pot and cook on high for 2 hours.

Nutrition: Calories 313 Fat 15.2 g Sodium 102 mg Carbohydrate 0.7 g Fiber 0.1 g Protein 44.2 g Sugars 0 g

558. Asparagus Smoked Salmon

Preparation Time: 15 minutes
Cooking Time: 5 hours
Servings: 6
Ingredients:

- 1 tablespoon extra-virgin olive oil
- 6 large eggs
- 1 cup heavy (whipping) cream
- 2 teaspoons chopped fresh dill, plus additional for garnish
- ½ teaspoon kosher salt
- ¼ teaspoon freshly ground black pepper
- 1½ cups shredded Havarti or Monterey Jack cheese
- 12 ounces asparagus, trimmed and sliced
- 6 ounces smoked salmon, flaked

Directions:

1. Brush butter into a cooker
2. Whisk in the heavy cream with eggs, dill, salt, and pepper.
3. Stir in the cheese and asparagus.
4. Gently fold in the salmon and then pour the mixture into the prepared insert.
5. Cover and cook on low or 3 hours on high.
6. Serve warm, garnished with additional fresh dill.

Nutrition: Calories 388 Fat 19 Carbs 1.0 Protein 21

559. Salmon with Caper Sauce

Preparation Time: 5 minutes
Cooking Time: 45 minutes.
Servings: 4
Ingredients:

- ½ cup dry white wine
- ½ cup water
- 1 yellow onion, thin sliced
- ½ teaspoon salt
- ¼ teaspoon black pepper
- 4 salmon steaks
- 2 tablespoons butter
- 2 tablespoons flour
- 1 cup chicken broth
- 2 teaspoons lemon juice
- 3 tablespoons capers

Directions:

1. Combine wine, water, onion, salt and black pepper in a crockpot; cover and cook on high for 20 minutes.
2. Add salmon steaks; cover and cook on high until salmon is tender or about 20 minutes.
3. To make the sauce, in a small skillet, melt butter over medium flame. Stir in flour and cook for 1 minute.
4. Pour in chicken broth and lemon juice; whisk for 1 to 2 minutes. Add capers; serve the sauce with salmon.

Nutrition: Calories: 234 Fat: 15 g Carbs: 2 g Protein: 12 g

560. Herbed Salmon Loaf with Sauce

Preparation Time: 5 minutes
Cooking Time: 5 hours.
Servings: 4
Ingredients:

For the Salmon Meatloaf:

- 1 cup fresh bread crumbs
- 1 can (7½ ounces) salmon, drained
- ¼ cup scallions, chopped
- ⅓ cup whole milk
- 1 egg
- 1 tablespoon fresh lemon juice
- 1 teaspoon dried rosemary
- 1 teaspoon ground coriander
- ½ teaspoon fenugreek
- 1 teaspoon mustard seed
- ½ teaspoon salt
- ¼ teaspoon white pepper
- ½ cup cucumber, chopped
- ½ cup reduced-fat plain yogurt
- ½ teaspoon dill weed
- Salt, to taste

Directions:

1. Line your crockpot with a foil.
2. Mix all ingredients for the salmon meatloaf until everything is well incorporated; form into loaf and place in the crockpot.
3. Cover with a suitable lid and cook on a low heat setting for 5 hours.
4. Combine all of the ingredients for the sauce; whisk to combine.
5. Serve your meatloaf with prepared sauce.

Nutrition: Calories: 145 Fat: 11 g Carbs: 2 g Protein: 11 g

Chapter 8. Poultry and Meat Recipes

561. Beef Corn Chili
Preparation Time: 8-10 minutes
Cooking Time: 30 minutes
Servings: 8
Ingredients:

- 2 small onions, chopped (finely)
- ¼ cup canned corn
- 1 tablespoon oil
- 10 ounces lean ground beef
- 2 small chili peppers, diced

Directions:

1. Take your instant pot and place over a dry kitchen surface; open its top lid and switch it on.
2. Press. "SAUTE."
3. In its Cooking pot, add and heat the oil.
4. Add the onions, chili pepper, and beef; cook for 2-3 minutes until turn translucent and softened.
5. Add the 3 cups water to the cooking pot; combine to mix well.
6. Close its top lid and make sure that its valve is closed to avoid spilling.
7. Press "MEAT/STEW." Adjust the timer to 20 minutes.
8. Press will slowly build up; let the added ingredients cook until the timer indicates zero.
9. Press "CANCEL." Now press "NPR" for natural release pressure. Instant pot will gradually release pressure for about 8-10 minutes.
10. Open the top lid; transfer the cooked recipe to serving plates.
11. Serve the recipe warm.

Nutrition: Calories: 94 Protein: 7 g Fat: 5 g Carbohydrates: 2 g

562. Balsamic Beef Dish
Preparation Time: 5 minutes
Cooking Time: 55 minutes
Servings: 8
Ingredients:

- 3 pounds chuck roast

- 3 cloves garlic, thinly sliced
- 1 tablespoon oil
- 1 teaspoon flavored vinegar
- ½ teaspoon pepper
- ½ teaspoon rosemary
- 1 tablespoon butter
- ½ teaspoon thyme
- ¼ cup balsamic vinegar
- 1 cup beef broth

Directions:

1. Cut slits in the roast and stuff garlic slices all over.
2. Take a bowl and add flavored vinegar, rosemary, pepper, thyme and rub the mixture over the roast.
3. Set your pot to sauté mode and add oil, allow the oil to heat up.
4. Add roast and brown both sides (5 minutes each side).
5. Take the roast out and keep it on the side.
6. Add butter, broth, balsamic vinegar and deglaze the pot.
7. Transfer the roast back and lock up the lid, cook on HIGH pressure for 40 minutes.
8. Perform a quick release.
9. Remove the lid and serve!

Nutrition: Calories: 393 Protein: 37 g Fat: 15 g Carbohydrates: 25 g

563. Soy Sauce Beef Roast
Preparation Time: 8 minutes
Cooking Time: 35 minutes
Servings: 2-3
Ingredients:

- ½ teaspoon beef bouillon
- 1½ teaspoon rosemary
- ½ teaspoon minced garlic
- 2 pounds roast beef
- ⅓ cup soy sauce

Directions:

1. Mix the soy sauce, bouillon, rosemary, and garlic together in a mixing bowl.
2. Place your instant pot over a dry kitchen platform. Open the top lid and plug it on.
3. Add the roast, bowl mix and enough water to cover the roast; gently stir to mix well.

4. Properly close the top lid; make sure that the safety valve is properly locked.
5. Press "MEAT/STEW" Cooking function; set pressure level to "HIGH" and set the cooking time to 35 minutes.
6. Allow the pressure to build to cook the ingredients.
7. After cooking time is over press the "CANCEL" setting. Find and press the "NPR" Cooking function. This setting is for the natural release of inside pressure, and it takes around 10 minutes to slowly release pressure.
8. Slowly open the lid, take out the cooked meat and shred it.
9. Add the shredded meat back in the potting mix and stir to mix well.
10. Take out the cooked recipe in serving containers. Serve warm.

Nutrition: Calories: 423 Protein: 21 g Fat: 14 g Carbohydrates: 12 g

564. Rosemary Beef Chuck Roast
Preparation Time: 5 minutes
Cooking Time: 45 minutes
Servings: 5-6
Ingredients:

- 3 pounds chuck beef roast
- 3 garlic cloves
- ¼ cup balsamic vinegar
- 1 sprig fresh rosemary
- 1 sprig fresh thyme
- 1 cup of water
- 1 tablespoon vegetable oil
- Salt and pepper to taste

Directions:

1. Cut slices in the beef roast and place the garlic cloves in them.
2. Coat the roast with herbs, black pepper, and salt.
3. Preheat your instant pot using the sauté setting and add the oil.
4. When warmed, add the beef roast and stir-cook until browned on all sides.

5. Add the remaining ingredients; stir gently.
6. Seal the lid and cook on high pressure for 40 minutes using the manual setting.
7. Let the pressure release naturally, about 10 minutes.
8. Uncover the instant pot; transfer the beef roast to the serving plates, slice and serve.

Nutrition: Calories: 542 Protein: 55.2 g Fat: 11.2 g Carbohydrates: 8.7 g

565. Pork Chops and Tomato Sauce

Preparation Time: 10 minutes
Cooking Time: 20 minutes
Servings: 4
Ingredients:
- 4 pork chops, boneless
- 1 tablespoon soy sauce
- ¼ teaspoon sesame oil
- 1½ cups tomato paste
- 1 yellow onion
- 8 mushrooms, sliced

Directions:
1. In a bowl, mix pork chops with soy sauce and sesame oil, toss and leave aside for 10 minutes.
2. Set your instant pot on sauté mode, add pork chops and brown them for 5 minutes on each side.
3. Add onion, stir and cook for 1-2 minutes more.
4. Add tomato paste and mushrooms, toss, cover, and cook on high for 8-9 minutes.
5. Divide everything between plates and serve.
6. Enjoy!

Nutrition: Calories: 300 Protein: 4 g Fat: 7 g Carbohydrates: 18 g

566. Pork Potato

Preparation Time: 8-10 minutes
Cooking Time: 25 minutes
Servings: 4
Ingredients:
- 10 ounces pork neck, fat remove and make small pieces
- 1 medium sweet potato, chopped
- 1 tablespoon oil

- 3 cups beef stock, low – sodium
- 1 onion, chopped (finely)

Directions:
1. Take your pot and place over a dry kitchen surface; open its top lid and switch it on.
2. Press "sauté." Grease the pot with some cooking oil.
3. Add the onions; cook for 2 minutes until turn translucent and softened.
4. Add the meat; stir-cook for 4-5 minutes to evenly brown.
5. Mix in the stock and potatoes.
6. Close its top lid and make sure that its valve is closed to avoid spillage.
7. Press "Manual." Adjust the timer to 20 minutes.
8. Pressure will slowly build up; let the added ingredients cook until the timer indicates zero.
9. Press "CANCEL." Now press "NPR" for natural release pressure. Instant pot will gradually release pressure for about 8-10 minutes.
10. Open the top lid transfer the cooked recipe to serving plates.
11. Serve the recipe warm.

Nutrition: Calories: 278 Protein: 18 g Fat: 18 g Carbohydrates: 12 g

567. Coffee Flavored Pork Ribs

Preparation Time: 3 minutes
Cooking Time: 40 minutes
Servings: 4
Ingredients:
- 1 rack baby back ribs
- 2 teaspoons sesame oil
- 3 tablespoons oyster sauce
- 1 teaspoon salt
- 1 teaspoon sugar
- 1 cup of water
- A ½ cup of liquid smoke
- 2 tablespoons instant coffee powder

Directions:
1. Add the listed ingredients to the pot.

2. Lock the lid and cook on MEAT/STEW mode for 40 minutes.
3. Release the pressure naturally over 10 minutes.
4. Serve and enjoy!

Nutrition: Calories: 898 Protein: 77 g Fat: 63 g Carbohydrates: 4 g

568. Slow Cooker Meatloaf Recipe

Preparation Time: 10 minutes
Cooking Time: 6 hours and 10 minutes
Servings: 8
Ingredients:
- 2 pounds ground bison
- 1 grated zucchini
- 2 large eggs
- Olive oil cooking spray – as required
- 1 Zucchini, shredded
- ½ cup parsley, fresh, finely chopped
- ½ cup parmesan cheese, shredded
- 3 tablespoons balsamic vinegar
- 4 cloves garlic, grated
- 2 tablespoons onion minced, dry
- 1 tablespoon dried oregano
- ½ teaspoon Ground black pepper
- ½ teaspoon Kosher salt

For the topping:
- ¼ cup shredded Mozzarella cheese
- ¼ cup ketchup without sugar
- ¼ cup freshly chopped parsley

Directions:
1. Stripe line the inside of a six-quart slow cooker with aluminum foil.
2. Spray non-stick cooking oil over it.
3. In a large bowl combine ground bison or extra lean ground sirloin, zucchini, eggs, parsley, balsamic vinegar, garlic, dried oregano, sea or kosher salt, minced dry onion, and ground black pepper.

4. Transfer this mixture into the slow cooker and form an oblong-shaped loaf.
5. Cover the cooker, set on low heat, and cook for 6 hours.
6. After cooking, open the cooker and spread ketchup all over the meatloaf.
7. Now, place the cheese above the ketchup as a new layer and close the slow cooker.
8. Let the meatloaf sit on these two layers for about 10 minutes or until the cheese starts to melt.
9. Garnish with fresh parsley and shredded Mozzarella cheese.

Nutrition: Calories: 320 Carbohydrate: 4 g Protein: 26 g Sugars: 2 g Fat: 20 g Dietary Fiber: 1 g Cholesterol: 131 mg Sodium: 403 mg Potassium: 507 mg

569. Slow Cooker Mediterranean Beef Hoagies

Preparation Time: 10 minutes
Cooking Time: 13 hours
Servings: 6
Ingredients:

- 3 pounds beef top round roast fatless
- ½ teaspoon onion powder
- ½ teaspoon black pepper
- 3 cups low sodium beef broth
- 4 teaspoons salad dressing mix
- 1 bay leaf
- 1 tablespoon garlic, minced
- 2 red bell peppers, thin strips cut
- 16 ounces pepperoncino
- 8 slices Sargento Provolone, thin
- 2 ounces gluten-free bread
- ½ teaspoon salt

For seasoning:

- 1½ tablespoon onion powder
- 1½ tablespoon garlic powder
- 2 tablespoons dried parsley
- 1 tablespoon stevia
- ½ teaspoon dried thyme
- 1 tablespoon dried oregano
- 2 tablespoons black pepper
- 1 tablespoon salt
- 6 cheese slices

Directions:
1. Pat dry the roast with a paper towel. Combine black pepper, onion powder and salt in a small bowl and rub the mixture over the roast. Place the seasoned roast into a slow cooker.
2. Add broth, salad dressing mix, bay leaf, and garlic to the slow cooker. Combine it gently. Cover the slow cooker and set to low cooking for 12 hours. After cooking, remove the bay leaf.
3. Take out the cooked beef and shred the beef meet. Put back the shredded beef and add bell peppers and. Add bell peppers and pepperoncino into the slow cooker. Cover the cooker and low cook for 1 hour. Before serving, top each of the bread with 3 ounces of the meat mixture. Top it with a cheese slice. The liquid gravy can be used as a dip.

Nutrition: Calories: 442 Carbohydrate: 37 g Protein: 49 g Sugars: 3.5 g Fat: 11.5 g Dietary Fiber: 4 g Cholesterol: 116 mg Sodium: 873 mg

570. Beef, Artichoke & Mushroom Stew

Preparation Time: 20 minutes
Cooking Time: 2 hours and 15 minutes
Servings: 6
Ingredients:
For Beef Marinade:

- 1 onion, chopped
- 1 garlic clove, crushed
- 2 tablespoons fresh thyme, hopped
- ½ cup dry red wine
- 2 tablespoons tomato puree
- 2 tablespoons olive oil
- 1 teaspoon cayenne pepper
- Pinch of salt and ground black pepper
- 1½ pounds beef stew meat, cut into large chunks

For Stew:

- 2 tablespoons olive oil
- 2 tablespoons all-purpose flour
- ½ cup water
- ½ cup dry red wine
- 12 ounces jar artichoke hearts, drained and cut into small chunks
- 4 ounces button mushrooms, sliced
- Salt and ground black pepper, as required

Directions:
1. For the marinade: in a large bowl, add all the ingredients except the beef and mix well.
2. Add the beef and coat with the marinade generously.
3. Refrigerate to marinate overnight.
4. Remove the beef from the bowl, reserving the marinade.
5. In a large pan, heat the oil and sear the beef in 2 batches for about 5 minutes or until browned.
6. With a slotted spoon, transfer the beef into a bowl.
7. In the same pan, add the reserved marinade, flour, water and wine and stir to combine.
8. Stir in the cooked beef and bring to a boil.
9. Reduce the heat to low and simmer, covered for about 2 hours, stirring occasionally.
10. Stir in the artichoke hearts and mushrooms and simmer for about 30 minutes.
11. Stir in the salt and black pepper and bring to a boil over high heat.
12. Remove from the eat ad serve hot.

Nutrition: Calories 367 Total Fat 16.6 g Saturated Fat 4 g Cholesterol 101 mg Total Carbs 9.6 g Sugar 2.2 g Fiber 3.1 g Sodium 292 mg Potassium 624 mg Protein 36.7 g

571. Beef & Tapioca Stew

Preparation Time: 20 minutes
Cooking Time: 1 hour and 45 minutes
Servings: 8
Ingredients:

- 1 tablespoon olive oil
- 2 pounds boneless beef chuck roast, cut into ¾-inch cubes
- 1 (14½-ounce) can diced tomatoes with juice
- ¼ cup quick-cooking tapioca
- 1 tablespoon honey
- 2 teaspoons ground cinnamon
- ¼ teaspoon garlic powder
- Ground black pepper, as required
- ¼ cup red wine vinegar
- 2 cups beef broth
- 2 cups sweet potato, peeled and cubed
- 2 medium onions, cut into thin wedges
- 2 cups prunes, pitted

Directions:

1. In a Dutch oven, heat 1 tablespoon of oil over medium-high heat and sear the beef cubes in 2 batches for bout 4-5 minutes or until browned.
2. Drain off the grease from the pan.
3. Stir in the tomatoes, tapioca, honey, cinnamon, garlic powder, black pepper, vinegar and broth and bring to a boil.
4. Reduce the heat to low and simmer, covered for about 1 hour, stirring occasionally.
5. Stir in the onions and sweet potato and simmer, covered for about 20-30 minutes.
6. Stir in the prunes and cook for about 3-5 minutes.
7. Serve hot.

Nutrition: Calories 675 Total Fat34.1 g Saturated Fat 13 g Cholesterol 117 mg Total Carbs 59.6 g Sugar 26 g Fiber 7.1 g Sodium 295 mg Potassium 1150 mg Protein 34.1 g

572. Beef Pizza

Preparation Time: 20 minutes
Cooking Time: 50 minutes
Servings: 10
Ingredients:
For Crust:

- 3 cups all-purpose flour
- 1 tablespoon sugar
- 2¼ teaspoons active dry yeast
- 1 teaspoon salt
- 2 tablespoons olive oil
- 1 cup warm water

For Topping:

- 1-pound ground beef
- 1 medium onion, chopped
- 2 tablespoons tomato paste
- 1 tablespoon ground cumin
- Salt and ground black pepper, as required
- ¼ cup water
- 1 cup fresh spinach, chopped
- 8 ounces artichoke hearts, quartered
- 4 ounces fresh mushrooms, sliced
- 2 tomatoes, chopped
- 4 ounces feta cheese, crumbled

Directions:
For the crust:

1. In the bowl of a stand mixer, fitted with the dough hook, add the flour, sugar, yeast and salt.
2. Add 2 tablespoons of the oil and warm water and knead until a smooth and elastic dough is formed.
3. Make a ball of the dough and set aside for about 15 minutes.
4. Place the dough onto a lightly floured surface and roll into a circle.
5. Place the dough into a lightly, greased round pizza pan and gently, press to fit.
6. Set aside for about 10-15 minutes.
7. Coat the crust with some oil.
8. Preheat the oven to 400°F.

For topping:

1. Heat a nonstick skillet over medium-high heat and cook the beef for about 4-5 minutes.
2. Add the onion and cook for about 5 minutes, stirring frequently.
3. Add the tomato paste, cumin, salt, black pepper and water and stir to combine.
4. Reduce the heat to medium and cook for about 5-10 minutes.
5. Remove from the heat and set aside.
6. Place the beef mixture over the pizza crust and top with the spinach, followed by the artichokes, mushrooms, tomatoes, and Feta cheese.
7. Bake for about 25-30 minutes or until the cheese is melted.
8. Remove from the oven and set aside for about 3-5 minutes before slicing.
9. Cut into desired-sized slices and serve.

Nutrition: Calories 309 Total Fat 8.7 g Saturated Fat 3.3 g Cholesterol 51 mg Total Carbs 36.4 g Sugar 3.7 g Fiber 3.3 g Sodium 421 mg Potassium 502 mg Protein 21.4 g

573. Beef & Bulgur Meatballs

Preparation Time: 20 minutes
Cooking Time: 28 minutes
Servings: 6
Ingredients:

- ¾ cup uncooked bulgur
- 1-pound ground beef
- ¼ cup shallots, minced
- ¼ cup fresh parsley, minced
- ½ teaspoon ground allspice
- ½ teaspoon ground cumin
- ½ teaspoon ground cinnamon
- ¼ teaspoon red pepper flakes, crushed
- Salt, as required
- 1 tablespoon olive oil

Directions:

1. In a large bowl of cold water, soak the bulgur for about 30 minutes.
2. Drain the bulgur well and then, squeeze with your

hands to remove the excess water.

3. In a food processor, add the bulgur, beef, shallot, parsley, spices and salt and pulse until a smooth mixture is formed.
4. Transfer the mixture into a bowl and refrigerate, covered for about 30 minutes.
5. Remove from the refrigerator and make equal-sized balls from the beef mixture.
6. In a large nonstick skillet, heat the oil over medium-high heat and cook the meatballs in 2 batches for about 13-14 minutes, flipping frequently.
7. Serve warm.

Nutrition: Calories 228 Total Fat 7.4 g Saturated Fat 2.2 g Cholesterol 68 mg Total Carbs 15 g Sugar 0.1 g Fiber 3.5 g Sodium 83 mg Potassium 420 mg Protein 25.4 g

574. Tasty Beef and Broccoli

Preparation Time: 10 minutes
Cooking Time: 15 minutes
Servings: 4
Ingredients:

- 1½ pounds flanks steak, cut into thin strips
- 1 tablespoon olive oil
- 1 tablespoon tamari sauce
- 1 cup beef stock
- 1-pound broccoli, florets separated

Directions:

1. In a bowl, mix steak strips with oil and tamari, toss and leave aside for 10 minutes.
2. Set your instant pot on sauté mode, add beef strips, and brown them for 4 minutes on each side.
3. Add stock, stir, cover pot again, and cook on high for 8 minutes.
4. Add broccoli, stir, cover pot again and cook on high for 4 minutes more.
5. Divide everything between plates and serve.
6. Enjoy!

Nutrition: Calories: 312 Protein: 4 g Fat: 5 g Carbohydrates: 20 g

575. Tomato Pork Paste

Preparation Time: 5-8 minutes
Cooking Time: 15 minutes
Servings: 4
Ingredients:

- 2 cups tomato puree
- 1 tablespoon red wine
- 1-pound lean ground pork
- 8 (10-oz.) pack paste of your choice, uncooked
- Salt and black pepper to taste
- 1 tablespoon vegetable oil

Directions:

1. Season the pork with black pepper and salt.
2. Place your instant pot over a dry kitchen platform. Open the top lid and plug it on.
3. Press the "SAUTE" Cooking function; add the oil and heat it.
4. In the pot, add the ground meat; stir-cook using a wooden spatula until turns evenly brown for 8-10 minutes.
5. Add the wine. Cook for 1-2 minutes.
6. Add the ingredients; gently stir to mix well.
7. Properly close the top lid; make sure that the safety valve is properly locked.
8. Press "MEAT/STEW" Cooking function; set pressure level to "HIGH" and set the cooking time to 6 minutes.
9. Allow the pressure to build to cook the ingredients.
10. After cooking time is over press the "CANCEL" setting. Find and press the "NPR" cooking function. This setting is for the natural release of inside pressure, and it takes around 10 minutes to slowly release pressure.
11. Slowly open the lid, take out the cooked recipe in serving containers. Serve warm.

Nutrition: Calories: 423 Protein: 36 g Fat: 34 g Carbohydrates: 14 g

576. Garlic Pulled Pork

Preparation Time: 5 minutes
Cooking Time: 1 hour and 40 minutes
Servings: 12
Ingredients:

- 4-pounds pork shoulder, boneless and cut into 3 pieces
- 2 tablespoons soy sauce
- 2 tablespoons brown sugar
- 1 cup chicken broth
- 10 cloves garlic, finely chopped
- 2 tablespoons butter, melted at room temperature

Directions:

1. In a mixing bowl, combine the broth, soy sauce, and brown sugar. Add the garlic and stir to combine.
2. Preheat your instant pot using the sauté setting and add the butter.
3. When warmed, add the pork pieces and stir-cook until browned on all sides.
4. Add the soy mix; stir gently.
5. Seal the lid and cook on high pressure for 90 minutes using the manual setting.
6. Let the pressure release naturally, about 10 minutes.
7. Uncover the instant pot; take out the meat and shred it using a fork.
8. Return the shredded meat to the instant pot and stir the mixture well.
9. Transfer to serving plates and serve.

Nutrition: Calories: 142 Protein: 11.2 g Fat: 8.2 g Carbohydrates: 3.5 g

577. Buttered Pork Chops

Preparation Time: 15 minutes
Cooking Time: 15 minutes
Servings: 4
Ingredients:

- 4 pork chops
- 1 teaspoon salt
- 2 tablespoons bacon grease
- 4 tablespoons butter
- Pepper

Directions:

1. If you are looking for a quick and easy meal, look no further than buttered

pork chops! Within twenty minutes, you'll be sitting down and enjoying your meal. You will want to start off this recipe by taking out your pork chops and seasoning them on either side. If you need more than a teaspoon of salt and pepper, feel free to season as desired.

2. Next, you are going to want to place your skillet over high heat and place the bacon grease and butter into the bottom.

3. Once the butter is melted and the grease is sizzling, pop the pork chops into the skillet and sear on either side for three to four minutes. In the end, the pork should be a nice golden color.

4. When the meat is cooked as desired, remove the skillet from the heat and enjoy your meal!

Nutrition: Calories: 450 Fats: 30 g Proteins: 45 g

578. Quick and Easy Pork Loin Roast

Preparation Time: 45 minutes
Cooking Time: 30 minutes
Servings: 6
Ingredients:

- 1 tablespoon bacon grease
- Salt
- 3 pounds pork loin
- Pepper

Directions:

1. Even with just four ingredients, you will be surprised how delicious this recipe will be! Before you start cooking, you will want to go ahead and heat your oven to 375°F.

2. As the oven is warming up, take out your baking pan and gently place the pork loin into the bottom. Once in place, go ahead and rub the salt and pepper all over the sides. Be sure that each side is coated to help even out the flavor over the loin.

3. Finally, pop the dish into the oven for one hour. At the end of this time, the meat should be cooked to your liking. Remember that you will want your meat to be slightly rare to get the most nutrients from it.

4. Remove the meat from the oven, allow it to cool for several minutes, and then your meat is ready to be enjoyed.

Nutrition: Calories: 520 Fats: 35 g Protein: 50 g

579. Cheese and Ham Roll-ups

Preparation Time: 20 minutes
Cooking Time: 15 minutes
Servings: 7
Ingredients:

- 2 eggs
- 1 cup ham, diced
- ½ cup cheddar cheese, shredded
- ¾ cup mozzarella cheese, shredded
- ½ cup parmesan cheese

Directions:

1. If you ever find yourself craving a snack while following the Carnivore Diet, this little recipe should do the trick! Start off by heating your oven to 375°F.

2. As the oven warms up, take out a mixing bowl and combine the egg and shredded cheeses together. Once the clumps are taken out, you can also add in the ham and give everything a good stir.

3. Now, you will want to take out a baking sheet and line it with parchment paper. When this is in place, divide your mixture onto the parchment paper for six or eight rolls.

4. When you are ready, place it into the oven and cook these for about twenty minutes. By the end, the cheese should create a brown crust.

5. If it looks like this, remove it from the oven, allow the

roll-ups to cool, and enjoy your quick and easy snack!

Nutrition: Calories: 200 Fats: 15 g Proteins: 15 g

580. Meat Cup Snacks

Preparation Time: 25 minutes
Cooking Time: 15 minutes
Servings: 4
Ingredients:

- 6 eggs
- 6 slices ham
- Pepper
- ½ cup shredded cheddar cheese

Directions:

1. Looking for another great snack? These will be perfect for breakfast, lunch, or dinner! Start off by heating the oven to 375°F. As it warms up, you can prep for this recipe by taking out a muffin tin and greasing it up with butter or bacon grease. If you want to avoid a mess, you can also use silicone muffin tins.

2. Once you are ready, take your slices of ham and line each hole with them, carefully placing them into a bottom.

3. When the ham is in place, get out a skillet and scramble the six eggs until they reach the desired consistency. Once cooked through, go ahead and scoop the scrambled egg into the muffin tin and place it on top of the ham.

4. For a final touch, sprinkle the egg with some shredded cheddar cheese. At this point, feel free to season these cups with salt and pepper. If not, they are going to taste delicious without any seasoning!

5. Finally, pop the muffin tin into your oven for about ten minutes. At the end of this time, the cheese should be melted and a nice golden color. If it looks like this, remove from the oven, allow to cool, and enjoy!

Nutrition: Calories: 250 Fats: 15 g Proteins: 20 g

581. Pork and Cheese Stuffed Peppers

Preparation Time: 30 minutes
Cooking Time: 25 minutes
Servings: 2
Ingredients:

- 2 sweet Italian peppers, deveined and halved
- ½ Spanish onion, finely chopped
- 1 cup marinara sauce
- ½ cup cheddar cheese, grated
- 4 ounces pork, ground

Directions:

1. Heat 1 tablespoon of canola oil in a saucepan over moderate heat. Then, sauté the onion for 3 to 4 minutes until tender and fragrant.
2. Add in the ground pork; cook for 3 to 4 minutes more. Add in Italian seasoning mix. Spoon the mixture into the pepper halves.
3. Spoon the marinara sauce into a lightly greased baking dish. Arrange the stuffed peppers in the baking dish.
4. Bake in the preheated oven at 395°F for 17 to 20 minutes. Top with cheddar cheese and continue to bake for about 5 minutes or until the top is golden brown. Bon appétit!

Nutrition: 313 Calories 21.3 g Fat 5.7 g Carbs 20.2 g Protein 1.9 g Fiber

582. Peppered Pork Rack

Preparation Time: 120 minutes
Cooking Time: 1 hour and 30 minutes
Servings: 6
Ingredients:

- Pepper
- 1 pork rib rack

Directions:

1. While simple, this peppered pork rack can become a staple in your new carnivore diet because it is easy to make and delicious! You'll want to start off by heating your oven only to 375°F.
2. As the oven warms up, you will want to prepare your rib rack. Be sure that you coat the roast with pepper seasoning. While a quarter of a cup of pepper may seem like a lot, you will want this much for maximum flavor.
3. When the meat is coated, place the roast into a baking dish, bones up. If you are ready to cook your meal, pop it into the oven for one hour and thirty minutes. Once it is cooked through, you can remove it from the oven and allow it to rest for around ten minutes.
4. Finally, cut the meat between the rib bones, and your meal is ready to be served!

Nutrition: Calories: 400 Fats: 15 g Proteins: 30 g

583. Pork Belly

Preparation Time: 30 minutes
Cooking Time: 1 hour and 30 minutes
Servings: 4
Ingredients:

- 2 pounds pork belly (2 Lbs.)
- Black Pepper
- 1 tablespoon butter

Directions:

1. As you can already tell, pork belly is high in fat and high in calories. The good news is that you are on the carnivore diet, and none of that matters; bring on the pork belly! To start off, you are going to want to heat your oven to 400°F.
2. To prepare your pork belly, you are going to want to score the belly skin. You will want to be careful not to cut the meat during this step, so take your time. When this is completed, go ahead and rub on the salt and pepper. You can use as much or as little seasoning as you desire!
3. When you are ready, place the pork belly into a roasting pan and place into the oven for thirty minutes. After this time has passed, you will want to turn the heat down to 320°F and then roast it for another twenty-five minutes per half-pound of meat.
4. Once the pork belly has cooked through, you have the option to switch on the broiler for a few minutes. By doing this, you can achieve a nice, crispy skin to dig into!
5. When your meat is cooked to the desired temperature, you will want to carefully remove the dish from your oven. I suggest waiting thirty minutes or so to allow the flavors to fully form in your pork belly. After that, you can slice up the meat, and your meal is ready to be served!

Nutrition: Calories: 1,200 Fats: 120 g Proteins: 20 g

584. Easy Pork Chops

Preparation Time: 10 minutes
Cooking Time: 20 or 50 minutes
Servings: 4
Ingredients:

- 4 pork chops, boneless
- 1 tablespoon extra-virgin olive oil
- 1 cup chicken stock, low-sodium
- A pinch of black pepper
- 1 teaspoon sweet paprika

Directions:

1. Heat up a pan while using the oil over medium-high heat, add pork chops, brown them for 5 minutes on either side, add paprika, black pepper and stock, toss, cook for fifteen minutes more, divide between plates, and serve by using a side salad.
2. Enjoy!

Nutrition: Calories: 272 Fat: 4 Fiber: 8 Carbs: 14 Protein: 17

585. Coffee BBQ Pork Belly

Preparation Time: 20 minutes
Cooking Time: 50 minutes
Servings: 4
Ingredients:

- 1½ cups beef stock
- Low-carb barbecue dry rub (as needed)

- 2 tablespoons Instant Espresso Powder
- 2 pounds pork belly
- 4 tablespoons olive oil

Directions:

1. Set the oven at 350° F.
2. Warm the beef stock in a small saucepan using medium heat until hot - not boiling.
3. Mix in the dry barbecue rub and espresso powder until well combined.
4. Place the pork belly, skin side up in a shallow dish and drizzle half of the oil over the top, rubbing it over the entire pork belly.
5. Pour the hot stock around the pork belly and cover the dish tightly with aluminum foil. Bake it for 45 minutes.
6. **Note:** Slice into eight thick slices or 16 slices if you like a crispy pork belly.
7. Warm the remaining olive oil in a skillet using med-high heat and sear each slice for three minutes per side or until the desired level of crispiness is reached.

Nutrition: Calories: 644 Protein: 24 g Fat: Content: 68 g Net Carbohydrates: 3 g

586. Mustard and Rosemary Pork Tenderloin

Preparation Time: 10 minutes
Cooking Time: 15 minutes plus 5 minutes resting time
Servings: 4
Ingredients:

- ½ cup fresh parsley leaves
- ¼ cup Dijon mustard
- 6 garlic cloves
- 3 tablespoons fresh rosemary leaves
- 3 tablespoons extra-virgin olive oil
- ½ teaspoon sea salt
- ¼ teaspoon freshly ground black pepper
- 1 (1½-pound) pork tenderloin

Directions:

1. Preheat the oven to 400°F.
2. In a blender or food processor, combine the parsley, mustard, garlic, rosemary, olive oil, salt, and pepper. Pulse in 1-second pulses, about 20 times, until paste forms. Rub this paste all over the tenderloin and put the pork on a rimmed baking sheet.
3. Bake the pork for about 15 minutes, or until it registers 165°F on an instant-read meat thermometer.
4. Let rest for 5 minutes, slice, and serve.

Nutrition: Calories: 362 Total Fat: 18 g Total Carbs: 5 g Sugar: 1 g Fiber: 2 g Protein: 2 g Sodium: 515 mg

587. Stuffed Pork Loin with Sun-Dried Tomato and Goat Cheese

Preparation Time: 15 minutes
Cooking Time: 40 minutes
Servings: 6
Ingredients:

- 1 to 1½ pounds pork tenderloin
- 1 cup crumbled goat cheese
- 4 ounces frozen spinach, thawed and well-drained
- 2 tablespoons chopped sun-dried tomatoes
- 2 tablespoons extra-virgin olive oil (or seasoned oil marinade from sun-dried tomatoes), plus ¼ cup, divided
- ½ teaspoon salt
- ½ teaspoon freshly ground black pepper
- Zucchini Noodles or sautéed greens, for serving

Directions:

1. Preheat the oven to 350°F. Cut cooking twine into eight (6-inch) pieces.
2. Cut the pork tenderloin in half lengthwise, leaving about an inch border, being careful to not cut all the way through to the other side. Open the tenderloin like a book to form a large rectangle. Place it between two pieces of parchment paper or plastic wrap and pound to about ¼-inch thickness with a meat mallet, rolling pin, or the back of a heavy spoon.
3. In a small bowl, combine the goat cheese, spinach, sun-dried tomatoes, 2 tablespoons olive oil, salt, and pepper and mix to incorporate well.
4. Spread the filling over the surface of the pork, leaving a 1-inch border from one long edge and both short edges. To roll, start from the long edge with filling and roll towards the opposite edge. Tie cooking twine around the pork to secure it closed, evenly spacing each of the eight pieces of twine along the length of the roll.
5. In a Dutch oven or large oven-safe skillet, heat ¼ cup olive oil over medium-high heat. Add the pork and brown on all sides. Remove from the heat, cover, and bake until the pork is cooked through, 45 to 75 minutes, depending on the thickness of the pork. Remove from the oven and let rest for 10 minutes at room temperature.
6. To serve, remove the twine and discard. Slice the pork into medallions and serve over Zucchini Noodles or sautéed greens, spooning the cooking oil and any bits of filling that fell out during cooking over top.

Nutrition: Calories: 270 Total Fat: 21 g Total Carbs: 2 g Net Carbs: 1 g Fiber: 1 g Protein: 20 g Sodium: 323 mg

588. Meatballs in Creamy Almond Sauce

Preparation Time: 15 minutes
Cooking Time: 35 minutes
Servings: 4-6
Ingredients:

- 8 ounces ground veal or pork
- 8 ounces ground beef
- ½ cup finely minced onion, divided
- 1 large egg, beaten

- ¼ cup almond flour
- 1½ teaspoons salt, divided
- 1 teaspoon garlic powder
- ½ teaspoon freshly ground black pepper
- ½ teaspoon ground nutmeg
- 2 teaspoons chopped fresh flat-leaf Italian parsley, plus ¼ cup, divided
- ½ cup extra-virgin olive oil, divided
- ¼ cup slivered almonds
- 1 cup dry white wine or chicken broth
- ¼ cup unsweetened almond butter

Directions:

1. In a large bowl, combine the veal, beef, ¼ cup onion, and the egg and mix well with a fork. In a small bowl, whisk together the almond flour, 1 teaspoon salt, garlic powder, pepper, and nutmeg. Add to the meat mixture along with 2 teaspoons chopped parsley and incorporate well. Form the mixture into small meatballs, about 1 inch in diameter, and place on a plate. Let sit for 10 minutes at room temperature.
2. In a large skillet, heat ¼ cup oil over medium-high heat. Add the meatballs to the hot oil and brown on all sides, cooking in batches if necessary, 2 to 3 minutes per side. Remove from skillet and keep warm.
3. In the hot skillet, sauté the remaining ¼ cup minced onion in the remaining ¼ cup olive oil for 5 minutes. Reduce the heat to medium-low and add the slivered almonds. Sauté until the almonds are golden, another 3 to 5 minutes.
4. In a small bowl, whisk together the white wine, almond butter, and remaining ½ teaspoon salt. Add to the skillet and bring to a boil, stirring constantly. Reduce the heat to low, return the meatballs to skillet, and cover. Cook

until the meatballs are cooked through, another 8 to 10 minutes.
5. Remove from the heat, stir in the remaining ¼ cup chopped parsley, and serve the meatballs warm and drizzled with almond sauce.

Nutrition: Calories: 449 Total Fat: 42 g Total Carbs: 3 g Net Carbs: 2 g Fiber: 1 g Protein: 16 g Sodium: 696 mg

589. Flank Steak with Orange-Herb Pistou

Preparation Time: 10 minutes
Cooking Time: 20 minutes
Servings: 4
Ingredients:

- 1-pound flank steak
- 8 tablespoons extra-virgin olive oil, divided
- 2 teaspoons salt, divided
- 1 teaspoon freshly ground black pepper, divided
- ½ cup chopped fresh flat-leaf Italian parsley
- ¼ cup chopped fresh mint leaves
- 2 garlic cloves, roughly chopped
- Zest and juice of 1 orange or 2 clementines
- 1 teaspoon red pepper flakes (optional)
- 1 tablespoon red wine vinegar

Directions:

1. Heat the grill to medium-high heat or, if using an oven, preheat to 400°F.
2. Rub the steak with 2 tablespoons olive oil and sprinkle with 1 teaspoon salt and ½ teaspoon pepper. Let sit at room temperature while you make the pistou.
3. In a food processor, combine the parsley, mint, garlic, orange zest and juice, remaining 1 teaspoon salt, red pepper flakes (if using), and remaining ½ teaspoon pepper. Pulse until finely chopped. With the processor running, stream in the red wine vinegar and remaining 6 tablespoons olive oil until well combined. This pistou will

be more oil-based than traditional basil pesto.
4. Cook the steak on the grill, 6 to 8 minutes per side. Remove from the grill and allow to rest for 10 minutes on a cutting board. If cooking in the oven, heat a large oven-safe skillet (cast iron works great) over high heat. Add the steak and sear, 1 to 2 minutes per side, until browned. Transfer the skillet to the oven and cook for 10 to 12 minutes, or until the steak reaches your desired temperature.
5. To serve, slice the steak and drizzle with the pistou.

Nutrition: Calories: 441 Total Fat: 36 g Total Carbs: 3 g Net Carbs: 3 g Fiber: 0 g Protein: 25 g Sodium: 1237 mg

590. Braised Short Ribs with Red Wine

Preparation Time: 10 minutes
Cooking Time: 2 minutes
Servings: 4
Ingredients:

- 1½ pounds boneless beef short ribs (if using bone-in, use 3½ pounds)
- 1 teaspoon salt
- ½ teaspoon freshly ground black pepper
- ½ teaspoon garlic powder
- ¼ cup extra-virgin olive oil
- 1 cup dry red wine (such as cabernet sauvignon or merlot)
- 2 to 3 cups beef broth, divided
- 4 sprigs rosemary

Directions:

1. Preheat the oven to 350°F.
2. Season the short ribs with salt, pepper, and garlic powder. Let sit for 10 minutes.
3. In a Dutch oven or oven-safe deep skillet, heat the olive oil over medium-high heat.
4. When the oil is very hot, add the short ribs and brown until dark in color, 2 to 3 minutes per side. Remove the meat from the oil and keep warm.

5. Add the red wine and 2 cups beef broth to the Dutch oven, whisk together, and bring to a boil. Reduce the heat to low and simmer until the liquid is reduced to about 2 cups, about 10 minutes.

6. Return the short ribs to the liquid, which should come about halfway up the meat, adding up to 1 cup of remaining broth if needed. Cover and braise until the meat is very tender, about 1½ to 2 hours.

7. Remove from the oven and let sit, covered, for 10 minutes before serving. Serve warm, drizzled with cooking liquid.

Nutrition: Calories: 792 Total Fat: 76 g Total Carbs: 2 g Net Carbs: 2 g Fiber: 0 g Protein: 25 g Sodium: 783 mg

591. Beef Kofta

Preparation Time: 10 minutes
Cooking Time: 15 minutes
Servings: 4
Ingredients:

- 1 pound ground beef
- ½ cup minced onions
- 1 tablespoon olive oil
- ½ teaspoon salt
- ½ teaspoon ground coriander
- ½ teaspoon ground cumin
- ¼ teaspoon ground cinnamon
- ¼ teaspoon allspice
- ¼ teaspoon dried mint leaves

Directions:

1. Grab a large bowl and add all the ingredients.
2. Stir well to combine then use your hands to shape into ovals or balls.
3. Carefully thread onto skewers then brush with oil.
4. Pop into the grill and cook uncovered for 15 minutes, turning often.
5. Serve and enjoy.

Nutrition: Calories: 216 Net carbs: 4 g Fat: 19 g Protein: 25 g

592. Spicy Beef with Olives and Feta

Preparation Time: 3 hours
Cooking Time: 6 hours
Servings: 6-8
Ingredients:

- 2 pounds stewing beef, cut into ½" pieces
- 2 (15-oz.) cans chili-seasoned diced tomatoes, undrained
- 1 cup assorted olives, pitted and halved
- ½ teaspoon salt
- ¼ teaspoon pepper
- 2 cups cooked basmati rice
- ½ cup crumbled feta cheese

Directions:

1. Open the lid of your slow cooker and add the beef, tomatoes and olives. Stir well.
2. Cover and cook on high for 5-6 hours or low for 8-9 hours until tender.
3. Season well then serve with the rice and feta cheese.
4. Serve and enjoy.

Nutrition: Calories: 380 Net carbs: 14 g Fat: 19 g Protein: 36 g

593. Best Ever Beef Stew

Preparation Time: 1 hour
Cooking Time: 2 hours
Servings: 6
Ingredients:

- 2 tablespoons olive oil
- 1⅓ pounds extra- lean diced beef
- 1 large onion, sliced
- 1½ tablespoons chopped rosemary
- 5 garlic cloves, sliced
- 2/3 cup red wine (or extra stock)
- 1 2/3 cups beef stock
- 1 (14-oz.) can cherry tomatoes
- 3 mixed peppers, deseeded and thickly sliced
- 2 (14-oz.) can butterbeans, rinsed and drained
- 1 (2.4-oz.) pouch pitted Kalamata olives

- 2 tablespoons corn flour

Directions:

1. Preheat the oven to 280°F.
2. Place a Dutch oven over medium heat and add 1 tablespoon oil.
3. Place the beef onto a flat surface, season well, and cook in two batches.
4. Remove and place onto a plate when cooked.
5. Add the remaining oil and cook the onion, rosemary and garlic for 5 minutes until soft.
6. Add a pinch of salt then pour in the wine, scraping and browned bits from the pan.
7. Add the beef stock, tomatoes and peppers, stir well.
8. Add the beef, cover and bring to a simmer.
9. Pop into the oven and leave to cook for 2 hours.
10. Add the butterbeans and olive and pop back into the oven for 30 minutes.
11. Find a small bowl and combine the corn starch with a little water.
12. Pour gently into the stew, stir well and simmer until thickened.
13. Serve and enjoy.

Nutrition: Calories: 337 Net carbs: 15 g Fat: 10 g Protein: 31 g

594. One-Pot Mediterranean Spiced Beef and Macaroni

Preparation Time: 25 minutes
Cooking Time: 10 minutes
Servings: 4
Ingredients:

- 2 tablespoons olive oil
- 1 pound ground beef
- 1 cup onion, diced
- 3 cloves garlic minced
- 1 teaspoon ground cinnamon
- ½ teaspoon kosher salt
- ¼ teaspoon cayenne pepper
- ¼ teaspoon ground cloves
- ½ cup red wine
- 2 Roma tomatoes diced

- 8 ounces can tomato sauce
- 2 cups macaroni or cavatappi noodles
- 2 cups beef broth
- ¼ cup parmesan cheese, grated

Directions:
1. Place a large pan over medium heat and add the olive oil.
2. Add the beef, onion and garlic and cook for 10 minutes or so until soft.
3. Drain away the remaining grease then add the cinnamon, cayenne and cloves.
4. Cook for 3-4 minutes then add the red wine, tomatoes and tomato sauce.
5. Simmer for 5 minutes then add the noodles and the broth. Stir together.
6. Reduce the heat to low, cover, and cook for 25 minutes until the noodles are cooked.
7. Top with parmesan and serve.

Nutrition: Calories: 643 Net carbs: 57 g Fat: 23 g Protein: 35 g

595. Beef and Cheese Gratin

Preparation Time: 5 minutes
Cooking Time: 15 minutes
Servings: 4
Ingredients:
- 1½ pounds steak mince
- 2/3 cup beef stock
- 3 ounces mozzarella or cheddar cheese, grated
- 3 ounces butter, melted
- 7 ounces breadcrumbs
- 1 tablespoon extra-virgin olive oil
- 1 x roast vegetable pack
- 1 x red onion, diced
- 1 x red pepper, diced
- 1 (14-oz.) can chop tomatoes
- 1 x zucchini, diced
- 3 cloves garlic, crushed
- 1 tablespoon Worcestershire sauce

For the topping:
- Fresh thyme

Directions:
1. Pop a skillet over medium heat and add the oil.
2. Add the red pepper, onion, zucchini and garlic. Cook for 5 minutes.
3. Add the beef and cook for five minutes.
4. Throw in the tinned tomatoes, beef stock and Worcestershire sauce then stir well.
5. Bring to the boil then simmer for 6 minutes.
6. Divide between the bowls and top with the thyme.
7. Serve and enjoy.

Nutrition: Calories: 678 Net carbs: 24 g Fat: 45 g Protein: 48 g

596. Beef Cacciatore

Preparation Time: 10 minutes
Cooking Time: 40 minutes
Servings: 5
Ingredients:
- 1 pound beef, cut into thin slices
- ¼ cup extra-virgin olive oil
- 1 onion, chopped
- 2 red bell peppers, chopped
- 1 orange bell pepper, chopped
- Salt and pepper, to taste
- 1 cup tomato sauce

Directions:
1. Place a skillet over medium heat and add the oil.
2. Add the meat and cook until browned.
3. Add the onions and peppers and cook for 3-5 minutes.
4. Throw in the tomato sauce, salt and pepper, stir well then bring to a simmer.
5. Cover and cook for 40 minutes until the meat is tender.
6. Pour off as much sauce as you can then whizz in a blender.
7. Pour back into the pan and heat again for 5 minutes.
8. Serve with pasta or rice and enjoy.

Nutrition: Calories: 428 Net carbs: 16 g Fat: 35 g Protein: 12 g

597. Greek Beef and Veggie Skewers

Preparation Time: 20 minutes
Cooking Time: 10 minutes
Servings: 6-8
Ingredients:
For the beef skewers:
- 1½ pounds skirt steak, cut into cubes
- 1 teaspoon grated lemon zest
- ½ teaspoon coriander seeds, ground
- ½ teaspoon salt
- 2 garlic cloves, chopped
- 2 tablespoons olive oil
- 2 bell peppers, seeded and cubed
- 4 small green zucchinis, cubed
- 24 cherry tomatoes
- 2 tablespoons extra-virgin olive oil

To serve:
- Store-bought hummus
- 1 lemon, cut into wedges

Directions:
1. Grab a large bowl and add all the ingredients. Stir well.
2. Cover and pop into the fridge for at least 30 minutes, preferably overnight.
3. Preheat the grill to high and oil the grate.
4. Take a medium bowl and add the peppers, zucchini, tomatoes and oil. Season well
5. Just before cooking, start threading everything onto the skewers. Alternate veggies and meat as you wish.
6. Pop into the grill and cook for 5 minutes on each side.
7. Serve and enjoy.

Nutrition: Calories: 938 Net carbs: 65 g Fat: 25 g Protein: 87 g

598. Pork Tenderloin with Orzo

Preparation Time: 10 minutes
Cooking Time: 20 minutes
Servings: 6
Ingredients:
- 1½ pounds pork tenderloin
- 1 teaspoon coarsely ground pepper

- tablespoons extra-virgin olive oil
- 3 quarts water
- 1¼ cups uncooked orzo pasta
- ¼ teaspoon salt
- 6 ounces fresh baby spinach
- 1 cup grape tomatoes, halved
- ¾ cup crumbled feta cheese

Directions:
1. Place the pork onto a flat surface and rub with the pepper.
2. Cut into the 1" cubes.
3. Place a skillet over medium heat and add the oil.
4. Add the pork and cook for 10 minutes until no longer pink.
5. Fill a Dutch oven with water and place over medium heat. Bring to a boil.
6. Stir in the orzo and cook uncovered for 8-10 minutes.
7. Stir through the spinach then drain.
8. Add the tomatoes to the pork, heat through then stir through orzo and cheese.
9. Serve and enjoy.

Nutrition: Calories: 372 Net carbs: 34 g Fat: 11 g Protein: 31 g

599. Grilled Pork Chops with Tomato Salad

Preparation Time: 15 minutes
Cooking Time: 15 minutes
Servings: 4
Ingredients:
For the pork chops:
- 4 (6-oz.) boneless pork chops
- 1 tablespoon canola oil
- 1-2 tablespoons dry rub pork seasoning
- 1 teaspoon dried oregano

For the tomato salad:
- 1 pound medium-size tomatoes, quartered
- 1 cup fresh Italian flat leaf parsley, leaves roughly chopped
- ⅓ cup sliced red onion
- ¼ cup capers

- 1 clove garlic, pressed or minced
- 2 tablespoons extra-virgin olive oil
- ½ lemon
- ½ teaspoon kosher salt
- ½ teaspoon freshly ground black pepper
- ½ cup feta cheese

Directions:
1. Preheat the grill to 350°F.
2. Brush the pork chops with oil and season well with the rub and oregano.
3. Leave to rest for 5-10 minutes as the grill warms.
4. Meanwhile, grab a large bowl and add the salad ingredients. Stir well and pop into the fridge until ready to be served.
5. Cook the pork chops for 10 minutes or so, turning halfway through.
6. Remove from the pan and leave to rest for five minutes before cutting.
7. Enjoy with the salad and chunks of feta.

Nutrition: Calories: 340 Net carbs: 6 g Fat: 20 g Protein: 31 g

600. Boneless Pork Chops with Summer Veggies

Preparation Time: 10 minutes
Cooking Time: 25 minutes
Servings: 4
Ingredients:
- 8 thin sliced center cut boneless pork chops
- ¾ teaspoon Montreal chicken seasoning
- 1 small zucchini, julienned
- 1 small yellow squash, julienned
- 1 cup halved grape tomatoes
- 1 tablespoon extra-virgin olive oil
- Salt and pepper, to taste
- ¼ teaspoon oregano
- 3 cloves garlic, thinly sliced
- Extra-virgin olive oil, to taste
- ¼ cup pitted and sliced Kalamata olives

- ¼ cup crumbled feta cheese
- Juice of ½ lemon
- 1 teaspoon grated lemon rind

Directions:
1. Preheat the oven to 450°F.
2. Grab a medium bowl and add the tomatoes, ½ tablespoon oil, ⅛ teaspoon salt, pepper and oregano. Stir well.
3. Place onto a baking sheet and pop into the oven for 10 minutes.
4. Add the sliced garlic and cook for 5 more minutes.
5. Remove from the oven and transfer to a large bowl.
6. Reduce the oven temperature to 200°F.
7. Place a large skillet over medium heat, add ½ tablespoon olive oil, the zucchini and a pinch of salt and cook for 5 minutes until tender.
8. Transfer the zucchini to the bowl with the tomatoes and pop into the oven to keep warm.
9. Add more oil to the skillet and cook half the pork chops for about 2 minutes on each side.
10. Pop onto a platter then repeat with the second half. Pop onto a platter.
11. Remove the veggies from the oven then add the olives, lemon and lemon rind. Stir well to combine.
12. Top the pork with the veggies, top with feta then serve and enjoy.

Nutrition: Calories: 230 Net carbs: 9 g Fat: 9 g Protein: 28 g

601. One-Skillet Mediterranean Pork and Rice

Preparation Time: 20 minutes
Cooking Time: 15 minutes
Servings: 4
Ingredients:
- ½ pound roasted garlic & herb loin filet, cut in strips
- 2 tablespoons extra-virgin olive oil

- 2 carrots, chopped
- 1 bell pepper, chopped
- 1 onion, chopped
- 3 cloves garlic, minced
- ½ teaspoon oregano
- 2 cups vegetable stock
- 1 cup basmati rice
- ½ cup garbanzo beans
- 10 black pitted olives
- 1 lemon fresh parsley, chopped
- Salt and pepper, to taste

Directions:
1. Find a large skillet, add the oil and pop over medium heat.
2. Add the pork and cook for five minutes until cooked through.
3. Transfer to a plate and pop to one side.
4. Add the carrots, bell pepper, onion and garlic and season well.
5. Cook for five minutes until the veggies are tender.
6. Add the rice and stir well.
7. Add the salt, pepper, oregano, lemon zest and stock.
8. Stir then bring to a boil.
9. Cover and simmer for 12-15 minutes until the rice is cooked.
10. Add the lemon juice and pork slices and stir well.
11. Add the garbanzo beans and olives and garnish with parsley.
12. Serve and enjoy.

Nutrition: Calories: 341 Net carbs: 50 g Fat: 4 g Protein: 19 g

602. Pork Tenderloin with Roasted Vegetables

Preparation Time: 30 minutes
Cooking Time: 30 minutes
Servings: 8
Ingredients:
- 2 (1½-lb.) pork tenderloins, halved crosswise
- 1 teaspoon ground coriander
- 1 teaspoon dried thyme
- 1 teaspoon granulated or powdered garlic
- 1 teaspoon coarse or kosher salt, plus extra to taste

- ½ teaspoon freshly ground black pepper, plus extra to taste
- 10 thyme sprigs
- 4 tablespoons olive oil
- 1 large red or yellow onion, peeled and cut into 1½" chunks
- 1 large fennel bulb., trimmed and cut into 1½" chunks
- 10 small white or red potatoes, chopped into chunks
- 2 jalapeno peppers, deseeded and sliced

Directions:
1. Preheat the oven to 425°F.
2. Find a small bowl and add the coriander, thyme, garlic, salt and pepper.
3. Stir well together then rub over the pork loins.
4. Pop a heavy skillet over high heat and add about 2 tablespoons of olive oil.
5. Add the pork and sear on all sides.
6. Find a medium bowl and add the onions, fennel, potatoes, jalapenos and remaining oil.
7. Season well then toss to combine.
8. Place onto a rimmed baking sheet.
9. Top with the pork, tuck in thyme then pop into the oven for 30 minutes.
10. Remove the pork from the oven and place on a plate, covered to keep warm.
11. Spread the vegetables out over the tin and pop back into the oven for another 20 minutes until golden.
12. Slice the pork and serve with the roasted vegetables.
13. Serve and enjoy.

Nutrition: Calories: 401 Net carbs: 40 g Fat: 12 g Protein: 34 g

603. Marinated Balsamic Pork Loin Skillet

Preparation Time: 20 minutes
Cooking Time: 15 minutes
Servings: 4-6
Ingredients:
- 1 pound pork tenderloin, sliced ½" thick

- ¼ cup balsamic vinegar
- ¼ cup extra-virgin olive oil
- ½ teaspoon smoked paprika or regular paprika
- 1 tablespoon honey (optional)
- ½ teaspoon minced garlic
- Salt and pepper, to taste
- ¼ teaspoon oregano
- ¼ teaspoon dried marjoram or rosemary
- 1 cup sliced red onion
- 2 ounces sliced olives
- 1 zucchini, thinly sliced
- Fresh basil

To serve:
- Paprika or red pepper flakes
- Mixed leafy greens

Directions:
1. Grab a large bowl and add the balsamic marinade ingredients then stir well to combine.
2. Place the lamb into the bowl, stir well then pop into the fridge for at least 30 minutes to marinate.
3. When you're ready to start cooking, place a skillet over medium heat. Add a drop of oil to prevent sticking then add the onion and cook for 5 minutes until soft.
4. Add the pork loin and remaining marinade, stir well then cook on medium for 5 minutes.
5. Flip the pork and add the olive and zucchini.
6. Cook for 5 minutes more until the pork is no longer pink.
7. Serve and enjoy.

Nutrition: Calories: 309 Net carbs: 7 g Fat: 19 g Protein: 26 g

604. Ground Pork and Beef Chili with Tomato and Basil

Preparation Time: 10 minutes
Cooking Time: 20 minutes
Servings: 5
Ingredients:
- 3 tablespoons olive oil
- 1 large onion, finely chopped
- 5 garlic cloves, finely chopped

- 1 teaspoon dried red chili flakes
- 2 red bell peppers, finely chopped
- 1 pound ground beef
- 1 pound ground pork
- ½ cup red wine
- 3 cups canned chopped tomatoes
- ½ cup roughly chopped fresh basil
- Salt and pepper

Directions:
1. Add the olive oil to a large sauté pan over a medium-high heat
2. Add the onions, garlic, chili, and bell peppers and stir as they soften together, for about 3 minutes
3. Add the pork and beef and stir as they turn from pink to brown
4. Add the wine and allow the alcohol to burn off for about 2 minutes
5. Add the tomatoes, basil, salt and pepper, cover and allow to simmer for about 15 minutes. If it appears to be drying out, add a little water!
6. Serve hot, with brown rice pasta, or a side salad

Nutrition: Calories: 589 Fat: 36.9 g Protein: 44.5 g Total carbs: 14.4 g Net carbs: 12.5 g

605. Meatballs in Fresh Tomato Sauce

Preparation Time: 15 minutes
Cooking Time: 25 minutes
Servings: 4
Ingredients:
Meatballs:
- 4 garlic cloves, crushed
- 1 onion, finely chopped
- 1 pound ground beef
- 1 teaspoon each dried oregano, thyme, and rosemary
- 1 egg
- ½ cup whole grain bread crumbs
- Salt and pepper

Sauce:
- 2 tablespoons olive oil
- 2 garlic cloves
- ½ onion, finely chopped
- ½ cup red wine
- 8 fresh tomatoes, chopped
- 2 tablespoons pure tomato paste
- ½ fresh red chili, finely chopped (optional)
- Salt and pepper
- ½ cup beef stock or water

To Servings:
- ½ cup dried whole grain pasta (per serving), boiled in salty water until soft, but with a little "bite"
- 1 cup broccoli (per serving), steamed

Directions:
1. Preheat the oven to 380°F and line a baking tray with baking paper
2. In a large bowl combine all of the meatball ingredients with clean hands, or a very sturdy wooden spoon
3. Roll the meatball mixture into golf ball-sized balls and place them onto the lined tray, pop the tray into the oven and cook the meatballs for about 25 minutes, turning once, until golden all around
4. Drizzle the olive oil into a large sauté pan over a medium-high heat
5. Add the garlic and onions to the pan and allow them to soften, as you stir, for about 2 minutes
6. Add the wine to the pan and allow to reduce for a few minutes
7. Add the tomatoes, tomato paste, chili, salt, and pepper and stir to combine
8. Allow the sauce to simmer and become rich for about 5 minutes, adding a little water or beef stock if it appears to be drying out
9. Add the cooked meatballs to the sauté pan and drench them in sauce
10. Serve the meatballs on sauce on a small bed of whole-grain pasta, with steamed broccoli on the side

Nutrition: Calories: 610 Fat: 22.4 g Protein: 38.1 g Total carbs: 64.9 g Net carbs: 54.2 g

606. Pork Medallions with Roasted Fennel

Preparation Time: 15 minutes
Cooking Time: 30 minutes
Servings: 4
Ingredients:
- 4 pork medallions
- 2 tablespoons olive oil
- 1 sprig fresh thyme
- 1 sprig fresh rosemary
- 1 pound fennel bulbs, cut into quarters, (lengthwise)
- 3 tablespoons olive oil
- Salt and pepper

Directions:
1. Preheat the oven to 450°F and line a baking tray with baking paper
2. Lay the fennel bulb. quarters onto the tray and rub with olive oil, salt and pepper. Slip the tray into the oven and roast the fennel for 30 minutes, turning once. We're aiming for soft, slightly caramelized, golden fennel quarters!
3. As the fennel is roasting: place a large skillet over a high medium-heat
4. Lay the pork medallions onto a large board and use a wooden spoon to gently "bash" them
5. Rub the pork on both sides with olive oil and sprinkle with salt and pepper
6. Lay the pork medallions onto the hot pan, nestle the thyme and rosemary between them, and sear on both sides for about 2 minutes or until each side is golden and the meat is cooked through but still juicy
7. Let the pork rest for a few minutes before serving with roasted fennel!

Nutrition: Calories: 439 Fat: 20.2 g Protein: 37.2 g Total carbs: 8.3 g Net carbs: 4.8 g

607. Stuffed Bell Peppers with Beef and Mushrooms

Preparation Time: 10 minutes
Cooking Time: 20 minutes
Servings: 4
Ingredients:

- 4 large red bell peppers, halved, seeds removed
- 1 tablespoon olive oil
- 2 garlic cloves, finely chopped
- 1 onion, finely chopped
- 1 pound ground beef
- 4 large Portobello mushrooms, finely chopped
- 1 tomato, finely chopped
- 1 teaspoon each dried thyme, oregano, and rosemary
- Salt and pepper
- Parmesan cheese (about 2-oz.)

Directions:

1. Preheat the oven to 400°F and line a baking tray with baking paper
2. Prep the bell peppers and lay them on the lined tray, set aside
3. Drizzle the olive oil into a large sauté pan over a medium-high heat
4. Add the garlic and onion and stir as they soften for a minute or two
5. Add the beef and mushrooms, stir to combine, and allow the beef to turn from pink to brown
6. Add the tomatoes, herbs, salt and pepper to the meat, stir, and leave to simmer for about 10 minutes. (Note: the beef and mushroom mixture will likely be quite wet, which is fine!)
7. Spoon the beef mixture into the awaiting bell pepper halves and grate a small scattering of parmesan cheese over each one
8. Bake for about 20 minutes or until the peppers are soft!

Nutrition: Calories: 363 Fat: 16.3 g Protein: 33.7 g Total carbs: 19.6 g Net carbs: 13.2 g

608. Seasoned Beef Kebabs

Preparation Time: 15 minutes
Cooking Time: 10 minutes
Servings: 6
Ingredients:

- 2 pounds beef fillet
- 1½ teaspoons salt
- 1 teaspoon freshly ground black pepper
- ½ teaspoon ground allspice
- ½ teaspoon ground nutmeg
- ⅓ cup extra-virgin olive oil
- 1 large onion, cut into 8 quarters
- 1 large red bell pepper, cut into 1-inch cubes

Directions:

1. Preheat a grill, grill pan, or lightly oiled skillet to high heat.
2. Cut the beef into 1-inch cubes and put them in a large bowl.
3. In a small bowl, mix together the salt, black pepper, allspice, and nutmeg.
4. Pour the olive oil over the beef and toss to coat the beef. Then evenly sprinkle the seasoning over the beef and toss to coat all pieces.
5. Skewer the beef, alternating every 1 or 2 pieces with a piece of onion or bell pepper.
6. To cook, place the skewers on the grill or skillet, and turn every 2 to 3 minutes until all sides have cooked to desired doneness, 6 minutes for medium-rare, 8 minutes for well done. Serve warm.

Nutrition: Calories: 485 Protein: 35 g Total Carbohydrates: 4 g Sugars: 2 g Fiber: 1 g Total Fat: 36 g Saturated Fat: 11 g Cholesterol: 114 mg Sodium: 1,453 mg

609. Grilled Skirt Steak over Traditional Mediterranean Hummus

Preparation Time: 10 minutes
Cooking Time: 10 minutes
Servings: 4
Ingredients:

- 1-pound skirt steak
- 1 teaspoon salt
- ½ teaspoon freshly ground black pepper
- 2 cups prepared hummus (see Creamy Traditional Hummus)
- 1 tablespoon extra-virgin olive oil
- ½ cup pine nuts

Directions:

1. Preheat a grill, grill pan, or lightly oiled skillet to medium heat.
2. Season both sides of the steak with salt and pepper.
3. Cook the meat on each side for 3 to 5 minutes; 3 minutes for medium, and 5 minutes on each side for well done. Let the meat rest for 5 minutes.
4. Slice the meat into thin strips.
5. Spread the hummus on a serving dish, and evenly distribute the beef on top of the hummus.
6. In a small saucepan, over low heat, add the olive oil and pine nuts. Toast them for 3 minutes, constantly stirring them with a spoon so that they don't burn.
7. Spoon the pine nuts over the beef and serve.

Nutrition: Calories: 602 Protein: 42 g Total Carbohydrates: 20 g Sugars: 1 g Fiber: 8 g Total Fat: 41 g Saturated Fat: 9 g Cholesterol: 68 mg Sodium: 1,141 mg

610. Spanish Pepper Steak

Preparation Time: 10 minutes
Cooking Time: 20 minutes
Servings: 4
Ingredients:

- 1-pound beef fillet
- 1 tablespoon smoked paprika
- ¼ cup extra-virgin olive oil
- 3 tablespoons garlic, minced
- 1½ teaspoons salt
- 1 large onion, sliced
- 2 large bell peppers, any color, sliced

Directions:

1. Cut the beef into thin strips. Season with paprika.

2. In a large skillet over medium heat, cook the olive oil, garlic, beef, and salt for 7 minutes, using tongs to toss.
3. Turn the heat to low and add in the onion. Cook for 7 minutes.
4. Add the bell peppers and cook for 6 minutes.

Nutrition: Calories: 441 Protein: 28g Total Carbohydrates: 12g Sugars: 4 g Fiber: 3 g Total Fat: 32 g Saturated Fat: 9 g Cholesterol: 85 mg Sodium: 1,529 mg

611. Grilled Kefta

Preparation Time: 10 minutes
Cooking Time: 5 minutes
Servings: 4
Ingredients:

- 1 medium onion
- ⅓ cup fresh Italian parsley
- 1-pound ground beef
- ¼ teaspoon ground cumin
- ¼ teaspoon cinnamon
- 1 teaspoon salt
- ½ teaspoon freshly ground black pepper

Directions:

1. Preheat a grill or grill pan to high.
2. Mince the onion and parsley in a food processor until finely chopped.
3. In a large bowl, using your hands, combine the beef with the onion mix, ground cumin, cinnamon, salt, and pepper.
4. Divide the meat into 6 portions. Form each portion into a flat oval.
5. Place the patties on the grill or grill pan and cook for 3 minutes on each side.

Nutrition: Calories: 203 Protein: 24 g Total Carbohydrates: 3 g Sugars: 1 g Fiber: 1 g Total Fat: 10 g Saturated Fat: 4 g Cholesterol: 70 mg Sodium: 655 mg

612. Tahini Beef and Potatoes

Preparation Time: 10 minutes
Cooking Time: 30 minutes
Servings: 4-6
Ingredients:

- 1-pound ground beef
- 2 teaspoons salt, divided
- ½ teaspoon freshly ground black pepper
- 1 large onion, finely chopped
- 10 medium golden potatoes
- 2 tablespoons extra-virgin olive oil
- 3 cups Greek yogurt
- 1 cup tahini
- 3 cloves garlic, minced
- 2 cups water

Directions:

1. Preheat the oven to 450°F.
2. In a large bowl, using your hands, combine the beef with 1 teaspoon salt, black pepper, and onion.
3. Form meatballs of medium size (about 1-inch), using about 2 tablespoons of the beef mixture. Place them in a deep 8-by-8-inch casserole dish.
4. Cut the potatoes into ¼-inch-thick slices. Toss them with olive oil.
5. Lay the potato slices flat on a lined baking sheet.
6. Put the baking sheet with the potatoes and the casserole dish with the meatballs in the oven and bake for 20 minutes.
7. In a large bowl, mix together the yogurt, tahini, garlic, remaining 1 teaspoon salt, and water; set aside.
8. Once you take the meatballs and potatoes out of the oven, use a spatula to transfer the potatoes from the baking sheet to the casserole dish with the meatballs, and leave the beef drippings in the casserole dish for added flavor.
9. Reduce the oven temperature to 375°F and pour the yogurt tahini sauce over the beef and potatoes. Return it to the oven for 10 minutes. Once baking is complete, serve warm with a side of rice or pita bread.

Nutrition: Calories: 1,078 Protein: 58 g Total Carbohydrates: 89 g Sugars: 12 g Fiber: 11 g Total Fat: 59

g Saturated Fat: 14 g Cholesterol: 94 mg Sodium: 1,368 mg

613. Mediterranean Pork Chops

Preparation Time: 20 minutes
Cooking Time: 10 minutes
Servings: 4
Ingredients:

- ¼ cup extra-virgin olive oil
- 1 teaspoon smoked paprika
- 2 tablespoons fresh thyme leaves
- 1 teaspoon salt
- 4 pork loin chops, ½-inch-thick

Directions:

1. In a small bowl, mix together the olive oil, paprika, thyme, and salt.
2. Put the pork chops in a plastic zip-top bag or a bowl and coat them with the spice mix. Let them marinate for 15 minutes.
3. Preheat a grill, grill pan, or lightly oiled skillet to high heat. Cook the pork chops for 4 minutes on each side. Serve with a Greek salad.

Nutrition: Calories: 282 Protein: 21 g Total Carbohydrates: 1 g Sugars: 0 g Fiber: 0 g Total Fat: 23 g Saturated Fat: 5 g Cholesterol: 55 mg Sodium: 832 mg

614. Pork Souvlaki

Preparation Time: 1 hour and 15 minutes
Cooking Time: 10 minutes
Servings: 4
Ingredients:

- 1 (1½-lb.) pork loin
- 2 tablespoons garlic, minced
- ⅓ cup extra-virgin olive oil
- ⅓ cup lemon juice
- 1 tablespoon dried oregano
- 1 teaspoon salt
- Pita bread and tzatziki, for serving (optional)

Directions:

1. Cut the pork into 1-inch cubes and put them into a bowl or plastic zip-top bag.
2. In a large bowl, mix together the garlic, olive oil, lemon juice, oregano, and salt.

3. Pour the marinade over the pork and let it marinate for at least 1 hour.
4. Preheat a grill, grill pan, or lightly oiled skillet to high heat. Using wood or metal skewers, thread the pork onto the skewers.
5. Cook the skewers for 3 minutes on each side, for 12 minutes in total.
6. Serve with pita bread and tzatziki sauce, if desired.

Nutrition: Calories: 416 Protein: 32 g Total Carbohydrates: 5 g Sugars: 1 g Fiber: 1 g Total Fat: 30 g Saturated Fat: 7 g Cholesterol: 82 mg Sodium: 1,184 mg

615. Coriander and Coconut Chicken

Preparation Time: 10 minutes
Cooking Time: 30 minutes
Servings: 4
Ingredients:

- 2 pounds chicken thighs, skinless, boneless and cubed
- 2 tablespoons olive oil
- Salt and black pepper to the taste
- 3 tablespoons coconut flesh, shredded
- 1½ teaspoons orange extract
- 1 tablespoon ginger, grated
- ¼ cup orange juice
- 2 tablespoons coriander, chopped
- 1 cup chicken stock
- ¼ teaspoon red pepper flakes

Directions:

1. Heat up a pan with the oil over medium-high heat, add the chicken, and brown for 4 minutes on each side.
2. Add salt, pepper and the rest of the ingredients, bring to a simmer and cook over medium heat for 20 minutes.
3. Divide the mix between plates and serve hot.

Nutrition: calories 297, fat 14.4, fiber 9.6, carbs 22, protein 25

616. Saffron Chicken Thighs and Green Beans

Preparation Time: 10 minutes
Cooking Time: 25 minutes
Servings: 4
Ingredients:

- 2 pounds chicken thighs, boneless and skinless
- 2 teaspoons saffron powder
- 1-pound green beans, trimmed and halved
- ½ cup Greek yogurt
- Salt and black pepper to the taste
- 1 tablespoon lime juice
- 1 tablespoon dill, chopped

Directions:

1. In a roasting pan, combine the chicken with the saffron, green beans and the rest of the ingredients, toss a bit, introduce in the oven and bake at 400°F for 25 minutes.
2. Divide everything between plates and serve.

Nutrition: calories 274, fat 12.3, fiber 5.3, carbs 20.4, protein 14.3

617. Bold Chorizo Paella

Preparation Time: 5 minutes
Cooking Time: 30 minutes
Servings: 4
Ingredients:

- 3 tablespoons extra-virgin olive oil
- large onion, chopped
- 2 cloves garlic, minced
- 2 tablespoons tomato paste
- 1 teaspoon paprika
- 1 teaspoon saffron thread
- 1-pound Spanish chorizo sausage
- 2 cups Bomba or Arborio rice
- 1½ teaspoons salt
- 5 cups water

Directions:

1. In a large, deep skillet over medium heat, cook the olive oil and onion for 3 to 5 minutes. Add garlic and cook for another minute.
2. Stir in the tomato paste, paprika, and saffron. Stir in the chorizo and rice, and cook for 3 minutes.

3. Add the salt and water. Stir to combine, turn heat to low, and let simmer for 10 minutes. Give the rice a gentle stir and cook for another 12 to 15 minutes.
4. Serve warm.

Nutrition: Calories: 747 Protein: 23 g Total Carbohydrates: 76 g Sugars: 2 g Fiber: 2 g Total Fat: 39 g Saturated Fat: 12 g Cholesterol: 80 mg Sodium: 1,593 mg

618. Moist Shredded Beef

Preparation Time: 10 minutes
Cooking Time: 20 minutes
Servings: 8
Ingredients:

- 2 lbs. beef chuck roast, cut into chunks
- ½ tablespoons dried red pepper
- 1 tablespoon Italian seasoning
- 1 tablespoon garlic, minced
- 2 tablespoons vinegar
- 14 ounces can fire-roasted tomatoes
- ½ cup bell pepper, chopped
- ½ cup carrots, chopped
- 1 cup onion, chopped
- 1 teaspoon salt

Directions:

1. Add all ingredients into the inner pot of the instant pot and set the pot on sauté mode.
2. Seal pot with lid and cook on high for 20 minutes.
3. Once done, release pressure using quick release. Remove lid.
4. Shred the meat using a fork.
5. Stir well and serve.

Nutrition: Calories 456 Fat 32.7 g Carbohydrates 7.7 g Sugar4.1 g Protein 31 g Cholesterol 118 mg

619. Hearty Beef Ragu

Preparation Time: 10 minutes
Cooking Time: 50 minutes
Servings: 4
Ingredients:

- 1½ lbs. beef steak, diced
- 1½ cup beef stock
- 1 tablespoon coconut amino
- 14 ounces can tomato, chopped
- ½ teaspoon ground cinnamon

- 1 teaspoon dried oregano
- 1 teaspoon dried thyme
- 1 teaspoon dried basil
- 1 teaspoon paprika
- 1 bay leaf
- 1 tablespoon garlic, chopped
- ½ teaspoon cayenne pepper
- 1 celery stick, diced
- 1 carrot, diced
- 1 onion, diced
- 2 tablespoons olive oil
- ¼ teaspoon pepper
- 1½ teaspoon sea salt

Directions:
1. Add oil into the instant pot and set the pot on sauté mode.
2. Add celery, carrots, onion, and salt and sauté for 5 minutes.
3. Add meat and remaining ingredients and stir everything well.
4. Seal pot with lid and cook on high for 30 minutes.
5. Once done, allow to release pressure naturally for 10 minutes then release remaining using quick release. Remove lid.
6. Shred meat using a fork. Set pot on sauté mode and cook for 10 minutes. Stir every 2-3 minutes.
7. Serve and enjoy.

Nutrition: Calories 435 Fat 18.1 g Carbohydrates 12.3 g Sugar 5.5 g Protein 54.4 g Cholesterol 152 mg

620. Dill Beef Brisket
Preparation Time: 10 minutes
Cooking Time: 50 minutes
Servings: 4
Ingredients:
- 2½ lbs. beef brisket, cut into cubes
- 2½ cups beef stock
- 2 tablespoons dill, chopped
- 1 celery stalk, chopped
- 1 onion, sliced
- 1 tablespoon garlic, minced
- Pepper
- Salt

Directions:
1. Add all ingredients into the inner pot of the instant pot and stir well.

2. Seal pot with lid and cook on high for 50 minutes.
3. Once done, allow to release pressure naturally for 10 minutes then release remaining using quick release. Remove lid.
4. Serve and enjoy.

Nutrition: Calories 556 Fat 18.1 g Carbohydrates 4.3 g Sugar 1.3 g Protein 88.5 g Cholesterol 253 mg

621. Tasty Beef Stew
Preparation Time: 10 minutes
Cooking Time: 30 minutes
Servings: 4
Ingredients:
- 2½ lbs. beef roast, cut into chunks
- 1 cup beef broth
- ½ cup balsamic vinegar
- 1 tablespoon honey
- ½ teaspoon red pepper flakes
- 1 tablespoon garlic, minced
- Pepper
- Salt

Directions:
1. Add all ingredients into the inner pot of the instant pot and stir well.
2. Seal pot with lid and cook on high for 30 minutes.
3. Once done, allow to release pressure naturally. Remove lid.
4. Stir well and serve.

Nutrition: Calories 562 Fat 18.1 g Carbohydrates 5.7 g Sugar 4.6 g Protein 87.4 g Cholesterol 253 mg

622. Meatloaf
Preparation Time: 10 minutes
Cooking Time: 35 minutes
Servings: 6
Ingredients:
- 2 lbs. ground beef
- 2 eggs, lightly beaten
- ¼ teaspoon dried basil
- 3 tablespoons olive oil
- ½ teaspoon dried sage
- 1½ teaspoon dried parsley
- 1 teaspoon oregano
- 2 teaspoons thyme
- 1 teaspoon rosemary
- Pepper
- Salt

Directions:
1. Pour 1½ cups of water into the instant pot then place the trivet in the pot.
2. Spray loaf pan with cooking spray.
3. Add all ingredients into the mixing bowl and mix until well combined.
4. Transfer the meat mixture into the prepared loaf pan and place the loaf pan on top of the trivet in the pot.
5. Seal pot with lid and cook on high for 35 minutes.
6. Once done, allow to release pressure naturally for 10 minutes then release remaining using quick release. Remove lid.
7. Serve and enjoy.

Nutrition: Calories 365 Fat 18 g Carbohydrates 0.7 g Sugar 0.1 g Protein 47.8 g Cholesterol 190 mg

623. Flavorful Beef Bourguignon
Preparation Time: 10 minutes
Cooking Time: 20 minutes
Servings: 4
Ingredients:
- 1½ lbs. beef chuck roast, cut into chunks
- 2/3 cup beef stock
- 2 tablespoons fresh thyme
- 1 bay leaf
- 1 teaspoon garlic, minced
- 8 ounces mushrooms, sliced
- 2 tablespoons tomato paste
- 2/3 cup dry red wine
- 1 onion, sliced
- 4 carrots, cut into chunks
- 1 tablespoon olive oil
- Pepper
- Salt

Directions:
1. Add oil into the instant pot and set the pot on sauté mode.
2. Add meat and sauté until brown. Add onion and sauté until softened.
3. Add remaining ingredients and stir well.
4. Seal pot with lid and cook on high for 12 minutes.

5. Once done, allow to release pressure naturally. Remove lid.
6. Stir well and serve.

Nutrition: Calories 744 Fat 51.3 g Carbohydrates 14.5 g Sugar 6.5 g Protein 48.1 g Cholesterol 175 mg

624. Delicious Beef Chili
Preparation Time: 10 minutes
Cooking Time: 35 minutes
Servings: 8
Ingredients:
- 2 lbs. ground beef
- 1 teaspoon olive oil
- 1 teaspoon garlic, minced
- 1 small onion, chopped
- 2 tablespoons chili powder
- 1 teaspoon oregano
- ½ teaspoon thyme
- 28 ounces can tomato, crushed
- 2 cups beef stock
- 2 carrots, chopped
- 3 sweet potatoes, peeled and cubed
- Pepper
- Salt

Directions:
1. Add oil into the instant pot and set the pot on sauté mode.
2. Add meat and cook until brown.
3. Add remaining ingredients and stir well.
4. Seal pot with lid and cook on high for 35 minutes.
5. Once done, allow to release pressure naturally. Remove lid.
6. Stir well and serve.

Nutrition: Calories 302 Fat 8.2 g Carbohydrates 19.2 g Sugar 4.8 g Protein 37.1 g Cholesterol 101 mg

625. Basic Meatballs
Preparation Time: 15 minutes
Cooking Time: 15 minutes
Servings: 4
Ingredients:
- 1 pound 90% lean ground beef
- 1 onion, finely chopped
- 1 garlic clove, minced
- 1 large egg, beaten
- ¼ cup Homemade Bread Crumbs or store-bought unseasoned bread crumbs

- 1 tablespoon Italian seasoning
- ½ teaspoon salt
- ¼ teaspoon freshly ground black pepper
- 2 tablespoons olive oil

Directions:
1. In a large bowl, combine the ground beef, onion, garlic, egg, bread crumbs, Italian seasoning, salt, and pepper. Use clean hands to mix until well blended.
2. Shape 1 tablespoon of the meatball mixture into a ball, and place on a large plate. Repeat with the remaining mixture to make about 20 meatballs.
3. In a large skillet over medium heat, heat the olive oil. When the oil is shimmering, add the meatballs and cook, covered, about 15 minutes, browning on all sides until a thermometer inserted into a meatball reads 155°F.
4. Serve warm or freeze for later. To freeze, store cooled meatballs in a freezer-safe container in the freezer for up to 2 months. To defrost, refrigerate overnight. Reheat meatballs in a saucepan along with some Basic Tomato Sauce: Bring the sauce to a boil, then lower and simmer for 10 to 15 minutes until the meatballs are warmed through. Single-serve portions can be reheated in the microwave on high for about 2 minutes.

Nutrition: Calories: 269 Total Fat: 15 g Saturated Fat: 5 g Protein: 26 g Carbohydrates: 6 g Fiber: 1 g Sodium: 427 mg

626. Olive and Feta Burgers
Preparation Time: 15 minutes
Cooking Time: 15 minutes
Servings: 4
Ingredients:
- 1 pound 90% lean ground beef
- ½ cup crumbled feta cheese
- ½ cup pitted Kalamata olives, chopped

- 1 garlic clove, minced
- 1 large egg, beaten
- ¼ cup Homemade Bread Crumbs or store-bought unseasoned bread crumbs
- ¼ teaspoon freshly ground black pepper
- 2 tablespoons olive oil

Directions:
1. In a large bowl, combine the ground beef, feta, olives, garlic, egg, bread crumbs, and pepper.
2. Use clean hands to evenly divide the mixture into 4 burger patties.
3. In a large skillet or grill pan over medium-high heat, heat the olive oil. When the oil is shimmering, add the patties and cook for 3 to 5 minutes on each side, until browned and cooked through.

Nutrition: Calories: 325 Total Fat: 21 g Saturated Fat: 8 g Protein: 28 g Carbohydrates: 5 g Fiber: 1 g Sodium: 388 mg

627. Meatloaf in a Pinch
Preparation Time: 15 minutes
Cooking Time: 1 hour
Servings: 8
Ingredients:
- Cooking spray
- 1½ pounds 90% lean ground beef
- 1 cup Homemade Barbecue Sauce or store-bought barbecue sauce, divided
- ¾ cup quick-cooking oats
- 1 onion, finely chopped
- 1 garlic clove, minced
- 1 large egg, beaten
- ½ teaspoon salt
- ¼ teaspoon freshly ground black pepper

Directions:
1. Preheat the oven to 350°F. Coat a 9-by-5-inch loaf pan with cooking spray.
2. In a large bowl, add the ground beef, ½ cup of barbecue sauce, and the oats, onion, garlic, egg, salt, and pepper. Use clean hands to mix until well combined.

3. Place the meat mixture into the prepared loaf pan, making sure the top is level. Pour the remaining ½ cup of barbecue sauce over the meatloaf, using a spatula or the back of a wooden spoon to evenly spread it.

4. Bake for about 1 hour, until a thermometer inserted into the center of the meatloaf reads 155°F.

5. Remove from the oven, and allow to cool for 10 minutes. Cut into 8 equal slices.

6. Serve warm or freeze for later. To freeze, store cooled meatloaf sliced in a freezer-safe container in the freezer for up to 2 months. To defrost, refrigerate overnight. Reheat individual portions in the microwave on high for 1 to 1½ minutes.

Nutrition: Calories: 244 Total Fat: 10 g Saturated Fat: 4 g Protein: 19 g Carbohydrates: 18 g Fiber: 1 g Sodium: 546 mg

628. Skirt Steak Fajitas

Preparation Time: 15 minutes, plus 30 minutes to marinate
Cooking Time: 15 minutes
Servings: 4
Ingredients:

- 2 tablespoons olive oil
- 1 garlic clove, minced
- 1½ teaspoons smoked paprika
- ½ teaspoon ground cumin
- ½ teaspoon salt, divided
- ¼ teaspoon freshly ground black pepper, divided
- 1¼ pounds skirt steak
- Cooking spray
- 2 yellow bell peppers, seeded and cut into ¼-inch strips
- 1 large onion, thinly sliced

Directions:

1. In a large bowl, whisk the olive oil, garlic, paprika, cumin, ¼ teaspoon of salt, and ⅛ teaspoon of pepper. Add the skirt steak and toss to evenly coat. Cover the

bowl and marinate in the refrigerator for at least 30 minutes and up to overnight.

2. Coat a large grill pan with cooking spray and heat over medium-high heat. Add the skirt steak and cook for 8 to 12 minutes, turning once, until it reaches an internal cooking temperature of 145°F.

3. Remove the steak from the grill pan and transfer to a cutting board to cool for 5 minutes.

4. Coat the grill pan again with cooking spray. Add the peppers and onion, and cook for about 5 minutes, until the vegetables soften.

5. Meanwhile, cut the steak into 1-inch strips.

6. Add the steak strips and the remaining ¼ teaspoon of salt and remaining ⅛ teaspoon of pepper to the pan with the vegetables, and toss to combine.

7. Serve warm or freeze for later. To freeze, place cooled meat and vegetables in a resalable container in the freezer for up to 2 months. To defrost, refrigerate overnight. Reheat on the stove-top over medium heat for 8 to 10 minutes, until heated through. Individual portions can be reheated in the microwave on high for 1½ to 2 minutes.

Nutrition: Calories: 367 Total Fat: 25 g Saturated Fat: 8 g Protein: 30 g Carbohydrates: 7 g Fiber: 2 g Sodium: 355 mg

629. Grilled Steak with Herb Sauce

Preparation Time: 10 minutes
Cooking Time: 20 minutes
Servings: 4
Ingredients:

- Cooking spray
- 1 (1¼-pound) sirloin steak
- ½ teaspoon salt
- ⅛ teaspoon freshly ground black pepper

- 1 cup roughly chopped fresh cilantro leaves and stems
- 2 tablespoons capers, drained
- 2 scallions, roughly chopped
- 2 tablespoons olive oil
- ¼ cup water
- Juice of 1 lemon
- 1 garlic clove, minced

Directions:

1. Preheat the oven to 400°F. Coat an ovenproof grill pan or skillet with cooking spray.

2. Sprinkle both sides of the steak with salt and pepper.

3. Heat the prepared grill pan over high heat. When the pan is hot, add the steak and cook on each side for 2 minutes. Place the pan in the oven and roast for about 12 minutes, until the steak reaches an internal temperature of 145°F.

4. Remove from the oven and transfer the steak to a cutting board to rest for 5 minutes.

5. Meanwhile, in a blender, add the cilantro, capers, scallions, olive oil, water, lemon juice, and garlic, and blend until almost smooth but still a little chunky.

6. Thinly slice the steak, and serve with the herb sauce.

Nutrition: Calories: 335 Total Fat: 23 g Saturated Fat: 7 g Protein: 30 g Carbohydrates: 2 g Fiber: 0 g Sodium: 493 mg

630. Beef Tenderloin with Red Wine Reduction

Preparation Time: 10 minutes
Cooking Time: 30 minutes
Servings: 4
Ingredients:

- Cooking spray
- 4 (5-oz.) beef tenderloin steaks
- ½ teaspoon salt, divided
- ¼ teaspoon freshly ground black pepper, divided
- 1 cup dry red wine
- 1 shallot, finely chopped

- 1 tablespoon tomato paste
- ½ cup low-sodium beef broth

Directions:

1. Coat a grill pan with cooking spray and heat over medium heat.
2. Sprinkle the steaks with ¼ teaspoon of salt and ⅛ teaspoon of pepper.
3. When the cooking spray is shimmering, place the steaks in the pan and cook for 7 to 10 minutes, turning once, until a thermometer inserted into the thickest part reads 145°F. Transfer the steaks to a platter.
4. In a small saucepan, add the wine, shallot, and tomato paste, and bring to a boil. Reduce heat and simmer for 8 minutes, stirring occasionally, until the liquid is reduced by about half. Add the beef broth and return the mixture to a boil. Reduce heat and simmer for another 8 minutes, until the liquid is again reduced by about half. Add the remaining ¼ teaspoon of salt and remaining ⅛ teaspoon of pepper, and stir to combine.
5. Top each steak with 3 tablespoons of red wine reduction.

Nutrition: Calories: 230 Total Fat: 10 g Saturated Fat: 4 g Protein: 31 g Carbohydrates: 3 g Fiber: 1 g Sodium: 425 mg

631. Slow Cooker Shredded Barbecue Beef

Preparation Time: 15 minutes
Cooking Time: 6 to 8 hours
Servings: 6
Ingredients:

- 1 (4-lb.) pot roast, like bottom round
- ½ cup Homemade Barbecue Sauce or bottled barbecue sauce
- ½ cup low-sodium beef broth

Directions:

1. Place the pot roast in a slow cooker and cover with the barbecue sauce and beef broth. Using the back of a wooden spoon or spatula, spread the barbecue sauce over the pot roast. Cover and cook on low for 6 to 8 hours, until a thermometer inserted into the center of the roast reads 145°F.
2. Remove the roast and transfer to a plate, reserving the sauce. Allow the roast to cool for 10 minutes.
3. Using two forks, shred the beef and place into a large bowl. Add the reserved sauce and toss to coat.
4. Serve warm or freeze for later. To freeze, store cooled beef in a freezer-safe container in the freezer for up to 2 months. To defrost, refrigerate overnight. Reheat in a saucepan over medium heat for 5 to 10 minutes, until the beef and sauce are warmed through. Single-serve portions can be reheated in the microwave on high for about 1½ minutes.

Nutrition: Calories: 434 Total Fat: 13 g Saturated Fat: 5 g Protein: 67 g; Carbohydrates: 8 g Fiber: 0 g Sodium: 464 mg

632. Slow Cooker Beef with Bell Peppers

Preparation Time: 10 minutes
Cooking Time: 6 to 8 hours
Servings: 6
Ingredients:

- 1 (2-lbs.) top round steak or London broil
- ½ teaspoon salt
- ¼ teaspoon freshly ground black pepper
- 1 large onion, thinly sliced
- 2 red bell peppers, seeded and cut into ¼-inch strips
- ¾ cup Basic Tomato Sauce or jarred tomato sauce
- ½ cup low-sodium beef broth

Directions:

1. Season the steak with salt and pepper, and place in the slow cooker. Top with the onion, peppers, tomato sauce, and broth. Stir to combine.
2. Cover and cook on low for 6 to 8 hours, until the beef, reaches an internal cooking temperature of 145°F.
3. Cut the steak into thin slices and serve warm or freeze for later. To freeze, place cooled steak with vegetables and liquid into a resealable container in the freezer for up to 2 months. To defrost, refrigerate overnight. Reheat in a large skillet on the stovetop for about 10 minutes, or reheat individual portions in the microwave on high for about 2 minutes.

Nutrition: Calories: 248 Total Fat: 9 g Saturated Fat: 3 g Protein: 34 g Carbohydrates: 6 g Fiber: 2 g Sodium: 386 mg

633. Pork Larb

Preparation Time: 10 minutes
Cooking Time: 15 minutes
Servings: 4
Ingredients:

- 1 tablespoon olive oil
- 1-pound ground pork
- ¼ cup Thai Dressing
- 3 shallots, thinly sliced
- ½ cup chopped fresh cilantro
- 24 Bibb lettuce leaves

Directions:

1. In a medium skillet over medium heat, heat the olive oil. When the oil is shimmering, add the ground pork and cook for 10 to 12 minutes, until browned, using a wooden spoon to break it up. Remove from heat and drain any liquid. Allow the pork to cool for 10 minutes.
2. Pour the Thai Dressing into a medium bowl. Add the cooked pork and toss to blend. Add the shallots and cilantro, and gently stir to incorporate.
3. Scoop 2 tablespoons of the meat into each of 24 lettuce leaves. Serve warm.

Nutrition: Calories: 402 Total Fat: 33 g Saturated Fat: 8 g Protein: 22 g;

Carbohydrates: 6 g Fiber: 1 g Sodium: 131 mg

634. Herbed Pork Meatballs

Preparation Time: 15 minutes
Cooking Time: 15 minutes
Servings: 4
Ingredients:

- 1-pound ground pork
- 1 onion, finely chopped
- 1 garlic clove, minced
- 1 large egg, beaten
- ½ cup whole-wheat panko bread crumbs
- ½ cup finely chopped fresh parsley
- ½ teaspoon salt
- ¼ teaspoon freshly ground black pepper
- 2 tablespoons olive oil

Directions:

1. In a large bowl, combine the ground pork, onion, garlic, egg, bread crumbs, parsley, salt, and pepper.
2. Shape 1 tablespoon of the pork mixture into a ball, and place on a large plate. Repeat with the remaining mixture to make about 20 meatballs.
3. In a large skillet over medium heat, heat the olive oil. When the oil is shimmering, add the meatballs and cook, covered, for about 15 minutes, browning on all sides until a thermometer inserted into a meatball reads 155°F.
4. Serve warm or freeze for later. To freeze, store cooled meatballs in a resalable container in the freezer for up to 2 months. To defrost, refrigerate overnight. Reheat the meatballs in a saucepan along with Basic Tomato Sauce: Bring the sauce to a boil, then lower and simmer for 10 to 15 minutes until the meatballs are warmed through. Single-serve portions of meatballs can be reheated in the microwave on high for about 2 minutes.

Nutrition: Calories: 365 Total Fat: 26 g Saturated Fat: 7 g Protein: 23 g Carbohydrates: 9 g Fiber: 1 g Sodium: 406 mg

635. Asian-Spiced Pork Loin

Preparation Time: 10 minutes, plus 30 minutes to marinate
Cooking Time: 50 minutes
Servings: 8
Ingredients:

- ⅓ cup low-sodium soy sauce
- 2 garlic cloves, minced
- 3 tablespoons Chinese five-spice powder
- 2 tablespoons light brown sugar
- 1 teaspoon cayenne pepper
- ½ teaspoon salt
- 1 (2-lbs.) pork loin, fat trimmed
- Cooking spray

Directions:

1. In a medium bowl, whisk together the soy sauce, garlic, Chinese five-spice powder, brown sugar, cayenne, and salt. Add the pork loin, and turn to evenly coat. Cover the bowl and marinate in the refrigerator for at least 30 minutes or up to overnight.
2. Preheat the oven to 400°F. Coat a baking sheet with cooking spray.
3. Transfer the pork to the baking sheet, discarding the marinade. Bake for 40 to 50 minutes, until a thermometer inserted into the thickest part of the loin reads 145°F.
4. Remove from the oven, and transfer to a cutting board to cool for 10 minutes. Cut into ¾-inch-thick slices.
5. Serve warm or freeze for later. To freeze, store cooled pork in a freezer-safe container in the freezer for up to 2 months. To defrost, refrigerate overnight. Reheat several slices in the microwave on high for 1 to 2 minutes.

Nutrition: Calories: 164 Total Fat: 5 g Saturated Fat: 2 g Protein: 25 g Carbohydrates: 5 g Fiber: 0 g Sodium: 502 mg

636. Pork Tenderloin with Apple-Tarragon Sauce

Preparation Time: 5 minutes
Cooking Time: 25 minutes
Servings: 4
Ingredients:

- 1 tablespoon olive oil
- 1 (1¼-lbs.) pork tenderloin
- 2 medium apples, cored and sliced
- 1 tablespoon unsalted butter
- 2 garlic cloves, minced
- 2 cups apple cider vinegar
- ½ teaspoon salt
- ⅛ teaspoon freshly ground black pepper
- 2 teaspoons chopped fresh tarragon

Directions:

1. Preheat the oven to 400°F.
2. In a large ovenproof skillet over medium heat, heat the olive oil. When the oil is shimmering, add the pork tenderloin and cook for about 8 minutes, turning occasionally, until browned on all sides.
3. Add the apple slices, and place the skillet in the oven. Bake for about 20 minutes, until the pork reaches a minimum internal temperature of 145°F. Place the pork on a cutting board to cool for 5 minutes. Transfer the apples to a plate, and set aside.
4. Carefully return the skillet to the stovetop over medium heat, and add the butter. When the butter is melted, add the garlic and cook until fragrant, 1 minute. Add the apple cider vinegar, and use a wooden spoon to scrape the pork bits from the bottom of the pan. Bring the mixture to a boil, then reduce heat and simmer for 2 minutes, until the flavors combine. Add the salt, pepper, and

tarragon, and stir to incorporate. Turn off the heat.

5. Thinly slice the cooled pork tenderloin, then return it to the skillet. Add the apples and toss to evenly coat. Transfer to a serving dish and serve warm.

Nutrition: Calories: 256 Total Fat: 9 g Saturated Fat: 3 g Protein: 29 g Carbohydrates: 13 g Fiber: 2 g Sodium: 641 mg

637. Miso-Garlic Pork Chops

Preparation Time: 10 minutes, plus 30 minutes to marinate
Cooking Time: 10 minutes
Servings: 4
Ingredients:

- ⅓ cup white miso
- ⅓ cup sake
- ⅓ cup mirin
- 2 teaspoons minced fresh ginger
- 1 garlic clove, minced
- 4 (5-oz.) boneless pork loin chops
- Cooking spray, or
- 1 tablespoon olive oil

Directions:

1. In a large bowl, mix the miso, sake, mirin, ginger, and garlic into a smooth paste.
2. Add the pork chops and turn to coat all sides with the glaze. Marinate in the refrigerator for at least 30 minutes or up to overnight.
3. Coat a grill pan with cooking spray and heat over medium heat. Alternatively, brush the grates of an outdoor grill with olive oil. When the pan or grill is hot, cook the pork chops for about 3 to 5 minutes on each side, until they reach an internal cooking temperature of 145°F.

Nutrition: Calories: 209 Total Fat: 4 g Saturated Fat: 1 g Protein: 32g; Carbohydrates: 12 g Fiber: 1 g Sodium: 932 mg

638. Slow Cooker Honey Mustard Pork with Pears

Preparation Time: 10 minutes
Cooking Time: 3 to 4 hours on high for 6 to 8 hours on low
Servings: 8
Ingredients:

- ¼ cup Homemade Honey Mustard
- ⅓ cup low-sodium chicken broth
- ½ teaspoon salt
- ¼ teaspoon freshly ground black pepper
- 1 (2-lbs.) boneless pork loin, fat trimmed
- 2 pears, peeled, cored, and thinly sliced
- 1 tablespoon cornstarch
- 2 tablespoons water

Directions:

1. In a small bowl, whisk together the honey mustard, broth, salt, and pepper.
2. Place the pork and pears in the slow cooker. Pour the honey mustard mixture over the top.
3. Cover and cook on high for 3 to 4 hours or on low for 6 to 8 hours.
4. Remove the pork from the slow cooker, retaining the pears and liquid, and transfer to a cutting board to cool for 10 minutes, then thinly slice.
5. In a small bowl, whisk together the cornstarch and water.
6. In a medium skillet over medium heat, heat the pears and liquid from the slow cooker. Add the cornstarch mixture and continue whisking for about 3 minutes, until the mixture thickens.
7. Serve the pork slices topped with the warm sauce, or freeze for later. To freeze, store cooled pork in a freezer-safe container in the freezer for up to 2 months. To defrost, refrigerate overnight. Reheat in a saucepan over medium heat for 5 to 10 minutes, until the pork and sauce are warmed through. Single-serve portions can be reheated in the microwave on high for about 1½ minutes.

Nutrition: Calories: 212 Total Fat: 8 g Saturated Fat: 2 g Protein: 24 g Carbohydrates: 9 g Fiber: 1 g Sodium: 368 mg

639. Slow Cooker Cranberry Pork Chops

Preparation Time: 10 minutes
Cooking Time: 3 hours on high or 6 hours on low
Servings: 4
Ingredients:

- 4 (5-oz.) boneless pork chops
- ½ teaspoon salt
- ¼ teaspoon freshly ground black pepper
- 1 onion, thinly sliced
- 1½ cups fresh or thawed frozen cranberries
- ½ cup apple juice
- ¼ cup balsamic vinegar
- 2 tablespoons honey

Directions:

1. Season both sides of the pork chops with salt and pepper.
2. In a slow cooker, add the pork chops, onion, and cranberries.
3. In a small bowl, whisk together the apple juice, balsamic vinegar, and honey. Pour over the pork chops.
4. Cover and cook on high for 3 hours or on low for 6 hours.
5. Serve warm or freeze for later. To freeze, store cooled pork chops with the sauce in a freezer-safe container in the freezer for up to 2 months. To defrost, refrigerate overnight. Reheat the pork chops and sauce in a saucepan over medium-high heat for about 10 minutes. Alternatively, reheat individual pork chops

with sauce in the microwave on high for about 2 minutes.

Nutrition: Calories: 278 Total Fat: 10 g Saturated Fat: 3 g Protein: 24 g; Carbohydrates: 21 g; Fiber 2 g Sodium: 361 mg

640. Chicken and Olives

Preparation Time: 10 minutes
Cooking Time: 15 minutes
Servings: 4
Ingredients:

- 4 chicken breasts, skinless and boneless
- 2 tablespoons garlic, minced
- 1 tablespoon oregano, dried
- Salt and black pepper to the taste
- 2 tablespoons olive oil
- ½ cup chicken stock
- Juice of 1 lemon
- 1 cup red onion, chopped
- 1½ cups tomatoes, cubed
- ¼ cup green olives, pitted and sliced
- 1 handful parsley, chopped

Directions:

1. Heat up a pan with the oil over medium-high heat, add the chicken, garlic, salt and pepper and brown for 2 minutes on each side.
2. Add the rest of the ingredients, toss, bring the mix to a simmer and cook over medium heat for 13 minutes.
3. Divide the mix between plates and serve.

Nutrition: Calories 135, Fat 5.8, Fiber 3.4, Carbs 12.1, Protein 9.6

641. Chicken Bake

Preparation Time: 10 minutes
Cooking Time: 30 minutes
Servings: 4
Ingredients:

- 1½ pounds chicken thighs, skinless, boneless and cubed
- 2 garlic cloves, minced
- 1 tablespoon oregano, chopped
- 2 tablespoons olive oil
- 1 tablespoon red wine vinegar
- ½ cup canned artichokes, drained and chopped
- 1 red onion, sliced

- 1-pound whole wheat fusilli pasta, cooked
- ½ cup canned white beans, drained and rinsed
- ½ cup parsley, chopped
- 1 cup mozzarella, shredded
- Salt and black pepper to the taste

Directions:

1. Heat up a pan with half of the oil over medium-high heat, add the meat and brown for 5 minutes.
2. Grease a baking pan with the rest of the oil, add the browned chicken, and the rest of the ingredients except the pasta and the mozzarella.
3. Spread the pasta all over and toss gently.
4. Sprinkle the mozzarella on top and bake at 425°F for 25 minutes.
5. Divide the bake between plates and serve.

Nutrition: Calories 195, Fat 5.8, Fiber 3.4, Carbs 12.1, Protein 11.6

642. Chicken and Artichokes

Preparation Time: 10 minutes
Cooking Time: 20 minutes
Servings: 4
Ingredients:

- 2 pounds chicken breast, skinless, boneless and sliced
- A pinch of salt and black pepper
- 4 tablespoons olive oil
- 8 ounces canned roasted artichoke hearts, drained
- 6 ounces sun-dried tomatoes, chopped
- 3 tablespoons capers, drained
- 2 tablespoons lemon juice

Directions:

1. Heat up a pan with half of the oil over medium-high heat, add the artichokes and the other ingredients except the chicken, stir and sauté for 10 minutes.
2. Transfer the mix to a bowl, heat up the pan again with the rest of the oil over medium-high heat, add the

meat and cook for 4 minutes on each side.
3. Return the veggie mix to the pan, toss, cook everything for 2-3 minutes more, divide between plates and serve.

Nutrition: Calories 552, Fat 28, Fiber 6, Carbs 33, Protein 43

643. Chicken Kebabs

Preparation Time: 30 minutes
Cooking Time: 20 minutes
Servings: 4
Ingredients:

- 2 chicken breasts, skinless, boneless and cubed
- 1 red bell pepper, cut into squares
- 1 red onion, roughly cut into squares
- 2 teaspoons sweet paprika
- 1 teaspoon nutmeg, ground
- 1 teaspoon Italian seasoning
- ¼ teaspoon smoked paprika
- A pinch of salt and black pepper
- ¼ teaspoon cardamom, ground
- Juice of 1 lemon
- 3 garlic cloves, minced
- ½ cup olive oil

Directions:

1. In a bowl, combine the chicken with the onion, the bell pepper and the other ingredients, toss well, cover the bowl and keep in the fridge for 30 minutes.
2. Assemble skewers with chicken, peppers and onions, place them on your preheated grill and cook over medium heat for 8 minutes on each side.
3. Divide the kebabs between plates and serve with a side salad.

Nutrition: Calories 262, Fat 14, Fiber 2, Carbs 14, Protein 20

644. Chili Chicken Mix

Preparation Time: 10 minutes
Cooking Time: 18 minutes
Servings: 4
Ingredients:

- 2 pounds chicken thighs, skinless and boneless
- 2 tablespoons olive oil
- 2 cups yellow onion, chopped

- 1 teaspoon onion powder
- 1 teaspoon smoked paprika
- 1 teaspoon chili pepper
- ½ teaspoon coriander seeds, ground
- 2 teaspoons oregano, dried
- 2 teaspoon parsley flakes
- 30 ounces canned tomatoes, chopped
- ½ cup black olives, pitted and halved

Directions:

1. Set the instant pot on Sauté mode, add the oil, heat it up, add the onion, onion powder and the rest of the ingredients except the tomatoes, olives and the chicken, stir and sauté for 10 minutes.
2. Add the chicken, tomatoes and olives put the lid on, and cook on high for 8 minutes.
3. Release the pressure naturally for 10 minutes, divide the mix into bowls and serve.

Nutrition: Calories 153, Fat 8, Fiber 2, Carbs 9, Protein 12

645. Chicken Pilaf

Preparation Time: 10 minutes
Cooking Time: 30 minutes
Servings: 4
Ingredients:

- 4 tablespoons avocado oil
- 2 pounds chicken breasts, skinless, boneless and cubed
- ½ cup yellow onion, chopped
- 4 garlic cloves, minced
- 8 ounces brown rice
- 4 cups chicken stock
- ½ cup kalamata olives, pitted
- ½ cup tomatoes, cubed
- 6 ounces baby spinach
- ½ cup feta cheese, crumbled
- A pinch of salt and black pepper
- 1 tablespoon marjoram, chopped
- 1 tablespoon basil, chopped

- Juice of ½ lemon & ¼ cup pine nuts, toasted

Directions:

1. Heat up a pot with 1 tablespoon avocado oil over medium-high heat, add the chicken, some salt and pepper, brown for 5 minutes on each side, and transfer to a bowl.
2. Heat up the pot again with the rest of the avocado oil over medium heat, add the onion and garlic and sauté for 3 minutes.
3. Add the rice, the rest of the ingredients except the pine nuts, also return the chicken, toss, bring to a simmer and cook over medium heat for 20 minutes.
4. Divide the mix between plates, top each serving with some pine nuts and serve.

Nutrition: Calories 283, Fat 12.5, Fiber 8.2, Carbs 21.5, Protein 13.4

646. Chicken and Sweet Potatoes

Preparation Time: 10 minutes
Cooking Time: 40 minutes
Servings: 6
Ingredients:

- 2 pounds chicken breasts, skinless, boneless and sliced
- 2 tablespoons harissa seasoning
- Juice of 1 lemon
- Zest of 1 lemon, grated
- ¼ cup olive oil
- Salt and black pepper to the taste
- 2 sweet potatoes, peeled and roughly cubed
- 1 sweet onion, chopped
- ½ cup feta cheese, crumbled
- ½ cup green olives, pitted and smashed

Directions:

1. In a roasting pan, combine the chicken with the seasoning and the rest of the ingredients except the cheese and the olives, toss and bake at 425°F for 40 minutes.

2. In a bowl, combine the cheese with the smashed olives and stir well.
3. Divide the chicken and sweet potatoes between plates, top each serving with the cheese and olives mix, and serve right away.

Nutrition: Calories 303, Fat 9.5, Fiber 9.2, Carbs 21.5, Protein 13.6

647. Chicken and Cashews Mix

Preparation Time: 10 minutes
Cooking Time: 30 minutes
Servings: 4
Ingredients:

- 1½ pounds chicken breasts, skinless, boneless and roughly cubed
- 4 spring onions, chopped
- 2 tablespoons olive oil
- 2 carrots, peeled and sliced
- ¼ cup mayonnaise
- ½ cup Greek yogurt
- 1 cup cashews, toasted and chopped
- A pinch of salt and black pepper

Directions:

1. Heat up a pan with the oil over medium-high heat, add the chicken and cook for 4 minutes on each side.
2. Add the onions, carrots and the rest of the ingredients except the cashews, toss, bring to a simmer and cook over medium heat for 20 minutes.
3. Divide the mix into bowls and serve with the cashews sprinkled on top.

Nutrition: Calories 304, Fat 13.2, Fiber 6.5, Carbs 19.1, Protein 15.4

648. Chicken, Corn and Peppers

Preparation Time: 5 minutes
Cooking Time: 1 hour
Servings: 4
Ingredients:

- 2 pounds chicken breast, skinless, boneless and cubed
- 2 tablespoons olive oil
- 2 garlic cloves, minced
- 1 red onion, chopped

- 2 red bell peppers, chopped
- ¼ teaspoon cumin, ground
- 2 cups corn
- ½ cup chicken stock
- 1 teaspoon chili powder
- ¼ cup cilantro, chopped

Directions:
1. Heat up a pot with the oil over medium-high heat, add the chicken and brown for 4 minutes on each side.
2. Add the onion and the garlic and sauté for 5 minutes more.
3. Add the rest of the ingredients, stir, bring to a simmer over medium heat and cook for 45 minutes.
4. Divide into bowls and serve.

Nutrition: Calories 332, Fat 16.1, Fiber 8.4, Carbs 25.4, Protein 17.4

649. Walnut Turkey and Peaches

Preparation Time: 10 minutes
Cooking Time: 1 hour
Servings: 4
Ingredients:
- 2 turkey breasts, skinless, boneless and sliced
- ¼ cup chicken stock
- 1 tablespoon walnuts, chopped
- 1 red onion, chopped
- Salt and black pepper to the taste
- 2 tablespoons olive oil
- 4 peaches, pitted and cut into quarters
- 1 tablespoon cilantro, chopped

Directions:
1. In a roasting pan greased with the oil, combine the turkey and the onion and the rest of the ingredients except the cilantro, introduce in the oven and bake at 390°F for 1 hour.
2. Divide the mix between plates, sprinkle the cilantro on top and serve.

Nutrition: Calories 500, Fat 14, Fiber 3, Carbs 15, Protein 10

650. Balsamic Turkey Bites and Apricots

Preparation Time: 5 minutes
Cooking Time: 1 hour
Servings: 4
Ingredients:
- 1 cup apricots, pitted and cubed
- ¼ cup chicken stock
- 1 big turkey breast, skinless, boneless and cubed
- 1 tablespoon balsamic vinegar
- 1 sweet onion, chopped
- ¼ teaspoon red pepper flakes
- 2 tablespoons olive oil
- Salt and black pepper to the taste
- 2 tablespoons parsley, chopped

Directions:
1. Heat up a pan with the oil over medium-high heat, add the turkey and brown for 3 minutes on each side.
2. Add the onion, pepper flakes and vinegar and cook for 5 minutes more.
3. Add the remaining ingredients except for the parsley, toss, introduce the pan in the oven and bake at 380°F for 50 minutes.
4. Divide the mix between plates and serve with the parsley sprinkled on top.

Nutrition: Calories 292, Fat 16.7, Fiber 8.6, Carbs 24.8, Protein 14.4

651. Chipotle Turkey and Tomatoes

Preparation Time: 10 minutes
Cooking Time: 1 hour
Servings: 4
Ingredients:
- 2 pounds cherry tomatoes, halved
- 3 tablespoons olive oil
- 1 red onion, roughly chopped
- 1 big turkey breast, skinless, boneless and sliced
- 3 garlic cloves, chopped
- 3 red chili peppers, chopped
- 4 tablespoons chipotle paste
- Zest of ½ lemon, grated
- Juice of 1 lemon
- Salt and black pepper to the taste

- 1 handful coriander, chopped

Directions:
1. Heat up a pan with the oil over medium-high heat, add the turkey slices, cook for 4 minutes on each side and transfer to a roasting pan.
2. Heat up the pan again over medium-high heat, add the onion, garlic and chili peppers and sauté for 2 minutes.
3. Add the chipotle paste, sauté for 3 minutes more and pour over the turkey slices.
4. Toss the turkey slices with the chipotle mix, also add the rest of the ingredients except the coriander, introduce in the oven and bake at 400°F for 45 minutes.
5. Divide everything between plates, sprinkle the coriander on top and serve.

Nutrition: Calories 264, Fat 13.2, Fiber 8.7, Carbs 23.9, Protein 33.2

652. Parmesan Chicken and Cream

Preparation Time: 10 minutes
Cooking Time: 25 minutes
Servings: 4
Ingredients:
- 1½ pounds chicken breasts, skinless, boneless and cubed
- 1 tablespoon olive oil
- 1 teaspoon coriander, ground
- 1 teaspoon parsley flakes
- 2 garlic cloves, minced
- 1 cup heavy cream
- Salt and black pepper to the taste
- ¼ cup parmesan cheese, grated
- 1 tablespoon basil, chopped

Directions:
1. Heat up a pan with the oil over medium-high heat, add the chicken, salt and pepper and cook for 3 minutes on each side.
2. Add the garlic and cook for 1 more minute.
3. Add the rest of the ingredients except the parmesan and basil, cook

everything over medium heat for 20 minutes, and divide between plates.

4. Sprinkle the basil and the parmesan on top and serve.

Nutrition: Calories 249, Fat 16.6, Fiber 7.5, Carbs 24.5, Protein 25.3

653. Oregano Chicken and Zucchini Pan

Preparation Time: 10 minutes
Cooking Time: 30 minutes
Servings: 4
Ingredients:

- 2 cups tomatoes, peeled and crushed
- 1½ pounds chicken breast, boneless, skinless and cubed
- 2 tablespoons olive oil
- Salt and black pepper to the taste
- 1 small yellow onion, sliced
- 2 garlic cloves, minced
- 2 zucchinis, sliced
- 2 tablespoons oregano, chopped
- 1 cup chicken stock

Directions:

1. Heat up a pan with the oil over medium-high heat, add the chicken, and brown for 3-minute on each side.
2. Add the onion and the garlic and sauté for 4 minutes more.
3. Add the rest of the ingredients except the oregano, bring to a simmer and cook over medium heat and cook for 20 minutes.
4. Divide the mix between plates, sprinkle the oregano on top and serve.

Nutrition: Calories 228, Fat 9.5, Fiber 9.1, Carbs 15.6, Protein 18.6

654. Creamy Chicken and Grapes

Preparation Time: 10 minutes
Cooking Time: 20 minutes
Servings: 4
Ingredients:

- 1½ pounds chicken breasts, skinless, boneless and cubed
- ½ cup almonds, chopped
- 1 cup green grapes, seedless and halved
- 2 tablespoons olive oil
- Salt and black pepper to the taste

- 1 cup heavy cream
- 1 tablespoon chives, chopped

Directions:

1. Heat up a pan with the oil over medium-high heat, add the chicken and brown for 3 minutes on each side.
2. Add the grapes and the rest of the ingredients, bring to a simmer and cook over medium heat for 15 minutes more.
3. Divide everything into bowls and serve.

Nutrition: calories

655. Tomato Chicken and Lentils

Preparation Time: 10 minutes
Cooking Time: 1 hour
Servings: 8
Ingredients:

- 2 tablespoons olive oil
- 2 celery stalks, chopped
- 1 red onion, chopped
- 2 tablespoons tomato paste
- 2 garlic cloves, chopped
- ½ cup chicken stock
- 2 cups French lentils
- 1-pound chicken thighs, boneless and skinless
- Salt and black pepper to the taste
- 1 tablespoon cilantro, chopped

Directions:

1. Heat up a Dutch oven with the oil over medium-high heat, add the onion and the garlic and sauté for 2 minutes.
2. Add the chicken and brown for 3 minutes on each side.
3. Add the rest of the ingredients except the cilantro, bring to a simmer, and cook over medium-low heat for 45 minutes.
4. Add the cilantro, stir, divide the mix into bowls and serve.

Nutrition: Calories 249, Fat 9.7, Fiber 11.9, Carbs 25.3, Protein 24.3

656. Turkey, Leeks and Carrots

Preparation Time: 10 minutes

Cooking Time: 1 hour
Servings: 4
Ingredients:

- 1 big turkey breast, skinless, boneless and cubed
- 2 tablespoons avocado oil
- Salt and black pepper to the taste
- 1 tablespoon sweet paprika
- ½ cup chicken stock
- 1 leek, sliced
- 1 carrot, sliced
- 1 yellow onion, chopped
- 1 tablespoon lemon juice
- 1 teaspoon cumin, ground
- 1 tablespoon basil, chopped

Directions:

1. Heat up a pan with the oil over medium-high heat, add the turkey and brown for 4 minutes on each side.
2. Add the leeks, carrot and the onion and sauté everything for 5 minutes more.
3. Add the rest of the ingredients, bring to a simmer and cook over medium heat for 40 minutes.
4. Divide the mix between plates and serve.

Nutrition: Calories 249, Fat 10.7, Fiber 11.9, Carbs 22.3, Protein 17.3

657. Herbed Chicken

Preparation Time: 10 minutes
Cooking Time: 40 minutes
Servings: 4
Ingredients:

- 2 chicken breasts, skinless, boneless and sliced
- 2 red onions, chopped
- 2 tablespoons olive oil
- 2 garlic cloves, minced
- ½ cup chicken stock
- 1 teaspoon oregano, dried
- 1 teaspoon basil, dried
- 1 teaspoon rosemary, dried
- 1 cup canned tomatoes, chopped
- Salt and black pepper to the taste

Directions:

1. Heat up a pot with the oil over medium-high heat, add

the chicken and brown for 4 minutes on each side.

2. Add the garlic and the onions and sauté for 5 minutes more.
3. Add the rest of the ingredients, bring to a simmer and cook over medium heat for 25 minutes.
4. Divide everything between plates and serve.

Nutrition: Calories 251, Fat 11.6, Fiber 15.5, Carbs 15.6, Protein 9.1

658. Chives Chicken and Radishes

Preparation Time: 10 minutes
Cooking Time: 30 minutes
Servings: 4
Ingredients:

- 2 chicken breasts, skinless, boneless and cubed
- Salt and black pepper to the taste
- 1 tablespoon olive oil
- 1 cup chicken stock
- ½ cup tomato sauce
- ½ pound red radishes, cubed
- 2 tablespoon chives, chopped

Directions:

1. Heat up a Dutch oven with the oil over medium-high heat, add the chicken and brown for 4 minutes on each side.
2. Add the rest of the ingredients except the chives, bring to a simmer and cook over medium heat for 20 minutes.
3. Divide the mix between plates, sprinkle the chives on top and serve.

Nutrition: Calories 277, Fat 15, Fiber 9.3, Carbs 20.9, Protein 33.2

659. Feta Chicken and Cabbage

Preparation Time: 10 minutes
Cooking Time: 25 minutes
Servings: 4
Ingredients:

- 2 chicken breasts, skinless, boneless and cut into strips
- 1 red cabbage, shredded
- 2 tablespoons olive oil

- Salt and black pepper to the taste
- 2 tablespoons balsamic vinegar
- 1½ cups tomatoes, cubed
- 1 tablespoon chives, chopped
- ¼ cup feta cheese, crumbled

Directions:

1. Heat up a pan with the oil over medium-high heat, add the chicken, and brown for 5 minutes.
2. Add the rest of the ingredients except the cheese, and cook over medium heat for 20 minutes stirring often.
3. Add the cheese, toss, divide everything between plates and serve.

Nutrition: Calories 277, Fat 15, Fiber 8.6, Carbs 14.9, Protein 14.2

660. Garlic Chicken and Endives

Preparation Time: 10 minutes
Cooking Time: 15 minutes
Servings: 4
Ingredients:

- 1-pound chicken breasts, skinless, boneless and cubed
- 2 endives, sliced
- 2 tablespoons olive oil
- 4 garlic cloves, minced
- ½ cup chicken stock
- 2 tablespoons parmesan, grated
- 1 tablespoon parsley, chopped
- Salt and black pepper to the taste

Directions:

1. Heat up a pan with the oil over medium-high heat, add the chicken and cook for 5 minutes.
2. Add the endives, garlic, the stock, salt and pepper, stir, bring to a simmer and cook over medium-high heat for 10 minutes.
3. Add the parmesan and the parsley, toss gently, divide everything between plates and serve.

Nutrition: Calories 280, Fat 9.2, Fiber 10.8, Carbs 21.6, Protein 33.8

661. Turkey and Chickpeas

Preparation Time: 5 minutes
Cooking Time: 5 hours
Servings: 4
Ingredients:

- 2 tablespoons avocado oil
- 1 big turkey breast, skinless, boneless and roughly cubed
- Salt and black pepper to the taste
- 1 red onion, chopped
- 15 ounces canned chickpeas, drained and rinsed
- 15 ounces canned tomatoes, chopped
- 1 cup kalamata olives, pitted and halved
- 2 tablespoons lime juice
- 1 teaspoon oregano, dried

Directions:

1. Heat up a pan with the oil over medium-high heat, add the meat and the onion, brown for 5 minutes, and transfer to a slow cooker.
2. Add the rest of the ingredients, put the lid on, and cook on High for 5 hours.
3. Divide between plates and serve right away!

Nutrition: Calories 352, Fat 14.4, Fiber 11.8, Carbs 25.1, Protein 26.4

662. Lime Turkey and Avocado Mix

Preparation Time: 10 minutes
Cooking Time: 1 hour and 10 minutes
Servings: 2
Ingredients:

- 2 tablespoons olive oil
- 1 turkey breast, boneless, skinless and halved
- 2 ounces cherry tomatoes, halved
- 1 handful coriander, chopped
- Juice of 1 lime
- Zest of 1 lime, grated
- Salt and black pepper to the taste
- 2 spring onions, chopped

- 2 avocadoes, pitted, peeled and cubed

Directions:
1. In a roasting pan, combine the turkey with the oil and the rest of the ingredients, introduce in the oven and bake at 370°F for 1 hour and 10 minutes.
2. Divide between plates and serve.

Nutrition: Calories 301, Fat 8.9, Fiber 10.2, Carbs 19.8, Protein 13.5

663. Turkey and Salsa Verde

Preparation Time: 10 minutes
Cooking Time: 50 minutes
Servings: 4
Ingredients:
- 1 big turkey breast, skinless, boneless and cubed
- 1½ cups Salsa Verde
- Salt and black pepper to the taste
- 1 tablespoon olive oil
- 1½ cups feta cheese, crumbled
- ¼ cup cilantro, chopped

Directions:
1. In a roasting pan greased with the oil combine the turkey with the salsa, salt and pepper and bake 400°F for 50 minutes.
2. Add the cheese and the cilantro, toss gently, divide everything between plates and serve.

Nutrition: Calories 332, Fat 15.4, Fiber 10.5, Carbs 22.1, Protein 34.5

664. Basil Turkey and Zucchinis

Preparation Time: 10 minutes
Cooking Time: 1 hour
Servings: 4
Ingredients:
- 2 tablespoons avocado oil
- 1-pound turkey breast, skinless, boneless and sliced
- Salt and black pepper to the taste
- 3 garlic cloves, minced
- 2 zucchinis, sliced
- 1 cup chicken stock
- ¼ cup heavy cream

- 2 tablespoons basil, chopped

Directions:
1. Heat up a pot with the oil over medium-high heat, add the turkey and brown for 5 minutes on each side.
2. Add the garlic and cook everything for 1 minute.
3. Add the rest of the ingredients except the basil, toss gently, bring to a simmer and cook over medium-low heat for 50 minutes.
4. Add the basil, toss, divide the mix between plates and serve.

Nutrition: Calories 262, Fat 9.8, Fiber 12.2, Carbs 25.8, Protein 14.6

665. Herbed Almond Turkey

Preparation Time: 10 minutes
Cooking Time: 40 minutes
Servings: 4
Ingredients:
- 1 big turkey breast, skinless, boneless and cubed
- 1 tablespoon olive oil
- ½ cup chicken stock
- 1 tablespoon basil, chopped
- 1 tablespoon rosemary, chopped
- 1 tablespoon oregano, chopped
- 1 tablespoon parsley, chopped
- 3 garlic cloves, minced
- ½ cup almonds, toasted and chopped
- 3 cups tomatoes, chopped

Directions:
1. Heat up a pan with the oil over medium-high heat, add the turkey and the garlic and brown for 5 minutes.
2. Add the stock and the rest of the ingredients, bring to a simmer over medium heat and cook for 35 minutes.
3. Divide the mix between plates and serve.

Nutrition: Calories 297, Fat 11.2, Fiber 9.2, Carbs 19.4, Protein 23.6

666. Duck and Tomato Sauce

Preparation Time: 10 minutes
Cooking Time: 2 hours
Servings: 4
Ingredients:
- 4 duck legs
- 2 yellow onions, sliced
- 4 garlic cloves, minced
- ¼ cup parsley, chopped
- A pinch of salt and black pepper
- 1 teaspoon herbs de Provence
- 1 cup tomato sauce
- 2 cups black olives, pitted and sliced

Directions:
1. In a baking dish, combine the duck legs with the onions, garlic and the rest of the ingredients, introduce in the oven and bake at 370°F for 2 hours.
2. Divide the mix between plates and serve.

Nutrition: Calories 300, Fat 13.5, Fiber 9.2, Carbs 16.7, Protein 15.2

667. Chicken and Mustard Sauce

Preparation Time: 10 minutes
Cooking Time: 26 minutes
Servings: 4
Ingredients:
- ⅓ cup mustard
- Salt and black pepper to the taste
- 1 red onion, chopped
- 1 tablespoon olive oil
- 1½ cups chicken stock
- 4 chicken breasts, skinless, boneless and halved
- ¼ teaspoon oregano, dried

Directions:
1. Heat up a pan with the stock over medium heat, add the mustard, onion, salt, pepper and oregano, whisk, bring to a simmer and cook for 8 minutes.
2. Heat up a pan with the oil over medium-high heat, add the chicken and brown for 3 minutes on each side.
3. Add the chicken to the pan with the sauce, toss, simmer everything for 12 minutes more, divide between plates and serve.

Nutrition: Calories 247, Fat 15.1, Fiber 9.1, Carbs 16.6, Protein 26.1

668. Cinnamon Duck Mix

Preparation Time: 10 minutes
Cooking Time: 20 minutes
Servings: 4
Ingredients:

- 4 duck breasts, boneless and skin scored
- Salt and black pepper to the taste
- 1 teaspoon cinnamon powder
- ½ cup chicken stock
- 3 tablespoons chives, chopped
- 2 tablespoons parsley, chopped
- 1 tablespoon olive oil
- 3 tablespoons balsamic vinegar
- 2 red onions, chopped

Directions:

1. Heat up a pan with the oil over medium-high heat, add the duck skin side down and cook for 5 minutes.
2. Add the cinnamon and the rest of the ingredients except the chives and cook for 5 minutes more.
3. Flip the duck breasts again, bring the whole mix to a simmer and cook over medium heat for 10 minutes.
4. Add the chives, divide everything between plates and serve.

Nutrition: Calories 310, Fat 13.5, Fiber 9.2, Carbs 16.7, Protein 15.2

669. Turkey, Artichokes and Asparagus

Preparation Time: 10 minutes
Cooking Time: 30 minutes
Servings: 4
Ingredients:

- 2 turkey breasts, boneless, skinless and halved
- 3 tablespoons olive oil
- 1½ pounds asparagus, trimmed and halved
- 1 cup chicken stock
- A pinch of salt and black pepper
- 1 cup canned artichoke hearts, drained

- ¼ cup kalamata olives, pitted and sliced
- 1 shallot, chopped
- 3 garlic cloves, minced
- 3 tablespoons dill, chopped

Directions:

1. Heat up a pan with the oil over medium-high heat, add the turkey and the garlic and brown for 4 minutes on each side.
2. Add the asparagus, the stock and the rest of the ingredients except the dill, bring to a simmer, and cook over medium heat for 20 minutes.
3. Add the dill, divide the mix between plates and serve.

Nutrition: Calories 291, Fat 16, Fiber 10.3, Carbs 22.8, Protein 34.5

670. Orange Duck and Celery

Preparation Time: 10 minutes
Cooking Time: 40 minutes
Servings: 4
Ingredients:

- 2 duck legs, boneless, skinless
- 1 tablespoon avocado oil
- 1 cup chicken stock
- Salt and black pepper to the taste
- 4 celery ribs, roughly chopped
- 2 garlic cloves, minced
- 1 red onion, chopped
- 2 teaspoons thyme, dried
- 2 tablespoons tomato paste
- Zest of 1 orange, grated
- Juice of 2 oranges
- 3 oranges, peeled and cut into segments

Directions:

1. Grease a roasting pan with the oil, add the duck legs, the stock, salt, pepper and the other ingredients, toss a bit, and bake at 450°F for 40 minutes.
2. Divide everything between plates and serve warm.

Nutrition: Calories 294, Fat 12.4, Fiber 11.3, Carbs 25.5, Protein 16.4

671. Duck and Blackberries

Preparation Time: 10 minutes
Cooking Time: 25 minutes
Servings: 4

Ingredients:

- 4 duck breasts, boneless and skin scored
- 2 tablespoons balsamic vinegar
- Salt and black pepper to the taste
- 1 cup chicken stock
- 4 ounces blackberries
- ¼ cup chicken stock
- 2 tablespoons avocado oil

Directions:

1. Heat up a pan with the avocado oil over medium-high heat, add duck breasts, skin side down and cook for 5 minutes.
2. Flip the duck, add the rest of the ingredients, bring to a simmer and cook over medium heat for 20 minutes.
3. Divide everything between plates and serve.

Nutrition: Calories 239, Fat 10.5, Fiber 10.2, Carbs 21.1, Protein 33.3

672. Ginger Duck Mix

Preparation Time: 10 minutes
Cooking Time: 1 hour and 50 minutes
Servings: 4
Ingredients:

- 4 duck legs, boneless
- 4 shallots, chopped
- 2 tablespoons olive oil
- 1 tablespoon ginger, grated
- 2 tablespoons rosemary, chopped
- 1 cup chicken stock
- 1 tablespoon chives, chopped

Directions:

1. In a roasting pan, combine the duck legs with the shallots and the rest of the ingredients except the chives, toss, introduce in the oven at 250°F and bake for 1 hour and 30 minutes.
2. Divide the mix between plates, sprinkle the chives on top and serve.

Nutrition: Calories 299, Fat 10.2, Fiber 9.2, Carbs 18.1, Protein 17.3

673. Duck, Cucumber and Mango Salad

Preparation Time: 10 minutes
Cooking Time: 50 minutes

Servings: 4

Ingredients:

- Zest of 1 orange, grated
- 2 big duck breasts, boneless and skin scored
- 2 tablespoons olive oil
- Salt and black pepper to the taste
- 1 tablespoon fish sauce
- 1 tablespoon lime juice
- 1 garlic clove, minced
- 1 Serrano chili, chopped
- 1 small shallot, sliced
- 1 cucumber, sliced
- 2 mangos, peeled and sliced
- ¼ cup oregano, chopped

Directions:

1. Heat up a pan with the oil over medium-high heat, add the duck breasts skin side down and cook for 5 minutes.
2. Add the orange zest, salt, pepper, fish sauce and the rest of the ingredients, bring to a simmer and cook over medium-low heat for 45 minutes.
3. Divide everything between plates and serve.

Nutrition: Calories 297, Fat 9.1, Fiber 10.2, Carbs 20.8, Protein 16.5

674. Duck and Orange Warm Salad

Preparation Time: 10 minutes
Cooking Time: 25 minutes
Servings: 4
Ingredients:

- 2 tablespoons balsamic vinegar
- 2 oranges, peeled and cut into segments
- 1 teaspoon orange zest, grated
- 1 tablespoon orange juice
- 3 shallots, minced
- 2 tablespoons olive oil
- Salt and black pepper to the taste
- 2 duck breasts, boneless and skin scored
- 2 cups baby arugula
- 2 tablespoons chives, chopped

Directions:

1. Heat up a pan with the oil over medium-high heat, add the duck breasts skin side down and brown for 5 minutes.
2. Flip the duck, add the shallot, and the other ingredients except for the arugula, orange and chives, and cook for 15 minutes more.
3. Transfer the duck breasts to a cutting board, cool down, cut into strips, and put in a salad bowl.
4. Add the remaining ingredients, toss and serve warm.

Nutrition: Calories 304, Fat 15.4, Fiber 12.6, Carbs 25.1, Protein 36.4

675. Creamy Coriander Chicken

Preparation Time: 10 minutes
Cooking Time: 55 minutes
Servings: 4
Ingredients:

- 2 chicken breasts, boneless, skinless and halved
- 2 tablespoons avocado oil
- ½ teaspoon hot paprika
- 1 cup chicken stock
- 1 tablespoon almonds, chopped
- 2 spring onions, chopped
- 2 garlic cloves, minced
- ¼ cup heavy cream
- 1 handful coriander, chopped
- Salt and black pepper to the taste

Directions:

1. Grease a roasting pan with the oil, add the chicken, paprika and the rest of the ingredients except the coriander and the heavy cream, toss, introduce in the oven and bake at 360°F for 40 minutes.
2. Add the cream and the coriander, toss, bake for 15 minutes more, divide between plates and serve.

Nutrition: Calories 225, Fat 8.9, Fiber 10.2, Carbs 20.8, Protein 17.5

676. Lemony Turkey and Pine Nuts

Preparation Time: 10 minutes
Cooking Time: 30 minutes
Servings: 4
Ingredients:

- 2 turkey breasts, boneless, skinless and halved
- A pinch of salt and black pepper
- 2 tablespoons avocado oil
- Juice of 2 lemons
- 1 tablespoon rosemary, chopped
- 3 garlic cloves, minced
- ¼ cup pine nuts, chopped
- 1 cup chicken stock

Directions:

1. Heat up a pan with the oil over medium-high heat, add the garlic and the turkey and brown for 4 minutes on each side.
2. Add the rest of the ingredients, bring to a simmer and cook over medium heat for 20 minutes.
3. Divide the mix between plates and serve with a side salad.

Nutrition: Calories 293, Fat 12.4, Fiber 9.3, Carbs 17.8, Protein 24.5

677. Creamy Chicken and Mushrooms

Preparation Time: 10 minutes
Cooking Time: 30 minutes
Servings: 4
Ingredients:

- 1 red onion, chopped
- 1 tablespoon olive oil
- 2 garlic cloves, minced
- 2 carrots chopped
- Salt and black pepper to the taste
- 1 tablespoon thyme, chopped
- 1½ cups chicken stock
- ½ pound Bella mushrooms, sliced
- 1 cup heavy cream
- 2 chicken breasts, skinless, boneless and cubed

- 2 tablespoons chives, chopped
- 1 tablespoon parsley, chopped

Directions:
1. Heat up a Dutch oven with the oil over medium-high heat, add the onion and the garlic and sauté for 5 minutes.
2. Add the chicken and the mushrooms, and sauté for 10 minutes more.
3. Add the rest of the ingredients except the chives and the parsley, bring to a simmer, and cook over medium heat for 15 minutes.
4. Add the chives and parsley, divide the mix between plates and serve.

Nutrition: Calories 275, Fat 11.9, Fiber 10.6, Carbs 26.7, Protein 23.7

678. Oregano Turkey and Peppers

Preparation Time: 10 minutes
Cooking Time: 1 hour
Servings: 4
Ingredients:

- 2 red bell peppers, cut into strips
- 2 green bell peppers, cut into strips
- 1 red onion, chopped
- 4 garlic cloves, minced
- ½ cup black olives, pitted and sliced
- 2 cups chicken stock
- 1 big turkey breast, skinless, boneless and cut into strips
- 1 tablespoon oregano, chopped
- ½ cup cilantro, chopped

Directions:
1. In a baking pan, combine the peppers with the turkey and the rest of the ingredients, toss, introduce in the oven at 400°F, and roast for 1 hour.
2. Divide everything between plates and serve.

Nutrition: Calories 229, Fat 8.9, Fiber 8.2, Carbs 17.8, Protein 33.6

679. Chicken and Mint Sauce

Preparation Time: 10 minutes
Cooking Time: 30 minutes
Servings: 4
Ingredients:

- 2½ tablespoons olive oil
- 2 pounds chicken breasts, skinless, boneless and halved
- 3 tablespoons garlic, minced
- 2 tablespoons lemon juice
- 1 tablespoon red wine vinegar
- ⅓ cup Greek yogurt
- 2 tablespoons mint, chopped
- A pinch of salt and black pepper

Directions:
1. In a blender, combine the garlic with the lemon juice and the other ingredients except the oil and the chicken and pulse well.
2. Heat up a pan with the oil over medium-high heat, add the chicken, and brown for 3 minutes on each side.
3. Add the mint sauce, introduce in the oven and bake everything at 370°F for 25 minutes.
4. Divide the mix between plates and serve.

Nutrition: Calories 278, Fat 12, Fiber 11.2, Carbs 18.1, Protein 13.3

680. Curry Chicken, Artichokes and Olives

Preparation Time: 5 minutes
Cooking Time: 7 hours
Servings: 6
Ingredients:

- 2 pounds chicken breasts, boneless, skinless and cubed
- 12 ounces canned artichoke hearts, drained
- 1 cup chicken stock
- 1 red onion, chopped
- 1 tablespoon white wine vinegar
- 1 cup kalamata olives, pitted and chopped
- 1 tablespoon curry powder
- 2 teaspoons basil, dried
- Salt and black pepper to the taste
- ¼ cup rosemary, chopped

Directions:
1. In your slow cooker, combine the chicken with the artichokes, olives and the rest of the ingredients, put the lid on, and cook on Low for 7 hours.
2. Divide the mix between plates and serve hot.

Nutrition: Calories 275, Fat 11.9, Fiber 7.6, Carbs 19.7, Protein 18.7

681. Turkey and Cranberry Sauce

Preparation Time: 10 minutes
Cooking Time: 50 minutes
Servings: 4
Ingredients:

- 1 cup chicken stock
- 2 tablespoons avocado oil
- ½ cup cranberry sauce
- 1 big turkey breast, skinless, boneless and sliced
- 1 yellow onion, roughly chopped
- Salt and black pepper to the taste

Directions:
1. Heat up a pan with the avocado oil over medium-high heat, add the onion and sauté for 5 minutes.
2. Add the turkey and brown for 5 minutes more.
3. Add the rest of the ingredients, toss, introduce in the oven at 350°F and cook for 40 minutes

Nutrition: Calories 382, Fat 12.6, Fiber 9.6, Carbs 26.6, Protein 17.6

Chapter 9. Side Dishes

682. Cherry Tomato Gratin
Preparation Time: 15 minutes
Cooking Time: 20 minutes
Servings: 4
Ingredients:
- 2 tablespoons olive oil,
- ½ cup cherry tomatoes halved
- ½ cup mayonnaise, Keto-friendly
- ½ cup vegan mozzarella cheese, cut into pieces
- 1 ounce (28-g.) vegan Parmesan cheese, shredded
- 1 tablespoon basil pesto
- Pepper and salt
- 1 cup watercress

Directions:
1. Let the oven heat up to 400°F. Grease a baking pan with olive oil.
2. Combine the cherry tomatoes, mayo, vegan Mozzarella cheese, ½ ounce (14-g.) of Parmesan cheese, basil pesto, salt, and black pepper baking pan.
3. Scatter with the remaining Parmesan.
4. **Baking Time:** 20 minutes
5. Remove them from the oven and divide among four plates. Top with watercress and olive oil, and slice to serve.

Nutrition: Calories: 254 Fat: 12.1g Fiber: 9.3 g Carbohydrates: 11.1 g Protein: 9.5 g

683. Fennel-Parmesan Farro
Preparation Time: 15 minutes
Cooking Time: 50 minutes
Servings: 4-6
Ingredients:
- ¼ cup minced fresh parsley
- 1 onion, chopped fine
- 1 ounce Parmesan cheese, grated (½ cup)
- 1 small fennel bulb, stalks discarded, bulb halved, cored, and chopped fine
- 1 teaspoon minced fresh thyme or ¼ teaspoon dried
- 1½ cups whole farro
- 2 teaspoons sherry vinegar
- 3 garlic cloves, minced
- 3 tablespoons extra-virgin olive oil
- Salt and pepper

Directions:
1. Bring 4 quarts of water to boil in a Dutch oven. Put in farro and 1 tablespoon salt, return to boil and cook until grains are soft with a slight chew, 15 to 30 minutes.
2. Drain farro, return to now-empty pot and cover to keep warm. Heat 2 tablespoons oil in a 12-inch frying pan on moderate heat until it starts to shimmer.
3. Put in onion, fennel, and ¼ teaspoon salt and cook, stirring intermittently, till they become tender, 8 to 10 minutes. Put in garlic and thyme and cook until aromatic, approximately half a minute.
4. Put in residual 1 tablespoon oil and farro and cook, stirring often, until heated through, approximately 2 minutes.
5. Remove from the heat, mix in Parmesan, parsley, and vinegar. Sprinkle with salt and pepper to taste. Serve.

Nutrition: Calories: 338 Carbs: 56 g Fat: 10 g Protein: 11 g

684. Creamy Zoodles
Preparation Time: 15 minutes
Cooking Time: 10 minutes
Servings: 4
Ingredients:
- 1¼ cups heavy whipping cream
- ¼ cup mayonnaise
- Salt and ground black pepper, as required
- 30 ounces zucchini, spiralized with blade C
- 3 ounces Parmesan cheese, grated
- 2 tablespoons fresh mint leaves
- 2 tablespoons butter, melted

Directions:
1. The heavy cream must be added to a pan then bring to a boil.
2. Lower the heat to low and cook until reduced in half.
3. Put in the pepper, mayo, and salt; cook until mixture is warm enough.
4. Add the zucchini noodles and gently stir to combine.
5. Stir in the Parmesan cheese.
6. Divide the zucchini noodles onto four serving plates and immediately drizzle with the melted butter.
7. Serve immediately.

Nutrition: Calories: 241 Fat: 11.4 g Fiber: 7.5 g Carbohydrates: 3.1 g Protein: 5.1 g

685. Black Bean Veggie Burger
Preparation Time: 15 minutes
Cooking Time: 20 minutes
Servings: 2
Ingredients:
- ½ onion (chopped small)
- 1 (14-oz.) can of black beans (well-drained)
- slices of bread (crumbled)
- ½ teaspoon of seasoned salt
- 1 teaspoon of garlic powder
- 1 teaspoon of onion powder
- ½ cup of almond flour
- Dash salt (to taste)
- Dash pepper (to taste)
- Oil for frying (divide)

Directions:
1. Combine onions and sauté and pour it into the small frying pan. Fry them until they are soft. This process usually takes between 3 and 5 minutes.
2. Get a large bowl. Mash the black beans inside it. Ensure that the beans are almost smooth.
3. Sauté your onions and crumble the bread.
4. In the bowl, add the sautéed onions, mashed black beans, crumbled bread, seasoned salt, garlic powder, and

onion powder. Ensure you mix to combine well.

5. Add some flour to the ingredients by adding a teaspoon per time. Stir everything together until it is well combined.
6. While mixing, make sure that it is very thick.
7. To achieve this, you may want to use your hand to work your flour well.
8. Make the mixed black beans into patties.
9. Ensure that each of the patties is approximately ½ inch thick.
10. The best way to do this is to make a ball with black beans.
11. After doing this, flatten the ball gently. Place your frying pan on medium-low heat. Add some oil.
12. Fry your black bean patties in the frying pan until it is slightly firm and lightly browned on each side. This usually takes about 3 minutes.
13. Ensure you adjust the head well because if the pan is too hot, the bean burgers will be brown in the middle and will not be well cooked in the middle.
14. To serve, assemble your veggie burgers and enjoy it with all the fixings.
15. You can also serve to get a plate, serve them with a little ketchup or hot sauce.
16. To increase the nutrition of the meal, you can add a nice green salad.

Nutrition: Calories: 376 Fat: 15.1 g Fiber: 12.9 g Carbohydrates: 9.4 g Protein: 11.6 g

686. Red Curry

Preparation Time: 20 minutes
Cooking Time: 15-20 minutes
Servings: 6
Ingredients:
- 1 cup broccoli florets
- 1 large handful of fresh spinach
- 4 tablespoons coconut oil
- ¼ medium onion
- 1 teaspoon garlic, minced
- 1 teaspoon fresh ginger, peeled and minced
- 2 teaspoons soy sauce
- 1 tablespoon red curry paste
- ½ cup coconut cream

Directions:
1. Add half the coconut oil to a saucepan and heat over medium-high heat.
2. When the oil is hot, put the onion in the pan and sauté for 3-4 minutes, until it is semi-translucent.
3. Sauté garlic, stirring, just until fragrant, about 30 seconds.
4. Lower the heat to medium-low and add broccoli florets. Sauté, stirring, for about 1-2 minutes.
5. Now, add the red curry paste. Sauté until the paste is fragrant, then mix everything.
6. Add the spinach on top of the vegetable mixture. When the spinach begins to wilt, add the coconut cream and stir.
7. Add the rest of the coconut oil, the soy sauce, and the minced ginger. Bring to a simmer for 5-10 minutes.
8. Serve hot.

Nutrition: Calories: 265 Fat: 7.1 g Fiber: 6.9 g Carbohydrates: 2.1 g Protein: 4.4 g

687. Sweet-And-Sour Tempeh

Preparation Time: 10 minutes
Cooking Time: 25 minutes
Servings: 4
Ingredients:
Tempeh:
- 1 package of tempeh
- ¾ cup of vegetable broth
- 2 tablespoons of soy sauce
- 2 tablespoons olive oil

Sauce:
- 1 can of pineapple juice
- 2 tablespoons of brown sugar
- ¼ cup of white vinegar
- 1 tablespoon of cornstarch
- 1 red bell pepper
- 1 chopped white onion

Directions:
1. Place a skillet on high heat. Pour in the vegetable broth and tempeh in it.
2. Add the soy sauce to the tempeh. Let it cook until it softens. This usually takes 10 minutes.
3. When it is well cooked, remove the tempeh and keep the liquid. We are going to use it for the sauce.
4. Put the tempeh in another skillet placed on medium heat.
5. Sauté it with olive oil and cook until the tempeh is browned. This should take 3 minutes.
6. Place a pot of the reserved liquid from the cooked tempeh on medium heat.
7. Add the pineapple juice, vinegar, brown sugar, and cornstarch. Stir everything together until it's well combined.
8. Let it simmer for 5 minutes.
9. Add the onion and pepper to the sauce.
10. Stir in until the sauce is thick.
11. Reduce the heat, add the cooked tempeh and pineapple chunks to the sauce. Leave it to simmer together.
12. Remove from heat and serve with any grain food of your choice.

Nutrition: Calories: 312 Fat: 10g Fiber: 4.1 g Carbohydrates: 2.1 g Protein: 5.2 g

688. Mexican Casserole with BlackBeans

Preparation Time: 20 minutes
Cooking Time: 20 minutes
Servings: 6
Ingredients:
- 2 cups of minced garlic cloves
- 2 cups of Monterey Jack and cheddar
- ¾ cup of salsa
- 2½ cups chopped red pepper
- 2 teaspoons ground cumin
- 2 cans black beans
- 12 corn tortillas

- 2 chopped tomatoes
- ½ cup of sliced black olives
- 2 cups of chopped onion

Directions:
1. Let the oven heat to 350°F.
2. Place a large pot over medium heat.
3. Pour the onion, garlic, pepper, cumin, salsa, and black beans in the pot — Cook the ingredients for 3 minutes, stirring frequently.
4. Arrange the tortillas in the baking dish.
5. Ensure they are well spaced and even overlapping the dish if necessary.
6. Spread half of the bean's mixture on the tortillas. Sprinkle with the cheddar.
7. Repeat the process across the tortillas until everything is well stuffed.
8. Cover the baking dish with foil paper and place in the oven.
9. Bake it for 15 minutes. Remove from the oven to cool down a bit.
10. Garnish the casserole with olives and tomatoes

Nutrition: Calories: 325 Fat: 9.4 g Fiber: 11.2 g Carbohydrates: 3.1 g Protein: 12.6 g

689. Baked Zucchini Gratin
Preparation Time: 25 minutes
Cooking Time: 30 minutes
Servings: 2
Ingredients:
- 1 large zucchini, cut into ¼-inch-thick slices
- Pink Himalayan salt
- 1-oz. Brie cheese, rind trimmed off
- 1 tablespoon butter
- Freshly ground black pepper
- ⅓ cup shredded Gruyere cheese
- ¼ cup crushed pork rinds

Directions:
1. Preheat the oven to 400°F.
2. When the zucchini has been "weeping" for about 30 minutes, in a small saucepan over medium-low heat, heat the Brie and butter, occasionally stirring, until the cheese has melted.

3. The mixture is thoroughly combined for about 2 minutes.
4. Arrange the zucchini in an 8-inch baking dish, so the zucchini slices are overlapping a bit.
5. Season with pepper.
6. Pour the Brie mixture over the zucchini, and top with the shredded Gruyere cheese.
7. Sprinkle the crushed pork rinds over the top.
8. Bake for about 25 minutes, until the dish is bubbling and the top is nicely browned, and serve.

Nutrition: Calories: 324 Fat: 11.5 g Fiber: 5.1 g Carbohydrates: 2.2 g Protein: 5.1 g

690. Veggie Greek Moussaka
Preparation Time: 20 minutes
Cooking Time: 30 minutes
Servings: 6
Ingredients:
- 2 large eggplants, cut into strips
- cup diced celery
- cup diced carrots
- small white onion, chopped
- eggs
- teaspoon olive oil
- cups grated Parmesan
- 1 cup ricotta cheese
- cloves garlic, minced
- teaspoon Italian seasoning blend
- Salt to taste

Sauce:
- ½ cups heavy cream
- ¼ cup butter, melted
- 1 cup grated mozzarella cheese
- 2 teaspoons Italian seasoning
- ¾ cup almond flour

Directions:
1. Preheat the oven to 350°F.
2. Lay the eggplant strips, sprinkle with salt, and let sit there to exude liquid. Heat olive oil heat and sauté the onion, celery, garlic, and carrots for 5 minutes.
3. Mix the eggs, 1 cup of Parmesan cheese, ricotta

cheese, and salt in a bowl; set aside.
4. Pour the heavy cream into a pot and bring to heat over a medium fire while continually stirring.
5. Stir in the remaining Parmesan cheese and one teaspoon of Italian seasoning. Turn the heat off and set aside.
6. To lay the moussaka, spread a small amount of the sauce at the bottom of the baking dish.
7. Pat dry the eggplant strips and make a single layer on the sauce.
8. A layer of ricotta cheese must be spread on the eggplants, sprinkle some veggies on it, and repeat everything
9. In a small bowl, evenly mix the melted butter, almond flour, and one teaspoon of Italian seasoning.
10. Spread the top of the moussaka layers with it and sprinkle the top with mozzarella cheese.
11. Bake for 25 minutes until the cheese is slightly burned. Slice the moussaka and serve warm.

Nutrition: Calories: 398 Fat: 15.1 g Fiber: 11.3 g Carbohydrates: 3.1 g Protein: 5.9 g

691. Gouda Cauliflower Casserole
Preparation Time: 15 minutes
Cooking Time: 15 minutes
Servings: 4
Ingredients:
- 2 heads cauliflower, cut into florets
- ⅓ cup butter, cubed
- 2 tablespoons melted butter
- 1 white onion, chopped
- Salt and black pepper to taste
- ¼ almond milk
- ½ cup almond flour
- 1½ cups grated gouda cheese

Directions:
1. Preheat oven to 350°F and put the cauliflower florets in

a large microwave-safe bowl.

2. Sprinkle with a bit of water, and steam in the microwave for 4 to 5 minutes.
3. Melt the ⅓ cup of butter in a saucepan over medium heat and sauté the onion for 3 minutes.
4. Add the cauliflower, season with salt and black pepper, and mix in almond milk. Simmer for 3 minutes.
5. Mix the remaining melted butter with almond flour.
6. Stir into the cauliflower as well as half of the cheese. Sprinkle the top with the remaining cheese and bake for 10 minutes until the cheese has melted and golden brown.
7. Plate the bake and serve with salad.

Nutrition: Calories: 349 Fat: 9.4 g Fiber: 12.1 g Carbohydrates: 4.1 g Protein: 10 g

692. Spinach and Zucchini Lasagna

Preparation Time: 15 minutes
Cooking Time: 30 minutes
Servings: 4
Ingredients:

- 2 zucchinis, sliced
- Salt and black pepper to taste
- 2 cups ricotta cheese
- 2 cups shredded mozzarella cheese
- 3 cups tomato sauce
- 1 cup baby spinach

Directions:

1. Let the oven heat to 375°F and grease a baking dish with cooking spray.
2. Put the zucchini slices in a colander and sprinkle with salt.
3. Let sit and drain liquid for 5 minutes and pat dry with paper towels.
4. Mix the ricotta, mozzarella cheese, salt, and black pepper to evenly combine and spread ¼ cup of the mixture in the bottom of the baking dish.
5. Layer ⅓ of the zucchini slices on top spread 1 cup

of tomato sauce over, and scatter a ⅓ cup of spinach on top. Repeat process.
6. Grease one end of foil with cooking spray and cover the baking dish with the foil.
7. Let it bake for about 35 minutes. And bake further for 5 to 10 minutes or until the cheese has a nice golden-brown color.
8. Remove the dish, sit for 5 minutes, make slices of the lasagna, and serve warm.

Nutrition: Calories: 376 Fat: 14.1 g Fiber: 11.3 g Carbohydrates: 2.1 g Protein: 9.5 g

693. Lemon Cauliflower "Couscous" with Halloumi

Preparation Time: 5 minutes
Cooking Time: 5 minutes
Servings: 2
Ingredients:

- 4 ounces halloumi, sliced
- cauliflower head, cut into small florets
- ¼ cup chopped cilantro
- ¼ cup chopped parsley
- ¼ cup chopped mint
- ½ lemon juiced
- Salt and black pepper to taste
- Sliced avocado to garnish

Directions:

1. Heat the pan and add oil
2. Add the halloumi and fry on both sides until golden brown, set aside. Turn the heat off.
3. Next, pour the cauliflower florets in a food processor and pulse until it crumbles and resembles couscous.
4. Transfer to a bowl and steam in the microwave for 2 minutes.
5. They should be slightly cooked but crunchy.
6. Stir in the cilantro, parsley, mint, lemon juice, salt, and black pepper.
7. Garnish the couscous with avocado slices and serve with grilled halloumi and vegetable sauce.

Nutrition: Calories: 312 Fat: 9.4 g Fiber: 11.9 g Carbohydrates: 1.2 g Protein: 8.5 g

694. Spicy Cauliflower Steaks with Steamed Green Beans

Preparation Time: 15 minutes
Cooking Time: 20 minutes
Servings: 4
Ingredients:

- 2 heads cauliflower, sliced lengthwise into 'steaks.'
- ¼ cup olive oil
- ¼ cup chili sauce
- 2 teaspoons erythritol
- Salt and black pepper to taste
- 2 shallots, diced
- bunch green beans, trimmed
- tablespoons fresh lemon juice
- 1 cup of water
- Dried parsley to garnish

Directions:

1. In a bowl or container, mix the olive oil, chili sauce, and erythritol.
2. Brush the cauliflower with the mixture. Grill for 6 minutes. Flip the cauliflower, cook further for 6 minutes.
3. Let the water boil, place the green beans in a sieve, and set over the steam from the boiling water.
4. Cover with a clean napkin to keep the steam trapped in the sieve.
5. Cook for 6 minutes.
6. After, remove to a bowl and toss with lemon juice.
7. Remove the grilled caulis to a plate; sprinkle with salt, pepper, shallots, and parsley. Serve with the steamed green beans.

Nutrition: Calories: 329 Fat: 10.4 g Fiber: 3.1 g Carbohydrates: 4.2 g Protein: 8.4 g

695. Cheesy Cauliflower Falafel

Preparation Time: 20 minutes
Cooking Time: 15 minutes
Servings: 4
Ingredients:

- head cauliflower, cut into florets
- ⅓ cup silvered ground almonds

- tablespoons cheddar cheese, shredded
- ½ teaspoon mixed spice
- Salt and chili pepper to taste
- tablespoons coconut flour
- fresh eggs
- tablespoons ghee

Directions:
1. Blend the florets in a blender until a grain meal consistency is formed.
2. Pour the rice in a bowl, add the ground almonds, mixed spice, salt, cheddar cheese, chili pepper, coconut flour, and mix until evenly combined.
3. Beat the eggs in a bowl until creamy in color and mix with the cauliflower mixture.
4. Shape ¼ cup each into patties.
5. Melt ghee and fry the patties for 5 minutes on each side to be firm and browned.
6. Remove onto a wire rack to cool, share into serving plates, and top with tahini sauce.

Nutrition: Calories: 287 Fat: 9.2 g Fiber: 4.1 g Carbohydrates: 3.2 g Protein: 13.2 g

696. Tofu Sesame Skewers with Warm Kale Salad
Preparation Time: 2 hours
Cooking Time: 25 minutes
Servings: 4
Ingredients:
- 14 ounces firm tofu
- 4 teaspoons sesame oil
- lemon, juiced
- tablespoons sugar-free soy sauce
- teaspoon garlic powder
- tablespoons coconut flour
- ½ cup sesame seeds
- Warm Kale Salad:
- cups chopped kale
- 2 teaspoons + 2 teaspoons olive oil
- white onion, thinly sliced
- cloves garlic, minced

- 1 cup sliced white mushrooms
- 1 teaspoon chopped rosemary
- Salt and black pepper to season
- 1 tablespoon balsamic vinegar

Directions:
1. In a bowl, mix sesame oil, lemon juice, soy sauce, garlic powder, and coconut flour.
2. Wrap the tofu in a paper towel, squeeze out as much liquid from it, and cut it into strips.
3. Stick on the skewers, height-wise.
4. Place onto a plate, pour the soy sauce mixture over, and turn in the sauce to be adequately coated.
5. Heat the griddle pan over high heat.
6. Pour the sesame seeds into a plate and roll the tofu skewers in the seeds for a generous coat.
7. Grill the tofu in the griddle pan to be golden brown on both sides, about 12 minutes.
8. Heat 2 tablespoons of olive oil in a skillet over medium heat and sauté onion to begin browning for 10 minutes with continuous stirring.
9. Add the remaining olive oil and mushrooms.
10. Continue cooking for 10 minutes. Add garlic, rosemary, salt, pepper, and balsamic vinegar.
11. Cook for 1 minute.
12. Put the kale in a salad bowl; when the onion mixture is ready, pour it on the kale and toss well.
13. Serve the tofu skewers with the warm kale salad and a peanut butter dipping sauce.

Nutrition: Calories: 276 Fat: 11.9 g Fiber: 9.4 g Carbohydrates: 21 g Protein: 10.3 g

697. Brussel Sprouts with Spiced Halloumi
Preparation Time: 20 minutes
Cooking Time: 30 minutes
Servings: 2
Ingredients:
- 10 ounces halloumi cheese, sliced
- tablespoons coconut oil
- ½ cup unsweetened coconut, shredded
- 1 teaspoon chili powder
- ½ teaspoon onion powder
- ½ pound Brussels sprouts, shredded
- 4 ounces butter
- Salt and black pepper to taste
- Lemon wedges for serving

Directions:
1. In a bowl, mix the shredded coconut, chili powder, salt, coconut oil, and onion powder.
2. Then, toss the halloumi slices in the spice mixture.
3. The grill pan must be heated then cook the coated halloumi cheese for 2-3 minutes.
4. Transfer to a plate to keep warm.
5. The half butter must be melted in a pan, add, and sauté the Brussels sprouts until slightly caramelized.
6. Then, season with salt and black pepper.
7. Dish the Brussels sprouts into serving plates with the halloumi cheese and lemon wedges.
8. Melt left butter and drizzle over the Brussels sprouts and halloumi cheese. Serve.

Nutrition: Calories: 276 Fat: 9.5 g Fiber: 9.1 g Carbohydrates: 4.1 g Protein: 5.4 g

698. Vegetable Patties
Preparation Time: 15 minutes
Cooking Time: 20 minutes
Servings: 4
Ingredients:
- tablespoons olive oil
- 1 onion, chopped
- 1 garlic clove, minced
- ½ head cauliflower, grated
- 1 carrot, shredded

- 1 tablespoon coconut flour
- ½ cup Gruyere cheese, shredded
- ½ cup Parmesan cheese, grated
- 3 eggs, beaten
- ½ teaspoon dried rosemary
- Salt and black pepper, to taste

Directions:
1. Cook onion and garlic in warm olive oil over medium heat, until soft, for about 3 minutes.
2. Stir in grated cauliflower and carrot and cook for a minute; allow cooling and set aside.
3. To the cooled vegetables, add the rest of the ingredients, form balls from the mixture, then press each ball to form a burger patty.
4. Set oven to 400°F and bake the burgers for 20 minutes.
5. Flip and bake for another 10 minutes or until the top becomes golden brown.

Nutrition: Calories: 315 Fat: 12.1 g Fiber: 8.6 g Carbohydrates: 3.3 g Protein: 5.8 g

699. Vegan Sandwich with Tofu & Lettuce Slaw
Preparation Time: 15 minutes
Cooking Time: 15minutes
Servings: 2
Ingredients:
- ¼ pound firm tofu, sliced
- 2 low carb buns
- 1 tablespoon olive oil

Marinade:
- 2 tablespoons olive oil
- Salt and black pepper to taste
- 1 teaspoon all-spice
- ½ tablespoons xylitol
- 1 teaspoon thyme, chopped
- 1 habanero pepper, seeded and minced
- 2 green onions, thinly sliced
- 1 garlic clove
- Lettuce slaw
- ½ small iceberg lettuce, shredded
- ½ carrot, grated
- ½ red onion, grated
- 2 teaspoons liquid stevia

- 1 tablespoon lemon juice
- 2 tablespoons olive oil
- ½ teaspoon Dijon mustard
- Salt and black pepper to taste

Directions:
1. Put the tofu slices in a bowl.
2. Blend the marinade ingredients for a minute.
3. Cover the tofu with this mixture and place in the fridge to marinate for 1 hour.
4. In a container, combine the lemon juice, stevia, olive oil, Dijon mustard, salt, and pepper.
5. Stir in the lettuce, carrot, and onion; set aside.
6. Heat oil, cook the tofu on both sides for 6 minutes in total.
7. Remove to a plate.
8. In the buns, add the tofu and top with the slaw. Close the buns and serve.

Nutrition: Calories: 315 Fat: 10.4 g Fiber: 15.1 g Carbohydrates: 9.4 g Protein: 8.4 g

700. Pumpkin and Cauliflower Curry
Preparation Time: 15 minutes
Cooking Time: 7 to 8 hours
Servings: 6
Ingredients:
- 1 tablespoon extra-virgin olive oil
- 4 cups coconut milk
- 1 cup diced pumpkin
- 1 cup cauliflower florets
- 1 red bell pepper, diced
- 1 zucchini, diced
- 1 sweet onion, chopped
- 1 teaspoon grated fresh ginger
- 1 teaspoon minced garlic
- 1 tablespoon curry powder
- 2 cups shredded spinach
- 1 avocado, diced, for garnish

Directions:
1. Lightly grease the insert of the slow cooker with olive oil.
2. Add the coconut milk, pumpkin, cauliflower, bell pepper, zucchini, onion,

ginger, garlic, and curry powder.
3. Cover and cook on low for 7 to 8 hours.
4. Stir in the spinach.
5. Garnish each bowl with a spoonful of avocado and serve.

Nutrition: Calories: 501 Fat: 44.0 g Protein: 7.0 g Carbs: 19.0 g Net carbs: 9.0 g Fiber: 10.0 g

701. Cauliflower Egg Bake
Preparation Time: 10 minutes
Cooking Time: 25 minutes
Servings: 6
Ingredients:
- 1½ pounds (680-g.) cauliflower, broken into small florets
- ½ cup Greek yogurt
- 4 eggs, beaten
- 6 ounces (170 g) ham, diced
- 1 cup Swiss cheese, preferably freshly grated

Directions:
1. Place the cauliflower into a deep saucepan; cover with water and bring to a boil over high heat; immediately reduce the heat to medium-low.
2. Let it simmer, covered, for approximately 6 minutes. Drain and mash with a potato masher.
3. Add in the yogurt, eggs and ham; stir until everything is well combined and incorporated.
4. Scrape the mixture into a lightly greased casserole dish. Top with the grated Swiss cheese and transfer to a preheated at 390°F (199°C) oven.
5. Bake for 15 to 20 minutes or until cheese bubbles and browns. Bon appétit!

Nutrition: Calories: 237 Fat: 13.6 g Protein: 20.2 g Carbs: 7.1 g Net carbs: 4.8 g Fiber: 2.3 g

702. Zucchini Casserole
Preparation Time: 15 minutes
Cooking Time: 45 minutes
Servings: 4
Ingredients:
- Nonstick cooking spray
- 2 cups zucchini, thinly sliced
- 2 tablespoons leeks, sliced

- ½ teaspoon salt
- Freshly ground black pepper, to taste
- ½ teaspoon dried basil
- ½ teaspoon dried oregano
- ½ cup Cheddar cheese, grated
- ¼ cup heavy cream
- 4 tablespoons Parmesan cheese, freshly grated
- 1tablespoon butter, room temperature
- 1 teaspoon fresh garlic, minced

Directions:

1. Start by preheating your oven to 370ºF (188ºC). Lightly grease a casserole dish with a nonstick cooking spray.
2. Place 1 cup of the zucchini slices in the dish; add 1 tablespoon of leeks; sprinkle with salt, pepper, basil, and oregano. Top with ¼ cup of Cheddar cheese. Repeat the layers one more time.
3. In a mixing dish, thoroughly whisk the heavy cream with Parmesan, butter, and garlic. Spread this mixture over the zucchini layer and cheese layers.
4. Place in the preheated oven and bake for about 40 to 45 minutes until the edges are nicely browned. Sprinkle with chopped chives, if desired. Bon appétit!

Nutrition: Calories: 156 Fat: 12.8 g Protein: 7.5 g Carbs: 3.6 g Net carbs: 2.8 g Fiber: 0.8 g

703. Chinese Cauliflower Rice with Eggs

Preparation Time: 7 minutes
Cooking Time: 8 minutes
Servings: 3
Ingredients:

- ½ pound (227-g.) fresh cauliflower
- 1 tablespoon sesame oil
- ½ cup leeks, chopped
- 1 garlic, pressed
- Sea salt and freshly ground black pepper, to taste
- ½ teaspoon Chinese five-spice powder
- 1 teaspoon oyster sauce

- ½ teaspoon light soy sauce
- 1 tablespoon Shaoxing wine
- 3 eggs

Directions:

1. Pulse the cauliflower in a food processor until it resembles rice.
2. Heat the sesame oil in a pan over medium-high heat; sauté the leeks and garlic for 2 to 3 minutes. Add the prepared cauliflower rice to the pan, along with salt, black pepper, and Chinese five-spice powder.
3. Next, add oyster sauce, soy sauce, and wine. Let it cook, stirring occasionally, until the cauliflower is crisp-tender, about 5 minutes.
4. Then, add the eggs to the pan; stir until everything is well combined. Serve warm and enjoy!

Nutrition: Calories: 132 Fat: 8.8 g Protein: 7.2 g Carbs: 6.2 g Net Carbs: 4.4 g Fiber: 1.8 g

704. Mushroom Stroganoff

Preparation Time: 5 minutes
Cooking Time: 10 minutes
Servings: 3
Ingredients:

- 2 tablespoons olive oil
- ½ shallot, diced
- 3 cloves garlic, chopped
- 12 ounces (340-g.) brown mushrooms, thinly sliced
- 2 cups tomato sauce

Directions:

1. Heat the olive oil in a stockpot over medium-high heat. Then, sauté the shallot for about 3 minutes until tender and fragrant.
2. Now, stir in the garlic and mushrooms and cook them for 1 minute more until aromatic.
3. Fold in the tomato sauce and bring to a boil; turn the heat to medium-low, cover, and continue to simmer for 5 to 6 minutes.
4. Salt to taste and serve over cauliflower rice if desired. Enjoy!

Nutrition: Calories: 137 Fat: 9.3 g Protein: 3.4 g Carbs: 7.1 g Net Carbs: 5.3 g Fiber: 1.8 g

705. Zucchini Fritters

Preparation Time: 10 minutes
Cooking Time: 5 minutes
Servings: 6
Ingredients:

- 1pound (454-g.) zucchini, grated and drained
- 1 egg
- 1 teaspoon fresh Italian parsley
- ½ cup almond meal
- ½ cup goat cheese, crumbled
- Sea salt and ground black pepper, to taste
- ½ teaspoon red pepper flakes, crushed
- 2 tablespoons olive oil

Directions:

1. Mix all ingredients, except for the olive oil, in a large bowl. Let it sit in your refrigerator for 30 minutes.
2. Heat the oil in a non-stick frying pan over medium heat; scoop the heaped tablespoons of the zucchini mixture into the hot oil.
3. Cook for 3 to 4 minutes; then, gently flip the fritters over and cook on the other side. Cook in a couple of batches.
4. Transfer to a paper towel to soak up any excess grease. Serve and enjoy!

Nutrition: Calories: 110 Fat: 8.8 g Protein: 5.8 g Carbs: 3.2 g Net Carbs: 2.2 g Fiber: 1.0 g

706. Cheese Stuffed Spaghetti Squash

Preparation Time: 15 minutes
Cooking Time: 50 to 60 minutes
Servings: 4
Ingredients:

- ½ pound (227 g) spaghetti squash, halved, scoop out seeds
- 1 teaspoon olive oil
- ½ cup Mozzarella cheese, shredded
- ½ cup cream cheese
- ½ cup full-fat Greek yogurt
- 2 eggs
- 1 garlic clove, minced
- ½ teaspoon cumin
- ½ teaspoon basil ½ teaspoon mint

- Sea salt and ground black pepper, to taste

Directions:

1. Place the squash halves in a baking pan; drizzle the insides of each squash half with olive oil.
2. Bake in the preheated oven at 370°F (188°C) for 45 to 50 minutes or until the interiors are easily pierced through with a fork
3. Now, scrape out the spaghetti squash "noodles" from the skin in a mixing bowl. Add the remaining ingredients and mix to combine well.
4. Carefully fill each of the squash halves with the cheese mixture. Bake at 350°F (180°C) for 5 to 10 minutes, until the cheese is bubbling and golden brown. Bon appétit!

Nutrition: Calories: 220 Fat: 17.6 g Protein: 9.0 g Carbs: 6.8 g Net Carbs: 5.9 g Fiber: 0.9 g

707. Cottage Kale Stir-Fry

Preparation Time: 10 minutes
Cooking Time: 10 minutes
Servings: 3
Ingredients:

- ½ tablespoon olive oil
- 1 teaspoon fresh garlic, chopped
- 9 ounces (255-g.) kale, torn into pieces
- ½ cup Cottage cheese, creamed
- ½ teaspoon sea salt

Directions:

1. Heat the olive oil in a saucepan over a moderate flame. Now, cook the garlic until just tender and aromatic.
2. Then, stir in the kale and continue to cook for about 10 minutes until all liquid evaporates.
3. Fold in the Cottage cheese and salt; stir until everything is heated through. Enjoy!

Nutrition: Calories: 94 Fat: 4.5 g Protein: 7.0 g Carbs: 6.2 g Net Carbs: 3.5 g Fiber: 2. 7 g

708. Herbed Eggplant and Kale Bake

Preparation Time: 20 minutes
Cooking Time: 40 minutes
Servings: 6
Ingredients:

- 1 (¾-lb. / 340-g.) eggplant, cut into ½-inch slices
- 1 tablespoon olive oil
- 1 tablespoon butter, melted
- 8 ounces (227-g.) kale leaves, torn into pieces
- 14 ounces (397-g.) garlic-and-tomato pasta sauce, without sugar
- ⅓ cup cream cheese
- 1 cup Asiago cheese, shredded
- ½ cup Gorgonzola cheese, grated
- 2 tablespoons ketchup, without sugar
- 1 teaspoon hot pepper
- 1 teaspoon basil
- 1 teaspoon oregano
- ½ teaspoon rosemary

Directions:

1. Place the eggplant slices in a colander and sprinkle them with salt. Allow it to sit for 2 hours. Wipe the eggplant slices with paper towels.
2. Brush the eggplant slices with olive oil; cook in a cast-iron grill pan until nicely browned on both sides, about 5 minutes.
3. Melt the butter in a pan over medium flame. Now, cook the kale leaves until wilted. In a mixing bowl, combine the three types of cheese.
4. Transfer the grilled eggplant slices to a lightly greased baking dish. Top with the kale. Then, add a layer of ½ of cheese blend.
5. Pour the tomato sauce over the cheese layer. Top with the remaining cheese mixture. Sprinkle with seasoning.
6. Bake in the preheated oven at 350°F (180°C) until cheese is bubbling and golden brown, about 35 minutes. Bon appétit!

Nutrition: Calories: 231 Fat: 18.6 g Protein: 10.5 g Carbs: 6.7 g Net Carbs: 4.3 g Fiber: 2.4 g

709. Broccoli and Cauliflower Mash

Preparation Time: 2 minutes
Cooking Time: 13 minutes
Servings: 3
Ingredients:

- ½ pound (227-g.) broccoli florets
- ½ pound (227-g.) cauliflower florets
- Kosher salt and ground black pepper, to season
- ½ teaspoon garlic powder
- 1 teaspoon shallot powder
- 4 tablespoons whipped cream cheese
- 1½ tablespoons butter

Directions:

1. Microwave the broccoli and cauliflower for about 13 minutes until they have softened completely. Transfer to a food processor and add in the remaining ingredients.
2. Process the ingredients until everything is well combined.
3. Taste and adjust the seasoning. Bon appétit!

Nutrition: Calories: 163 Fat: 12.8 g Protein: 4.7 g Carbs: 7.2 g Net Carbs: 3.7 g Fiber: 3.5 g

710. Cheesy Stuffed Peppers

Preparation Time: 15 minutes
Cooking Time: 40 minutes
Servings: 4
Ingredients:

- 2 tablespoons olive oil
- 4 red bell peppers, halved and seeded
- 1 cup ricotta cheese
- ½ cup gorgonzola cheese, crumbled
- 2 cloves garlic, minced
- 1½ cups tomatoes, chopped
- 1 teaspoon dried basil
- Salt and black pepper, to taste
- ½ teaspoon oregano

Directions:

1. Let the oven heat up to 350°F.
2. In a bowl, mix garlic, tomatoes, gorgonzola, and ricotta cheeses.

3. Stuff the pepper halves and remove them to the baking dish. Season with oregano, salt, cayenne pepper, black pepper, and basil.
4. **Baking Time:** 40 minutes

Nutrition: Calories: 295 Fat: 12.4 g Fiber: 10.1 g Carbohydrates: 5.4 g Protein: 13.2 g

711.   Creamy Spinach

Preparation Time: 5 minutes
Cooking Time: 5 minutes
Servings: 4
Ingredients:

- 1 tablespoon butter, room temperature
- 1 clove garlic, minced
- 10 ounces (283-g.) spinach
- ½ teaspoon garlic salt
- ¼ teaspoon ground black pepper, or more to taste
- ½ teaspoon cayenne pepper
- 3 ounces (85-g.) cream cheese
- ½ cup double cream

Directions:

1. Melt the butter in a saucepan that is preheated over medium heat. Once hot. Cook garlic for 30 seconds.
2. Now, add the spinach; cover the pan for 2 minutes to let the spinach wilt. Season with salt, black pepper, and cayenne pepper
3. Stir in cheese and cream; stir until the cheese melts. Serve immediately.

Nutrition: Calories: 167 Fat: 15.1 g Protein: 4.4 g Carbs: 5.0 g Net Carbs: 3.3 g Fiber: 1.7 g

712.   Fried Cabbage

Preparation Time: 10 minutes
Cooking Time: 15 minutes
Servings: 3
Ingredients:

- 4 ounces (113-g.) bacon, diced
- 1 medium-sized onion, chopped
- 2 cloves garlic, minced
- ½ teaspoon caraway seeds
- 1 bay laurel
- ½ teaspoon cayenne pepper
- 1 pound (454-g.) red cabbage, shredded

- ¼ teaspoon ground black pepper, to season
- 1 cup beef bone broth

Directions:

1. Heat up a nonstick skillet over a moderate flame. Cook the bacon for 3 to 4 minutes, stirring continuously; set aside.
2. In the same skillet, sauté the onion for 2 to 3 minutes or until it has softened. Now, sauté the garlic and caraway seeds for 30 seconds more or until aromatic.
3. Then, add in the remaining ingredients and stir to combine. Reduce the temperature to medium-low, cover, and cook for 10 minutes longer; stirring periodically to ensure even cooking.
4. Serve in individual bowls, garnished with the reserved bacon. Enjoy!

Nutrition: Calories: 242 Fat: 22.2 g Protein: 6.5 g Carbs: 6.8 g Net Carbs: 4.9 g Fiber: 1.9 g

713.   Cumin Green Cabbage Stir-Fry

Preparation Time: 10 minutes
Cooking Time: 20 minutes
Servings: 2
Ingredients:

- 2 tablespoons olive oil
- 1 (1-inch) piece fresh ginger, grated
- ½ teaspoon cumin seeds
- 1 shallot, chopped
- ½ cup chicken stock
- ¾ pound (340-g.) green cabbage, sliced
- ¼ teaspoon turmeric powder
- ½ teaspoon coriander powder
- Kosher salt and cayenne pepper, to taste

Directions:

1. Heat the olive oil in a saucepan over medium heat; then, sauté the ginger and cumin seeds until fragrant.
2. Add in the shallot and continue sautéing an additional 2 to 3 minutes or until just tender and

aromatic. Pour in the chicken stock to deglaze the pan.
3. Add the cabbage wedges, turmeric, coriander, salt, and cayenne pepper. Cover and cook for 15 to 18 minutes or until your cabbage has softened. Make sure to stir occasionally.
4. Serve in individual bowls and enjoy!

Nutrition: Calories: 169 Fat: 13.0 g Protein: 2.6 g Carbs: 7.0 g Net Carbs: 2.9 g Fiber: 4.1 g

714.   Greek Veggie Briam

Preparation Time: 10 minutes
Cooking Time: 30 minutes
Servings: 4
Ingredients:

- ⅓ cup good-quality olive oil, divided
- 1 onion, thinly sliced
- 1 tablespoon minced garlic
- ¾ small eggplant, diced
- 2 zucchinis, diced
- 2 cups chopped cauliflower
- 1 red bell pepper, diced
- 2 cups diced tomatoes
- 2 tablespoons chopped fresh parsley
- 2 tablespoons chopped fresh oregano
- Sea salt, for seasoning
- Freshly ground black pepper, for seasoning
- 1½ cups crumbled feta cheese
- ¼ cup pumpkin seeds

Directions:

1. Preheat the oven. Set the oven to broil and lightly grease a 9-by-13-inch casserole dish with olive oil.
2. Sauté the aromatics in a medium stockpot over medium heat, warm 3 tablespoons of the olive oil. Add the onion and garlic and sauté until they've softened for about 3 minutes.
3. Sauté the vegetables. Stir in the eggplant, cook, stirring occasionally.
4. Add the zucchini, cauliflower, and red bell

pepper and cook for 5 minutes.

5. Stir in the tomatoes, parsley, and oregano and cook, stirring it from time to time, until the vegetables are tender, about 10 minutes. Season it with salt and pepper.

6. Broil. Put vegetable mix in the casserole dish and top with the crumbled feta. Broil until the cheese is melted.

7. Serve. Divide the casserole between four plates and top it with the pumpkin seeds. Drizzle with the remaining olive oil.

Nutrition: Calories: 341 Fat: 5.1 g Fiber: 11 g Carbohydrates: 1.2 g

715. Braised Cream Kale
Preparation Time: 4 minutes
Cooking Time: 11 minutes
Servings: 5
Ingredients:

- 2 tablespoons olive oil
- 1 shallot, chopped
- 6 cups kale, torn into pieces
- ½ teaspoon fresh garlic, minced
- 2 tablespoons dry white wine
- ¼ teaspoon red pepper flakes, crushed
- Sea salt and ground black pepper, to taste
- ½ cup double cream

Directions:

1. Heat the olive oil in a large, heavy-bottomed sauté pan over moderate heat. Now, sauté the shallot until it is tender or about 4 minutes.

2. Stir in the kale and continue to cook for 2 minutes more. Remove any excess liquid and stir in the garlic; continue to cook for a minute or so.

3. Add a splash of wine to deglaze the pan. Then, add the red pepper, salt, black pepper, and double cream to the pan.

4. Turn the heat to simmer. Continue to simmer, covered, for a further 4

minutes. Serve warm and enjoy!

Nutrition: Calories: 130 Fat: 10.5 g Protein: 3.7 g Carbs: 6.1 g Net Carbs: 3.1 g Fiber: 3.0 g

716. White Wine-Dijon Brussels Sprouts
Preparation Time: 10 minutes
Cooking Time: 10 minutes
Servings: 3
Ingredients:

- 6 ounces (170-g.) smoked bacon, diced
- 12 Brussels sprouts, trimmed and halved
- ¼ teaspoon ground bay leaf
- ¼ teaspoon dried oregano
- ¼ teaspoon dried sage
- ¼ teaspoon freshly cracked black pepper, or more to taste
- Sea salt, to taste
- ½ cup dry white wine
- 1 teaspoon Dijon mustard

Directions:

1. Heat up a nonstick skillet over medium-high heat. Once hot, cook the bacon for 1 minute.

2. Add the Brussels sprouts and seasoning and continue sautéing, adding white wine and stirring until the bacon is crisp and the Brussels sprouts are tender. It will take about 9 minutes.

3. Then, stir in the mustard, remove from the heat, and serve immediately. Enjoy!

Nutrition: Calories: 298 Fat: 22.4 g Protein: 9.6 g Carbs: 6.4 g Net Carbs: 3.4 g Fiber: 3.0 g

717. Paprika Riced Cauliflower
Preparation Time: 4 minutes
Cooking Time: 6 minutes
Servings: 4
Ingredients:

- 1 tablespoon butter
- 1 pound (454-g.) cauliflower florets
- 2 cloves garlic, minced
- 1 tablespoon smoked paprika
- Flaky salt, to taste

Directions:

1. Melt the butter in a frying pan over a moderate flame.

2. Pulse the cauliflower in your food processor until your cauliflower has broken down into rice-sized chunks for approximately 6 seconds.

3. Add the cauliflower rice to the frying pan and cook, covered, for 5 minutes. Stir in the garlic and smoked paprika. Continue to sauté an additional minute or so.

4. Season with salt to taste and serve immediately. Bon appétit!

Nutrition: Calories: 57 Fat: 3.2 g Protein: 2.3 g Carbs: 6.1 g Net Carbs: 3.8 g Fiber: 2.3 g

718. Wax Beans with Tomato-Mustard Sauce
Preparation Time: 9 minutes
Cooking Time: 6 minutes
Servings: 4
Ingredients:

- 1 tablespoon butter
- 2 garlic cloves, thinly sliced
- ½ pound (227-g.) wax beans, trimmed
- ½ cup tomato sauce
- 2 tablespoons dry white wine
- ½ teaspoon mustard seeds
- Sea salt and ground black pepper, to taste

Directions:

1. Melt the butter in a saucepan over a medium-high flame. Now, sauté the garlic until aromatic but not browned.

2. Stir in the wax beans, tomato sauce, wine, and mustard seeds. Season with salt and black pepper to taste.

3. Turn the heat to medium-low, partially cover, and continue to cook for 6 minutes longer or until everything is heated through. Bon appétit!

Nutrition: Calories: 56 Fat: 3.5 g Protein: 1.5 g Carbs: 6.0 g Net Carbs: 3.8 g Fiber: 2.2 g

719. Leek, Mushroom, and Zucchini Stew

Preparation Time: 5 minutes
Cooking Time: 15 minutes
Servings: 4
Ingredients:

- ½ cup leeks, chopped
- 1 pound (454-g.) brown mushrooms, chopped
- 1 teaspoon garlic, minced
- 1 medium-sized zucchini, diced
- 2 ripe tomatoes, puréed

Directions:

1. Heat up a lightly greased soup pot over medium-high heat. Now, sauté the leeks until just tender about 3 minutes.
2. Stir in the mushrooms, garlic, and zucchini. Continue to sauté for an additional 2minutes or until tender and aromatic.
3. Add in the tomatoes and 2cups of water. Season with Sazón spice, if desired. Reduce the temperature to simmer and continue to cook, covered, for 10 to 12minutes more. Bon appétit!

Nutrition: Calories: 108 Fat: 7.5 g Protein: 3.1 g Carbs: 7.0 g Net Carbs: 4.5 g Fiber: 2.5 g

720. Almond and Rind Crusted Zucchini Fritters

Preparation Time: 13 minutes
Cooking Time: 2minutes
Servings: 2
Ingredients:

- 2 tablespoons olive oil
- 3 eggs, whisked
- 1 teaspoon garlic, pressed
- ½ pound (227-g.) zucchini, grated
- ⅓ cup almond meal
- 2 tablespoons pork rinds
- ¼ teaspoon paprika
- Sea salt and ground black pepper, to taste
- ½ cup Swiss cheese, shredded

Directions:

1. Add the grated zucchini to a colander. Add ½ teaspoon of salt, toss and let it sit for 10 minutes. After that, drain the zucchini completely using a cheese cloth.
2. Heat the olive oil in a skillet over medium-high flame. In a mixing bowl, combine the zucchini with the remaining ingredients until everything is well incorporated.
3. Make the fritters, flattening them with a spatula; cook for 2minutes on both sides. Bon appétit!

Nutrition: Calories: 462 Fat: 36.0 g Protein: 27.5 g Carbs: 7.6 g Net Carbs: 4.8 g Fiber: 2.8 g

721. Spiced Cauliflower Cheese Bake

Preparation Time: 20 minutes
Cooking Time: 20 minutes
Servings: 4
Ingredients:

- ½ teaspoon butter, melted
- 1 (½-lb. / 227-g.) head cauliflower, broken into florets
- ½ cup Swiss cheese, shredded
- ½ cup Mexican blend cheese, room temperature
- ½ cup Greek yogurt
- 1 cup cooked ham, chopped
- 1 roasted chili pepper, chopped
- ½ teaspoon porcini powder
- 1 teaspoon garlic powder
- 1 teaspoon shallot powder
- ½ teaspoon cayenne pepper
- ¼ teaspoon dried sage
- ½ teaspoon dried oregano
- Sea salt and ground black pepper, to taste

Directions:

1. Start by preheating your oven to 340°F (171°C). Then, coat the bottom and sides of a casserole dish with ½ teaspoon of melted butter.
2. Empty the cauliflower into a pot and cover it with water. Let it cook for 6 minutes until it is nice and tender (mashable). Mash the prepared cauliflower with a potato ricer press or potato masher.
3. Now, stir in the cheese; stir until the cheese has melted. Add Greek yogurt, chopped ham, roasted pepper, and spices.
4. Place the mixture in the prepared casserole dish; bake in the preheated oven for 20 minutes. Let it sit for about 10 minutes before cutting. Serve and enjoy!

Nutrition: Calories: 189 Fat: 11.3 g Protein: 14.9 g Carbs: 5.7 g Net Carbs: 4.6 g Fiber: 1.1 g

722. Roasted Asparagus

Preparation Time: 10 minutes
Cooking Time: 15 minutes
Servings: 5
Ingredients:

- 4 tablespoons butter, melted
- 4 tablespoons Pecorino Romano cheese, grated
- 1½ pounds (680-g.) asparagus, trimmed
- ½ teaspoon cayenne pepper
- Sea salt and cracked black pepper, to taste
- 1 tablespoon Sriracha sauce
- 1 tablespoon fresh cilantro, roughly chopped

Directions:

1. Toss your asparagus with the melted butter, cheese, cayenne pepper, salt, black pepper, and Sriracha sauce; toss until well coated.
2. Place the asparagus on a roasting pan. Roast in the preheated oven at 420°F (216°C) for 10 minutes.
3. Rotate the pan and continue to cook for an additional 4 to 5 minutes. Serve immediately garnished with fresh cilantro. Bon appétit!

Nutrition: Calories: 141 Fat: 11.5 g Protein: 5.6 g Carbs: 5.5 g Net Carbs: 2.6 g Fiber: 2.9 g

723. Mozzarella Italian Peppers

Preparation Time: 7 minutes
Cooking Time: 13 minutes
Servings: 5
Ingredients:

- 4 tablespoons canola oil
- 1 yellow onion, sliced
- 1⅓ pounds (605-g.) Italian peppers, deveined and sliced

- 1 teaspoon Italian seasoning mix
- Sea salt and cayenne pepper, to season
- 2 balls buffalo mozzarella, drained and halved

Directions:
1. Heat the canola oil in a saucepan over a medium-low flame. Now, sauté the onion until just tender and translucent.
2. Add in the peppers and spices. Cook for about 13 minutes, adding a splash of water to deglaze the pan.
3. Divide between serving plates; top with cheese and serve immediately. Enjoy!

Nutrition: Calories: 175 Fat: 11.0 g Protein: 10.4 g Carbs: 7.0 g Net Carbs: 5.1 g Fiber: 1.9 g

724. Queso Fresco Avocado Salsa

Preparation Time: 5 minutes
Cooking Time: 0 minutes
Servings: 4
Ingredients:
- 2 tomatoes, diced
- 3 scallions, chopped
- 1 poblano pepper, chopped
- 1 garlic clove, minced
- 2 ripe avocados, peeled, pitted and diced
- 1 tablespoon extra-virgin olive oil
- 2 tablespoons fresh lime juice
- Sea salt and ground black pepper, to season
- ¼ cup queso fresco, crumbled

Directions:
1. Place the tomatoes, scallions, poblano pepper, garlic and avocado in a serving bowl. Drizzle olive oil and lime juice over everything.
2. Season with salt and black pepper.
3. To serve, top with crumbled queso fresco and enjoy!

Nutrition: Calories: 189 Fat: 16.0 g Protein: 3.6 g Carbs: 6.9 g Net Carbs: 2.7 g Fiber: 4.2 g

725. Indian White Cabbage Stew

Preparation Time: 8 minutes
Cooking Time: 22 minutes
Servings: 3
Ingredients:
- 6 ounces (170-g.) Goan chorizo sausage, sliced
- 2 cloves garlic, finely chopped
- 1 teaspoon Indian spice blend
- 1 pound (454-g.) white cabbage, outer leaves removed and finely shredded
- ¾ cup cream of celery soup

Directions:
1. Heat a large-sized wok over a moderate flame. Now, sear the Goan chorizo sausage until no longer pink; reserve.
2. Cook the garlic and Indian spice blend in the pan drippings until they are aromatic. Now, stir in the cabbage and cream of celery soup.
3. Turn the temperature to medium-low, cover, and continue simmering for an additional 22minutes or until tender and heated through.
4. Add the reserved Goan chorizo sausage; ladle into individual bowls and serve. Enjoy!

Nutrition: Calories: 236 Fat: 17.7 g Protein: 9.8 g Carbs: 6.1 g Net Carbs: 3.7 g Fiber: 2.4 g

726. Baked Eggplant Rounds

Preparation Time: 10 minutes
Cooking Time: 35 minutes
Servings: 6
Ingredients:
- 1 pound (454-g.) eggplant, peeled and sliced
- 2 teaspoons Italian seasoning blend
- ½ teaspoon cayenne pepper
- ½ teaspoon salt
- 1½ cups marinara sauce
- 1 cup Mozzarella cheese
- 2 tablespoons fresh basil leaves, snipped

Directions:
1. Begin by preheating your oven to 380ºF (193ºC). Line a baking pan with parchment paper.
2. Now, arrange the eggplant rounds on the baking pan. Season with the Italian blend, cayenne pepper, and salt.
3. Bake for 25 to 28 minutes, flipping the rounds halfway through baking time.
4. Next, remove from the oven and top with the marinara sauce and Mozzarella cheese.
5. Bake for 6 to 8 minutes more until Mozzarella is bubbling. Garnish with fresh basil leaves just before serving.

Nutrition: Calories: 92 Fat: 4.8 g Protein: 5.2 g Carbs: 5.2 g Net Carbs: 2.3 g Fiber: 2.9 g

727. Fennel Avgolemono

Preparation Time: 10 minutes
Cooking Time: 20 minutes
Servings: 6
Ingredients:
- 2 tablespoons olive oil
- 1 celery stalk, chopped
- 1 pound (454 g) fennel bulbs, sliced
- 1 garlic clove, minced
- 1 bay laurel
- 1 thyme sprig
- 2 cups chicken stock
- Sea salt and ground black pepper, to season
- 2 eggs
- 1 tablespoon freshly squeezed lemon juice

Directions:
1. Heat the olive oil in a heavy-bottomed pot over a medium-high flame. Now, sauté the celery and fennel until they have softened but not browned, about 8 minutes.
2. Add in the garlic, bay laurel, and thyme sprig; continue sautéing until aromatic an additional minute or so.
3. Add the chicken stock, salt, and black pepper to the pot. Bring to a boil. Reduce the heat to medium-low and let

it simmer, partially covered for approximately 13 minutes.

4. Discard the bay laurel and then, blend your soup with an immersion blender.
5. Whisk the eggs and lemon juice; gradually pour 2 cups of the hot soup into the egg mixture, whisking constantly.
6. Return the soup to the pot and continue stirring for a few minutes or just until thickened. Serve warm.

Nutrition: Calories: 85 Fat: 6.2 g Protein: 2.8 g Carbs: 6.0 g Net Carbs: 3.5 g Fiber: 2.5 g

728. Spinach and Butternut Squash Stew

Preparation Time: 10 minutes
Cooking Time: 30 minutes
Servings: 4
Ingredients:

- 2 tablespoons olive oil
- 1 Spanish onion, peeled and diced
- 1 garlic clove, minced
- ½ pound (227-g.) butternut squash, diced
- 1 celery stalk, chopped
- 3 cups vegetable broth
- Kosher salt and freshly cracked black pepper, to taste
- 4 cups baby spinach
- 4 tablespoons sour cream

Directions:

1. Heat the olive oil in a soup pot over a moderate flame. Now, sauté the Spanish onion until tender and translucent.
2. Then, cook the garlic until just tender and aromatic.
3. Stir in the butternut squash, celery, broth, salt, and black pepper. Turn the heat to simmer and let it cook, covered, for 30 minutes.
4. Fold in the baby spinach leaves and cover with the lid; let it sit in the residual heat until the baby spinach wilts completely.
5. Serve dolloped with cold sour cream. Enjoy!

Nutrition: Calories: 150 Fat: 11.6 g Protein: 2.5 g Carbs: 6.8 g Net Carbs: 4.5 g Fiber: 2.3 g

729. Broccoli Cheese

Preparation Time: 10 minutes
Cooking Time: 15 minutes
Servings: 5
Ingredients:

- 3 tablespoons olive oil
- 1 teaspoon garlic, minced
- 1½ pounds (680-g.) broccoli florets
- ½ teaspoon flaky salt
- ½ teaspoon ground black pepper
- ½ teaspoon paprika
- ½ cup cream of mushrooms soup
- 6 ounces (170-g.) Swiss cheese, shredded

Directions:

1. Heat 1 tablespoon of the olive oil in a nonstick frying pan over a moderate flame. Then, sauté the garlic until just tender and fragrant.
2. Preheat your oven to 390°F (199°C). Now, brush the sides and bottom of a casserole dish with 1 tablespoon of olive oil.
3. Parboil the broccoli in salted water until it is crisp-tender; discard any excess water and transfer the boiled broccoli florets to the prepared casserole dish. Scatter the sautéed garlic around the broccoli florets.
4. Drizzle the remaining tablespoon of olive oil; sprinkle the salt, black pepper, and paprika over your broccoli. Pour in the cream of mushroom soup.
5. Top with the Swiss cheese and bake for approximately 18 minutes until the cheese bubbled all over. Bon appétit!

Nutrition: Calories: 180 Fat: 10.3 g Protein: 13.5 g Carbs: 7.6 g Net Carbs: 4.0 g Fiber: 3.6 g

730. Za'atar Chanterelle Stew

Preparation Time: 15 minutes
Cooking Time: 50 minutes
Servings: 4
Ingredients:

- ½ teaspoon Za'atar spice
- 4 tablespoons olive oil
- ½ cup shallots, chopped
- 2 bell peppers, chopped
- 1 poblano pepper, finely chopped
- 8 ounces (227-g.) Chanterelle mushroom, sliced
- ½ teaspoon garlic, minced
- Sea salt and freshly cracked black pepper, to taste
- 1 cup tomato purée & 3 cups vegetable broth
- 1 bay laurel

Directions:

1. Combine the Za'atar with 3 tablespoons of olive oil in a small saucepan. Cook over a moderate flame until hot; make sure not to burn the zaatar. Set aside for 1 hour to cool and infuse.
2. In a heavy-bottomed pot, heat the remaining tablespoon of olive oil. Now, sauté the shallots and bell peppers until just tender and fragrant.
3. Stir in the poblano pepper, mushrooms, and garlic; continue to sauté until the mushrooms have softened.
4. Next, add in the salt, black pepper, tomato purée, broth, and bay laurel. Once your stew begins to boil, turn the heat down to a simmer.
5. Let it simmer for about 40 minutes until everything is thoroughly cooked. Ladle into individual bowls and drizzle each serving with Za'atar oil. Bon appétit!

Nutrition: Calories: 156 Fat: 13.8 g Protein: 1.4 g Carbs: 6.0 g Net Carbs: 3.1 g Fiber: 2.9 g

731. Duo-Cheese Broccoli Croquettes

Preparation Time: 10 minutes
Cooking Time: 10 minutes
Servings: 5
Ingredients:

- 1 pound (454-g.) broccoli florets
- 1 tablespoon fresh parsley, minced
- ½ teaspoon paprika
- Sea salt and ground black pepper, to taste
- 3 eggs
- 1 cup Romano cheese, preferably freshly grated
- 5 ounces (142-g.) Swiss cheese, sliced
- 2 tablespoons olive oil

Directions:

1. Pulse the broccoli florets in your food processor until small rice-sized pieces are formed.
2. Mix the chopped broccoli florets with parsley, paprika, salt, pepper, eggs, and Romano cheese. Shape the mixture into bite-sized balls; flatten the balls with your hands or fork.
3. Heat the olive oil in a frying pan over a moderate flame.
4. Cook for 4 to 5 minutes; turn over, top with the Swiss cheese, and continue to cook on the other side for a further 4 minutes or until thoroughly cooked. Bon appétit!

Nutrition: Calories: 324 Fat: 24.1 g Protein: 19.9 g Carbs: 5.8 g Net Carbs: 3.5 g Fiber: 2.3 g

732. Bell Pepper and Tomato Sataraš

Preparation Time: 5 minutes
Cooking Time: 15 minutes
Servings: 3
Ingredients:

- 3 teaspoons olive oil
- 1 onion, chopped
- 2 garlic cloves, minced
- 3 bell peppers, deveined and sliced
- 1 tomato, puréed

Directions:

1. Heat the olive oil in a saucepan over moderate flame. Then, sweat the onion until translucent.
2. Stir in the garlic and bell peppers and sauté for 2 minutes more or until aromatic. Stir in the puréed tomato.
3. Cover, reduce the temperature to medium-low, and continue to cook for 12 minutes or until the peppers have softened and the cooking liquid has evaporated.
4. Salt to taste and serve in individual bowls. Bon appétit!

Nutrition: Calories: 84 Fat: 4.6 g Protein: 1.6 g Carbs: 6.5 g Net Carbs: 4.7 g Fiber: 1.8 g

733. Provençal Ratatouille

Preparation Time: 15 minutes
Cooking Time: 35 minutes
Servings: 6
Ingredients:

- 2 tablespoons olive oil
- 2 garlic cloves, finely minced
- 1 red pepper, sliced
- 1 yellow pepper, sliced
- 1 green pepper, sliced
- 1 shallot, sliced
- 1 large-sized zucchini, sliced
- 3 tomatoes, sliced
- 1 cup vegetable broth
- Sea salt, to taste
- ½ teaspoon dried oregano
- ½ teaspoon dried parsley flakes
- ½ teaspoon paprika
- ½ teaspoon ground black pepper & eggs

Directions:

1. Start by preheating your oven to 400°F (205°C). Brush the sides and bottom of a baking pan with olive oil.
2. Layer all vegetables into the prepared pan and cover tightly with foil. Pour in the vegetable broth. Season with salt, oregano, parsley, paprika, and ground black pepper.
3. Bake for about 25 minutes.
4. Create six indentations in the hot ratatouille. Break an egg into each indentation. Bake until the eggs are set or about 9 minutes. Enjoy!

Nutrition: Calories: 440 Fat: 45.0 g Protein: 6.4 g Carbs: 5.6 g Net Carbs: 4.6 g Fiber: 1.0 g

734. Mozzarella Roasted Peppers

Preparation Time: 5 minutes
Cooking Time: 15 minutes
Servings: 4
Ingredients:

- 2 teaspoons olive oil
- 4 Italian sweet peppers, deveined and halved
- Salt and black pepper, to taste
- ¼ teaspoon red pepper flakes
- 8 ounces (227-g.) Mozzarella cheese

Directions:

1. Put your oven on broil. Drizzle the pepper halves with olive oil. Season the peppers with salt, black pepper, and red pepper flakes.
2. Top the pepper halves with Mozzarella cheese. Arrange the stuffed peppers on a parchment-lined baking tray.
3. Roast for 12 to 15 until the cheese is browned on top and the peppers are tender and blistered. Bon appétit!

Nutrition: Calories: 215 Fat: 15.1 g Protein: 13.5 g Carbs: 6.7 g Net Carbs: 4.7 g Fiber: 2.0 g

735. Italian Tomato and Cheese Stuffed Peppers

Preparation Time: 15 minutes
Cooking Time: 10 minutes
Servings: 2
Ingredients:

- 1 tablespoon canola oil
- 1 garlic clove, pressed
- ½ cup celery, finely chopped
- ½ Spanish onion, finely chopped
- 4 ounces (113-g.) pork, ground
- Sea salt, to taste
- 1 teaspoon Italian seasoning mix

- 2 sweet Italian peppers, deveined and halved
- 1 large-sized Roma tomato, puréed
- ½ cup Cheddar cheese, grated

Directions:
1. Heat the canola oil in a sauté pan over medium-high heat. Now, sauté the garlic, celery, and onion until they have softened.
2. Stir in the ground pork and cook for a further 3 minutes or until no longer pink. Sprinkle with salt and Italian seasoning mix. Divide the filling mixture between the pepper halves.
3. Add the puréed tomato to a lightly greased baking dish; place the stuffed peppers in the baking dish.
4. Bake in the preheated oven at 390°F (199°C) for 20 minutes. Top with the Cheddar cheese and bake an additional 4 to 6 minutes or until the cheese is bubbling. Serve warm and enjoy!

Nutrition: Calories: 312 Fat: 21.4 g Protein: 20.2 g Carbs: 5.7 g Net Carbs: 3.8 g Fiber: 1.9 g

736. Mushroom Mélange

Preparation Time: 10 minutes
Cooking Time: 15 minutes
Servings: 6
Ingredients:
- 4 tablespoons olive oil
- 1 bell pepper, sliced
- ½ cup leeks, finely diced
- 2 cloves garlic, smashed
- 2 pounds (907-g.) brown mushrooms, sliced
- 2 cups chicken broth
- 1 cup tomato sauce
- ½ teaspoon dried oregano
- ½ teaspoon chili powder
- ½ teaspoon paprika
- ½ teaspoon ground black pepper
- Sea salt, to taste

Directions:
1. Heat the oil in a heavy-bottomed pot over medium-high flame. Now, sauté bell pepper along with the leeks for about 5 minutes.

2. Stir in the garlic and mushrooms, and continue sautéing an additional minute or so. Add in a splash of chicken broth to deglaze the bottom of the pan.
3. After that, add in the tomato sauce and seasonings. Bring to a boil and immediately reduce the heat to simmer.
4. Partially cover and cook for 8 to 10 minutes more or until the mushrooms are cooked through.
5. Ladle into individual bowls and serve with cauli rice if desired. Bon appétit!

Nutrition: Calories: 124 Fat: 9.2 g Protein: 4.6 g Carbs: 5.8 g Net Carbs: 4.3 g Fiber: 1.5 g

737. Green Cabbage with Tofu

Preparation Time: 5 minutes
Cooking Time: 15 minutes
Servings: 3
Ingredients:
- 6 ounces (170-g.) tofu, diced
- ½ shallot, chopped
- 2 garlic cloves, finely chopped
- 1 (1½-lbs. / 680-g.) head green cabbage, cut into strips
- ½ cup vegetable broth

Directions:
1. Heat up a lightly oiled sauté pan over moderate heat. Now, cook the tofu until brown and crisp; set aside.
2. Then, sauté the shallot and garlic until just tender and fragrant. Add in the green cabbage and beef bone broth; stir to combine.
3. Reduce the heat to medium-low and continue cooking for an additional 13 minutes. Season with salt to taste, top with reserved tofu and serve warm. Bon appétit!

Nutrition: Calories: 168 Fat: 11.7 g Protein: 10.5 g Carbs: 5.2 g Net Carbs: 2.9 g Fiber: 2.3 g

738. Mushroom and Bell Pepper Omelet

Preparation Time: 5 minutes
Cooking Time: 5 minutes
Servings: 4
Ingredients:
- 2 tablespoons olive oil
- 1 cup Chanterelle mushrooms, chopped
- 2 bell peppers, chopped
- 1 white onion, chopped
- eggs

Directions:
1. Heat the olive oil in a nonstick skillet over moderate heat. Now, cook the mushrooms, peppers, and onion until they have softened.
2. In a mixing bowl, whisk the eggs until frothy. Add the eggs to the skillet, reduce the heat to medium-low, and cook approximately 5 minutes until the center starts to look dry. Do not overcook.
3. Taste and season with salt to taste. Bon appétit!

Nutrition: Calories: 240 Fat: 17.5 g Protein: 12.3 g Carbs: 6.1 g Net Carbs: 4.3 g Fiber: 1.8 g

739. Parmigiano-Reggiano Cheese Broiled Avocados

Preparation Time: 10 minutes
Cooking Time: 5 minutes
Servings: 6
Ingredients:
- 3 avocados, pitted and halved
- ½ teaspoon red pepper flakes, crushed
- ½ teaspoon Himalayan salt
- 3 tablespoons extra-virgin olive oil
- tablespoons Parmigiano-Reggiano cheese, grated

Directions:
1. Begin by preheating your oven for broil.
2. Then, cut a crisscross pattern about ¾ of the way through on each avocado half with a sharp knife.

3. Sprinkle red pepper and salt over the avocado halves. Drizzle olive oil over them and top with the grated Parmigiano-Reggiano cheese.
4. Transfer the avocado halves to a roasting pan and cook under the broiler for approximately 5 minutes. Enjoy!

Nutrition: Calories: 196 Fat: 18.8 g Protein: 2.6 g Carbs: 6.4 g Net Carbs: 1.9 g Fiber: 4.5 g

740. Romaine Lettuce Boats

Preparation Time: 10 minutes
Cooking Time: 3 minutes
Servings: 4
Ingredients:

- ½ pound (227-g.) pork sausage, sliced
- 1 green bell pepper, deveined and chopped
- 1 garlic clove, minced
- ½ cup tomato purée
- ¼ teaspoon ground black pepper
- ½ teaspoon fennel seeds
- Himalayan salt, to taste
- 1 head romaine lettuce, separated into leaves
- 2 scallions, chopped

Directions:

1. Preheat a nonstick frying pan over a moderate flame. Then, sear the pork sausage until no longer pink, crumbling with a fork.
2. Stir in the bell pepper and garlic, and continue sautéing an additional minute or so or until fragrant.
3. Fold in the tomato purée. Season with black pepper, fennel seeds, and salt. Stir well and continue to cook for 2minutes more; remove from the heat.
4. Arrange the lettuce boats on a serving platter. Then, top each boat with the sausage mixture. Garnish with scallions and serve immediately. Bon appétit!

Nutrition: Calories: 231 Fat: 18.1 g Protein: 10.2 g Carbs: 5.6 g Net Carbs: 3.5 g Fiber: 2.1 g

741. Gruyère Celery Boats

Preparation Time: 10 minutes
Cooking Time: 35 minutes
Servings: 2
Ingredients:

- 1 jalapeño pepper, deveined and minced
- ¼ teaspoon sea salt
- ¼ teaspoon ground black pepper
- 1 teaspoon granulated garlic
- 3 tablespoons scallions, minced
- ½ teaspoon caraway seeds
- 2 ounces (57-g.) Gruyère cheese
- 3 celery stalks, halved

Directions:

1. In a mixing bowl, thoroughly combine the minced jalapeño with sea salt, black pepper, garlic, scallions, caraway seeds, and Gruyère cheese.
2. Spread this mixture over the celery stalks. Then, arrange them on a parchment-lined baking tray.
3. Roast in the preheated oven at 360°F (182°C) for 35 minutes or until cooked through.

Nutrition: Calories: 195 Fat: 17.1 g Protein: 2.5 g Carbs: 7.0 g Net Carbs: 2.0 g Fiber: 5.0 g

742. Peasant Stir-Fry

Preparation Time: 10 minutes
Cooking Time: 20 minutes
Servings: 5
Ingredients:

- 2 tablespoons olive oil
- 1 yellow onion, sliced
- 3 garlic cloves, halved
- 8 bell peppers, deveined and cut into strips
- 1 tomato, chopped
- ½ teaspoon ground black pepper
- ½ teaspoon paprika
- ½ teaspoon kosher salt
- 2 eggs

Directions:

1. Heat the olive oil in a frying pan over medium-low heat. Now, sweat the onion for 3 to 4 minutes or until tender.
2. Now, stir in the garlic and peppers; continue sautéing for 5 minutes. Then, add in the tomato, black pepper, paprika, and kosher salt.
3. Partially cover and continue to cook for a further 6 to 8 minutes.
4. Fold in the eggs and stir fry for another 5 minutes. Serve warm and enjoy!

Nutrition: Calories: 115 Fat: 7.5 g Protein: 3.4 g Carbs: 6.0 g Net Carbs: 4.5 g Fiber: 1.5 g

743. Cauliflower Soup

Preparation Time: 4 minutes
Cooking Time: 15 minutes
Servings: 4
Ingredients:

- 2 green onions, chopped
- ½ teaspoon ginger-garlic paste
- 1 celery stalk, chopped
- 1 pound (454-g.) cauliflower florets
- 3 cups vegetable broth

Directions:

1. Heat up a lightly oiled soup pot over a medium-high flame. Now, sauté the green onions until they have softened.
2. Stir in the ginger-garlic paste, celery, cauliflower, and vegetable broth; bring to a rapid boil. Turn the heat to medium-low.
3. Continue to simmer for 13 minutes more or until heated through; heat off.
4. Puree the soup in your blender until creamy and uniform. Enjoy!

Nutrition: Calories: 70 Fat: 1.6 g Protein: 6.2 g Carbs: 7.0 g Net Carbs: 4.0 g Fiber: 3.0 g

744. Avocado Sauced Cucumber Noodles

Preparation Time: 15 minutes
Cooking Time: 0 minutes
Servings: 2
Ingredients:

- ½ teaspoon sea salt
- 1 cucumber, spiralized
- 1 California avocado, pitted, peeled and mashed
- 1 tablespoon olive oil
- ½ teaspoon garlic powder

- ½ teaspoon paprika
- 1 tablespoon fresh lime juice

Directions:

1. Toss your cucumber with salt and let it sit for 30 minutes; discard the excess water and pat dry.
2. In a mixing bowl, thoroughly combine the avocado with olive oil, garlic powder, paprika, and lime juice.
3. Add the sauce to the cucumber noodles and serve immediately. Bon appétit!

Nutrition: Calories: 195 Fat: 17.2 g Protein: 2.6 g Carbs: 7.6 g Net Carbs: 3.0 g Fiber: 4.6 g

745. Zucchini Noodles with Mushroom Sauce

Preparation Time: 10 minutes
Cooking Time: 10 minutes
Servings: 3
Ingredients:

- 1½ tablespoons olive oil
- 3 cups button mushrooms, chopped
- 2 cloves garlic, smashed
- 1 cup tomato purée
- 1 pound (454-g.) zucchini, spiralized
- Salt and ground black pepper, to taste
- ⅓ cup Pecorino Romano cheese, preferably freshly grated

Directions:

1. Heat the olive oil in a saucepan over a moderate flame. Then, cook the mushrooms until tender and fragrant or about 4 minutes.
2. Stir in the garlic and continue to sauté for an additional 30 seconds or until just tender and aromatic. Fold in the tomato purée and zucchini.
3. Reduce the heat to medium-low, partially cover, and let it cook for about 6 minutes or until heated through. Season with salt and black pepper to taste.
4. Divide your zoodles and sauce between serving plates. Top with Pecorino

Romano cheese and serve warm. Bon appétit!

Nutrition: Calories: 161 Fat: 10.5 g Protein: 10.0 g Carbs: 7.4 g Net Carbs: 4.0 g Fiber: 3.4 g

746. Goat Cheese Eggplant Casserole

Preparation Time: 10 minutes
Cooking Time: 25 minutes
Servings: 3
Ingredients:

- 1 (1-lb. / 454-g) eggplant, cut into rounds
- 2 bell peppers, deveined and quartered
- 2 vine-ripe tomatoes, sliced
- 3 tablespoons olive oil
- Sea salt and freshly ground black pepper, to taste
- ½ teaspoon red pepper flakes, crushed
- ½ teaspoon sumac
- ½ cup sour cream
- 1½ cups goat cheese
- 2 tablespoons green onions, chopped

Directions:

1. Place your eggplant and peppers in a baking pan. Top with the sliced tomatoes. Drizzle olive oil over the vegetables.
2. Season with salt, black pepper, crushed red pepper, and sumac. Bake in the preheated oven at 420°F (216°C) for 15 minutes. Rotate the pan and bake for an additional 10 minutes.
3. Top with sour cream and goat cheese. Garnish with green onions and serve. Enjoy!

Nutrition: Calories: 476 Fat: 41.4 g Protein: 18.4 g Carbs: 7.2 g Net Carbs: 3.6 g Fiber: 3.6 g

747. Mushroom Red Wine Chili

Preparation Time: 10 minutes
Cooking Time: 15 minutes
Servings: 3
Ingredients:

- 3 ounces (85-g.) bacon, diced
- 1 brown onion, chopped
- 2 cloves garlic, minced
- ¾ pound (340-g.) brown mushrooms, sliced

- 3 tablespoons dry red wine
- ½ teaspoon freshly ground black pepper
- 1 teaspoon chili powder
- 2 bay laurels
- Sea salt, to taste

Directions:

1. Heat a soup pot over a medium-high flame and fry the bacon; once the bacon is crisp, remove from the pot and reserve.
2. Now, cook the brown onion and garlic until they have softened or about 6 minutes. Stir in the mushrooms and sauté them for 3 to 4 minutes longer.
3. Turn the heat to simmer; add the other ingredients and continue to cook for 10 minutes more, until most of the cooking liquid has evaporated.
4. Ladle into bowls and top with the reserved bacon. Bon appétit!

Nutrition: Calories: 160 Fat: 11.3 g Protein: 6.9 g Carbs: 6.0 g Net Carbs: 4.7 g Fiber: 1.3 g

748. Minutes Vegetarian Pasta

Preparation Time: 5 minutes
Cooking Time: 16 minutes
Servings: 4
Ingredients:

- 3 shallots, chopped
- ¼ teaspoon red pepper flakes
- ¼ cup vegan parmesan cheese
- 2 tablespoons olive oil
- 2 garlic cloves, minced
- 8-ounce spinach leaves
- 8-ounce linguine pasta
- 1 pinch salt
- 1 pinch black pepper

Directions:

1. Boil salted water in a large pot and add pasta.
2. Cook for about 6 minutes and drain the pasta in a colander.
3. Heat olive oil over medium heat in a large skillet and add the shallots.
4. Cook for about 5 minutes until soft and caramelized

and stir in the spinach, garlic, red pepper flakes, salt and black pepper.

5. Cook for about 5 minutes and add pasta and 2 ladles of pasta water.
6. Stir in the parmesan cheese and dish out in a bowl to serve.

Nutrition: Calories: 25; Fat: 2.0 g Protein: 5.2 g Carbohydrates: 5.3 g Fiber: 4 g; Sodium: 18 mg

749. Chipotle, Pinto, and Green Bean and Corn Succotash

Preparation Time: 5 minutes
Cooking Time: 10 minutes
Servings: 2
Ingredients:

- 2 tablespoons extra-virgin olive oil
- 1½ cups fresh or frozen corn
- 1 cup green beans, chopped
- 2 green onions, white and green parts, sliced
- ½ tablespoon minced garlic
- 1 medium tomato, chopped
- 1 teaspoon chili powder
- ½ teaspoon chipotle powder
- ½ teaspoon ground cumin
- 1 (14-oz.) can pinto beans, drained and rinsed
- 1 teaspoon sea salt, or to taste

Directions:

1. Heat the olive oil in a large skillet over medium heat. Add the corn, green beans, green onions, and garlic and stir for 5 minutes.
2. Add the tomato, chili powder, chipotle powder, and cumin and stir for 3 minutes, until the tomato starts to soften.
3. In a bowl, mash some of the pinto beans with a fork. Add all of the beans to the skillet and stir for 2 minutes, until the beans are heated through.
4. Remove from the heat and stir in the salt. Serve hot or warm.

Nutrition: Calories: 391 Total Fat: 16 g Total Carbs: 53 g Fiber: 15 g

Sugar: 4 g Protein: 15 g Sodium: 253 mg

750. Broccoli Salad

Preparation Time: 5 minutes
Cooking Time: 25 minutes
Servings: 6
Ingredients:

- 2 tablespoons sherry vinegar
- ¼ cup olive oil
- 2 teaspoons fresh thyme, chopped
- 1 teaspoon Dijon mustard
- 1 teaspoon honey
- Salt to taste
- 8 cups broccoli florets, steamed or roasted
- 2 red onions, sliced thinly
- ½ cup Parmesan cheese, shaved
- ¼ cup pecans, toasted and chopped

Directions:

1. Mix the sherry vinegar, olive oil, thyme, mustard, honey and salt in a bowl.
2. In a serving bowl, combine the broccoli florets and onions.
3. Drizzle the dressing on top.
4. Sprinkle with the pecans and Parmesan cheese before serving.

Nutrition: Calories 199 Fat 17.4 g Saturated fat 2.9 g carbohydrates 7.5 g Fiber 2.8 g Protein 5.2 g

751. Potato Carrot Salad

Preparation Time: 15 minutes
Cooking Time: 10 minutes
Servings: 6
Ingredients:

- Water
- 6 potatoes, sliced into cubes
- 3 carrots, sliced into cubes
- 1 tablespoon milk
- 1 tablespoon Dijon mustard
- ¼ cup mayonnaise
- Pepper to taste
- 2 teaspoons fresh thyme, chopped
- 1 stalk celery, chopped
- 2 scallions, chopped
- 1 slice turkey bacon, cooked crispy and crumbled

Directions:

1. Fill your pot with water.
2. Place it over medium-high heat.

3. Boil the potatoes and carrots for 10 minutes or until tender.
4. Drain and let cool.
5. In a bowl, mix the milk mustard, mayo, pepper and thyme.
6. Stir in the potatoes, carrots and celery.
7. Coat evenly with the sauce.
8. Cover and refrigerate for 4 hours.
9. Top with the scallions and turkey bacon bits before serving.

Nutrition: Calories 106 Fat 5.3 g Saturated fat 1 g Carbohydrates 12.6 g Fiber 1.8g Protein 2 g

752. Mixed Vegetable Medley

Preparation Time: 5 minutes
Cooking Time: 20 minutes
Servings: 2
Ingredients:

- 1 stick (½ cup) unsalted butter, divided
- 1 large potato, cut into ½-inch dice
- 1 onion, chopped
- ½ tablespoon minced garlic
- 1 cup green beans, chopped
- 2 ears fresh sweet corn, kernels removed
- 1 red bell pepper, seeded and cut into strips
- 2 cups sliced white mushrooms
- Salt
- Freshly ground black pepper

Directions:

1. Heat half of the butter in a large nonstick skillet over medium-high heat. When the butter is frothy, add the potato and cook, stirring frequently, for 15 minutes, until golden.
2. Turn the heat down slightly if the butter begins to burn.
3. Add the remaining butter, turn down the heat to medium, and add the onion, garlic, green beans, and corn. Cook, stirring frequently, for 5 minutes.
4. Add the red bell pepper and mushrooms. Stir for another 5 minutes, until the

vegetables are tender and the mushrooms have browned but are still plump. Add more butter, if necessary.

5. Remove from heat and season with salt and pepper. Serve hot.

Nutrition: Calories: 688 Total Fat: 48 g Total Carbs: 63 g Fiber: 11 g Sugar: 11 g Protein: 11 g Sodium: 360 mg

753. Spicy Lentils with Spinach

Preparation Time: 5 minutes
Cooking Time: 25 minutes
Servings: 4
Ingredients:

- 1 cup dried red lentils, well-rinsed
- 2½ cups water
- 1 tablespoon extra-virgin olive oil
- 1 tablespoon minced garlic
- 1 teaspoon ground cumin
- ½ teaspoon ground coriander
- ½ teaspoon turmeric
- ¼ teaspoon cayenne pepper
- 1 medium tomato, chopped
- 1 (16-oz.) package spinach
- 1 teaspoon salt
- Freshly ground black pepper

Directions:

1. In a medium saucepan, bring the lentils and water to a boil.
2. Partially cover the pot, reduce the heat to medium, and simmer, stirring occasionally, until the lentils are tender, about 15 minutes.
3. Drain the lentils and set aside.
4. In a large nonstick skillet, heat the olive oil over medium heat. When hot, add garlic, cumin, coriander, turmeric, and cayenne. Sauté for 2 minutes.
5. Stir in the tomato and cook for another 3 to 5 minutes, until the tomato begins to break apart and the mixture thickens somewhat.

6. Add handfuls of the spinach at a time, stirring until wilted.
7. Stir in the drained lentils and cook for another few minutes.
8. Season with salt and freshly ground black pepper and serve hot.

Nutrition: Calories: 237 Total Fat: 5 g Total Carbs: 35 g Fiber: 18 g Sugar: 2 g Protein: 16 g Sodium: 677 mg

754. Parmesan Asparagus

Preparation Time: 10 minutes
Cooking Time: 5 minutes
Servings: 2
Ingredients:

- 1 egg, lightly beaten
- 10 asparagus spears, trimmed and cut woody ends
- 1 tablespoon heavy cream
- ⅓ cup parmesan cheese, grated
- ⅓ cup almond flour
- ½ teaspoon paprika

Directions:

1. Spray Air Fryer basket with cooking spray.
2. In a shallow dish, whisk together egg and cream until good mix.
3. In a separate dish, mix together almond flour, parmesan cheese, paprika, and salt.
4. Dip asparagus spear into the egg mixture then coat with almond flour mixture.
5. Place coated asparagus into the Air Fryer basket and cook at 350°F for 5 minutes.

Nutrition: Calories 166 Fat 11.3 g Carbohydrates 7 g Sugar 2.7 g Protein 12.3 g Cholesterol 105 mg

755. Greek Vegetables

Preparation Time: 10 minutes
Cooking Time: 20 minutes
Servings: 4
Ingredients:

- 1 carrot, sliced
- 1 parsnip, sliced
- 1 green bell pepper, chopped
- 1 courgette, chopped
- ¼ cup cherry tomatoes, cut in half

- 6 tablespoons olive oil
- 2 teaspoons garlic puree
- 1 teaspoon mustard
- 1 teaspoon mixed herbs
- Pepper
- Salt

Directions:

1. Add cherry tomatoes, carrot, parsnip, bell pepper, and courgette into the Air Fryer basket.
2. Drizzle olive oil over vegetables and cook at 350°F for 15 minutes.
3. In a mixing bowl, mix together the remaining ingredients. Add vegetables into the mixing bowl and toss well.
4. Return vegetables to the Air Fryer basket and cook at 400°F for 5 minutes more.
5. Serve and enjoy.

Nutrition: Calories 66 Fat 1.5 g Carbohydrates 12.7 g Sugar 5.3 g Protein 1.8 g Cholesterol 1 mg

756. Lemon Garlic Cauliflower

Preparation Time: 10 minutes
Cooking Time: 10 minutes
Servings: 2
Ingredients:

- 3 cups cauliflower
- 1 tablespoon fresh parsley, chopped
- ½ teaspoon lemon juice
- 1 tablespoon pine nuts
- ½ teaspoon dried oregano
- 1½ teaspoon olive oil
- Pepper
- Salt

Directions:

1. Add cauliflower, oregano, oil, pepper, and salt into the mixing bowl and toss well.
2. Add cauliflower into the Air Fryer basket and cook at 375°F for 10 minutes.
3. Transfer cauliflower into the serving bowl. Add pine nuts, parsley, and lemon juice and toss well.
4. Serve and enjoy.

Nutrition: Calories 99 Fat 6.7 g Carbohydrates 8.9 g Sugar 3.8 g Protein 3.7 g Cholesterol 0 mg

757. Balsamic Brussels Sprouts

Preparation Time: 10 minutes
Cooking Time: 20 minutes
Servings: 4
Ingredients:

- 1 pound brussels sprouts, remove ends and cut in half
- 1 tablespoon balsamic vinegar
- 2 tablespoons olive oil
- Pepper
- Salt

Directions:

1. Add brussels sprouts, vinegar, oil, pepper, and salt into the mixing bowl and toss well.
2. Add brussels sprouts into the Air Fryer basket and cook at 360°F for 15-20 minutes. Toss halfway through.
3. Serve and enjoy.

Nutrition: Calories 110 Fat 7.4 g Carbohydrates 10.4 g Sugar 2.5 g Protein 3.9 g Cholesterol 0 mg

758. Flavorful Butternut Squash

Preparation Time: 10 minutes
Cooking Time: 15 minutes
Servings: 4
Ingredients:

- 4 cups butternut squash, cut into 1-inch pieces
- 1 teaspoon Chinese five-spice powder
- 1 tablespoon Truvia
- 2 tablespoons olive oil

Directions:

1. Add butternut squash and remaining ingredients into the mixing bowl and mix well.
2. Add butternut squash into the Air Fryer basket and cook at 400°F for 15 minutes. Shake basket halfway through.
3. Serve and enjoy.

Nutrition: Calories 83 Fat 7.1 g Carbohydrates 6.7 g Sugar 2.2 g Protein 0.6 g Cholesterol 0 mg

759. Crispy Green Beans

Preparation Time: 10 minutes
Cooking Time: 10 minutes
Servings: 4
Ingredients:

- 2 cups green beans, ends trimmed
- 2 tablespoons parmesan cheese, shredded
- 1 tablespoon fresh lemon juice
- 1 teaspoon Italian seasoning
- 2 teaspoons olive oil
- ¼ teaspoon salt

Directions:

1. Preheat the Cosori Air Fryer to 400°F.
2. Brush green beans with olive oil and season with Italian seasoning and salt.
3. Place green beans into the Air Fryer basket and cook for 8-10 minutes. Shake basket 2-3 times.
4. Transfer green beans to a serving plate.
5. Pour lemon juice over beans and sprinkle shredded cheese on top of beans.
6. Serve and enjoy.

Nutrition: Calories 64 Fat 4.3 g Carbohydrates 4.4 g Sugar 1 g Protein 3.3 g Cholesterol 6 mg

760. Roasted Zucchini

Preparation Time: 10 minutes
Cooking Time: 10 minutes
Servings: 4
Ingredients:

- 2 medium zucchini, cut into 1-inch slices
- 1 teaspoon lemon zest
- 1 tablespoon olive oil
- Pepper
- Salt

Directions:

1. Toss zucchini with lemon zest, oil, pepper, and salt.
2. Arrange zucchini slices into the Air Fryer basket and cook at 350°F for 10 minutes. Turn halfway through.
3. Serve and enjoy.

Nutrition: Calories 46 Fat 3.7 g Carbohydrates 3.4 g Sugar 1.7 g Protein 1.2 g Cholesterol 0 mg

761. Air Fried Carrots, Zucchini & Squash

Preparation Time: 10 minutes
Cooking Time: 35 minutes
Servings: 2
Ingredients:

- 1 pound yellow squash, cut into ¾-inch half-moons
- 1 pound zucchini, cut into ¾-inch half-moons
- ½ pound carrots, peeled and cut into 1-inch pieces
- 6 teaspoons olive oil
- 1 tablespoon tarragon, chopped
- Pepper
- Salt

Directions:

1. In a bowl, toss carrots with 2 teaspoons of oil. Add carrots into the Air Fryer basket and cook at 400°F for 5 minutes.
2. In a mixing bowl, toss squash, zucchini, remaining oil, pepper, and salt.
3. Add squash and zucchini mixture into the Air Fryer basket with carrots and cook for 30 minutes. Shake basket 2-3 times.
4. Sprinkle with tarragon and serve.

Nutrition: Calories 176 Fat 17.3 g Carbohydrates 6.2 g Sugar 3.2 g Protein 2.5 g Cholesterol 0 mg

762. Crispy & Spicy Eggplant

Preparation Time: 10 minutes
Cooking Time: 20 minutes
Servings: 4
Ingredients:

- 1 eggplant, cut into 1-inch pieces
- ½ teaspoon Italian seasoning
- 1 teaspoon paprika
- ½ teaspoon red pepper
- 1 teaspoon garlic powder
- 2 tablespoons olive oil

Directions:

1. Add eggplant and remaining ingredients into the bowl and toss well.
2. Spray Air Fryer basket with cooking spray.
3. Add eggplant into the Air Fryer basket and cook at

375°F for 20 minutes. Shake basket halfway through.

4. Serve and enjoy.

Nutrition: Calories 99 Fat 7.5 g Carbohydrates 8.7 g Sugar 4.5 g Protein 1.5 g Cholesterol 0 mg

763. Curried Eggplant Slices

Preparation Time: 10 minutes
Cooking Time: 10 minutes
Servings: 4
Ingredients:

- 1 large eggplant, cut into ½-inch slices
- 1 garlic clove, minced
- 1 tablespoon olive oil
- ½ teaspoon curry powder
- ⅛ teaspoon turmeric
- Salt

Directions:

1. Preheat the Cosori Air Fryer to 300°F.
2. In a small bowl, mix together oil, garlic, curry powder, turmeric, and salt and rub all over eggplant slices.
3. Add eggplant slices into the Air Fryer basket and cook for 10 minutes or until lightly browned.
4. Serve and enjoy.

Nutrition: Calories 61 Fat 3.8 g Carbohydrates 7.2 g Sugar 3.5 g Protein 1.2 g Cholesterol 0 mg

764. Spiced Green Beans

Preparation Time: 10 minutes
Cooking Time: 10 minutes
Servings: 2
Ingredients:

- 2 cups green beans
- ⅛ teaspoon ground allspice
- ¼ teaspoon ground cinnamon
- ½ teaspoon dried oregano
- 2 tablespoons olive oil
- ¼ teaspoon ground coriander
- ¼ teaspoon ground cumin
- ⅛ teaspoon cayenne pepper
- ½ teaspoon salt

Directions:

1. Add all ingredients into the medium bowl and toss well.
2. Spray Air Fryer basket with cooking spray.
3. Add green beans into the Air Fryer basket and cook at

370°F for 10 minutes. Shake basket halfway through

4. Serve and enjoy.

Nutrition: Calories 158 Fat 14.3 g Carbohydrates 8.6 g Sugar 1.6 g Protein 2.1 g Cholesterol 0 mg

765. Air Fryer Basil Tomatoes

Preparation Time: 10 minutes
Cooking Time: 25 minutes
Servings: 4
Ingredients:

- 4 large tomatoes, halved
- 1 garlic clove, minced
- 1 tablespoon vinegar
- 1 tablespoon olive oil
- 2 tablespoons parmesan cheese, grated
- ½ teaspoon fresh parsley, chopped
- 1 teaspoon fresh basil, minced
- Pepper
- Salt

Directions:

1. Preheat the Cosori Air Fryer to 320°F.
2. In a bowl, mix together oil, basil, garlic, vinegar, pepper, and salt. Add tomatoes and stir to coat.
3. Place tomato halves into the Air Fryer basket and cook for 20 minutes.
4. Sprinkle parmesan cheese over tomatoes and cook for 5 minutes more.
5. Serve and enjoy.

Nutrition: Calories 87 Fat 5.4 g Carbohydrates 7.7 g Sugar 4.8 g Protein 3.9 g Cholesterol 5 mg

766. Air Fryer Ratatouille

Preparation Time: 10 minutes
Cooking Time: 15 minutes
Servings: 6
Ingredients:

- 1 eggplant, diced
- 1 onion, diced
- 3 tomatoes, diced
- 1 red bell pepper, diced
- 1 green bell pepper, diced
- 1 tablespoon vinegar
- 2 tablespoons olive oil
- 2 tablespoons herb de Provence
- 2 garlic cloves, chopped
- Pepper

- Salt

Directions:

1. Preheat the Cosori Air Fryer to 400°F.
2. Add all ingredients into the bowl and toss well and transfer into the Air Fryer safe dish.
3. Place dish into the Air Fryer basket and cook for 15 minutes. Stir halfway through.
4. Serve and enjoy.

Nutrition: Calories 91 Fat 5 g Carbohydrates 11.6 g Sugar 6.4 g Protein 1.9 g Cholesterol 0 mg

767. Garlicky Cauliflower Florets

Preparation Time: 10 minutes
Cooking Time: 20 minutes
Servings: 4
Ingredients:

- 5 cups cauliflower florets
- ½ teaspoon cumin powder
- ½ teaspoon ground coriander
- 6 garlic cloves, chopped
- 4 tablespoons olive oil
- ½ teaspoon salt

Directions:

1. Add cauliflower florets and remaining ingredients into the large mixing bowl and toss well.
2. Add cauliflower florets into the Air Fryer basket and cook at 400°F for 20 minutes. Shake basket halfway through.
3. Serve and enjoy.

Nutrition: Calories 159 Fat 14.2 g Carbohydrates 8.2 g Sugar 3.1 g Protein 2.8 g Cholesterol 0 mg

768. Parmesan Brussels Sprouts

Preparation Time: 10 minutes
Cooking Time: 12 minutes
Servings: 4
Ingredients:

- 1 pound Brussels sprouts, remove stems and halved
- ¼ cup parmesan cheese, grated
- 2 tablespoons olive oil
- Pepper

- Salt

Directions:
1. Preheat the Cosori Air Fryer to 350°F.
2. In a mixing bowl, toss Brussels sprouts with oil, pepper, and salt.
3. Transfer Brussels sprouts into the Air Fryer basket and cook for 12 minutes. Shake basket halfway through.
4. Sprinkle with parmesan cheese and serve.

Nutrition: Calories 129 Fat 8.7 g Carbohydrates 10.6 g Sugar 2.5 g Protein 5.9 g Cholesterol 4 mg

769. Flavorful Tomatoes

Preparation Time: 10 minutes
Cooking Time: 15 minutes
Servings: 4
Ingredients:
- 4 Roma tomatoes, sliced, removeseeds pithy portion
- 1 tablespoon olive oil
- ½ teaspoon dried thyme
- 2 garlic cloves, minced
- Pepper
- Salt

Directions:
1. Preheat the Cosori Air Fryer to 390°F.
2. Toss sliced tomatoes with oil, thyme, garlic, pepper, and salt.
3. Arrange sliced tomatoes into the Air Fryer basket and cook for 15 minutes.
4. Serve and enjoy.

Nutrition: Calories 55 Fat 3.8 g Carbohydrates 5.4 g Sugar 3.3 g Protein 1.2 g Cholesterol 0 mg

770. Healthy Roasted Carrots

Preparation Time: 10 minutes
Cooking Time: 12 minutes
Servings: 4
Ingredients:
- 2 cups carrots, peeled and chopped
- 1 teaspoon cumin
- 1 tablespoon olive oil
- ¼ fresh coriander, chopped

Directions:
1. Toss carrots with cumin and oil and place them into the Air Fryer basket.

2. Cook at 390°F for 12 minutes.
3. Garnish with fresh coriander and serve.

Nutrition: Calories 55 Fat 3.6 g Carbohydrates 5.7 g Sugar 2.7 g Protein 0.6 g Cholesterol 0 mg

771. Curried Cauliflower with Pine Nuts

Preparation Time: 10 minutes
Cooking Time: 10 minutes
Servings: 4
Ingredients:
- 1 small cauliflower head, cut into florets
- 2 tablespoons olive oil
- ¼ cup pine nuts, toasted
- 1 tablespoon curry powder
- ¼ teaspoon salt

Directions:
1. Preheat the Cosori Air Fryer to 350°F.
2. In a mixing bowl, toss cauliflower florets with oil, curry powder, and salt.
3. Add cauliflower florets into the Air Fryer basket and cook for 10 minutes. Shake basket halfway through.
4. Transfer cauliflower into the serving bowl. Add pine nuts and toss well.
5. Serve and enjoy.

Nutrition: Calories 139 Fat 13.1 g Carbohydrates 5.5 g Sugar 1.9 g Protein 2.7 g Cholesterol 0 mg

772. Thyme Sage Butternut Squash

Preparation Time: 10 minutes
Cooking Time: 12 minutes
Servings: 4
Ingredients:
- 2 pounds butternut squash, cut into chunks
- 1 teaspoon fresh thyme, chopped
- 1 tablespoon fresh sage, chopped
- 1 tablespoon olive oil
- Pepper
- Salt

Directions:
1. Preheat the Cosori Air Fryer to 390°F.
2. In a mixing bowl, toss butternut squash with thyme, sage, oil, pepper, and salt.

3. Add butternut squash into the Air Fryer basket and cook for 10 minutes. Shake basket well and cook for 2 minutes more.
4. Serve and enjoy.

Nutrition: Calories 50 Fat 3.8 g Carbohydrates 4.2 g Sugar 2.5 g Protein 1.4 g Cholesterol 0 mg

773. Grilled Cauliflower

Preparation Time: 15 minutes
Cooking Time: 40 minutes
Servings: 4
Ingredients:
- 1 large head of cauliflower, leaves removed and stem trimmed
- Salt, as required
- 4 tablespoons unsalted butter
- ¼ cup hot sauce
- 1 tablespoon ketchup
- 1 tablespoon soy sauce
- ½ cup mayonnaise
- 2 tablespoons white miso
- 1 tablespoon fresh lemon juice
- ½ teaspoon ground black pepper
- 2 scallions, thinly sliced

Directions:
1. Sprinkle the cauliflower with salt evenly.
2. Arrange the cauliflower head in a large microwave-safe bowl.
3. With a plastic wrap, cover the bowl.
4. With a knife, pierce the plastic a few times to vent.
5. Microwave on high for about 5 minutes.
6. Remove from the microwave and set aside to cool slightly.
7. In a small saucepan, add butter, hot sauce, ketchup and soy sauce over medium heat and cook for about 2-3 minutes, stirring occasionally.
8. Brush the cauliflower head with warm sauce evenly.
9. Place the water tray in the bottom of the Power XL Smokeless Electric Grill.
10. Place about 2 cups of lukewarm water into the water tray.
11. Place the drip pan over the water tray and then arrange the heating element.

12. Now, place the grilling pan over the heating element.
13. Set the temperature settings according to the manufacturer's directions.
14. Cover the grill with a lid and let it preheat.
15. After preheating, remove the lid and grease the grilling pan.
16. Place the cauliflower head over the grilling pan.
17. Cover with the lid and cook for about 10 minutes.
18. Turn the cauliflower over and brush with warm sauce.
19. Cover with the lid and cook for about 25 minutes, flipping and brushing with warm sauce after every 10 minutes.
20. In a bowl, place the mayonnaise, miso, lemon juice, and pepper and beat until smooth.
21. Spread the mayonnaise mixture onto a plate and arrange the cauliflower on top.

Nutrition: Calories 261 Total Fat 22 g Saturated Fat 8.9 g Cholesterol 38 mg Sodium 1300 mg Total Carbs 15.1 g Fiber 2.5 g Sugar 5.4 g Protein 3.3 g

774. Stuffed Zucchini
Preparation Time: 20 minutes
Cooking Time: 24 minutes
Servings: 6
Ingredients:
- 3 medium zucchinis, sliced in half lengthwise
- 1 teaspoon vegetable oil
- 3 cups corn, cut off the cob
- 1 cup Parmesan cheese, shredded
- 2/3 cup sour cream
- ¼ teaspoon hot sauce
- Olive oil cooking spray

Directions:
1. Cut the ends off the zucchini and slice in half lengthwise.
2. Scoop out the pulp from each half of zucchini, leaving the shell.

For the filling:
1. In a large pan of boiling water, add the corn over medium heat and cook for about 5-7 minutes.
2. Drain the corn and set aside to cool.

3. In a large bowl, add corn, half of the parmesan cheese, sour cream and hot sauce and mix well.
4. Spray the zucchini shells with cooking spray evenly.
5. Place the water tray in the bottom of the Power XL Smokeless Electric Grill.
6. Place about 2 cups of lukewarm water into the water tray.
7. Place the drip pan over the water tray and then arrange the heating element.
8. Now, place the grilling pan over the heating element.
9. Set the temperature settings according to the manufacturer's directions.
10. Cover the grill with a lid and let it preheat.
11. After preheating, remove the lid and grease the grilling pan.
12. Place the zucchini halves over the grilling pan, flesh side down.
13. Cover with the lid and cook for about 8-10 minutes.
14. Remove the zucchini halves from the grill.
15. Spoon filling into each zucchini half evenly and sprinkle with remaining parmesan cheese.
16. Place the zucchini halves over the grilling pan.
17. Cover with the lid and cook for about 8 minutes.
18. Serve hot.

Nutrition: Calories 198 Total Fat 10.8 g Saturated Fat 6 g Cholesterol 21 mg Sodium 293 mg Total Carbs 19.3 g Fiber 3.2 g Sugar 4.2 g Protein 9.6 g

775. Vinegar Veggies
Preparation Time: 15 minutes
Cooking Time: 10 minutes
Servings: 4
Ingredients:
- 3 golden beets, trimmed, peeled and sliced thinly
- 3 carrots, peeled and sliced lengthwise
- 1 cup zucchini, sliced
- 1 onion, sliced
- ½ cup yam, sliced thinly
- 2 tablespoon fresh rosemary

- 1 garlic clove, minced
- Salt and ground black pepper, as required
- 3 tablespoons vegetable oil
- 2 teaspoons balsamic vinegar

Directions:
1. Place all ingredients in a bowl and toss to coat well.
2. Refrigerate to marinate for at least 30 minutes.
3. Place the water tray in the bottom of the Power XL Smokeless Electric Grill.
4. Place about 2 cups of lukewarm water into the water tray.
5. Place the drip pan over the water tray and then arrange the heating element.
6. Now, place the grilling pan over the heating element.
7. Plugin the Power XL Smokeless Electric Grill and press the 'Power' button to turn it on.
8. Then press the 'Fan" button.
9. Set the temperature settings according to the manufacturer's directions.
10. Cover the grill with a lid and let it preheat.
11. After preheating, remove the lid and grease the grilling pan.
12. Place the vegetables over the grilling pan.
13. Cover with the lid and cook for about 5 minutes per side.
14. Serve hot.

Nutrition: Calories 184 Total Fat 10.7 g Saturated Fat 2.2 g Cholesterol 0 mg Sodium 134 mg Total Carbs 21.5 g Fiber 4.9 g Sugar 10 g Protein 2.7 g

776. Garlicky Mixed Veggies
Preparation Time: 15 minutes
Cooking Time: 8 minutes
Servings: 4
Ingredients:
- 1 bunch fresh asparagus, trimmed
- 6 ounces fresh mushrooms, halved
- 6 Campari tomatoes, halved

- 1 red onion, cut into 1-inch chunks
- 3 garlic cloves, minced
- 2 tablespoons olive oil
- Salt and ground black pepper, as required

Directions:
1. In a large bowl, add all ingredients and toss to coat well.
2. Place the water tray in the bottom of the Power XL Smokeless Electric Grill.
3. Place about 2 cups of lukewarm water into the water tray.
4. Place the drip pan over the water tray and then arrange the heating element.
5. Now, place the grilling pan over the heating element.
6. Plugin the Power XL Smokeless Electric Grill and press the 'Power' button to turn it on.
7. Then press the 'Fan" button.
8. Set the temperature settings according to the manufacturer's directions.
9. Cover the grill with a lid and let it preheat.
10. After preheating, remove the lid and grease the grilling pan.
11. Place the vegetables over the grilling pan.
12. Cover with the lid and cook for about 8 minutes, flipping occasionally.

Nutrition: Calories 137 Total Fat 7.7 g Saturated Fat 1.1 g Cholesterol 0 mg Sodium 54 mg Total Carbs 15.6 g Fiber 5.6 g Sugar 8.9 g Protein 5.8 g

777. Mediterranean Veggies

Preparation Time: 5 minutes
Cooking Time: 10 minutes
Servings: 4
Ingredients:
- 1 cup mixed bell peppers, chopped
- 1 cup eggplant, chopped
- 1 cup zucchini, chopped
- 1 cup mushrooms, chopped
- ½ cup onion, chopped
- ½ cup sun-dried tomato vinaigrette dressing

Directions:
1. In a large bowl, add all ingredients and toss to coat well.
2. Refrigerate to marinate for about 1 hour.
3. Place the water tray in the bottom of the Power XL Smokeless Electric Grill.
4. Place about 2 cups of lukewarm water into the water tray.
5. Place the drip pan over the water tray and then arrange the heating element.
6. Now, place the grilling pan over the heating element.
7. Plugin the Power XL Smokeless Electric Grill and press the 'Power' button to turn it on.
8. Then press the 'Fan" button.
9. Set the temperature settings according to the manufacturer's directions.
10. Cover the grill with a lid and let it preheat.
11. After preheating, remove the lid and grease the grilling pan.
12. Place the vegetables over the grilling pan.
13. Cover with the lid and cook for about 8-10 minutes, flipping occasionally.

Nutrition: Calories 159 Total Fat 11.2 g Saturated Fat 2 g Cholesterol 0 mg Sodium 336 mg Total Carbs 12.3 g Fiber 1.9 g Sugar 9.5 g Protein 1.6 g

778. Marinated Veggie Skewers

Preparation Time: 20 minutes
Cooking Time: 10 minutes
Servings: 4
Ingredients:
For Marinade:
- 2 garlic cloves, minced
- 2 teaspoons fresh basil, minced
- 2 teaspoons fresh oregano, minced
- ½ teaspoon cayenne pepper
- Sea Salt and ground black pepper, as required
- 2 tablespoons fresh lemon juice
- 2 tablespoons olive oil

For Veggies:
- 2 large zucchinis, cut into thick slices
- 8 large button mushrooms, quartered
- 1 yellow bell pepper, seeded and cubed
- 1 red bell pepper, seeded and cubed

Directions:
For the marinade:
1. In a large bowl, add all the ingredients and mix until well combined.
2. Add the vegetables and toss to coat well.
3. Cover and refrigerate to marinate for at least 6-8 hours.
4. Remove the vegetables from the bowl and thread onto pre-soaked wooden skewers.
5. Place the water tray in the bottom of the Power XL Smokeless Electric Grill.
6. Place about 2 cups of lukewarm water into the water tray.
7. Place the drip pan over the water tray and then arrange the heating element.
8. Now, place the grilling pan over the heating element.
9. Plugin the Power XL Smokeless Electric Grill and press the 'Power' button to turn it on.
10. Then press the 'Fan" button.
11. Set the temperature settings according to the manufacturer's directions. Cover the grill with a lid and let it preheat.
12. After preheating, remove the lid and grease the grilling pan.
13. Place the skewers over the grilling pan. Cover with the lid and cook for about 8-10 minutes, flipping occasionally. Serve hot.

Nutrition: Calories 122 Total Fat 7.8 g Saturated Fat 1.2 g Cholesterol 0 mg Sodium 81 mg Total Carbs 12.7 g Fiber 3.5 g Sugar 6.8g Protein 4.3 g

779. Pineapple & Veggie Skewers

Preparation Time: 20 minutes
Cooking Time: 15 minutes
Servings: 6
Ingredients:

- ⅓ cup olive oil
- 1½ teaspoons dried basil
- ¾ teaspoon dried oregano
- Salt and ground black pepper, as required
- 2 zucchinis, cut into 1-inch slices
- 2 yellow squash, cut into 1-inch slices
- ½ pound whole fresh mushrooms
- 1 red bell pepper, cut into chunks
- 1 red onion, cut into chunks
- 12 cherry tomatoes
- 1 fresh pineapple, cut into chunks

Directions:

1. In a bowl, add oil, herbs, salt and black pepper and mix well.
2. Thread the veggies and pineapple onto pre-soaked wooden skewers.
3. Brush the veggies and pineapple with the oil mixture evenly.
4. Place the water tray in the bottom of the Power XL Smokeless Electric Grill.
5. Place about 2 cups of lukewarm water into the water tray.
6. Place the drip pan over the water tray and then arrange the heating element.
7. Now, place the grilling pan over the heating element.
8. Plugin the Power XL Smokeless Electric Grill and press the 'Power' button to turn it on.
9. Then press the 'Fan" button.
10. Set the temperature settings according to the manufacturer's directions.
11. Cover the grill with a lid and let it preheat.
12. After preheating, remove the lid and grease the grilling pan.
13. Place the skewers over the grilling pan.
14. Cover with the lid and cook for about 10-15 minutes, flipping occasionally.
15. Serve hot.

Nutrition: Calories 220 Total Fat 11.9 g Saturated Fat 1.7 g Cholesterol 0 mg Sodium 47 mg Total Carbs 30 g Fiber 5 g Sugar 20.4 g Protein 4.3 g

780. Buttered Corn

Preparation Time: 10 minutes
Cooking Time: 20 minutes
Servings: 6
Ingredients:

- 6 fresh whole corn on the cob
- ½ cup butter, melted
- Salt, as required

Directions:

1. Husk the corn and remove all the silk.
2. Brush each corn with melted butter and sprinkle with salt.
3. Place the water tray in the bottom of the Power XL Smokeless Electric Grill.
4. Place about 2 cups of lukewarm water into the water tray.
5. Place the drip pan over the water tray and then arrange the heating element.
6. Now, place the grilling pan over the heating element.
7. Plugin the Power XL Smokeless Electric Grill and press the 'Power' button to turn it on.
8. Then press the 'Fan" button.
9. Set the temperature settings according to the manufacturer's directions.
10. Cover the grill with a lid and let it preheat.
11. After preheating, remove the lid and grease the grilling pan.
12. Place the corn over the grilling pan.
13. Cover with the lid and cook for about 20 minutes, rotating after every 5 minutes and brushing with butter once halfway through.
14. Serve warm.

Nutrition: Calories 268 Total Fat 17.2 g Saturated Fat 10 g Cholesterol 41 mg Sodium 159 mg Total Carbs 29 g Fiber 4.2 g Sugar 5 g Protein 5.2 g

781. Guacamole

Preparation Time: 15 minutes
Cooking Time: 4 minutes
Servings: 4
Ingredients:

- 2 ripe avocados, halved and pitted
- 2 teaspoons vegetable oil
- 3 tablespoons fresh lime juice
- 1 garlic clove, crushed
- ¼ teaspoon ground chipotle chili
- Salt, as required
- ¼ cup red onion, chopped finely
- ¼ cup fresh cilantro, chopped finely

Directions:

1. Brush the cut sides of each avocado half with oil.
2. Place the water tray in the bottom of the Power XL Smokeless Electric Grill.
3. Place about 2 cups of lukewarm water into the water tray.
4. Place the drip pan over the water tray and then arrange the heating element.
5. Now, place the grilling pan over the heating element.
6. Plugin the Power XL Smokeless Electric Grill and press the 'Power' button to turn it on.
7. Then press the 'Fan" button.
8. Set the temperature settings according to the manufacturer's directions.
9. Cover the grill with a lid and let it preheat.
10. After preheating, remove the lid and grease the grilling pan.
11. Place the avocado halves over the grilling pan, cut side down.
12. Cook, uncovered for about 2-4 minutes.
13. Transfer the avocados onto the cutting board and let them cool slightly.

14. Remove the peel and transfer the flesh into a bowl.
15. Add the lime juice, garlic, chipotle and salt and with a fork, mash until almost smooth.
16. Stir in onion and cilantro and refrigerate, covered for about 1 hour before serving.

Nutrition: Calories 230 Total Fat 21.9 g Saturated Fat 4.6g Cholesterol 0 mg Sodium 46 mg Total Carbs 9.7 g Fiber 6.9 g Sugar 0.8 g Protein 2.1 g

782. Potato Latke

Preparation Time: 15 minutes
Cooking Time: 10 minutes
Servings: 6
Ingredients:

- 3 eggs, beaten
- 1 onion, grated
- 1½ teaspoons baking powder
- Salt and pepper to taste
- 2 pounds potatoes, peeled and grated
- ¼ cup all-purpose flour
- 4 tablespoons vegetable oil
- Chopped onion chives

Directions:

1. Prep your oven to 400°F.
2. Scourge eggs, onion, baking powder, salt and pepper.
3. Squeeze moisture from the shredded potatoes using a paper towel.
4. Add potatoes to the egg mixture.
5. Stir in the flour.
6. Fill the oil into a pan over medium heat.
7. Cook a small amount of the batter for 3 to 4 minutes per side.
8. Repeat. Garnish with the chives.

Nutrition: 266 Calories 34.6g Carbohydrates 7.6g Protein

783. Broccoli Rabe

Preparation Time: 15 minutes
Cooking Time: 15 minutes
Servings: 8
Ingredients:

- 2 oranges, sliced in half
- 1 pound broccoli rabe
- 2 tablespoons sesame oil, toasted
- Salt and pepper to taste

- 1 tablespoon sesame seeds, toasted

Directions:

1. Fill the oil into a pan over medium heat.
2. Add the oranges and cook until caramelized.
3. Transfer to a plate.
4. Put the broccoli in the pan and cook for 8 minutes.
5. Squeeze the oranges to release juice in a bowl.
6. Stir in the oil, salt and pepper.
7. Coat the broccoli rabe with the mixture.
8. Sprinkle seeds on top.

Nutrition: 59 Calories 4.1g Carbohydrates 2.2g Protein

784. Shrimp Veggie Pasta Salad

Preparation Time: 50 minutes
Cooking Time: 10 minutes
Servings: 6
Ingredients:

- 1 pound shrimp, peeled and deveined
- 8 ounces asparagus, sliced
- Salt and pepper to taste
- 12 ounces farfalle, penne or macaroni pasta, cooked
- 2 tablespoons parsley, chopped
- ½ cup shallots, sliced thinly
- ¼ cup Parmesan cheese, grated
- 2 tablespoons freshly squeezed lemon juice
- ½ cup mayonnaise
- 2 teaspoons garlic, minced
- 1 teaspoon Worcestershire sauce
- 1 teaspoon Dijon mustard
- 1 lemon, sliced into wedges

Directions:

1. Preheat your oven to 400°F.
2. Arrange the shrimp and asparagus in a baking pan.
3. Season with salt and pepper.
4. Roast in the oven for 10 minutes.
5. Let cool. Transfer to a bowl.
6. Stir in the cooked pasta, parsley and shallots.
7. Sprinkle the Parmesan cheese on top.
8. In another bowl, combine the lemon juice,

mayonnaise, garlic, Worcestershire sauce and Dijon mustard.
9. Add this mixture to the pasta salad.
10. Toss to coat evenly.
11. Refrigerate for at least 30 minutes before serving.
12. Garnish with lemon wedges.

Nutrition: Calories 429 Fat 17.1 g Saturated fat 2.8 g Carbohydrates 45.6 g Fiber 7.2 g Protein 25 g

785. Pea Salad

Preparation Time: 40 minutes
Cooking Time: 0 minute
Servings: 6
Ingredients:

- 1 cup chickpeas, rinsed and drained
- 1½ cups peas, divided
- Salt to taste
- 3 tablespoons olive oil
- ½ cup buttermilk
- Pepper to taste
- 8 cups pea greens
- 3 carrots, shaved
- 1 cup snow peas, trimmed

Directions:

1. Add the chickpeas and half of the peas to your food processor.
2. Season with salt.
3. Pulse until smooth. Set aside.
4. In a bowl, toss the remaining peas in oil, milk, salt and pepper.
5. Transfer the mixture to your food processor.
6. Process until pureed.
7. Transfer this mixture to a bowl.
8. Arrange the pea greens on a serving plate.
9. Top with the shaved carrots and snow peas.
10. Stir in the pea and milk dressing.
11. Serve with the reserved chickpea hummus.

Nutrition: Calories 214 Fat 8.6 g Saturated fat 1.5 g Carbohydrates 27.3 g Fiber 8.4 g Protein 8 g

786. Snap Pea Salad

Preparation Time: 1 hour
Cooking Time: 0 minute
Servings: 6
Ingredients:

- 2 tablespoons mayonnaise

- ¾ teaspoon celery seed
- ¼ cup cider vinegar
- 1 teaspoon yellow mustard
- 1 tablespoon sugar
- Salt and pepper to taste
- 4 ounces radishes, sliced thinly
- 12 ounces sugar snap peas, sliced thinly

Directions:
1. In a bowl, combine the mayonnaise, celery seeds, vinegar, mustard, sugar, salt and pepper.
2. Stir in the radishes and snap peas.
3. Refrigerate for 30 minutes.

Nutrition: Calories 69 Fat 3.7 g Saturated fat 0.6 g Carbohydrates 7.1 g Fiber 1.8 g Protein 2 g

787. Pinto and Green Bean Fry with Couscous

Preparation Time: 5 minutes
Cooking Time: 15 minutes
Servings: 4
Ingredients:
- ½ cup water
- ⅓ cup couscous (semolina or whole-wheat)
- 2 tablespoons extra-virgin olive oil
- 1 small onion, chopped
- ½ tablespoon minced garlic
- 1 cup green beans, cut into 1-inch pieces
- 1 cup fresh or frozen corn
- 1½ teaspoons chili powder
- ½ teaspoon ground cumin
- 1 large tomato, finely chopped
- 1 (14-oz.) can pinto beans, drained and rinsed
- 1 teaspoon salt

Directions:
1. Bring the water to a boil in a small saucepan. Remove from the heat and stir in the couscous. Cover the pan and let sit for 10 minutes.
2. Gently fluff the couscous with a fork.
3. While the couscous is cooking, heat the olive oil in a large skillet over medium heat. Add the onion and garlic and stir for 1 minute.

4. Add the green beans and stir for 4 minutes, until they begin to soften.
5. Add the corn, stir for another 2 minutes, then add the chili powder and cumin, and stir to coat the vegetables.
6. Add the tomato and simmer for 3 or 4 minutes. Stir in the pinto beans and couscous and cook for 3 to 4 minutes, until everything is heated throughout. Stir often.
7. Stir in the salt and serve hot or warm.

Nutrition: Calories: 267 Total Fat: 8 g Total Carbs: 41 g Fiber: 10 g Sugar: 4 g Protein: 10 g Sodium: 601 mg

788. Indonesian-Style Spicy Fried Tempeh Strips

Preparation Time: 5 minutes
Cooking Time: 20 minutes
Servings: 4
Ingredients:
- 1 cup sesame oil, or as needed
- 1 (12-oz.) package tempeh, cut into narrow 2-inch strips
- 2 medium onions, sliced
- 1½ tablespoons tomato paste
- 3 teaspoons tamari or soy sauce
- 1 teaspoon dried red chili flakes
- ½ teaspoon brown sugar
- 2 tablespoons lime juice

Directions:
1. Heat the sesame oil in a large wok or saucepan over medium-high heat. Add more sesame oil as needed to raise the level to at least 1 inch.
2. As soon as the oil is hot but not smoking, add the tempeh slices and cook, stirring frequently, for 10 minutes, until a light golden color on all sides.
3. Add the onions and stir for another 10 minutes, until the tempeh and onions are brown and crispy.
4. Remove with a slotted spoon and add to a large

bowl lined with several sheets of paper towel.
5. While the tempeh and onions are cooking, whisk together the tomato paste, tamari or soy sauce, red chili flakes, brown sugar, and lime juice in a small bowl.
6. Remove the paper towel from the large bowl and pour the sauce over the tempeh strips. Mix well to coat.

Nutrition: Calories: 317 Total Fat: 23 g Total Carbs: 15 g Sugar: 4 g Protein: 17 g Sodium: 266 mg

789. Cucumber Tomato Chopped Salad

Preparation Time: 15 minutes
Cooking Time: 0 minute
Servings: 6
Ingredients:
- ½ cup light mayonnaise
- 1 tablespoon lemon juice
- 1 tablespoon fresh dill, chopped
- 1 tablespoon chives, chopped
- ½ cup feta cheese, crumbled
- Salt and pepper to taste
- 1 red onion, chopped
- 1 cucumber, diced
- 1 radish, diced
- 3 tomatoes, diced
- Chives, chopped

Directions:
1. Combine the mayo, lemon juice, fresh dill, chives, feta cheese, salt and pepper in a bowl.
2. Mix well.
3. Stir in the onion, cucumber, radish and tomatoes.
4. Coat evenly.
5. Garnish with the chopped chives.

Nutrition: Calories 187 Fat 16.7 g Saturated fat 4.1 g Carbohydrates 6.7 g Fiber 2 g Protein 3.3 g

790. Zucchini Pasta Salad

Preparation Time: 4 minutes
Cooking Time: 0 minute
Servings: 15
Ingredients:
- 5 tablespoons olive oil
- 2 teaspoons Dijon mustard

- 3 tablespoons red-wine vinegar
- 1 clove garlic, grated
- 2 tablespoons fresh oregano, chopped
- 1 shallot, chopped
- ¼ teaspoon red pepper flakes
- 16 ounces zucchini noodles
- ¼ cup Kalamata olives, pitted
- 3 cups cherry tomatoes, sliced in half
- ¾ cup Parmesan cheese, shaved

Directions:
1. Mix the olive oil, Dijon mustard, red-wine vinegar, garlic, oregano, shallot and red pepper flakes in a bowl.
2. Stir in the zucchini noodles.
3. Sprinkle on top the olives, tomatoes and Parmesan cheese.

Nutrition: Calories 299 Fat 24.7 g Saturated fat 5.1 g Carbohydrates 11.6 g Fiber 2.8 g Protein 7 g

791. Fried Rice and Vegetables

Preparation Time: 5 minutes
Cooking Time: 25 minutes
Servings: 4
Ingredients:

- ¾ cup uncooked short- or long-grain white rice
- 1½ cups water
- 2 tablespoons sesame oil, divided
- 2 large eggs, lightly beaten
- 2 carrots, diced
- 4 ounces (1¼ cups) sliced white mushrooms
- 1 tablespoon minced garlic
- 6 green onions, white and green parts, sliced and divided
- 2 tablespoons tamari or soy sauce
- ½ cup frozen green peas, defrosted

Directions:
1. Rinse the rice and add to a small saucepan. Add the water and bring to a boil.
2. Reduce the heat to low, cover, and simmer for 15 minutes, until the water is

absorbed. Fluff with a fork and set aside.
3. While the rice is cooking, heat ½ tablespoon of the sesame oil in a large saucepan or wok over medium heat.
4. Add the eggs and cook without stirring for 5 minutes, until the egg is dry. Remove to a plate and cut into small strips. Set aside.
5. Return the saucepan or wok to the heat. Heat the remaining 2½ tablespoons of sesame oil. Add the carrots and stir for 2 minutes.
6. Add the mushrooms, garlic, and white parts of the green onions. Stir for 3 more minutes.
7. Add the cooked rice and tamari or soy sauce. Cook, stirring frequently, for 10 minutes, until the rice is sticky.
8. Toss in the green parts of the green onions, peas, and egg and stir to mix. Remove from the heat and serve hot with extra tamari or soy sauce, if desired.

Nutrition: Calories: 271 Total Fat: 10 g Total Carbs: 37 g Fiber: 3 g Sugar: 4 g Protein: 9 g Sodium: 567 mg

792. Spanish-Style Saffron Rice with Black Beans

Preparation Time: 5 minutes
Cooking Time: 25 minutes
Servings: 4
Ingredients:

- 2 cups vegetable stock
- ¼ teaspoon saffron threads (optional)
- 1½ tablespoons extra-virgin olive oil
- 1 small red or yellow onion, halved and thinly sliced
- 1 tablespoon minced garlic
- 1 teaspoon turmeric
- 2 teaspoons paprika
- 1 cup long-grain white rice, well-rinsed
- 1 (14-oz.) can black beans, drained and rinsed
- ½ cup green beans, halved or quartered

- 1 small red bell pepper, chopped
- 1 teaspoon salt

Directions:
1. In a small pot, heat the vegetable stock until boiling. Add the saffron, if using, and remove from the heat.
2. Meanwhile, heat the olive oil in a large nonstick skillet over medium heat.
3. Add the onion, garlic, turmeric, paprika, and rice and stir to coat.
4. Pour in the stock, and mix in the black beans, green beans, and red bell pepper.
5. Bring to a boil, reduce the heat to medium-low, cover, and simmer until the rice is tender and most of the liquid has been absorbed, about 20 minutes.
6. Stir in the salt and serve hot.

Nutrition: Calories: 332 Total Fat: 5 g Total Carbs: 63 g Fiber: 9 g Sugar: 2 g Protein: 11 g Sodium: 658 mg

793. Egg Avocado Salad

Preparation Time: 10 minutes
Cooking Time: 0 minute
Servings: 4
Ingredients:

- 1 avocado
- 6 hard-boiled eggs, peeled and chopped
- 1 tablespoon mayonnaise
- 2 tablespoons freshly squeezed lemon juice
- ¼ cup celery, chopped
- 2 tablespoons chives, chopped
- Salt and pepper to taste

Directions:
1. Add the avocado to a large bowl.
2. Mash the avocado using a fork.
3. Stir in the egg and mash the eggs.
4. Add the mayo, lemon juice, celery, chives, salt and pepper.
5. Chill in the refrigerator for at least 30 minutes before serving.

Nutrition: Calories 224 Fat 18 g Saturated fat 3.9 g Carbohydrates 6.1 g Fiber 3.6 g Protein 10.6 g

794. Pepper Tomato Salad

Preparation Time: 1 hour and 25 minutes
Cooking Time: 0 minute
Servings: 8
Ingredients:

- 2 tablespoons balsamic vinegar
- 2 tablespoons olive oil
- ½ teaspoon Dijon mustard
- 2 teaspoons fresh basil leaves, chopped
- 1 tablespoon fresh chives, chopped
- 1 teaspoon sugar
- Pepper to taste
- 2 cups yellow bell peppers, sliced into rings
- 1 cups orange bell pepper, sliced into rings
- 4 tomatoes, sliced into rounds
- ¼ cup blue cheese, crumbled

Directions:

1. Mix the vinegar, olive oil, mustard, basil, chives, sugar and pepper in a bowl.
2. Arrange the tomatoes and pepper rings on a serving plate.
3. Sprinkle the crumbled blue cheese on top.
4. Drizzle with the dressing.
5. Chill in the refrigerator for 1 hour before serving.

Nutrition: Calories 116 Fat 7 g Saturated fat 2 g Carbohydrates 11 g Fiber 2 g Protein 3 g

795. Simple Lemon Dal

Preparation Time: 5 minutes
Cooking Time: 25 minutes
Servings: 4
Ingredients:
For the lentils:

- 1 cup dried red lentils, well-rinsed
- 2½ cups water
- ½ teaspoon turmeric
- ½ teaspoon ground cumin
- 2 tablespoons lemon juice
- ⅓ cup fresh parsley, chopped
- 1 teaspoon salt

For finishing:

- 1 tablespoon extra-virgin olive oil
- 2 teaspoons minced garlic
- ½ teaspoon dried red chili flakes or ¼ teaspoon cayenne pepper

Directions:

1. Add the lentils to a medium saucepan and pour in the water. Stir in the turmeric and cumin and bring to a boil.
2. Reduce the heat to medium-low, cover, and simmer, stirring occasionally, for 20 minutes, until the lentils are soft and the mixture has thickened.
3. Stir in the lemon juice, parsley, and salt, and remove the pan from the heat.
4. In a small saucepan, heat the oil over medium-high heat. When hot, add the garlic and red chili flakes or cayenne and stir for 1 minute.
5. Quickly pour the oil into the cooked lentils, cover, and let sit for 5 minutes.
6. Stir the lentils and serve immediately.

Nutrition: Calories: 207 Total Fat: 4 g Total Carbs: 30 g Fiber: 15 g Sugar: 1 g Protein: 13 g Sodium: 589 mg

796. Cauliflower Latke

Preparation Time: 15 minutes
Cooking Time: 30 minutes
Servings: 4
Ingredients:

- 12 ounces cauliflower rice, cooked
- 1 egg, beaten
- ⅓ cup cornstarch
- Salt and pepper to taste
- ¼ cup vegetable oil, divided
- Chopped onion chives

Directions:

1. Squeeze excess water from the cauliflower rice using paper towels.
2. Place the cauliflower rice in a bowl.
3. Stir in the egg and cornstarch.
4. Season with salt and pepper.
5. Fill 2 tablespoons of oil into a pan over medium heat.
6. Add 2 to 3 tablespoons of the cauliflower mixture into the pan.
7. Cook for 3 minutes on each side.
8. Repeat until you've used up the rest of the batter.
9. Garnish with chopped chives.

Nutrition: 209 Calories 1.9 g Fiber 3.4 g Protein

797. Penne with Veggies

Preparation Time: 5 minutes
Cooking Time: 25 minutes
Servings: 6
Ingredients:

- 2 teaspoons olive oil & 2 cloves garlic, crushed and minced
- ½ cup shallots, chopped
- 2 tablespoons dry white wine
- 1 cup Brussels sprouts, trimmed and chopped
- 6 cups bok choy, chopped
- 6 cups cooked penne pasta
- 1 tablespoon vegetable oil spread
- Salt and pepper to taste
- 2 teaspoons dried Italian seasoning
- 3 tablespoons Parmesan cheese, grated

Directions:

1. Pour the oil into a pan over medium heat.
2. Cook the garlic and shallots for 3 minutes.
3. Pour in the wine.
4. Scrape the browned bits using a wooden spoon.
5. Stir in the Brussels sprouts.
6. Cook for 3 minutes.
7. Stir in the bok choy and cook for 2 to 3 minutes.
8. Toss the pasta in the veggies.
9. Add the vegetable oil to the mix.
10. Season with salt, pepper and Italian seasoning.
11. Sprinkle the Parmesan cheese on top.

Nutrition: Calories 127 Fat 4 g Saturated fat 1 g Carbohydrates 17 g Fiber 3 g Protein 6 g

798. Marinated Veggie Salad

Preparation Time: 4 hours and 30 minutes
Cooking Time:
Servings: 6
Ingredients:

- 1 zucchini, sliced
- 4 tomatoes, sliced into wedges
- ¼ cup red onion, sliced thinly
- 1 green bell pepper, sliced
- 2 tablespoons fresh parsley, chopped
- 2 tablespoons red-wine vinegar
- 2 tablespoons olive oil
- 1 clove garlic, minced
- 1 teaspoon dried basil
- 2 tablespoons water
- Pine nuts, toasted and chopped

Directions:

1. In a bowl, combine the zucchini, tomatoes, red onion, green bell pepper and parsley.
2. Pour the vinegar and oil into a glass jar with a lid.
3. Add the garlic, basil and water.
4. Seal the jar and shake well to combine.
5. Pour the dressing into the vegetable mixture.
6. Cover the bowl.
7. Marinate in the refrigerator for 4 hours.
8. Garnish with the pine nuts before serving.

Nutrition: Calories 65 Fat 4.7 g Saturated fat 0.7 g Carbohydrates 5.3 g Fiber 1.2 g Protein 0.9 g

799. Roasted Brussels Sprouts

Preparation Time: 30 minutes
Cooking Time: 20 minutes
Servings: 4
Ingredients:

- 1 pound Brussels sprouts, sliced in half
- 1 shallot, chopped
- 1 tablespoon olive oil
- Salt and pepper to taste
- 2 teaspoons balsamic vinegar

- ¼ cup pomegranate seeds
- ¼ cup goat cheese, crumbled

Directions:

1. Preheat your oven to 400°F.
2. Coat the Brussels sprouts with oil.
3. Sprinkle with salt and pepper.
4. Transfer to a baking pan.
5. Roast in the oven for 20 minutes.
6. Drizzle with vinegar.
7. Sprinkle with the seeds and cheese before serving.

Nutrition: 117 Calories 4.8 g Fiber 5.8 g Protein

800. Brussels Sprouts & Cranberries

Preparation Time: 10 minutes
Cooking Time: 0 minute
Servings: 6
Ingredients:

- 3 tablespoons lemon juice
- ¼ cup olive oil
- Salt and pepper to taste
- 1 pound Brussels sprouts, sliced thinly
- ¼ cup dried cranberries, chopped
- ½ cup pecans, toasted and chopped
- ½ cup Parmesan cheese, shaved

Directions:

1. Mix the lemon juice, olive oil, salt and pepper in a bowl.
2. Toss the Brussels sprouts, cranberries and pecans in this mixture.
3. Sprinkle the Parmesan cheese on top.

Nutrition: 245 Calories 6.4 g Protein 5 g Fiber

801. Arugula Salad

Preparation Time: 15 minutes
Cooking Time: 0 minute
Servings: 4
Ingredients:

- 6 cups fresh arugula leaves
- 2 cups radicchio, chopped
- ¼ cup low-fat balsamic vinaigrette
- ¼ cup pine nuts, toasted and chopped

Directions:

1. Arrange the arugula leaves in a serving bowl.
2. Sprinkle the radicchio on top.
3. Drizzle with the vinaigrette.
4. Sprinkle the pine nuts on top.

Nutrition: Calories 85 Fat 6.6 g Saturated Fat 0.5 Carbohydrates 5.1 g Fiber 1 g Protein 2.2 g

802. Mediterranean Salad

Preparation Time: 20 minutes
Cooking Time: 5 minutes
Servings: 2
Ingredients:

- 2 teaspoons balsamic vinegar
- 1 tablespoon basil pesto
- 1 cup lettuce
- ¼ cup broccoli florets, chopped
- ½ cup zucchini, chopped
- ¼ cup tomato, chopped
- ¼ cup yellow bell pepper, chopped
- 2 tablespoons feta cheese, crumbled

Directions:

1. Arrange the lettuce on a serving platter.
2. Top with broccoli, zucchini, tomato and bell pepper.
3. In a bowl, mix the vinegar and pesto.
4. Drizzle the dressing on top.
5. Sprinkle the feta cheese and serve.

Nutrition: Calories 100 Fat 6 g Saturated Fat 1 g Carbohydrates 7 g Protein 4 g

Chapter 10. Vegetarian Dishes

803. Vegetarian Chili with Avocado Cream

Preparation Time: 15 minutes
Cooking Time: 25 minutes
Servings: 8
Ingredients:

- 2 tablespoons olive oil
- ½ onion, finely chopped
- tablespoon minced garlic
- jalapeño peppers, chopped
- red bell pepper, diced
- teaspoon ground cumin
- tablespoons chili powder
- cups pecans, chopped
- cups canned diced tomatoes and their juice

Topping:

- 1 cup sour cream
- 1 avocado, diced
- 2 tablespoons fresh cilantro, chopped

Directions:

1. Heat olive oil.
2. Toss in the onion, garlic, jalapeño peppers, and red bell pepper, then sauté for about 4 minutes until tender.
3. Put in the chili powder and cumin and stir for 30 seconds.
4. Fold in the pecans, tomatoes, and their juice, then bring to a boil.
5. Simmer uncovered for about 20 minutes to infuse the flavors, stirring occasionally.
6. Remove from the heat to eight bowls.
7. Evenly top each bowl of chili with sour cream, diced avocado, and fresh cilantro.

Nutrition: Calories: 318 Fat: 14.4 g Fiber: 17.5g Carbohydrates: 9.5g Protein: 14g

804. Eggs with Zucchini Noodles

Preparation Time: 10 minutes
Cooking Time: 11 minutes
Servings: 2
Ingredients:

- 2 tablespoons extra-virgin olive oil

- 3 zucchinis, cut with a spiralizer
- 4 eggs
- Salt and black pepper to the taste
- A pinch of red pepper flakes
- Cooking spray
- 1 tablespoon basil, chopped

Directions:

1. In a bowl, combine the zucchini noodles with salt, pepper and olive oil and toss well.
2. Grease a baking sheet with cooking spray and divide the zucchini noodles into 4 nests.
3. Crack an egg on top of each nest, sprinkle salt, pepper and pepper flakes on top and bake at 350°F for 11 minutes.
4. Divide the mix between plates, sprinkle the basil on top and serve.

Nutrition: Calories 296, Fat 23.6, Fiber 3.3, Carbs 10.6, Protein 14.7

805. Roasted Root Veggies

Preparation Time: 20 minutes
Cooking Time: 1 hour and 30 minutes
Servings: 6
Ingredients:

- 2 tablespoons olive oil
- 1 head garlic, cloves separated and peeled
- 1 large turnip, peeled and cut into ½-inch pieces
- 1 medium-sized red onion, cut into ½-inch pieces
- 1½ pounds beets, trimmed but not peeled, scrubbed and cut into ½-inch pieces
- 1½ pounds Yukon gold potatoes, unpeeled, cut into ½-inch pieces
- 2½ pounds butternut squash, peeled, seeded, cut into ½-inch pieces

Directions:

1. Grease 2 rimmed and large baking sheets. Preheat oven to 425°F.

2. In a large bowl, mix all ingredients thoroughly.
3. Into the two baking sheets, evenly divide the root vegetables, spread in one layer.
4. Season generously with pepper and salt.
5. Pop into the oven and roast for 1 hour and 15 minutes or until golden brown and tender.
6. Remove from oven and let it cool for at least 15 minutes before serving.

Nutrition: Calories: 298; Carbs: 61.1g; Protein: 7.4g; Fat: 5.0g

806. Rustic Vegetable and Brown Rice Bowl

Preparation Time: 15 minutes
Cooking Time: 10 minutes
Servings: 4
Ingredients:

- Nonstick cooking spray
- 2 cups broccoli florets
- 2 cups cauliflower florets
- 1 (15-oz.) can chickpeas, drained and rinsed
- 1 cup carrots sliced 1 inch thick
- 2 to 3 tablespoons extra-virgin olive oil, divided
- Salt and freshly ground black pepper
- 2 to 3 tablespoons sesame seeds, for garnish
- 2 cups cooked brown rice

For the dressing:

- 3 to 4 tablespoons tahini
- 2 tablespoons honey
- 1 lemon, juiced
- 1 garlic clove, minced
- Salt
- Freshly ground black pepper

Directions:

1. Preheat the oven to 400°F. Spray two baking sheets with cooking spray.
2. Cover the first baking sheet with broccoli and cauliflower and the second with chickpeas and carrots. Toss each sheet with half of the oil and season with salt

and pepper before placing in the oven.

3. Cook the carrots and chickpeas for 10 minutes, leaving the carrots still just crisp, and the broccoli and cauliflower for 20 minutes, until tender. Stir each halfway through cooking.
4. To make the dressing, in a small bowl, mix the tahini, honey, lemon juice, and garlic. Season with salt and pepper and set aside.
5. Divide the rice into individual bowls, then layer with vegetables and drizzle dressing over the dish.

Nutrition: Calories: 192; Carbs: 12.7g; Protein: 3.8g; Fat: 15.5g

807. Roasted Brussels Sprouts and Pecans

Preparation Time: 10 minutes
Cooking Time: 15 minutes
Servings: 4
Ingredients:

- 1½ pounds fresh Brussels sprouts
- 4 tablespoons olive oil
- 4 cloves of garlic, minced
- 3 tablespoons water
- Salt and pepper to taste
- ½ cup chopped pecans

Directions:

1. Place all ingredients in the Instant Pot.
2. Combine all ingredients until well combined.
3. Close the lid and make sure that the steam release vent is set to "Venting."
4. Press the "Slow Cook" button and adjust the cooking time to 3 hours.
5. Sprinkle with a dash of lemon juice if desired.

Nutrition: Calories: 161; Carbs: 10.2g; Protein: 4.1g; Fat: 13.1g

808. Roasted Vegetables and Zucchini Pasta

Preparation Time: 10 minutes
Cooking Time: 7 minutes
Servings: 2
Ingredients:

- ¼ cup raw pine nuts
- 4 cups leftover vegetables
- 2 garlic cloves, minced

- 1 tablespoon extra-virgin olive oil
- 4 medium zucchinis, cut into long strips resembling noodles

Directions:

1. Heat oil in a large skillet over medium heat and sauté the garlic for 2 minutes.
2. Add the leftover vegetables and place the zucchini noodles on top. Let it cook for five minutes. Garnish with pine nuts.

Nutrition: Calories: 288; Carbs: 23.6g; Protein: 8.2g; Fat: 19.2g

809. Sautéed Collard Greens

Preparation Time: 10 minutes
Cooking Time: 0 minute
Servings: 4
Ingredients:

- 1-pound fresh collard greens, cut into 2-inch pieces
- 1 pinch red pepper flakes
- 3 cups chicken broth
- 1 teaspoon pepper
- 1 teaspoon salt
- 2 cloves garlic, minced
- 1 large onion, chopped
- 3 slices bacon
- 1 tablespoon olive oil

Directions:

1. Using a large skillet, heat oil on medium-high heat. Sauté bacon until crisp. Remove it from the pan and crumble it once cooled. Set it aside.
2. Using the same pan, sauté onion and cook until tender. Add garlic until fragrant. Add the collard greens and cook until they start to wilt.
3. Pour in the chicken broth and season with pepper, salt and red pepper flakes. Reduce the heat to low and simmer for 45 minutes.

Nutrition: Calories: 20; Carbs: 3.0g; Protein: 1.0g; Fat: 1.0g

810. Balsamic Bulgur Salad

Preparation Time: 30 minutes
Cooking Time: 0 minutes
Servings: 4
Ingredients:

- 1 cup bulgur
- 2 cups hot water
- 1 cucumber, sliced

- A pinch of sea salt and black pepper
- 2 tablespoons lemon juice
- 2 tablespoons balsamic vinegar
- ¼ cup olive oil

Directions:

1. In a bowl, mix bulgur with the water, cover, leave aside for 30 minutes, fluff with a fork, and transfer to a salad bowl.
2. Add the rest of the ingredients, toss and serve.

Nutrition: Calories 171, Fat 5.1g, Fiber 6.1g, Carbs 11.3g, Protein 4.4g

811. Savoy Cabbage with Coconut Cream Sauce

Preparation Time: 5 minutes
Cooking Time: 20 minutes
Servings: 4
Ingredients:

- 3 tablespoons olive oil
- 1 onion, chopped
- 4 cloves of garlic, minced
- 1 head savoy cabbage, chopped finely
- 2 cups bone broth
- 1 cup coconut milk, freshly squeezed
- 1 bay leaf
- Salt and pepper to taste
- 2 tablespoons chopped parsley

Directions:

1. Heat oil in a pot for 2 minutes.
2. Stir in the onions, bay leaf, and garlic until fragrant, around 3 minutes.
3. Add the rest of the ingredients, except for the parsley and mix well.
4. Cover pot, bring to a boil, and let it simmer for 5 minutes or until cabbage is tender to taste.
5. Stir in parsley and serve.

Nutrition: Calories: 195; Carbs: 12.3g; Protein: 2.7g; Fat: 19.7g

812. Slow Cooked Buttery Mushrooms

Preparation Time: 10 minutes
Cooking Time: 10 minutes
Servings: 2
Ingredients:

- 2 tablespoons butter

- 2 tablespoons olive oil
- 3 cloves of garlic, minced
- 16 ounces fresh brown mushrooms, sliced
- 7 ounces fresh shiitake mushrooms, sliced
- A dash of thyme
- Salt and pepper to taste

Directions:
1. Heat the butter and oil in a pot.
2. Sauté the garlic until fragrant, around 1 minute.
3. Stir in the rest of the ingredients and cook until soft, around 9 minutes.

Nutrition: Calories: 192; Carbs: 12.7g; Protein: 3.8g; Fat: 15.5g

813. Radish and Corn Salad

Preparation Time: 10 minutes
Cooking Time: 0 minutes
Servings: 2
Ingredients:
- 1 tablespoon lemon juice
- 1 jalapeno, chopped
- 2 tablespoons olive oil
- ¼ teaspoon oregano, dried
- A pinch of sea salt and black pepper
- 2 cups fresh corn
- 6 radishes, sliced

Directions:
1. In a salad bowl, combine the corn with the radishes and the rest of the ingredients, toss and serve cold.

Nutrition: Calories 134, Fat 4.5g, Fiber 1.8g, Carbs 4.1g, Protein 1.9g

814. Arugula and Corn Salad

Preparation Time: 10 minutes
Cooking Time: 0 minutes
Servings: 4
Ingredients:
- 1 red bell pepper, thinly sliced
- 2 cups corn
- Juice of 1 lime
- Zest of 1 lime, grated
- 8 cups baby arugula
- A pinch of sea salt and black pepper

Directions:
1. In a salad bowl, mix the corn with the arugula and

the rest of the ingredients, toss and serve cold.

Nutrition: Calories 172, Fat 8.5g, Fiber 1.8g, Carbs 5.1g, Protein 1.4g

815. Steamed Squash Chowder

Preparation Time: 20 minutes
Cooking Time: 40 minutes
Servings: 4
Ingredients:
- 3 cups chicken broth
- 2 tablespoons ghee
- 1 teaspoon chili powder
- ½ teaspoon cumin
- 1½ teaspoon salt
- 2 teaspoons cinnamon
- 3 tablespoons olive oil
- 2 carrots, chopped
- 1 small yellow onion, chopped
- 1 green apple, sliced and cored
- 1 large butternut squash, peeled, seeded, and chopped to ½-inch cubes

Directions:
1. In a large pot on medium-high fire, melt ghee.
2. Once the ghee is hot, sauté onions for 5 minutes or until soft and translucent.
3. Add olive oil, chili powder, cumin, salt, and cinnamon. Sauté for half a minute.
4. Add chopped squash and apples.
5. Sauté for 10 minutes while stirring once in a while.
6. Add broth, cover, and cook on medium fire for twenty minutes or until apples and squash are tender.
7. With an immersion blender, puree chowder. Adjust consistency by adding more water.
8. Add more salt or pepper depending on desire.
9. Serve and enjoy.

Nutrition: Calories: 228; Carbs: 17.9g; Protein: 2.2g; Fat: 18.0g

816. Steamed Zucchini-Paprika

Preparation Time: 15 minutes
Cooking Time: 30 minutes
Servings: 2
Ingredients:
- 4 tablespoons olive oil

- 3 cloves of garlic, minced
- 1 onion, chopped
- 3 medium-sized zucchinis, sliced thinly
- A dash of paprika
- Salt and pepper to taste

Directions:
1. Place all ingredients in the Instant Pot.
2. Give a good stir to combine all ingredients.
3. Close the lid and make sure that the steam release valve is set to "Venting."
4. Press the "Slow Cook" button and adjust the cooking time to 4 hours.
5. Halfway through the cooking time, open the lid and give a good stir to brown the other side.

Nutrition: Calories: 93; Carbs: 3.1g; Protein: 0.6g; Fat: 10.2g

817. Orange and Cucumber Salad

Preparation Time: 10 minutes
Cooking Time: 0 minutes
Servings: 4
Ingredients:
- 2 cucumbers, sliced
- 1 orange, peeled and cut into segments
- 1 cup cherry tomatoes, halved
- 1 small red onion, chopped
- 3 tablespoons olive oil
- 4½ teaspoon balsamic vinegar
- Salt and black pepper to the taste
- 1 tablespoon lemon juice

Directions:
1. In a bowl, mix the cucumbers with the orange and the rest of the ingredients, toss and serve cold.

Nutrition: Calories 102, Fat 7.5g, Fiber 3g, Carbs 6.1g, Protein 3.4g

818. Parsley and Corn Salad

Preparation Time: 10 minutes
Cooking Time: 0 minutes
Servings: 4
Ingredients:
- 1½ teaspoon balsamic vinegar
- 2 tablespoons lime juice
- 2 tablespoons olive oil

- A pinch of sea salt and black pepper
- Black pepper to the taste
- 4 cups corn
- ½ cup parsley, chopped
- 2 spring onions, chopped

Directions:
1. In a salad bowl, combine the corn with the onions and the rest of the ingredients, toss and serve cold.

Nutrition: Calories 121, Fat 9.5g, Fiber 1.8g, Carbs 4.1g, Protein 1.9g

819. Stir Fried Brussels sprouts and Carrots

Preparation Time: 10 minutes
Cooking Time: 15 minutes
Servings: 6
Ingredients:
- 1 tablespoon cider vinegar
- ⅓ cup water
- 1 pound Brussels sprouts, halved lengthwise
- 1 pound carrots cut diagonally into ½-inch thick lengths
- 3 tablespoons unsalted butter, divided
- 2 tablespoons chopped shallot
- ½ teaspoon pepper
- ¾ teaspoon salt

Directions:
1. On medium-high fire, place a nonstick medium fry pan and heat 2 tablespoons butter.
2. Add shallots and cook until softened, around one to two minutes while occasionally stirring.
3. Add pepper salt, Brussels sprouts and carrots. Stir fry until vegetables start to brown on the edges, around 3 to 4 minutes.
4. Add water, cook and cover.
5. After 5 to 8 minutes, or when veggies are already soft, add the remaining butter.
6. If needed season with more pepper and salt to taste.
7. Turn off fire, transfer to a platter, serve and enjoy.

Nutrition: Calories: 98; Carbs: 13.9g; Protein: 3.5g; Fat: 4.2g

820. Stir Fried Eggplant

Preparation Time: 10 minutes
Cooking Time: 30 minutes
Servings: 2
Ingredients:
- 1 teaspoon cornstarch + 2 tablespoons water, mixed
- 1 teaspoon brown sugar
- 2 tablespoons oyster sauce
- 1 tablespoon fish sauce
- 2 tablespoons soy sauce
- ½ cup fresh basil
- 2 tablespoons oil
- ¼ cup water
- 2 cups Chinese eggplant, spiral
- 1 red chili & 6 cloves garlic, minced
- ½ purple onion, sliced thinly
- 1 (3-oz.) package medium-firm tofu, cut into slivers

Directions:
1. Prepare sauce by mixing cornstarch and water in a small bowl. In another bowl mix brown sugar, oyster sauce and fish sauce and set aside.
2. On medium-high fire, place a large nonstick saucepan and heat 2 tablespoons of oil. Sauté chili, garlic and onion for 4 minutes. Add tofu, stir fry for 4 minutes.
3. Add eggplant noodles and stir fry for 10 minutes. If the pan dries up, add water in small amounts to moisten the pan and cook noodles.
4. Pour in the sauce and mix well. Once simmering, slowly add cornstarch mixer while continuing to mix vigorously. Once the sauce thickens add fresh basil and cook for a minute.
5. Remove from fire, transfer to a serving plate and enjoy.

Nutrition: Calories: 369; Carbs: 28.4g; Protein: 11.4g; Fat: 25.3g

821. Tomato and Avocado Salad

Preparation Time: 10 minutes
Cooking Time: 0 minutes
Servings: 4
Ingredients:
- 1 pound cherry tomatoes, cubed

- 2 avocados, pitted, peeled and cubed
- 1 sweet onion, chopped
- A pinch of sea salt and black pepper
- 2 tablespoons lemon juice
- 1½ tablespoons olive oil
- 1 handful basil, chopped

Directions:
1. In a salad bowl, mix the tomatoes with the avocados and the rest of the ingredients, toss and serve right away.

Nutrition: Calories 148, Fat 7.8g, Fiber 2.9g, Carbs 5.4g, Protein 5.5g

822. Corn and Tomato Salad

Preparation Time: 10 minutes
Cooking Time: 0 minutes
Servings: 4
Ingredients:
- 2 avocados, pitted, peeled and cubed
- 1-pint mixed cherry tomatoes, halved:
- 2 tablespoons avocado oil
- 1 tablespoon lime juice
- ½ teaspoon lime zest, grated
- A pinch of salt and black pepper
- ¼ cup dill, chopped

Directions:
1. In a salad bowl, mix the avocados with the tomatoes and the rest of the ingredients, toss and serve cold.

Nutrition: Calories 188, Fat 7.3g, Fiber 4.9g, Carbs 6.4g, Protein 6.5g

823. Summer Vegetables

Preparation Time: 20 minutes
Cooking Time: 1 hour and 40 minutes minute
Servings: 6
Ingredients:
- 1 teaspoon dried marjoram
- ⅓ cup Parmesan cheese
- 1 small eggplant, sliced into ¼-inch thick circles
- 1 small summer squash, peeled and sliced diagonally into the ¼-inch thickness
- 3 large tomatoes, sliced into ¼-inch thick circles

- ½ cup dry white wine
- ½ teaspoon freshly ground pepper, divided
- ½ teaspoon salt, divided
- 5 cloves garlic, sliced thinly
- 2 cups leeks, sliced thinly
- 4 tablespoons extra-virgin olive oil, divided

Directions:

1. On medium fire, place a large nonstick saucepan and heat 2 tablespoons of oil.
2. Sauté garlic and leeks for 6 minutes or until garlic is starting to brown. Season with pepper and salt, ¼ teaspoon each.
3. Pour in the wine and cook for another minute. Transfer to a 2-quart baking dish.
4. In the baking dish, layer in the alternating pattern the eggplant, summer squash, and tomatoes. Do this until the dish is covered with vegetables. If there are excess vegetables, store for future use.
5. Season with remaining pepper and salt. Drizzle with remaining olive oil and pop in a preheated 425°F oven.
6. Bake for 75 minutes. Remove from oven and top with marjoram and cheese.
7. Return to oven and bake for 15 minutes more or until veggies are soft and edges are browned.
8. Allow to cool for at least 5 minutes before serving.

Nutrition: Calories: 150; Carbs: 11.8g; Protein: 3.3g; Fat: 10.8g

824. Stir Fried Bok Choy

Preparation Time: 5 minutes
Cooking Time: 13 minutes
Servings: 4
Ingredients:

- 3 tablespoons coconut oil
- 4 cloves of garlic, minced
- 1 onion, chopped
- 2 heads bok choy, rinsed and chopped
- 2 teaspoons coconut aminos

- Salt and pepper to taste
- 2 tablespoons sesame oil
- 2 tablespoons sesame seeds, toasted

Directions:

1. Heat the oil in a pot for 2 minutes.
2. Sauté the garlic and onions until fragrant, around 3 minutes.
3. Stir in the bok choy, coconut aminos, salt and pepper.
4. Cover pan and cook for 5 minutes.
5. Stir and continue cooking for another 3 minutes.
6. Drizzle with sesame oil and sesame seeds on top before serving.

Nutrition: Calories: 358; Carbs: 5.2g; Protein: 21.5g; Fat: 28.4g

825. Beans and Cucumber Salad

Preparation Time: 10 minutes
Cooking Time: 0 minutes
Servings: 4
Ingredients:

- 15 ounces canned great northern beans, drained and rinsed
- 2 tablespoons olive oil
- ½ cup baby arugula
- 1 cup cucumber, sliced
- 1 tablespoon parsley, chopped
- 2 tomatoes, cubed
- A pinch of sea salt and black pepper
- 2 tablespoons balsamic vinegar

Directions:

1. In a bowl, mix the beans with the cucumber and the rest of the ingredients, toss and serve cold.

Nutrition: Calories 233, Fat 9g, Fiber 6.5g, Carbs 13g, Protein 8g

826. Minty Olives and Tomatoes Salad

Preparation Time: 10 minutes
Cooking Time: 0 minutes
Servings: 4
Ingredients:

- 1 cup kalamata olives, pitted and sliced
- 1 cup black olives, pitted and halved

- 1 cup cherry tomatoes, halved
- 4 tomatoes, chopped
- 1 red onion, chopped
- 2 tablespoons oregano, chopped
- 1 tablespoon mint, chopped
- 2 tablespoons balsamic vinegar
- ¼ cup olive oil
- 2 teaspoons Italian herbs, dried
- A pinch of sea salt and black pepper

Directions:

1. In a salad bowl, mix the olives with the tomatoes and the rest of the ingredients, toss and serve cold.

Nutrition: Calories 190, Fat 8.1g, Fiber 5.8g, Carbs 11.6g, Protein 4.6g

827. Summer Veggies in Instant Pot

Preparation Time: 10 minutes
Cooking Time: 7 minutes
Servings: 6
Ingredients:

- 2 cups okra, sliced
- 1 cup grape tomatoes
- 1 cup mushroom, sliced
- 1½ cups onion, sliced
- 2 cups bell pepper, sliced
- 2½ cups zucchini, sliced
- 2 tablespoons basil, chopped
- 1 tablespoon thyme, chopped
- ½ cups balsamic vinegar
- ½ cups olive oil
- Salt and pepper

Directions:

1. Place all ingredients in the Instant Pot.
2. Stir the contents and close the lid.
3. Close the lid and press the Manual button.
4. Adjust the cooking time to 7 minutes.
5. Do quick pressure release.
6. Once cooled, evenly divide into serving size, keep in your preferred container, and refrigerate until ready to eat.

Nutrition: Calories 233; Carbs: 7g; Protein: 3g; Fat: 18g

828. Sumptuous Tomato Soup

Preparation Time: 10 minutes
Cooking Time: 30 minutes
Servings: 2
Ingredients:

- Pepper and salt to taste
- 2 tablespoons tomato paste
- 1½ cups vegetable broth
- 1 tablespoon chopped parsley
- 1 tablespoon olive oil
- 5 garlic cloves
- ½ medium yellow onion
- 4 large ripe tomatoes

Directions:

1. Preheat oven to 350°F.
2. Chop onion and tomatoes into thin wedges. Place on a rimmed baking sheet. Season with parsley, pepper, salt, and olive oil. Toss to combine well. Hide the garlic cloves inside tomatoes to keep it from burning.
3. Pop in the oven and bake for 30 minutes.
4. On medium pot, bring vegetable stock to a simmer. Add tomato paste.
5. Pour baked tomato mixture into the pot. Continue simmering for another 10 minutes.
6. With an immersion blender, puree soup.
7. Adjust salt and pepper to taste before serving.

Nutrition: Calories: 179; Carbs: 26.7g; Protein: 5.2g; Fat: 7.7g

829. Superfast Cajun Asparagus

Preparation Time: 10 minutes
Cooking Time: 8 minutes
Servings: 2
Ingredients:

- 1 teaspoon cajun seasoning
- 1-pound asparagus
- 1 teaspoon olive oil

Directions:

1. Snap the asparagus and make sure that you use the tender part of the vegetable.
2. Place a large skillet on the stovetop and heat on high for a minute.
3. Then grease skillet with cooking spray and spread asparagus in one layer.
4. Cover skillet and continue cooking on high for 5 to eight minutes.
5. Halfway through cooking time, stir the skillet and then cover and continue to cook.
6. Once done cooking, transfer to plates, serve, and enjoy!

Nutrition: Calories: 81; Carbs: 0g; Protein: 0g; Fat: 9g

830. Sweet and Nutritious Pumpkin Soup

Preparation Time: 20 minutes
Cooking Time: 40 minutes
Servings: 8
Ingredients:

- 1 teaspoon chopped fresh parsley
- ½ cup half and half
- ½ teaspoon chopped fresh thyme
- 1 teaspoon salt
- 4 cups pumpkin puree
- 6 cups vegetable stock, divided
- 1 clove garlic, minced
- 1 1-inch piece gingerroot, peeled and minced
- 1 cup chopped onion

Directions:

1. On medium-high fire, place a heavy-bottomed pot and for 5 minutes heat ½ cup vegetable stock, ginger, garlic and onions or until veggies are tender.
2. Add remaining stock and cook for 30 minutes.
3. Season with thyme and salt.
4. With an immersion blender, puree soup until smooth.
5. Turn off fire and mix in half and half.
6. Transfer pumpkin soup into 8 bowls, garnish with parsley, serve and enjoy.

Nutrition: Calories: 58; Carbs: 6.6g; Protein: 5.1g; Fat: 1.7g

831. Sweet Potato Puree

Preparation Time: 10 minutes
Cooking Time: 15 minutes
Servings: 6
Ingredients:

- 2 pounds sweet potatoes, peeled
- 1½ cups water

- 5 Medjool dates, pitted and chopped

Directions:

1. Place all ingredients in a pot.
2. Close the lid and allow to boil for 15 minutes until the potatoes are soft.
3. Drain the potatoes and place in a food processor together with the dates.
4. Pulse until smooth.
5. Place in individual containers.
6. Put a label and store in the fridge.
7. Allow to thaw at room temperature before heating in the microwave oven.

Nutrition: Calories: 619; Carbs: 97.8g; Protein: 4.8g; Fat: 24.3g;

832. Sweet Potatoes Oven Fried

Preparation Time: 10 minutes
Cooking Time: 30 minutes
Servings: 7
Ingredients:

- 1 small garlic clove, minced
- 1 teaspoon grated orange rind
- 1 tablespoon fresh parsley, chopped finely
- ¼ teaspoon pepper
- ¼ teaspoon salt
- 1 tablespoon olive oil
- 4 medium sweet potatoes, peeled and sliced to the ¼-inch thickness

Directions:

1. In a large bowl mix well pepper, salt, olive oil and sweet potatoes.
2. In a greased baking sheet, in a single layer arrange sweet potatoes.
3. Pop in a preheated 400oF oven and bake for 15 minutes, turnover potato slices, and return to oven. Bake for another 15 minutes or until tender.
4. Meanwhile, mix well in a clove of small bowl garlic, orange rind and parsley, sprinkle over cooked potato slices and serve.
5. You can store baked sweet potatoes in a lidded container and just

microwave whenever you want to eat it. Do consume within 3 days.

Nutrition: Calories: 176; Carbs: 36.6g; Protein: 2.5g; Fat: 2.5g

833. Tasty Avocado Sauce over Zoodles

Preparation Time: 10 minutes
Cooking Time: 10 minutes
Servings: 2
Ingredients:

- 1 zucchini peeled and spiralized into noodles
- 4 tablespoons pine nuts
- 2 tablespoons lemon juice
- 1 avocado peeled and pitted
- 12 sliced cherry tomatoes
- ⅓ cup water
- 1¼ cup basil
- Pepper and salt to taste

Directions:

1. Make the sauce in a blender by adding pine nuts, lemon juice, avocado, water, and basil. Pulse until smooth and creamy. Season with pepper and salt to taste. Mix well.
2. Place zoodles in the salad bowl. Pour over the avocado sauce and toss well to coat.
3. Add cherry tomatoes, serve, and enjoy.

Nutrition: Calories: 313; Protein: 6.8g; Carbs: 18.7g; Fat: 26.8g

834. Tomato Basil Cauliflower Rice

Preparation Time: 5 minutes
Cooking Time: 10 minutes
Servings: 4
Ingredients:

- Salt and pepper to taste
- Dried parsley for garnish
- ¼ cup tomato paste
- ½ teaspoon garlic, minced
- ½ teaspoon onion powder
- ½ teaspoon marjoram
- 1½ teaspoon dried basil
- 1 teaspoon dried oregano
- 1 large head of cauliflower
- 1 teaspoon oil

Directions:

1. Cut the cauliflower into florets and place in the food processor.

2. Pulse until it has a coarse consistency similar to rice. Set aside.
3. In a skillet, heat the oil and sauté the garlic and onion for three minutes. Add the rest of the ingredients. Cook for 8 minutes.

Nutrition: Calories: 106; Carbs: 15.1g; Protein: 3.3g; Fat: 5.0g

835. Vegan Sesame Tofu and Eggplants

Preparation Time: 10 minutes
Cooking Time: 20 minutes
Servings: 4
Ingredients:

- 5 tablespoons olive oil
- 1-pound firm tofu, sliced
- 3 tablespoons rice vinegar
- 2 teaspoons Swerve sweetener
- 2 whole eggplants, sliced
- ¼ cup soy sauce
- Salt and pepper to taste
- 4 tablespoons toasted sesame oil
- ¼ cup sesame seeds
- 1 cup fresh cilantro, chopped

Directions:

1. Heat the oil in a pan for 2 minutes.
2. Pan fry the tofu for 3 minutes on each side.
3. Stir in the rice vinegar, sweetener, eggplants, and soy sauce. Season with salt and pepper to taste.
4. Cover and cook for 5 minutes on medium fire. Stir and continue cooking for another 5 minutes.
5. Toss in the sesame oil, sesame seeds, and cilantro.
6. Serve and enjoy.

Nutrition: Calories: 616; Carbs: 27.4g; Protein: 23.9g; Fat: 49.2g

836. Vegetarian Coconut Curry

Preparation Time: 10 minutes
Cooking Time: 30 minutes
Servings: 4
Ingredients:

- 4 tablespoons coconut oil
- 1 medium onion, chopped
- 1 teaspoon minced garlic

- 1 teaspoon minced ginger
- 1 cup broccoli florets
- 2 cups fresh spinach leaves
- 2 teaspoons fish sauce
- 1 tablespoon garam masala
- ½ cup coconut milk
- Salt and pepper to taste

Directions:

1. Heat oil in a pot.
2. Sauté the onion and garlic until fragrant, around 3 minutes.
3. Stir in the rest of the ingredients, except for spinach leaves.
4. Season with salt and pepper to taste.
5. Cover and cook on medium fire for 5 minutes.
6. Stir and add spinach leaves. Cover and cook for another 2 minutes.
7. Turn off the fire and let it sit for two more minutes before serving.

Nutrition: Calories: 210; Carbs: 6.5g; Protein: 2.1g; Fat: 20.9g

837. Veggie Lo Mein

Preparation Time: 10 minutes
Cooking Time: 4 minutes
Servings: 6
Ingredients:

- 2 tablespoons olive oil
- 5 cloves of garlic, minced
- 2-inch knob of ginger, grated
- 8 ounces mushrooms, sliced
- ½ pound zucchini, spiralized
- 1 carrot, julienned
- 1 spring green onions, chopped
- 3 tablespoons coconut aminos
- Salt and pepper to taste
- 1 tablespoon sesame oil

Directions:

1. Heat the oil in a skillet and sauté the garlic and ginger until fragrant.
2. Stir in the mushrooms, zucchini, carrot, and green onions.
3. Season with coconut aminos, salt and pepper.

213

4. Close the lid and allow to simmer for 5 minutes.
5. Drizzle with sesame oil last.
6. Place in individual containers.
7. Put a label and store in the fridge.
8. Allow to thaw at room temperature before heating in the microwave oven.

Nutrition: Calories 288; Carbs: 48.7g; Protein: 7.6g; Fat: 11g;

838. Veggie Jamaican Stew

Preparation Time: 15 minutes
Cooking Time: 30 minutes
Servings: 4
Ingredients:

- 1 tablespoon cilantro, chopped
- 1 teaspoon salt
- 1 teaspoon pepper
- 1 tablespoon lime juice
- 2 cups collard greens, sliced
- 3 cups carrots, cut into bite-sized chunks
- ½ yellow plantain, cut into bite-sized pieces
- 1 cup okra, cut into ½" pieces
- 2 cups potatoes, cut into bite-sized cubes
- 2 cups taro, cut into bite-sized cubes
- 2 cups pumpkin, cut into bite-sized cubes
- 2 cups water
- 2 cups coconut milk
- 2 bay leaves
- 3 green onions, white bottom removed
- ½ teaspoon dried thyme
- ½ teaspoon ground allspice
- 4 garlic cloves, minced
- 1 onion, chopped
- 1 tablespoon olive oil

Directions:

1. On medium fire, place a stockpot and heat oil. Sauté onions for 4 minutes or until translucent and soft. Add thyme, allspice and garlic. Sauté for a minute.
2. Pour in water and coconut milk and bring to a simmer.

Add bay leaves and green onions.
3. Once simmering, slow fire to keep the broth at a simmer and add taro and pumpkin. Cook for 5 minutes.
4. Add potatoes and cook for three minutes.
5. Add carrots, plantain and okra. Mix and cook for five minutes.
6. Then remove and fish for thyme sprigs, bay leaves and green onions and discard.
7. Add collard greens and cook for four minutes or until bright green and darker in color.
8. Turn off fire, add pepper, salt and lime juice to taste. Once it tastes good, mix well, transfer to a serving bowl, serve and enjoy.

Nutrition: Calories: 531; Carbs: 59.7g; Protein: 8.3g; Fat: 32.7g

839. Vegetable Soup Moroccan Style

Preparation Time: 10 minutes
Cooking Time: 10 minutes
Servings: 6
Ingredients:

- ½ teaspoon pepper
- 1 teaspoon salt
- 2 ounces whole-wheat orzo
- 1 large zucchini, peeled and cut into ¼-inch cubes
- 8 sprigs fresh cilantro, plus more leaves for garnish
- 12 sprigs flat-leaf parsley, plus more for garnish
- A pinch of saffron threads
- 2 stalks celery leaves included, sliced thinly
- 2 carrots, diced
- 2 small turnips, peeled and diced
- 1 (14-oz.) can dice tomatoes
- 6 cups water
- 1 pound lamb stew meat, trimmed and cut into ½-inch cubes
- 2 teaspoons ground turmeric
- 1 medium onion, diced finely

- 2 tablespoons extra-virgin olive oil

Directions:

1. On medium-high fire, place a large Dutch oven and heat oil.
2. Add turmeric and onion, stir fry for two minutes.
3. Add meat and sauté for 5 minutes.
4. Add saffron, celery, carrots, turnips, tomatoes and juice, and water.
5. With a kitchen string, tie cilantro and parsley sprigs together and into the pot.
6. Cover and bring to a boil. Once boiling reduces fire to a simmer and continue to cook for 45 to 50 minutes or until meat is tender.
7. Once the meat is tender, stir in zucchini. Cover and cook for 8 minutes.
8. Add orzo; cook for 10 minutes or until soft.
9. Remove and discard cilantro and parsley sprigs.
10. Season with pepper and salt.
11. Transfer to a serving bowl and garnish with cilantro and parsley leaves before serving.

Nutrition: Calories: 268; Carbs: 12.9g; Protein: 28.1g; Fat: 11.7g

840. Veggie Ramen Miso Soup

Preparation Time: 5 minutes
Cooking Time: 20 minutes
Servings: 1
Ingredients:

- 2 teaspoons thinly sliced green onion
- A pinch of salt
- ½ teaspoon Shoyu
- 2 tablespoons mellow white miso
- 1 cup zucchini, cut into angel hair spirals
- ½ cup thinly sliced cremini mushrooms
- ½ medium carrot, cut into angel hair spirals
- ½ cup baby spinach leaves – optional
- 2¼ cups water

- ½ box of medium-firm tofu, cut into ¼-inch cubes
- 1 hardboiled egg

Directions:
1. In a small bowl, mix ¼ cup of water and miso. Set aside.
2. In a small saucepan on medium-high fire, bring to a boil 2 cups water, mushrooms, tofu and carrots. Add salt, Shoyu and miso mixture. Allow to boil for 5 minutes. Remove from fire and add green onion, zucchini and baby spinach leaves if using.
3. Let soup stand for 5 minutes before transferring to individual bowls. Garnish with ½ of hardboiled egg per bowl, serve and enjoy.

Nutrition: Calories: 335; Carbs: 19.0g; Protein: 30.6g; Fat: 17.6g

841. Yummy Cauliflower Fritters

Preparation Time: 10 minutes
Cooking Time: 15 minutes
Servings: 6
Ingredients:

- 1 large cauliflower head, cut into florets
- 2 eggs, beaten
- ½ teaspoon turmeric
- ½ teaspoon salt
- ¼ teaspoon black pepper
- 6 tablespoons coconut oil

Directions:
1. Place the cauliflower florets in a pot with water.
2. Bring to a boil and drain once cooked.
3. Place the cauliflower, eggs, turmeric, salt, and pepper into the food processor.
4. Pulse until the mixture becomes coarse.
5. Transfer into a bowl. Using your hands, form six small flattened balls and place in the fridge for at least 1 hour until the mixture hardens.
6. Heat the oil in a skillet and fry the cauliflower patties for 3 minutes on each side
7. Place in individual containers.

8. Put a label and store in the fridge.
9. Allow to thaw at room temperature before heating in the microwave oven.

Nutrition: Calories 157; Carbs: 2.8g; Protein: 3.9g; Fat: 15.3g; Fiber: 0.9g

842. Zucchini Garlic Fries

Preparation Time: 15 minutes
Cooking Time: 20 minutes
Servings: 6
Ingredients:

- ¼ teaspoon garlic powder
- ½ cup almond flour
- 2 large egg whites, beaten
- 3 medium zucchinis, sliced into fry sticks
- Salt and pepper to taste

Directions:
1. Preheat oven to 400°F.
2. Mix all ingredients in a bowl until the zucchini fries are well coated.
3. Place fries on a cookie sheet and spread evenly.
4. Put in oven and cook for 20 minutes.
5. Halfway through cooking time, stir fries.

Nutrition: Calories: 11; Carbs: 1.1g; Protein: 1.5g; Fat: 0.1g

843. Zucchini Pasta with Mango-Kiwi Sauce

Preparation Time: 5 minutes
Cooking Time: 20 minutes
Servings: 2
Ingredients:

- 1 teaspoon dried herbs – optional
- ½ cup Raw Kale leaves, shredded
- 2 small dried figs
- 3 Medjool dates
- 4 medium kiwis
- 2 big mangos, seed discarded
- 2 cup zucchini, spiralized
- ¼ cup roasted cashew

Directions:
1. On a salad bowl, place kale then topped with zucchini noodles and sprinkle with dried herbs. Set aside.
2. In a food processor, grind to a powder the cashews.

Add figs, dates, kiwis and mangoes then puree to a smooth consistency.
3. Pour over zucchini pasta, serve and enjoy.

Nutrition: Calories: 530; Carbs: 95.4g; Protein: 8.0g; Fat: 18.5g

844. Quinoa with Almonds and Cranberries

Preparation Time: 10 minutes
Cooking Time: 15 minutes
Servings: 4
Ingredients:

- 2 cups cooked quinoa
- ⅓ teaspoon cranberries or currants
- ¼ cup sliced almonds
- 2 garlic cloves, minced
- 1¼ teaspoon salt
- ½ teaspoon ground cumin
- ½ teaspoon turmeric
- ¼ teaspoon ground cinnamon
- ¼ teaspoon freshly ground black pepper

Directions:
1. In a large bowl, toss the quinoa, cranberries, almonds, garlic, salt, cumin, turmeric, cinnamon, and pepper and stir to combine. Enjoy alone or with roasted cauliflower.

Nutrition: Calories: 430; Carbs: 65.4g; Protein: 8.0g; Fat: 15.5g

845. Mediterranean Baked Chickpeas

Preparation Time: 15 minutes
Cooking Time: 15 minutes
Servings: 6
Ingredients:

- 1 tablespoon extra-virgin olive oil
- ½ medium onion, chopped
- 3 garlic cloves, chopped
- 2 teaspoons smoked paprika
- ¼ teaspoon ground cumin
- 4 cups halved cherry tomatoes
- 2 (15-oz.) cans chickpeas, drained and rinsed
- ½ cup plain, unsweetened, full-fat Greek yogurt, for serving
- 1 cup crumbled feta, for serving

Directions:

1. Preheat the oven to 425°F.
2. In an oven-safe sauté pan or skillet, heat the oil over medium heat and sauté the onion and garlic. Cook for about 5 minutes, until softened and fragrant. Stir in the paprika and cumin and cook for 2 minutes. Stir in the tomatoes and chickpeas.
3. Bring to a simmer for 5 to 10 minutes before placing in the oven.
4. Roast in the oven for 25 to 30 minutes, until bubbling and thickened. To serve, top with Greek yogurt and feta.

Nutrition: Calories: 330; Carbs: 75.4g; Protein: 9.0g; Fat: 18.5g

846. Falafel Bites
Preparation Time: 10 minutes
Cooking Time: 15 minutes
Servings: 4
Ingredients:

- 1 2/3 cups falafel mix
- 1¼ cups water
- Extra-virgin olive oil spray
- 1 tablespoon Pickled Onions (optional)
- 1 tablespoon Pickled Turnips (optional)
- 2 tablespoons Tzatziki Sauce (optional)

Directions:

1. In a large bowl, carefully stir the falafel mix into the water. Mix well. Let stand 15 minutes to absorb the water. Form the mix into 1-inch balls and arrange on a baking sheet.
2. Preheat the broiler to high.
3. Take the balls and flatten slightly with your thumb (so they won't roll around on the baking sheet). Spray with olive oil, and then broil for 2 to 3 minutes on each side, until crispy and brown.
4. To fry the falafel, fill a pot with ½ inch of cooking oil and heat over medium-high heat to 375°F. Fry the balls for about 3 minutes, until brown and crisp. Drain on paper towels and serve with pickled onions, pickled turnips, and tzatziki sauce (if using).

Nutrition: Calories: 530; Carbs: 95.4g; Protein: 8.0g; Fat: 18.5g

847. Quick Vegetable Kebabs
Preparation Time: 15 minutes
Cooking Time: 20 minutes
Servings: 6
Ingredients:

- 4 medium red onions, peeled and sliced into 6 wedges
- 4 medium zucchinis, cut into 1-inch-thick slices
- 4 bell peppers, cut into 2-inch squares
- 2 yellow bell peppers, cut into 2-inch squares
- 2 orange bell peppers, cut into 2-inch squares
- 2 beefsteak tomatoes, cut into quarters
- 3 tablespoons herbed oil

Directions:

1. Preheat the oven or grill to medium-high or 350°F.
2. Thread 1-piece red onion, zucchini, different colored bell peppers, and tomatoes onto a skewer. Repeat until the skewer is full of vegetables, up to 2 inches away from the skewer end, and continue until all skewers are complete.
3. Put the skewers on a baking sheet and cook in the oven for 10 minutes or grill for 5 minutes on each side. The vegetables will be done with they reach your desired crunch or softness.
4. Remove the skewers from heat and drizzle with herbed oil.

Nutrition: Calories: 235; Carbs: 30.4g; Protein: 8.0g; Fat: 14.5g

848. Tortellini in Red Pepper Sauce
Preparation Time: 15 minutes
Cooking Time: 10 minutes
Servings: 4
Ingredients:

- 1 (16-oz.) container fresh cheese tortellini (usually green and white pasta)
- 1 (16-oz.) jar roasted red peppers, drained
- 1 teaspoon garlic powder
- ¼ cup tahini
- 1 tablespoon red pepper oil (optional)

Directions:

1. Bring a large pot of water to a boil and cook the tortellini according to package directions.
2. In a blender, combine the red peppers with the garlic powder and process until smooth. Once blended, add the tahini until the sauce is thickened. If the sauce gets too thick, add up to 1 tablespoon red pepper oil (if using).
3. Once tortellini are cooked, drain and leave the pasta in a colander. Add the sauce to the bottom of the empty pot and heat for 2 minutes. Then, add the tortellini back into the pot and cook for 2 more minutes. Serve and enjoy!

Nutrition: Calories: 530; Carbs: 95.4g; Protein: 8.0g; Fat: 18.5g

849. Freekeh, Chickpea, and Herb Salad
Preparation Time: 15 minutes
Cooking Time: 10 minutes
Servings: 6
Ingredients:

- 1 (15-oz.) can chickpeas, rinsed and drained
- 1 cup cooked freekeh
- 1 cup thinly sliced celery
- 1 bunch scallions, both white and green parts, finely chopped
- ½ cup chopped fresh flat-leaf parsley
- ¼ cup chopped fresh mint
- 3 tablespoons chopped celery leaves
- ½ teaspoon kosher salt
- ⅓ cup extra-virgin olive oil
- ¼ cup freshly squeezed lemon juice
- ¼ teaspoon cumin seeds
- 1 teaspoon garlic powder

Directions:

1. In a large bowl, combine the chickpeas, freekeh, celery,

scallions, parsley, mint, celery leaves, and salt and toss lightly.

2. In a small bowl, whisk together the olive oil, lemon juice, cumin seeds, and garlic powder. Once combined, add to freekeh salad.

Nutrition: Calories: 230; Carbs: 25.4g; Protein: 8.0g; Fat: 18.5g

850. Kate's Warm Mediterranean Farro Bowl

Preparation Time: 15 minutes
Cooking Time: 10 minutes
Servings: 4
Ingredients:

- ⅓ cup extra-virgin olive oil
- ½ cup chopped red bell pepper
- ⅓ cup chopped red onions
- 2 garlic cloves, minced
- 1 cup zucchini, cut in ½-inch slices
- ½ cup canned chickpeas, drained and rinsed
- ½ cup coarsely chopped artichokes
- 3 cups cooked farro & Salt
- Freshly ground black pepper
- ¼ cup sliced olives, for serving (optional)
- ½ cup crumbled feta cheese, for serving (optional)
- 2 tablespoons fresh basil, chiffonade, for serving (optional)
- 3 tablespoons balsamic reduction, for serving (optional)

Directions:

1. In a large sauté pan or skillet, heat the oil over medium heat and sauté the pepper, onions, and garlic for about 5 minutes, until tender.
2. Add the zucchini, chickpeas, and artichokes, then stir and continue to sauté vegetables, approximately 5 more minutes, until just soft.

3. Stir in the cooked farro, tossing to combine and cooking enough to heat through. Season with salt and pepper and remove from the heat.
4. Transfer the contents of the pan into the serving vessels or bowls.
5. Top with olives, feta, and basil (if using). Drizzle with balsamic reduction (if using) to finish.

Nutrition: Calories: 530; Carbs: 95.4g; Protein: 8.0g; Fat: 13.5g

851. Creamy Chickpea Sauce with Whole-Wheat Fusilli

Preparation Time: 15 minutes
Cooking Time: 20 minutes
Servings: 4
Ingredients:

- ¼ cup extra-virgin olive oil
- ½ large shallot, chopped
- 5 garlic cloves, thinly sliced
- 1 (15-oz.) can chickpeas, drained and rinsed, reserving ½ cup canning liquid
- Pinch red pepper flakes
- 1 cup whole-grain fusilli pasta
- ¼ teaspoon salt
- ⅛ teaspoon freshly ground black pepper
- ¼ cup shaved fresh Parmesan cheese
- ¼ cup chopped fresh basil
- 2 teaspoons dried parsley
- 1 teaspoon dried oregano
- Red pepper flakes

Directions:

1. In a medium pan, heat the oil over medium heat, and sauté the shallot and garlic for 3 to 5 minutes, until the garlic is golden. Add ¾ of the chickpeas plus 2 tablespoons of liquid from the can, and bring to a simmer.
2. Remove from the heat, transfer into a standard blender, and blend until smooth. At this point, add the remaining chickpeas.

Add more reserved chickpea liquid if it becomes thick.

3. Bring a large pot of salted water to a boil and cook pasta until al dente, about 8 minutes. Reserve ½ cup of the pasta water, drain the pasta and return it to the pot.
4. Add the chickpea sauce to the hot pasta and add up to ¼ cup of the pasta water. You may need to add more pasta water to reach your desired consistency.
5. Place the pasta pot over medium heat and mix occasionally until the sauce thickens. Season with salt and pepper.
6. Serve, garnished with Parmesan, basil, parsley, oregano, and red pepper flakes.

Nutrition: Calories: 230; Carbs: 20.4g; Protein: 8.0g; Fat: 18.5g

852. Linguine and Brussels sprouts

Preparation Time: 10 minutes
Cooking Time: 25 minutes
Servings: 4
Ingredients:

- 8 ounces whole-wheat linguine
- ⅓ cup, plus 2 tablespoons extra-virgin olive oil, divided
- 1 medium sweet onion, diced
- 2 to 3 garlic cloves, smashed
- 8 ounces Brussels sprouts, chopped
- ½ cup chicken stock, as needed
- ⅓ cup dry white wine
- ½ cup shredded Parmesan cheese
- 1 lemon, cut in quarters

Directions:

1. Bring a large pot of water to a boil and cook the pasta according to package directions. Drain, reserving 1 cup of the pasta water. Mix the cooked pasta with 2 tablespoons of olive oil, then set aside.
2. In a large sauté pan or skillet, heat the remaining ⅓ cup of olive oil on medium

heat. Add the onion to the pan and cook for about 5 minutes, until softened. Add the smashed garlic cloves and cook for 1 minute, until fragrant.

3. Add the Brussels sprouts and cook covered for 15 minutes. Add chicken stock as needed to prevent burning. Once Brussels sprouts have wilted and are fork-tender, add white wine and cook down for about 7 minutes, until reduced.
4. Add the pasta to the skillet and add the pasta water as needed.
5. Serve with the Parmesan cheese and lemon for squeezing over the dish right before eating.

Nutrition: Calories: 530; Carbs: 95.4g; Protein: 5.0g; Fat: 16.5g

853. Peppers and Lentils Salad
Preparation Time: 10 minutes
Cooking Time: 0 minutes
Servings: 4
Ingredients:

- 14 ounces canned lentils, drained and rinsed
- 2 spring onions, chopped
- 1 red bell pepper, chopped
- 1 green bell pepper, chopped
- 1 tablespoon fresh lime juice
- ⅓ cup coriander, chopped
- 2 teaspoons balsamic vinegar

Directions:

1. In a salad bowl, combine the lentils with the onions, bell peppers and the rest of the ingredients, toss and serve.

Nutrition: Calories 200, Fat 2.45g, Fiber 6.7g, Carbs 10.5g, Protein 5.6g

854. Cashews and Red Cabbage Salad
Preparation Time: 10 minutes
Cooking Time: 0 minutes
Servings: 4
Ingredients:

- 1 pound red cabbage, shredded

- 2 tablespoons coriander, chopped
- ½ cup cashews, halved
- 2 tablespoons olive oil
- 1 tomato, cubed
- A pinch of salt and black pepper
- 1 tablespoon white vinegar

Directions:

1. In a salad bowl, combine the cabbage with the coriander and the rest of the ingredients, toss and serve cold.

Nutrition: Calories 210, Fat 6.3g, Fiber 5.2g, Carbs 5.5g, Protein 8g

855. Apples and Pomegranate Salad
Preparation Time: 10 minutes
Cooking Time: 0 minutes
Servings: 4
Ingredients:

- 3 big apples, cored and cubed
- 1 cup pomegranate seeds
- 3 cups baby arugula
- 1 cup walnuts, chopped
- 1 tablespoon olive oil
- 1 teaspoon white sesame seeds
- 2 tablespoons apple cider vinegar
- Salt and black pepper to the taste

Directions:

1. In a bowl, mix the apples with the arugula and the rest of the ingredients, toss and serve cold.

Nutrition: Calories 160, Fat 4.3g, Fiber 5.3g, Carbs 8.7g, Protein 10g

856. Cranberry Bulgur Mix
Preparation Time: 10 minutes
Cooking Time: 0 minutes
Servings: 4
Ingredients:

- 1½ cups hot water
- 1 cup bulgur
- Juice of ½ lemon
- 4 tablespoons cilantro, chopped
- ½ cup cranberries, chopped
- 1½ teaspoon curry powder
- ¼ cup green onions, chopped
- ½ cup red bell peppers, chopped

- ½ cup carrots, grated
- 1 tablespoon olive oil
- A pinch of salt and black pepper

Directions:

1. Put bulgur into a bowl, add the water, stir, cover, leave aside for 10 minutes, fluff with a fork, and transfer to a bowl.
2. Add the rest of the ingredients, toss, and serve cold.

Nutrition: Calories 300, Fat 6.4g, Fiber 6.1g, Carbs 7.6g, Protein 13g

857. Chickpeas, Corn and Black Beans Salad
Preparation Time: 10 minutes
Cooking Time: 0 minutes
Servings: 4
Ingredients:

- 1½ cups canned black beans, drained and rinsed
- ½ teaspoon garlic powder
- 2 teaspoons chili powder
- A pinch of sea salt and black pepper
- 1½ cups canned chickpeas, drained and rinsed
- 1 cup baby spinach
- 1 avocado, pitted, peeled and chopped
- 1 cup corn kernels, chopped
- 2 tablespoons lemon juice
- 1 tablespoon olive oil
- 1 tablespoon apple cider vinegar
- 1 teaspoon chives, chopped

Directions:

1. In a salad bowl, combine the black beans with the garlic powder, chili powder and the rest of the ingredients, toss and serve cold.

Nutrition: Calories 300, Fat 13.4g, Fiber 4.1g, Carbs 8.6g, Protein 13g

858. Olives and Lentils Salad
Preparation Time: 10 minutes
Cooking Time: 0 minutes
Servings: 2
Ingredients:

- ⅓ cup canned green lentils, drained and rinsed
- 1 tablespoon olive oil

- 2 cups baby spinach
- 1 cup black olives, pitted and halved
- 2 tablespoons sunflower seeds
- 1 tablespoon Dijon mustard
- 2 tablespoons balsamic vinegar
- 2 tablespoons olive oil

Directions:
1. In a bowl, mix the lentils with the spinach, olives and the rest of the ingredients, toss and serve cold.

Nutrition: Calories 279, Fat 6.5g, Fiber 4.5g, Carbs 9.6g, Protein 12g

859. Lime Spinach and Chickpeas Salad

Preparation Time: 10 minutes
Cooking Time: 0 minutes
Servings: 4
Ingredients:

- 16 ounces canned chickpeas, drained and rinsed
- 2 cups baby spinach leaves
- ½ tablespoons lime juice
- 2 tablespoons olive oil
- 1 teaspoon cumin, ground
- A pinch of sea salt and black pepper
- ½ teaspoon chili flakes

Directions:
1. In a bowl, mix the chickpeas with the spinach and the rest of the ingredients, toss and serve cold.

Nutrition: Calories 240, Fat 8.2g, Fiber 5.3g, Carbs 11.6g, Protein 12g

860. Whipped Potatoes

Preparation Time: 20 minutes
Cooking Time: 35 minutes
Servings: 10
Ingredients:

- 4 cups water
- 3 pounds potatoes, sliced into cubes
- 3 cloves garlic, crushed
- 6 tablespoons butter
- 2 bay leaves
- 10 sage leaves
- ½ cup Greek yogurt
- ¼ cup low-Fat milk

Directions:

1. Cook potatoes in water for 30 minutes.
2. Drain.
3. Cook garlic in butter for 1 minute over medium heat.
4. Add the sage and cook for 5 more minutes.
5. Discard the garlic.
6. Use a fork to mash the potatoes.
7. Whip using an electric mixer while gradually adding the butter, yogurt, and milk.
8. Season with salt.

Nutrition: 169 Calories 22g Carbohydrates 4.2g Protein

861. Jalapeno Rice Noodles

Preparation Time: 10 minutes
Cooking Time: 25 minutes
Servings: 4
Ingredients:

- ¼ cup soy sauce
- 1 tablespoon brown sugar
- 2 teaspoons sriracha
- 3 tablespoons lime juice
- 8 ounces rice noodles
- 3 teaspoons toasted sesame oil
- 1 package extra-firm tofu, pressed
- 1 onion, sliced
- 2 cups green cabbage, shredded
- 1 small jalapeno, minced
- 1 red bell pepper, sliced
- 1 yellow bell pepper, sliced
- 3 garlic cloves, minced
- 3 scallions, sliced
- 1 cup Thai basil leaves, roughly chopped
- Lime wedges for serving

Directions:
1. Fill a suitably-sized pot with salted water and boil it on high heat.
2. Add pasta to the boiling water and cook until it is al dente, then rinse under cold water.
3. Put the lime juice, soy sauce, sriracha, and brown sugar in a bowl then mix well.
4. Place a large wok over medium heat then add 1 teaspoon sesame oil.
5. Toss in tofu and stir for 5 minutes until golden-brown.

6. Transfer the golden-brown tofu to a plate and add 2 teaspoons oil to the wok.
7. Stir in scallions, garlic, peppers, cabbage, and onion.
8. Sauté for 2 minutes, then add cooked noodles and prepared sauce.
9. Cook for 2 minutes, then garnish with lime wedges and basil leaves.
10. Serve fresh.

Nutrition: Calories:45 Fat:2.5g Protein:4g Carbohydrates:9g Fiber:4g Sugar:3g Sodium: 20mg

862. Sautéed Cabbage

Preparation Time: 8 minutes
Cooking Time: 12 minutes
Servings: 8
Ingredients:

- ¼ cup butter
- 1 onion, sliced thinly
- 1 head cabbage, sliced into wedges
- Salt and pepper to taste
- Crumbled crispy bacon bits

Directions:
1. Add the butter to a pan over medium-high heat.
2. Cook the onion for 1 minute, stirring frequently.
3. Season with salt and pepper.
4. Add the cabbage and cook while stirring for 12 minutes.
5. Sprinkle with the crispy bacon bits.

Nutrition: Calories 77 Fat 5.9 g Saturated fat 3.6 g Carbohydrates 6.1 g Fiber 2.4 g Protein 1.3 g

863. Southwest Style Salad

Preparation Time: 10 minutes
Cooking Time: 0 minutes
Servings: 3
Ingredients:

- ½ cup dry black beans
- ½ cup dry chickpeas
- ⅓ cup purple onion, diced
- 1 red bell pepper, pitted, sliced
- 4 cups mixed greens, fresh or frozen, chopped
- 1 cup cherry tomatoes, halved or quartered
- 1 medium avocado, peeled, pitted, and cubed

- 1 cup sweet kernel corn, canned, drained
- ½ teaspoon chili powder
- ¼ teaspoon cumin
- ¼ tsp Salt
- ¼ tsp pepper
- 2 teaspoons olive oil
- 1 tablespoon vinegar

Directions:
1. Prepare the black beans and chickpeas according to the method.
2. Put all of the ingredients into a large bowl.
3. Toss the mix of veggies and spices until combined thoroughly.
4. Store, or serve chilled with some olive oil and vinegar on top!

Nutrition: Calories 635 Total Fat 19.9g Saturated Fat 3.6g Cholesterol 0mg Sodium 302mg Total Carbohydrate 95.4g Dietary Fiber 28.1g Total Sugars 18.8g Protein 24.3g Vitamin D 0mcg Calcium 160mg Iron 7mg Potassium 1759mg

864. Rainbow Soba Noodles
Preparation Time: 10 minutes
Cooking Time: 20 minutes
Servings: 4
Ingredients:
- 8 ounces tofu, pressed and crumbled
- 1 teaspoon olive oil
- ½ teaspoon red pepper flakes
- 10 ounces package buckwheat soba noodles, cooked
- 1 package broccoli slaw
- 2 cups cabbage, shredded
- ¼ cup very red onion, thinly sliced

Peanut Sauce:
- ¼ cup peanut butter
- ¾ cup hot water
- 2 tablespoons apple cider vinegar
- 1 tablespoon maple syrup
- 1–2 garlic cloves, minced
- 1 lime, zest, and juice
- Salt and crushed red pepper flakes, to taste
- Cilantro, for garnish
- Crushed peanuts, for garnish

Directions:
1. Crumble tofu on a baking sheet and toss in 1 teaspoon oil and 1 teaspoon red pepper flakes.
2. Bake the tofu for 20 minutes at 400°F in a preheated oven.
3. Meanwhile, whisk peanut butter with hot water, garlic cloves, maple syrup, cider vinegar, lime zest, salt, lime juice, and pepper flakes in a large bowl.
4. Toss in cooked noodles, broccoli slaw, cabbages, and onion.
5. Mix well, then stir in tofu, cilantro, and peanuts.
6. Enjoy.

Nutrition: Calories:45 Fat: 2.5g Protein: 4g Carbohydrates: 9g Fiber: 4g Sugar: 3g Sodium: 20mg

865. Grilled Fajitas with Jalapeño Sauce
Preparation Time: 10 minutes
Cooking Time: 25 minutes
Servings: 4
Ingredients:
Marinade:
- ¼ cup olive oil
- ¼ cup lime juice
- 2 garlic cloves, minced
- 1 teaspoon chili powder
- 1 teaspoon ground cumin
- 1 teaspoon dried oregano
- ½ teaspoon salt
- ½ teaspoon black pepper

Jalapeño Sauce:
- 6 jalapeno peppers stemmed, halved, and seeded
- 1–2 teaspoons olive oil
- 1 cup raw cashews, soaked and drained
- ½ cup almond milk
- ¼ cup water
- ¼ cup lime juice
- 2 teaspoons agaves
- ½ cup fresh cilantro
- Salt, to taste

Grilled Vegetables:
- ½ pound asparagus spears, trimmed
- 2 large portobello mushrooms, sliced
- 1 large zucchini, sliced

- 1 red bell pepper, sliced
- 1 red onion, sliced

Directions:
1. Dump all the ingredients for the marinade in a large bowl.
2. Toss in all the veggies and mix well to marinate for 1 hour.
3. Meanwhile, prepare the sauce and brush the jalapenos with oil.
4. Grill the jalapenos for 5 minutes per side until slightly charred.
5. Blend the grilled jalapenos with other ingredients for the sauce in a blender.
6. Transfer this sauce to a separate bowl and keep it aside.
7. Now grill the marinated veggies in the grill until soft and slightly charred on all sides.
8. Pour the prepared sauce over the grilled veggies.
9. Serve.

Nutrition: Calories: 663 Total Fat: 68g Carbs: 20g Net Carbs: 10g Fiber: 2g Protein: 4g

866. Shaved Brussel Sprout Salad
Preparation Time: 25 minutes
Cooking Time: 0 minutes
Servings: 4
Ingredients:
Dressing:
- 1 tablespoon brown mustard
- 1 tablespoon maple syrup
- 2 tablespoons apple cider vinegar
- 2 tablespoons extra-virgin olive oil
- ½ tablespoons garlic minced

Salad:
- ½ cup dry red kidney beans
- ¼ cup dry chickpeas
- 2 cups Brussel sprouts
- 1 cup purple onion
- 1 small sour apple
- ½ cup slivered almonds, crushed

- ½ cup walnuts, crushed
- ½ cup cranberries, dried
- ¼ teaspoon Salt
- ¼ teaspoon pepper

Directions:
1. Prepare the beans according to the method.
2. Combine all dressing ingredients in a bowl and stir well until combined.
3. Refrigerate the dressing for up to one hour before serving.
4. Using a grater, mandolin, or knife to thinly slice each Brussel sprout. Repeat this with the apple and onion.
5. Take a large bowl to mix the chickpeas, beans, sprouts, apples, onions, cranberries, and nuts.
6. Drizzle the cold dressing over the salad to coat.
7. Serve with salt and pepper to taste, or, store for later!

Nutrition: Calories 432 Total Fat 23.5g Saturated Fat 2.2g Cholesterol 0mg Sodium 197mg Total Carbohydrate 45.3g Dietary Fiber 12.4g Total Sugars 14g Protein 15.9g Vitamin D 0mcg Calcium 104mg Iron 4mg Potassium 908mg

867. Colorful Protein Power Salad

Preparation Time: 20 minutes
Cooking Time: 0 minutes
Servings: 2
Ingredients:
- ½ cup dry quinoa
- 2 cups dry navy beans
- 1 green onion, chopped
- 2 teaspoons garlic, minced
- 3 cups green or purple cabbage, chopped
- 4 cups kale, fresh or frozen, chopped
- 1 cup shredded carrot, chopped
- 2 tablespoons extra-virgin olive oil
- 1 teaspoon lemon juice
- ¼ teaspoon Salt
- ¼ teaspoon pepper

Directions:

1. Prepare the quinoa according to the recipe.
2. Prepare the beans according to the method.
3. Heat 1 tablespoon of the olive oil in a frying pan over medium heat.
4. Add the chopped green onion, garlic, and cabbage, and sauté for 2-3 minutes.
5. Add the kale, the remaining 1 tablespoon of olive oil, and salt. Lower the heat and cover until the greens have wilted, around 5 minutes. Remove the pan from the stove and set aside.
6. Take a large bowl and mix the remaining ingredients with the kale and cabbage mixture once it has cooled down. Add more salt and pepper to taste.
7. Mix until everything is distributed evenly.
8. Serve topped with a dressing, or, store for later!

Nutrition: Calories 1100 Total Fat 19.9g Saturated Fat 2.7g Cholesterol 0mg Sodium 420mg Total Carbohydrate 180.8g Dietary Fiber 60.1g Total Sugars 14.4g Protein 58.6g Vitamin D 0mcg Calcium 578mg Iron 16mg Potassium 3755mg

868. Grilled Ratatouille Kebabs

Preparation Time: 10 minutes
Cooking Time: 20 minutes
Servings: 6
Ingredients:
- 3 tablespoons soy sauce
- 3 tablespoons balsamic vinegar
- 1 teaspoon dried thyme leaves
- 2 tablespoons extra-virgin olive oil

Veggies:
- 1 zucchini, diced
- ½ red onion, diced
- ½ red capsicum, diced
- 2 tomatoes, diced
- 1 small eggplant, diced
- 8 button mushrooms, diced

Directions:

1. Toss the veggies with soy sauce, olive oil, thyme, and balsamic vinegar in a large bowl.
2. Thread the veggies alternately on the wooden skewers and reserve the remaining marinade.
3. Marinate these skewers for 1 hour in the refrigerator.
4. Preheat the grill over medium heat.
5. Grill the marinated skewers for 5 minutes per side while basting with the reserved marinade.
6. Serve fresh.

Nutrition: Calories: 166 Total Fat: 17g Carbs: 5g Net Carbs: 3g Fiber: 1g Protein: 1g

869. Tofu Hoagie Rolls

Preparation Time: 10 minutes
Cooking Time: 20 minutes
Servings: 6
Ingredients:
- ½ cup vegetable broth
- ¼ cup hot sauce
- 1 tablespoon vegan butter
- 1 (16-oz.) package tofu, pressed and diced
- 4 cups cabbage, shredded
- 2 medium apples, grated
- 1 medium shallot, grated
- 6 tablespoons vegan mayonnaise
- 1 tablespoon apple cider vinegar
- Salt and black pepper
- 4 (6-inch) hoagie rolls, toasted

Directions:

1. In a saucepan, combine broth with butter and hot sauce and bring to a boil.
2. Add tofu and reduce the heat to a simmer.
3. Cook for 10 minutes then remove from heat and let sit for 10 minutes to marinate.
4. Toss cabbage and the rest of the ingredients in a salad bowl.
5. Prepare and set up a grill on medium heat.
6. Drain the tofu and grill for 5 minutes per side.
7. Lay out the toasted hoagie rolls and add grilled tofu to each hoagie

8. Add the cabbage mixture evenly between them then close it.
9. Serve.

Nutrition: Calories: 111 Total Fat: 11g Carbs: 5g Net Carbs: 1g Fiber: 0g Protein: 1g

870. Edamame & Ginger Citrus Salad

Preparation Time: 15 minutes
Cooking Time: 0 minutes
Servings: 3
Ingredients:
Dressing:

- ¼ cup orange juice
- 1 teaspoon lime juice
- ½ tablespoons maple syrup
- ½ teaspoon ginger, finely minced
- ½ tablespoons sesame oil

Salad:

- ½ cup dry green lentils
- 2 cups carrots, shredded
- 4 cups kale, fresh or frozen, chopped
- 1 cup edamame, shelled
- 1 tablespoon roasted sesame seeds
- 2 teaspoons mint, chopped
- Salt and pepper to taste
- 1 small avocado, peeled, pitted, diced

Directions:

1. Prepare the lentils according to the method.
2. Combine the orange and lime juices, maple syrup, and ginger in a small bowl. Mix with a whisk while slowly adding the sesame oil.
3. Add the cooked lentils, carrots, kale, edamame, sesame seeds, and mint to a large bowl.
4. Add the dressing and stir well until all the ingredients are coated evenly.
5. Store or serve topped with avocado and an additional sprinkle of mint.

Nutrition: Calories 507 Total Fat 23.1g Saturated Fat 4g Cholesterol 0mg Sodium 303mg Total Carbohydrate 56.8g Dietary Fiber 21.6g Total Sugars 8.4g Protein 24.6g

Vitamin D 0mcg Calcium 374mg Iron 8mg Potassium 1911mg

871. Taco Tempeh Salad

Preparation Time: 25 minutes
Cooking Time: 0 minutes
Servings: 3
Ingredients:

- 1 cup dry black beans
- 1 8-oz. package tempeh
- 1 tablespoon lime or lemon juice
- 2 tablespoons extra-virgin olive oil
- 1 teaspoon maple syrup
- ½ teaspoon chili powder
- ¼ teaspoon cumin
- ¼ teaspoon paprika
- 1 large bunch of kale, fresh or frozen, chopped
- 1 large avocado, peeled, pitted, diced
- ½ cup salsa
- ¼ teaspoon salt
- ¼ teaspoon pepper

Directions:

1. Prepare the beans according to the method.
2. Cut the tempeh into ¼-inch cubes, place in a bowl, and then add the lime or lemon juice, 1 tablespoon of olive oil, maple syrup, chili powder, cumin, and paprika.
3. Stir well and let the tempeh marinate in the fridge for at least 1 hour, up to 12 hours.
4. Heat the remaining 1 tablespoon of olive oil in a frying pan over medium heat.
5. Add the marinated tempeh mixture and cook until brown and crispy on both sides, around 10 minutes.
6. Put the chopped kale in a bowl with the cooked beans and prepared tempeh.
7. Store, or serve the salad immediately, topped with salsa, avocado, and salt and pepper to taste.

Nutrition: Calories 627 Total Fat 31.7g Saturated Fat 6.1g Cholesterol 0mg Sodium 493mg Total Carbohydrate 62.7g Dietary Fiber 16g Total Sugars 4.5g Protein 31.4g

Vitamin D 0mcg Calcium 249mg Iron 7mg Potassium 1972mg

872. Black Bean Wrap with Hummus

Preparation Time: 5 minutes
Cooking Time: 30 minutes
Servings: 2 Wraps
Ingredients:

- 1 Poblano pepper, roasted
- ½ packet spinach
- 1 onion, chopped
- 2 whole-grain wraps
- ½ can black beans
- 1 bell pepper, seeded & chopped
- 4 ounces mushrooms, sliced
- ½ cup corn
- 8 ounces red bell pepper hummus, roasted

Directions:

1. First, preheat the oven to 450°F.
2. Next, spoon in oil to a heated skillet and stir in the onion.
3. Cook them for 2 to 3 minutes or until softened.
4. After that, stir in the bell pepper and sauté for another 3 minutes.
5. Then, add mushrooms and corn to the skillet. Sauté for 2 minutes.
6. In the meantime, spread the hummus over the wraps.
7. Now, place the sautéed vegetables, spinach, Poblano strips, and beans.
8. Roll them into a burrito and place on a baking sheet with the seam side down.
9. Finally, bake them for 9 to 10 minutes.
10. Serve them warm.

Nutrition: Calories: 293, Proteins: 13.7g, Carbs: 42.8g, Fat: 8.8g

873. Black-Eyed Peas and Corn Salad

Preparation Time: 30 minutes
Cooking Time: 50 minutes
Servings: 4
Ingredients:

- 2½ cups cooked black-eyed peas
- 3 ears corn, kernels removed
- 1 medium ripe tomato, diced

- ½ medium red onion, peeled and diced small
- ½ red bell pepper, deseeded and diced small
- 1 jalapeño pepper, deseeded and minced
- ½ cup finely chopped cilantro
- ¼ cup plus 2 tablespoons balsamic vinegar
- 3 cloves garlic, peeled and minced
- 1 teaspoon toasted and ground cumin seeds

Directions:
1. Stir together all the ingredients in a large bowl and refrigerate for about 1 hour, or until well chilled.
2. Serve chilled.

Nutrition: Calories: 247 Fat: 1.8g Carbs: 47.6g Protein: 12.9g Fiber: 11.7g

874. Grilled Avocado with Tomatoes

Preparation Time: 10 minutes
Cooking Time: 15 minutes
Servings: 6
Ingredients:

- 3 avocados, halved and pitted
- 3 limes, wedged
- 1½ cups grape tomatoes
- 1 cup fresh corn
- 1 cup onion, chopped
- 3 serrano peppers
- 2 garlic cloves, peeled
- ¼ cup cilantro leaves, chopped
- 1 tablespoon olive oil
- Salt and black pepper to taste

Directions:
1. Prepare and set a grill over medium heat.
2. Brush the avocado with oil and grill it for 5 minutes per side.
3. Meanwhile, toss the garlic, onion, corn, tomatoes, and pepper on a baking sheet.
4. At 550°F, roast the vegetables for 5 minutes.

5. Toss the veggie mix and stir in salt, cilantro, and black pepper.
6. Mix well then fill the grilled avocadoes with the mixture.
7. Garnish with lime.
8. Serve.

Nutrition: Calories: 56 Total Fat: 6g Carbs: 3g Net Carbs: 1g Fiber: 0g Protein: 1g

875. Grilled Tofu with Chimichurri Sauce

Preparation Time: 10 minutes
Cooking Time: 12 minutes
Servings: 4
Ingredients:

- 2 tablespoons plus 1 teaspoon olive oil
- 1 teaspoon dried oregano
- 1 cup parsley leaves
- ½ cup cilantro leaves
- 2 Fresno peppers, seeded and chopped
- 2 tablespoons white wine vinegar
- 2 tablespoons water
- 1 tablespoon fresh lime juice
- Salt and black pepper
- 1 cup couscous, cooked
- 1 teaspoon lime zest
- ¼ cup toasted pumpkin seeds
- 1 cup fresh spinach, chopped
- 1 (15½ -oz.) can kidney beans, rinsed and drained
- 1 (14 to 16-oz.) block tofu, diced
- 2 summer squashes, diced
- 3 spring onions, quartered

Directions:
1. In a saucepan, heat 2 tablespoons of oil and add oregano over medium heat.
2. After 30 seconds add parsley, chili pepper, cilantro, lime juice, 2 tablespoons water, vinegar, salt and black pepper.
3. Mix well then blend in a blender.
4. Add the remaining oil, pumpkin seeds, beans and

spinach and cook for 3 minutes.
5. Stir in couscous and adjust seasoning with salt and black pepper.
6. Prepare and set up a grill on medium heat.
7. Thread the tofu, squash, and onions on the skewer in an alternating pattern.
8. Grill these skewers for 4 minutes per side while basting with the green sauce.
9. Serve the skewers on top of the couscous with green sauce.
10. Enjoy.

Nutrition: Calories: 813 Total Fat: 83g Carbs: 25g Net Carbs: 11g Fiber: 1g Protein: 7g

876. Lebanese Potato Salad

Preparation Time: 5 minutes
Cooking Time: 10 minutes
Servings: 4
Ingredients:

- 1-pound Russet potatoes
- 1½ tablespoons extra-virgin olive oil
- 2 scallions, thinly sliced
- Freshly ground pepper to taste
- 2 tablespoons lemon juice
- ¼ teaspoon salt or to taste
- 2 tablespoons fresh mint leaves, chopped

Directions:
1. Place a saucepan half-filled with water over medium heat. Add salt and potatoes and cook for 10 minutes until tender. Drain the potatoes and place in a bowl of cold water. When cool enough to handle, peel and cube the potatoes. Place in a bowl.

To make the dressing:
2. Add oil, lemon juice, salt and pepper in a bowl and whisk well. Drizzle dressing over the potatoes. Toss well.
3. Add scallions and mint and toss well.
4. Divide into 4 plates and serve.

Nutrition: Calories 129 Total Fat 5.5g Saturated Fat 0.9g Cholesterol 0mg Sodium 158mg Total Carbohydrate 18.8g Dietary Fiber 3.2g Total Sugars 1.6g Protein 2.2g Vitamin D 0mcg Calcium 22mg Iron 1mg Potassium 505mg

877. Chickpea and Spinach Salad

Preparation Time: 5 minutes
Cooking Time: 0 minutes
Servings: 4
Ingredients:

- 2 cans (14½ oz. each) chickpeas, drained, rinsed
- 7 ounces' vegan feta cheese, crumbled or chopped
- 1 tablespoon lemon juice
- ⅓ -½ cup olive oil
- ½ teaspoon salt or to taste
- 4-6 cups spinach, torn
- ½ cup raisins
- 2 tablespoons honey
- 1-2 teaspoons ground cumin
- 1 teaspoon chili flakes

Directions:

1. Add cheese, chickpeas and spinach into a large bowl.

To make the dressing:

2. Add the rest of the ingredients into another bowl and mix well.
3. Pour dressing over the salad. Toss well and serve.

Nutrition: Calories 822 Total Fat 42.5g Saturated Fat 11.7g Cholesterol 44mg Sodium 910mg Total Carbohydrate 89.6g Dietary Fiber 19.7g Total Sugars 32.7g Protein 29g Vitamin D 0mcg Calcium 417mg Iron 9mg Potassium 1347mg

878. Indian Tomato and Garbanzo Stew

Preparation Time: 15 minutes
Cooking Time: 50 minutes
Servings: 4 to 6
Ingredients:

- 1 large onion, quartered and thinly sliced
- 1-inch fresh ginger, peeled and minced
- 2 cloves garlic, peeled and minced
- 1 teaspoon curry powder
- 1 teaspoon cumin seeds
- 1 teaspoon black mustard seeds
- 1 teaspoon coriander seeds,
- 1½ pounds (680-g.) tomatoes, deseeded and puréed
- 1 red bell pepper, cut into ½-inch dice
- 1 green bell pepper, cut into ½-inch dice
- 3 cups cooked garbanzo beans
- 1 tablespoon garam masala
- ⅓ cup water

Directions:

1. Heat the water in a medium saucepan over medium-low heat. Add the onion, ginger, garlic, curry powder, and seeds to the pan. Sauté for about 10 minutes, or until the onion is tender, stirring frequently.
2. Add the tomatoes and simmer, uncovered, for 10 minutes. Add the peppers and garbanzo beans. Reduce the heat. Cover and simmer for 30 minutes, stirring occasionally. Stir in the garam masala and serve.

Nutrition: Calories: 100 Fat: 1.2g Carbs: 20.9g Protein: 5.1g Fiber: 7.0g

879. Simple Baked Navy Beans

Preparation Time: 10 minutes
Cooking Time: 2½ to 3 hours
Servings: 8
Ingredients:

- 1½ cups navy beans
- 8 cups water
- 1 bay leaf
- ½ cup finely chopped green bell pepper
- ½ cup finely chopped onion
- 1 teaspoon minced garlic
- ½ cup unsweetened tomato purée
- 3 tablespoons molasses
- 1 tablespoon fresh lemon juice

Directions:

1. Preheat the oven to 300°F (150°C).
2. Place the beans and water in a large pot, along with the bay leaf, green pepper, onion and garlic. Cover and cook for 1½ to 2 hours, or until the beans are softened. Remove from the heat and drain, reserving the cooking liquid. Discard the bay leaf.
3. Transfer the mixture to a casserole dish with a cover. Stir in the remaining ingredients and 1 cup of the reserved cooking liquid. Bake in the oven for 1 hour, covered. Stir occasionally during baking and add a little more cooking liquid if needed to keep the beans moist.
4. Serve warm.

Nutrition: Calories: 162 Fat: 0.6g Carbs: 31.3g Protein: 9.1g Fiber: 6.4g

880. Black Bean Buda Bowl

Preparation Time: 10 minutes
Cooking Time: 10 minutes
Servings: 4
Ingredients:

- ½-pound black beans, soaked overnight and drained
- 2 cups brown rice, cooked
- 1 medium-sized onion, thinly sliced
- 1 cup bell pepper, seeded and sliced
- 1 jalapeno pepper, seeded and sliced
- 2 cloves garlic, minced
- 1 cup arugula
- 1 cup baby spinach
- 1 teaspoon lime zest
- 1 tablespoon Dijon mustard
- ¼ cup red wine vinegar
- ¼ cup extra-virgin olive oil
- 2 tablespoons agave syrup
- Flaky sea salt and ground black pepper, to taste
- ¼ cup fresh Italian parsley, roughly chopped

Directions:

1. Cover the soaked beans with a fresh change of cold water and bring to a boil. Let it boil for about 10 minutes. Turn the heat to a simmer and continue to cook for 50 to 55 minutes or until tender.

2. To serve, divide the beans and rice between serving bowls; top with the vegetables.
3. A small mixing dish thoroughly combines the lime zest, mustard, vinegar, olive oil, agave syrup, salt and pepper. Drizzle the vinaigrette over the salad.
4. Garnish with fresh Italian parsley. Bon appétit!

Nutrition: Calories: 365; Fat: 14.1g; Carbs: 45.6g; Protein: 15.5g

881. Grilled Seitan with Creole Sauce

Preparation Time:10 minutes
Cooking Time: 14 minutes
Servings: 4
Ingredients:
Grilled Seitan Kebabs:
- 4 cups seitan, diced
- 2 medium onions, diced into squares
- 8 bamboo skewers
- 1 can coconut milk
- 2½ tablespoons creole spice
- 2 tablespoons tomato paste
- 2 cloves of garlic

Creole Spice Mix:
- 2 tablespoons paprika
- 12 dried peri chili peppers
- 1 tablespoon salt
- 1 tablespoon freshly ground pepper
- 2 teaspoons dried thyme
- 2 teaspoons dried oregano

Directions:
1. Prepare the creole seasoning by blending all its ingredients and preserve in a sealable jar.
2. Thread seitan and onion on the bamboo skewers in an alternating pattern.
3. On a baking sheet, mix coconut milk with creole seasoning, tomato paste and garlic.
4. Soak the skewers in the milk marinade for 2 hours.
5. Prepare and set up a grill over medium heat.
6. Grill the skewers for 7 minutes per side.
7. Serve.

Nutrition: Calories: 407 Total Fat: 42g Carbs: 13g Net Carbs: 6g Fiber: 1g Protein: 4g

882. Green Beans Gremolata

Preparation Time: 15 minutes
Cooking Time: 5 minutes
Servings: 6
Ingredients:
- 1-pound fresh green beans
- 3 garlic cloves, minced
- Zest of 2 oranges
- 3 tablespoons minced fresh parsley
- 2 tablespoons pine nuts
- 3 tablespoons olive oil
- Sea salt
- Freshly ground black pepper

Directions:
1. Boil water over high heat. Cook green beans for 3 minutes. Drain r and rinse with cold water to stop the cooking.
2. Blend garlic, orange zest, and parsley.
3. In a huge sauté pan over medium-high heat, toast the pine nuts in the dry, hot pan for 3 minutes. Remove from the pan and set aside.
4. Cook olive oil in the same pan until it shimmers. Add the beans and cook, -stirring frequently, until heated through, about 2 minutes. Take the pan away from the heat and add the parsley mixture and pine nuts. Season with salt and pepper. Serve immediately.

Nutrition: 98 Calories 2g Fiber 3g Protein

883. Spinach & Dill Pasta Salad

Preparation Time: 5 minutes
Cooking Time: 0 minutes
Servings: 4
Ingredients:
For salad:
- 3 cups cooked whole-wheat fusilli
- 2 cups cherry tomatoes, halved
- ½ cup vegan cheese, shredded
- 4 cups spinach, chopped
- 2 cups edamame, thawed
- 1 large red onion, finely chopped

For dressing:
- 2 tablespoons white wine vinegar
- ½ teaspoon dried dill
- 2 tablespoons extra-virgin olive oil
- Salt to taste
- Pepper to taste

Directions:
To make the dressing:
1. Add all the ingredients for dressing into a bowl and whisk well. Set aside for a while for the flavors to set in.

To make the salad:
1. Add all the ingredients of the salad to a bowl. Toss well.
2. Drizzle dressing on top. Toss well.
3. Divide into 4 plates and serve.

Nutrition: Calories 684 Total Fat 33.6g Saturated Fat 4.6g Cholesterol 4mg Sodium 632mg Total Carbohydrate 69.5g Dietary Fiber 12g Total Sugars 6.4g Protein 31.7g Vitamin D 0mcg Calcium 368mg Iron 8mg Potassium 1241mg

884. Vinegary Black Beans

Preparation Time: 10 minutes
Cooking Time: 2 hours
Servings: 8
Ingredients:
- 1 pound (454-g.) black beans, soaked overnight and drained
- 10 ½ cups water, divided
- 1 green bell pepper, cut in half
- 1 onion, finely chopped
- 1 green bell pepper, finely chopped
- 4 cloves garlic, pressed
- 1 tablespoon maple syrup (optional)
- 1 tablespoon Mrs. Dash seasoning
- 1 bay leaf
- ¼ teaspoon dried oregano
- 2 tablespoons cider vinegar

Directions:
1. Place the beans, 10 cups of water, and green bell pepper

in a large pot. Cook over medium heat for about 45 minutes, or until the green pepper is tendered. Remove the green pepper and discard.

2. Meanwhile, in a different pot, combine the onion, chopped green pepper, garlic and the remaining ½ cup of water. Sauté for 15 to 20 minutes, or until soft.

3. Add 1 cup of the cooked beans to the pot with vegetables. Mash the beans and vegetables with a potato masher. Add to the pot with the beans, maple syrup (if desired), Mrs. Dash, bay leaf and oregano. Cover and cook over low heat for 1 hour.

4. Drizzle in the vinegar and continue to cook for another hour.

5. Serve warm.

Nutrition: Calories: 226 Fat: 0.9g Carbs: 42.7g Protein: 12.9g Fiber: 9.9g

885. Spiced Lentil Burgers

Preparation Time: 10 minutes
Cooking Time: 43 minutes
Servings: 4
Ingredients:

- ¼ cup minced onion
- 1 clove garlic, minced
- 2 tablespoons water
- 1 cup chopped boiled potatoes
- 1 cup cooked lentils
- 2 tablespoons minced fresh parsley
- 1 teaspoon onion powder
- 1 teaspoon minced fresh basil
- 1 teaspoon dried dill
- 1 teaspoon paprika

Directions:

1. Preheat the oven to 350°F (180°C).

2. In a pot, sauté the onion and garlic in the water for about 3 minutes, or until soft.

3. Combine the lentils and potatoes in a large bowl and mash together well. Add the cooked onion and garlic and the remaining ingredients to the lentil-potato mixture and stir until well combined.

4. Form the mixture into four patties and place on a nonstick baking sheet. Bake in the oven for 20 minutes. Turnover and bake for an additional 20 minutes.

5. Serve hot.

Nutrition: Calories: 101 Fat: 0.4g Carbs: 19.9g Protein: 5.5g Fiber: 5.3g

886. Middle Eastern Chickpea Stew

Preparation Time: 10 minutes
Cooking Time: 10 minutes
Servings: 4
Ingredients:

- 1 onion, chopped
- 1 chili pepper, chopped
- 2 garlic cloves, chopped
- 1 teaspoon mustard seeds
- 1 teaspoon coriander seeds
- 1 bay leaf
- ½ cup tomato puree
- 2 tablespoons olive oil
- 1 celery with leaves, chopped
- 2 medium carrots, trimmed and chopped
- 2 cups vegetable broth
- 1 teaspoon ground cumin
- 1 small-sized cinnamon stick
- 16 ounces canned chickpeas, drained
- 2 cups Swiss chard, torn into pieces

Directions:

1. In your blender or food processor, blend the onion, chili pepper, garlic, mustard seeds, coriander seeds, bay leaf and tomato puree into a paste.

2. In a stockpot, heat the olive oil until sizzling. Now, cook the celery and carrots for about 3 minutes or until they've softened. Add in the paste and continue to cook for a further 2 minutes.

3. Then, add vegetable broth, cumin, cinnamon and chickpeas; bring it to a gentle boil.

4. Turn the heat to simmer and let it cook for 6 minutes; fold in Swiss chard

and continue to cook for 4 to 5 minutes more or until the leaves wilt. Serve hot and enjoy!

Nutrition: Calories: 305; Fat: 11.2g; Carbs: 38.6g; Protein: 12.7g

887. Lentil and Tomato Dip

Preparation Time: 10 minutes
Cooking Time: 10 minutes
Servings: 4
Ingredients:

- 16 ounces' lentils, boiled and drained
- 4 tablespoons sun-dried tomatoes, chopped
- 1 cup tomato paste
- 4 tablespoons tahini
- 1 teaspoon stone-ground mustard
- 1 teaspoon ground cumin
- ¼ teaspoon ground bay leaf
- 1 teaspoon red pepper flakes
- Sea salt and ground black pepper, to taste

Directions:

1. Blitz all the ingredients in your blender or food processor until your desired consistency is reached.

2. Place in your refrigerator until ready to serve.

3. Serve with toasted pita wedges or vegetable sticks. Enjoy!

Nutrition: Calories: 144; Fat: 4.5g; Carbs: 20.2g; Protein: 8.1g

888. Minted Peas

Preparation Time: 5 minutes
Cooking Time: 5 minutes
Servings: 4
Ingredients:

- 1 tablespoon olive oil
- 4 cups peas, fresh or frozen (not canned)
- ½ teaspoon sea salt
- Freshly ground black pepper
- 3 tablespoons chopped fresh mint

Direction:

1. In a large sauté pan, cook olive oil over medium-high heat until hot. Add the peas and cook for about 5 minutes. Remove the pan from heat. Stir in the salt,

season with pepper, and stir in the mint. Serve hot.

Nutrition: 90 Calories 5g Fiber 8g Protein

889. Sweet and Spicy Brussels Sprout Hash

Preparation Time: 10 minutes
Cooking Time: 15 minutes
Servings: 4
Ingredients:

- 3 tablespoons olive oil
- 2 shallots, thinly sliced
- 1½ pounds Brussel sprouts
- 3 tablespoons apple cider vinegar
- 1 tablespoon pure maple syrup
- ½ teaspoon sriracha sauce (or to taste)
- Sea salt
- Freshly ground black pepper

Directions:

1. In a pan, cook olive oil over medium-high heat until it shimmers. Mix the shallots and Brussels sprouts and cook, stirring frequently, until the -vegetables soften and begin to turn golden brown, about 10 minutes. Stir in the vinegar, using a spoon to scrape any browned bits from the pan's bottom. Stir in the maple syrup and Sriracha.
2. Simmer, stirring frequently, until the liquid reduces, 3 to 5 minutes. Season and serve immediately.

Nutrition: 97 Calories 4g Fiber 7g Protein

890. Italian Veggie Salad

Preparation Time: 10 minutes
Cooking Time: 0 minutes
Servings: 8
Ingredients:
For salad:

- 1 cup fresh baby carrots, quartered lengthwise
- 1 celery rib, sliced
- 3 large mushrooms, thinly sliced
- 1 cup cauliflower florets, bite-sized, blanched
- 1 cup broccoli florets, blanched
- 1 cup thinly sliced radish
- 4-5 ounces' hearts of romaine salad mix to serve

For dressing:

- ½ package Italian salad dressing mix
- 3 tablespoons white vinegar
- 3 tablespoons water
- 3 tablespoons olive oil
- 3-4 pepperoncino, chopped

Directions:
To make the salad:

1. Add all the ingredients of the salad except hearts of romaine to a bowl and toss.

To make the dressing:

2. Add all the ingredients of the dressing in a small bowl. Whisk well.
3. Pour dressing over salad and toss well. Refrigerate for a couple of hours.
4. Place romaine in a large bowl. Place the chilled salad over it and serve.

Nutrition: Calories 84 Total Fat 6.7g Saturated Fat 1.2g Cholesterol 3mg Sodium 212mg Total Carbohydrate 5g Dietary Fiber 1.4g Total Sugars 1.6g Protein 2g Vitamin D 31mcg Calcium 27mg Iron 1mg Potassium 193mg

891. Pecan-Maple Granola

Preparation Time: 5 minutes
Cooking Time: 50 minutes
Servings: 4
Ingredients:

- 1½ cups rolled oats
- ¼ cup maple syrup (optional)
- ¼ cup pecan pieces
- 1 teaspoon vanilla extract
- ½ teaspoon ground cinnamon

Directions:

1. Preheat the oven to 300°F (150°C). Line a baking sheet with parchment paper.
2. In a large bowl, stir together all the ingredients until the oats and pecan pieces are completely coated.
3. Spread the mixture on the baking sheet in an even layer. Bake in the oven for 20 minutes, stirring once halfway through cooking.
4. Remove from the oven and allow to cool on the countertop for 30 minutes before serving.

Nutrition: Calories: 221 Fat: 17.2g Carbs: 5.1g Protein: 4.9g Fiber: 3.8g

892. Bean and Summer Squash Sauté

Preparation Time: 10 minutes
Cooking Time: 15 to 16 minutes
Servings: 4
Ingredients:

- 1 medium red onion, peeled and thinly sliced
- 4 yellow squash, cut into ½-inch rounds
- 4 medium zucchinis, cut into ½-inch rounds
- 1 (15-oz. / 425-g) can navy beans, drained and rinsed
- 2 cups corn kernels
- Zest of 2 lemons
- 1 cup finely chopped basil
- Salt, to taste (optional)
- Freshly ground black pepper, to taste

Directions:

1. Place the onion in a large saucepan and sauté over medium heat for 7 to 8 minutes. Add water 1 to 2 tablespoons at a time to keep the onion from sticking to the pan.
2. Add the squash, zucchini, beans, and corn and cook for about 8 minutes, or until the squash is softened.
3. Remove from the heat. Stir in the lemon zest and basil. Season with salt (if desired) and pepper.
4. Serve hot.

Nutrition: Calories: 298 Fat: 2.2g Carbs: 60.4g Protein: 17.2g Fiber: 13.6g

893. Creamed Green Pea Salad

Preparation Time: 10 minutes
Cooking Time: 10 minutes
Servings: 4
Ingredients:

- 2 (14½-oz.) cans green peas, drained
- ½ cup vegan mayonnaise
- 1 teaspoon Dijon mustard
- 2 tablespoons scallions, chopped
- 3 pickles, chopped

- ½ cup marinated mushrooms, chopped and drained
- ½ teaspoon garlic, minced
- Sea salt and ground black pepper, to taste

Directions:
1. Place all the ingredients in a salad bowl. Gently stir to combine.
2. Place the salad in your refrigerator until ready to serve.
3. Bon appétit!

Nutrition: Calories: 154; Fat: 6.7g; Carbs: 17.3g; Protein: 6.9g

894. Middle Eastern Za'atar Hummus
Preparation Time: 10 minutes
Cooking Time: 10 minutes
Servings: 4
Ingredients:
- 10 ounces' chickpeas, boiled and drained
- ¼ cup tahini
- 2 tablespoons extra-virgin olive oil
- 2 tablespoons sun-dried tomatoes, chopped
- 1 lemon, freshly squeezed
- 2 garlic cloves, minced
- Kosher salt and ground black pepper, to taste
- ½ teaspoon smoked paprika
- 1 teaspoon Za'atar

Directions:
1. Blitz all the ingredients in your food processor until creamy and uniform.
2. Place in your refrigerator until ready to serve.
3. Bon appétit!

Nutrition: Calories: 140; Fat: 8.5g; Carbs: 12.4g; Protein: 4

895. Glazed Curried Carrots
Preparation Time: 5 minutes
Cooking Time: 15 minutes
Servings: 6
Ingredients:
- 1-pound carrots
- 2 tablespoons olive oil
- 2 tablespoons curry powder
- 2 tablespoons pure maple syrup
- Juice of ½ lemon

Directions:
1. Cook carrots with water over medium-high heat for

10 minutes. Drain and return them to the pan over medium-low heat.
2. Stir in olive oil, curry powder, maple syrup, and lemon juice. Cook, stirring constantly, until the liquid reduces, about 5 minutes. Season well and serve immediately.

Nutrition: 91 Calories 5g Fiber 9g Protein

896. Pepper Medley
Preparation Time: 10 minutes
Cooking Time: 15 minutes
Servings: 4
Ingredients:
- 3 tablespoons olive oil
- 1 red bell pepper, sliced
- 1 orange bell pepper, sliced
- 1 yellow bell pepper, sliced
- 1 green bell pepper, sliced
- 2 garlic cloves, minced
- 3 tablespoons red wine vinegar
- 2 tablespoons chopped fresh basil

Directions:
1. Warm up olive oil over medium-high heat. Stir in the bell peppers and cook, stir, for 7 to 10 minutes. Cook garlic for 30 seconds. Add the vinegar, using a spoon to scrape any browned bits off the bottom of the pan.
2. Simmer until the vinegar reduces, 2 to 3 minutes. Season. Stir in the basil and serve immediately.

Nutrition: 96 Calories 3g Fiber 5g Protein

897. Spinach and Mashed Tofu Salad
Preparation Time: 20 minutes
Cooking Time: 0 minutes
Servings: 4
Ingredients:
- 2 (8-oz.) blocks firm tofu, drained
- 4 cups baby spinach leaves
- 4 tablespoons cashew butter
- 1½ tablespoons soy sauce
- 1 tablespoon ginger, chopped
- 1 teaspoon red miso paste

- 2 tablespoons sesame seeds
- 1 teaspoon organic orange zest
- 1 teaspoon nori flakes
- 2 tablespoons water

Directions:
1. Use paper towels to absorb any excess water left in the tofu before crumbling both blocks into small pieces.
2. In a large bowl, combine the mashed tofu with the spinach leaves.
3. Mix the remaining ingredients in another small bowl and, if desired, add the optional water for a smoother dressing.
4. Pour this dressing over the mashed tofu and spinach leaves.
5. Transfer the bowl to the fridge and allow the salad to chill for up to one hour. Doing so will guarantee a better flavor. Or, the salad can be served right away. Enjoy!

Nutrition: Calories 623 Total Fat 30.5g Saturated Fat 5.8g Cholesterol 0mg Sodium 2810mg Total Carbohydrate 48g Dietary Fiber 5.9g Total Sugars 3g Protein 48.4g Vitamin D 0mcg Calcium 797mg Iron 22mg Potassium 2007mg

898. Peppery Black Beans
Preparation Time: 10 minutes
Cooking Time: 33 to 34 minutes
Servings: 4
Ingredients:
- 1 red bell pepper, deseeded and chopped
- 1 medium yellow onion, peeled and chopped
- 2 jalapeño peppers, deseeded and minced
- 4 cloves garlic, peeled and minced
- 1 tablespoon thyme
- 1 tablespoon curry powder
- 1½ teaspoons ground allspice
- 1 teaspoon freshly ground black pepper
- 1 (15-oz. / 425-g) can diced tomatoes

- 2 cups cooked black beans

Directions:

1. Add the red bell pepper and onion to a saucepan and sauté over medium heat for 10 minutes, or until the onion is softened. Add water 1 to 2 tablespoons at a time to keep the vegetables from sticking to the pan.
2. Stir in the jalapeño peppers, garlic, thyme, curry powder, allspice and black pepper. Cook for 3 to 4 minutes, then add the tomatoes and black beans. Cook over medium heat for 20 minutes, covered.
3. Serve immediately.

Nutrition: Calories: 283 Fat: 1.7g Carbs: 52.8g Protein: 17.4g Fiber: 19.8g

899. Walnut, Coconut, and Oat Granola

Preparation Time: 15 minutes
Cooking Time: 1 hour and 40 minutes
Servings: 4
Ingredients:

- 1 cup chopped walnuts
- 1 cup unsweetened, shredded coconut
- 2 cups rolled oats
- 1 teaspoon ground cinnamon
- 2 tablespoons hemp seeds
- 2 tablespoons ground flaxseeds
- 2 tablespoons chia seeds
- ¾ teaspoon salt (optional)
- ¼ cup maple syrup
- ¼ cup water
- 1 teaspoon vanilla extract
- ½ cup dried cranberries

Directions:

1. Preheat the oven to 250°F (120°C). Line a baking sheet with parchment paper.
2. Mix the walnuts, coconut, rolled oats, cinnamon, hemp seeds, flaxseeds, chia seeds, and salt (if desired) in a bowl.
3. Combine the maple syrup and water in a saucepan. Bring to a boil over medium

heat, then pour in the bowl of walnut mixture.

4. Add the vanilla extract to the bowl of mixture. Stir to mix well. Pour the mixture into the baking sheet, then level with a spatula so the mixture coats the bottom evenly.
5. Place the baking sheet in the preheated oven and bake for 90 minutes or until browned and crispy. Stir the mixture every 15 minutes.
6. Remove the baking sheet from the oven. Allow to cool for 10 minutes, then serve with dried cranberries on top.

Nutrition: Calories: 1870 Fat: 115.8g Carbs: 238.0g Protein: 59.8g Fiber: 68.9g

900. Traditional Indian Rajma Dal

Preparation Time: 10 minutes
Cooking Time: 10 minutes
Servings: 4
Ingredients:

- 3 tablespoons sesame oil
- 1 teaspoon ginger, minced
- 1 teaspoon cumin seeds
- 1 teaspoon coriander seeds
- 1 large onion, chopped
- 1 celery stalk, chopped
- 1 teaspoon garlic, minced
- 1 cup tomato sauce
- 1 teaspoon garam masala
- ½ teaspoon curry powder
- 1 small cinnamon stick
- 1 green chili, seeded and minced
- 2 cups canned red kidney beans, drained
- 2 cups vegetable broth
- Kosher salt and ground black pepper, to taste

Directions:

1. In a saucepan, heat the sesame oil over medium-high heat; now, sauté the ginger, cumin seeds and coriander seeds until fragrant or about 30 seconds or so.
2. Add in the onion and celery and continue to sauté for 3

minutes more until they've softened.

3. Add in the garlic and continue to sauté for 1 minute longer.
4. Stir the remaining ingredients into the saucepan and turn the heat to a simmer. Continue to cook for 10 to 12 minutes or until thoroughly cooked. Serve warm and enjoy!

Nutrition per serving: Calories: 443; Fat: 19.2g; Carbs: 52.2g; Protein: 18.1g

901. Red Kidney Bean Salad

Preparation Time: 10 minutes
Cooking Time: 10 minutes
Servings: 4
Ingredients:

- ¾-pound red kidney beans, soaked overnight
- 2 bell peppers, chopped
- 1 carrot, trimmed and grated
- 3 ounces frozen or canned corn kernels, drained
- 3 heaping tablespoons scallions, chopped
- 2 cloves garlic, minced
- 1 red chile pepper, sliced
- ½ cup extra-virgin olive oil
- 2 tablespoons apple cider vinegar
- 2 tablespoons fresh lemon juice
- Sea salt and ground black pepper, to taste
- 2 tablespoons fresh cilantro, chopped
- 2 tablespoons fresh parsley, chopped
- 2 tablespoons fresh basil, chopped

Directions:

1. Cover the soaked beans with a fresh change of cold water and bring to a boil. Let it boil for about 10 minutes. Turn the heat to a simmer and continue to cook for 50 to 55 minutes or until tender.
2. Allow your beans to cool completely, then, transfer them to a salad bowl.

3. Add in the remaining ingredients and toss to combine well. Bon appétit!

Nutrition: Calories: 443; Fat: 19.2g; Carbs: 52.2g; Protein: 18.1g

902. Garlicky Red Wine Mushrooms

Preparation Time: 10 minutes
Cooking Time: 15 minutes
Servings: 4
Ingredients:

- 3 tablespoons olive oil
- 2 cups sliced mushrooms
- 3 garlic cloves, minced
- ½ cup red wine
- 1 tablespoon dried thyme

Directions:

1. Cook olive oil over medium-high heat until it shimmers. Mix in the mushrooms and sit, untouched, until they release their liquid and begin to brown, about 5 minutes. Stir the mushrooms occasionally, cooking until softened and golden brown, about 5 minutes more. Cook garlic. Add the red wine and thyme, using a wooden spoon to scrape any browned bits off the pan's bottom.
2. Adjust heat to medium. Cook for 5 minutes. Season well and serve.

Nutrition: 98 Calories 4 g Fiber 6 g Protein

903. Sautéed Citrus Spinach

Preparation Time: 10 minutes
Cooking Time: 10 minutes
Servings: 4
Ingredients:

- 2 tablespoons olive oil
- 1 shallot, chopped
- 2 garlic cloves, minced
- 10 ounces baby spinach
- Zest and juice of 1 orange

Directions:

1. Cook olive oil over medium-high heat. Cook the shallot for 3 minutes. Cook garlic for 30 seconds.
2. Add the spinach, orange juice, and orange zest. Cook for 2 minutes. Season with salt and pepper. Serve warm.

Nutrition: 91 Calories 4 g Fiber 7 g Protein

904. Super Summer Salad

Preparation Time: 10 minutes
Cooking Time: 0 minutes
Servings: 2
Ingredients:
Dressing:

- 1 tablespoon olive oil
- ¼ cup chopped basil
- 1 teaspoon lemon juice
- ¼ teaspoon salt
- 1 medium avocado, halved, diced
- ¼ cup water

Salad:

- ¼ cup dry chickpeas
- ¼ cup dry red kidney beans
- 4 cups raw kale, shredded
- 2 cups Brussel sprouts, shredded
- 2 radishes, thinly sliced
- 1 tablespoon walnuts, chopped
- 1 teaspoon flax seeds
- Salt and pepper to taste

Directions:

1. Prepare the chickpeas and kidney beans according to the method.
2. Soak the flax seeds according to the method, and then drain excess water.
3. Prepare the dressing by adding the olive oil, basil, lemon juice, salt, and half of the avocado to a food processor or blender, and pulse at low speed.
4. Keep adding small amounts of water until the dressing is creamy and smooth.
5. Transfer the dressing to a small bowl and set it aside.
6. Combine the kale, Brussel sprouts, cooked chickpeas, kidney beans, radishes, walnuts, and remaining avocado in a large bowl and mix thoroughly.
7. Store the mixture, or, serve with the dressing and flax seeds, and enjoy!

Nutrition: Calories 266 Total Fat 26.6g Saturated Fat 5.1g Cholesterol 0mg Sodium 298mg Total Carbohydrate 8.8g Dietary Fiber 6.8g Total Sugars 0.6g Protein 2g Vitamin D 0mcg Calcium 19mg Iron 1mg Potassium 500mg

905. Ritzy Fava Bean Ratatouille

Preparation Time: 15 minutes
Cooking Time: 40 minutes
Servings: 4
Ingredients:

- 1 medium red onion, peeled and thinly sliced
- 2 tablespoons low-sodium vegetable broth
- 1 large eggplant, stemmed and cut into ½-inch dice
- 1 red bell pepper, seeded and diced
- 2 cups cooked fava beans
- 2 Roma tomatoes, chopped
- 1 medium zucchini, diced
- 2 cloves garlic, peeled and finely chopped
- ¼ cup finely chopped basil
- Salt, to taste (optional)
- Ground black pepper, to taste

Directions:

1. Add the onion to a saucepan and sauté for 7 minutes or until caramelized.
2. Add the vegetable broth, eggplant and red bell pepper to the pan and sauté for 10 more minutes.
3. Add the fava beans, tomatoes, zucchini, and garlic to the pan and sauté for an additional 5 minutes.
4. Reduce the heat to medium-low. Put the pan lid on and cook for 15 minutes or until the vegetables are soft. Stir the vegetables halfway through.
5. Transfer them onto a large serving plate. Sprinkle with basil, salt (if desired), and black pepper before serving.

Nutrition: Calories: 114 Fat: 1.0g Carbs: 24.2g Protein: 7.4g Fiber: 10.3g

906. Peppers and Black Beans with Brown Rice

Preparation Time: 15 minutes
Cooking Time: 20 minutes
Servings: 4
Ingredients:

- 2 jalapeño peppers, diced
- 1 red bell pepper, seeded and diced
- 1 medium yellow onion, peeled and diced
- 2 tablespoons low-sodium vegetable broth
- 1 teaspoon toasted and ground cumin seeds
- 1½ teaspoons toasted oregano
- 5 cloves garlic, peeled and minced
- 4 cups cooked black beans
- Salt, to taste (optional)
- Ground black pepper, to taste
- 3 cups cooked brown rice
- 1 lime, quartered
- 1 cup chopped cilantro

Directions:

1. Add the jalapeño peppers, bell pepper, and onion to a saucepan and sauté for 7 minutes or until the onion is well browned and caramelized.
2. Add vegetable broth, cumin, oregano, and garlic to the pan and sauté for 3 minutes or until fragrant.
3. Add the black beans and sauté for 10 minutes or until the vegetables are tender. Sprinkle with salt (if desired) and black pepper halfway through.
4. Arrange the brown rice on a platter, then top with the cooked vegetables. Garnish with lime wedges and cilantro before serving.

Nutrition: Calories: 426 Fat: 2.6g Carbs: 82.4g Protein: 20.2g Fiber: 19.5g

907. Anasazi Bean and Vegetable Stew

Preparation Time: 10 minutes
Cooking Time: 10 minutes
Servings: 4
Ingredients:

- 1 cup Anasazi beans, soaked overnight and drained
- 3 cups roasted vegetable broth
- 1 bay laurel
- 1 thyme sprig, chopped
- 1 rosemary sprig, chopped
- 3 tablespoons olive oil
- 1 large onion, chopped
- 2 celery stalks, chopped
- 2 carrots, chopped
- 2 bell peppers, seeded and chopped
- 1 green chili pepper, seeded and chopped
- 2 garlic cloves, minced
- Sea salt and ground black pepper, to taste
- 1 teaspoon cayenne pepper
- 1 teaspoon paprika

Directions:

1. In a saucepan, bring the Anasazi beans and broth to a boil. Once boiling, turn the heat to a simmer. Add in the bay laurel, thyme and rosemary; let it cook for about 50 minutes or until tender.
2. Meanwhile, in a heavy-bottomed pot, heat the olive oil over medium-high heat. Now, sauté the onion, celery, carrots and peppers for about 4 minutes until tender.
3. Add in the garlic and continue to sauté for 30 seconds more or until aromatic.
4. Add the sautéed mixture to the cooked beans. Season with salt, black pepper, cayenne pepper and paprika.
5. Continue to simmer, stirring periodically, for 10 minutes more or until everything is cooked through. Bon appétit!

Nutrition: Calories: 444; Fat: 15.8g; Carbs: 58.2g; Protein: 20.2g

908. Easy and Hearty Shakshuka

Preparation Time: 10 minutes
Cooking Time: 10 minutes
Servings: 4
Ingredients:

- 2 tablespoons olive oil
- 1 onion, chopped
- 2 bell peppers, chopped
- 1 poblano pepper, chopped
- 2 cloves garlic, minced
- 2 tomatoes, pureed
- Sea salt and black pepper, to taste
- 1 teaspoon dried basil
- 1 teaspoon red pepper flakes
- 1 teaspoon paprika
- 2 bay leaves
- 1 cup chickpeas, soaked overnight, rinsed and drained
- 3 cups vegetable broth
- 2 tablespoons fresh cilantro, roughly chopped

Directions:

1. Heat the olive oil in a saucepan over medium heat. Once hot, cook the onion, peppers and garlic for about 4 minutes, until tender and aromatic.
2. Add in the pureed tomato tomatoes, sea salt, black pepper, basil, red pepper, paprika and bay leaves.
3. Turn the heat to a simmer and add in the chickpeas and vegetable broth. Cook for 45 minutes or until tender.
4. Taste and adjust seasonings. Spoon your Shakshuka into individual bowls and serve garnished with fresh cilantro. Bon appétit!

Nutrition: Calories: 324; Fat: 11.2g; Carbs: 42.2g; Protein: 15.8g

909. Lemon Broccoli Rabe

Preparation Time: 10 minutes
Cooking Time: 10 minutes
Servings: 4
Ingredients:

- 8 cups water
- Sea salt
- 2 bunches broccoli rabe, chopped
- 3 tablespoons olive oil
- 3 garlic cloves, minced
- Pinch of cayenne pepper
- Zest of 1 lemon

Directions:

1. Boil 8 cups of water. Sprinkle a pinch of salt and the broccoli rabe. Cook until the broccoli rabe is

slightly softened, about 2 minutes. Drain.

2. Heat olive oil over medium-high heat. Cook the garlic for 30 seconds. Stir in the broccoli rabe, cayenne, and lemon zest. Season with salt and black pepper. Serve immediately.

Nutrition: 99 Calories 7g Fiber 11g Protein

910. Spicy Swiss Chard
Preparation Time: 10 minutes
Cooking Time: 10 minutes
Servings: 4
Ingredients:

- 2 tablespoons olive oil
- 1 onion, chopped
- 2 bunches Swiss chard
- 3 garlic cloves, minced
- ½ teaspoon red pepper flakes (or to taste)
- Juice of ½ lemon

Directions:

1. In a big pot, cook olive oil over medium-high heat until it shimmers. Cook the onion and chard stems for 5 minutes.
2. Cook chard leaves for 1 minute. Stir in the garlic and pepper flakes. Cover and cook for 5 minutes. Stir in the lemon juice. Season with salt and serve immediately.

Nutrition: 94 Calories 5g Fiber 7g Protein

911. Roasted Almond Protein Salad
Preparation Time: 30 minutes
Cooking Time: 0 minutes
Servings: 4
Ingredients:

- ½ cup dry quinoa
- ½ cup dry navy beans
- ½ cup dry chickpeas
- ½ cup raw whole almonds
- 1 teaspoon extra-virgin olive oil
- ½ teaspoon salt
- ½ teaspoon paprika
- ½ teaspoon cayenne
- Dash of chili powder
- 4 cups spinach, fresh or frozen

- ¼ cup purple onion, chopped

Directions:

1. Prepare the quinoa according to the recipe. Store in the fridge for now.
2. Prepare the beans according to the method. Store in the fridge for now.
3. Toss the almonds, olive oil, salt, and spices in a large bowl, and stir until the ingredients are evenly coated.
4. Put a skillet over medium-high heat, and transfer the almond mixture to the heated skillet.
5. Roast while stirring until the almonds are browned, around 5 minutes. You may hear the ingredients pop and crackle in the pan as they warm up. Stir frequently to prevent burning.
6. Turn off the heat and toss the cooked and chilled quinoa and beans, onions, spinach, or mixed greens in the skillet. Stir well before transferring the roasted almond salad to a bowl.
7. Enjoy the salad with a dressing of choice, or, store for later!

Nutrition: Calories 347 Total Fat 10.5g Saturated Fat 1g Cholesterol 0mg Sodium 324mg Total Carbohydrate 49.2g Dietary Fiber 14.7g Total Sugars 4.7g Protein 17.2g Vitamin D 0mcg Calcium 139mg Iron 5mg Potassium 924mg

912. Black-Eyed Pea, Beet, and Carrot Stew
Preparation Time: 15 minutes
Cooking Time: 40 minutes
Servings: 2
Ingredients:

- ½ cup black-eyed peas, soaked in water overnight
- 3 cups water
- 1 large beet, peeled and cut into ½-inch pieces (about ¾ cup)
- 1 large carrot, peeled and cut into ½-inch pieces (about ¾ cup)
- ¼ teaspoon turmeric

- ¼ teaspoon toasted and ground cumin seeds
- ⅛ teaspoon asafetida
- ¼ cup finely chopped parsley
- ¼ teaspoon cayenne pepper
- ¼ teaspoon salt (optional)
- ½ teaspoon fresh lime juice

Directions:

1. Pour the black-eyed peas and water into a pot, then cook over medium heat for 25 minutes.
2. Add the beet and carrot to the pot and cook for 10 more minutes. Add more water if necessary.
3. Add the turmeric, cumin, asafetida, parsley, and cayenne pepper to the pot and cook for an additional 6 minutes or until the vegetables are soft. Stir the mixture periodically. Sprinkle with salt, if desired.
4. Drizzle the lime juice on top before serving in a large bowl.

Nutrition: calories: 84 | fat: 0.7g | carbs: 16.6g | protein: 4.1g | fiber: 4.5g

913. Koshari
Preparation Time: 15 minutes
Cooking Time: 2 hours 10 minutes
Servings: 6
Ingredients:

- 1 cup green lentils, rinsed
- 3 cups water
- Salt, to taste (optional)
- 1 large onion, peeled and minced
- 2 tablespoons low-sodium vegetable broth
- 4 cloves garlic, peeled and minced
- ½ teaspoon ground allspice
- 1 teaspoon ground coriander
- 1 teaspoon ground cumin
- 2 tablespoons tomato paste
- ½ teaspoon crushed red pepper flakes
- 3 large tomatoes, diced
- 1 cup cooked medium-grain brown rice

- 1 cup whole-grain elbow macaroni, cooked, drained, and kept warm
- 1 tablespoon brown rice vinegar

Directions:

1. Put the lentils and water in a saucepan, and sprinkle with salt, if desired. Bring to a boil over high heat. Reduce the heat to medium, then put the pan lid on and cook for 45 minutes or until the water is mostly absorbed. Pour the cooked lentils into the bowl and set aside.
2. Add the onion to a nonstick skillet, then sauté over medium heat for 15 minutes or caramelized.
3. Add vegetable broth and garlic to the skillet and sauté for 3 minutes or until fragrant.
4. Add the allspice, coriander, cumin, tomato paste, and red pepper flakes to the skillet and sauté for an additional 3 minutes until aromatic.
5. Add the tomatoes to the skillet and sauté for 15 minutes or until the tomatoes are wilted. Sprinkle with salt, if desired.
6. Arrange the cooked brown rice on the bottom of a large platter, then top the rice with macaroni, and then spread the lentils over. Pour the tomato mixture and brown rice vinegar over before serving.

Nutrition: Calories: 201 Fat: 1.6g Carbs: 41.8g Protein: 6.5g Fiber: 3

914. Old-Fashioned Chili

Preparation Time: 10 minutes
Cooking Time: 10 minutes
Servings: 4
Ingredients:

- ¾-pound red kidney beans, soaked overnight
- 2 tablespoons olive oil
- 1 onion, chopped
- 2 bell peppers, chopped
- 1 red chili pepper, chopped
- 2 ribs celery, chopped

- 2 cloves garlic, minced
- 2 bay leaves
- 1 teaspoon ground cumin
- 1 teaspoon thyme, chopped
- 1 teaspoon black peppercorns
- 20 ounces' tomatoes, crushed
- 2 cups vegetable broth
- 1 teaspoon smoked paprika
- Sea salt, to taste
- 2 tablespoons fresh cilantro, chopped
- 1 avocado, pitted, peeled and sliced

Directions:

1. Cover the soaked beans with a fresh change of cold water and bring to a boil. Let it boil for about 10 minutes. Turn the heat to a simmer and continue to cook for 50 to 55 minutes or until tender.
2. In a heavy-bottomed pot, heat the olive oil over medium heat. Once hot, sauté the onion, bell pepper and celery.
3. Sauté the garlic, bay leaves, ground cumin, thyme and black peppercorns for about 1 minute or so.
4. Add in the diced tomatoes, vegetable broth, paprika, salt and cooked beans. Let it simmer, stirring periodically, for 25 to 30 minutes or until cooked through.
5. Serve garnished with fresh cilantro and avocado. Bon appétit!

Nutrition: Calories: 514; Fat: 16.4g; Carbs: 72g; Protein: 25.8g

915. Easy Red Lentil Salad

Preparation Time: 10 minutes
Cooking Time: 10 minutes
Servings: 4
Ingredients:

- ½ cup red lentils, soaked overnight and drained
- 1½ cups water
- 1 sprig rosemary
- 1 bay leaf
- 1 cup grape tomatoes, halved

- 1 cucumber, thinly sliced
- 1 bell pepper, thinly sliced
- 1 clove garlic, minced
- 1 onion, thinly sliced
- 2 tablespoons fresh lime juice
- 4 tablespoons olive oil
- Sea salt and ground black pepper, to taste

Directions:

1. Add the red lentils, water, rosemary and bay leaf to a saucepan and bring to a boil over high heat. Then, turn the heat to a simmer and continue to cook for 20 minutes or until tender.
2. Place the lentils in a salad bowl and let them cool completely.
3. Add in the remaining ingredients and toss to combine well. Serve at room temperature or well-chilled.
4. Bon appétit!

Nutrition: Calories: 295; Fat: 18.8g; Carbs: 25.2g; Protein: 8.5g

916. Quinoa and Chickpea Vegetable Bowls

Preparation Time: 15 minutes
Cooking Time: 15 minutes
Servings: 4
Ingredients:

- 1 cup red dry quinoa, rinsed and drained
- 2 cups low-sodium vegetable soup
- 2 cups fresh spinach
- 2 cups finely shredded red cabbage
- 1 (15-oz. / 425-g) can chickpeas, drained and rinsed
- 1 ripe avocado, thinly sliced
- 1 cup shredded carrots
- 1 red bell pepper, thinly sliced
- 4 tablespoons Mango Sauce
- ½ cup fresh cilantro, chopped

Mango Sauce:

- 1 mango, diced
- ¼ cup fresh lime juice

- ½ teaspoon ground turmeric
- 1 teaspoon finely minced fresh ginger
- ¼ teaspoon sea salt
- Pinch of ground red pepper
- 1 teaspoon pure maple syrup
- 2 tablespoons extra-virgin olive oil

Directions:
1. Pour the quinoa and vegetable soup into a saucepan. Bring to a boil. Reduce the heat to low. Cover and cook for 15 minutes or until tender. Fluffy with a fork.
2. Meanwhile, combine the ingredients for the mango sauce in a food processor. Pulse until smooth.
3. Divide the quinoa, spinach, and cabbage into 4 serving bowls, then top with chickpeas, avocado, carrots, and bell pepper.
4. Dress them with the mango sauce and spread with cilantro. Serve immediately.

Nutrition: Calories: 366 Fat: 11.1g Protein: 15.5g Carbs: 55.6g

917. Papaya, Jicama, and Peas Rice Bowl

Preparation Time: 15 minutes
Cooking Time: 45 minutes
Servings: 4
Ingredients:
Sauce:
- Juice of ¼ lemon
- 2 teaspoons chopped fresh basil
- 1 tablespoon raw honey
- 1 tablespoon extra-virgin olive oil
- Sea salt, to taste

Rice:
- 1½ cups wild rice
- 2 papayas, peeled, seeded, and diced
- 1 jicama, peeled and shredded
- 1 cup snow peas, julienned
- 2 cups shredded cabbage

- 1 scallion, white and green parts, chopped

Directions:
1. Combine the ingredients for the sauce in a bowl. Stir to mix well. Set aside until ready to use. Pour the wild rice in a saucepan, then pour in enough water to cover. Bring to a boil.
2. Reduce the heat to low, then simmer for 45 minutes or until the wild rice is soft and plump. Drain and transfer to a large serving bowl.
3. Top the rice with papayas, jicama, peas, cabbage, and scallion. Pour the sauce over and stir to mix well before serving.

Nutrition: Calories: 446 Fat: 7.9g Protein: 13.1g Carbs: 85.8g

918. Italian Baked Beans

Preparation Time: 5 minutes
Cooking Time: 15 minutes
Servings: 6
Ingredients:
- 2 teaspoons extra-virgin olive oil
- ½ cup minced onion (about ¼ onion)
- 1 (12-oz.) can low-sodium tomato paste
- ¼ cup red wine vinegar
- 2 tablespoons honey
- ¼ teaspoon ground cinnamon
- ½ cup water
- 2 (15-oz.) cans cannellini or great northern beans, undrained

Directions:
1. In a medium saucepan over medium heat, heat the oil. Add the onion and cook for 5 minutes, stirring frequently.
2. Add the tomato paste, vinegar, honey, cinnamon, and water, and mix well. Turn the heat to low. Drain and rinse one can of the beans in a colander and add to the saucepan.
3. Pour the entire second can of beans (including the liquid) into the saucepan. Let it cook for 10 minutes,

stirring occasionally, and serve.
4. Ingredient tip: Switch up this recipe by making new variations of the homemade ketchup. Instead of the cinnamon, try ¼ teaspoon of smoked paprika and 1 tablespoon of hot sauce. Serve.

Nutrition: Calories: 236 Fat: 3g Carbohydrates: 42g Protein: 10g

919. Cannellini Bean Lettuce Wraps

Preparation Time: 15 minutes
Cooking Time: 10 minutes
Servings: 4
Ingredients:
- 1 tablespoon extra-virgin olive oil
- ½ cup diced red onion (about ¼ onion)
- ¾ cup chopped fresh tomatoes (about 1 medium tomato)
- ¼ teaspoon freshly ground black pepper
- 1 (15-oz.) can cannellini or great northern beans, drained and rinsed
- ¼ cup finely chopped fresh curly parsley
- ½ cup Lemony Garlic Hummus or ½ cup prepared hummus
- 8 romaine lettuce leaves

Directions:
1. In a large skillet over medium heat, heat the oil. Add the onion and cook for 3 minutes, stirring occasionally.
2. Add the tomatoes and pepper and cook for 3 more minutes, stirring occasionally. Add the beans and cook for 3 more minutes, stirring occasionally. Remove from the heat, and mix in the parsley.
3. Spread 1 tablespoon of hummus over each lettuce leaf. Evenly spread the warm bean mixture down the center of each leaf.
4. Fold one side of the lettuce leaf over the filling lengthwise, then fold over

the other side to make a wrap and serve.

Nutrition: Calories: 211 Fat: 8g Carbohydrates: 28g Protein: 10g

920. Israeli Eggplant, Chickpea, and Mint Sauté

Preparation Time: 5 minutes
Cooking Time: 20 minutes
Servings: 6
Ingredients:

- Nonstick cooking spray
- 1 medium globe eggplant (about 1 pound), stem removed
- 1 tablespoon extra-virgin olive oil
- 2 tablespoons freshly squeezed lemon juice (from about 1 small lemon)
- 2 tablespoons balsamic vinegar
- 1 teaspoon ground cumin
- ¼ teaspoon kosher or sea salt
- 1 (15-oz.) can chickpeas, drained and rinsed
- 1 cup sliced sweet onion (about ½ medium Walla Walla or Vidalia onion)
- ¼ cup loosely packed chopped or torn mint leaves
- 1 tablespoon sesame seeds, toasted if desired
- 1 garlic clove, finely minced (about ½ teaspoon)

Directions:

1. Place one oven rack about 4 inches below the broiler element. Turn the broiler to the highest setting to preheat. Spray a large, rimmed baking sheet with nonstick cooking spray.
2. On a cutting board, cut the eggplant lengthwise into four slabs (each piece should be about ½- to ⅛-inch thick). Place the eggplant slabs on the prepared baking sheet. Set aside.
3. In a small bowl, whisk together the oil, lemon juice, vinegar, cumin, and salt. Brush or drizzle 2

tablespoons of the lemon dressing over both sides of the eggplant slabs. Reserve the remaining dressing.

4. Broil the eggplant directly under the heating element for 4 minutes, flip them, then broil for another 4 minutes, until golden brown.
5. While the eggplant is broiling, in a serving bowl, combine the chickpeas, onion, mint, sesame seeds, and garlic. Add the reserved dressing, and gently mix to incorporate all the ingredients.
6. When the eggplant is done, using tongs, transfer the slabs from the baking sheet to a cooling rack and cool for 3 minutes.
7. When slightly cooled, place the eggplant on a cutting board and slice each slab crosswise into ½-inch strips.
8. Add the eggplant to the serving bowl with the onion mixture. Gently toss everything together, and serve warm or at room temperature.

Nutrition: Calories: 159 Fat: 4g Carbohydrates: 26g Protein: 6g

921. Mediterranean Lentils and Rice

Preparation Time: 5 minutes
Cooking Time: 25 minutes
Servings: 4
Ingredients:

- 2¼ cups low-sodium or no-salt-added vegetable broth
- ½ cup uncooked brown or green lentils
- ½ cup uncooked instant brown rice
- ½ cup diced carrots (about 1 carrot)
- ½ cup diced celery (about 1 stalk)
- 1 (2¼ -oz.) can sliced olives, drained (about ½ cup)
- ¼ cup diced red onion (about ⅛ onion)
- ¼ cup chopped fresh curly-leaf parsley
- 1½ tablespoons extra-virgin olive oil

- 1 tablespoon freshly squeezed lemon juice (from about ½ small lemon)
- 1 garlic clove, minced (about ½ teaspoon)
- ¼ teaspoon kosher or sea salt
- ¼ teaspoon freshly ground black pepper

Directions:

1. In a medium saucepan over high heat, bring the broth and lentils to a boil, cover, and lower the heat to medium-low. Cook for 8 minutes.
2. Raise the heat to medium, and stir in the rice. Cover the pot and cook the mixture for 15 minutes, or until the liquid is absorbed. Remove the pot from the heat and let it sit, covered, for 1 minute, then stir.
3. While the lentils and rice are cooking, mix together the carrots, celery, olives, onion, and parsley in a large serving bowl.
4. In a small bowl, whisk together the oil, lemon juice, garlic, salt, and pepper. Set aside. When the lentils and rice are cooked, add them to the serving bowl.
5. Pour the dressing on top, and mix everything together. Serve warm or cold, or store in a sealed container in the refrigerator for up to 7 days.

Nutrition: Calories: 230 Fat: 8g Carbohydrates: 34g Protein: 8g

922. Spring Soup with Gourmet Grains

Preparation Time: 10 minutes
Cooking Time: 25 minutes
Servings: 2
Ingredients:

- 2 tablespoons olive oil
- 1-pc small onion, diced
- 6-cups chicken broth, homemade (refer to the recipe of Avgolemono Soup)
- 1-bay leaf
- ½-cup of fresh dill, chopped (divided)

- ⅓-cup Italian or Arborio whole grain rice
- 1-cup asparagus, chopped
- 1-cup carrots, diced
- 1½-cups cooked chicken, de-boned and diced or shredded
- ½-lemon, juice
- 1-pc large egg
- 2 tablespoons water
- Kosher salt and fresh pepper to taste
- Fresh chives, minced for garnish

Directions:

1. Heat the olive oil and sauté the onions for 5 minutes in a large stockpot placed over medium heat. Pour in the chicken broth.
2. Add the bay leaf and half of the dill. Bring to a boil.
3. Add rice and turn the heat to medium-low. Simmer for 10 minutes.
4. Add the asparagus and carrots. Cook for 15 minutes until the vegetables are tender and the rice cooks through.
5. Add the cooked shredded chicken. Continue simmer over low heat.
6. In the meantime, combine the lemon juice and egg with water in a mixing bowl.
7. Take ½-cup of the simmering stock and pour it on the lemon-egg mixture, whisking gradually to prevent eggs from curdling.
8. Pour the lemon-egg broth into the stockpot, still whisking gradually. Soon as the soup thickens, turn off the heat
9. Remove the bay leaf, and discard. Add the remaining dill, salt, and pepper.
10. To serve, ladle the creamy soup into bowls and garnish with minced chives.

Nutrition: Calories: 252.8, Fats: 8g, Dietary Fiber: 0.3g, Carbohydrates: 19.8g, Protein: 25.6g

923. Minestrone Chickpeas and Macaroni Casserole

Preparation Time: 15 minutes
Cooking Time: 7 hours & 25 minutes
Servings: 5
Ingredients:

- 1 (15-oz. / 425-g.) can chickpeas, drained and rinsed
- 1 (28-oz. / 794-g.) can diced tomatoes, with the juice
- 1 (6-oz. / 170-g.) can no-salt-added tomato paste
- 3 medium carrots, sliced
- 3 cloves garlic, minced
- 1 medium yellow onion, chopped
- 1 cup low-sodium vegetable soup
- ½ teaspoon dried rosemary
- 1 teaspoon dried oregano
- 2 teaspoons maple syrup
- ½ teaspoon sea salt
- ¼ teaspoon ground black pepper
- ½ pound (227-g.) fresh green beans, trimmed and cut into bite-size pieces
- 1 cup macaroni pasta
- 2 ounces (57-g.) Parmesan cheese, grated

Directions:

1. Except for the green beans, pasta, and Parmesan cheese, combine all the ingredients in the slow cooker and stir to mix well. Put the slow cooker lid on and cook on low for 7 hours.
2. Fold in the pasta and green beans. Put the lid on and cook on high for 20 minutes or until the vegetable are soft and the pasta is al dente.
3. Pour them in a large serving bowl and spread with Parmesan cheese before serving.

Nutrition: Calories: 349 Fat: 6.7g Protein: 16.5g Carbs: 59.9g

924. Spiced Soup with Lentils & Legumes

Preparation Time: 15 minutes
Cooking Time: 35 minutes
Servings: 2
Ingredients:

- 2 tablespoons extra-virgin olive oil
- 2-cloves garlic, minced
- 4-pcs large celery stalks, diced
- 2-pcs large onions, diced
- 6-cups water
- 1 teaspoon cumin
- ¾ teaspoon turmeric
- ½ teaspoon cinnamon
- ½ teaspoon fresh ginger, grated
- 1-cup dried lentils, rinsed and sorted
- 1 (16-oz.) can chickpeas (garbanzo beans), drained and rinsed
- 3-pcs ripe tomatoes, cubed
- ½-lemon, juice
- ½ cup fresh cilantro or parsley, chopped
- Salt

Directions:

1. Heat the olive oil and sauté the garlic, celery, and onion for 5 minutes in a large stockpot placed over medium heat.
2. Pour in the water. Add the spices and lentils. Cover the stockpot and simmer for 40 minutes until the lentils are tender.
3. Add the chickpeas and tomatoes. (Pour more water and additional spices, if desired.) Simmer for 15 minutes over low heat.
4. Pour in the lemon juice and stir the soup. Add the cilantro or parsley and salt to taste.

Nutrition: Calories: 123, Fats: 3g, Dietary Fiber: 5g, Carbohydrates: 19g, Protein: 5g

925. Brown Rice Pilaf with Golden Raisins

Preparation Time: 5 minutes
Cooking Time: 15 minutes
Servings: 6
Ingredients:

- 1 tablespoon extra-virgin olive oil
- 1 cup chopped onion (about ½ medium onion)
- ½ cup shredded carrot (about 1 medium carrot)
- 1 teaspoon ground cumin
- ½ teaspoon ground cinnamon
- 2 cups instant brown rice
- 1¾ cups 100% orange juice
- ¼ cup water
- 1 cup golden raisins
- ½ cup shelled pistachios
- Chopped fresh chives (optional)

Directions:

1. In a medium saucepan over medium-high heat, heat the oil. Add the onion and cook for 5 minutes, stirring frequently.
2. Add the carrot, cumin, and cinnamon, and cook for 1 minute, stirring frequently. Stir in the rice, orange juice, and water.
3. Bring to a boil, cover, then lower the heat to medium-low. Simmer for 7 minutes, or until the rice is cooked through and the liquid is absorbed. Stir in the raisins, pistachios, and chives (if using) and serve.

Nutrition: Calories: 320 Fat: 7g Carbohydrates: 61g Protein: 6g

926. Ritzy Veggie Chili

Preparation Time: 15 minutes
Cooking Time: 5 hours
Servings: 4
Ingredients:

- 1 (28-oz. / 794-g.) can chopped tomatoes, with the juice
- 1 (15-oz. / 425-g.) can black beans, drained and rinsed
- 1 (15-oz. / 425-g.) can redly beans, drained and rinsed
- 1 medium green bell pepper, chopped
- 1 yellow onion, chopped
- 1 tablespoon onion powder
- 1 teaspoon paprika
- 1 teaspoon cayenne pepper
- 1 teaspoon garlic powder
- ½ teaspoon sea salt
- ½ teaspoon ground black pepper
- 1 tablespoon olive oil
- 1 large Hass avocado, pitted, peeled, and chopped, for garnish

Directions:

1. Combine all the ingredients, except for the avocado, in the slow cooker. Stir to mix well.
2. Put the slow cooker lid on and cook on high for 5 hours or until the vegetables are tender and the mixture has a thick consistency.
3. Pour the chili into a large serving bowl. Allow to cool for 30 minutes, then spread with chopped avocado and serve.

Nutrition: Calories: 633 Fat: 16.3g Protein: 31.7g Carbs: 97.0g

927. Spicy Italian Bean Balls with Marinara

Preparation Time: 15 minutes
Cooking Time: 30 minutes
Servings: 2-4
Ingredients:

Bean Balls:

- 1 tablespoon extra-virgin olive oil
- ½ yellow onion, minced
- 1 teaspoon fennel seeds
- 2 teaspoons dried oregano
- ½ teaspoon crushed red pepper flakes
- 1 teaspoon garlic powder
- 1 (15-oz. / 425-g.) can white beans (cannellini or navy), drained and rinsed
- ½ cup whole-grain bread crumbs
- Sea salt and ground black pepper, to taste

Marinara:

- 1 tablespoon extra-virgin olive oil
- 3 garlic cloves, minced
- Handful basil leaves
- 1 (28-oz. / 794-g.) can chop tomatoes with juice reserved
- Sea salt, to taste

Directions:

1. Preheat the oven to 350°F (180°C). Line a baking sheet with parchment paper. Heat the olive oil in a nonstick skillet over medium heat until shimmering.
2. Add the onion and sauté for 5 minutes or until translucent. Sprinkle with fennel seeds, oregano, red pepper flakes, and garlic powder, then cook for 1 minute or until aromatic.
3. Pour the sautéed mixture into a food processor and add the beans and bread crumbs. Sprinkle with salt and ground black pepper, then pulse to combine well and the mixture holds together.
4. Shape the mixture into balls with a 2-ounce (57-g.) cookie scoop, then arrange the balls on the baking sheet.
5. Bake in the preheated oven for 30 minutes or until lightly browned. Flip the balls halfway through the cooking time.
6. While baking the beanballs, heat the olive oil in a saucepan over medium-high heat until shimmering. Add the garlic and basil and sauté for 2 minutes or until fragrant.
7. Fold in the tomatoes and juice. Bring to a boil. Reduce the heat to low. Put the lid on and simmer for 15 minutes. Sprinkle with salt.
8. Transfer the beanballs to a large plate and baste with marinara before serving.

Nutrition: Calories: 351 Fat: 16.4g Protein: 11.5g Carbs: 42.9g

928. Baked Rolled Oat with Pears and Pecans

Preparation Time: 15 minutes
Cooking Time: 30 minutes
Servings: 6
Ingredients:

- 2 tablespoons coconut oil, melted, plus more for greasing the pan
- 3 ripe pears, cored and diced
- 2 cups unsweetened almond milk
- 1 tablespoon pure vanilla extract
- ¼ cup pure maple syrup
- 2 cups gluten-free rolled oats
- ½ cup raisins
- ¾ cup chopped pecans
- ¼ teaspoon ground nutmeg
- 1 teaspoon ground cinnamon
- ½ teaspoon ground ginger
- ¼ teaspoon sea salt

Directions:

1. Preheat the oven to 350°F (180°C). Grease a baking dish with melted coconut oil, then spread the pears in a single layer on the baking dish evenly.
2. Combine the almond milk, vanilla extract, maple syrup, and coconut oil in a bowl. Stir to mix well.
3. Combine the remaining ingredients in a separate large bowl. Stir to mix well. Fold the almond milk mixture in the bowl, then pour the mixture over the pears.
4. Place the baking dish in the preheated oven and bake for 30 minutes or until lightly browned and set. Serve immediately.

Nutrition: Calories: 479 Fat: 34.9g Protein: 8.8g Carbs: 50.1g

929. Brown Rice Pilaf with Pistachios and Raisins

Preparation Time: 15 minutes
Cooking Time: 15 minutes
Servings: 6
Ingredients:

- 1 tablespoon extra-virgin olive oil
- 1 cup chopped onion
- ½ cup shredded carrot
- ½ teaspoon ground cinnamon
- 1 teaspoon ground cumin
- 2 cups brown rice
- 1¾ cups pure orange juice
- ¼ cup water
- ½ cup shelled pistachios
- 1 cup golden raisins
- ½ cup chopped fresh chives

Directions:

1. Heat the olive oil in a saucepan over medium-high heat until shimmering. Add the onion and sauté for 5 minutes or until translucent.
2. Add the carrots, cinnamon, and cumin, then sauté for 1 minute or until aromatic.
3. Pour in the brown rice, orange juice, and water. Bring to a boil. Reduce the heat to medium-low and simmer for 7 minutes or until the liquid is almost absorbed.
4. Transfer the rice mixture to a large serving bowl, then spread with pistachios, raisins, and chives. Serve immediately.

Nutrition: Calories: 264 Fat: 7.1g Protein: 5.2g Carbs: 48.9g

Chapter 11. Soup Recipes

930. Basic Recipe for Vegetable Broth

Preparation Time: 10 minutes
Cooking Time: 60 minutes
Servings: makes 2 quarts
Ingredients:

- 8 cups water
- 1 onion, chopped
- 4 garlic cloves, crushed
- 2 celery stalks, chopped
- Pinch of salt
- 1 carrot, chopped
- Dash of pepper
- 1 potato, medium & chopped
- 1 tablespoon soy sauce
- 3 bay leaves

Directions:

1. To make the vegetable broth, you need to place all of the ingredients in a deep saucepan.
2. Heat the pan over medium-high heat. Bring the vegetable mixture to a boil.
3. Once it starts boiling, lower the heat to medium-low and allow it to simmer for at least an hour or so. Cover it with a lid.
4. When the time is up, pass it through a filter and strain the vegetables, garlic, and bay leaves.
5. Allow the stock to cool completely and store in an air-tight container.

Nutrition: Calories: 44 kcal Fat: 0.6g Carbs: 9.7g Protein: 0.9g

931. Cucumber Dill Gazpacho

Preparation Time: 10 minutes
Cooking Time: 2 hours
Servings: 4
Ingredients:

- 4 large cucumbers, peeled, deseeded, and chopped
- ⅛ teaspoon salt
- 1 teaspoon chopped fresh dill + more for garnishing
- 2 tablespoons freshly squeezed lemon juice

- 1½ cups green grape, seeds removed
- 3 tablespoons extra-virgin olive oil
- 1 garlic clove, minced

Directions:

1. Add all the ingredients to a food processor and blend until smooth.
2. Pour the soup into serving bowls and chill for 1 to 2 hours.
3. Garnish with dill and serve chilled.

Nutrition: Calories: 236 kcal Fat: 1.8g Carbs: 48.3g Protein: 7g

932. Red Lentil Soup

Preparation Time: 5 minutes
Cooking Time: 25 minutes
Servings: makes 6 cups
Ingredients:

- 2 tablespoons nutritional yeast
- 1 cup red lentil, washed
- ½ tablespoons garlic, minced
- 4 cups vegetable stock
- 1 teaspoon salt
- 2 cups kale, shredded
- 3 cups mixed vegetables

Directions:

1. To start with, place all ingredients needed to make the soup in a large pot.
2. Heat the pot over medium-high heat and bring the mixture to a boil.
3. Once it starts boiling, lower the heat to low. Allow the soup to simmer.
4. Simmer it for 1o to 15 minutes or until cooked.
5. Serve and enjoy.

Nutrition: Calories: 212 kcal Fat: 11.9g Carbs: 31.7g Protein: 7.3g

933. Spinach and Kale Soup

Preparation Time: 5 minutes
Cooking Time: 5 minutes
Servings: 2
Ingredients:

- 3 ounces vegan butter
- 1 cup fresh spinach, chopped coarsely
- 1 cup fresh kale, chopped coarsely

- 1 large avocado
- 3 tablespoons chopped fresh mint leaves
- 3½ cups coconut cream
- 1 cup vegetable broth
- Salt and black pepper to taste
- 1 lime, juiced

Directions:

1. Melt the vegan butter in a medium pot over medium heat and sauté the kale and spinach until wilted, 3 minutes. Turn the heat off.
2. Stir in the remaining ingredients and using an immersion blender, puree the soup until smooth.
3. Dish the soup and serve warm.

Nutrition: Calories 380 Fat 10 g Protein 20 g Carbohydrates 30 g

934. Coconut and Grilled Vegetable Soup

Preparation Time: 10 minutes
Cooking Time: 45 minutes
Servings: 4
Ingredients:

- 2 small red onions cut into wedges
- 2 garlic cloves
- 10 ounces butternut squash, peeled and chopped
- 10 ounces pumpkins, peeled and chopped
- 4 tablespoons melted vegan butter
- Salt and black pepper to taste
- 1 cup of water
- 1 cup unsweetened coconut milk
- 1 lime juiced
- ¾ cup vegan mayonnaise
- Toasted pumpkin seeds for garnishing

Directions:

1. Preheat the oven to 400°F.
2. On a baking sheet, spread the onions, garlic, butternut squash, and pumpkins and drizzle half of the butter on top. Season with salt, black

pepper, and rub the seasoning well onto the vegetables. Roast in the oven for 45 minutes or until the vegetables are golden brown and softened.

3. Transfer the vegetables to a pot; add the remaining ingredients except for the pumpkin seeds and using an immersion blender puree the ingredients until smooth.

4. Dish the soup, garnish with the pumpkin seeds and serve warm.

Nutrition: Calories 290 Fat 10 g Protein 30 g Carbohydrates 0 g

935. Celery Dill Soup

Preparation Time: 5 Minutes
Cooking Time: 25 Minutes
Servings: 4
Ingredients:

- 2 tablespoons coconut oil
- ½ pound celery root, trimmed
- 1 garlic clove
- 1 medium white onion
- ¼ cup fresh dill, roughly chopped
- 1 teaspoon cumin powder
- ¼ teaspoon nutmeg powder
- 1 small head cauliflower, cut into florets
- 3½ cups seasoned vegetable stock
- 5 ounces vegan butter
- Juice from 1 lemon
- ¼ cup coconut cream
- Salt and black pepper to taste

Directions:

1. Melt the coconut oil in a large pot and sauté the celery root, garlic, and onion until softened and fragrant, 5 minutes.

2. Stir in the dill, cumin, and nutmeg, and stir-fry for 1 minute. Mix in the cauliflower and vegetable stock. Allow the soup to boil for 15 minutes and turn the heat off.

3. Add the vegan butter and lemon juice, and puree the

soup using an immersion blender.

4. Stir in the coconut cream, salt, black pepper, and dish the soup.

5. Serve warm.

Nutrition: Calories 320 Fat 10 g Protein 20 g Carbohydrates 30 g

936. Broccoli Fennel Soup

Preparation Time: 15 minutes
Cooking Time: 10 minutes
Servings: 4
Ingredients:

- 1 fennel bulb, white and green parts coarsely chopped
- 10 ounces broccoli, cut into florets
- 3 cups vegetable stock
- Salt and freshly ground black pepper
- 1 garlic clove
- 1 cup dairy-free cream cheese
- 3 ounces vegan butter
- ½ cup chopped fresh oregano

Directions:

1. In a medium pot, combine the fennel, broccoli, vegetable stock, salt, and black pepper. Bring to a boil until the vegetables soften, 10 to 15 minutes.

2. Stir in the remaining ingredients and simmer the soup for 3 to 5 minutes.

3. Adjust the taste with salt and black pepper, and dish the soup.

4. Serve warm.

Nutrition: Calories 240 Fat 0 g Protein 0 g Carbohydrates 20 g

937. Tofu Goulash Soup

Preparation Time: 35 minutes
Cooking Time: 20 minutes
Servings: 4
Ingredients:

- 4¼ ounces vegan butter
- 1 white onion, chopped
- 2 garlic cloves, minced
- 1½ cups butternut squash
- 1 red bell pepper, deseeded and chopped
- 1 tablespoon paprika powder
- ¼ teaspoon red chili flakes
- 1 tablespoon dried basil

- ½ tablespoon crushed cardamom seeds
- Salt and black pepper to taste
- 1½ cups crushed tomatoes
- 3 cups vegetable broth
- 1½ teaspoon red wine vinegar
- Chopped parsley to serve

Directions:

1. Place the tofu between two paper towels and allow draining of water for 30 minutes. After, crumble the tofu and set aside.

2. Melt the vegan butter in a large pot over medium heat and sauté the onion and garlic until the veggies are fragrant and soft, 3 minutes.

3. Stir in the tofu and cook until golden brown, 3 minutes.

4. Add the butternut squash, bell pepper, paprika, red chili flakes, basil, cardamom seeds, salt, and black pepper. Cook for 2 minutes to release some flavor and mix in the tomatoes and 2 cups of vegetable broth.

5. Close the lid, bring the soup to a boil, and then simmer for 10 minutes.

6. Stir in the remaining vegetable broth, the red wine vinegar, and adjust the taste with salt and black pepper.

7. Dish the soup, garnish with the parsley and serve warm.

Nutrition: Calories 320 Fat 10 g Protein 10 g Carbohydrates 20 g

938. Pesto Pea Soup

Preparation Time: 10 minutes
Cooking Time: 20 minutes
Servings: 4
Ingredients:

- 2 cups water
- 8 ounces tortellini
- ¼ cup pesto
- 1 onion, small & finely chopped
- 1 pound peas, frozen
- 1 carrot, medium & finely chopped

- 1¾ cup vegetable broth, less sodium
- 1 celery rib, medium & finely chopped

Directions:
1. To start with, boil the water in a large pot over medium-high heat.
2. Next, stir in the tortellini to the pot and cook it following the packet's instructions.
3. In the meantime, cook the onion, celery, and carrot in a deep saucepan along with the water and broth.
4. Cook the celery-onion mixture for 6 minutes or until softened.
5. Now, spoon in the peas and allow it to simmer while keeping it uncovered.
6. Cook the peas for few minutes or until they are bright green and soft.
7. Then, spoon in the pesto to the pea's mixture. Combine well.
8. Pour the mixture into a high-speed blender and blend for 2 to 3 minutes or until you get a rich, smooth soup.
9. Return the soup to the pan. Spoon in the cooked tortellini.
10. Finally, pour into a serving bowl and top with more cooked peas if desired.

Tip: If desired, you can season it with Maldon salt at the end.
Nutrition: Calories 100 Fat 0 g Protein 0 g Carbohydrates 0 g

939. Tofu and Mushroom Soup

Preparation Time: 15 minutes
Cooking Time: 10 minutes
Servings: 4
Ingredients:
- 2 tablespoons olive oil
- 1 garlic clove, minced
- 1 large yellow onion, finely chopped
- 1 teaspoon freshly grated ginger
- 1 cup vegetable stock

- 2 small potatoes, peeled and chopped
- ¼ teaspoon salt
- ¼ teaspoon black pepper
- 2 (14-oz.) silken tofu, drained and rinsed
- 2/3 cup baby Bella mushrooms, sliced
- 1 tablespoon chopped fresh oregano
- 2 tablespoons chopped fresh parsley to garnish

Directions:
1. Heat the olive oil in a medium pot over medium heat and sauté the garlic, onion, and ginger until soft and fragrant.
2. Pour in the vegetable stock, potatoes, salt, and black pepper. Cook until the potatoes soften, 12 minutes.
3. Stir in the tofu and using an immersion blender, puree the ingredients until smooth.
4. Mix in the mushrooms and simmer with the pot covered until the mushrooms warm up while occasionally stirring to ensure that the tofu doesn't curdle, 7 minutes.
5. Stir oregano, and dish the soup.
6. Garnish with the parsley and serve warm.

Nutrition: Calories 310 Fat 10 g Protein 40.0 g Carbohydrates 0 g

940. Moroccan Vermicelli Vegetable Soup

Preparation Time: 5 minutes
Cooking Time: 35 minutes
Servings: 4 to 6
Ingredients:
- 1 tablespoon olive oil
- 1 small onion, chopped
- 1 large carrot, chopped
- 1 celery rib, chopped
- 3 small zucchinis, cut into ¼-inch dice
- 1 (28-oz.) can diced tomatoes, drained
- 2 tablespoons tomato paste

- 1½ cups cooked or 1 (15½-oz.) can chickpeas, drained and rinsed
- 2 teaspoons smoked paprika
- 1 teaspoon ground cumin
- 1 teaspoon za'atar spice (optional)
- ¼ teaspoon ground cayenne
- 6 cups vegetable broth, homemade (see light vegetable broth) or store-bought, or water
- Salt
- 4 ounces' vermicelli
- 2 tablespoons minced fresh cilantro, for garnish

Directions:
1. In a large soup pot, heat the oil over medium heat. Add the onion, carrot, and celery. Cover and cook until softened, about 5 minutes. Stir in the zucchini, tomatoes, tomato paste, chickpeas, paprika, cumin, za'atar, and cayenne.
2. Add the broth and salt to taste. Bring to a boil, then reduce heat to low and simmer, uncovered, until the vegetables are tender, about 30 minutes.
3. Shortly before serving, stir in the vermicelli and cook until the noodles are tender, about 5 minutes. Ladle the soup into bowls, garnish with cilantro, and serve.

Nutrition: Calories: 236 kcal Fat: 1.8g Carbs: 48.3g Protein: 7g

941. Moroccan Vegetable Stew

Preparation Time: 5 minutes
Cooking Time: 35 minutes
Servings: 4
Ingredients:
- 1 tablespoon olive oil
- 2 medium yellow onions, chopped
- 2 medium carrots, cut into ½-inch dice
- ½ teaspoon ground cumin
- ½ teaspoon ground cinnamon or allspice
- ½ teaspoon ground ginger

- ½ teaspoon sweet or smoked paprika
- ½ teaspoon saffron or turmeric
- 1 (14½ -oz.) can diced tomatoes, undrained
- 8 ounces green beans, trimmed and cut into 1 -inch pieces
- 2 cups peeled, seeded, and diced winter squash
- 1 large russet or another baking potato, peeled and cut into ½-inch dice
- 1½ cups vegetable broth
- 1½ cups cooked or 1 (15½ - oz.) can chickpeas, drained and rinsed
- ¾ cup frozen peas
- ½ cup pitted dried plums (prunes)
- 1 teaspoon lemon zest
- Salt and freshly ground black pepper
- ½ cup pitted green olives
- 1 tablespoon minced fresh cilantro or parsley, for garnish
- ½ cup toasted slivered almonds, for garnish

Directions:
1. In a large saucepan, heat the oil over medium heat. Add the onions and carrots, cover, and cook for 5 minutes. Stir in the cumin, cinnamon, ginger, paprika, and saffron. Cook, uncovered, stirring, for 30 seconds.
2. Add the tomatoes, green beans, squash, potato, and broth and bring to a boil. Reduce heat to low, cover, and simmer until the vegetables are tender, about 20 minutes.
3. Add the chickpeas, peas, dried plums, and lemon zest. Season with salt and pepper to taste. Stir in the olives and simmer, uncovered, until the flavors are blended, about 10 minutes. Sprinkle with cilantro and almonds and serve immediately.

Nutrition: Calories: 71 kcal Fat: 2.8g Carbs: 9.8g Protein: 3.7g

942. Avocado Cucumber Soup

Preparation Time: 20 minutes
Cooking Time: 0 minutes
Servings: 3
Ingredients:
- 1 large cucumber, peeled and sliced
- ¾ cup water
- ¼ cup lemon juice
- 2 garlic cloves
- 6 green onion
- 2 avocados, pitted
- ½ teaspoon black pepper
- ½ teaspoon pink salt

Directions:
1. Add all ingredients into the blender and blend until smooth and creamy.
2. Place in refrigerator for 30 minutes.
3. Stir well and serve chilled.

Nutrition: Calories: 127 kcal Fat: 6.6g Carbs: 13g Protein: 0.7g

943. Garden Vegetable Stew

Preparation Time: 5 minutes
Cooking Time: 60 minutes
Servings: 4
Ingredients:
- 2 tablespoons olive oil
- 1 medium red onion, chopped
- 1 medium carrot, cut into ¼-inch slices
- ½ cup dry white wine
- 2 medium new potatoes, unpeeled and cut into 1-inch pieces
- 1 medium red bell pepper, cut into ½-inch dice
- 1½ cups vegetable broth
- 1 tablespoon minced fresh savory or 1 teaspoon dried

Directions:
1. In a large saucepan, heat the oil over medium heat. Add the onion and carrot, cover, and cook until softened, 7 minutes. Add the wine and cook, uncovered, for 5 minutes. Stir in the potatoes, bell pepper, and broth and bring to a boil.

Reduce the heat to medium and simmer for 15 minutes.
2. Add the zucchini, yellow squash, and tomatoes. Season with salt and black pepper to taste, cover, and simmer until the vegetables are tender, 20 to 30 minutes. Stir in the corn, peas, basil, parsley, and savory. Taste, adjusting seasonings if necessary. Simmer to blend flavors, about 10 minutes more. Serve immediately.

Nutrition: Calories: 219 kcal Fat: 4.5g Carbs: 38.2g Protein: 6.4g

944. Lemon and Egg Pasta Soup

Preparation Time: 15 minutes
Cooking Time: 0 minutes
Servings: 2
Ingredients:
- 4 ounces ditalini pasta
- 4 cups fat-free and low-sodium chicken broth
- 2 large whole eggs
- ½ cup fresh lemon juice
- 4 tablespoons chopped fresh parsley
- 1 lemon, thinly sliced for garnish
- Salt and freshly ground pepper to taste

Directions:
1. Place a medium saucepan on medium-high heat. Add chicken broth to it and bring it to a boil, stirring it a couple of times.
2. Bring down the heat to low and allow the broth to simmer for about 5 minutes. Take the saucepan off the heat.
3. Take a bowl and add the eggs to it. Beat them well, add the lemon juice, and beat the eggs again
4. Use a ladle to transfer a single serving of the chicken broth into the egg bowl. Mix them well and then transfer the entire contents of the bowl into the saucepan.
5. Heat the soup while ensuring that the heat is still at a low. Keep an eye out on the eggs because they tend

to curdle and you need to prevent that from happening by gently stirring the soup.

6. Add salt and pepper to taste, if preferred.
7. Serve hot and garnish with lemon slices and parsley.

Nutrition: Calories: 161 Protein: 10 g Fat: 2 g Carbohydrate: 65 g

945. Roasted Vegetable Soup

Preparation Time: 15 minutes
Cooking Time: 20 minutes
Servings: 2
Ingredients:

- 1 tablespoon olive oil
- 5 garlic cloves, peeled
- 0.3-pound potatoes diced (1 cm thick)
- 2 yellow bell peppers, diced
- ½ teaspoons fresh rosemary, finely chopped
- 1 carrot, halved lengthwise and cut into 1 cm piece
- 1 red onion, in chunks
- 0.4 quarts carrot juice
- 0.3-pound Italian tomatoes, diced
- 1 teaspoon fresh tarragon
- Salt and pepper, to taste

Directions:

1. Preheat oven to 400°F.
2. In a baking tray place potatoes, peppers, garlic, carrot, onion, and tomatoes. Drizzle with olive oil and roast for 10-15 minutes.
3. In a saucepan add carrot juice, tarragon; let boil a little.
4. Add all roasted vegetables and stir well. Let it simmer for a few minutes.
5. Season with salt, pepper, and rosemary. Mix well.
6. Serve and enjoy.

Nutrition: Calories – 318, Fat – 97 g, Carbs – 60 g, Protein – 1.7 g

946. Mediterranean Tomato Soup

Preparation Time: 5 minutes
Cooking Time: 30 minutes
Servings: 2
Ingredients:

- 2 red bell peppers, unseeded, chopped
- 2 medium onions, chopped
- 2-3 garlic cloves, minced
- 7-8 tomatoes, chopped
- 0.4 quarts chicken broth
- Salt and pepper, to taste
- 3 tablespoons olive oil
- 1 tablespoon vinegar

Directions:

1. Heat oil in a saucepan and cook onion, garlic, and bell peppers for 5-6 minutes or until bell peppers are roasted well.
2. Add tomatoes, salt, pepper, and vinegar; stir fry for 4-5 minutes.
3. Add chicken broth and cover with lid. Let it cook for about 20 minutes on low heat.
4. When tomatoes are cooked well, puree the soup with the help of an electric beater.
5. Simmer for 1-2 minutes.
6. Add to a serving dish and top with desired herbs.
7. Serve and enjoy.

Nutrition: Calories – 318, Fat – 97 g, Carbs – 60 g, Protein – 1.7 g

947. Tomato and Cabbage Puree Soup

Preparation Time: 5 minutes
Cooking Time: 30 minutes
Servings: 2
Ingredients:

- 0.6 lb. tomatoes, chopped
- 3-4 garlic cloves, minced
- 0.2 lb. cabbage, chopped
- 4 tablespoons olive oil
- 1 red onion, chopped
- Salt and pepper, to taste
- Spice mix of choice
- 4 quarts of vegetable broth

Directions:

1. Heat oil in a saucepan and cook onion, garlic, and cabbage for about 4-5 minutes. Make sure that cabbage is nicely softened.
2. Add tomatoes and stir fry until liquid is reduced and tomatoes are dissolved.
3. Add salt, pepper, spice mix, and vegetable broth.
4. Cover the saucepan with a lid and let the mixture cook on low flame for about 30 minutes.
5. Puree the soup with the help of an electric beater.
6. Serve and enjoy.

Nutrition: Calories – 218, Fat – 15 g, Carbs – 220 g. Protein – 2 g

948. Athenian Avgolemono Sour Soup

Preparation Time: 20 minutes
Cooking Time: 50 minutes
Servings: 2
Ingredients:

- 8-cups water
- 1-pc whole chicken, cut into pieces
- Salt and pepper
- 1-cup whole grain rice
- 4-pcs eggs, separated
- 2-pcs lemons, juice
- ¼-cup fresh dill, minced
- Dill sprigs and lemon slices for garnish

Directions:

1. Pour the water into a large pot. Add the chicken pieces, and cover the pot. Simmer for an hour
2. Remove the cooked chicken pieces from the pot and take 2-cups of the chicken broth. Set aside and let it cool
3. Bring to a boil the remaining. Add salt and pepper to taste. Add the rice and cover the pot. Simmer for 20 minutes
4. Meanwhile, de-bone the cooked chicken and tear the flesh into small pieces. Set aside.
5. Work on the separated egg whites and yolks: whisk the egg whites until stiff; whisk the yolks with the lemon juice.
6. Pour the egg yolk mixture into the egg white mixture. Whisk well until fully combined.
7. Add gradually the reserved 2-cups of chicken broth to the mixture, whisking constantly to prevent the eggs from curdling.
8. After fully incorporating the egg mixture and chicken

broth, pour this mixture into the simmering broth and rice. Add the dill, and stir well. Simmer further without bringing it to a boil.

9. Add the chicken pieces to the soup. Mix until fully combined.

10. To serve, ladle the soup in bowls and sprinkle with fresh ground pepper. Garnish with lemon slices and dill sprigs.

Nutrition: Calories: 122.4, Fats: 1.2g, Dietary Fiber: 0.2g, Carbohydrates: 7.5g, Protein: 13.7g

949. Italian Bean Soup

Preparation Time: 15 minutes
Cooking Time: 15 minutes
Servings: 2
Ingredients:

- 1 tablespoon virgin olive oil
- 1 onion (diced)
- 2 garlic cloves (minced)
- 2 cups tomato sauce (homemade or 1 can of low-sodium organic canned tomato sauce)
- 3 cups cooked cannellini beans (or about 24 ounces of canned beans that have been drained and rinsed)
- 1 tablespoon basil (dried)
- ½ teaspoon oregano
- ¼ teaspoon black pepper

Directions:

1. Take a large soup or stockpot and place it on your stove. Turn the heat all the way up to medium-high and pour in the virgin olive oil.

2. Allow the oil to heat slightly before adding your diced onions to the pot. Sautee for 3 minutes and then adds the garlic. Let the flavors come together for 2 minutes.

3. Add the cannellini beans, basil, oregano, and black pepper to the pot. Stir everything together then pour over the tomato sauce.

4. Allow the sauce to come to a steady simmer. Reduce the heat to medium-low. Cover

your pot so the flavors can simmer together for 5 minutes.

5. Uncover the pot and allow the aroma to fill your kitchen. Then, take a ladle and fill your soup bowls! Grab a soup spoon and enjoy

Nutrition: Calories – 164, Carbs - 25.6 g, Protein - 8.1 g, Fat - 3.8 g

950. Red Soup, Seville Style

Preparation Time: 15 minutes
Cooking Time: 15 minutes
Servings: 2
Ingredients:

- 2 ounces stale bread, crusts removed
- 3 tablespoons further virgin olive oil
- 3 tablespoons fortified wine vinegar
- 2 garlic cloves, crushed
- 2 teaspoon salt
- Teaspoon cayenne pepper pinch of cumin
- Little red onion, chopped
- Pound ripe tomatoes, peeled, seeded, and chopped
- Cucumber, peeled, seeded, and chopped
- Red peppers, cored, seeded, and chopped
- Cups ice water

For the garnish:

- 4 tablespoons red peppers, cored, seeded, and finely chopped
- 4 tablespoons finely cut cucumber
- 4 tablespoons finely cut purple onion
- 2 tablespoons finely cut contemporary mint leaves

Directions:

1. First of all, you should Soak the bread into the water and after that squeeze dry.

2. Place in a blender or kitchen appliance

3. With the vegetable oil, vinegar, garlic, salt, and spices and method to a sleek cream.

4. Add the onion, tomatoes, cucumber, and peppers and

½ the drinking water and still method the vegetables till sleek.

5. Pour into a soup serving dish and add the remaining water.

6. Chill totally before serving. Place the garnishes in little dishes and serve with the soup.

Nutrition: Calories: 123, Fats: 3g, Dietary Fiber: 5g, Carbohydrates: 19g, Protein: 5g

951. Garlic Soup

Preparation Time: 15 minutes
Cooking Time: 0 minutes
Servings: 2
Ingredients:

- 5 cups water
- head garlic, unpeeled
- sprigs fresh thyme
- tablespoons further virgin olive oil
- Salt
- freshly ground black pepper
- 2 egg yolks
- Slices of bread, gently toasted

Directions:

1. Bring the water to boil with the garlic and thyme and simmer for twenty minutes.

2. Take away the garlic and peel. Place the flesh in an exceedingly bowl and mash with a fork.

3. Step by step add the vegetable oil and blend well. Return to the soup.

4. Take away the thyme and after that, you should Season it with salt & black pepper.

5. Beat the egg yolks in another bowl and step by step add a ladleful of the soup.

6. Combine well and stir into the soup. Simmer for some minutes, however, don't let it boil or the soup can curdle.

7. Place the slices of toasts in individual bowls and pour over the soup. Serve at once.

Nutrition: Calories: 123, Fats: 3g, Dietary Fiber: 5g, Carbohydrates: 19g, Protein: 5g

952. Dalmatian Cabbage, Potato, And Pea Soup

Preparation Time: 15 minutes
Cooking Time: 15 minutes
Servings: 2
Ingredients:

- 4 tablespoons further virgin olive oil
- Medium onion, chopped
- Carrots, coarsely grated
- Medium potatoes, peeled and diced into little items inexperienced cabbage, shredded
- Cup contemporary shelled peas or frozen petit pois
- Quart water
- Salt
- Freshly ground black pepper

Directions:

1. Heat the vegetable oil in an exceedingly massive pot and cook the onion over moderate heat for three minutes.
2. Add the carrots, potatoes, and cabbage and still cook for an additional five minutes.
3. Add the peas and water and produce to a boil.
4. Cowl and simmer for thirty-five to forty minutes or till the vegetables are tender and also the soup is fairly thick.
5. Finally, you must season it with salt & black pepper and serve hot.

Nutrition: Calories: 123, Fats: 3g, Dietary Fiber: 5g, Carbohydrates: 19g, Protein: 5g

953. Green Creamy Soup

Preparation Time: 10 minutes
Cooking Time: 30 minutes
Servings: 2
Ingredients:

- 5 ounces fresh green beans, thinly sliced
- 8 ounces fresh Brussels sprouts, sliced
- 5 cups low-sodium, fat-free vegetable broth
- 1½ cups frozen peas, defrosted

- 4 tablespoons olive oil
- 1 white onion, chopped
- 1 tablespoon freshly squeezed lemon juice
- 4 cloves fresh garlic, minced
- 1 large leek, slice both white parts and sliced green parts thinly but keep them separate
- 1 teaspoon ground coriander
- 1 cup low-fat milk
- Salt and freshly ground pepper to taste
- Croutons for garnish

Directions:

1. Take out a large skillet and place it over low heat. Add the olive oil and allow the oil to heat up slightly.
2. Add onion and garlic. Cook them until they turn fragrant and soft. Make sure that you do not allow them to turn brown.
3. Add the green parts of the Brussels sprouts, leek, and green beans to the skillet. Add the broth and mix the ingredients well. Bring the broth to a boil. When it starts boiling, lower the heat and let simmer for about 12 minutes.
4. Add lemon juice, peas, and coriander. Let the broth continue to simmer for another 10 minutes, or until the vegetables become tender.
5. Remove the broth mixture from heat and allow it to cool slightly. Transfer the mixture to a blender and pulse until they turn smooth.
6. Take out a saucepan and add the white parts of the leek. Add the blended mixture into the saucepan. Place the saucepan over medium-high heat and allow the soup to boil. Reduce the heat to low and allow the soup to simmer for about 5 minutes
7. Take out another bowl and add flour and milk. Whisk

them until they turn smooth.
8. Add salt and pepper to taste, if preferred.

Nutrition: Calories: 163 calories Protein: 4 g Fat: 8 g Carbohydrate: 15 g

954. Orzo and Lemon Chicken Soup

Preparation Time: 10 minutes
Cooking Time: 40 minutes
Servings: 2
Ingredients:

- 12 ounces skinless, boneless chicken breasts
- 1 tablespoon olive oil
- ½ cup chopped celery
- ½ cup chopped white onion
- 6 cups low-sodium, fat-free chicken broth
- ½ cup sliced carrot
- ½ cup orzo
- ¼ cup chopped fresh dill
- Salt and freshly ground pepper to taste
- Lemon halves

Directions:

1. Take out a large pot and place it over medium heat. Add olive oil to it and allow it to heat.
2. Add celery and onion. Cook them until the onions are fragrant and the celery is soft.
3. Add chicken, chicken broth, and carrot to the mixture. Add salt and pepper to taste, if preferred.
4. Increase the temperature to medium-high heat and allow the broth to boil. When it starts boiling, reduce heat and allow the soup to simmer for about 20 minutes, or until the chicken is cooked.
5. Take out the chicken from the pot, transfer it to a bowl and allow it to cool. Cover the pot so that the ingredients inside are simmering. When the chicken is sufficiently cool, shred the chicken into small pieces.

6. Open the cover of the pot and add orzo. Increase the heat to medium-high and allow the broth to boil for about 8 minutes. Make sure that the cover is back on the pot during the boiling process.

7. Remove pot from heat and add dill and the shredded chicken broth.

8. Squeeze lemon juice into the broth. Serve immediately.

Nutrition: Calories: 248 calories Protein: 25 g Fat: 4 g Carbohydrate: 23 g

955. Chilled Avocado Soup

Preparation Time: 50 minutes
Cooking Time: 0 minutes
Servings: 2
Ingredients:

- 3 medium ripe avocados, halved, seeded, peeled, and cut into chunks
- 2 cloves fresh garlic, minced
- 2 cups low-sodium, fat-free chicken broth, divided
- ½ cucumber, peeled and chopped
- ½ cup chopped white onion
- ¼ cup finely diced carrot
- Thin avocado slices for garnish
- Paprika to sprinkle
- Salt and freshly ground pepper to taste
- Hot red pepper sauce to taste

Directions:

1. Place 6 bowls into the freezer and allow them to chill for half an hour.

2. In the meantime, take out your blender and add garlic, cucumber, avocados, onion, carrot, and 1 cup broth. Blend all the ingredients together until they turn smooth.

3. Add the remaining broth. Add the salt and pepper and hot sauce to taste, if preferred.

4. Blend all the ingredients again until they are smooth.

5. Take out the chilled bowls and pour the blended ingredients into them.

6. This time, place the bowls in the refrigerator for another 1 hour.

7. When you are ready to serve, top the soup with paprika and slices of avocado.

8. Serve chilled.

Nutrition: Calories: 255 calories Protein: 4 g Fat: 22 g Carbohydrate: 15 g

956. Broccoli and Potato Soup

Preparation Time: 10 minutes
Cooking Time: 25 minutes
Servings: 2
Ingredients:

- 2 cups escarole leaves, rinsed and drained
- 3 tablespoons all-purpose flour
- 3 cups fresh broccoli florets
- 3 scallions, sliced
- 2 cups smoked Gouda cheese, shredded and more for garnish
- 2 cups low-sodium, fat-free chicken broth
- 1 cup almond milk
- 3 medium red-gold potatoes, chopped
- 2 cloves fresh garlic, minced
- Salt and freshly ground pepper to taste

Directions:

1. Take out a large pot and place it over medium-high heat. Add potatoes, garlic, and chicken broth. Bring the mixture to a boil and reduce the heat to low. Allow the mixture to simmer for a while until you notice the potatoes begin to soften

2. Use a fork and mash the potatoes slightly.

3. Add broccoli, milk, and scallions. Continue to heat to a simmer until broccoli turns tender and crispy.

4. Bring down the heat to low and then add the Gouda cheese. Continue stirring

until the sauce thickens and the cheese melts.

5. Add salt and pepper for seasoning, if preferred. Serve the soup in 4 equal portions.

6. Add additional cheese and escarole as toppings.

Nutrition: Calories: 350 calories Protein: 17 g Fat: 14 g Carbohydrate: 42 g

957. Tortellini and Vegetable Soup

Preparation Time: 10 minutes
Cooking Time: 30 minutes
Servings: 2
Ingredients:

- 32 ounces low-sodium, fat-free chicken broth
- 3 cups fresh chicken-filled tortellini
- 1 large white onion, chopped
- 4 cloves fresh garlic, chopped
- 3 celery stalks, chopped
- 1 teaspoon minced chives
- 2 (14½ -oz.) cans diced tomatoes, undrained
- 2 tablespoons olive oil
- 1 teaspoon dried sweet basil
- 1 cup frozen corn
- 1 teaspoon dried thyme
- 1 cup chopped carrot
- 1 cup frozen cut green beans
- 1 cup diced raw potato

Directions:

1. Take out a large pot and place it over medium heat. Add garlic, onion, celery, and olive oil. Sauté until you notice the onion and garlic become fragrant and soft.

2. Add potato, basil, carrot, beans, broth, thyme, corn, and chives. Increase the heat to medium-high and then bring the broth to a boil.

3. When it starts boiling, reduce the heat and cover the pot. Allow the mixture to simmer for about 15 minutes, or until the vegetables become tender.

4. Add tortellini and tomatoes. Remove the cover and allow the soup to simmer

uncovered for about 5 minutes.

5. Serve hot.

Nutrition: Calories: 213 calories Protein: 7 g Fat: 7 g Carbohydrate: 26 g

958. Traditional Oyster Soup

Preparation Time: 5 minutes
Cooking Time: 30 minutes
Servings: 2
Ingredients:

- 2 pints (about 32-oz.) freshly shucked oysters, undrained
- 4 tablespoons olive oil
- 1 cup finely chopped celery
- 3 (12-oz.) cans of low-fat evaporated milk
- 6 tablespoons minced shallots
- 2 pinches of cayenne pepper (add more if you like more spice)
- Toasted bread squares
- Salt and freshly ground pepper to taste

Directions:

1. Start with the oysters. Drain the liquid from them in a small bowl. Set the liquid aside since we are going to use it. Place the oysters separately.
2. Run the liquid through a strainer to remove any solid materials.
3. Take out a large pot and place it over medium heat. Add olive oil into it. Toss in oysters, celery, and shallots.
4. Allow the ingredients to simmer for about 5 minutes, or until you notice the edges of the oysters begin to curl.
5. Take a separate pot (or pan) and then heat the oyster liquid and milk. When the mixture is sufficiently warm, then pour it over the oysters. Stir all the ingredients together.
6. Add salt and pepper, and cayenne pepper to taste.
7. Serve soup warm with toasted bread squares as toppings or on the side.

Nutrition: Calories: 311 calories Protein: 23 g Fat: 11 g Carbohydrate: 22 g

959. Eggplant Soup

Preparation Time: 10 minutes
Cooking Time: 30 minutes
Servings: 2
Ingredients:

- 3 tablespoons olive oil
- 1 (14-oz.) can low-sodium tomato and basil pasta sauce
- ½ cup chopped white onion
- 2 tablespoons Italian bread crumbs
- 2 cloves fresh garlic, minced
- 2 cups low sodium, fat-free chicken broth
- ½ cup shredded reduced-fat mozzarella cheese
- 1 small eggplant, halved and sliced thinly (about 2 cups)
- 2 tablespoons freshly grated parmesan cheese for garnish

Directions:

1. Preheat the oven to 500°F. We are aiming for a broiling temperature. An oven's broiling temperature is anywhere from 500°F to 550°F.
2. If you feel that you want to increase the temperature, feel free to do so when you place the dish in the oven.
3. Take out a nonstick pan and place it over medium heat. Add olive oil into the pan and allow it to heat. Add the eggplant and cook for about 5 minutes, stirring occasionally.
4. Add garlic and onion and continue cooking until you notice the eggplant turn into a golden-brown color.
5. Add broth and sauce. Increase the heat to medium-high and then allow the mixture to boil.
6. When it starts boiling, lower the heat to a simmer. Continue to cook until the soup thickens.
7. Take out a baking tray and line it with tin foil. Use 2 oven-safe crock bowls and place them on the tray. Split the soup into equal portions and pour them into the bowls.
8. Top with bread crumbs, mozzarella cheese, and a sprinkling of parmesan cheese.
9. Allow the dish to broil for about 2 to 3 minutes, or until cheese has melted and turned golden.
10. Serve hot.

Nutrition: Calories: 274 calories Protein: 9 g Fat: 17 g Carbohydrate: 23 g

960. Tortellini and Spinach Soup

Preparation Time: 5 minutes
Cooking Time: 20 minutes
Servings: 2
Ingredients:

- 4 cups low-sodium, fat-free chicken broth
- ¼ teaspoon ground pepper
- 2 cups coarsely chopped fresh spinach leaves
- 4 scallions, chopped
- 5 ounces fresh cheese-filled tortellini
- 2 cloves fresh garlic, minced
- Freshly grated parmesan cheese

Directions:

1. Take a large pot and place it on medium heat. Add broth and stir for half a minute. Add garlic, scallions, and pepper and increase the heat to medium-high.
2. Allow the broth to boil and when it starts boiling, bring the heat back to medium.
3. Add the tortellini and cook for 10 minutes. Toss in the spinach and cook for an additional 5 minutes, or until the pasta becomes tender.
4. Transfer the soup equally to 4 bowls. Top it with parmesan cheese, if preferred.

Nutrition: Calories: 97 calories Protein: 6 g Fat: 4 g Carbohydrate: 14 g

961. Spicy Vegetable Soup

Preparation Time: 10 minutes
Cooking Time: 20 minutes
Servings: 2
Ingredients:

- 1 (14-oz.) can fiery roasted diced tomatoes, undrained
- 4 cups fresh cauliflower florets

- 1 cup frozen baby peas
- 2 teaspoons curry powder
- ½ teaspoon cumin
- 1 tablespoon finely chopped Serrano chili pepper
- 1 cup frozen corn
- Cooked couscous
- 2 cloves fresh garlic, finely minced
- 1 (15-oz.) can chickpeas, drained
- ¾ cup solid packed canned pumpkin mash
- ¾ cup water
- Salt and freshly ground pepper to taste

Directions:

1. Take a pot and place it over medium-high heat. Cover it partially with water and add the cauliflower florets into it.
2. Bring the water to a boil and then place the cover on the pot. Allow the florets to steam until they are tender.
3. Remove the pot from the heat and drain the florets well. Cut them into small pieces and set aside.
4. Take out a non-stick skillet and place it over medium heat. In a large, non-stick skillet over medium heat, add cumin and curry powder until fragrant. Add chili pepper, garlic, pumpkin, tomatoes with juices, chickpeas, and water.
5. Allow the ingredients to reach a boil and then lower the heat. Let them simmer for about a minute before you add the salt and pepper to taste, if you prefer. Keep the ingredients simmering for another 15 minutes.
6. Add the corn and peas and let the ingredients simmer for another 5 minutes.
7. Remove from the heat and serve the soup separately with couscous or serve it over the couscous. You can also make use of brown rice instead of couscous.

Nutrition: Calories: 228 calories Protein: 12 g Fat: 2 g Carbohydrate: 43 g

962. Cheesy Keto Zucchini Soup

Preparation Time: 15 minutes
Cooking Time: 20 minutes
Servings: 2
Ingredients:

- ½ medium onion, peeled and chopped
- 1 cup bone broth
- 1 tablespoon coconut oil
- 1½ zucchinis, cut into chunks
- ½ tablespoon nutrition al yeast
- Dash of black pepper
- ½ tablespoon parsley, chopped, for garnish
- ½ tablespoon coconut cream, for garnish

Directions:

1. Melt the coconut oil in a large pan over medium heat and add onions. Sauté for about 3 minutes and add zucchinis and bone broth.
2. Reduce the heat to simmer for about 15 minutes and cover the pan. Add nutritional yeast and transfer to an immersion blender.
3. Blend until smooth and season with black pepper. Top with coconut cream and parsley to serve.

Nutrition: Calories: 154 Carbs: 8.9g Fats: 8.1g Proteins: 13.4g

963. Spring Soup with Poached Egg

Preparation Time: 15 minutes
Cooking Time: 10 minutes
Servings: 2
Ingredients:

- 32 ounces vegetable broth
- 2 eggs
- 1 head romaine lettuce, chopped
- Salt, to taste

Directions:

1. Bring the vegetable broth to a boil and reduce the heat. Poach the eggs for 5 minutes in the broth and remove them into 2 bowls.
2. Stir in romaine lettuce into the broth and cook for 4 minutes. Dish out in a bowl and serve hot.

Nutrition: Calories: 158 Carbs: 6.9g Fats: 7.3g Proteins: 15.4g

964. Mint Avocado Chilled Soup

Preparation Time: 15 minutes
Cooking Time: 0 minutes
Servings: 2
Ingredients:

- 2 romaine lettuce leaves
- 1 Tablespoon lime juice
- 1 medium ripe avocado
- 1 cup coconut milk, chilled
- 20 fresh mint leaves
- Salt to taste

Directions:

1. Put all the ingredients in a blender and blend until smooth. Refrigerate for about 10 minutes and serve chilled.

Nutrition: Calories: 432 Carbs: 16.1g Fats: 42.2g Proteins: 5.2g

965. Easy Butternut Squash Soup

Preparation Time: 15 minutes
Cooking Time: 1 hour & 35 minutes
Servings: 4
Ingredients:

- 1 small onion, chopped
- 4 cups chicken broth
- 1 butternut squash
- 3 tablespoons coconut oil
- Salt, to taste
- Nutmeg and pepper, to taste

Directions:

1. Put oil and onions in a large pot and add onions. Sauté for about 3 minutes and add chicken broth and butternut squash.
2. Simmer for about 1 hour on medium heat and transfer into an immersion blender. Pulse until smooth and season with salt, pepper and nutmeg.
3. Return to the pot and cook for about 30 minutes. Dish out and serve hot.

Nutrition: Calories: 149 Carbs: 6.6g Fats: 11.6g Proteins: 5.4g

966. Cauliflower, Leek & Bacon Soup

Preparation Time: 15 minutes
Cooking Time: 1 hour & 31 minutes
Servings: 4
Ingredients:

- 4 cups chicken broth
- ½ cauliflower head, chopped
- 1 leek, chopped
- Salt and black pepper, to taste
- 5 bacon strips

Directions:

1 Put the cauliflower, leek and chicken broth into the pot and cook for about 1 hour on medium heat. Transfer into an immersion blender and pulse until smooth.

2 Return the soup into the pot and microwave the bacon strips for 1 minute. Cut the bacon into small pieces and put into the soup.

3 Cook on for about 30 minutes on low heat. Season with salt and pepper and serve.

Nutrition: Calories: 185 Carbs: 5.8g Fats: 12.7g Proteins: 10.8g

967. Swiss Chard Egg Drop Soup

Preparation Time: 15 minutes
Cooking Time: 10 minutes
Servings: 4
Ingredients:

- 3 cups bone broth
- 2 eggs, whisked
- 1 teaspoon ground oregano
- 3 tablespoons butter
- 2 cups Swiss chard, chopped
- 2 tablespoons coconut aminos
- 1 teaspoon ginger, grated
- Salt and black pepper, to taste

Directions:

1 Heat the bone broth in a saucepan and add whisked eggs while stirring slowly. Add the swiss chard, butter, coconut aminos, ginger,

oregano, and salt and black pepper. Cook for about 10 minutes and serve hot.

Nutrition: Calories: 185 Carbs: 2.9g Fats: 11g Proteins: 18.3g

968. Mushroom Spinach Soup

Preparation Time: 15 minutes
Cooking Time: 10 minutes
Servings: 4
Ingredients:

- 1 cup spinach, cleaned and chopped
- 100 g mushrooms, chopped
- 1 onion
- 6 garlic cloves
- ½ teaspoon red chili powder
- Salt and black pepper, to taste
- 3 tablespoons buttermilk
- 1 teaspoon almond flour
- 2 cups chicken broth
- 3 tablespoons butter
- ¼ cup fresh cream for garnish

Directions:

1 Heat butter in a pan and add onions and garlic. Sauté for about 3 minutes and add spinach, salt and red chili powder.

2 Sauté for about 4 minutes and add mushrooms. Transfer into a blender and blend to make a puree. Return to the pan and add buttermilk and almond flour for a creamy texture.

3 Mix well and simmer for about 2 minutes. Garnish with fresh cream and serve hot.

Nutrition: Calories: 160 Carbs: 7g Fats: 13.3g Proteins: 4.7g

969. Delicate Squash Soup

Preparation Time: 15 minutes
Cooking Time: 27 minutes
Servings: 5
Ingredients:

- 1½ cups beef bone broth
- 1 small onion, peeled and grated.
- ½ teaspoon sea salt
- ¼ teaspoon poultry seasoning

- 2 small Delicata Squash, chopped
- 2 garlic cloves, minced
- 2 tablespoons olive oil
- ¼ teaspoon black pepper
- 1 small lemon, juiced
- 5 tablespoons sour cream

Directions:

1 Put Delicata Squash and water in a medium pan and bring to a boil. Reduce the heat and cook for about 20 minutes. Drain and set aside.

2 Put olive oil, onions, garlic and poultry seasoning in a small saucepan. Cook for about 2 minutes and add broth. Allow it to simmer for 5 minutes and remove from heat.

3 Whisk in the lemon juice and transfer the mixture to a blender. Pulse until smooth and top with sour cream.

Nutrition: Calories: 109 Carbs: 4.9g Fats: 8.5g Proteins: 3g

970. Broccoli Soup

Preparation Time: 15 minutes
Cooking Time: 37 minutes
Servings: 6
Ingredients:

- 3 tablespoons ghee
- 5 garlic cloves
- 1 teaspoon sage
- ¼ teaspoon ginger
- 2 cups broccoli
- 1 small onion
- 1 teaspoon oregano
- ½ teaspoon parsley
- Salt and black pepper, to taste
- 6 cups vegetable broth
- 4 tablespoons butter

Directions:

1 Put ghee, onions, spices and garlic in a pot and cook for 3 minutes. Add broccoli and cook for about 4 minutes. Add vegetable broth, cover and allow it to simmer for about 30 minutes.

2 Transfer into a blender and blend until smooth. Add the

butter to give it a creamy delicious texture and flavor

Nutrition: Calories: 183 Carbs: 5.2g Fats: 15.6g Proteins: 6.1g

971. Apple Pumpkin Soup

Preparation Time: 15 minutes
Cooking Time: 39 minutes
Servings: 8
Ingredients:

- 1 apple, chopped
- 1 whole kabocha pumpkin, peeled, seeded and cubed
- 1 cup almond flour
- ¼ cup ghee
- 1 pinch cardamom powder
- 2 quarts water
- ¼ cup coconut cream
- 1 pinch ground black pepper

Directions:

1. Heat ghee in the bottom of a heavy pot and add apples. Cook for about 5 minutes on a medium flame and add pumpkin.
2. Sauté for about 3 minutes and add the almond flour. Sauté for about 1 minute and add water. Lower the flame and cook for about 30 minutes.
3. Transfer the soup into an immersion blender and blend until smooth. Top with coconut cream and serve.

Nutrition: Calories: 186 Carbs: 10.4g Fats: 14.9g Proteins: 3.7g

972. Keto French Onion Soup

Preparation Time: 15 minutes
Cooking Time: 335 minutes
Servings: 6
Ingredients:

- 5 tablespoons butter
- 500 g brown onion medium
- 4 drops liquid stevia
- 4 tablespoons olive oil
- 3 cups beef stock

Directions:

1. Put the butter and olive oil in a large pot over medium-low heat and add onions and salt. Cook for about 5 minutes and stir in stevia.
2. Cook for another 5 minutes and add beef stock. Reduce the heat to low and simmer for about 25 minutes. Dish

out into soup bowls and serve hot.

Nutrition: Calories: 198 Carbs: 6g Fats: 20.6g Proteins: 2.9g

973. Cauliflower and Thyme Soup

Preparation Time: 15 minutes
Cooking Time: 13 minutes
Servings: 6
Ingredients:

- 2 teaspoons thyme powder
- 1 head cauliflower
- 3 cups vegetable stock
- ½ teaspoon matcha green tea powder
- 3 tablespoons olive oil
- Salt and black pepper, to taste
- 5 garlic cloves, chopped

Directions:

1. Put the vegetable stock, thyme and matcha powder to a large pot over medium-high heat and bring to a boil. Add cauliflower and cook for about 10 minutes.
2. Meanwhile, put the olive oil and garlic in a small saucepan and cook for about 1 minute. Add the garlic, salt and black pepper and cook for about 2 minutes.
3. Transfer into an immersion blender and blend until smooth. Dish out and serve immediately.

Nutrition: Calories: 79 Carbs: 3.8g Fats: 7.1g Proteins: 1.3g

974. Homemade Thai Chicken Soup

Preparation Time: 15 minutes
Cooking Time: 8 hours
Servings: 12
Ingredients:

- 1 lemongrass stalk, cut into large chunks
- 5 thick slices of fresh ginger
- 1 whole chicken
- 20 fresh basil leaves
- 1 lime, juiced
- 1 tablespoon salt

Directions:

1. Place the chicken, 10 basil leaves, lemongrass, ginger, salt and water into the slow cooker. Cook for about 8 hours on low and dish out

into a bowl. Stir in fresh lime juice and basil leaves to serve.

Nutrition: Calories: 255 Carbs: 1.2g Fats: 17.6g Proteins: 25.2g

975. Chicken Kale Soup

Preparation Time: 15 minutes
Cooking Time: 6 hours & 15 minutes
Servings: 6
Ingredients:

- 2 pounds chicken breast, skinless
- ⅓ cup onion
- 1 tablespoon olive oil
- 14 ounces chicken bone broth
- ½ cup olive oil
- 4 cups chicken stock
- ¼ cup lemon juice
- 5 ounces baby kale leaves
- Salt, to taste

Directions:

1. Season chicken with salt and black pepper. Heat olive oil over medium heat in a large skillet and add seasoned chicken.
2. Reduce the temperature and cook for about 15 minutes. Shred the chicken and place in the crockpot. Process the chicken broth and onions in a blender and blend until smooth.
3. Pour into crockpot and stir in the remaining ingredients. Cook on low for about 6 hours, stirring once while cooking.

Nutrition: Calories: 261 Carbs: 2g Fats: 21g Proteins: 14.1g

976. Chicken Veggie Soup

Preparation Time: 15 minutes
Cooking Time: 1 hour & 30 minutes
Servings: 6
Ingredients:

- 5 chicken thighs
- 12 cups water
- 1 tablespoon adobo seasoning
- 4 celery ribs
- 1 yellow onion

- 1½ teaspoons whole black peppercorns
- 6 sprigs fresh parsley
- 2 teaspoons coarse sea salt
- 2 carrots
- 6 mushrooms, sliced
- 2 garlic cloves
- 1 bay leaf
- 3 sprigs fresh thyme

Directions:

1. Put water, chicken thighs, carrots, celery ribs, onion, garlic cloves and herbs in a large pot. Bring to a boil and reduce the heat to low.
2. Cover the pot and simmer for about 30 minutes. Dish out the chicken and shred it, removing the bones. Put the bones back into the pot and simmer for about 20 minutes.
3. Strain the broth, discarding the chunks, and put the liquid back into the pot. Bring it to a boil and simmer for about 30 minutes.
4. Put the mushrooms in the broth and simmer for about 10 minutes. Dish out to serve hot.

Nutrition: Calories: 250 Carbs: 6.4g Fats: 8.9g Proteins: 35.1g

977. Chicken Mulligatawny Soup

Preparation Time: 15 minutes
Cooking Time: 0 minutes
Servings: 10
Ingredients:

- 1½ tablespoons curry powder
- 3 cups celery root, diced
- 2 tablespoons Swerve
- 10 cups chicken broth
- 5 cups chicken, chopped and cooked
- ¼ cup apple cider
- ½ cup sour cream
- ¼ cup fresh parsley, chopped
- 2 tablespoons butter
- Salt and black pepper, to taste

Directions:

1. Combine the broth, butter, chicken, curry powder, celery root and apple cider in a large soup pot. Bring to a boil and simmer for about 30 minutes.
2. Stir in Swerve, sour cream, fresh parsley, salt and black pepper. Dish out and serve hot.

Nutrition: Calories: 215 Carbs: 7.1g Fats: 8.5g Proteins: 26.4g

978. Buffalo Ranch Chicken Soup

Preparation Time: 15 minutes
Cooking Time: 0 minutes
Servings: 4
Ingredients:

- 2 tablespoons parsley
- 2 celery stalks, chopped
- 6 tablespoons butter
- 1 cup heavy whipping cream
- 4 cups chicken, cooked and shredded
- 4 tablespoons ranch dressing
- ¼ cup yellow onions, chopped
- 8 ounces cream cheese
- 8 cups chicken broth
- 7 hearty bacon slices, crumbled

Directions:

1. Heat butter in a pan and add chicken. Cook for about 5 minutes and add 1½ cups water. Cover and cook for about 10 minutes.
2. Put the chicken and rest of the ingredients into the saucepan except parsley and cook for about 10 minutes. Top with parsley and serve hot.

Nutrition: Calories: 444 Carbs: 4g Fats: 34g Proteins: 28g

979. Traditional Chicken Soup

Preparation Time: 15 minutes
Cooking Time: 0 minutes
Servings: 6
Ingredients:

- 3 pounds chicken
- 4 quarts water
- 4 stalks celery
- ⅓ large red onion

- 1 large carrot
- 3 garlic cloves
- 2 thyme sprigs
- 2 rosemary sprigs
- Salt and black pepper, to taste

Directions:

1. Put water and chicken in the stockpot on medium-high heat. Bring to a boil and allow it to simmer for about 10 minutes.
2. Add onion, garlic, celery, salt and pepper and simmer on medium-low heat for 30 minutes. Add thyme and carrots and simmer on low for another 30 minutes.
3. Dish out the chicken and shred the pieces, removing the bones. Return the chicken pieces to the pot and add rosemary sprigs. Simmer for about 20 minutes at low heat and dish out to serve.

Nutrition: Calories: 357 Carbs: 3.3g Fats: 7g Proteins: 66.2g

980. Chicken Noodle Soup

Preparation Time: 15 minutes
Cooking Time: 0 minutes
Servings: 6
Ingredients:

- 1 onion, minced
- 1 rib celery, sliced
- 3 cups chicken, shredded
- 3 eggs, lightly beaten
- 1 green onion, for garnish
- 2 tablespoons coconut oil
- 1 carrot, peeled and thinly sliced
- 2 teaspoons dried thyme
- 2½ quarts homemade bone broth
- ¼ cup fresh parsley, minced
- Salt and black pepper, to taste

Directions:

1. Heat coconut oil over medium-high heat in a large pot and add onions, carrots, and celery. Cook for about 4 minutes and stir in the bone broth, thyme and chicken.
2. Simmer for about 15 minutes and stir in parsley. Pour beaten eggs into the

soup in a slow steady stream.

3   Remove soup from heat and let it stand for about 2 minutes. Season with salt and black pepper and dish out to serve.

Nutrition: Calories: 226 Carbs: 3.5g Fats: 8.9g Proteins: 31.8g

981.   Chicken Cabbage Soup
Preparation Time: 15 minutes
Cooking Time: 26 minutes
Servings: 8
Ingredients:

- 2 celery stalks
- 2 garlic cloves, minced
- 4 ounces butter
- 6 ounces mushrooms, sliced
- 2 tablespoons onions, dried and minced
- 1 teaspoon salt
- 8 cups chicken broth
- 1 medium carrot
- 2 cups green cabbage, sliced into strips
- 2 teaspoons dried parsley
- ¼ teaspoon black pepper
- 1½ rotisserie chickens, shredded

Directions:

1   Melt butter in a large pot and add celery, mushrooms, onions and garlic into the pot. Cook for about 4 minutes and add broth, parsley, carrot, salt and black pepper.

2   Simmer for about 10 minutes and add cooked chicken and cabbage. Simmer for an additional 12 minutes until the cabbage is tender. Dish out and serve hot.

Nutrition: Calories: 184 Carbs: 4.2g Fats: 13.1g Proteins: 12.6g

982.   Carrot and Red Lentil Soup
Preparation Time: 5 minutes
Cooking Time: 20-30 minutes
Servings: 2
Ingredients:

- 2 onions, minced
- 2 tablespoons dried parsley flakes
- 2 teaspoons ground allspice
- 2 teaspoons ground cumin
- 2 teaspoons ground turmeric

- 1-½ teaspoon salt & 1 teaspoon garlic powder
- 1 teaspoon ground cardamom
- 1 teaspoon ground cinnamon
- 1 teaspoon pepper
- 0.6 lb. Dried red lentils
- 1 medium carrot, finely chopped
- 1 celery rib, finely chopped
- 1 tablespoon olive oil
- 4 quarts of vegetable broth

Directions:

1   In a saucepan add olive oil, onion, carrots, and salt; cook for a few seconds.

2   Add red lentils, pepper, cardamom, garlic, cinnamon, celery, turmeric, cumin, all spices, parsley, and pepper; mix well.

3   Add vegetable broth and cover with a lid. Let it cook on low flame for 20-25 minutes or until the lentil is tender.

4   Serve and enjoy.

Nutrition: Calories – 318, Fat – 97 g, Carbs – 60 g, Protein – 1.7 g

983.   White Bean Soup
Preparation Time: 5 minutes
Cooking Time: 35 minutes
Servings: 2
Ingredients:

- 1 tablespoon virgin olive oil
- 1 red onion (chopped)
- 1 garlic clove (minced)
- 1 celery stalk (chopped)
- 1 cup spinach (fresh, finely chopped)
- 1 tablespoon lemon juice (fresh squeezed)
- 2 (16-oz.) cans white kidney beans (drained, rinsed)
- 2 cups chicken broth (or a 14-oz. can of low-sodium chicken broth)
- ¼ teaspoon thyme (dried)
- ½ teaspoon black pepper
- 1½ cups water

Directions:

1   Place a large saucepan on your stove. Add the virgin olive oil to your pan and turn the heat to medium-

high. Add the celery, chopped onions, and minced garlic to the pan and allow them to cook for 5 minutes.

2   Add the white kidney beans, chicken broth, water, thyme, and black pepper to the saucepan.

3   Allow the liquid to come to a boil, then reduce heat to medium-low and let the soup simmer for 15 minutes.

4   Transfer two cups of the bean and vegetables from the saucepan to a bowl. Use a slotted spoon to get as little of the liquid as possible. Set the bowl to the side.

5   Use an emulsion blender to blend the remaining soup mixture in the saucepan. You want to get a nice smooth consistency.

6   If you do not have an emulsion blender you can use a regular stand-alone blender. Just work in batches to blend everything. Once everything has been thoroughly blended, return back to your saucepan.

7   Add the 2 cups of beans and vegetable mixture that you removed earlier back into the soup. Bring the soup back up to a boil, stirring occasionally.

8   Add the spinach to the soup; after 2 minutes it should begin to wilt.

9   Turn the heat all the way off, and then stirs in the lemon juice just before serving.

Nutrition: Calories – 185, Carbs - 23.8 g, Protein - 10.1 g, Fat - 5.2 g

984.   Peas Soup
Preparation Time: 10 minutes
Cooking Time: 25 minutes
Servings: 2
Ingredients:

- ¼ cup long-grain rice
- 4 cups chicken stock
- ½ cup Cheddar cheese, peas

- ¼ teaspoon ground black pepper
- ½ teaspoon Italian seasonings

Directions:

1 Heat a saucepan with the stock.
2 Add all ingredients except Cheddar cheese and bring the soup to boil.
3 Then add cheese and stir it well.
4 Cook the soup for 5 minutes over low heat.

Nutrition: 95 calories 5.4g protein 6.1g carbohydrates

985. Sweet Potato Soup

Preparation Time: 10 minutes
Cooking Time: 1 hour and 40 minutes
Servings: 6

Ingredients:

- 4 big sweet potatoes
- 28 ounces veggie stock
- A pinch of black pepper
- ¼ teaspoon nutmeg, ground
- ⅓ cup low-sodium heavy cream

Directions:

1 Put the sweet potatoes on a lined baking sheet, bake them at 350°F for 1 hour and 30 minutes, cool them down, peel, roughly chop them, and put them in a pot.
2 Add stock, nutmeg, cream, and pepper pulse well using an immersion blender, heat the soup over medium heat, cook for 10 minutes, ladle into bowls and serve. Enjoy!

Nutrition: Calories: 110 Carbs: 23g Fat: 1g Protein: 2g Sodium 140 mg

986. White Mushrooms Soup

Preparation Time: 10 minutes
Cooking Time: 25 minutes
Servings: 2

Ingredients:

- 4 ounces white mushrooms, chopped
- ¼ cup Cheddar cheese, shredded
- ½ cup white onion, diced
- 1 teaspoon cayenne pepper
- 2 cups of water

Directions:

1 Melt the 1 tablespoon olive oil in the pan and add onion and mushrooms.
2 Cook the vegetables for 5 minutes over medium heat.
3 Then add cayenne pepper and water.
4 Simmer the soup for 10 minutes.
5 Add Cheddar cheese and stir the soup until the cheese is melted.
6 Remove the soup from the heat.

Nutrition: 142 calories 5.7g protein 5.2g carbohydrates

987. Lamb Soup

Preparation Time: 10 minutes
Cooking Time: 35 minutes
Servings: 2

Ingredients:

- 9 ounces lamb sirloin, sliced
- 5 cups of water
- 1 cup cauliflower, chopped
- 1 teaspoon dried dill
- 2 tablespoons tomato paste

Directions:

1 Preheat the pan well and add lamb sirloin.
2 Roast it for 1 minute per side.
3 Then add water, ½ teaspoon of ground black pepper, and dried dill.
4 Cook the meat for 20 minutes, covered.
5 Then add tomato paste and cauliflower. Stir the soup.
6 Cook the soup for 10 minutes.

Nutrition: 144 calories 19g protein 3.2g carbohydrates

988. Lemon Zest Soup

Preparation Time: 10 minutes
Cooking Time: 15 minutes
Servings: 2

Ingredients:

- 2 tablespoons lemon juice
- ½ teaspoon lemon zest, grated
- ¼ cup long-grain rice
- 4 cups chicken stock
- 1 celery stalk, chopped

Directions:

1 Boil chicken stock then add rice, cook for 10 minutes.
2 Then add lemon zest and celery stalk. Cook the soup for 3 minutes more.
3 After this, add lemon juice and boil it for 2 minutes.

Nutrition: 109 calories 3.2g protein 20.6g carbohydrates

989. Pumpkin Soup

Preparation Time: 30 minutes
Cooking Time: 8 minutes
Servings: 2

Ingredients:

- 1 onion, chopped
- 2 cups sweet potato, chopped
- 30 ounces pumpkin puree
- 1-quart chicken stock
- 1 teaspoon garlic powder

Directions:

1 Add all the ingredients to the Instant Pot.
2 Seal the pot.
3 Press the manual button.
4 Cook at high pressure for 8 minutes.
5 Release the pressure quickly.
6 Transfer the contents into a blender.
7 Pulse until smooth.
8 Season with salt and pepper.

Nutrition: 186 Calories 1.4g Fat 10.2g Fiber

990. Bacon & Potato Soup

Preparation Time: 36 minutes
Cooking Time: 12 minutes
Servings: 2

Ingredients:

- 4 slices bacon, sliced in half
- ½ cup onion, chopped
- 1½ lb. Potatoes, diced
- 2 cups chicken stock
- ½ cup sour cream

Directions:

1 Pour 1 tablespoon olive oil into the Instant Pot.
2 Add the bacon and cook until crispy.
3 Drain in a paper towel and then chop.
4 Add the onion and cook for 2 minutes.
5 Add the potatoes and stock.
6 Cover the pot.

7   Set it to manual.

8   Cook at high pressure for 10 minutes.

9   Release the pressure naturally.

10 Transfer the contents to a blender.

11 Puree until smooth.

12 Stir in the sour cream.

13 Top with the crispy bacon bits.

Nutrition: 195 Calories 9.6g Fat 7.6g Protein

991. Lemon Chicken Soup

Preparation Time: 18 minutes
Cooking Time: 11 minutes
Servings: 2
Ingredients:

- 3 chicken breast fillets
- 1 onion, diced
- 1 teaspoon garlic powder
- 2 tablespoons lemon juice
- 6 cups chicken stock

Directions:

1   Situate all the ingredients except the lemon juice in the Instant Pot.

2   Mix well.

3   Choose a manual setting.

4   Cook at high pressure for 10 minutes.

5   Release the pressure naturally.

6   Remove the chicken and shred.

7   Put it back to the pot and press sauté.

8   Stir in the lemon juice.

9   Season with salt and pepper.

Nutrition: 238 Calories 9.1g Fat 33g Protein

992. Artichoke Soup

Preparation Time: 15 minutes
Cooking Time: 15 minutes
Servings: 2
Ingredients:

- pound capital of Israel artichokes
- tablespoons further virgin olive oil
- massive onion, thinly sliced
- 2-pound potatoes, bare-assed and diced
- 5 cups of water
- A grating of nutmeg salt

- Freshly ground black pepper
- tablespoons Petroselinum crispum, finely chopped

Directions:

1   Scrub the Jerusalem artichokes and peel them thinly, cutting away any stringy roots or tips. Heat the vegetable oil

2   In an exceedingly massive cooking pan and cook the onion over moderate heat till it's clear.

3   Add the capital of Israel artichokes and potatoes and simmer for five minutes, stirring once or double

4   Therefore, the vegetables cook equally. Add the water and produce to a boil.

5   Cowl and simmer for twenty minutes or till the vegetables are tender.

6   You should force it thru a sieve or puree in a total liquidizer.Come back to the pan and warmth totally.

7   Finally, you should Season it with nutmeg, salt, & black pepper. Serve hot, fancy with parsley.

Nutrition: Calories: 123, Fats: 3g, Dietary Fiber: 5g, Carbohydrates: 19g, Protein: 5g

993. Dalmatian Potato Soup

Preparation Time: 15 minutes
Cooking Time: 15 minutes
Servings: 2
Ingredients:

- Pound potatoes
- Tablespoons further virgin olive oil
- Massive onion, chopped
- Ripe plum tomatoes, peeled, seeded, and chopped
- Bay leaf
- Cups water
- Tablespoons butter
- Tablespoons Petroselinum crispum, finely chopped
- Tablespoons contemporary basil leaves, cut salt
- Freshly ground black pepper

Directions:

1   Peel and dice the potatoes heat the vegetable oil.

2   In an exceedingly large pot and cook the onion over moderate heat till it's clear.

3   Add the potatoes, tomatoes, bay leaf, and water, and produce to a boil. Cover and simmer for half-hour.

4   Remove the herb. Force the soup through a sieve or puree in an exceeding liquidizer.

5   Come back to the pot and warmth totally. Add the butter, parsley, and basil, and after that, you should Season it with salt & black pepper.

6   Simmer for five minutes and serve hot.

Nutrition: Calories: 123, Fats: 3g, Dietary Fiber: 5g, Carbohydrates: 19g, Protein: 5g

994. Pumpkin Soup with Rice and Spinach

Preparation Time: 15 minutes
Cooking Time: 15 minutes
Servings: 2
Ingredients:

- 3 small pumpkins, concerning one pound
- 2 tablespoons extra-virgin olive oil
- Medium onion, chopped
- Leek, white half only
- Medium potatoes, bare-assed and diced
- Cups vegetable stock or water
- Cups milk
- 1 bay leaf
- A sprig of thyme
- A grating of nutmeg
- Salt
- Freshly ground black pepper
- Cup Arborio rice
- 2-pound spinach
- Tablespoons butter
- Freshly grated Parmesan cheese

Directions:

1   Slice the pumpkin. Stop the skin and take away the seeds and pith.

2   Dice the flesh into little items. Heat the vegetable oil in an exceedingly massive

cooking pan and cook the onion and leek over moderate heat till they're softened.

3 Add the pumpkin, potatoes, stock or water, milk, and herbs and produce to a boil. Cowl and simmer for 30 minutes or till the vegetables are tender. Season with nutmeg, salt, and black pepper.

4 Remove the herb and thyme. You should force it via a sieve or puree in an exceeding liquidizer.

5 Return to the pot, adding a touch of a lot of water if the soup is simply too thick. Rouse a boil.

6 Add the rice and cook for twenty a lot of minutes or till the rice is tender but still firm.

7 Meanwhile, wash the spinach carefully and cook in an exceedingly lined pan over moderate heat for five minutes or till it is simply tender. Drain well and chop coarsely.

8 Melt ½ the butter in an exceedingly cooking pan and cook the spinach over delicate heat for three or four minutes.

9 Augment the soup. Stir within the remaining butter and serve hot with cheese on the facet.

Nutrition: Calories: 123, Fats: 3g, Dietary Fiber: 5g, Carbohyd rates: 19g, Protein: 5g

995. Nettle Soup
Preparation Time: 15 minutes
Cooking Time: 15 minutes
Servings: 2
Ingredients:
- 6 ounces nettles
- 3 tablespoons further virgin olive oil
- 2 medium onions, sliced
- Pound potatoes, bare-assed and diced
- 5 cups water
- Cup crème Fraiche
- Salt
- Freshly ground black pepper

Directions:

1 Wash the nettles fastidiously and put aside.

2 Heat the olive oil in an exceedingly massive cooking pan and cook the onions over moderate heat for five minutes.

3 Add the nettles, potatoes, and water, and produce to a boil.

4 Cover and simmer for half-hour. Force through a sieve or puree in an exceeding liquidizer.

5 Return to the cooking pan and warmth totally.

6 Stir within the crème Fraiche and after that, you should Season it with salt & black pepper.

Nutrition: 195 Calories 9.6g Fat 7.6g Protein

996. Wild Mushroom Soup
Preparation Time: 15 minutes
Cooking Time: 15 minutes
Servings: 2
Ingredients:
- Pound mixed wild mushrooms
- 4 tablespoons further virgin olive oil
- Spanish onion, chopped
- Ripe plum tomatoes, peeled, seeded, and chopped
- 5 cups vegetable broth or water
- Salt
- Freshly ground black pepper

For the picada:
- 15 blanched almonds
- Slice white bread concerning one in. Thick (crust removed)
- 1-2 tablespoons further virgin olive oil
- Garlic cloves, crushed
- Pinch of saffron powder

Directions:

1 To build the soup, wash the mushrooms fastidiously and wipe dry.

2 Cut them into three or four items consistent with their size and heat the vegetable oil

3 In an exceedingly massive pan and cook the onion over delicate heat for

concerning ten minutes or till it starts to show golden.

4 Add the tomatoes and still cook till any liquid is gaseous and also the tomatoes are reduced to a pulp.

5 Stir within the mushrooms.

6 Cowl and simmer for a quarter-hour, stirring from time to time therefore the mushrooms cook equally.

7 You should add the broth & convey to a boil. Simmer, uncovered, for twenty minutes. After that, you should Season it with salt & black pepper.

8 To build the picada, toast the almonds in an exceedingly 350°F kitchen appliance until they're golden chop coarsely.

9 Heat one or a pair of tablespoons of vegetable oil in an exceedingly small cooking pan.

10 And fry the bread till it's golden on each side drain on a paper towel and withdraw little items or crush or grind the almonds, deep-fried bread, garlic, and saffron with a mortar and pestle

11 In an exceeding kitchen appliance, till all the ingredients type a sleek, thick paste.

12 Mix with a tablespoon or 2 of the soup into the picada, then stir the mixture into the soup.

13 Place a slice of bread on the lowest of 4 man or woman soup bowls. Pour the new soup over the bread and serve.

Nutrition: 195 Calories 9.6g Fat 7.6g Protein

997. Tomato and Alimentary Paste Soup
Preparation Time: 15 minutes
Cooking Time: 15 minutes
Servings: 2
Ingredients:
- 3 tablespoons further virgin olive oil
- Massive onion, chopped
- Garlic cloves, finely chopped

- 1-2 red chili peppers, cored, seeded, and finely chopped
- Cup canned plum tomatoes, forced through a sieve or pureed in a food processor
- Bunch Petroselinum crispum, finely chopped
- 6 cups water
- Ounces fine alimentary paste or (angel hair)
- Salt

Directions:

1. Heat the vegetable oil in an exceedingly massive pot and cook the onion over moderate heat till it's softened.
2. Add the garlic and chili peppers and cook for two a lot of minutes.
3. Add the tomato puree and parsley and cook for a further five minutes.
4. Pour within the water and produce to a boil. Simmer for ten minutes.
5. Increase the warmth. Once the soup is boiling, come by the alimentary paste and cook till it's tender however still firm.
6. Finally, you need to Season it with salt and serve hot.

Nutrition: Calories: 123, Fats: 3g, Dietary Fiber: 5g, Carbohydrates: 19g, Protein: 5g

998. Sorrel Soup

Preparation Time: 15 minutes
Cooking Time: 15 minutes
Servings: 2
Ingredients:

- 1-pound sorrel
- 3 tablespoons butter
- 3 tablespoons flour
- 5 cups quandary (or .05 water and half milk)
- A grating of nutmeg
- Salt
- Freshly ground black pepper

Directions:

1. Wash the sorrel fastidiously and take away the stalks and larger ribs.
2. Heat the butter in an exceedingly massive cooking pan and add the sorrel.

3. Cover and cook over a delicate heat till the sorrel has softened into a puree.
4. Stir within the flour and cook for two minutes.
5. Gradually add the new water, stirring perpetually, till the soup is slightly thickened.
6. Simmer for twenty minutes. Finally, you must season it with nutmeg, salt, and black pepper.

999. Summer Vegetable Soup

Preparation Time: 15 minutes
Cooking Time: 15 minutes
Servings: 2
Ingredients:

- medium eggplant (about ~ pound)
- Pound zucchini
- Red, green, or yellow bell peppers
- Cup further virgin olive oil
- Massive onion, thinly sliced
- Celery stalks, diced
- Pound waxy potatoes, peeled and diced
- 2-pound ripe plum tomatoes, peeled, seeded, and chopped
- Cups water
- 2 tablespoons torn basil leaves
- Salt
- Freshly ground black pepper
- Freshly grated pecorino or Parmesan cheese

Directions:

1. Peel and dice the eggplant. Trim the ends of the zucchini and withdraw rounds.
2. Cut the peppers into quarters and take away the cores and seeds. Withdraw skinny strips and heat the vegetable oil
3. In an exceedingly massive pot and cook the onion, celery, and potatoes over a coffee heat for ten minutes
4. Stirring from time to time therefore the vegetables cook equally.

5. Add the eggplant, zucchini, and peppers, cover, and cook for an additional ten minutes.
6. Add the tomatoes and cook, uncovered, for 10 more minutes.
7. Pour within the water and produce to a boil.
8. Cowl and simmer for fifteen to 20 minutes or till the vegetables are tender.
9. The soup ought to be terribly thick, almost a stew.
10. Add the basil and simmer for two or three minutes.
11. After that, you should Season it with salt & black pepper. Serve hot with cheese on the facet.

Nutrition: Calories: 123, Fats: 3g, Dietary Fiber: 5g, Carbohydrates: 19g, Protein: 5g

1000. Tuscan Black Cabbage Soup

Preparation Time: 15 minutes
Cooking Time: 15 minutes
Servings: 2
Ingredients:

- Pound Tuscan black cabbage
- Tablespoons further virgin olive oil
- Large onion, thinly sliced
- Celery stalk, thinly sliced
- Carrot, diced
- Medium potato, bare-assed and diced
- 5 cups vegetable broth or water
- Salt
- Freshly ground black pepper
- Slices wheaten bread
- Garlic cloves, peeled, and cut in half
- Freshly grated Parmesan cheese

Directions:

1. Wash the cabbage and take away the stalks. Withdraw skinny strips and heat the vegetable oil
2. In an exceedingly massive pot and cook the onion, celery, carrot, and potato for three minutes.

3 Add the cabbage and broth and bring to a boil cowl and simmer for one hour and you should After that you should Season it with salt & black pepper.

4 Meanwhile, place the slices of bread on a baking receptacle and toast

5 In an exceedingly preheated 375°F kitchen appliance till they're golden.

6 Take away from the kitchen appliance and rub every slice with garlic.

7 Place the slices of bread into individual soup bowls and pour the new soup over them.

8 Serve at once with cheese on the facet.

Nutrition: Calories: 123, Fats: 3g, Dietary Fiber: 5g, Carbohydrates: 19g, Protein: 5g

1001. Potato Leek Soup

Preparation Time: 10 minutes
Cooking Time: 20 minutes
Servings: 5
Ingredients:

- 4 tablespoons of olive oil
- 3 leeks
- 3 cups of onions, diced
- 1 pound of potatoes, diced
- 4 garlic cloves, chopped
- 1 tablespoon of thyme
- 6 cups of veggie stock
- ½ teaspoon of pepper
- 1 teaspoon of salt
- ½ cup of plant-based sour cream
- 2 tablespoons of chives, for garnishing

Directions:

1 Cut the leeks in half length. Slice them into ¼-inch rounds.

2 Heat oil over medium heat in a pot or oven.

3 Add the leeks and sauté for 8 minutes.

4 Add the garlic. Sauté for 3 minutes more.

5 Add the thyme, potatoes, and stock. Boil. Turn the heat to a simmer for 20

minutes. Your potatoes should be tender.

6 Add the pepper and salt.

7 Blend in batches to make it very silky and smooth.

8 Return your soup to the pot. Simmer over low heat.

9 Stir the sour cream in. Serve with the chives.

Nutrition: Calories 224 Carbohydrates 31g Cholesterol 10mg Fat 13g Protein 4g Sugar 4g Fiber 4g Sodium 337mg

1002. Lentil Beet Soup

Preparation Time: 10 minutes
Cooking Time: 30 minutes
Servings: 2
Ingredients:

- 1 shallot, chopped
- 2 teaspoons of olive oil
- 3 cloves of garlic, chopped
- 4 cups of water
- ½ cup of dry whole lentils
- 2 teaspoons of cumin
- 1 teaspoon of salt
- 1 lemon
- 2-3 cups of beets, grated
- Cilantro or parsley for garnishing

Directions:

1 Heat oil over medium heat in a pot. Sauté the shallot for 2 minutes.

2 Add the garlic. Sauté for 2 minutes more.

3 Add the beets, lentils, water, cumin, and salt. Cook for half an hour.

4 Squeeze the juice of one lemon when your lentils are tender.

5 Divide among two bowls. Top with the dill and grated beets.

Nutrition: Calories 329 Carbohydrates 53g Cholesterol 0mg Fat 9g Protein 16g Sugar 13g Fiber 11g Sodium 308mg

Chapter 12. Snacks and Smoothies

1003. Tomato Olive Salsa
Preparation Time: 15 minutes
Cooking Time: 5 Minutes
Servings: 4
Ingredients:

- 2 cups olives, pitted and chopped
- ¼ cup fresh parsley, chopped
- ¼ cup fresh basil, chopped
- 2 tablespoons green onion, chopped
- 1 cup grape tomatoes, halved
- 1 tablespoon olive oil
- 1 tablespoon vinegar
- Pepper
- Salt

Directions:

1. Add all ingredients into the inner pot of the instant pot and stir well. Seal pot with lid and cook on high for 5 minutes.
2. Once done, allow to release pressure naturally for 5 minutes then release remaining using quick release. Remove lid. Stir well and serve.

Nutrition: Calories 119 Fat 10.8 g Carbohydrates 6.5 g Protein 1.2 g

1004. Thin-Crust Flatbread
Preparation Time: 15 minutes
Cooking Time: 25 minutes
Servings: 2
Ingredients:

- 2 cup all-purpose flour
- ¾ cup lukewarm water
- 1 teaspoon instant yeast
- 1½ teaspoon salt
- 1 tablespoon olive oil
- 1 garlic clove, crushed
- ¼ teaspoon sea salt
- ½ tomato, thinly sliced
- ¼ yellow beet, thinly sliced
- ½ Meyer lemon, thinly sliced
- ¼ potato, thinly sliced
- 1 radish, thinly sliced
- ½ burrata mozzarella ball, dotted all over flatbread
- 1 tablespoon fresh tarragon, chopped

Directions:

1. Mix yeast and water in a bowl and stir to dissolve the yeast. Add salt and flour to the bowl and mix well.
2. Turn the dough onto a clear surface. Knead well for 5 minutes. If the dough is sticky, add 1 tablespoon flour at a time. Let the dough rise for 1½ hours. Cover with a bowl. Preheat the oven to 375°F.
3. Roll out the flatbread. Brush olive oil over it. Rub crushed garlic over it. Sprinkle with sea salt. Lay toppings over it as you like.
4. Dollop cheese over it. Sprinkle with pinches of salt. Place in the oven and bake for 25 minutes. Top with tarragon. Serve.

Nutrition: Calories: 150 Carbs: 27g Fat: 2g Protein: 7g

1005. Smoked Salmon Goat Cheese Endive Bites
Preparation Time: 15 minutes
Cooking Time: 0 minutes
Servings: 4
Ingredients:

- 1 package herbed goat cheese
- 3 endive heads
- 1 package smoked salmon

Directions:

1. Pull the leaves apart from endives and cut the ends off of them. Add goat cheese to endive leaves. Add salmon slices on top of the goat cheese. Serve.

Nutrition: Calories: 46 Carbs: 1g Fat: 3g Protein: 3g

1006. Hummus Peppers
Preparation Time: 15 minutes
Cooking Time: 0 minutes
Servings: 12
Ingredients:

- 6 baby bell peppers, halved lengthwise
- 10 ounces hummus
- ¼ cup kalamata olives, pitted and chopped
- ¼ cup reduced-fat crumbled feta
- parsley

Directions:

1. Place sliced bell peppers on a plate and add 2 tablespoons of hummus to each. Add feta, olives and parsley. Serve.

Nutrition: Calories: 70 Carbs: 4g Fat: 5g Protein: 2g

1007. Loaded Mediterranean Hummus
Preparation Time: 15 minutes
Cooking Time: 0 minutes
Servings: 2 cups
Ingredients:

- 1 tablespoon olive oil
- 2 cups hummus
- 1 teaspoon paprika
- 1 cup olives, sliced
- ½ red bell pepper, sliced
- 2 tablespoons pine nuts
- 2 tablespoons cilantro, chopped
- ¼ cup feta cheese, crumbled

Directions:

1. Add hummus to a serving dish. Add paprika and olive oil. Add olives, red bell pepper, feta cheese, pine nuts and cilantro, then mix well. Serve.

Nutrition: Calories: 70 Carbs: 4g Fat: 5g Protein: 2g

1008. Warm Beef and Lentil Salad
Preparation Time: 10 minutes
Cooking Time: 15 minutes
Servings: 4
Ingredients:

- 1 large piece of steak, (rump steak is great), about 1 lb., room temperature
- 1 tablespoon olive oil
- Salt and pepper
- 3 cups canned brown lentils, (3 cups once drained)
- ½ red onion, finely chopped
- 3 ounces feta cheese, crumbled
- ½ cup finely chopped parsley

- ⅓ cup finely chopped mint
- Juice of 1 lemon
- 3 tablespoons olive oil

Directions:
1. Place a skillet over a high heat
2. Rub the steak with olive oil and sprinkle with salt and pepper
3. Lay the steak onto the hot skillet and sear on both sides until golden, but still blushing in the center (medium-rare), leave to rest while you prepare the salad
4. In a large salad bowl, toss the lentils, onion, feta, parsley, mint, lemon juice, and olive oil
5. Slice the warm steak into thin slices and lay on top of the salad, or divide individually when serving

Nutrition: Calories: 442 Fat: 21.3 grams Protein: 39.3 grams Total carbs: 24.8 grams Net carbs: 18.4 grams

1009. Lighter Lasagna

Preparation Time: 20 minutes
Cooking Time: 1 hour
Servings: 6
Ingredients:

- 2 tablespoons olive oil
- 1 onion, finely chopped
- 4 garlic cloves, finely chopped
- 1½ pounds ground beef
- ⅓ cup red wine
- 2 cups canned chopped tomatoes
- 1 teaspoon dried chili flakes
- 1 teaspoon each dried oregano, thyme, and rosemary
- Salt and pepper
- 12 sheets (12 halves or 6 whole sheets) fresh lasagna (enough to create three layers across the entire dish)
- 1 large handful of fresh basil
- 5 ounces fresh mozzarella, torn

Directions:
1. Add the olive oil to a large sauté pan over a medium-high heat

2. Add the onion and garlic to the pan and stir as they soften for about 2 minutes
3. Add the beef and stir as it turns from pink to brown
4. Add the red wine and allow the alcohol to burn off for about 2 minutes
5. Add the tomatoes, chili flakes, herbs, salt and pepper and stir to combine
6. Leave to simmer for about 30 minutes until thick and rich in flavor
7. Preheat the oven to 400°Fahrenheit and have a lasagna dish waiting by
8. Layer the lasagna in this fashion: start with a layer of beef mixture on the bottom, then a layer of pasta, then a few torn basil leaves, repeat until everything has been used, and the top layer is beef sauce (it's not meant to be super tidy, just throw it all together as you please, as long as it's roughly even!)
9. Finish with the torn Mozzarella and a few extra basil leaves
10. Bake in the oven for about 30 minutes or until everything is golden and bubbling

Nutrition: Calories: 714 Fat: 34 grams Protein: 50.5 grams Total carbs: 47.1 grams Net carbs: 41 grams

1010. Smoky Loaded Eggplant Dip

Preparation Time: 15 minutes
Cooking Time: 20 minutes
Servings: 6
Ingredients:

- 1 large eggplant
- 1½ tablespoon Greek yogurt
- 2 tablespoon tahini paste
- 1 garlic clove, chopped
- 1 tablespoon lemon juice
- 1½ teaspoon sumac
- ¾ teaspoon Aleppo pepper
- toasted pine nuts
- salt and pepper
- 1 tomato, diced
- ½ English cucumber, diced
- lemon juice
- parsley

- olive oil

Directions:
1. Add parsley, cucumber and tomato to a bowl. Season with ½ teaspoon sumac, salt and pepper. Add lemon juice and olive oil. Toss and set aside.
2. Turn a gas burner on high and turn eggplant on it every 5 minutes with a tong until charred and crispy, for 20 minutes. Remove from the heat and let cool.
3. Peel the skin off the eggplant and discard the stem. Transfer eggplant flesh to a colander and drain for 5 minutes.
4. Transfer flesh to a blender. Add yogurt, tahini paste, garlic, lemon juice, salt, pepper, Aleppo pepper and sumac. Blend for 2 pulses to combine.
5. Transfer to a bowl. Cover and refrigerate for 30 minutes. Bring it to room temperature and add olive oil on top. Add pine nuts. Add a salad on top and serve.

Nutrition: Calories: 40 Carbs: 3g Fat: 4g Protein: 0g

1011. Peanut Butter Banana Greek Yogurt Bowl

Preparation Time: 15 minutes
Cooking Time: 0 minutes
Servings: 4
Ingredients:

- 2 medium bananas, sliced
- 4 cups vanilla Greek yogurt
- ¼ cup peanut butter
- 1 teaspoon nutmeg
- ¼ cup flax seed meal

Directions:
1. Divide the yogurt equally among 4 bowls and add banana slices to it. Add peanut butter to a bowl and microwave for 40 seconds.
2. Add 1 tablespoon peanut butter to each bowl. Add nutmeg and flaxseed meal to each bowl. Serve.

Nutrition: Calories: 110 Carbs: 13g Fat: 0g Protein: 15g

1012. Roasted Chickpeas

Preparation Time: 15 minutes
Cooking Time: 30 minutes
Servings: 2
Ingredients:

- 2 tablespoons extra-virgin olive oil
- 2 (15-oz.) cans chickpeas
- 2 teaspoon red wine vinegar
- 2 teaspoon lemon juice
- 1 teaspoon dried oregano
- ½ teaspoon garlic powder
- 1 teaspoon kosher salt
- ½ teaspoon black pepper, cracked

Directions:

1 Preheat the oven to 425°F and line a baking sheet with parchment paper. Drain, rinse and dry chickpeas and put on a baking sheet.

2 Roast for 10 minutes, then remove from the oven. Turn chickpeas and roast for 10 minutes. Add the remaining ingredients to a bowl and mix well.

3 Add chickpeas to it and mix to coat well. Transfer coated chickpeas back to the oven and roast for 10 minutes. Cool completely. Serve.

Nutrition: Calories: 191 Carbs: 27g Fat: 1g Protein: 9g

1013. Savory Feta Spinach and Sweet Red Pepper Muffins

Preparation Time: 15 minutes
Cooking Time: 25 minutes
Servings: 12
Ingredients:

- 2 eggs
- 2 ¾ cups all-purpose flour
- ¼ cup sugar
- 1 teaspoon paprika
- 2 teaspoons baking powder
- ¾ cup low-fat milk
- ½ cup extra-virgin olive oil
- ¾ cup feta, crumbled
- ⅓ cup jarred Florina peppers, drained and patted dry
- ¾ teaspoon salt
- 1¼ cups spinach, thinly sliced

Directions:

1 Preheat the oven to 375°F. Mix sugar, flour, baking powder, paprika and salt in a bowl. Mix eggs, olive oil and milk in another bowl.

2 Add wet ingredients to dry and mix until blended. Add spinach, feta and peppers and mix well.

3 Line a muffin pan with liners and add the mixture to them equally. Bake for 25 minutes. Let cool for 10 minutes. Remove from the tray. Cool for 2 hours and serve.

Nutrition: Calories: 295 Carbs: 27g Fat: 18g Protein: 8g

1014. Baked Whole-Grain Lavash Chips with Dip

Preparation Time: 15 minutes
Cooking Time: 6 minutes
Servings: 4
Ingredients:

- 3 teaspoons oil
- 3 California lavash whole-grain lavash flatbreads, cut into 16 squares
- 1 ripe avocado
- ½ cup cashews, soaked overnight, drained and rinsed
- ½ cup parsley, chopped
- 2 garlic cloves
- ½ cup kalamata olive brine
- ¼ cup tahini
- 1 lemon juice
- salt and pepper
- cherry tomatoes

Directions:

1 Blend cashews, avocado, garlic and parsley in a blender. Add lemon juice, olive brine, tahini and blend well. Season. Transfer to a bowl and add parsley. Set aside.

2 Preheat the oven to 400°F and place lavash squares on top. Add little oil on both sides of each square. Bake for 6 minutes and remove from the oven Let cool.

3 Chop cherry tomatoes. Serve chips with tomatoes and dip.

Nutrition: Calories: 557 Carbs: 33g Fat: 30g Protein: 35g

1015. Quinoa Granola

Preparation Time: 15 minutes
Cooking Time: 35 minutes
Servings: 7
Ingredients:

- 1 cup old fashioned rolled oats
- 2 cups raw almonds, chopped
- ½ cup white quinoa, uncooked
- 1 tablespoon coconut sugar
- 3½ tablespoon coconut oil
- ¼ cup maple syrup
- A pinch of sea salt

Directions:

1 Preheat the oven to 340°F. Add quinoa, oats, almonds, sugar and salt to a bowl. Mix well. Add maple syrup and coconut oil to a pan. Heat over medium heat for 3 minutes, whisking along.

2 Add dry ingredients and stir to coat well. Place on a baking sheet and spread. Bake for 20 minutes. Remove from the oven and toss the granola.

3 Turn the pan around and bake for 8 minutes more. Cool completely and serve.

Nutrition: Calories: 274 Carbs: 38g Fat: 11g Protein: 9g

1016. Greek Yogurt Spinach Artichoke Dip

Preparation Time: 15 minutes
Cooking Time: 30 minutes
Servings: 16
Ingredients:

- 10 ounces package frozen spinach, thawed
- 1⅓ cups plain Greek yogurt
- 1 (4-oz.) can artichoke hearts, drained and chopped
- 2 garlic cloves, minced
- 6 ounces feta, crumbled
- ⅓ cup parmesan, shredded
- 2/3 cup mozzarella, shredded

Directions:

1 Preheat the oven to 350°F and grease a 1-quart casserole dish. Set aside. Drain out the liquid from

spinach completely. Add spinach to a bowl.

2　Add the remaining ingredients and mix well. Transfer the mixture to a baking dish. Add more parmesan and mozzarella. Bake for 30 minutes. Serve.

Nutrition: Calories: 50 Carbs: 2g Fat: 5g Protein: 2g

1017. Fig Smoothie with Cinnamon

Preparation Time: 5 minutes
Cooking Time: 0 minutes
Servings: 1
Ingredients:

- 1 large ripe fig
- 3 dessertspoons porridge oats
- 3 rounded dessertspoons Greek yogurt
- ½ teaspoon ground cinnamon
- 200 ml orange juice
- 3 ice cubes

Directions:

1　Wash and dry the fig. Chop. Add all ingredients to a blender. Blend well. Serve.

Nutrition: Calories: 152 Carbs: 32g Fat: 3g Protein: 3g

1018. Smoked Salmon, Avocado and Cucumber Bites

Preparation Time: 15 minutes
Cooking Time: 0 minutes
Servings: 12
Ingredients:

- 1 large avocado, peeled and pit removed
- 1 medium cucumber
- ½ tablespoon lime juice
- 6 ounces smoked salmon
- chives
- black pepper

Directions:

1　Cut the cucumber into ¼ inch thick slices. Place flat on a plate. Add lime juice, avocado to a bowl and mash well.

2　Spread avocado on each cucumber slice and add a slice of smoked salmon on top. Add chives and black pepper on top. Serve.

Nutrition: Calories: 216 Carbs: 6g Fat: 10g Protein: 27g

1019. Baked Root Vegetable Chips with Buttermilk-Parsley Dipping Sauce

Preparation Time: 15 minutes
Cooking Time: 40 minutes
Servings: 2
Ingredients:

- 6 tablespoons buttermilk
- 7 ounces cup 2% Greek yogurt
- 2 tablespoons parsley, minced
- 2 garlic cloves, minced
- 1 teaspoon honey
- 1 teaspoon lemon zest
- Salt
- 1 large parsnip
- 1 medium turnip
- 1 medium golden beet
- 1 medium red beet
- 2 tablespoons olive oil
- 1 teaspoon garlic powder
- ½ teaspoon dried thyme
- ½ teaspoon ground cumin
- ¼ teaspoon kosher salt

Directions:

1　Whisk the first 7 ingredients in a bowl and mix until combined. Cover and refrigerate. Preheat the oven to 400°F. Mix dried thyme, oil, garlic powder, ground cumin and kosher salt in a bowl.

2　Peel all of the root vegetables and slice them ⅛ inch thick. Brush oil on both sides of chips, place slices on a wire rack, and place the wire rack on 2 baking sheets.

3　Place baking sheets in the oven and bake until crispy. Check on them every 20 minutes and remove once done. Serve with sauce.

Nutrition: Calories: 506 Carbs: 67g Fat: 26g Protein: 3g

1020. Spicy Red Lentil Dip

Preparation Time: 15 minutes
Cooking Time: 20 minutes
Servings: 6
Ingredients:

- 1 cup red lentils, picked over and rinsed
- 1 teaspoon onion powder
- 2 teaspoons curry powder

- ¼ teaspoon turmeric
- ½ teaspoon cumin
- ½ teaspoon garam masala
- 1 teaspoon sea salt
- ¼ teaspoon black pepper
- Crackers

Directions:

1　Add red lentils to a pan and cover with water by one inch. Bring to a boil and reduce the heat to medium-low. Cook for 20 minutes. Mash lentils.

2　Add all spices and mix well. Serve with crackers.

Nutrition: Calories: 79 Carbs: 0g Fat: 5g Protein: 3g

1021. Cucumber Hummus Sandwiches

Preparation Time: 15 minutes
Cooking Time: 0 minutes
Servings: 1
Ingredients:

- 10 round slices English cucumber
- 5 teaspoons hummus

Directions:

1　Add 1 teaspoon hummus to a slice of cucumber and top with another cucumber. Repeat with the rest. Serve.

Nutrition: Calories: 108 Carbs: 13g Fat: 5g Protein: 3g

1022. Fig & Honey Yogurt

Preparation Time: 15 minutes
Cooking Time: 0 minutes
Servings: 1
Ingredients:

- 3 dried figs, sliced
- 2 teaspoons honey
- 2/3 cup low-fat plain yogurt

Directions:

1　Add yogurt to a bowl and top with honey and figs. Serve.

Nutrition: Calories: 240 Carbs: 29g Fat: 9g Protein: 7g

1023. Peach Caprese Skewers

Preparation Time: 15 minutes
Cooking Time: 0 minutes
Servings: 1
Ingredients:

- ½ cup cherry tomatoes
- 1 medium peach, sliced
- ¼ cup baby mozzarella balls
- 4 fresh basil leaves

Directions:
1 Put peach slices, tomatoes, basil and mozzarella balls on skewers. Serve.

Nutrition: Calories: 103 Carbs: 10g Fat: 4g Protein: 7g

1024. Tomato-Basil Skewers

Preparation Time: 15 minutes
Cooking Time: 0 minutes
Servings: 16
Ingredients:
- 16 cherry tomatoes
- 16 small mozzarella balls
- 16 fresh basil leaves
- Extra-virgin olive oil
- Salt and black pepper

Directions:
1 Put basil, tomatoes and mozzarella balls on skewers. Add oil and season with salt and pepper. Serve.

Nutrition: Calories: 106 Carbs: 3g Fat: 7g Protein: 7g

1025. Fig & Ricotta Toast

Preparation Time: 15 minutes
Cooking Time: 5 minutes
Servings: 1
Ingredients:
- 1 slice whole-grain bread, ½ "thick
- 1 teaspoon honey
- ¼ cup part-skim ricotta cheese
- 1 teaspoon sliced almonds, roasted
- 1 fresh fig
- Pinch of sea salt

Directions:
1 Toast bread. Add cheese, figs and almonds on top. Add honey and season with salt. Serve.

Nutrition: Calories: 240 Carbs: 36g Fat: 8g Protein: 8g

1026. Meatballs Platter

Preparation Time: 10 minutes
Cooking Time: 15 minutes
Servings: 4
Ingredients:
- 1-pound beef meat, ground
- ¼ cup panko breadcrumbs
- A pinch of salt and black pepper
- 3 tablespoons red onion, grated
- ¼ cup parsley, chopped
- 2 garlic cloves, minced
- 2 tablespoons lemon juice
- Zest of 1 lemon, grated
- 1 egg
- ½ teaspoon cumin, ground
- ½ teaspoon coriander, ground
- ¼ teaspoon cinnamon powder
- 2 ounces feta cheese, crumbled
- Cooking spray

Directions:
1 In a bowl, blend the beef with the breadcrumbs, salt, pepper and the rest of the ingredients except the cooking spray, stir well and shape medium balls out of this mix.
2 Arrange the meatballs on a baking sheet lined with parchment paper, grease them with cooking spray and bake at 450°F for 15 minutes.
3 Position the meatballs on a platter and serve as a snack.

Nutrition: Calories: 300, Fat: 15.4, Fiber: 6.4, Carbs: 22.4, Protein: 35

1027. Artichoke Flatbread

Preparation Time: 10 minutes
Cooking Time: 15 minutes
Servings: 4
Ingredients:
- 5 tablespoons olive oil
- 2 garlic cloves, minced
- 2 tablespoons parsley, chopped
- 2 round whole wheat flatbreads
- 4 tablespoons parmesan, grated
- ½ cup mozzarella cheese, grated
- 14 ounces canned artichokes, drained and quartered
- 1 cup baby spinach, chopped
- ½ cup cherry tomatoes, halved
- ½ teaspoon basil, dried
- Salt and black pepper to the taste

Directions:

1 In a bowl, mix the parsley with the garlic and 4 tablespoons oil, whisk well, and spread this over the flatbreads.
2 Sprinkle the mozzarella and half of the parmesan.
3 In a bowl, mix the artichokes with the spinach, tomatoes, basil, salt, pepper and the rest of the oil, toss and divide over the flatbreads as well.
4 Sprinkle the remaining parmesan on top, arrange the flatbreads on a baking sheet lined with parchment paper and bake at 425°F for 15 minutes.
5 Serve a snack.

Nutrition: Calories: 223, Fat: 11.2, Fiber: 5.34, Carbs: 15.5, Protein: 7.4

1028. Triple Berry Banana Smoothie

Preparation Time: 5 minutes
Cooking Time: 0 minutes
Servings: 2
Ingredients:
- ½ cup strawberries
- 2 tablespoons agave syrup
- ½ cup raspberries
- 1 burro banana, peeled
- ½ cup blueberries
- 1 cup spring water

Directions:
1 Plug in a high-speed food processor or blender and add all the ingredients to its jar.
2 Cover the blender jar with its lid and then pulse for 40 to 60 seconds until smooth.
3 Divide the drink between two glasses and then serve.

Nutrition: 130 Calories; 1.5 g Fats; 5 g Protein; 26 g Carbohydrates; 4 g Fiber;

1029. Raspberry, Peach and Walnuts Smoothie

Preparation Time: 5 minutes
Cooking Time: 0 minutes
Servings: 2
Ingredients:
- ½ of peach
- ½ cup raspberries
- 1½ tablespoons walnuts

- 2 tablespoons agave syrup
- ½ tablespoon Bromide Plus Powder
- 2 cups spring water

Extra:

- ¼ teaspoon salt
- ⅛ teaspoon cayenne pepper

Directions:

1. Plug in a high-speed food processor or blender and add all the ingredients to its jar.
2. Cover the blender jar with its lid and then pulse for 40 to 60 seconds until smooth.
3. Divide the drink between two glasses and then serve.

Nutrition: 165 Calories; 0.3 g Fats; 12 g Protein; 18.7 g Carbohydrates; 2.5 g Fiber;

1030. Smoothie with Strawberries and Coconut

Preparation Time: 5 minutes
Cooking Time: 10 minutes
Servings: 2
Ingredients:

- 1½ cup Dr. Sebi's Herbal Tea
- ¼ cup soft-jelly coconut, shredded
- ½ cup strawberries
- 2 tablespoons agave syrup

Directions:

1. Plug in a high-speed food processor or blender and add all the ingredients to its jar.
2. Cover the blender jar with its lid and then pulse for 40 to 60 seconds until smooth.
3. Divide the drink between two glasses and then serve.

Nutrition: 168 Calories; 2.5 g Fats; 2 g Protein; 38 g Carbohydrates; 4.5 g Fiber;

1031. Nutty Date Papaya Smoothie

Preparation Time: 5 minutes
Cooking Time: 0 minutes
Servings: 2
Ingredients:

- 1 papaya, deseeded
- 3 dates, pitted
- 1 burro banana, peeled

- ¼ of key lime, juiced
- 1 tablespoon Bromide Plus Powder

Extra:

- 1 cup spring water

Directions:

1. Plug in a high-speed food processor or blender and add all the ingredients to its jar.
2. Cover the blender jar with its lid and then pulse for 40 to 60 seconds until smooth.
3. Divide the drink between two glasses and then serve.

Nutrition: 152 Calories; 3.6 g Fats; 2.4 g Protein; 33 g Carbohydrates; 5 g Fiber

1032. Cucumber and Coconut Smoothie

Preparation Time: 5 minutes
Cooking Time: 0 minutes
Servings: 2
Ingredients:

- 1 burro banana, peeled
- ½ of cucumber, deseeded
- ½ teaspoon Bromide Plus Powder
- ½ cup soft-jelly coconut water
- ½ cup Dr. Sebi's Herbal Tea

Directions:

1. Plug in a high-speed food processor or blender and add all the ingredients to its jar.
2. Cover the blender jar with its lid and then pulse for 40 to 60 seconds until smooth.
3. Divide the drink between two glasses and then serve.

Nutrition: 138 Calories; 5 g Fats; 3 g Protein; 22 g Carbohydrates; 3 g Fiber;

1033. Hearty Berry Smoothie

Preparation Time: 5 minutes
Cooking Time: 0 minutes
Servings: 2
Ingredients:

- ¼ cup strawberries
- ¼ cup blueberries
- ¼ cup blackberries
- ¼ cup raspberries
- 2 tablespoons walnuts

Extra:

- 1 tablespoon of Bromide Plus Powder
- 2/3 cup spring water

Directions:

1. Plug in a high-speed food processor or blender and add all the ingredients to its jar.
2. Cover the blender jar with its lid and then pulse for 40 to 60 seconds until smooth.
3. Divide the drink between two glasses and then serve.

Nutrition: 180 Calories; 8 g Fats; 4 g Protein; 25 g Carbohydrates; 5 g Fiber;

1034. Dandelion Green Smoothie

Preparation Time: 5 minutes
Cooking Time: 0 minutes
Servings: 2
Ingredients:

- 1 cup dandelion greens
- ½ of cucumber, deseeded
- 1 apple, cored, deseeded
- 1 burro banana, peeled
- ½ tablespoon walnuts

Extra:

- ½ teaspoon Bromide Plus Powder
- 1 cup soft-jelly coconut milk

Directions:

1. Plug in a high-speed food processor or blender and add all the ingredients to its jar.
2. Cover the blender jar with its lid and then pulse for 40 to 60 seconds until smooth.
3. Divide the drink between two glasses and then serve.

Nutrition: 317 Calories; 11 g Fats; 10 g Protein; 42 g Carbohydrates; 7 g Fiber;

1035. Cantaloupe Smoothie

Preparation Time: 5 minutes
Cooking Time: 0 minutes
Servings: 2
Ingredients:

- 1 cantaloupe, peeled, deseeded, sliced
- ½ cup Dr. Sebi Herbal Tea
- ½ of burro banana, peeled
- ½ cup soft-jelly coconut water

Directions:

1. Plug in a high-speed food processor or blender and add all the ingredients to its jar.
2. Cover the blender jar with its lid and then pulse for 40 to 60 seconds until smooth.
3. Divide the drink between two glasses and then serve.

Nutrition: 114.7 Calories; 0.6 g Fats; 1.8 g Protein; 27.8 g Carbohydrates; 1 g Fiber;

1036. Watermelon Refresher
Preparation Time: 5 minutes
Cooking Time: 0 minutes
Servings: 2
Ingredients:
- 1 watermelon, peeled, deseeded, cubed
- 1 tablespoon date
- ½ of key lime, juiced, zest
- 2 cups soft-jelly coconut water

Directions:
1. Place watermelon pieces in a high-speed food processor or blender, add lime zest and juice, add date and then pulse until smooth.
2. Take two tall glasses, fill them with watermelon mixture until two-third full, and then pour in coconut water.
3. Stir until mixed and then serve.

Nutrition: 55 Calories; 1.3 g Fats; 0.9 g Protein; 9.9 g Carbohydrates; 7 g Fiber;

1037. Smoothie Snack
Preparation Time: 5 minutes
Cooking Time: 0 minutes
Servings: 2
Ingredients:
- 1 burro banana, peeled
- 1½ cup mixed berries
- 1 mango, peeled, destoned, chopped
- 2 tablespoons walnut milk, homemade
- 1 tablespoon walnut butter, homemade

Extra:
- 2 tablespoons agave syrup

Directions:
1. Plug in a high-speed food processor or blender, add burro banana and berries and then pulse at low speed

until small pieces of fruits remain in the jar.
2. Add milk, butter, and agave syrup, pulse until combined, and then divide the mixture evenly between two bowls.
3. Top evenly with mango slices and some more berries and then serve.

Nutrition: 338 Calories; 9.6 g Fats; 8.6 g Protein; 64.3 g Carbohydrates; 12.1 g Fiber;

1038. Smoothie with Nuts
Preparation Time: 5 minutes
Cooking Time: 0 minutes
Servings: 2
Ingredients:
- ½ of burro banana, peeled
- ½ cup figs
- 2 strawberries
- ¼ cup Brazil nuts
- 1 cup spring water

Directions:
1. Plug in a high-speed food processor or blender and add all the ingredients to its jar.
2. Cover the blender jar with its lid and then pulse for 40 to 60 seconds until smooth.
3. Divide the drink between two glasses and then serve.

Nutrition: 234 Calories; 2 g Fats; 6.1 g Protein; 53.1 g Carbohydrates; 5.8 g Fiber;

1039. Watercress Detox Smoothie
Preparation Time: 5 minutes
Cooking Time: 0 minutes
Servings: 2
Ingredients:
- ½ cup watercress
- ½ of avocado, peeled, pitted
- 1 key lime, juiced
- 1 cup soft-jelly coconut milk, homemade
- 1 teaspoon Bromide Plus Powder

Directions:
1. Plug in a high-speed food processor or blender and add all the ingredients to its jar.
2. Cover the blender jar with its lid and then pulse for 40 to 60 seconds until smooth.
3. Divide the drink between two glasses and then serve.

Nutrition: 146 Calories; 10.5 g Fats; 7 g Protein; 7.5 g Carbohydrates; 2.5 g Fiber;

1040. Mango and Orange Smoothie
Preparation Time: 5 minutes
Cooking Time: 0 minutes
Servings: 2
Ingredients:
- ½ of a large mango, peeled, destoned, cubed
- 1 key lime, juiced
- 1 orange, peeled
- 1 tablespoon agave syrup
- 1 tablespoon grapeseed oil

Extra:
- 1 cup herbal tea

Directions:
1. Plug in a high-speed food processor or blender and add all the ingredients to its jar.
2. Cover the blender jar with its lid and then pulse for 40 to 60 seconds until smooth.
3. Divide the drink between two glasses and then serve.

Nutrition: 163 Calories; 3.4 g Fats; 1 g Protein; 32 g Carbohydrates; 6 g Fiber;

1041. Green Smoothie with Apple and Blueberries
Preparation Time: 5 minutes
Cooking Time: 0 minutes
Ingredients:
- 1 cup blueberries
- 1 apple, cored
- 1 cup turnip greens
- ¼ cup Brazil nuts
- ½ tablespoon agave syrup

Extra:
- 1 cup walnut milk, homemade

Directions:
1. Plug in a high-speed food processor or blender and add all the ingredients to its jar.
2. Cover the blender jar with its lid and then pulse for 40 to 60 seconds until smooth.
3. Divide the drink between two glasses and then serve.

Nutrition: 215 Calories; 1.1 g Fats; 2.3 g Protein; 48 g Carbohydrates; 8.3 g Fiber;

1042. Nutty Sea Moss Smoothie

Preparation Time: 10 minutes
Cooking Time: 0 minutes
Servings: 2
Ingredients:

- 33 g sea moss, rinsed
- 1 tablespoon coconut nectar
- 2 cups spring water, warmed
- 1 cup walnut milk, unsweetened

Extra:

- ¼ cup dates

Directions:

1. Place rinsed seaweed in a medium bowl, pour in the water, and let it soak for a minimum of 4 hours until thickened slightly.
2. Drain the soaked sea moss, transfer into a food processor, pulse until the smooth paste comes together, and then refrigerate until required.
3. When ready to drink, transfer 8 tablespoons of sea moss paste into a food processor, add remaining Ingredients: and then pulse until smooth.
4. Divide the drink evenly between two glasses and then serve.

Nutrition: 100.5 Calories; 0.1 g Fats; 1.7 g Protein; 22.5 g Carbohydrates; 3.5 g Fiber;

1043. Zucchini and Avocado Smoothie

Preparation Time: 5 minutes
Cooking Time: 0 minutes
Servings: 2
Ingredients:

- 3 tablespoons hemp seeds
- ⅓ cup diced zucchini
- 1 cup dandelion greens
- ¼ of a large avocado, peeled, pitted
- 1¼ cup walnut milk, homemade

Directions:

1. Plug in a high-speed food processor or blender and add all the ingredients to its jar.
2. Cover the blender jar with its lid and then pulse for 40 to 60 seconds until smooth.

3. Divide the drink between two glasses and then serve.

Nutrition: 165 Calories; 6.8 g Fats; 8.5 g Protein; 17.3 g Carbohydrates; 5.5 g Fiber;

1044. Blueberry-Pie Smoothie

Preparation Time: 5 minutes
Cooking Time: 0 minutes
Servings: 2
Ingredients:

- ¼ cup cooked amaranth
- 1 cup blueberries
- 1 teaspoon Bromide Plus Powder
- 1 burro banana, peeled
- 1 tablespoon walnut butter, homemade

Extra:

- 2 tablespoons date
- 2 cups soft-jelly coconut milk, homemade

Directions:

1. Plug in a high-speed food processor or blender and add all the ingredients to its jar.
2. Cover the blender jar with its lid and then pulse for 40 to 60 seconds until smooth.
3. Divide the drink between two glasses and then serve.

Nutrition: 302 Calories; 3 g Fats; 11 g Protein; 60 g Carbohydrates; 7 g Fiber;

1045. Cucumber and Basil Cleansing Drink

Preparation Time: 5 minutes
Cooking Time: 0 minutes
Servings: 2
Ingredients:

- 4 cucumbers, deseeded
- 1 bunch of basil leaves
- 2 key limes, juiced
- ½ teaspoon Bromide Plus Powder
- 2 cups soft-jelly coconut water

Directions:

1. Plug in a high-speed food processor or blender and add all the ingredients to its jar.

2. Cover the blender jar with its lid and then pulse for 40 to 60 seconds until smooth.
3. Divide the drink between two glasses and then serve.

Nutrition: 56.1 Calories; 0.5 g Fats; 0.9 g Protein; 12 g Carbohydrates; 2 g Fiber;

1046. Banana, Pear and Coconut Smoothie

Preparation Time: 5 minutes
Cooking Time: 0 minutes
Servings: 2
Ingredients:

- 1 burro banana, peeled
- 2 cups chopped kale
- 1 pear, diced
- 1 cup of soft-jelly coconut water

Directions:

1. Plug in a high-speed food processor or blender and add all the ingredients to its jar.
2. Cover the blender jar with its lid and then pulse for 40 to 60 seconds until smooth.
3. Divide the drink between two glasses and then serve.

Nutrition: 90 Calories; 0 g Fats; 1 g Protein; 24 g Carbohydrates; 3 g Fiber;

1047. Watermelon and Raspberries Smoothie

Preparation Time: 5 minutes
Cooking Time: 0 minutes
Servings: 2
Ingredients:

- 1 cup watermelon chunks
- ½ cup raspberries
- 1 key lime, juiced
- ¼ cup cucumber, deseeded, diced
- ½ cup soft-jelly coconut water

Directions:

1. Plug in a high-speed food processor or blender and add all the ingredients to its jar.
2. Cover the blender jar with its lid and then pulse for 40 to 60 seconds until smooth.
3. Divide the drink between two glasses and then serve.

Nutrition: 110 Calories; 1 g Fats; 3.4 g Protein; 26 g Carbohydrates; 7 g Fiber;

1048. Papaya and Quinoa Smoothie

Preparation Time: 5 minutes
Cooking Time: 10 minutes
Servings: 2
Ingredients:

- 2 cups papaya cubes
- 2 tablespoons date
- 1 cup cooked quinoa or amaranth
- 2 teaspoons Bromide Plus Powder
- 2 cups hemp milk, homemade

Directions:

1 Plug in a high-speed food processor or blender and add all the ingredients to its jar.
2 Cover the blender jar with its lid and then pulse for 40 to 60 seconds until smooth.
3 Divide the drink between two glasses and then serve.

Nutrition: 224.6 Calories; 7.7 g Fats; 7 g Protein; 33.7 g Carbohydrates; 3.5 g Fiber;

1049. Avocado and Cucumber Smoothie

Preparation Time: 5 minutes
Cooking Time: 0 minutes
Servings: 2
Ingredients:

- 1 burro banana, peeled
- ¼ of an avocado
- ¼ of a cucumber
- 1 tablespoon agave syrup
- ½ cup herbal tea

Extra:

- 1 tablespoon chopped walnuts
- 1 cup soft-jelly coconut milk, homemade

Directions:

1 Plug in a high-speed food processor or blender and add all the ingredients to its jar.
2 Cover the blender jar with its lid and then pulse for 40 to 60 seconds until smooth.
3 Divide the drink between two glasses and then serve.

Nutrition: 103 Calories; 4.5 g Fats; 1.6 g Protein; 16.2 g Carbohydrates; 2.5 g Fiber;

1050. Orange and Banana Drink

Preparation Time: 5 minutes
Cooking Time: 0 minutes
Servings: 2
Ingredients:

- ½ of a burro banana, peeled
- 3 oranges, peeled
- 1½ tablespoons Date
- ½ teaspoon Bromide Plus Powder
- 1 cup of soft-jelly coconut water

Directions:

1 Plug in a high-speed food processor or blender and add all the ingredients to its jar.
2 Cover the blender jar with its lid and then pulse for 40 to 60 seconds until smooth.
3 Divide the drink between two glasses and then serve.

Nutrition: 138.5 Calories; 0.6 g Fats; 1.5 g Protein; 35.1 g Carbohydrates; 4.7 g Fiber;

1051. Lettuce, Banana and Berries Smoothie

Preparation Time: 5 minutes
Cooking Time: 0 minutes
Servings: 2
Ingredients:

- ½ of a burro banana
- ¼ cup blueberries
- 1 cup Romaine lettuce
- 2 tablespoons key lime juice
- ½ cup soft jelly coconut water

Directions:

1 Plug in a high-speed food processor or blender and add all the ingredients to its jar.
2 Cover the blender jar with its lid and then pulse for 40 to 60 seconds until smooth.
3 Divide the drink between two glasses and then serve.

Nutrition: 147 Calories; 0.8 g Fats; 3.3 g Protein; 36 g Carbohydrates; 4 g Fiber;

Chapter 13. Pizza Recipes

1052. Pizza Bianca

Preparation Time: 10 minutes
Cooking Time: 10 minutes
Servings: 2
Ingredients:

- 2 tablespoons olive oil
- 4 eggs
- 2 tablespoons water
- 1 jalapeño pepper, diced
- ¼ cup mozzarella cheese, shredded
- 2 chives, chopped
- 2 cups egg Alfredo sauce
- ½ teaspoon oregano
- ½ cup mushrooms, sliced

Directions:

1. Preheat oven to 360°F.
2. In a bowl, whisk eggs, water, and oregano. Heat the olive oil in a large sk illet.
3. The egg mixture must be poured in then let it cook until set, flipping once.
4. Remove and spread the alfredo sauce and jalapeño pepper all over.
5. Top with mozzarella cheese, mushrooms and chives. Let it bake for 10 minutes

Nutrition: Calories: 314 Fat: 15.6g Fiber: 10.3g Carbohydrates: 5.9 g Protein: 10.4g

1053. Eggplant Pizza with Tofu

Preparation Time: 15 minutes
Cooking Time: 45 minutes
Servings: 2
Ingredients:

- 2 eggplants, sliced
- ⅓ cup butter, melted
- 2 garlic cloves, minced
- red onion
- 12 ounces tofu, chopped
- oz tomato sauce
- Salt and black pepper to taste
- ½ teaspoon cinnamon powder
- 1 cup Parmesan cheese, shredded
- ¼ cup dried oregano

Directions:

1. Let the oven heat to 400°F. Lay the eggplant slices on a baking sheet and brush with some butter. Bake in the oven until lightly browned, about 20 minutes.
2. Heat the remaining butter in a skillet; sauté garlic and onion until fragrant and soft, about 3 minutes.
3. Stir in the tofu and cook for 3 minutes. Add the tomato sauce, salt and black peppe r. Simmer for 10 minutes.
4. Sprinkle with Parmesan cheese and oregano. Bake for 10 minutes.

Nutrition: Calories: 321 Fat: 11.3g Fiber: 8.4g Carbohydrates: 4.3 g Protein: 10.1g

1054. Naan Bread Pizza

Preparation Time: 15 minutes
Cooking Time: 0 minutes
Servings: 1
Ingredients:

- 1 naan bread, toasted
- 1 teaspoon hummus
- ½ cucumber, chopped
- ½ tomato, chopped
- ¼ teaspoon capers, canned

Directions:

1. Spread the naan bread with hummus and top with cucumber, tomato, and capers. Serve.

Nutrition: Calories 97 Protein 3.6 g Carbohydrates 17.5g Fat 1.8g

1055. Thin Crust Low Carb Pizza

Preparation Time: 15 minutes
Cooking Time: 25 minutes
Servings: 6
Ingredients:

- 2 tablespoons tomato sauce
- ⅛ teaspoon black pepper
- ⅛ teaspoon chili flakes
- 1 piece low-carb pita bread
- 2 ounces low-moisture mozzarella cheese
- ⅛ teaspoon garlic powder

Toppings:

- Bacon, roasted red peppers, spinach, olives, pesto, artichokes, salami, pepperoni, roast beef, prosciutto, avocado, ham, chili paste, Sriracha

Directions:

1. Warm the oven to 450°F, then oiled a baking dish. Mix tomato sauce, black pepper, chili flakes, and garlic powder in a bowl and keep aside.
2. Place the low-carb pita bread in the oven and bake for about 2 minutes. Remove from the oven and spread the tomato sauce on it.
3. Add mozzarella cheese and top with your favorite toppings. Bake again for 3 minutes and dish out.

Nutrition: Calories: 254 Carbs: 12.9g Fats: 16g Proteins: 19.3g

1056. BBQ Chicken Pizza

Preparation Time: 15 minutes
Cooking Time: 30 minutes
Servings: 4
Ingredients:

- Dairy-Free Pizza Crust
- 6 tablespoons Parmesan cheese
- 6 large eggs
- 3 tablespoons psyllium husk powder
- Salt and black pepper, to taste
- 1½ teaspoons Italian seasoning

Toppings:

- 6 ounces rotisserie chicken, shredded
- 4 ounces cheddar cheese
- 1 tablespoon mayonnaise
- 4 tablespoons tomato sauce
- 4 tablespoons BBQ sauce

Directions:

1. Warm the oven to 400°F and grease a baking dish. Place all Pizza Crust ingredients in an immersion blender and blend until smooth.

2 Spread dough mixture onto the baking dish and transfer it to the oven. Bake for about 10 minutes and top with favorite toppings. Bake for about 3 minutes and dish out.

Nutrition: Calories: 356 Carbs: 2.9g Fats: 24.5g Proteins: 24.5g

1057. Buffalo Chicken Crust Pizza

Preparation Time: 15 minutes
Cooking Time: 25 minutes
Servings: 6
Ingredients:
- 1 cup whole milk mozzarella, shredded
- 1 teaspoon dried oregano
- 2 tablespoons butter
- 1-pound chicken thighs, boneless and skinless
- 1 large egg
- ¼ teaspoon black pepper
- ¼ teaspoon salt
- 1 stalk celery
- 3 tablespoons Franks Red Hot Original
- 1 stalk green onion
- 1 tablespoon sour cream
- 1-ounce bleu cheese, crumbled

Directions:
1 Warm the oven to 400°F and grease a baking dish. Process chicken thighs in a food processor until smooth.
2 Transfer to a large bowl and add egg, ½ cup of shredded mozzarella, oregano, black pepper, and salt to form a dough.
3 Spread the chicken dough in the baking dish and transfer to the oven. Bake for about 25 minutes and keep aside.
4 Meanwhile, heat butter and add celery, and cook for about 4 minutes—Mix Franks Red Hot Original with the sour cream in a small bowl.
5 Spread the sauce mixture over the crust, layer with the cooked celery and remaining ½ cup of mozzarella and the bleu cheese. Bake again within 10 minutes, until the cheese is melted.

Nutrition: Calories: 172 Carbs: 1g Fats: 12.9g Proteins: 13.8g

1058. Fresh Bell Pepper Basil Pizza

Preparation Time: 15 minutes
Cooking Time: 25 minutes
Servings: 3
Ingredients:
Pizza Base:
- ½ cup almond flour
- 2 tablespoons cream cheese
- 1 teaspoon Italian seasoning
- ½ teaspoon black pepper
- 6 ounces mozzarella cheese
- 2 tablespoons psyllium husk
- 2 tablespoons fresh Parmesan cheese
- 1 large egg
- ½ teaspoon salt

Toppings:
- 4 ounces cheddar cheese, shredded
- ¼ cup Marinara sauce
- 2/3 medium bell pepper
- 1 medium vine tomato
- 3 tablespoons basil, fresh chopped

Directions:
1 Warm the oven to 400°F and grease a baking dish. Microwave mozzarella cheese for about 30 seconds and top with the remaining pizza crust.
2 Add the remaining pizza ingredients to the cheese and mix. Flatten the dough and transfer to the oven.
3 Bake for about 10 minutes. Remove, and top the pizza with the toppings and bake for another 10 minutes. Remove pizza from the oven and allow to cool.

Nutrition: Calories: 411 Carbs: 6.4g Fats: 31.3g Proteins: 22.2g

1059. Caramelized Onion and Goat Cheese Pizza

Preparation Time: 1 hour & 15 minutes
Cooking Time: 30 minutes
Servings: 4
Ingredients:
For the crust:
- 2 cups flour
- 1 cup lukewarm water
- 1 pinch of sugar
- 1 teaspoon active dry yeast
- ¾ teaspoon salt
- 2 tablespoons olive oil

For the topping:
- 2 tablespoons butter
- 2 red onions, thinly sliced
- Salt and black pepper to taste
- 1 cup crumbled goat cheese
- 1 tablespoon almond milk
- 1 cup fresh curly endive, chopped

Directions:
1 Sift the flour and salt in a bowl and stir in yeast. Mix lukewarm water, olive oil, and sugar in another bowl. Add the wet mixture to the dry mixture and whisk until you obtain a soft dough.
2 Place the dough on a lightly floured work surface and knead it thoroughly for 4-5 minutes until elastic. Transfer the dough to a greased bowl.
3 Cover with cling film and leave to rise for 50-60 minutes in a warm place until doubled in size. Roll out the dough to a thickness of around 12 inches.
4 Preheat the oven to 400°F. Line a pizza pan with parchment paper. Melt the butter in a large skillet and stir in the onions.
5 Reduce the heat to low, season the onions with salt, black pepper, and cook with frequent stirring until caramelized, 15 to 20 minutes. Turn the heat.
6 In a medium bowl, mix the goat cheese with the almond milk and spread on the crust. Top with the caramelized onions. Bake in the oven for 10 minutes and take out after. Top with the curly endive, slice, and serve warm.

Nutrition: Calories 317 Fats 20g Carbs 1g Protein 28g

1060. Vegetarian Spinach-Olive Pizza

Preparation Time: 15 minutes
Cooking Time: 25 minutes
Servings: 4
Ingredients:
For the crust:
- ½ cup almond flour

- ¼ teaspoon salt
- 2 tablespoons ground psyllium husk
- 1 tablespoon olive oil
- 1 cup lukewarm water

For the topping:
- ½ cup tomato sauce
- ½ cup baby spinach
- 1 cup grated mozzarella cheese
- 1 teaspoon dried oregano
- 3 tablespoons sliced black olives

Directions:
1 Preheat the oven to 400°F. Line a baking sheet with parchment paper. In a medium bowl, mix the almond flour, salt, psyllium powder, olive oil, and water until dough forms.
2 Spread the mixture on the pizza pan and bake in the oven until crusty, 10 minutes. When ready, remove the crust and spread the tomato sauce on top.
3 Add the spinach, mozzarella cheese, oregano, and olives. Bake until the cheese melts, 15 minutes. Take out of the oven, slice and serve warm.

Nutrition: Calories 95 Fats 4.3g Carbs 1.8g Protein 9.7g

1061. Chicken Bacon Ranch Pizza

Preparation Time: 1 hour & 15 minutes
Cooking Time: 20 minutes
Servings: 4
Ingredients:
For the crust:
- 2 cups flour
- 1 cup lukewarm water
- 1 pinch of sugar
- 1 teaspoon active dry yeast
- ¾ teaspoon salt
- 2 tablespoons olive oil

For the ranch sauce:
- 1 tablespoon butter
- 2 garlic cloves, minced
- 1 tablespoon cream cheese
- ¼ cup half and half
- 1 tablespoon dry Ranch seasoning mix

For the topping:
- 3 bacon slices, chopped

- 2 chicken breasts
- Salt and black pepper to taste
- 1 cup grated mozzarella cheese
- 6 fresh basil leaves

Directions:
1 Sift the flour and salt in a bowl and stir in yeast. Mix lukewarm water, olive oil, and sugar in another bowl. Add the wet mixture to the dry mixture and whisk until you obtain a soft dough.
2 Place the dough on a lightly floured work surface and knead it thoroughly for 4-5 minutes until elastic. Transfer the dough to a greased bowl.
3 Cover with cling film and leave to rise for 50-60 minutes in a warm place until doubled in size. Roll out the dough to a thickness of around 12 inches.
4 Preheat the oven to 400°F. Line a pizza pan with parchment paper. In a bowl, mix the sauce's ingredients butter, garlic, cream cheese, half and half, and ranch mix. Set aside.
5 Heat a grill pan over medium heat and cook the bacon until crispy and brown, 5 minutes. Transfer to a plate and set aside.
6 Season the chicken with salt, pepper and grill in the pan on both sides until golden brown, 10 minutes. Remove to a plate, allow cooling, and cut into thin slices.
7 Spread the ranch sauce on the pizza crust, followed by the chicken and bacon, and then, mozzarella cheese and basil. Bake for 5 minutes or until the cheese melts. Slice and serve warm.

Nutrition: Calories 528 Fats 27.8g Carbs 4.9g Protein 61.2g

1062. Chicken Pizza

Preparation Time: 1 minute
Cooking Time: 10 minutes
Servings: 4
Ingredients:
- 2 flatbreads
- 1 tablespoon Greek vinaigrette
- ½ cup feta cheese, crumbled

- ¼ cup Parmesan cheese, grated
- ½ cup water-packed artichoke hearts, rinsed, drained and chopped
- ½ cup olives, pitted and sliced
- ½ cup cooked chicken breast strips, chopped
- ⅛ teaspoon dried basil
- ⅛ teaspoon dried oregano
- Pinch of ground black pepper
- 1 cup part-skim mozzarella cheese, shredded

Directions:
1 Preheat the oven to 400°F. Arrange the flatbreads onto a large ungreased baking sheet and coat each with vinaigrette.
2 Top with feta, followed by the Parmesan, veggies and chicken. Sprinkle with dried herbs and black pepper. Top with mozzarella cheese evenly.
3 Bake for about 8-10 minutes or until cheese is melted. Remove from the oven and set aside for about 1-2 minutes before slicing. Cut each flatbread into 2 pieces and serve.

Nutrition: Calories 393 Fat 22 g Carbs 20.6 g Protein 28.9 g

1063. Shrimp Pizza

Preparation Time: 15 minutes
Cooking Time: 10 minutes
Servings: 1
Ingredients:
- 2 tablespoons spaghetti sauce
- 1 tablespoon pesto sauce
- 1 (6-inch) pita bread
- 2 tablespoons mozzarella cheese, shredded
- 5 cherry tomatoes, halved
- ⅛ cup bay shrimp
- Pinch of garlic powder
- Pinch of dried basil

Directions:
1 Preheat the oven to 325°F. Lightly, grease a baking sheet. In a bowl, mix together the spaghetti sauce and pesto. Spread the pesto

mixture over the pita bread in a thin layer.

2 Top the pita bread with the cheese, followed by the tomatoes and shrimp. Sprinkle with garlic powder and basil.

3 Arrange the pita bread onto the prepared baking sheet and bake for about 7-10 minutes.

4 Remove from the oven and set aside for about 3-5 minutes before slicing. Cut into desired-sized slices and serve.

Nutrition: Calories 482 Fat 18.9 g Carbs 44.5 g Protein 33.4 g

1064. Veggie Pizza

Preparation Time: 20 minutes
Cooking Time: 12 minutes
Servings: 6
Ingredients:

- 1 (12-inch) prepared pizza crust
- ¼ teaspoon Italian seasoning
- ¼ teaspoon red pepper flakes, crushed
- 1 cup goat cheese, crumbled
- 1 (14-oz.) can quartered artichoke hearts
- 3 plum tomatoes, sliced into ¼-inch thick size
- 6 kalamata olives, pitted and sliced
- ¼ cup fresh basil, chopped

Directions:

1 Preheat the oven to 450°F. Grease a baking sheet. Sprinkle the pizza crust with Italian seasoning and red pepper flakes evenly.

2 Place the goat cheese over crust evenly, leaving about ½-inch of the sides. With the back of a spoon, gently press the cheese downwards.

3 Place the artichoke, tomato and olives on top of the cheese. Arrange the pizza crust onto the prepared baking sheet.

4 Bake for about 10-12 minutes or till cheese becomes bubbly. Remove from oven and sprinkle with

the basil. Cut into equal-sized wedges and serve.

Nutrition: Calories 381 Fat 16.1 g Carbs 42.4 g Protein 19.4 g

1065. Bread Machine Pizza Dough

Preparation Time: 15 minutes
Cooking Time: 24 minutes
Servings: 6
Ingredients:

- 1 cup of beer
- 2 tablespoons butter
- 2 tablespoons sugar
- 1 teaspoon of salt
- 2½ cups of all-purpose flour
- 2¼ teaspoons of yeast

Directions:

1 Place beer, butter, sugar, salt, flour, and yeast in a bread maker in the order recommended by the manufacturer. Select the Paste setting and press Start.

2 Remove the dough from the bread maker once the cycle is complete. Roll or press the dough to cover a prepared pizza dish.

3 Brush lightly with olive oil. Cover and let stand for 15 minutes. Preheat the oven to 250°C (400°F).

4 Spread the sauce and garnish on the dough. Bake until the crust is a little brown and crispy on the outside, about 24 minutes.

Nutrition: Calories: 101 Carbs: 18g Fat: 2g Protein: 3g

1066. Pizza Crust

Preparation Time: 15 minutes
Cooking Time: 15-20 minutes
Servings: 15
Ingredients:

- 7/8 cup warm water
- ¾ teaspoon salt
- 2 tablespoons olive oil
- 2½ cups all-purpose flour
- 2 teaspoons white sugar
- 2 teaspoons active dry yeast

Directions:

1 Set the bread machine to adjust the dough and start the machine. Tap the dough into a rolling pan or a 12-inch greased round pizza

pan. Let stand for 10 minutes.

2 Preheat the oven to 205°C (400°F). Spread the pizza sauce on the dough. Sprinkle the toppings over the sauce. Bake for 15-20 minutes, or until the crust is golden brown.

Nutrition: Calories: 170 Carbs: 27g Fat: 5g Protein: 4g

1067. Pizza Buns

Preparation Time: 15 minutes
Cooking Time: 41 minutes
Servings: 8
Ingredients:

- 8 hamburger buns, divided
- 1-pound ground beef
- ⅓ cup onion, minced
- 1 (15-oz.) jar pizza sauce
- ⅓ cup grated Parmesan cheese
- 2¼ teaspoon Italian herbs
- 1 teaspoon garlic powder
- ¼ cup onion powder
- ⅛ teaspoon ground crushed red pepper flakes
- 1 teaspoon bell pepper
- 2 cups grated mozzarella cheese

Directions:

1 Place the oven rack about 6 centimeters from the heat source. Place the buns on a baking sheet. Grill for about 1 minute until they are toasted. Set aside.

2 Set the oven to 350°F (175°C). In a frying skillet over medium heat, cook and mix the minced beef until it is golden and crumbly, about 10 minutes. Drain the excess fat and stir in the onion.

3 Cook and mix the beef mixture until the onion is transparent, about 5 minutes longer, then add the pizza sauce, parmesan cheese, Italian herbs, garlic powder, onion powder, ground red pepper flakes bell pepper.

4 Bring the sauce to a boil and simmer for 10 to 15 minutes

to mix the flavors, stirring often.

5   Pour the beef sauce over the baking sheet and cover each loaf with about ¼ cup grated mozzarella cheese.

6   Put the rolls back in the oven and bake for about 10 minutes, until the cheese is bubbling and light brown.

Nutrition: Calories: 307 Carbs: 50g Fat: 6g Protein: 11g

1068. Brick Oven Pizza (Brooklyn Style)

Preparation Time: 16 hours & 15 minutes

Cooking Time: 6 minutes

Servings: 18

Ingredients:

- 1 teaspoon of active dry yeast
- ¼ cup of warm water
- 1 cup of cold water
- 1 teaspoon of salt
- 3 cups of bread flour
- 6 ounces low-mozzarella cheese, minced
- ½ cup of crushed canned tomatoes without salt
- ¼ teaspoon of fresh pepper
- ½ teaspoon dried oregano
- 3 tablespoons extra-virgin olive oil
- 6 fresh basil leaves, torn

Directions:

1   Scatter the yeast over the warm water in a large bowl. Let stand for 5 minutes to check. Stir in salt and cold water, and then add about 1 cup of flour at a time.

2   When the dough is thick enough to be removed from the bowl, knead it on a floured surface until smooth, about 10 minutes.

3   Divide it in two and form a tight ball. Coat the balls with olive oil and leave them in a sealed container for at least 16 hours. Remove the dough from the fridge one hour before use.

4   Preheat the oven with a pizza stone on the lowest rack at 550°F. Lightly dust a pizza skin with flour.

5   Use a dough ball at a time, sprinkle the dough lightly with flour, and gradually stretch it until it is approximately 14 inches in diameter, about the pizza stone's size. Place on the floured tin.

6   Place thin slices of mozzarella on the crust and then chop a generous amount of black pepper.

7   Sprinkle with dried oregano. Arrange the crushed tomatoes randomly and leave empty areas. Sprinkle with olive oil.

8   Make sure the dough comes off the skin with a quick jerk. Place the skin's tip on the back of the preheated pizza stone and remove it to leave the pizza on the stone.

9   Bake in the preheated oven for 4 to 6 minutes or until the crust starts to brown. Remove from the oven by sliding the skin under the pizza.

10   Randomly sprinkle some basil leaves on the pizza. Cut into segments and serve.

Nutrition: Calories: 310 Carbs: 29g Fat: 13g Protein: 15g

1069. Valentine Pizza

Preparation Time: 15 minutes

Cooking Time: 15-20 minutes

Servings: 12

Ingredients:

- 3 cups of bread flour
- 1 (0.25-oz.) active dry yeast cover
- 1¼ cup of warm water
- 3 tablespoons chopped fresh rosemary
- 3 tablespoons extra-virgin olive oil, divided
- 1 can of pizza sauce (14oz.)
- 3 cups grated mozzarella cheese
- 2 ripe tomatoes
- 15 slices of vegetarian pepperoni
- 1 can (2.25-oz.) sliced black olives, sliced
- 1 zucchini, sliced

Directions:

1   Place the bread flour, yeast, water, and 2 tablespoons of olive oil in the bread maker in the order recommended by the manufacturer.

2   Select the Paste setting. Press Start. When the dough is ready, knead the rosemary into the dough.

3   Divide the dough into three servings. Shape each heart shaped piece about ½ inch thick. Brush with remaining olive oil, then spread a thin layer of pizza sauce on each pizza.

4   Sprinkle cheese over pizza sauce and arrange on top with tomatoes, zucchini, pepperoni, and sliced olives. Bake for about 15 to 20 minutes.

Nutrition: Calories: 119 Carbs: 14g Fat: 5g Protein: 1g

1070. Pizza Muffins

Preparation Time: 15 minutes

Cooking Time: 15-20 minutes

Servings: 12

Ingredients:

- 2½ cups flour
- ½ teaspoon baking powder
- ½ teaspoon dried oregano
- 2 tablespoons white sugar
- ½ teaspoon salt
- 1 teaspoon dried basil leaves
- 3 sun-dried tomatoes
- 2½ cups of cheddar cheese, grated, divided
- 4 green onions, minced
- 1 beaten egg
- 1½ cup buttermilk

Directions:

1   Preheat the oven to 190°C. Grease the muffin cups or double them with muffin paper. Combine flour baking powder, baking powder, salt, basil, oregano, and sugar in a large bowl in a large bowl.

2   Stir until everything is well mixed. Mix tomatoes, 1.5 cups of cheese, and onions. In another bowl, whisk the egg, pick up buttermilk and stir until smooth.

3   Place the dough halfway in the muffin pans. Sprinkle the remaining cup of cheese over the muffins.

4   Bake in the preheated oven for 15 to 20 minutes until a toothpick in the middle of the muffin comes out clean.

Nutrition: Calories: 100 Carbs: 18g Fat: 0g Protein: 6g

1071. Pub Pizza

Preparation Time: 15 minutes
Cooking Time: 12-15 minutes
Servings: 1
Ingredients:

- 1 small (4-inch) pita bread
- ¼ cup pizza sauce
- 4 slices cooked ham
- ¼ cup pineapple chunks, drained
- 4 slices Monterey Jack cheese

Directions:

1   Preheat the oven to 250°C (400°F). Place the pita bread on a small baking sheet. Cover with pizza sauce, ham, and pieces of pineapple garnish with Monterey Jack cheese.

2   Bake in the preheated oven for 12 to 15 minutes, until cheese, is melted and light brown.

Nutrition: Calories: 276 Carbs: 31g Fat: 11g Protein: 12g

1072. Alfredo Chicken Pita Pizza

Preparation Time: 15 minutes
Cooking Time: 20 minutes
Servings: 4
Ingredients:

- 2 tablespoons olive oil, divided
- 6 small frozen chicken fillets, thawed and sliced
- 1 pinch of salt with garlic or to taste
- ¼ cup of garlic hummus
- 4 pita bread & 4 teaspoons of basil pesto
- ½ cup of prepared Alfredo sauce
- 1 cup of freshly chopped spinach leaves
- 1 jar of marinated artichoke hearts
- ¾ cup mozzarella cheese & ¾ cup crumbled feta cheese

- ½ cup grated Parmesan cheese
- ½ cup sliced fresh mushrooms

Directions:

1   Preheat the oven to 175°C (350°F). Heat 1 tablespoon of olive oil in a frying pan over medium-high heat.

2   Season the chicken with garlic salt; cook and stir the hot oil until it is no longer pink in the middle, in 5 minutes. Set aside to cool.

3   Spread 1 tablespoon of hummus on one side of each pita bread almost to the edges. Cover with layers of pesto and alfredo sauce.

4   Sprinkle a layer of chopped spinach on the Alfredo sauce; garnish with equal Servings of chicken, artichoke hearts, feta cheese, mozzarella, parmesan cheese, and mushrooms.

5   Sprinkle the pizzas with the remaining olive oil. Bake for 15 minutes.

Nutrition: Calories: 305 Carbs: 13g Fat: 14g Protein: 36g

1073. Miniature Pizzas

Preparation Time: 15 minutes
Cooking Time: 12-15 minutes
Servings: 20
Ingredients:

- 1-pound ground beef
- 1 pound of fresh minced pork sausage
- 1 chopped onion
- 10 grams of processed American cheese, diced
- 32 grams of cocktail rye bread

Directions:

1   Preheat the oven to 175°C (350° F). Brown ground beef and sausages.

2   Mix the onion in the sausage and beef mixture and cook until done. Pour the fat into the pan. Add the melted cheese to the mixture. Keep cooking until the cheese has melted.

3   Place spoons full of the mixture on each slice of

bread. Bake 12 to 15 minutes.

Nutrition: Calories: 190 Carbs: 22g Fat: 10g Protein: 2g

1074. Easy Pizza with a Pinch

Preparation Time: 15 minutes
Cooking Time: 45 minutes
Servings: 8
Ingredients:

- 8 hot-dog buns
- 2 cups of tomato sauce
- 3 teaspoons of minced garlic
- 3 teaspoons dried Italian herbs
- 1 tablespoon sweet pepper
- 1 tablespoon Kosher salt
- 1 teaspoon ground black pepper
- 1 pound of sweet Italian sausages
- 2 tablespoons extra-virgin olive oil
- 1 cup of grated mozzarella cheese
- ½ cup grated Parmesan cheese
- fresh oregano sprigs (optional)
- Ground red pepper (optional)

Directions:

1   For the sauce, mix tomato sauce, garlic, pepper, salt, and pepper in a pan over medium heat.

2   When the sauce is bubbling, place on low heat and stir. Cover and simmer for 15 minutes on low heat.

3   Crumble the Italian sausages in a pan and cook them over medium heat until they are no longer pink about 15 minutes. Drain on kitchen paper. Set aside.

4   Preheat the oven to 400°F. Combine olive oil, garlic, and 1 teaspoon in a small bowl. Put the hot dog bun on baking trays with aluminum foil.

5   Cover the buns with the olive oil mixture. Grill for about 5 minutes, until the edges start to brown.

Remove the pan from the oven and brush each sandwich with hot tomato sauce.

6. Garnish with golden Italian sausages, sliced pepperoni, mozzarella, and parmesan cheese.

7. Put the pan in the oven and bake for 5 to 10 minutes, at 400°F, or until the cheese is bubbling. Serve garnished with fresh oregano leaves and chopped red pepper, if desired.

Nutrition: Calories: 377 Carbs: 60g Fat: 7g Protein: 15g

1075. Basil & Artichoke Pizza

Preparation Time: 1 hours & 15 minutes
Cooking Time: 24 minutes
Servings: 4
Ingredients:

- 1 cup canned passata
- 2 cups flour
- 1 cup lukewarm water
- 1 pinch of sugar
- 1 teaspoon active dry yeast
- ¾ teaspoon salt
- 2 tablespoons olive oil
- 1½ cups frozen artichoke hearts
- ¼ cup grated Asiago cheese
- ½ onion, minced
- 3 garlic cloves, minced
- 1 tablespoon dried oregano
- 1 cup sun-dried tomatoes, chopped
- ½ teaspoon red pepper flakes
- 5-6 basil leaves, torn

Directions:

1. Sift the flour and salt in a bowl and stir in yeast. Mix lukewarm water, olive oil, and sugar in another bowl. Add the wet mixture to the dry mixture and whisk until you obtain a soft dough.
2. Place the dough on a lightly floured work surface and knead it thoroughly for 4-5 minutes until elastic. Transfer the dough to a greased bowl.

3. Cover with cling film and leave to rise for 50-60 minutes in a warm place until doubled in size. Roll out the dough to a thickness of around 12 inches.
4. Preheat oven to 400°F. Warm oil in a saucepan over medium heat and sauté onion and garlic for 3-4 minutes. Mix in tomatoes and oregano and bring to a boil.
5. Decrease the heat and simmer for another 5 minutes. Transfer the pizza crust to a baking sheet. Spread the sauce all over and top with artichoke hearts and sun-dried tomatoes.
6. Scatter the cheese and bake for 15 minutes until golden. Top with red pepper flakes and basil leaves and serve sliced.

Nutrition: Calories 254 Fat 9.5g Carbs 34.3g Protein 8g

1076. Balsamic-Glazed Pizza with Arugula & Olives

Preparation Time: 1 hour & 20 minutes
Cooking Time: 20 minutes
Servings: 4
Ingredients:

- 2 cups flour
- 1 cup lukewarm water
- 1 pinch of sugar
- 1 teaspoon active dry yeast
- 2 tablespoons olive oil
- 2 tablespoons honey
- ½ cup balsamic vinegar
- 4 cups arugula
- Salt and black pepper to taste
- 1 cup mozzarella cheese, grated
- ¾ teaspoon dried oregano
- 6 black olives, drained

Directions:

1. Sift the flour and ¾ teaspoon of salt in a bowl and stir in yeast. Mix lukewarm water, olive oil, and sugar in another bowl. Add the wet mixture to the

dry mixture and whisk until you obtain a soft dough.
2. Place the dough on a lightly floured work surface and knead it thoroughly for 4-5 minutes until elastic. Transfer the dough to a greased bowl.
3. Cover with cling film and leave to rise for 50-60 minutes in a warm place until doubled in size. Roll out the dough to a thickness of around 12 inches.
4. Place the balsamic vinegar and honey in a saucepan over medium heat and simmer for 5 minutes until syrupy. Preheat oven to 390°F.
5. Transfer the pizza crust to a baking sheet and sprinkle with oregano and mozzarella cheese; bake for 10-15 minutes.
6. Remove the pizza from the oven and top with arugula. Sprinkle with balsamic glaze and black olives and serve.

Nutrition: Calories 350 Fat 15.4g Carbs 47.1g Protein 6.4g

1077. Pepperoni Fat Head Pizza

Preparation Time: 1 hour & 20 minutes
Cooking Time: 15 minutes
Servings: 4
Ingredients:

- 2 cups flour
- 1 cup lukewarm water
- 1 pinch of sugar
- 1 teaspoon active dry yeast
- ¾ teaspoon salt
- 2 tablespoons olive oil
- 1 teaspoon dried oregano
- 2 cups mozzarella cheese
- 1 cup sliced pepperoni

Directions:

1. Sift the flour and salt in a bowl and stir in yeast. Mix lukewarm water, olive oil, and sugar in another bowl. Add the wet mixture to the dry mixture and whisk until you obtain a soft dough.
2. Place the dough on a lightly floured work surface and

knead it thoroughly for 4-5 minutes until elastic. Transfer the dough to a greased bowl.

3 Cover with cling film and leave to rise for 50-60 minutes in a warm place until doubled in size. Roll out the dough to a thickness of around 12 inches.

4 Preheat oven to 400 F. Line a round pizza pan with parchment paper. Spread the dough on the pizza pan and top with the mozzarella cheese, oregano, and pepperoni slices.

5 Bake in the oven for 15 minutes or until the cheese melts. Remove the pizza, slice and serve.

Nutrition: Calories 229 Fats 7.1g Carbs 0.4g Protein 36.4g

1078. Extra Cheesy Pizza

Preparation Time: 15 minutes
Cooking Time: 28 minutes
Servings: 4
Ingredients:
For the crust:

- ½ cup almond flour
- ¼ teaspoon salt
- 2 tablespoons ground psyllium husk
- 1 tablespoon olive oil
- 1 cup lukewarm water

For the topping:

- ½ cup sugar-free pizza sauce
- 1 cup sliced mozzarella cheese
- 1 cup grated mozzarella cheese
- 3 tablespoons grated Parmesan cheese
- 2 teaspoon Italian seasoning

Directions:

1 Preheat the oven to 400°F. Line a baking sheet with parchment paper. In a medium bowl, mix the almond flour, salt, psyllium powder, olive oil, and lukewarm water until dough forms.

2 Spread the mixture on the pizza pan and bake in the oven until crusty, 10 minutes. When ready,

remove the crust and spread the pizza sauce on top.

3 Add the sliced mozzarella, grated mozzarella, Parmesan cheese, and Italian seasoning. Bake in the oven for 18 minutes or until the cheeses melt. Serve warm.

Nutrition: Calories 193 Fats 10.2g Carbs 3.2g Protein 19.5g

1079. Spanish-Style Pizza de Jamon

Preparation Time: 1 hour & 15 minutes
Cooking Time: 15 minutes
Servings: 4
Ingredients:
For the crust:

- 2 cups flour
- 1 cup lukewarm water
- 1 pinch of sugar
- 1 teaspoon active dry yeast
- ¾ teaspoon salt
- 2 tablespoons olive oil

For the topping:

- ½ cup tomato sauce
- ½ cup sliced mozzarella cheese
- 4 ounces jamon serrano, sliced
- 7 fresh basil leaves

Directions:

1 Sift the flour and salt in a bowl and stir in yeast. Mix lukewarm water, olive oil, and sugar in another bowl. Add the wet mixture to the dry mixture and whisk until you obtain a soft dough.

2 Place the dough on a lightly floured work surface and knead it thoroughly for 4-5 minutes until elastic. Transfer the dough to a greased bowl.

3 Cover with cling film and leave to rise for 50-60 minutes in a warm place until doubled in size. Roll out the dough to a thickness of around 12 inches.

4 Preheat the oven to 400°F. Line a pizza pan with parchment paper. Spread the tomato sauce on the crust.

5 Arrange the mozzarella slices on the sauce and then the Jamon serrano. Bake for 15 minutes or until the cheese melts. Remove from the oven and top with the basil. Slice and serve warm.

Nutrition: Calories 160 Fats 6.2g Carbs 0.5g Protein 21.9g

1080. Spicy & Smoky Pizza

Preparation Time: 1 hour & 15 minutes
Cooking Time: 20 minutes
Servings: 4
Ingredients:
For the crust:

- 2 cups flour
- 1 cup lukewarm water
- 1 pinch of sugar
- 1 teaspoon active dry yeast
- ¾ teaspoon salt
- 2 tablespoons olive oil

For the topping:

- 1 tablespoon olive oil
- 1 cup sliced chorizo
- ¼ cup sugar-free marinara sauce
- 1 cup sliced smoked mozzarella cheese
- 1 jalapeño pepper, deseeded and sliced
- ¼ red onion, thinly sliced

Directions:

1 Sift the flour and salt in a bowl and stir in yeast. Mix lukewarm water, olive oil, and sugar in another bowl. Add the wet mixture to the dry mixture and whisk until you obtain a soft dough.

2 Place the dough on a lightly floured work surface and knead it thoroughly for 4-5 minutes until elastic. Transfer the dough to a greased bowl.

3 Cover with cling film and leave to rise for 50-60 minutes in a warm place until doubled in size. Roll out the dough to a thickness of around 12 inches.

4 Preheat the oven to 400°F. Line a pizza pan with parchment paper. Heat the olive oil and cook the

chorizo until brown, 5 minutes.

5 Spread the marinara sauce on the crust, top with the mozzarella cheese, chorizo, jalapeño pepper, and onion.

6 Bake in the oven until the cheese melts, 15 minutes. Remove from the oven, slice, and serve warm.

Nutrition: Calories 302 Fats 17g Carbs 1.4g Protein 31.6g

1081. Turkey Pizza with Pesto Topping

Preparation Time: 15 minutes
Cooking Time: 30 minutes
Servings: 4
Ingredients:
Pizza Crust:

- 3 cups flour
- 3 tablespoons olive oil
- ⅓ teaspoon salt
- 3 large eggs

Pesto Chicken Topping:

- ½ pound turkey ham, chopped
- 2 tablespoons cashew nuts
- Salt and black pepper to taste
- 1½ tablespoons olive oil
- 1 green bell pepper, seeded and sliced
- 1½ cups basil pesto
- 1 cup mozzarella cheese, grated
- 1½ tablespoons Parmesan cheese, grated
- 1½ tablespoons fresh basil leaves
- A pinch of red pepper flakes

Directions:

1 In a bowl, mix flour, 3 tablespoons of olive oil, salt, and eggs until a dough form. Mold the dough into a ball and place it in between two full parchment papers on a flat surface.

2 Roll it out into a circle of a ¼ -inch thickness. After, slide the pizza dough into the pizza pan and remove the parchment paper. Place the pizza pan in the oven and bake the dough for 20 minutes at 350°F.

3 Once the pizza bread is ready, remove it from the oven, fold and seal the ext ra inch of dough at its edges to make a crust around it.

4 Apply 2/3 of the pesto on it and sprinkle half of the mozzarella cheese too. Toss the chopped turkey ham in the remaining pesto and spread it on top of the pizza.

5 Sprinkle with the remaining mozzarella, bell peppers, and cashew nuts, and put the pizza back in the oven to bake for 9 minutes.

6 When it is ready, remove from the oven to cool slightly, garnish with the basil leaves and sprinkle with parmesan cheese and red pepper flakes. Slice and serve.

Nutrition: Calories 684 Fat 54g Carbs 22g Protein 31.5g

1082. Baby Spinach Pizza with Sweet Onion

Preparation Time: 1 hour & 15 minutes
Cooking Time: 53 minutes
Servings: 4
Ingredients:
For the crust:

- 2 cups flour
- 1 cup lukewarm water
- 1 pinch of sugar
- 1 teaspoon active dry yeast
- ¾ teaspoon salt
- 2 tablespoons olive oil

For the caramelized onion:

- 1 onion, sliced
- 1 teaspoon sugar
- 2 tablespoons olive oil
- ½ teaspoon salt

For the pizza:

- ¼ cup shaved Pecorino Romano cheese
- 2 tablespoons olive oil
- ½ cup grated mozzarella cheese
- 1 cup baby spinach
- ¼ cup chopped fresh basil leaves
- ½ red bell pepper, sliced

Directions:

1 Sift the flour and salt in a bowl and stir in yeast. Mix lukewarm water, olive oil, and sugar in another bowl. Add the wet mixture to the dry mixture and whisk until you obtain a soft dough.

2 Place the dough on a lightly floured work surface and knead it thoroughly for 4-5 minutes until elastic. Transfer the dough to a greased bowl.

3 Cover with cling film and leave to rise for 50-60 minutes in a warm place until doubled in size. Roll out the dough to a thickness of around 12 inches.

4 Warm olive oil in a skillet over medium heat and sauté onion with salt and sugar for 3 minutes. Lower the heat and brown for 20-35 minutes until caramelized. Preheat oven to 390°F.

5 Transfer the pizza crust to a baking sheet. Drizzle the crust with olive oil and top with onion. Cover with bell pepper and mozzarella. Bake for 10-15 minutes. Serve topped with baby spinach, basil, and Pecorino cheese.

Nutrition: Calories 399 Fat 22.7g Carbs 42.9g Protein 8.1g

1083. Italian Mushroom Pizza

Preparation Time: 1 hour & 15 minutes
Cooking Time: 25 minutes
Servings: 4
Ingredients:
For the crust:

- 2 cups flour
- 1 cup lukewarm water
- 1 pinch of sugar
- 1 teaspoon active dry yeast
- ¾ teaspoon salt
- 2 tablespoons olive oil

For the topping:

- 1 teaspoon olive oil
- 2 medium cremini mushrooms, sliced
- 1 garlic clove, minced

- ½ cup sugar-free tomato sauce
- 1 teaspoon sugar
- 1 bay leaf
- 1 teaspoon dried oregano
- 1 teaspoon dried basil
- Salt and black pepper to taste
- ½ cup grated mozzarella cheese
- ½ cup grated Parmesan cheese
- 6 black olives, pitted and sliced

Directions:

1. Sift the flour and salt in a bowl and stir in yeast. Mix lukewarm water, olive oil, and sugar in another bowl. Add the wet mixture to the dry mixture and whisk until you obtain a soft dough.
2. Place the dough on a lightly floured work surface and knead it thoroughly for 4-5 minutes until elastic. Transfer the dough to a greased bowl.
3. Cover with cling film and leave to rise for 50-60 minutes in a warm place until doubled in size. Roll out the dough to a thickness of around 12 inches.
4. Preheat the oven to 400°F. Line a pizza pan with parchment paper. Heat the olive oil in a medium skillet and sauté the mushrooms until softened, 5 minutes. Stir in the garlic and cook until fragrant, 30 seconds.
5. Mix in the tomato sauce, sugar, bay leaf, oregano, basil, salt, and black pepper. Cook for 2 minutes and turn the heat off.
6. Spread the sauce on the crust, top with the mozzarella and Parmesan cheeses, and then, the olives. Bake in the oven until the cheese melts, 15 minutes. Remove the pizza, slice, and serve warm.

Nutrition: Calories 203 Fats 8.6g Carbs 2.6g Protein 24.3g

1084. Broccoli-Pepper Pizza

Preparation Time: 15 minutes
Cooking Time: 20 minutes
Servings: 4
Ingredients:
For the crust:

- ½ cup almond flour
- ¼ teaspoon salt
- 2 tablespoons ground psyllium husk
- 1 tablespoon olive oil
- 1 cup lukewarm water

For the topping:

- 1 tablespoon olive oil
- 1 cup sliced fresh mushrooms
- 1 white onion, thinly sliced
- 3 cups broccoli florets
- 4 garlic cloves, minced
- ½ cup pizza sauce
- 4 tomatoes, sliced
- 1½ cup grated mozzarella cheese
- ½ cup grated Parmesan cheese

Directions:

1. Preheat the oven to 400°F. Line a baking sheet with parchment paper. In a bowl, mix the almond flour, salt, psyllium powder, olive oil, and lukewarm water until dough forms.
2. Spread the mixture on the pizza pan and bake in the oven until crusty, 10 minutes. When ready, remove the crust and allow cooling.
3. Heat olive oil in a skillet and sauté the mushrooms, onion, garlic, and broccoli until softened, 5 minutes.
4. Spread the pizza sauce on the crust and top with the broccoli mixture, tomato, mozzarella and Parmesan cheeses. Bake for 5 minutes.

Nutrition: Calories 180 Fats 9g Carbs 3.6g Protein 17g

1085. White Pizza with Prosciutto and Arugula

Preparation Time: 10 minutes
Cooking Time: 15 minutes
Servings: 6
Ingredients:

- 1-pound prepared pizza dough

- ½ cup ricotta cheese
- 1 tablespoon garlic, minced
- 1 cup grated mozzarella cheese
- 3 ounces prosciutto, thinly sliced
- ½ cup fresh arugula
- ½ teaspoon freshly ground black pepper

Directions:

1. Preheat the oven to 450°F. Roll out the pizza dough on a floured surface. Put the pizza dough on a parchment-lined baking sheet or pizza sheet. Put the dough in the oven and bake for 8 minutes.
2. In a small bowl, mix together the ricotta, garlic, and mozzarella. Remove the pizza dough from the oven and spread the cheese mixture over the top.
3. Bake for another 5 to 6 minutes. Top the pizza with prosciutto, arugula, and pepper; serve warm.

Nutrition: Calories: 273 Protein: 12.3g Carbs: 34g Fat: 11g

1086. Za'atar Pizza

Preparation Time: 10 minutes
Cooking Time: 15 minutes
Servings: 5
Ingredients:

- 1 sheet puff pastry
- ¼ cup extra-virgin olive oil
- ⅓ cup za'atar seasoning

Directions:

1. Preheat the oven to 350°F. Put the puff pastry on a parchment-lined baking sheet. Cut the pastry into desired slices.
2. Brush the pastry with olive oil. Sprinkle with the zaatar. Put the pastry in the oven and bake for 10 to 12 minutes or until edges are lightly browned and puffed up. Serve warm or at room temperature.

Nutrition: Calories: 153 Protein: 10.3g Carbs: 21g Fat: 10g

1087. Broccoli Cheese Burst Pizza

Preparation Time: 20 minutes
Cooking Time: 5 minutes
Servings: 6
Ingredients:

- 1 cup mozzarella cheese, shredded
- 2/3 cup ricotta cheese
- 2 teaspoons avocado oil
- 1 large whole-wheat pizza crust
- ¼ cup basil, chopped
- 1½ cups broccoli florets, chopped
- ½ teaspoon garlic powder
- Cornmeal (for dusting)
- 1½ cups corn kernels
- Ground black pepper and salt, to taste

Directions:

1 Preheat your oven to 400°F. Take a baking sheet, line it with parchment paper. Grease it with some avocado oil. Spread some cornmeal over the baking sheet

2 In a mixing bowl, combine the corn, broccoli, ricotta, mozzarella, scallions, garlic powder, basil, black pepper and salt.

3 Place the pizza crust on the baking sheet. Add the topping mixture on top and bake until the top is light brown, for 12-15 minutes. Slice and serve warm!

Nutrition: Calories 417 Fat 11g Carbs 53g Protein 19g

1088. Mozzarella Bean Pizza

Preparation Time: 10 minutes
Cooking Time: 15 minutes
Servings: 6
Ingredients:

- 2 tablespoons cornmeal
- 1 cup mozzarella
- ⅓ cup barbecue sauce
- 1 Roma tomato, diced
- 1 cup black beans
- 1 cup corn kernels
- 1 medium whole-wheat pizza crust

Directions:

1 Preheat your oven to 400°F. Take a baking sheet, line it with parchment paper. Grease it with some avocado oil. Spread some cornmeal over the baking sheet.

2 In a bowl, mix together the tomatoes, corn and beans. Place the pizza crust on the baking sheet.

3 Spread the sauce on top; add the topping, and top with the cheese and bake until the cheese melts and the crust edges are golden-brown for 12-15 minutes. Slice and serve warm.

Nutrition: Calories 223 Fat 14g Carbs 41g Protein 8g

1089. Pizza Dough Without Yeast in Milk

Preparation Time: 5 minutes
Cooking Time: 1 hour
Servings: 5
Ingredients:

- 2 cups wheat flour
- 125 ml milk
- 1 teaspoon salt
- 2 pieces chicken egg
- 2 tablespoons sunflower oil

Directions:

1 Making pizza dough without yeast in milk is quite simple. The recipe is designed to prepare a dough, which is enough for two, but only large, baking sheets.

2 Combine flour and salt in one bowl. And in the second butter, milk and eggs, mix well and combine the contents of two bowls in one large container.

3 Wait a few minutes for the whole liquid consistency to soak in the flour, and start mixing the dough. It will take about 15 minutes. Dough, in finished form, should be elastic, soft and smooth.

4 Then you need to take a kitchen towel, of course clean and soak it in water. As a result, it should be moist, but not wet. Excess fluid must be squeezed out. Wrap the dough in a towel, leave to lie down for 20 minutes.

5 After waiting for the set time, remove the dough and, sprinkling flour on the countertop, roll out, but only very thinly.

6 Place it on a baking sheet and lay out the filling prepared according to your taste preferences. As a result, the finished dough will have an effect that is easy, of course, of puff pastry and has a crispy taste.

Nutrition: Calories: 453 Protein: 10.3g Carbs: 30.4g Fat: 14.3g

1090. Ideal Pizza Dough (On A Large Baking Sheet)

Preparation Time: 10 minutes
Cooking Time: 1 hour
Servings: 5
Ingredients:

- 13 ounces wheat flour
- 1½ teaspoons salt
- 1,799 teaspoons dry yeast
- 1 teaspoon sugar
- 200 ml water
- 1 tablespoon olive oil
- 1½ teaspoons dried Basil

Directions:

1 We cultivate yeast in warm water. There you can add a spoonful of sugar, so the yeast will begin to work faster. Leave them for 10 minutes.

2 Sift the flour through a sieve (leave 2 oz. for the future) in a deep bowl. Add salt, basil, mix. Pour water with yeast into the cavity in the flour and mix thoroughly with a fork.

3 Somewhere in the middle of the process, when the dough becomes less than one whole, add olive oil. When the dough is ready, cover with a damp towel and put in the heat for 30 minutes.

4 Now just lay it on a flour-dusted surface and roll out

the future pizza to a thickness of 2-3 mm.

5   The main rule of pizza is the maximum possible temperature, minimum time. Therefore, feel free to set the highest temperature that is available in your oven.

Nutrition: Calories: 193 Protein: 10.3g Carbs: 34g Fat: 9.3g

1091. Vegetable Oil Pizza Dough

Preparation Time: 10 minutes
Cooking Time: 1 hour
Servings: 3
Ingredients:

- 1 cup wheat flour
- 1 cup water
- Salt to taste
- 1 tablespoon vegetable oil
- 10 g Dry yeast

Directions:

1   We mix water and yeast, leave for 40 minutes so that they disperse. You can add a tablespoon of sugar.
2   Then pour in the oil, add the flour; knead well, and put in a warm place to increase the volume by 2 times.

Nutrition: Calories: 223 Protein: 10.3g Carbs: 9.4g Fat: 5.3g

1092. Pizza Dough on Yogurt

Preparation Time: 10 minutes
Cooking Time: 30 minutes
Servings: 5
Ingredients:

- 9 ounces natural yogurt
- 5 tablespoons vegetable oil
- ½ teaspoon salt
- 2½ cups heat flour
- 1 teaspoon baking powder

Directions:

1   Mix flour, baking powder and salt. Add yogurt and butter, mix everything thoroughly. Preheat the oven to 190°C.
2   Lubricate the pan with oil. Roll the dough very thinly and transfer to a baking sheet. Put the filling to taste. Bake for 10-15 minutes.

Nutrition: Calories: 336 Protein: 10.3g Carbs: 24g Fat: 13.3g

1093. Eggplant Pizza

Preparation Time: 10 minutes
Cooking Time: 30 minutes
Servings: 6
Ingredients:

- Eggplants (1 large or 2 medium)
- Olive oil (.33 cup)
- Black pepper & salt (as desired)
- Marinara sauce - store-bought/homemade (1.25 cups)
- Shredded mozzarella cheese (1.5 cups)
- Cherry tomatoes (2 cups - halved)
- Torn basil leaves (.5 cup)

Directions:

1   Heat the oven to reach 400°F. Prepare a baking sheet with a layer of parchment baking paper.
2   Slice the end/ends off of the eggplant and them it into ¾-inch slices. Arrange the slices on the prepared sheet and brush both sides with olive oil. Dust with pepper and salt to your liking.
3   Roast the eggplant until tender (10 to 12 minutes.).
4   Transfer the tray from the oven and add two tablespoons of sauce on top of each section. Top it off with the mozzarella and three to five tomato pieces on top.
5   Bake it until the cheese is melted. The tomatoes should begin to blister in about five to seven more minutes. Take the tray from the oven. Serve hot and garnish with a dusting of basil.

Nutrition: Protein: 8 g Fat: 20 g Carbs: 25 g Calories: 257

1094. Mediterranean Whole Wheat Pizza

Preparation Time: 5 minutes
Cooking Time: 25 minutes
Servings: 4
Ingredients:

- Whole-wheat pizza crust (1)

- Basil pesto (4 oz. jar)
- Artichoke hearts (.5 cup)
- Kalamata olives (2 tablespoons)
- Pepperoncini (2 tablespoons drained)
- Feta cheese (.25 cup)

Directions:

1   Program the oven to 450°F. Drain and pull the artichokes to pieces. Slice/chop the pepperoncini and olives.
2   Arrange the pizza crust onto a floured work surface and cover it using pesto. Arrange the artichoke, pepperoncini slices, and olives over the pizza. Lastly, crumble and add the feta.
3   Bake in the hot oven until the cheese has melted, and it has a crispy crust for 10-12 minutes.

Nutrition: Calories: 277 Protein: 9.7 g Carbs: 24 g Fat: 18.6 g

1095. Fruit Pizza

Preparation Time: 15 minutes
Cooking Time: 0 minutes
Servings: 4
Ingredients:

- 4 watermelon slices
- 1-ounce blueberries
- 2 ounces goat cheese, crumbled
- 1 teaspoon fresh parsley, chopped

Directions:

1   Put the watermelon slices on the plate in one layer. Then sprinkle them with blueberries, goat cheese, and fresh parsley.

Nutrition: Calories 69 Protein 4.4g Carbohydrates 1.4g Fat 5.1g

1096. Sprouts Pizza

Preparation Time: 15 minutes
Cooking Time: 15 minutes
Servings: 6
Ingredients:

- 4 ounces wheat flour, whole grain
- 2 tablespoons olive oil
- ¼ teaspoon baking powder
- 5 ounces chicken fillet, boiled

- 2 ounces mozzarella cheese, shredded
- 1 tomato, chopped
- 2 ounces bean sprouts

Directions:

1 Make the pizza crust: mix wheat flour, olive oil, baking powder, and knead the dough. Roll it up in the shape of pizza crust and transfer into the pizza mold.

2 Then sprinkle it with chopped tomato, shredded chicken, and Mozzarella. Bake the pizza at 365F for 15 minutes. Sprinkle the cooked pizza with bean sprouts and cut into servings.

Nutrition: Calories 184 Protein 11.9g Carbohydrates 15.6g Fat 8.2g

1097. Cheese Pinwheels

Preparation Time: 15 minutes
Cooking Time: 25 minutes
Servings: 6
Ingredients:

- 1 teaspoon chili flakes
- ½ teaspoon dried cilantro
- 1 egg, beaten
- 1 teaspoon cream cheese
- 1 ounce Cheddar cheese, grated
- 6 ounces pizza dough

Directions:

1 Roll up the pizza dough and cut into 6 squares. Sprinkle the dough with dried cilantro, cream cheese, and Cheddar cheese.

2 Roll the dough in the shape of pinwheels, brush with beaten egg and bake in the preheated to 365°F oven for 25 minutes or until the pinwheels are light brown.

Nutrition: Calories 16 Protein 3.8g Carbohydrates 12.1g Fat 11.2g

1098. Ground Meat Pizza

Preparation Time: 15 minutes
Cooking Time: 35 minutes
Servings: 4
Ingredients:

- 7 ounces ground beef
- 1 teaspoon tomato paste
- ½ teaspoon ground black pepper

- 2 egg whites, whisked
- ½ cup Mozzarella cheese, shredded
- 1 teaspoon fresh basil, chopped

Directions:

1 Line the baking tray with baking paper. Preheat the oven to 370°F. Mix all ingredients except Mozzarella in the mixing bowl.

2 Then place the mixture in the tray and flatten it to get a thick layer. Top the pizza with Mozzarella cheese and bake in the oven for 35 minutes. Then cut the cooked pizza into servings.

Nutrition: Calories 113 Protein 18g Carbohydrates 0.7g Fat 3.8g

1099. Quinoa Flour Pizza

Preparation Time: 15 minutes
Cooking Time: 15 minutes
Servings: 6
Ingredients:

- 1-ounce pumpkin puree
- 3 tablespoons quinoa flour
- ½ teaspoon dried oregano
- 1 cup Mozzarella cheese, shredded
- 1 tomato, chopped
- 1 teaspoon olive oil

Directions:

1 Mix pumpkin puree, quinoa flour, and olive oil. Knead the dough. Roll it up in the shape of pizza crust and transfer in the lined with a baking paper baking tray.

2 Then top the pizza crust with tomato, oregano, and Mozzarella cheese. Bake the pizza at 365F for 15 minutes.

Nutrition: Calories 38 Protein 2g Carbohydrates 3.3g Fat 1.8g

1100. Artichoke Pizza

Preparation Time: 15 minutes
Cooking Time: 20 minutes
Servings: 4
Ingredients:

- 7 ounces pizza crust
- 5 ounces artichoke hearts, canned, drained, chopped

- 1 teaspoon fresh basil, chopped
- 1 tomato, sliced
- 1 cup Monterey Jack cheese, shredded

Directions:

1 Line the pizza mold with baking paper. Then put the pizza crust inside. Top it with sliced tomato, canned artichoke hearts, and basil.

2 Then top the pizza with Monterey Jack cheese and transfer to the preheated to 365°F oven. Cook the pizza for 20 minutes.

Nutrition: Calories 247 Protein 12.1g Carbohydrates 28.2g Fat 10.2g

Chapter 14. Dessert Recipes

1101. Traditional Olive Oil Cake with Figs

Preparation Time: 45 minutes
Cooking Time: 0 minutes
Servings: 2
Ingredients:

- ½-pound cooking apples, peeled, cored, and chopped
- 2 tablespoons fresh lemon juice
- 2½ cups all-purpose flour
- 1 teaspoon baking powder
- ¼ teaspoon sea salt
- ½ teaspoon ground cinnamon
- A pinch of grated nutmeg
- ¾ cup granulated sugar
- ½ cup extra-virgin olive oil
- 2 eggs
- ½ cup dried figs, chopped
- 2 tablespoons walnuts, chopped

Directions:

1. Begin by preheating your oven to 350°F.
2. Toss the chopped apples with lemon juice and set them aside.
3. Then, thoroughly combine the flour, baking powder, sea salt, cinnamon, and nutmeg.
4. Then, beat the sugar and olive oil using your mixer at low speed.
5. Gradually fold in the eggs, one at a time, and continue to mix for a few minutes more until it has thickened.
6. Add the wet mixture to the dry ingredients and stir until you get a thick batter. Fold in the figs and walnuts and stir to combine well.
7. Spoon the batter into a parchment-lined baking pan and level the top using a wooden spoon.
8. Bake in the preheated oven for about 40 minutes or until the tester comes out dry and clean. Let it cool on a wire rack before slicing and serving. Bon appétit!

Nutrition: Calories: 339; Fat: 15.6g; Carbs: 44.7g; Protein: 6.4g

1102. Mascarpone and Fig Crostini

Preparation Time: 10 minutes
Cooking Time: 10 minutes
Servings: 6-8
Ingredients:

- 1 long French baguette
- 4 tablespoons (½ stick) salted butter, melted
- 1 (8-oz.) tub mascarpone cheese
- 1 (12-oz.) jar fig jam or preserves

Directions:

1. Preheat the oven to 350°F. Slice the bread into ¼-inch-thick slices. Layout the sliced bread on a single baking sheet and brush each slice with the melted butter.
2. Put the single baking sheet in the oven and toast the bread for 5 to 7 minutes, just until golden brown.
3. Let the bread cool slightly. Spread about a teaspoon or so of the mascarpone cheese on each piece of bread. Top with a teaspoon or so of the jam. Serve immediately.

Nutrition: Calories 445 Fat 24g Carbs 48g Protein 3g

1103. Traditional Mediterranean Lokum

Preparation Time: 25 minutes
Cooking Time: 0 minutes
Servings: 20
Ingredients:

- 1-ounce confectioners' sugar
- 3½ ounces cornstarch
- 20 ounces caster sugar
- 4 ounces pomegranate juice
- 16 ounces cold water
- 3 tablespoons gelatin, powdered

Directions:

1. Line a baking sheet with parchment paper.
2. Mix the confectioners' sugar and 2 ounces of cornstarch until well combined.
3. In a saucepan, heat the caster sugar, pomegranate juice and water over low heat.
4. In a mixing bowl, combine 4 ounces of cold water with the remaining cornstarch. Stir the mixture into the sugar syrup.
5. Slowly and gradually, add in the powdered gelatin and whisk until smooth and uniform.
6. Bring the mixture to a boil, turn the heat to medium and continue to cook for another 18 minutes, whisking constantly, until the mixture has thickened.
7. Scrape the mixture into the baking sheet and allow it to set in your refrigerator.
8. Cut your lokum into cubes and coat with the confectioners' sugar mixture. Bon appétit!

Nutrition: Calories: 208; Fat: 0.5g; Carbs: 54.4g; Protein: 0.2g

1104. Mixed Berry and Fig Compote

Preparation Time: 20 minutes
Cooking Time: 0 minutes
Servings: 5
Ingredients:

- 2 cups mixed berries
- 1 cup figs, chopped
- 4 tablespoons pomegranate juice
- ½ teaspoon ground cinnamon
- ½ teaspoon crystallized ginger
- ½ teaspoon vanilla extract
- 2 tablespoons honey

Directions:

1. Place the fruit, pomegranate juice, ground cinnamon, crystallized ginger, vanilla extract in a saucepan; bring to medium heat.

2 Turn the heat to a simmer and continue to cook for about 11 minutes, stirring occasionally to combine well. Add in the honey and stir to combine.

3 Remove from the heat and keep in your refrigerator. Bon appétit!

Nutrition: Calories: 150; Fat: 0.5g; Carbs: 36.4g; Protein: 1.4g

1105. Creamed Fruit Salad

Preparation Time: 10 minutes
Cooking Time: 0 minutes
Servings: 2
Ingredients:

- 1 orange, peeled and sliced
- 2 apples, pitted and diced
- 2 peaches, pitted and diced
- 1 cup seedless grapes
- ¾ cup Greek-style yogurt, well-chilled
- 3 tablespoons honey

Directions:

1 Divide the fruits between dessert bowls.

2 Top with the yogurt. Add a few drizzles of honey to each serving and serve well-chilled.

3 Bon appétit!

Nutrition: Calories: 250; Fat: 0.7g; Carbs: 60g; Protein: 6.4g

1106. Almond Cookies

Preparation Time: 5 minutes
Cooking Time: 10 minutes
Servings: 4-6
Ingredients:

- ½ cup sugar
- 8 tablespoons (1 stick) room temperature salted butter
- 1 large egg
- 1½ cups all-purpose flour
- 1 cup ground almonds or almond flour

Directions:

1 Preheat the oven to 375°F. Using a mixer, cream together the sugar and butter. Add the egg and mix until combined.

2 Alternately add the flour and ground almonds, ½ cup at a time, while the mixer is on slow.

3 Once everything is combined, line a baking sheet with parchment paper. Drop a tablespoon of dough on the baking sheet, keeping the cookies at least 2 inches apart.

4 Put the single baking sheet in the oven and bake just until the cookies start to turn brown around the edges for about 5 to 7 minutes.

Nutrition: Calories 604 Fat 36g Carbs 63g Protein 11g

1107. Crunchy Sesame Cookies

Preparation Time: 10 minutes
Cooking Time: 15 minutes
Servings: 14-16
Ingredients:

- 1 cup sesame seeds, hulled
- 1 cup sugar
- 8 tablespoons (1 stick) salted butter, softened
- 2 large eggs
- 1¼ cups flour

Directions:

1 Preheat the oven to 350°F. Toast the sesame seeds on a baking sheet for 3 minutes. Set aside and let cool.

2 Using a mixer, cream together the sugar and butter. Put the eggs one at a time until well-blended. Add the flour and toasted sesame seeds and mix until well-blended.

3 Drop a spoonful of cookie dough onto a baking sheet and form them into round balls, about 1-inch in diameter, similar to a walnut.

4 Put in the oven and bake for 5 to 7 minutes or until golden brown. Let the cookies cool and enjoy.

Nutrition: Calories 218 Fat 12g Carbs 25g Protein 4g

1108. Mini Orange Tarts

Preparation Time: 45 minutes
Cooking Time: 0 minutes
Servings: 2
Ingredients:

- 1 cup coconut flour

- ½ cup almond flour
- A pinch of grated nutmeg
- A pinch of sea salt
- ¼ teaspoon ground cloves
- ¼ teaspoon ground anise
- 1 cup brown sugar
- 6 eggs
- 2 cups heavy cream
- 2 oranges, peeled and sliced

Directions:

1 Begin by preheating your oven to 350°F.

2 Thoroughly combine the flour with spices. Stir in the sugar, eggs, and heavy cream. Mix again to combine well.

3 Divide the batter into six lightly greased ramekins.

4 Top with the oranges and bake in the preheated oven for about 40 minutes until the clafoutis is just set. Bon appétit!

Nutrition: Calories: 398; Fat: 28.5g; Carbs: 24.9g; Protein: 11.9g

1109. Traditional Kalo Prama

Preparation Time: 45 minutes
Cooking Time: 0 minutes
Servings: 2
Ingredients:

- 2 large eggs
- ½ cup Greek yogurt
- ½ cup coconut oil
- ½ cup sugar
- 8 ounces semolina
- 1 teaspoon baking soda
- 2 tablespoons walnuts, chopped
- ¼ teaspoon ground nutmeg
- ¼ teaspoon ground anise
- ½ teaspoon ground cinnamon
- 1 cup water
- 1½ cups caster sugar
- 1 teaspoon lemon zest
- 1 teaspoon lemon juice

Directions:

1 Thoroughly combine the eggs, yogurt, coconut oil, and sugar. Add in the semolina, baking soda, walnuts, nutmeg, anise, and cinnamon.

2 Let it rest for 1½ hours.

3 Bake in the preheated oven at 350°F for approximately 40 minutes or until a tester inserted in the center of the cake comes out dry and clean.

4 Transfer to a wire rack to cool completely before slicing.

5 Meanwhile, bring the water and caster sugar to a full boil; add in the lemon zest and lemon juice, and turn the heat to a simmer; let it simmer for about 8 minutes or until the sauce has thickened slightly.

6 Cut the cake into diamonds and pour the syrup over the top; allow it to soak for about 2 hours. Bon appétit!

Nutrition: Calories: 478; Fat: 22.5g; Carbs: 62.4g; Protein: 8.2g

1110. Turkish-Style Chocolate Halva

Preparation Time: 20 minutes
Cooking Time: 0 minutes
Servings: 2
Ingredients:

- ½ cup water
- 2 cups sugar
- 2 cups tahini
- ¼ teaspoon cardamom
- ¼ teaspoon cinnamon
- A pinch of sea salt
- 6 ounces dark chocolate, broken into chunks

Directions:

1 Bring the water to a full boil in a small saucepan. Add in the sugar and stir. Let it cook, stirring occasionally, until a candy thermometer registers 250°F. Heat off.

2 Stir in the tahini. Continue to stir with a wooden spoon just until halva comes together in a smooth mass; do not overmix your halva.

3 Add in the cardamom, cinnamon, and salt; stir again to combine well. Now, scrape your halva into a parchment-lined square pan.

4 Microwave the chocolate until melted; pour the melted chocolate over your halva and smooth the top.

5 Let it cool to room temperature; cover tightly with a plastic wrap and place in your refrigerator for at least 2 hours. Bon appétit!

Nutrition: Calories: 388; Fat: 27.5g; Carbs: 31.6g; Protein: 7.9g

1111. Rice Pudding with Dried Figs

Preparation Time: 45 minutes
Cooking Time: 0 minutes
Servings: 2
Ingredients:

- 3 cups milk
- 1 cup water
- 2 tablespoons sugar
- ⅓ cup white rice, rinsed
- 1 tablespoon honey
- 4 dried figs, chopped
- ½ teaspoon cinnamon
- ½ teaspoon rose water

Directions:

1 In a deep saucepan, bring the milk, water and sugar to a boil until the sugar has dissolved.

2 Stir in the rice, honey, figs, raisins, cinnamon, and turn the heat to a simmer; let it simmer for about 40 minutes, stirring periodically to prevent your pudding from sticking.

3 Afterward, stir in the rose water. Divide the pudding between individual bowls and serve. Bon appétit!

Nutrition: Calories: 228; Fat: 6.1g; Carbs: 35.1g; Protein: 7.1g

1112. Fruit Kabobs with Yogurt Deep

Preparation Time: 10 minutes
Cooking Time: 0 minutes
Servings: 2
Ingredients:

- 8 clementine orange segments
- 8 medium-sized strawberries
- 8 pineapple cubes
- 8 seedless grapes
- ½ cup Greek-style yogurt
- ½ teaspoon vanilla extract
- 2 tablespoons honey

Directions:

1 Thread the fruits onto 4 skewers.

2 In a mixing dish, thoroughly combine the yogurt, vanilla, and honey.

3 Serve alongside your fruit kabobs for dipping. Bon appétit!

Nutrition: Calories: 98; Fat: 0.2g; Carbs: 20.7g; Protein: 2.8g

1113. Stuffed Dried Figs

Preparation Time: 20 Minutes
Cooking Time: 0 Minutes
Servings: 4
Ingredients:

- 12 dried figs
- 2 tablespoons thyme honey
- 2 tablespoons sesame seeds
- 24 walnut halves

Directions:

1 Cut off the tough stalk ends of the figs.

2 Slice open each fig.

3 Stuff the fig openings with two walnut halves and close

4 Arrange the figs on a plate, drizzle with honey, and sprinkle the sesame seeds on it.

5 Serve.

Nutrition: Calories: 110kcal Carbs: 26 Fat: 3g, Protein: 1g

1114. Feta Cheesecake

Preparation Time: 30 Minutes
Cooking Time: 90 Minutes
Servings: 12
Ingredients:

- 2 cups graham cracker crumbs (about 30 crackers)
- ½ teaspoon ground cinnamon
- 6 tablespoons unsalted butter, melted
- ½ cup sesame seeds, toasted
- 12 ounces cream cheese, softened
- 1 cup crumbled feta cheese
- 3 large eggs & 1 cup of sugar
- 2 cups plain yogurt
- 2 tablespoons grated lemon zest & 1 teaspoon vanilla

Directions:

1 Set the oven to 350°F.

2 Mix the cracker crumbs, butter, cinnamon, and sesame seeds with a fork. Move the combination to a springform pan and spread until it is even. Refrigerate.

3   In a separate bowl, mix the cream cheese and feta. With an electric mixer, beat both kinds of cheese together. Add the eggs one after the other, beating the mixture with each new addition. Add sugar, then keep beating until creamy. Mix in yogurt, vanilla, and lemon zest.

4   Bring out the refrigerated springform and spread the batter on it. Then place it in a baking pan. Pour water in the pan till it is halfway full.

5   Bake for about 50 minutes. Remove cheesecake and allow it to cool. Refrigerate for at least 4 hours.

6   It is done. Serve when ready.

Nutrition: Calories: 98kcal Carbs: 7g Fat: 7g Protein: 3g

1115. No-Bake Chocolate Squares

Preparation Time: 10 minutes
Cooking Time: 0 minutes
Servings: 2
Ingredients:

- 8 ounces bittersweet chocolate
- 1 cup tahini paste
- ¼ cup almonds, chopped
- ¼ cup walnuts, chopped

Directions:

1   Microwave the chocolate for about 30 seconds or until melted. Stir in the tahini, almonds, and walnuts.

2   Spread the batter into a parchment-lined baking pan. Place in your refrigerator until set, for about 3 hours.

3   Cut into squares and serve well-chilled. Bon appétit!

Nutrition: Calories: 198; Fat: 13g; Carbs: 17.3g; Protein: 4.6g

1116. Greek Parfait with Mixed Berries

Preparation Time: 10 minutes
Cooking Time: 0 minutes
Servings: 2
Ingredients:

- 2 cups Greek yogurt
- 2 cups mixed berries
- ½ cup granola

Directions:

1   Alternate layers of mixed berries, granola, and yogurt until two dessert bowls are filled completely.

2   Cover and place in your refrigerator until you're ready to serve. Bon appétit!

Nutrition: Calories: 238; Fat: 16.7g; Carbs: 53g; Protein: 21.6g

1117. Greek-Style Chocolate Semifreddo

Preparation Time: 15 minutes
Cooking Time: 0 minutes
Servings: 2
Ingredients:

- 3 ounces dark chocolate, broken into chunks
- 1 teaspoon vanilla extract
- A pinch of grated nutmeg
- A pinch of sea salt
- 1 cup heavy cream, divided
- 2 egg whites, at room temperature
- ½ cup caster sugar
- 4 tablespoons water
- ½ cup plain Greek yogurt
- 1 tablespoon brandy
- 2 tablespoons dark chocolate curls, to decorate

Directions:

1   In a glass bowl, thoroughly combine the chocolate, vanilla, nutmeg, and sea salt.

2   In a small saucepan, bring the cream to a simmer. Pour the hot cream over the chocolate mixture and stir until everything is well incorporated.

3   Place in your refrigerator for about 1 hour.

4   Now, mix the egg whites at high speed until soft peaks form.

5   Dissolve the sugar in water over medium-low heat until a candy thermometer registers 250°F or until the syrup has thickened.

6   Now, pour the syrup into the beaten egg whites and continue to beat until glossy. Fold in the chilled chocolate mixture, Greek

yogurt, and brandy; mix again until everything is well combined.

7   Freeze your dessert for at least 3 hours. Then, let it sit at room temperature for about 15 minutes before slicing and serving. Top with the chocolate curls. Bon appétit!

Nutrition: Calories: 517; Fat: 27.7g; Carbs: 61g; Protein: 6.8g

1118. Traditional Italian Cake with Almonds

Preparation Time: 45 minutes
Cooking Time: 0 minutes
Servings: 2
Ingredients:

- 4 ripe peaches, peeled, pitted, and sliced
- 1 tablespoon fresh lemon juice
- 2¼ cups all-purpose flour
- 1 teaspoon baking soda
- ½ teaspoon baking powder
- A pinch of grated nutmeg
- A pinch of sea salt
- ½ teaspoon ground cloves
- ½ teaspoon ground cinnamon
- ½ cup olive oil
- 1⅓ cups sugar
- 3 eggs, at room temperature
- 1 cup Greek yogurt
- 1 teaspoon pure vanilla extract
- ½ cup almonds, chopped

Directions:

1   Begin by preheating your oven to 350°F. Toss the peaches with lemon juice and set them aside.

2   Then, thoroughly combine the dry ingredients.

3   Then, beat the olive oil and sugar using your mixer at low speed.

4   Gradually fold in the eggs, one at a time, and continue to mix for a few minutes more until it has thickened. Add in the yogurt and vanilla, and mix again.

5   Add the wet mixture to the dry ingredients and stir until you get a thick batter. Fold in the almonds and stir to combine well.

6   Spoon the batter into a parchment-lined baking pan and level the top using a wooden spoon.

7   Bake in the preheated oven for about 40 minutes or until a tester comes out dry and clean. Let it cool on a wire rack before slicing and serving. Bon appétit!

Nutrition: Calories: 407; Fat: 14.7g; Carbs: 61.4g; Protein: 6.6g

1119. Pear Croustade

Preparation Time: 30 minutes
Cooking Time: 60 minutes
Servings: 10
Ingredients:

- 1 cup plus 1 tablespoon all-purpose flour, divided
- 4½ tablespoons sugar, divided
- ⅛ teaspoon salt
- 6 tablespoons unsalted butter, chilled, cut into ½ inch cubes
- 1 large-sized egg, separated
- 1½ tablespoons ice-cold water
- 3 firm, ripe pears (Bosc), peeled, cored, sliced into ¼ inch slices 1 tablespoon fresh lemon juice
- ⅓ teaspoon ground allspice
- 1 teaspoon anise seeds

Directions:

1   Pour 1 cup of flour, 1½ tablespoons of sugar, butter, and salt into a food processor and combine the ingredients by pulsing.

2   Whisk the yolk of the egg and ice water in a separate bowl. Mix the egg mixture with the flour mixture. It will form a dough, wrap it, and set aside for an hour.

3   Set the oven to 400°F.

4   Mix the pear, sugar, leftover flour, allspice, anise seed, and lemon juice in a large bowl to make a filling.

5   Arrange the filling on the center of the dough.

6   Bake for about 40 minutes. Cool for about 15 minutes before serving.

Nutrition: Calories: 498kcal Carbs: 32g Fat: 32g Protein: 18g

1120. Loukoumades (Fried Honey Balls)

Preparation Time: 20 minutes
Cooking Time: 45 minutes
Servings: 10
Ingredients:

- 2 cups of sugar
- 1 cup of water
- 1 cup honey
- 1½ cups tepid water
- 1 tablespoon brown sugar
- ¼ cup of vegetable oil
- 1 tablespoon active dry yeast
- 1½ cups all-purpose flour, 1 cup cornstarch, ½ teaspoon salt
- Vegetable oil for frying
- 1½ cups chopped walnuts
- ¼ cup ground cinnamon

Directions:

1   Boil the sugar and water on medium heat. Add honey after 10 minutes. cool and set aside.

2   Mix the tepid water, oil, brown sugar,' and yeast in a large bowl. Allow it to sit for 10 minutes. In a distinct bowl, blend the flour, salt, and cornstarch. With your hands mix the yeast and the flour to make a wet dough. Cover and set aside for 2 hours.

3   Fry in oil at 350°F. Use your palm to measure the sizes of the dough as they are dropped into the frying pan. Fry each batch for about 3-4 minutes.

4   Immediately the loukoumades are done frying, drop them in the prepared syrup.

5   Serve with cinnamon and walnuts.

Nutrition: Calories: 355kcal Carbs: 64g Fat: 7g Protein: 6g

1121. Crème Caramel

Preparation Time: 60 minutes
Cooking Time: 60 minutes
Servings: 12
Ingredients:

- 5 cups of whole milk
- 2 teaspoons vanilla extract
- 8 large egg yolks
- 4 large-sized eggs
- 2 cups sugar, divided

- ¼ cup of water

Directions:

1   Preheat the oven to 350°F

2   Heat the milk with medium heat wait for it to be scalded.

3   Mix 1 cup of sugar and eggs in a bowl and add it to the eggs.

4   With a nonstick pan on high heat, boil the water and remaining sugar. Do not stir, instead whirl the pan. When the sugar forms caramel, divide it into ramekins.

5   Divide the egg mixture into the ramekins and place in a baking pan. Increase water to the pan until it is half full. Bake for 30 minutes.

6   Remove the ramekins from the baking pan, cool, then refrigerate for at least 8 hours.

7   Serve.

Nutrition: Calories: 110 kcal Carbs: 21g Fat: 1g Protein: 2g

1122. Galaktoboureko

Preparation Time: 30 minutes
Cooking Time: 90 minutes
Servings: 12
Ingredients:

- 4 cups sugar, divided
- 1 tablespoon fresh lemon juice
- 1 cup of water
- 1 tablespoon plus 1½ teaspoons grated lemon zest, divided into 10 cups
- Room temperature whole milk
- 1 cup plus 2 tablespoons unsalted butter, melted and divided into 2
- Tablespoons vanilla extract
- 7 large-sized eggs & 1 cup of fine semolina
- 1 package phyllo, thawed and at room temperature

Directions:

1   Preheat the oven to 350°F

2   Mix 2 cups of sugar, lemon juice, 1½ teaspoons of lemon zest, and water. Boil over medium heat. Set aside.

3   Mix the milk, 2 tablespoons of butter, and vanilla in a pot and put on medium heat. Remove from heat when milk is scalded

4   Mix the eggs and semolina in a bowl, then add the mixture to the scalded milk. Put the egg-milk mixture on medium heat. Stir until it forms a custard-like material.

5   Brush butter on each sheet then arrange all over the baking pan until everywhere is covered. Spread the custard on the bottom pile of phyllo

6   Arrange the buttered phyllo all over the top of the custard until every inch is covered.

7   Bake for about 40 minutes. cover the top of the pie with all the prepared syrup. Serve.

Nutrition: Calories: 393kcal Carbs: 55g Fat: 15g Protein: 8g

1123. Kourabiedes Almond Cookies

Preparation Time: 20 minutes
Cooking Time: 50 minutes
Servings: 20
Ingredients:

- 1½ cups unsalted butter, clarified, at room temperature 2 cups
- Confectioners' sugar, divided
- 1 large egg yolk
- 2 tablespoons brandy
- 1½ teaspoons baking powder
- 1 teaspoon vanilla extract
- 5 cups all-purpose flour, sifted
- 1 cup roasted almonds, chopped

Directions:

1   Preheat the oven to 350°F

2   Thoroughly mix butter and ½ cup of sugar in a bowl. Add in the egg after a while. Create a brandy mixture by mixing the brandy and baking powder. Add the mixture to the egg, add vanilla, then keep beating

until the ingredients are properly blended

3   Add flour and almonds to make a dough.

4   Roll the dough to form crescent shapes. You should be able to get about 40 pieces. Place the pieces on a baking sheet, then bake in the oven for 25 minutes.

5   Allow the cookies to cool, then coat them with the remaining confectioner's sugar.

6   Serve.

Nutrition: Calories: 102kcal Carbs: 10g Fat: 7g Protein: 2g

1124. Revani Syrup Cake

Preparation Time: 30 minutes
Cooking Time: 3 hours
Servings: 24
Ingredients:

- 1 tablespoon unsalted butter
- 2 tablespoons all-purpose flour
- 1 cup ground rusk or bread crumbs
- 1 cup fine semolina flour
- ¾ cup ground toasted almonds
- 3 teaspoons baking powder
- 16 large eggs
- 2 tablespoons vanilla extract
- 3 cups of sugar, divided
- 3 cups of water
- 5 (2-inch) strips lemon peel, pith removed
- 3 tablespoons fresh lemon juice
- 1 ounce of brandy

Directions:

1   Preheat the oven to 350°F. Grease the baking pan with 1 tablespoon of butter and flour.

2   Mix the rusk, almonds, semolina, baking powder in a bowl.

3   In another bowl, mix the eggs, 1 cup of sugar, vanilla, and whisk with an electric mixer for about 5 minutes. Add the semolina mixture to the eggs and stir.

4   Pour the stirred batter into the greased baking pan and place in the preheated oven.

5   With the remaining sugar, lemon peels, and water make the syrup by boiling the mixture on medium heat. Add the lemon juice after 6 minutes, then cook for 3 minutes. Remove the lemon peels and set the syrup aside.

6   After the cake is done in the oven, spread the syrup over the cake.

7   Cut the cake as you please and serve.

Nutrition: Calories: 348kcal Carbs: 55g Fat: 9g Protein: 5g

1125. Almonds and Oats Pudding

Preparation Time: 10 minutes
Cooking Time: 15 minutes
Servings: 4
Ingredients:

- 1 tablespoon lemon juice
- Zest of 1 lime
- 1½ cups of almond milk
- 1 teaspoon almond extract
- ½ cup oats
- 2 tablespoons stevia
- ½ cup silver almonds, chopped

Directions:

1   In a pan, blend the almond milk plus the lime zest and the other ingredients, whisk, bring to a simmer and cook over medium heat for 15 minutes.

2   Split the mix into bowls then serve cold.

Nutrition: Calories 174 Fat 12.1 Fiber 3.2 Carbs 3.9 Protein 4.8

1126. Mediterranean Tomato Salad with Feta and Fresh Herbs

Preparation Time: 10 minutes
Cooking Time: 15 minutes
Servings: 2
Ingredients:

- 5 diced tomatoes
- 2 ounces crumbled feta cheese
- ½ cup chopped fresh dill

- ½ cup diced onion
- 6 chopped mint leaves
- ½ teaspoon paprika
- 3 tablespoons olive oil
- 2 tablespoons minced garlic
- 2 teaspoons lemon juice
- 2 teaspoons white wine vinegar
- Salt and black pepper, to taste

Directions:
1 Combine the onions, tomatoes, herbs and garlic in a bowl, then season with your spices (salt, black pepper, paprika).
2 To create the dressing, in a separate bowl first mix together the olive oil, vinegar, and lemon juice.
3 Top with feta cheese

Nutrition: Calories: 125, Protein: 2 g, Carbohydrates: 8 g, Fat: 9g

1127. Quinoa Bowl with Yogurt, Dates, And Almonds

Preparation Time: 10 minutes
Cooking Time: 15 minutes
Servings: 2
Ingredients:
- 1½ cups water
- 1 cup quinoa
- 2 cinnamon sticks
- 1-inch knob of ginger, peeled
- ¼ teaspoon kosher salt
- 1 cup plain Greek yogurt
- ½ cup dates, pitted and chopped
- ½ cup almonds (raw or roasted), chopped
- 2 teaspoons honey (optional)

Directions:
- Bring the water, quinoa, cinnamon sticks, ginger, and salt to a boil in a medium saucepan over high heat.
- Reduce the heat to a simmer and cover; simmer for 10 to 12 minutes. Remove the cinnamon sticks and ginger. Fluff with a fork.
- Add the yogurt, dates, and almonds to the quinoa and mix together. Divide evenly among 4 bowls and garnish

with ½ teaspoon honey per bowl, if desired.
- Use any nuts or seeds you like in place of the almonds.

Nutrition: Calories: 125, Protein: 2 g, Carbohydrates: 8 g, Fat: 9g

1128. Almond Butter Banana Chocolate Smoothie

Preparation Time: 5 minutes
Cooking Time: 30 minutes
Servings: 2
Ingredients:
- ¾ cup almond milk
- ½ medium banana, preferably frozen
- ¼ cup frozen blueberries
- 1 tablespoon almond butter
- 1 tablespoon unsweetened cocoa powder
- 1 tablespoon chia seeds

Directions:
1 In a blender or Vitamix, add all the ingredients. Blend to combine.
2 Peanut butter, sunflower seed butter, and other nut butter are good choices to replace the almond butter

Nutrition: Calories: 125, Protein: 2 g, Carbohydrates: 8 g, Fat: 9g

1129. Ekmek Kataifi

Preparation Time: 30 Minutes
Cooking Time: 45 Minutes
Servings: 10
Ingredients:
- 1 cup of sugar
- 1 cup of water
- 2 (2-inch) strips lemon peel, pith removed
- 1 tablespoon fresh lemon juice
- ½ cup plus 1 tablespoon unsalted butter, melted
- ½ pound frozen kataifi pastry, thawed, at room temperature
- 2½ cups whole milk
- ½ teaspoon ground mastiha
- 2 large eggs
- ¼ cup fine semolina
- 1 teaspoon of cornstarch
- ¼ cup of sugar
- ½ cup sweetened coconut flakes

- 1 cup whipping cream
- 1 teaspoon vanilla extract
- 1 teaspoon powdered milk
- 3 tablespoons of confectioners' sugar
- ½ cup chopped unsalted pistachios

Directions:
1 Set the oven to 350°F. Grease the baking pan with 1 tablespoon of butter.
2 Put a pot on medium heat, then add water, sugar, lemon juice, lemon peel. Leave to boil for about 10 minutes. Reserve.
3 Untangle the kataifi, coat with the leftover butter, then place in the baking pan.
4 Mix the milk and mastiha, then place it on medium heat. Remove from heat when the milk is scalded, then cool the mixture.
5 Mix the eggs, cornstarch, semolina, and sugar in a bowl, stir thoroughly, then whisk the cooled milk mixture into the bowl.
6 Transfer the egg and milk mixture to a pot and place on heat. Wait for it to thicken like custard, then add the coconut flakes and cover it with a plastic wrap. Cool.
7 Spread the cooled custard-like material over the kataifi. Place in the refrigerator for at least 8 hours.
8 Strategically remove the kataifi from the pan with a knife. Take it away in such a way that the mold faces up.
9 Whip a cup of cream, add 1 teaspoon of vanilla, 1 teaspoon of powdered milk, and 3 tablespoons of sugar. Spread the mixture all over the custard, wait for it to harden, then flip and add the leftover cream mixture to the kataifi side.
10 Serve.

Nutrition: Calories: 649kcal Carbs: 37g Fat: 52g Protein: 11g

1130. Strawberry Rhubarb Smoothie

Preparation Time: 8 minutes
Cooking Time: 0 minutes
Servings: 2
Ingredients:

- 1 cup strawberries, fresh & sliced
- 1 rhubarb stalk, chopped
- 2 tablespoons honey, raw
- 3 ice cubes
- ⅛ teaspoon ground cinnamon
- ½ cup Greek yogurt, plain

Directions:

1. Start by getting out a small saucepan and fill it with water. Place it over high heat to bring it to a boil, and then add in your rhubarb.
2. Boil for three minutes before draining and transferring it to a blender.
3. In your blender add in your yogurt, honey, cinnamon and strawberries. Blend until smooth, and then add in your ice.
4. Blend until there are no lumps and it's thick. Enjoy cold.

Nutrition: Calories: 295, Protein: 6 g, Fat: 8 g, Carbs: 56 g

1131. Walnut & Date Smoothie
Preparation Time: 10 minutes
Cooking Time: 0 minutes
Servings: 2
Ingredients:

- 4 dates, pitted
- ½ cup milk
- 2 cups Greek yogurt, plain
- ½ cup walnuts
- ½ teaspoon cinnamon, ground
- ½ teaspoon vanilla extract, pure
- 2-3 ice cubes

Directions:

1. Blend everything together until smooth, and then serve chilled.

Nutrition: Calories: 385, Protein: 21 g, Fat: 17 g, Carbs: 35 g

1132. Vanilla Apple Compote
Preparation Time: 10 minutes

Cooking Time: 15 minutes
Servings: 2
Ingredients:

- 3 cups apples, cored and cubed
- 1 teaspoon vanilla
- ¾ cup coconut sugar
- 1 cup of water
- 2 tablespoons fresh lime juice

Directions:

1. Add all ingredients into the inner pot of the instant pot and stir well.
2. Seal pot with lid and cook on high for 15 minutes.
3. Once done, allow to release pressure naturally for 10 minutes then release remaining using quick release. Remove lid.
4. Stir and serve.

Nutrition: Calories 76 Fat 0.2 g Carbohydrates 19.1 g Sugar 11.9 g Protein 0.5 g Cholesterol 0 mg

1133. Apple Dates Mix
Preparation Time: 10 minutes
Cooking Time: 15 minutes
Servings: 2
Ingredients:

- 4 apples, cored and cut into chunks
- 1 teaspoon vanilla
- 1 teaspoon cinnamon
- ½ cup dates, pitted
- 1½ cups apple juice

Directions:

1. Add all ingredients into the inner pot of the instant pot and stir well.
2. Seal pot with lid and cook on high for 15 minutes.
3. Once done, allow to release pressure naturally for 10 minutes then release remaining using quick release. Remove lid.
4. Stir and serve.

Nutrition: Calories 226 Fat 0.6 g Carbohydrates 58.6 g Sugar 46.4 g Protein 1.3 g Cholesterol 0 mg

1134. Lemon Pear Compote
Preparation Time: 10 minutes

Cooking Time: 15 minutes
Servings: 2
Ingredients:

- 3 cups pears, cored and cut into chunks
- 1 teaspoon vanilla
- 1 teaspoon liquid stevia
- 1 tablespoon lemon zest, grated
- 2 tablespoons lemon juice

Directions:

1. Add all ingredients into the inner pot of the instant pot and stir well.
2. Seal pot with lid and cook on high for 15 minutes.
3. Once done, allow to release pressure naturally for 10 minutes then release remaining using quick release. Remove lid.
4. Stir and serve.

Nutrition: Calories 50 Fat 0.2 g Carbohydrates 12.7 g Sugar 8.1 g Protein 0.4 g Cholesterol 0 mg

1135. Strawberry Stew
Preparation Time: 10 minutes
Cooking Time: 15 minutes
Servings: 2
Ingredients:

- 12 ounces fresh strawberries, sliced
- 1 teaspoon vanilla
- 1½ cups water
- 1 teaspoon liquid stevia
- 2 tablespoons lime juice

Directions:

1. Add all ingredients into the inner pot of the instant pot and stir well.
2. Seal pot with lid and cook on high for 15 minutes.
3. Once done, allow to release pressure naturally for 10 minutes then release remaining using quick release. Remove lid.
4. Stir and serve.

Nutrition: Calories 36 Fat 0.3 g Carbohydrates 8.5 g Sugar 4.7 g Protein 0.7 g Cholesterol 0 mg

1136. Oat and Fruit Parfait
Preparation Time: 10 minutes
Cooking Time: 10 minutes

Servings: 2

Ingredients:

- ½ cup whole-grain rolled or quick-cooking oats (not instant)
- ½ cup walnut pieces
- 1 teaspoon honey
- 1 cup sliced fresh strawberries
- 1½ cups (12-oz.) vanilla low-fat Greek yogurt
- Fresh mint leaves for garnish

Directions:

1 Preheat the oven to 300°F.
2 Spread the oats and walnuts in a single layer on a baking sheet
3 Toast the oats and nuts just until you begin to smell the nuts, 10 to 12 minutes. Remove the pan from the oven and set aside.
4 In a small microwave-safe bowl, heat the honey just until warm, about 30 seconds. Add the strawberries and stir to coat.
5 Place 1 tablespoon of the strawberries in the bottom of each of 2 dessert dishes or 8-ounce glasses.
6 Add a portion of yogurt and then a portion of oats and repeat the layers until the containers are full, ending with the berries. Serve immediately or chill until ready to eat.

Nutrition: Calories: 385, Protein: 21 g, Fat: 17 g, Carbs: 35 g

1137. Watermelon Feta & Balsamic Pizza

Preparation Time: 5 minutes
Cooking Time: 15 minutes
Servings: 4

Ingredients:

- Watermelon (1-inch thick from the center)
- Crumbled feta cheese (1 oz.)
- Sliced Kalamata olives (5-6)
- Mint leaves (1 teaspoon)
- Balsamic glaze (.5 tablespoons)

Directions:

1 Slice the widest section of the watermelon in half.

Then, slice each half into four wedges. Serve on a round pie dish like a pizza round and cover with the olives, cheese, mint leaves, and glaze.

Nutrition: Calories: 90 Protein: 2 g Fat: 3 g Carbs 5 g

1138. Banana Dessert with Chocolate Chips

Preparation Time: 20 minutes
Cooking Time: 30 minutes
Servings: 24

Ingredients:

- 2/3 cup white sugar
- ¾ cup butter
- 2/3 cup brown sugar
- 1 egg, beaten
- 1 teaspoon vanilla extract
- 1 cup banana puree
- 1¾ cup flour
- 2 teaspoons baking powder
- ½ teaspoon salt
- 1 cup semi-sweet chocolate chips

Directions:

1 Preheat oven at 350°F. In a bowl, add the sugars and butter and beat until lightly colored. Add the egg and vanilla. Add the banana puree and stir.
2 In another bowl mix baking powder, flour, and salt. Add this mixture to the butter mixture. Stir in the chocolate chips.
3 Prepare a baking pan and place the dough onto it. Bake for 20 minutes and let it cool for 5 minutes before slicing into equal squares.

Nutrition: Calories 174 Fat 8.2g Carbs 25.2g Protein 1.7g

1139. Cranberry and Pistachio Biscotti

Preparation Time: 20 minutes
Cooking Time: 60 minutes
Servings: 4

Ingredients:

- ¼ cup light olive oil
- ¾ cup white sugar
- 2 teaspoons vanilla extract
- ½ teaspoon almond extract
- 2 eggs

- 1¾ cup all-purpose flour
- ¼ teaspoon salt
- 1 teaspoon baking powder
- ½ cup dried cranberries
- 1½ cup pistachio nuts

Directions:

1 Preheat the oven at 300°F. Combine olive oil and sugar in a bowl and mix well. Add eggs, almond and vanilla extracts, stir.
2 Add baking powder, salt, and flour. Add cranberries and nuts, mix. Divide the dough in half — form two 12 x 2-inch logs on a parchment baking sheet.
3 Set in the oven and bake for 35 minutes or until the blocks are golden brown. Set from oven and allow to cool for about 10 minutes.
4 Set the oven to 275°F. Cut diagonal trunks into ¾-inch-thick slices. Place on the sides of the baking sheet covered with parchment. Bake for about 8 - 10 minutes or until dry. You can serve it both hot and cold.

Nutrition: Calories 92 Fat 4.3g Carbs 11.7g Protein 2.1g

1140. Minty Watermelon Salad

Preparation Time: 10 minutes
Cooking Time: 0 minutes
Servings: 6-8

Ingredients:

- 1 medium watermelon
- 1 cup fresh blueberries
- 2 tablespoons fresh mint leaves
- 2 tablespoons lemon juice
- ⅓ cup honey

Directions:

1 Cut the watermelon into 1-inch cubes. Put them in a bowl. Evenly distribute the blueberries over the watermelon. Chop the mint leaves and then put them into a separate bowl.
2 Add the lemon juice and honey to the mint and whisk together. Drizzle the mint dressing over the

watermelon and blueberries. Serve cold.

Nutrition: Calories 238 Fat 1g Carbs 61g Protein 4g

1141. Date and Nut Balls

Preparation Time: 10 minutes
Cooking Time: 10 minutes
Servings: 6-8
Ingredients:

- 1 cup walnuts or pistachios
- 1 cup unsweetened shredded coconut
- 14 Medjool dates, pits removed
- 8 tablespoons (1 stick) butter, melted

Directions:

1   Preheat the oven to 350°F. Put the nuts on a baking sheet. Toast the nuts for 5 minutes.
2   Put the shredded coconut on a clean baking sheet; toast just until it turns golden brown, about 3 to 5 minutes (coconut burns fast so keep an eye on it). Once done, remove it from the oven and put it in a shallow bowl.
3   Inside a food processor with a chopping blade, put the nuts until they have a medium chop. Put the chopped nuts into a medium bowl.
4   Add the dates and melted butter to the food processor and blend until the dates become a thick paste.
5   Pour the chopped nuts into the food processor with the dates and pulse just until the mixture is combined, about 5 to 7 pulses. Remove the mixture from the food processor and scrape it into a large bowl.
6   To make the balls, spoon 1 to 2 tablespoons of the date mixture into the palm of your hand and roll around between your hands until you form a ball.
7   Put the ball on a clean, lined baking sheet. Repeat this until all of the mixtures are formed into balls.
8   Roll each ball in the toasted coconut until the outside of the ball is coated, put the ball back on the baking sheet, and repeat.
9   Put all the balls into the fridge for 20 minutes before serving so that they firm up. You can also store any leftovers inside the fridge in an airtight container.

Nutrition: Calories 489 Fat 35g Carbs 48g Protein 5g

1142. Creamy Rice Pudding

Preparation Time: 5 minutes
Cooking Time: 45 minutes
Servings: 6
Ingredients:

- 1¼ cups long-grain rice
- 5 cups whole milk
- 1 cup sugar
- 1 tablespoon of rose water/orange blossom water
- 1 teaspoon cinnamon

Directions:

1   Rinse the rice under cold water for 30 seconds. Add the rice, milk, and sugar to a large pot. Bring to a gentle boil while continually stirring.
2   Lessen the heat to low and then let simmer for 40 to 45 minutes, stirring every 3 to 4 minutes so that the rice does not stick to the bottom of the pot.
3   Add the rosewater at the end and simmer for 5 minutes. Divide the pudding into 6 bowls. Sprinkle the top with cinnamon. Let it cool for over an hour before serving. Store in the fridge.

Nutrition: Calories 394 Fat 7g Carbs 75g Protein 9g

1143. Ricotta-Lemon Cheesecake

Preparation Time: 5 minutes
Cooking Time: 1 hour
Servings: 8-10
Ingredients:

- 2 (8-oz.) packages full-fat cream cheese
- 1 (16-oz.) container full-fat ricotta cheese
- 1½ cups granulated sugar
- 1 tablespoon lemon zest
- 5 large eggs
- Nonstick cooking spray

Directions:

1   Preheat the oven to 350°F. Blend together the cream cheese and ricotta cheese. Blend in the sugar and lemon zest. Blend in the eggs; drop in 1 egg at a time, blend for 10 seconds, and repeat.
2   Put a 9-inch springform pan with parchment paper and nonstick spray. Wrap the bottom of the pan with foil. Pour the cheesecake batter into the pan.
3   To make a water bath, get a baking or roasting pan larger than the cheesecake pan. Fill the roasting pan about ⅓ of the way up with warm water.
4   Put the cheesecake pan into the water bath. Put the whole thing in the oven and let the cheesecake bake for 1 hour.
5   After baking is complete, remove the cheesecake pan from the water bath and remove the foil. Let the cheesecake cool for 1 hour on the countertop. Then put it in the fridge to cool for at least 3 hours before serving.

Nutrition: Calories 489 Fat 31g Carbs 42g Protein 15g

1144. Blueberry-Blackberry Ice Pops

Preparation Time: 5 minutes + 2 hours to freeze
Cooking Time: 0 minutes
Servings: 2
Ingredients:

- ½ (13½ -oz.) can coconut cream, ¾ cup unsweetened full-fat coconut milk, or ¾ cup heavy (whipping) cream
- 2 teaspoons Swerve natural sweetener or 2 drops liquid stevia
- ½ teaspoon vanilla extract
- ¼ cup mixed blueberries and blackberries

Directions:

1   Add together the coconut cream, sweetener, and vanilla. Add the mixed

berries, and then pulse just a few times. Pour it into ice pop molds and freeze for at least about 2 hours before serving.

Nutrition: Calories: 165 Carbohydrates: 4g Protein: 1g Fat: 17g

1145. Strawberry-Lime Ice Pops

Preparation Time: 5 minutes + 2 hours to freeze

Cooking Time: 0 minutes

Servings: 4

Ingredients:

- ½ (13½ -oz.) can coconut cream, ¾ cup unsweetened full-fat coconut milk, or ¾ cup heavy (whipping) cream
- 2 teaspoons Swerve natural sweetener or 2 drops liquid stevia
- 1 tablespoon freshly squeezed lime juice
- ¼ cup hulled and sliced strawberries (fresh or frozen)

Directions:

1   Mix together the coconut cream, sweetener, and lime juice in a blender. Add the strawberries, and pulse just a few times so the strawberries retain their texture.
2   Pour into ice pop molds, and freeze for at least 2 hours before serving.

Nutrition: Calories: 166 Carbohydrates: 5g Protein: 1g Fat: 17g

1146. Crockpot Keto Chocolate Cake

Preparation Time: 20 minutes

Cooking Time: 3 hours

Servings: 12

Ingredients:

- ¾ cup stevia sweetener
- 1½ cup almond flour
- ¼ teaspoon baking powder
- ¼ cup protein powder, chocolate, or vanilla flavor
- 2/3 cup unsweetened cocoa powder
- ¼ teaspoon salt
- ½ cup unsalted butter, melted

- 4 large eggs
- ¾ cup heavy cream
- 1 teaspoon vanilla extract

Directions:

1   Grease the ceramic inserts of the Crockpot. In a bowl, mix the sweetener, almond flour, protein powder, cocoa powder, salt, and baking powder.
2   Add the butter, eggs, cream, and vanilla extract. Pour the batter into the Crockpot and cook on low for 3 hours. Allow to cool before slicing.

Nutrition: Calories: 253 Carbohydrates: 5.1g Protein: 17.3g Fat: 29.5g

1147. Chocolate Lava Cake

Preparation Time: 30 minutes

Cooking Time: 3 hours

Servings: 12

Ingredients:

- 1½ cup stevia sweetener, divided
- ½ cup almond flour
- 5 tablespoons unsweetened cocoa powder
- ½ teaspoon salt
- 1 teaspoon baking powder
- 3 whole eggs
- 3 egg yolks
- ½ cup butter, melted
- 1 teaspoon vanilla extract
- 2 cups hot water
- 4 ounces sugar-free chocolate chips

Directions:

1   Grease the inside of the Crockpot. In a bowl, mix the stevia sweetener, almond flour, cocoa powder, salt, and baking powder.
2   In another bowl, mix the eggs, egg yolks, butter, and vanilla extract. Pour in the hot water. Pour the wet ingredients into the dry ingredients and fold to create a batter.
3   Add the chocolate chips last. Pour into the greased Crockpot and cook on low for 3 hours. Allow to cool before serving.

Nutrition: Calories: 157 Carbohydrates: 5.5g Protein: 10.6g Fat: 13g

1148. Semolina Cake with Almonds

Preparation Time: 60 minutes

Cooking Time: 0 minutes

Servings: 2

Ingredients:

- 2 cups Greek yogurt
- 1 cup full-fat milk
- ½ cup coconut oil
- 1½ cups powdered sugar
- 2 cups semolina
- 1 cup shredded coconut
- 1 teaspoon baking soda
- 1 teaspoon baking powder
- 1 tablespoon pure vanilla extract
- ¼ teaspoon ground cinnamon
- ½ cup almonds, slivered

Directions:

1   Thoroughly combine the yogurt, milk, coconut oil, and sugar. Add in the semolina, shredded coconut, baking soda, baking powder, vanilla, and cinnamon.
2   Let it rest for 1½ hours.
3   Bake in the preheated oven at 350°F for approximately 40 minutes or until a tester inserted in the center of the cake comes out dry and clean.
4   Transfer to a wire rack to cool completely before slicing and serving. Garnish with almonds and serve. Bon appétit!

Nutrition: Calories: 404; Fat: 16.4g; Carbs: 54.8g; Protein: 8.3g

1149. Romantic Mug Cakes

Preparation Time: 5 minutes

Cooking Time: 0 minutes

Servings: 2

Ingredients:

- 2 eggs
- 1½ tablespoons butter, melted
- 4 tablespoons full-fat milk
- 1 tablespoon rose water
- ¼ teaspoon ground cinnamon
- ⅛ teaspoon grated nutmeg
- A pinch of coarse sea salt

- 4 tablespoons all-purpose flour
- ½ teaspoon baking powder
- 2 tablespoons cocoa powder
- 2 tablespoons powdered sugar
- 1 teaspoon grated orange zest

Directions:

1 Whisk the eggs, melted butter, milk, rose water, cinnamon, nutmeg, and salt.
2 Add in the flour, baking powder, cocoa powder, and sugar. Spoon the batter into two mugs.
3 Microwave for 1 minute 30 seconds and top with the grated orange zest. Bon appétit!

Nutrition: Calories: 264; Fat: 14.4g; Carbs: 25.5g; Protein: 10.1g

1150. Pistachio and Tahini Halva

Preparation Time: 15 minutes
Cooking Time: 0 minutes
Servings: 2
Ingredients:

- ½ cup water
- ½-pound sugar
- 10 ounces tahini, at room temperature
- A ping of sea salt
- ½ teaspoon vanilla paste
- ½ teaspoon crystal citric acid
- ⅓ cup shelled pistachios, chopped

Directions:

1 Bring the water to a full boil in a small saucepan. Add in the sugar and stir. Let it cook, stirring occasionally, until a candy thermometer registers 250°F. Heat off.
2 Stir in the tahini. Continue to stir with a wooden spoon just until halva comes together in a smooth mass; do not overmix your halva.
3 Add in the remaining ingredients and stir again to combine well. Now, scrape your halva into a parchment-lined square pan and smooth the top.

4 Let it cool to room temperature; cover tightly with a plastic wrap and place in your refrigerator for at least 2 hours.

Nutrition: Calories: 464; Fat: 28.4g; Carbs: 49.5g; Protein: 9.4g

1151. Authentic Greek Rizogalo

Preparation Time: 40 minutes
Cooking Time: 0 minutes
Servings: 2
Ingredients:

- 1½ cups water
- ¼ cup rice
- 2 cups whole milk
- ¼ cup sugar & a pinch of sea salt
- A pinch of grated nutmeg
- 1 egg, whisked
- 1 tablespoon butter
- ½ teaspoon vanilla extract
- ¼ teaspoon ground cloves
- 1 teaspoon orange zest, grated
- ½ ground cinnamon

Directions:

1 Bring the water and rice to a boil in a saucepan. Immediately turn the heat to a simmer.
2 Let it simmer, stirring occasionally, until most of the water has been absorbed, about 30 minutes.
3 Add in the milk, sugar, salt, and nutmeg, and bring to a boil again.
4 Add about 1 cup of the warm mixture to the beaten egg and whisk to combine well.
5 Turn the heat to low; add in the egg mixture and continue simmering, stirring constantly, until the pudding has thickened.
6 Stir in the butter, vanilla, cloves, orange zest, and cinnamon, and serve at room temperature. Enjoy!

Nutrition: Calories: 247; Fat: 10.4g; Carbs: 29.1g; Protein: 8g

1152. Greek Frozen Yogurt Dessert

Preparation Time: 10 minutes

Cooking Time: 0 minutes
Servings: 2
Ingredients:

- ½ pineapple, diced
- 2 cups Greek-style yogurt, frozen
- 3 ounces almonds, slivered

Directions:

1 Divide the pineapple between two dessert bowls. Spoon the yogurt over it.
2 Top with the slivered almonds.
3 Cover and place in your refrigerator until you're ready to serve. Bon appétit!

Nutrition: Calories: 307; Fat: 14.4g; Carbs: 29.1g; Protein: 18g

1153. Salted Pistachio and Tahini Truffles

Preparation Time: 5 minutes
Cooking Time: 0 minutes
Servings: 2
Ingredients:

- ½ cup pure agave syrup
- ½ cup dates, pitted and soaked
- ⅓ cup tahini
- ⅓ cup shelled pistachios, roasted and salted
- 1 teaspoon pure vanilla extract
- ½ teaspoon ground cinnamon
- A pinch of sea salt
- 2 tablespoons carob powder
- 2 tablespoons cocoa powder
- 2 cups rolled oats

Directions:

1 In your food processor, mix all of the above ingredients, except for the oats, until well combined.
2 Add in the rolled oats and stir with a wooden spoon.
3 Roll the mixture into small balls and place in your refrigerator until ready to serve. Bon appétit!

Nutrition: Calories: 224; Fat: 9.5g; Carbs: 38.7g; Protein: 7.4g

1154. Apple and Berries Ambrosia

Preparation Time: 15 minutes
Cooking Time: 0 minutes

Servings: 4

Ingredients:

- 2 cups unsweetened coconut milk, chilled
- 2 tablespoons raw honey
- 1 apple, peeled, cored, and chopped
- 2 cups fresh raspberries
- 2 cups fresh blueberries

Directions:

1. Spoon the chilled milk in a large bowl, then mix in the honey. Stir to mix well.
2. Then mix in the remaining ingredients. Stir to coat the fruits well and serve immediately.

Nutrition: Calories: 386 Fat: 21.1g Protein: 4.2g Carbs: 45.9g

1155. Banana, Cranberry, and Oat Bars

Preparation Time: 15 minutes
Cooking Time: 40 minutes
Servings: 16 bars

Ingredients:

- 2 tablespoon extra-virgin olive oil
- 2 medium ripe bananas, mashed
- ½ cup almond butter
- ½ cup maple syrup
- ⅓ cup dried cranberries
- 1½ cups old-fashioned rolled oats
- ¼ cup oat flour
- ¼ cup ground flaxseed
- ¼ teaspoon ground cloves
- ½ cup shredded coconut
- ½ teaspoon ground cinnamon
- 1 teaspoon vanilla extract

Directions:

1. Preheat the oven to 400ºF (205ºC). Line an 8-inch square pan with parchment paper, then grease with olive oil.
2. Combine the mashed bananas, almond butter, and maple syrup in a bowl. Stir to mix well. Mix in the remaining ingredients and stir to mix well until thick and sticky.

3. Spread the mixture evenly on the square pan with a spatula, then bake in the preheated oven for 40 minutes or until a toothpick inserted in the center comes out clean.
4. Remove them from the oven and slice into 16 bars to serve.

Nutrition: Calories: 145 Fat: 7.2g Protein: 3.1g Carbs: 18.9g

1156. Berry and Rhubarb Cobbler

Preparation Time: 15 minutes
Cooking Time: 35 minutes
Servings: 8

Ingredients:

Cobbler:

- 1 cup fresh raspberries & 2 cups fresh blueberries
- 1 cup sliced (½-inch) rhubarb pieces
- 1 tablespoon arrowroot powder
- ¼ cup unsweetened apple juice
- 2 tablespoons melted coconut oil
- ¼ cup raw honey

Topping:

- 1 cup almond flour
- 1 tablespoon arrowroot powder
- ½ cup shredded coconut
- ¼ cup raw honey & ½ cup coconut oil

Directions:

1. Preheat the oven to 350ºF (180ºC). Grease a baking dish with melted coconut oil. Combine the ingredients for the cobbler in a large bowl. Stir to mix well. Spread the mixture in a single layer on the baking dish. Set aside.
2. Combine the almond flour, arrowroot powder, and coconut in a bowl. Stir to mix well. Fold in the honey and coconut oil. Stir with a fork until the mixture crumbled.
3. Spread the topping over the cobbler, then bake in the preheated oven for 35

minutes or until frothy and golden brown. Serve immediately.

Nutrition: Calories: 305 Fat: 22.1g Protein: 3.2g Carbs: 29.8g

1157. Citrus Cranberry and Quinoa Energy Bites

Preparation Time: 15 minutes
Cooking Time: 0 minutes
Servings: 12 bites

Ingredients:

- 2 tablespoons almond butter
- 2 tablespoons maple syrup
- ¾ cup cooked quinoa
- 1 tablespoon dried cranberries
- 1 tablespoon chia seeds
- ¼ cup ground almonds
- ¼ cup sesame seeds, toasted
- Zest of 1 orange
- ½ teaspoon vanilla extract

Directions:

1. Line a baking sheet with parchment paper. Combine the butter and maple syrup in a bowl. Stir to mix well.
2. Fold in the remaining ingredients and stir until the mixture holds together and smooth. Divide the mixture into 12 equal parts, then shape each part into a ball.
3. Arrange the balls on the baking sheet, then refrigerate for at least 15 minutes. Serve chilled.

Nutrition: Calories: 110 Fat: 10.8g Protein: 3.1g Carbs: 4.9g

1158. Chocolate, Almond, and Cherry Clusters

Preparation Time: 15 minutes
Cooking Time: 3 minutes
Servings: 10 clusters

Ingredients:

- 1 cup dark chocolate (60% cocoa or higher), chopped
- 1 tablespoon coconut oil
- ½ cup dried cherries
- 1 cup roasted salted almonds

Directions:

1. Line a baking sheet with parchment paper. Melt the chocolate and coconut oil in

a saucepan for 3 minutes. Stir constantly.

2   Turn off the heat and mix in the cherries and almonds. Drop the mixture on the baking sheet with a spoon. Place the sheet in the refrigerator and chill for at least 1 hour or until firm. Serve chilled.

Nutrition: Calories: 197 Fat: 13.2g Protein: 4.1g Carbs: 17.8g

1159. Chocolate and Avocado Mousse

Preparation Time: 15 minutes
Cooking Time: 5 minutes
Servings: 4-6
Ingredients:

- 8 ounces (227-g.) dark chocolate (60% cocoa or higher), chopped
- ¼ cup unsweetened coconut milk
- 2 tablespoons coconut oil
- 2 ripe avocados, deseeded
- ¼ cup raw honey
- Sea salt, to taste

Directions:

1   Put the chocolate in a saucepan. Pour in the coconut milk and add the coconut oil. Cook for 3 minutes or until the chocolate and coconut oil melt. Stir constantly.

2   Put the avocado in a food processor, then drizzle with honey and melted chocolate. Pulse to combine until smooth.

3   Pour the mixture into a serving bowl, then sprinkle with salt. Refrigerate to chill for 30 minutes and serve.

Nutrition: Calories: 654 Fat: 46.8g Protein: 7.2g Carbs: 55.9g

1160. Coconut Blueberries with Brown Rice

Preparation Time: 15 minutes
Cooking Time: 10 minutes
Servings: 4
Ingredients:

- 1 cup fresh blueberries
- 2 cups unsweetened coconut milk
- 1 teaspoon ground ginger
- ¼ cup maple syrup
- Sea salt, to taste
- 2 cups cooked brown rice

Directions:

1   Put all the ingredients, except for the brown rice, in a pot. Stir to combine well. Cook over medium-high heat for 7 minutes or until the blueberries are tender.

2   Pour in the brown rice and cook for 3 more minutes or until the rice is soft. Stir constantly. Serve immediately.

Nutrition: Calories: 470 Fat: 24.8g Protein: 6.2g Carbs: 60.1g

1161. Easy Blueberry and Oat Crisp

Preparation Time: 15 minutes
Cooking Time: 20 minutes
Servings: 4
Ingredients:

- 2 tablespoons coconut oil, melted, plus additional for greasing
- 4 cups fresh blueberries
- Juice of ½ lemon
- 2 teaspoons lemon zest
- ¼ cup maple syrup
- 1 cup gluten-free rolled oats
- ½ cup chopped pecans
- ½ teaspoon ground cinnamon
- Sea salt, to taste

Directions:

1   Preheat the oven to 350°F (180°C). Grease a baking sheet with coconut oil. Combine the blueberries, lemon juice and zest, and maple syrup in a bowl. Stir to mix well, then spread the mixture on the baking sheet.

2   Combine the remaining ingredients in a small bowl. Stir to mix well. Pour the mixture over the blueberry mixture.

3   Bake in the preheated oven for 20 minutes or until the oats are golden brown. Serve immediately with spoons.

Nutrition: Calories: 496 Fat: 32.9g Protein: 5.1g Carbs: 50.8g

1162. Glazed Pears with Hazelnuts

Preparation Time: 15 minutes
Cooking Time: 20 minutes
Servings: 4

Ingredients:

- 4 pears, peeled, cored, and quartered lengthwise
- 1 cup apple juice
- 1 tablespoon grated fresh ginger
- ½ cup pure maple syrup
- ¼ cup chopped hazelnuts

Directions:

1   Put the pears in a pot, then pour in the apple juice. Bring to a boil over medium-high heat, then reduce the heat to medium-low. Stir constantly.

2   Cover and simmer for an additional 15 minutes or until the pears are tender.

3   Meanwhile, combine the ginger and maple syrup in a saucepan. Bring to a boil over medium-high heat. Stir frequently. Turn off the heat and transfer the syrup to a small bowl and let sit until ready to use.

4   Transfer the pears to a large serving bowl with a slotted spoon, then top the pears with syrup. Spread the hazelnuts over the pears and serve immediately.

Nutrition: Calories: 287 Fat: 3.1g Protein: 2.2g Carbs: 66.9g

1163. Lemony Blackberry Granita

Preparation Time: 15 minutes
Cooking Time: 0 minutes
Servings: 4
Ingredients:

- 1 pound (454-g.) fresh blackberries
- 1 teaspoon chopped fresh thyme
- ¼ cup freshly squeezed lemon juice
- ½ cup raw honey
- ½ cup water

Directions:

1   Put all the ingredients in a food processor, then pulse to purée. Pour the mixture through a sieve into a baking dish. Discard the seeds that remain in the sieve.

2 Put the baking dish in the freezer for 2 hours. Remove the dish from the refrigerator and stir to break any frozen parts.

3 Return the dish back to the freezer for an hour, then stir to break any frozen parts again. Return the dish to the freezer for 4 hours until the granita is completely frozen.

4 Remove it from the freezer and mash to serve.

Nutrition: Calories: 183 Fat: 1.1g Protein: 2.2g Carbs: 45.9g

1164. Yogurt Dip

Preparation Time: 10 minutes
Cooking Time: 0 minutes
Servings: 6
Ingredients:

- 2 cups Greek yogurt
- 2 tablespoons pistachios, toasted and chopped
- A pinch of salt and white pepper
- 2 tablespoons mint, chopped
- 1 tablespoon kalamata olives, pitted and chopped
- ¼ cup zaatar spice
- ¼ cup pomegranate seeds
- ⅓ cup olive oil

Directions:

1 Mix the yogurt with the pistachios and the rest of the ingredients, whisk well, divide into small cups and serve with pita chips on the side.

Nutrition: Calories 294 Fat 18g Carbohydrates 2g Protein 10g

1165. Stuffed Avocado

Preparation Time: 10 minutes
Cooking Time: 0 minutes
Servings: 2
Ingredients:

- 1 avocado, halved and pitted
- 10 ounces canned tuna, drained
- 2 tablespoons sun-dried tomatoes, chopped
- 1½ tablespoon basil pesto
- 2 tablespoons black olives, pitted and chopped
- Salt and black pepper to the taste

- 2 teaspoons pine nuts, toasted and chopped
- 1 tablespoon basil, chopped

Directions:

1 Mix the tuna with the sun-dried tomatoes and the rest of the ingredients except the avocado and stir. Stuff the avocado halves with the tuna mix and serve as an appetizer.

Nutrition: Calories 233 Fat 9g Carbohydrates 11.4g Protein 5.6g

1166. Wrapped Plums

Preparation Time: 5 minutes
Cooking Time: 0 minutes
Servings: 8
Ingredients:

- 2 ounces prosciutto, cut into 16 pieces
- 4 plums, quartered
- 1 tablespoon chives, chopped
- A pinch of red pepper flakes, crushed

Directions:

1 Wrap each plum quarter in a prosciutto slice, arrange them all on a platter, sprinkle the chives and pepper flakes all over and serve.

Nutrition: Calories 30 Fat 1g Carbohydrates 4g Protein 2g

1167. Mini Nuts and Fruits Crumble

Preparation Time: 15 minutes
Cooking Time: 15 minutes
Servings: 6
Ingredients:
Topping:

- ¼ cup coarsely chopped hazelnuts
- 1 cup coarsely chopped walnuts
- 1 teaspoon ground cinnamon
- Sea salt, to taste
- 1 tablespoon melted coconut oil

Filling:

- 6 fresh figs, quartered
- 2 nectarines, pitted and sliced
- 1 cup fresh blueberries
- 2 teaspoons lemon zest
- ½ cup raw honey

- 1 teaspoon vanilla extract

Directions:

1 Combine the ingredients for the topping in a bowl. Stir to mix well. Set aside until ready to use.

2 Preheat the oven to 375°F (190°C). Combine the ingredients for the fillings in a bowl. Stir to mix well. Divide the filling into six ramekins, then divide and top with nut topping.

3 Bake in the preheated oven for 15 minutes or until the topping is lightly browned and the filling is frothy. Serve immediately.

Nutrition: Calories: 336 Fat: 18.8g Protein: 6.3g Carbs: 41.9g

1168. Mint Banana Chocolate Sorbet

Preparation Time: 4 hours & 5 minutes
Cooking Time: 0 minutes
Servings: 1
Ingredients:

- 1 frozen banana
- 1 tablespoon almond butter
- 2 tablespoons minced fresh mint
- 2 to 3 tablespoons dark chocolate chips (60% cocoa or higher)
- 2 to 3 tablespoons goji (optional)

Directions:

1 Put the banana, butter, and mint in a food processor. Pulse to purée until creamy and smooth. Add the chocolate and goji, then pulse several more times to combine well.

2 Pour the mixture in a bowl or a ramekin, then freeze for at least 4 hours before serving chilled.

Nutrition: Calories: 213 Fat: 9.8g Protein: 3.1g Carbs: 2.9g

1169. Pecan and Carrot Cake

Preparation Time: 15 minutes
Cooking Time: 45 minutes
Servings: 12
Ingredients:

- ½ cup coconut oil, at room temperature, plus more for greasing the baking dish
- 2 teaspoons pure vanilla extract
- ¼ cup pure maple syrup
- 6 eggs
- ½ cup coconut flour
- 1 teaspoon baking powder
- 1 teaspoon baking soda
- ½ teaspoon ground nutmeg
- 1 teaspoon ground cinnamon
- ⅛ teaspoon sea salt
- ½ cup chopped pecans
- 3 cups finely grated carrots

Directions:

1. Preheat the oven to 350°F (180°C). Grease a 13-by-9-inch baking dish with coconut oil. Combine the vanilla extract, maple syrup, and ½ cup of coconut oil in a large bowl. Stir to mix well.
2. Break the eggs in the bowl and whisk to combine well. Set aside. Combine the coconut flour, baking powder, baking soda, nutmeg, cinnamon, and salt in a separate bowl. Stir to mix well.
3. Make a well in the center of the flour mixture, then pour the egg mixture into the well. Stir to combine well.
4. Add the pecans and carrots to the bowl and toss to mix well. Pour the mixture into a single layer on the baking dish.
5. Bake in the preheated oven for 45 minutes or until puffed and the cake spring back when lightly press with your fingers.
6. Remove the cake from the oven. Allow to cool for at least 15 minutes, then serve.

Nutrition: Calories: 255 Fat: 21.2g Protein: 5.1g Carbs: 12.8g

1170. Raspberry Yogurt Basted Cantaloupe

Preparation Time: 15 minutes
Cooking Time: 0 minutes
Servings: 6

Ingredients:

- 2 cups fresh raspberries, mashed
- 1 cup plain coconut yogurt
- ½ teaspoon vanilla extract
- 1 cantaloupe, peeled and sliced
- ½ cup toasted coconut flakes
-

Directions:

1. Combine the mashed raspberries with yogurt and vanilla extract in a small bowl. Stir to mix well.
2. Place the cantaloupe slices on a platter, then top with the raspberry mixture and spread with toasted coconut. Serve immediately.

Nutrition: Calories: 75 Fat: 4.1g Protein: 1.2g Carbs: 10.9g

1171. Simple Apple Compote

Preparation Time: 15 minutes
Cooking Time: 10 minutes
Servings: 4

Ingredients:

- 6 apples, peeled, cored, and chopped
- ¼ cup raw honey
- 1 teaspoon ground cinnamon
- ¼ cup apple juice
- Sea salt, to taste

Directions:

1. Put all the ingredients in a stockpot. Stir to mix well, then cook over medium-high heat for 10 minutes or until the apples are glazed by honey and lightly saucy. Stir constantly. Serve immediately.

Nutrition: Calories: 246 Fat: 0.9g Protein: 1.2g Carbs: 66.3g

1172. Peanut Butter and Chocolate Balls

Preparation Time: 45 minutes
Cooking Time: 0 minutes
Servings: 15 balls

Ingredients:

- ¾ cup creamy peanut butter
- ¼ cup unsweetened cocoa powder
- 2 tablespoons softened almond butter
- ½ teaspoon vanilla extract

- 1¾ cups maple sugar

Directions:

1. Line a baking sheet with parchment paper. Combine all the ingredients in a bowl. Stir to mix well.
2. Divide the mixture into 15 parts and shape each part into a 1-inch ball. Arrange the balls on the baking sheet and refrigerate for at least 30 minutes, then serve chilled.

Nutrition: Calories: 146 Fat: 8.1g Protein: 4.2g Carbs: 16.9g

1173. Spiced Sweet Pecans

Preparation Time: 15 minutes
Cooking Time: 17 minutes
Servings: 4

Ingredients:

- 1 cup pecan halves
- 3 tablespoons almond butter
- 1 teaspoon ground cinnamon
- ½ teaspoon ground nutmeg
- ¼ cup raw honey
- ¼ teaspoon sea salt

Directions:

1. Preheat the oven to 350°F (180°C). Line a baking sheet with parchment paper. Combine all the ingredients in a bowl. Stir to mix well, then spread the mixture in the single layer on the baking sheet with a spatula.
2. Bake in the preheated oven for 16 minutes or until the pecan halves are well browned. Serve immediately.

Nutrition: Calories: 324 Fat: 29.8g Protein: 3.2g Carbs: 13.9g

1174. Lemon Crockpot Cake

Preparation Time: 15 minutes
Cooking Time: 3 hours
Servings: 8

Ingredients:

- ½ cup coconut flour
- 1½ cup almond flour
- 3 tablespoons Stevia sweetener
- 2 teaspoon baking powder
- ½ teaspoon Xanthan gum
- ½ cup whipping cream
- ½ cup butter, melted

- 1 tablespoon Juice, freshly squeezed
- Zest from one large lemon
- 2 eggs

Directions:

1. Grease the inside of the Crockpot with butter or cooking spray. Mix together coconut flour, almond flour, stevia, baking powder, and xanthan gum in a bowl.
2. In another bowl, combine the whipping cream, butter, lemon juice, lemon zest, and eggs. Mix until well combined.
3. Pour the wet ingredients into the dry ingredients gradually and fold to create a smooth batter. Spread the batter in the Crockpot and cook on low for 3 hours

Nutrition: Calories: 350 Carbohydrates: 11.1g Protein: 17.6g Fat: 32.6g

1175. Lemon and Watermelon Granita

Preparation Time: 10 minutes + 3 hours to freeze
Cooking Time: 0 minutes
Servings: 4
Ingredients:

- 4 cups watermelon cubes
- ¼ cup honey
- ¼ cup freshly squeezed lemon juice

Directions:

1. In a blender, combine the watermelon, honey, and lemon juice. Purée all the ingredients, then pour into a 9-by-9-by-2-inch baking pan and place in the freezer.
2. Every 30 to 60 minutes, run a fork across the frozen surface to fluff and create ice flakes. Freeze for about 3 hours total and serve.

Nutrition: Calories: 153 Carbohydrates: 39g Protein: 2g Fat: 1g

1176. Crazy Chocolate Cake

Preparation Time: 15 minutes
Cooking Time: 35 minutes
Servings: 12
Ingredients:

For the cake:

- Cooking spray, for greasing
- 1½ cups all-purpose flour
- 1 cup granulated sugar
- ¼ cup Dutch process cocoa powder
- 1 teaspoon baking soda
- ½ teaspoon salt
- 1 teaspoon white vinegar
- 5 tablespoons vegetable oil
- 1 teaspoon vanilla extract
- 1 cup water

For the frosting:

- 6 cups powdered sugar
- 1 cup cocoa powder
- 2 cups vegan butter, softened
- 1 teaspoon vanilla extract
- 1 pinch salt

Directions:

1. For the cake, warm your oven to 350°F. Grease or spray an 8-inch square baking dish or a 9-inch round cake pan.
2. In a large bowl, combine the flour, sugar, cocoa powder, baking soda, and salt. Add the vinegar, vegetable oil, vanilla extract, and water directly to the dry ingredients. Stir the batter until no lumps remain.
3. Put the batter into the greased dish and bake for 35 minutes or until a toothpick inserted into the center comes out clean.
4. Once the cake is baked, cool it in the pan for 10 minutes. Transfer it to a plate and refrigerate for about 30 minutes, then frost.
5. For the frosting, mix the powdered sugar plus cocoa powder in a large bowl. Beat the vegan butter on medium-high speed until pale and creamy using an electric hand mixer or a stand mixer with the paddle attachment.
6. Reduce the mixer speed to medium and add the powdered sugar and cocoa mix, ½ cup at a time, mixing well between each addition

(about 5 minutes total). Add the vanilla extract and salt and mix at high speed for 1 minute.

Nutrition: Calories: 831 Fat: 44 g Carbs: 111 g Protein: 5 g

1177. Chunky Chocolate Peanut Butter Balls

Preparation Time: 15 minutes
Cooking Time: 0 minutes
Servings: 6
Ingredients:

- ½ cup crunchy peanut butter
- 1½ cups shredded coconut, divided
- 1 cup rolled oats
- ½ cup ground flaxseed
- ¼ cup chia seeds
- ½ cup dairy-free mini chocolate chips
- ⅓ cup maple syrup
- 1 teaspoon vanilla extract

Directions:

1. Melt the peanut butter in a microwave-safe dish for 15 to 20 seconds. In a large bowl, combine 1 cup of the shredded coconut, the rolled oats, ground flaxseed, chia seeds, and chocolate chips.
2. Pour in the melted peanut butter, maple syrup, and vanilla extract. Stir well to combine. Refrigerate within 15 to 20 minutes, until chilled enough that the mixture sticks together when pressed but not so cold that the peanut butter hardens.
3. Place the remaining ½ cup of shredded coconut into a shallow dish. Spoon out 2 tablespoons of the mixture at a time and roll into 1-inch balls.
4. Roll the balls in the remaining ½ cup of shredded coconut to coat. Refrigerate for up to a week.

Nutrition: Calories: 528 Fat: 35 g Carbs: 47 g Protein: 12 g

1178. Chocolate Peanut Butter Crispy Bars

Preparation Time: 45 minutes
Cooking Time: 0 minutes
Servings: 6-8

Ingredients:
- 1 cup dates
- 1 cup raw cashews
- ¼ cup Dutch process cocoa powder
- 1 teaspoon vanilla extract
- 1½ cups crunchy peanut butter
- 2 cups dairy-free chocolate chips
- 1 cup all-natural smooth peanut butter
- 3 cups puffed rice cereal

Directions:
1   Prepare an 8-inch square baking dish lined using parchment paper. Set aside. Soak the dates in a bowl of warm water for 10 minutes. Drain and pat dry.
2   In a food processor or blender, combine the dates, cashews, cocoa powder, and vanilla extract and process to form a thick dough.
3   Press into the baking dish. Cover with the crunchy peanut butter, spreading it into an even layer. Refrigerate for 5 minutes.
4   In a large microwave-safe bowl, combine the chocolate chips and smooth peanut butter. Microwave in 30-second increments, stirring in between, until smooth. Remove from the microwave and stir in the puffed rice cereal, mixing to coat.
5   Pour the puffed rice mixture over the chunky peanut butter layer in the baking dish and press flat. Refrigerate for at least 30 minutes. Remove then cut into squares.

Nutrition: Calories: 977 Fat: 66 g Carbs: 83 g Protein: 26 g

1179. Cranberry Orange Pound Cake

Preparation Time: 15 minutes
Cooking Time: 50 minutes
Servings: 6-8

Ingredients:
- 2 cups fresh cranberries
- 2 tablespoons, plus 1⅓ cups sugar, divided
- 1 cup plain coconut yogurt
- 1 large banana, mashed
- 2 teaspoons grated orange zest
- 1 teaspoon vanilla extract
- ½ cup vegetable oil
- 1½ cups all-purpose flour
- 2 teaspoons baking powder
- ½ teaspoon salt
- ⅓ cup, plus 2 tablespoons freshly squeezed orange juice
- 1 cup powdered sugar

Directions:
1   Preheat the oven to 350°F. Grease a standard-size loaf pan. Line the bottom with parchment paper lengthwise, letting some hang over the edges. Set aside.
2   Mix the cranberries and 2 tablespoons of granulated sugar in a food processor or blender until coarsely chopped. Set aside.
3   In a large bowl, whisk together the yogurt, 1 cup of sugar, the banana, orange zest, vanilla extract, and oil. Stir in the cranberry mixture.
4   Mix the flour, baking powder, plus salt in a medium bowl. Incorporate the dry mixture into the wet mixture until smooth.
5   Pour the batter into the loaf pan and bake for 50 minutes, or until a toothpick inserted in the center comes out clean.
6   While the cake bakes, make the orange simple syrup. Mix the rest of the ⅓ cup of sugar plus ⅓ cup of orange juice in a small saucepan over medium heat. Simmer until your sugar dissolves and the syrup is clear. Set aside.
7   Remove the cake from the oven and let cool for 10 minutes. Remove from the loaf pan and place on a wire rack on top of a rimmed baking sheet to catch the syrup. Pour the simple syrup over the cake. Let cool completely.
8   Make the orange glaze. Whisk the powdered sugar and the remaining 2 tablespoons of orange juice in a medium bowl until no lumps remain. Drizzle over the cooled cake. Serve and store leftovers in an airtight container.

Nutrition: Calories: 536 Fat: 15 g Carbs: 99 g Protein: 3 g

1180. Strawberry Rhubarb Coffee Cake

Preparation Time: 15 minutes
Cooking Time: 45 minutes
Servings: 6-8
Ingredients:
For the filling:
- 2 cups rhubarb, thinly sliced
- 2 cups strawberries, sliced
- 1 tablespoon lemon juice
- 2/3 cup granulated sugar
- 3 tablespoons cornstarch

For the cake:
- 1½ cups all-purpose flour
- ¼ teaspoon baking soda
- 1 teaspoon baking powder
- ¼ teaspoon salt
- ¼ cup vegan butter, softened
- ¾ cup granulated sugar
- ½ cup coconut yogurt
- 1 banana, mashed
- 1 teaspoon vanilla extract

For the topping:
- ¾ cup all-purpose flour
- ½ cup granulated sugar
- ½ teaspoon ground cinnamon
- ¼ teaspoon ground nutmeg
- 5 tablespoons melted butter

Directions:
For the filling:
1   Set a medium saucepan over medium heat. Add the rhubarb, strawberries, lemon juice, sugar, and cornstarch and stir to combine.
2   Simmer, then adjust to low and continue simmering until thickened, stirring often, for 5 to 7 minutes.

Remove the filling from heat and let cool.

For the cake:

3   Preheat the oven to 350°F. Mix the flour, baking soda, baking powder, plus salt in a small bowl. Set aside.

4   Combine the butter plus sugar using an electric hand mixer and a large bowl or a stand mixer with the paddle attachment and beat on high until light and fluffy, about 5 minutes.

5   Put the yogurt, banana, plus vanilla extract and beat until combined. Adjust the speed to low then slowly add the dry mixture until fully incorporated.

6   Pour the batter evenly into a prepared 9-inch springform pan. Top with cooled strawberry-rhubarb filling and set aside.

For the topping:

7   combine the flour, sugar, cinnamon, nutmeg, and butter in a medium bowl. Stir to form a crumble topping. Sprinkle evenly over the filling.

8   Bake within 45 minutes or until a toothpick inserted in the center comes out clean and the topping is browned. Let cool for 10 minutes and serve or store in an airtight container.

Nutrition: Calories: 479 Fat: 14 g Carbs: 86 g Protein: 5 g

1181. Apple Crumble

Preparation Time: 15 minutes
Cooking Time: 25 minutes
Servings: 6
Ingredients:
For the filling:

- 4 to 5 apples, cored and chopped (about 6 cups)
- ½ cup unsweetened applesauce, or ¼ cup water
- 2 to 3 tablespoons unrefined sugar (coconut, date, sucanat, maple syrup)
- 1 teaspoon ground cinnamon
- Pinch sea salt

For the crumble:

- 2 tablespoons almond butter, or cashew or sunflower seed butter
- 2 tablespoons maple syrup
- 1½ cups rolled oats
- ½ cup walnuts, finely chopped
- ½ teaspoon ground cinnamon
- 2 to 3 tablespoons unrefined granular sugar (coconut, date, sucanat)

Directions:

1   Preheat the oven to 350°F. Put the apples and applesauce in an 8-inch-square baking dish, and sprinkle with sugar, cinnamon, and salt. Toss to combine.

2   In a medium bowl, mix together the nut butter and maple syrup until smooth and creamy. Add the oats, walnuts, cinnamon, and sugar and stir to coat, using your hands if necessary.

3   Sprinkle the topping over the apples, and put the dish in the oven. Bake for 20 to 25 minutes, or until the fruit is soft and the topping is lightly browned.

Nutrition: Calories: 356 Fat: 17g Carbs: 49g Protein: 7g

1182. Cashew-Chocolate Truffles

Preparation Time: 15 minutes
Cooking Time: 0 minutes
Servings: 12
Ingredients:

- 1 cup raw cashews, soaked/dipped in water overnight
- ¾ cup pitted dates
- 2 tablespoons coconut oil
- 1 cup unsweetened shredded coconut, divided
- 1 to 2 tablespoons cocoa powder, to taste

Directions:

1   In a food processor, combine the cashews, dates, coconut oil, ½ cup of shredded coconut, and cocoa powder.

2   Pulse until fully incorporated; it will resemble chunky cookie dough. Spread the remaining ½ cup of shredded coconut on a plate.

3   Form the mixture into tablespoon-size balls and roll on the plate to cover with the shredded coconut. Transfer to a parchment paper-lined plate or baking sheet. Repeat to make 12 truffles.

4   Place the truffles in the refrigerator for 1 hour to set. Transfer the truffles to a storage container or freezer-safe bag and seal.

Nutrition: Calories 238 Fat: 18g Protein: 3g Carbohydrates: 16g

1183. Banana Chocolate Cupcakes

Preparation Time: 15 minutes
Cooking Time: 20 minutes
Servings: 12
Ingredients:

- 3 medium bananas
- 1 cup non-dairy milk
- 2 tablespoons almond butter
- 1 teaspoon apple cider vinegar
- 1 teaspoon pure vanilla extract
- 1¼ cups whole-grain flour
- ½ cup rolled oats
- ¼ cup coconut sugar (optional)
- 1 teaspoon baking powder
- ½ teaspoon baking soda
- ½ cup unsweetened cocoa powder
- ¼ cup chia seeds, or sesame seeds
- Pinch sea salt
- ¼ cup dark chocolate chips, dried cranberries, or raisins (optional)

Directions:

1   Preheat the oven to 350°F. Lightly grease the cups of two 6-cup muffin tins or line with paper muffin cups.

2 Put the bananas, milk, almond butter, vinegar, and vanilla in a blender and purée until smooth. Or stir together in a large bowl until smooth and creamy.

3 Put the flour, oats, sugar (if using), baking powder, baking soda, cocoa powder, chia seeds, salt, and chocolate chips in another large bowl, and stir to combine.

4 Mix together the wet and dry ingredients, stirring as little as possible. Spoon into muffin cups, then bake within 20 to 25 minutes.

5 Remove the cupcakes then let it cool fully before taking out of the muffin tins, since they'll be very moist.

Nutrition: Calories: 215 Fat: 6g Carbs: 39g Protein: 6g

1184. Minty Fruit Salad

Preparation Time: 15 minutes
Cooking Time: 5 minutes
Servings: 4
Ingredients:

- ¼ cup lemon juice (about 2 small lemons)
- 4 teaspoons maple syrup or agave syrup
- 2 cups chopped pineapple
- 2 cups chopped strawberries
- 2 cups raspberries
- 1 cup blueberries
- 8 fresh mint leaves

Directions:

1 Beginning with 1 mason jar, add 1 tablespoon of lemon juice, 1 teaspoon of maple syrup, ½ cup of pineapple, ½ cup of strawberries, ½ cup of raspberries, ¼ cup of blueberries, and 2 mint leaves.

2 Repeat to fill 3 more jars. Close the jars tightly with lids. Place the airtight jars in the refrigerator for up to 3 days.

Nutrition: Calories: 138 Fat: 1g Protein: 2g Carbohydrates: 34g

1185. Mango Coconut Cream Pie

Preparation Time: 50 minutes
Cooking Time: 0 minutes
Servings: 8

Ingredients:
For the crust:

- ½ cup rolled oats
- 1 cup cashews
- 1 cup soft pitted dates

For the filling:

- 1 cup canned coconut milk
- ½ cup water
- 2 large mangos, peeled and chopped, or about 2 cups frozen chunks
- ½ cup unsweetened shredded coconut

Directions:

1 Put all the crust fixings in a food processor and pulse until it holds together. Press the mixture down firmly into an 8-inch pie or springform pan.

2 Put the all-filling ingredients in a blender and purée until smooth (about 1 minute). It should be very thick, so you may have to stop and stir until it's smooth.

3 Put the filling into the crust, use a rubber spatula to smooth the top, and put the pie in the freezer until set, about 30 minutes. Once frozen, it should be set out for about 15 minutes to soften before serving.

4 Top with a batch of Coconut Whipped Cream scooped on top of the pie once it's set. Finish it off with a sprinkling of toasted shredded coconut.

Nutrition: Calories: 427 Fat: 28g Carbs: 45g Protein: 8g

1186. Cherry-Vanilla Rice Pudding

Preparation Time: 15 minutes
Cooking Time: 30 minutes
Servings: 4-6
Ingredients:

- 1 cup short-grain brown rice
- 1¾ cups nondairy milk, plus more as needed
- 1½ cups water
- 4 tablespoons unrefined sugar or pure maple syrup (use 2 tablespoons if you use

sweetened milk), plus more as needed

- 1 teaspoon vanilla extract (use ½ teaspoon if you use vanilla milk)
- Pinch salt
- ¼ cup dried cherries or ½ cup fresh or frozen pitted cherries

Directions:

1 In your electric pressure cooker's cooking pot, combine the rice, milk, water, sugar, vanilla, and salt. High pressure for 30 minutes. Select High Pressure for 30 minutes.

2 Let the pressure release naturally, within 20 minutes. Unlock and remove the lid.

3 Stir in the cherries and put the lid back on loosely for about 10 minutes. Serve, adding more milk or sugar, as desired.

Nutrition: Calories: 177 Fat: 1g Protein: 3g Carbs: 2g

1187. Lime in the Coconut Chia Pudding

Preparation Time: 30 minutes
Cooking Time: 0 minutes
Servings: 4
Ingredients:

- Zest and juice of 1 lime
- 1 (14-oz.) can coconut milk
- 1 to 2 dates, or 1 tablespoon coconut or other unrefined sugar, or 1 tablespoon maple syrup, or 10 to 15 drops of pure liquid stevia
- 2 tablespoons chia seeds, whole or ground
- 2 teaspoons matcha green tea powder (optional)

Directions:

1 Blend all the ingredients in a blender until smooth. Chill in the fridge within 20 minutes, then serve topped with one or more of the topping ideas.

2 Try blueberries, blackberries, sliced strawberries, Coconut Whipped Cream, or toasted unsweetened coconut.

Nutrition: Calories: 226 Fat: 20g Carbs: 13g Protein: 3g

1188. Mint Chocolate Chip Sorbet

Preparation Time: 5 minutes
Cooking Time: 0 minutes
Servings: 1
Ingredients:

- 1 frozen banana
- 1 tablespoon almond butter/peanut butter, or other nut or seed butter
- 2 tablespoons fresh mint, minced
- ¼ cup or less non-dairy milk (only if needed)
- 2 to 3 tablespoons non-dairy chocolate chips, or cocoa nibs
- 2 to 3 tablespoons goji berries (optional)

Directions:

1. Put the banana, almond butter, and mint in a food processor or blender and purée until smooth.
2. Add the non-dairy milk if needed to keep blending (but only if needed, as this will make the texture less solid).
3. Pulse the chocolate chips and goji berries (if using) into the mix so they're roughly chopped up.

Nutrition: Calories: 212 Fat: 10g Carbs: 31g Protein: 3g

1189. Peach-Mango Crumble

Preparation Time: 15 minutes
Cooking Time: 6 minutes
Servings: 4-6
Ingredients:

- 3 cups chopped fresh or frozen peaches
- 3 cups chopped fresh or frozen mangos
- 4 tablespoons unrefined sugar or pure maple syrup, divided
- 1 cup gluten-free rolled oats
- ½ cup shredded coconut, sweetened or unsweetened
- 2 tablespoons coconut oil or vegan margarine

Directions:

1. In a 6- to 7-inch round baking dish, toss together the peaches, mangos, and 2 tablespoons of sugar. In a food processor, combine the oats, coconut, coconut oil, and remaining 2 tablespoons of sugar.
2. Pulse until combined. (If you use maple syrup, you'll need less coconut oil. Start with just the syrup and add oil if the mixture isn't sticking together.) Sprinkle the oat mixture over the fruit mixture.
3. Cover the dish with aluminum foil. Put a trivet in the bottom of your electric pressure cooker's cooking pot and pour in a cup or two of water.
4. Using a foil sling or silicone helper handles, lower the pan onto the trivet. High pressure for 6 minutes.
5. Select High Pressure for 6 minutes; then quickly release the pressure. Unlock and remove the lid.
6. Let cool for a few minutes before carefully lifting out the dish with oven mitts or tongs. Scoop out portions to serve.

Nutrition: Calories: 321 Fat: 18g Protein: 4g Carbs: 7g

1190. Zesty Orange-Cranberry Energy Bites

Preparation Time: 25 minutes
Cooking Time: 0 minutes
Servings: 12
Ingredients:

- 2 tablespoons almond butter, or cashew or sunflower seed butter
- 2 tablespoons maple syrup, or brown rice syrup
- ¾ cup cooked quinoa
- ¼ cup sesame seeds, toasted
- 1 tablespoon chia seeds
- ½ teaspoon almond extract, or vanilla extract
- Zest of 1 orange
- 1 tablespoon dried cranberries
- ¼ cup ground almonds

Directions:

1. In a medium bowl, mix together the nut or seed butter and syrup until smooth and creamy. Stir in the rest of the fixings, and mix to make sure the consistency is holding together in a ball. Form the mix into 12 balls.
2. Place them on a baking sheet lined with parchment or waxed paper and put in the fridge to set for about 15 minutes.
3. If your balls aren't holding together, it's likely because of the moisture content of your cooked quinoa. Add more nut or seed butter mixed with syrup until it all sticks together.

Nutrition: Calories: 109 Fat: 7g Carbs: 11g Protein: 3g

1191. "Frosty" Chocolate Shake

Preparation Time: 40 minutes
Cooking Time: 0 minutes
Servings: 2
Ingredients:

- 1 cup heavy (whipping) cream/coconut cream
- 2 tablespoons unsweetened cocoa powder
- 1 tablespoon almond butter
- 1 teaspoon vanilla extract
- 5 or 6 drops liquid stevia

Directions:

1. Beat the cream in a medium bowl or using a stand mixer until fluffy, 3 to 4 minutes. Add the cocoa powder, almond butter, vanilla, and stevia.
2. Beat the mixture for an additional 2 to 3 minutes, or until the mixture has the consistency of whipped cream. Place the bowl in the freezer for 25 to 30 minutes before serving.

Nutrition: Calories: 493 Fat: 49g Protein: 5g Carbs: 8g

1192. French Vanilla Ice Cream with Hot Fudge

Preparation Time: 10 minutes

Cooking Time: 0 minutes
Servings: 2
Ingredients:

- 1¼ cups heavy (whipping) cream, divided
- ¼ cup unsweetened almond milk
- ½ cup Swerve sweetener, divided
- 1½ teaspoons vanilla extract, divided
- 2 ounces unsweetened chocolate, chopped

Directions:

1   Put a bread loaf pan in the freezer to chill for about 20 minutes. In a medium bowl, combine ¾ cup of cream, almond milk, ¼ cup of Swerve, and ½ teaspoon of vanilla.

2   Mix with a handheld electric mixer for 2 minutes, or until the sweetener has dissolved. Pour the ice-cream mixture into the chilled loaf pan.

3   Place the pan in the freezer. Every half hour, remove the pan, scrape down the sides, and whisk the mixture for about 1 minute. It will get thicker and thicker each time you whisk it.

4   While the ice cream is in the freezer, combine the remaining ½ cup of cream, the remaining ¼ cup of Swerve, and the chocolate in a double boiler over medium-low heat.

5   Stir just until the chocolate melts, and then remove the mixture from the heat. Stir in the rest of the 1 teaspoon of vanilla.

6   After 3½ to 4 hours, the ice cream will be thick enough to eat. Scrape down the sides for the last time and scoop out to serve. Pour the warm sauce over the ice cream.

Nutrition: Calories: 719 Fat: 71g Protein: 7g Carbs: 13g

1193. Almond-Date Energy Bites

Preparation Time: 25 minutes
Cooking Time: 0 minutes

Servings: 24
Ingredients:

- 1 cup dates, pitted
- 1 cup unsweetened shredded coconut
- ¼ cup chia seeds
- ¾ cup ground almonds
- ¼ cup cocoa nibs, or non-dairy chocolate chips

Directions:

1   Purée everything in a food processor until crumbly and sticking together, pushing down the sides whenever necessary to keep it blending.

2   Form the mix into 24 balls and place them on a baking sheet lined with parchment or waxed paper. Put in the fridge to set for about 15 minutes.

Nutrition: Calories: 152 Fat: 11g Carbs: 13g Protein: 3g

1194. Coconut and Almond Truffles

Preparation Time: 15 minutes
Cooking Time: 0 minutes
Servings: 8
Ingredients:

- 1 cup pitted dates
- 1 cup almonds
- ½ cup sweetened cocoa powder, plus extra for coating
- ½ cup unsweetened shredded coconut
- ¼ cup pure maple syrup
- 1 teaspoon vanilla extract
- 1 teaspoon almond extract
- ¼ teaspoon sea salt

Directions:

1   In the bowl of a food processor, combine all the ingredients and process until smooth. Chill the mixture for about 1 hour.

2   Roll the batter into balls then roll it in cocoa powder to coat. Serve immediately or keep chilled until ready to serve.

Nutrition: Calories: 74 Carbs: 8g Fat: 4g Protein: 1g

1195. Chocolate Macaroons

Preparation Time: 15 minutes

Cooking Time: 15 minutes
Servings: 8
Ingredients:

- 1 cup unsweetened shredded coconut
- 2 tablespoons cocoa powder
- 2/3 cup coconut milk
- ¼ cup agave
- Pinch of sea salt

Directions:

1   Preheat the oven to 350°F. Line a baking sheet with parchment paper. In a medium saucepan, cook all the fixings over -medium-high heat until a firm dough is formed. Scoop the dough into balls and place on the baking sheet.

2   Bake for 15 minutes, remove from the oven and let cool on the baking sheet. Serve cooled macaroons.

Nutrition: Calories: 141 Carbs: 1g Fat: 8g Protein: 1g

1196. Chocolate Pudding

Preparation Time: 5 minutes
Cooking Time: 0 minutes
Servings: 1
Ingredients:

- 1 banana
- 2 to 4 tablespoons nondairy milk
- 2 tablespoons unsweetened cocoa powder
- 2 tablespoons sugar (optional)
- ½ ripe avocado or 1 cup silken tofu (optional)

Directions:

1   In a small blender, combine the banana, milk, cocoa powder, sugar (if using), and avocado (if using). Purée until smooth. Alternatively, in a small bowl, mash the banana very well, and stir in the remaining ingredients.

Nutrition: Calories: 244 Protein: 4g Fat: 3g Carbohydrates: 59g

1197. Lime and Watermelon Granita

Preparation Time: 6 hours & 15 minutes
Cooking Time: 0 minutes
Servings: 4

Ingredients:

- 8 cups seedless -watermelon chunks
- juice of 2 limes or 2 tablespoons prepared lime juice
- ½ cup sugar
- strips of lime zest, for garnish

Directions:

1. Mix the watermelon, lime juice, plus sugar in a blender or food processor and process until smooth. After processing, stir well to combine both batches.
2. Pour the mixture into a 9-by-13-inch glass dish. Freeze for 2 to 3 hours. Remove then use a fork to scrape the top layer of ice. Leave the shaved ice on top and return to the freezer.
3. In another hour, remove from the freezer and repeat. Do this a few more times until all the ice is scraped up. Serve frozen, garnished with strips of lime zest.

Nutrition: Calories: 70 Carbs: 18g Fat: 0g Protein: 1g

1198. Mint Chocolate Fat Bombs

Preparation Time: 15 minutes
Cooking Time: 0 minutes
Servings: 6
Ingredients:

- 2/3 cup coconut oil, melted
- 1 tablespoon erythritol, granulated
- ¼ teaspoon peppermint extract
- 2 tablespoons unsweetened cocoa powder

Directions:

1. Mix the coconut oil, erythritol, and peppermint extract in a small mixing bowl. Use a silicone mold and fill six of the cups only halfway with the mixture.
2. Place the mold in the refrigerator for 5 minutes. Add the cocoa powder to the remaining mixture and stir well.
3. Pour a cocoa layer on top of each peppermint layer and

place the mold back in the refrigerator until set.

4. Use a butter knife to remove the bombs from the mold (they should just pop right out) and place them in a resealable freezer bag. Store in the refrigerator or freezer.

Nutrition: Calories: 229 Fat: 25g Protein: 0g Carbs: 1g

1199. Spiced Apple Chia Pudding

Preparation Time: 35 minutes
Cooking Time: 0 minutes
Servings: 1
Ingredients:

- ½ cup unsweetened applesauce
- ¼ cup non-dairy milk or canned coconut milk
- 1 tablespoon chia seeds
- 1½ teaspoons sugar
- Pinch ground cinnamon or pumpkin pie spice

Directions:

1. Stir the applesauce, milk, chia seeds, sugar, and cinnamon in a small bowl. Enjoy as is, or let sit for 30 minutes so the chia seeds soften and expand.

Nutrition: Calories: 153 Protein: 3g Fat: 5g Carbohydrates: 26g

1200. Graham Pancakes

Preparation Time: 15 minutes
Cooking Time: 4 minutes
Servings: 6
Ingredients:

- 2 cups whole-wheat flour (about 11-oz.)
- 2 teaspoons baking powder
- ½ teaspoon baking soda
- 2 tablespoons date sugar
- ¾ teaspoon salt, optional
- 2½ cups unsweetened oat milk
- 2 tablespoons lemon juice
- ¼ cup unsweetened applesauce
- 2 teaspoons vanilla extract

Directions:

1. Combine the flour, baking powder and soda, date sugar, and salt (if desired) in a large bowl.

2. Make a well in the middle of the flour mixture, then add the oat milk, lemon juice, applesauce, and vanilla extract. Whisk the mixture until smooth and thick.
3. Make a pancake: Pour ¼ cup of the mixture in a nonstick skillet, then cook for 4 minutes. Flip the pancake halfway through the cooking time or until the first side is golden brown. Repeat with the remaining mixture. Transfer the pancakes to a plate and serve warm.

Nutrition: Calories: 208 Fat: 3.1g Carbs: 38.9g Protein: 8.7g

1201. Belgian Gold Waffles

Preparation Time: 15 minutes
Cooking Time: 5-6 minutes
Servings: 4
Ingredients:

- 2 cups soy flour (about 10-oz.)
- 1 tablespoon baking powder
- ¼ teaspoon baking soda
- 3 tablespoons cornstarch
- 2 tablespoons date sugar
- ½ teaspoon salt, optional
- 2 cups unsweetened soy milk
- 1 tablespoon lemon juice
- 1 teaspoon vanilla extract
- ¼ cup unsweetened applesauce

Directions:

1. Preheat the waffle iron. Combine the soy flour, baking powder and soda, cornstarch, date sugar, and salt (if desired) in a large bowl.
2. Make your well in the middle of the flour mixture, then add the soy milk, lemon juice, vanilla extract, and applesauce. Whisk the mixture until smooth and thick.
3. Add 1 cup of the mixture to the preheated waffle iron and cook for 5 to 6 minutes or until golden brown. Serve immediately. Repeat with the remaining mixture.

Nutrition: Calories: 292 Fat: 8.0g Carbs: 34.6g Protein: 23.9g

1202. Peach and Raspberry Crisp

Preparation Time: 50 minutes
Cooking Time: 30-35 minutes
Servings: 6
Ingredients:
Filling:

- 2½ pounds peaches, peeled, halved, pitted, and cut into ½-inch wedges
- ¼ cup maple sugar (about 1¾ ounces)
- ⅛ teaspoon salt, optional
- 1 tablespoon lemon juice
- 2 tablespoons ground tapioca
- 1 teaspoon vanilla extract
- 2 cups raspberries (about 10 ounces)

Topping:

- ½ cup soy flour (about 2½-oz.)
- ¼ teaspoon ground cinnamon
- ¼ teaspoon ground ginger
- ¼ cup date sugar (about1¾ oz.)
- ¼ cup maple sugar (about 1¾ oz.)
- ¼ teaspoon salt, optional
- ¼ cup unsweetened applesauce
- ½ cup chopped pecans
- ½ cup rolled oats (about 1½-oz.)
- 2 tablespoons water

Directions:
Make the filling:

1 Warm your oven to 400°F. Line a baking dish with parchment paper.
2 Put the peaches, maple sugar, and salt in a large bowl. Toss to combine well. Let stand for 30 minutes. Toss periodically.
3 Drain the peaches in a colander. Reserve 2 tablespoons of juice remain in the bowl and discard the extra juice.
4 Move the drained peaches back to the bowl. Add the lemon juice, tapioca, vanilla, and reserved peach juice. Toss to combine well.
5 Arrange the peaches and raspberries in the single layer on the baking dish.

Make the topping:

6 Put the soy flour, cinnamon, ginger, date sugar, maple sugar, and salt (if desired) in a food processor. Blitz for 15 seconds to combine well.
7 Add the applesauce to the mixture and blitz 10 times until it becomes wet sand. Add the pecans, oats, and water and blitz 15 times until smooth. Pour the batter into a large bowl then refrigerate for 20 minutes.
8 Spread the topping over the peaches and raspberries in the baking dish, then bake in the preheated oven for 30 to 35 minutes or until crispy and golden brown.
9 Flip the peaches and raspberries halfway through the cooking time. Remove the dish from the oven. Allow to cool within 30 minutes and serve.

Nutrition: Calories: 294 Fat: 7.9g Carbs: 55.9g Protein: 7.7g

1203. Chia Pudding with Coconut and Fruits

Preparation Time: 15 minutes
Cooking Time: 0 minutes
Servings: 4
Ingredients:

- 2 cups unsweetened soy milk
- 1½ teaspoons vanilla extract
- ½ cup chia seeds
- 2 tablespoons maple syrup
- ¼ teaspoon salt, optional
- ¼ cup flaked coconut, toasted
- 2 cups strawberries, avocado slices, and banana slices mix

Directions:
For the pudding:

1 Combine the soy milk, vanilla extract, chia seeds, maple syrup, and salt (if desired) in a bowl. Stir to mix well. Wrap your bowl in plastic then refrigerate for at least 8 hours.
2 Serve the pudding with coconut flakes and fruit mix on top.

Nutrition: Calories: 303 Fat: 14.7g Carbs: 36.0g Protein: 9.5g

1204. Orange and Cranberry Quinoa Bites

Preparation Time: 25 minutes
Cooking Time: 0 minutes
Servings: 12
Ingredients:

- 2 tablespoons almond butter
- 2 tablespoons maple syrup (optional)
- Zest of 1 orange
- 1 tablespoon dried cranberries
- ¾ cup cooked quinoa
- ¼ cup ground almonds
- 1 tablespoon chia seeds
- ¼ cup sesame seeds, toasted
- ½ teaspoon vanilla extract

Directions:

1 Mix the almond butter and maple syrup (if desired) in a medium bowl until smooth. Stir in the remaining ingredients, and mix to hold together in a ball.
2 Divide and form the mixture into 12 balls. Put them on a baking sheet lined with parchment paper. Put in the fridge to set for about 15 minutes. Serve chilled.

Nutrition: Calories: 109 Fat: 11.0g Carbs: 5.0g Protein: 3.0g

1205. Orange Glazed Bananas

Preparation Time: 15 minutes
Cooking Time: 4 minutes
Servings: 6-8
Ingredients:

- ⅓ cup fresh orange juice
- 6 ripe bananas, peeled and sliced
- 1 teaspoon vanilla extract
- ½ teaspoon ground cinnamon

Directions:

1 Put the orange juice in a saucepan and warm over

medium heat. Add the sliced bananas and cook for 2 minutes.

2 Add the vanilla and cinnamon and continue to cook until the moisture is absorbed, about another 2 minutes. Serve warm.

Nutrition: Calories: 98 Fat: 0.4g Carbs: 24.7g Protein: 1.2g

1206. Pear Squares

Preparation Time: 40 minutes
Cooking Time: 50 minutes
Servings: 24 squares
Ingredients:
Filling:

- 1 (1-lb.) can pears, with juice
- 2 cups chopped dried pears
- ¾ cup pitted dates
- ¼ cup tapioca
- 1 teaspoon orange extract

Crust:

- ½ cup pitted dates
- 1½ cups water
- ½ cup whole-wheat flour
- 1½ cups regular rolled oats
- ⅛ teaspoon salt (optional)
- 1 teaspoon vanilla extract

Topping:

- 1 cup regular rolled oats

Directions:

1 Put the canned pears and juice in a food processor and process until puréed. Transfer to a saucepan. Add the dried pears, dates, and tapioca. Simmer, covered, for 20 minutes. Add the orange extract and set aside.

2 Warm your oven to 375°F. Combine the dates plus water in a food processor and process until finely ground.

3 In a bowl, combine the date water (reserve ¼ cup), flour, oats, salt (if desired), and vanilla. Press into a baking dish and bake for 10 minutes.

4 Meanwhile, toss the remaining rolled oats with the reserved date water. Spoon the filling over the crust. Sprinkle, the oat topping over the filling.

5 Bake in the preheated oven within 20 minutes, or until firm. Cool and cut into 2-inch squares before serving.

Nutrition: Calories: 112 Fat: 0.8g Carbs: 27.5g Protein: 2.2g

1207. Prune, Grapefruit, and Orange Compote

Preparation Time: 15 minutes
Cooking Time: 4 minutes
Servings: 4
Ingredients:

- 1 cup pitted prunes
- ¾ cup fresh orange juice
- 1 tablespoon maple syrup (optional)
- 2 (1-lb.) cans unsweetened grapefruit sections, drained
- 2 (11-lb.) cans unsweetened mandarin oranges, drained

Directions:

1 Put the prunes, orange juice, and maple syrup (if desired) in a saucepan. Bring to a boil, reduce the heat, and cook gently for 1 minute. Remove from the heat and cool.

2 Combine the mixture with grapefruit and mandarin oranges. Stir to mix. Cover and refrigerate for at least 2 hours before serving.

Nutrition: Calories: 303 Fat: 0.7g Carbs: 77.2g Protein: 4.3g

1208. Pumpkin Pie Squares

Preparation Time: 15 minutes
Cooking Time: 30 minutes
Servings: 16 squares
Ingredients:

- 1 cup unsweetened almond milk
- 1 teaspoon vanilla extract
- 7 ounces dates, pitted and chopped
- 1¼ cups old-fashioned rolled oats
- 2 teaspoons pumpkin pie spice
- 1 (15-oz.) can pure pumpkin

Directions:

1 Warm your oven to 375°F (190°C). Put the parchment paper in a baking pan. Stir together the milk and vanilla in a bowl. Soak the dates in

it for 15 minutes, or until the dates become softened.

2 Add the rolled oats to a food processor and pulse the oats into flour. Remove the oat flour from the food processor bowl and whisk together with the pumpkin pie spice in a different bowl.

3 Place the milk mixture into the food processor and process until smooth. Add the flour mixture and pumpkin to the food processor and pulse until the mixture has broken down into a chunky paste consistency.

4 Transfer the batter to the prepared pan and smooth the top with a silicone spatula. Bake within 30 minutes, or until a toothpick inserted in the center of the pie comes out clean. Let cool completely before cutting into squares. Serve cold.

Nutrition: Calories: 68 Fat: 0.9g Carbs: 16.8g Protein: 2.3g

1209. Apple Crisp

Preparation Time: 15 minutes
Cooking Time: 40 minutes
Servings: 6
Ingredients:

- ½ cup vegan butter
- 6 large apples, diced large
- 1 cup dried cranberries
- 2 tablespoons granulated sugar
- 2 teaspoons ground cinnamon, divided
- ¼ teaspoon ground nutmeg
- ¼ teaspoon ground ginger
- 2 teaspoons lemon juice
- 1 cup all-purpose flour
- 1 cup rolled oats
- 1 cup brown sugar
- ¼ teaspoon salt

Directions:

1 Preheat the oven to 350°F. Oiled an 8-inch square baking dish with butter or cooking spray.

2   Make the filling. In a large bowl, combine the apples, cranberries, granulated sugar, 1 teaspoon of cinnamon, nutmeg, ginger, and lemon juice. Toss to coat. Transfer the apple mixture to the prepared baking dish.

3   Make the topping. In the same large bowl, now empty, combine the all-purpose flour, oats, brown sugar, and salt. Stir to combine.

4   Add the butter and, using a pastry cutter (or two knives moving in a crisscross pattern), cut the butter into the flour and oat mixture until the butter is the size of small peas.

5   Spread the topping over the apples evenly, patting down slightly. Bake for 40 minutes or until golden and bubbly.

Nutrition: Calories: 488 Fat: 9 g Carbs: 101 g Protein: 5 g

1210. Secret Ingredient Chocolate Brownies

Preparation Time: 15 minutes
Cooking Time: 35 minutes
Servings: 6-8
Ingredients:

- ¾ cup flour
- ¼ teaspoon baking soda
- ¼ teaspoon salt
- ⅓ cup vegan butter
- ¾ cup sugar
- 2 tablespoons water
- 1¼ cups semi-sweet or dark dairy-free chocolate chips
- 6 tablespoons aquafaba, divided
- 1 teaspoon vanilla extract

Directions:

1   Preheat the oven to 325°F. Line a 9-inch square baking pan with parchment or grease well. In a large bowl, combine the flour, baking soda, and salt. Set aside.

2   In a medium saucepan over medium-high heat, combine the butter, sugar, and water. Bring to a boil, stirring

occasionally. Remove then stir in the chocolate chips.

3   Whisk in 3 tablespoons of aquafaba until thoroughly combined. Add the vanilla extract and the remaining 3 tablespoons of aquafaba, and whisk until mixed.

4   Add the chocolate mixture into the flour mixture and stir until combined. Pour in an even layer into the prepared pan.

5   Bake for 35 minutes, until the top, is set but the brownie jiggles slightly when shaken. Allow to cool completely, 45 minutes to 1 hour, before removing and serving.

Nutrition: Calories: 369 Fat: 19 g Carbs: 48 g Protein: 4 g

1211. Chocolate Chip Pecan Cookies

Preparation Time: 15 minutes
Cooking Time: 16 minutes
Servings: 30 cookies
Ingredients:

- ¾ cup pecan halves, toasted
- 1 cup vegan butter & ½ teaspoon salt
- ½ cup powdered sugar
- 2 teaspoons vanilla extract
- 2 cups all-purpose flour
- 1 cup mini dairy-free chocolate chips, such as Enjoy Life brand

Directions:

1   Preheat the oven to 350°F. Prepare a large rimmed baking sheet lined using parchment paper.

2   In a small skillet over medium heat, toast the pecans until warm and fragrant, about 2 minutes. Remove from the pan. Once these are cool, chop them into small pieces.

3   Combine the butter, salt, and powdered sugar, and cream using an electric hand mixer or a stand mixer fitted with a paddle attachment on high speed for 3 to 4 minutes, until light and fluffy. Add the vanilla

extract and beat for 1 minute.

4   Turn the mixer on low and slowly add the flour, ½ cup at a time, until a dough form. Put the chocolate chips plus pecans, and mix until just incorporated.

5   Using your hands, a large spoon, or a 1-inch ice cream scoop, drop 1-inch balls of dough on the baking sheet, spaced 1 inch apart. Gently press down on the cookies to flatten them slightly.

6   Bake for 12 to 14 minutes until just golden around the edges. Cool on the baking sheet within 5 minutes before transferring them to a wire rack to cool. Serve or store in an airtight container.

Nutrition: Calories: 152 Fat: 11 g Carbs: 13 g Protein: 2 g

1212. Peanut Butter Chip Cookies

Preparation Time: 15 minutes
Cooking Time: 15 minutes
Servings: 12-15
Ingredients:

- 1 tablespoon ground flaxseed
- 3 tablespoons hot water
- 1 cup rolled oats
- 1 teaspoon baking soda
- 1 teaspoon ground cinnamon
- ¼ teaspoon salt
- 1 ripe banana, mashed
- ¼ cup maple syrup
- ½ cup all-natural smooth peanut butter
- 1 tablespoon vanilla extract
- ½ cup dairy-free chocolate chips

Directions:

1   Preheat the oven to 350°F. Prepare a large rimmed baking sheet lined using parchment paper.

2   Make a flaxseed egg by combining the ground flaxseed and hot water in a small bowl. Stir and let it sit for 5 minutes until thickened.

3　In a medium bowl, combine the oats, baking soda, cinnamon, and salt. Set aside.

4　Mash the banana then put the maple syrup, peanut butter, flaxseed egg, and vanilla extract in a large bowl. Stir to combine.

5　Add the dry batter into the wet batter and stir until just incorporated (do not overmix). Gently fold in the chocolate chips.

6　Using a large spoon or 2-inch ice cream scoop, drop the cookie dough balls onto the baking sheet. Flatten them slightly.

7　Bake within 12 to 15 minutes or until the bottoms and edges are slightly browned. Serve or store in an airtight container.

Nutrition: Calories: 192 Fat: 12 g Carbs: 17 g Protein: 6 g

1213. No-Bake Chocolate Coconut Energy Balls

Preparation Time: 15 minutes
Cooking Time: 0 minutes
Servings: 9
Ingredients:

- ¼ cup dry roasted or raw pumpkin seeds
- ¼ cup dry roasted or raw sunflower seeds
- ½ cup unsweetened shredded coconut
- 2 tablespoons chia seeds
- ¼ teaspoon salt
- 1½ tablespoons Dutch process cocoa powder
- ¼ cup rolled oats
- 2 tablespoons coconut oil, melted
- 6 pitted dates
- 2 tablespoons all-natural almond butter

Directions:

1　Combine the pumpkin seeds, sunflower seeds, coconut, chia seeds, salt, cocoa powder, and oats in a food processor or blender.

Pulse until the mix is coarsely crumbled.

2　Add the coconut oil, dates, and almond butter. Pulse until the batter is combined and sticks when squeezed between your fingers.

3　Scoop out 2 tablespoons of the mix at a time and roll them into 1½-inch balls with your hands. Place them spaced apart on a freezer-safe plate and freeze for 15 minutes.

4　Remove from the freezer and keep refrigerated in an airtight container for up to 4 days.

Nutrition: Calories: 230 Fat: 12 g Carbs: 27 g Protein: 5 g

Chapter 15. Additional Recipes

1214.

1215. Duck and Orange Sauce

Preparation Time: 10 minutes
Cooking Time: 5 hours
Servings: 6
Ingredients:

- 2 medium ducks, fat trimmed
- 1 tablespoon olive oil
- 1 cup water
- Salt and black pepper to taste
- 2 tomatoes, chopped
- 2 carrots, chopped
- 2 celery stalks, chopped
- 1 leek, chopped
- 2 garlic cloves, minced
- 1 yellow onion, chopped
- 2 bay leaves
- 3 tablespoons white flour
- 1 teaspoon thyme, dried
- 2 tablespoons tomato paste
- 1-quart chicken stock
- Juice of 2 oranges
- 3 oranges, peeled and cut into segments
- ⅓ cup sugar
- 2 tablespoons currant jelly
- ⅓ cup cider vinegar
- 2 tablespoons cold butter

Directions:

1. Pierce the duck skin, season all over with salt and pepper. Arrange them in a roasting pan, add the water, and bake in the oven at 450°F for 20 minutes.
2. Reduce heat to 350°F, turn the ducks and bake them for 30 minutes more.
3. Turn ducks again and roast them for 30 minutes more. Meanwhile, heat a pan with the oil over high heat, add carrots, celery, leek, tomatoes, garlic, onion, thyme and bay leaves, stir and cook for 10 minutes.
4. Add tomato paste, flour, the wine and the stock gradually, bring to a boil, reduce heat to medium-low, simmer for 50 minutes, take off the heat and strain the sauce into a bowl.
5. Heat a small pan over medium-high heat, add vinegar and sugar, stir and cook for 4 minutes.
6. Add orange juice and currant jelly, stir and bring to a boil. Add strained sauce, salt and pepper, stir and cook for 8 minutes.
7. Add butter gradually and stir well again. Take ducks out of the oven, turn them, place in the oven again and cook for 40 more minutes. Take ducks out of the oven again, place them under preheated broiler and broil them for 3 minutes.
8. Transfer ducks to a platter and keep them warm.
9. Heat up juices from the pan in a saucepan over medium heat, take off the heat and strain them into a bowl.
10. Add this to orange sauce and stir. Arrange the orange segments next to the ducks and serve with orange sauce on top.

Nutrition: Calories 342, Fat: 13g, Fiber: 4g, Carbs: 17g, Protein: 12g

1216. Brown Rice, Chicken and Scallions

Preparation Time: 10 minutes
Cooking Time: 30 minutes
Servings: 4
Ingredients:

- 1½ cups brown rice
- 3 cups chicken stock
- 2 tablespoon balsamic vinegar
- 1-pound chicken breast, boneless, skinless and cubed
- 6 scallions, chopped
- Salt and black pepper to the taste
- 1 tablespoon sweet paprika
- 2 tablespoons avocado oil

Directions:

1. Heat up a pan with the oil over medium-high heat, add the chicken, and brown for 5 minutes.
2. Add the scallions and sauté for 5 minutes more.
3. Add the rice and the rest of the ingredients, bring to a simmer and cook over medium heat for 20 minutes.
4. Stir the mix, divide everything between plates and serve.

Nutrition: Calories 300, Fat 9.2, Fiber 11.8, Carbs 18.6, Protein 23.8

1217. Peanut and Chives Chicken Mix

Preparation Time: 10 minutes
Cooking Time: 25 minutes
Servings: 4
Ingredients:

- 4 chicken breast halves, skinless and boneless
- Salt and black pepper to the taste
- 2 tablespoons olive oil
- 2 tablespoons peanuts, chopped
- 1 tablespoon chives, chopped
- ½ cup tomato sauce
- ½ cup chicken stock

Directions:

1. Heat up a pan with the oil over medium-high heat, add the chicken, and brown for 4 minutes on each side.
2. Add the rest of the ingredients, bring to a simmer and cook over medium heat for 16 minutes.
3. Divide the mix between plates and serve.

Nutrition: Calories 294, Fat 12.1, Fiber 9.2, Carbs 25.6, Protein 35.4

1218. Chicken and Ginger Cucumbers Mix

Preparation Time: 10 minutes
Cooking Time: 20 minutes
Servings: 4
Ingredients:

- 4 chicken breasts, boneless, skinless and cubed

- 2 cucumbers, cubed
- Salt and black pepper to the taste
- 1 tablespoon ginger, grated
- 1 tablespoon garlic, minced
- 2 tablespoons balsamic vinegar
- 3 tablespoons olive oil
- ¼ teaspoon chili paste
- ½ cup chicken stock
- ½ tablespoon lime juice
- 1 tablespoon chives, chopped

Directions:

1 Heat up a pan with the oil over medium-high heat, add the chicken, and brown for 3 minutes on each side.

2 Add the cucumbers, salt, pepper and the rest of the ingredients except the chives, bring to a simmer and cook over medium heat for 15 minutes.

3 Divide the mix between plates and serve with the chives sprinkled on top.

Nutrition: Calories 288, Fat 9.5, Fiber 12.1, Carbs 25.6, Protein 28.6

1219. Chicken Wings and Dates Mix

Preparation Time: 10 minutes
Cooking Time: 1 hour
Servings: 6
Ingredients:

- 12 chicken wings, halved
- 2 garlic cloves, minced
- Juice of 1 lime
- Zest of 1 lime
- 2 tablespoons avocado oil
- 1 cup dates, pitted and halved
- 1 teaspoon cumin, ground
- Salt and black pepper to the taste
- ½ cup chicken stock
- 1 tablespoon chives, chopped

Directions:

1 In a roasting pan, combine the chicken wings with the garlic, lime juice and the rest of the ingredients, toss, introduce in the oven and bake at 360°F for 1 hour.

2 Divide everything between plates and serve with a side salad.

Nutrition: Calories 294, Fat 19.4, Fiber 11.8, Carbs 21.4, Protein 17.5

1220. Sage Turkey Mix

Preparation Time: 10 minutes
Cooking Time: 40 minutes
Servings: 4
Ingredients:

- 1 big turkey breast, skinless, boneless and roughly cubed
- Juice of 1 lemon
- 2 tablespoons avocado oil
- 1 red onion, chopped
- 2 tablespoons sage, chopped
- 1 garlic clove, minced
- 1 cup chicken stock

Directions:

1 Heat up a pan with the avocado oil over medium-high heat, add the turkey, and brown for 3 minutes on each side.

2 Add the rest of the ingredients, bring to a simmer and cook over medium heat for 35 minutes.

3 Divide the mix between plates and serve with a side dish.

Nutrition: Calories 382, Fat 12.6, Fiber 9.6, Carbs 16.6, Protein 33.2

1221. Chicken and Apples Mix

Preparation Time: 10 minutes
Cooking Time: 40 minutes
Servings: 4
Ingredients:

- ½ cup chicken stock
- 1 red onion, sliced
- ½ cup tomato sauce
- 2 green apples, cored and chopped
- 1-pound breast, skinless, boneless and cubed
- 1 teaspoon thyme, chopped
- 1½ tablespoons olive oil
- 1 tablespoon chives, chopped

Directions:

1 In a roasting pan, combine the chicken with the tomato sauce, apples and the rest of

the ingredients except the chives, introduce the pan in the oven and bake at 425°F for 40 minutes.

2 Divide the mix between plates, sprinkle the chives on top and serve.

Nutrition: Calories 292, Fat 16.1, Fiber 9.4, Carbs 15.4, Protein 16.4

1222. Turmeric Chicken and Eggplant Mix

Preparation Time: 10 minutes
Cooking Time: 30 minutes
Servings: 4
Ingredients:

- 2 cups eggplant, cubed
- Salt and black pepper to the taste
- 2 tablespoons olive oil
- 1 cup yellow onion, chopped
- 2 tablespoons garlic, minced
- 2 tablespoons hot paprika
- 1 teaspoon turmeric powder
- 1½ tablespoons oregano, chopped
- 1 cup chicken stock
- 1-pound chicken breast, skinless, boneless and cubed
- 1 cup half and half
- 1 tablespoon lemon juice

Directions:

1 Heat up a pan with the oil over medium-high heat, add the chicken, and brown for 4 minutes on each side.

2 Add the eggplant, onion and garlic and sauté for 5 minutes more.

3 Add the rest of the ingredients, bring to a simmer and cook over medium heat for 16 minutes.

4 Divide the mix between plates and serve.

Nutrition: Calories 392, Fat 11.6, Fiber 8.3, Carbs 21.1, Protein 24.2

1223. Turkey and Asparagus Mix

Preparation Time: 10 minutes
Cooking Time: 30 minutes
Servings: 4
Ingredients:

- 1 bunch asparagus, trimmed and halved

- 1 big turkey breast, skinless, boneless and cut into strips
- 1 teaspoon basil, dried
- 2 tablespoons olive oil
- A pinch of salt and black pepper
- ½ cup tomato sauce
- 1 tablespoon chives, chopped

Directions:

1. Heat up a pan with the oil over medium-high heat, add the turkey, and brown for 4 minutes.
2. Add the asparagus and the rest of the ingredients except the chives, bring to a simmer and cook over medium heat for 25 minutes.
3. Add the chives, divide the mix between plates and serve.

Nutrition: Calories 337, Fat 21.2, Fiber 10.2, Carbs 21.4, Protein 17.6

1224. Chicken Salad and Mustard Dressing

Preparation Time: 10 minutes
Cooking Time: 0 minutes
Servings: 8
Ingredients:

- 1 cup rotisserie chicken, skinless, boneless and cubed
- ½ cup sun-dried tomatoes, chopped
- ½ cup marinated artichoke hearts, drained and chopped
- 1 cucumber, chopped
- ⅓ cup kalamata olives, pitted and sliced
- 2 cups baby arugula
- ¼ cup parsley, chopped
- 1 avocado, peeled, pitted and cubed
- ½ cup feta cheese, crumbled
- 4 tablespoons red wine vinegar
- 2 tablespoons Dijon mustard
- 1 teaspoon basil, dried
- 1 garlic clove, minced
- 2 teaspoons honey
- ½ cup olive oil
- Salt and black pepper to the taste

- 3 tablespoons lemon juice

Directions:

1. In a salad bowl, mix the chicken with the tomatoes, artichokes, cucumber, olives, arugula, parsley and avocado and toss.
2. In a different bowl, mix the vinegar with the mustard and the remaining ingredients except for the cheese, whisk well, add to the salad, and toss.
3. Sprinkle the cheese on top and serve.

Nutrition: Calories 326, Fat 21.7, Fiber 1.7, Carbs 24.9, Protein 8.8

1225. Thyme Chicken and Potatoes

Preparation Time: 10 minutes
Cooking Time: 50 minutes
Servings: 4
Ingredients:

- 1 tablespoon olive oil
- 4 garlic cloves, minced
- A pinch of salt and black pepper
- 2 teaspoons thyme, dried
- 12 small red potatoes, halved
- 2 pounds chicken breast, skinless, boneless and cubed
- 1 cup red onion, sliced
- ¾ cup chicken stock
- 2 tablespoons basil, chopped

Directions:

1. In a baking dish greased with the oil, add the potatoes, chicken and the rest of the ingredients, toss a bit, introduce in the oven and bake at 400°F for 50 minutes.
2. Divide between plates and serve.

Nutrition: Calories 281, Fat 9.2, Fiber 10.9, Carbs 21.6, Protein 13.6

1226. Chicken and Celery Quinoa Mix

Preparation Time: 10 minutes
Cooking Time: 50 minutes
Servings: 4
Ingredients:

- 4 chicken things, skinless and boneless

- 1 tablespoon olive oil
- Salt and black pepper to the taste
- 2 celery stalks, chopped
- 2 spring onions, chopped
- 2 cups chicken stock
- ½ cup cilantro, chopped
- ½ cup quinoa
- 1 teaspoon lime zest, grated

Directions:

1. Heat up a pot with the oil over medium-high heat, add the chicken, and brown for 4 minutes on each side.
2. Add the onion and the celery, stir and sauté everything for 5 minutes more.
3. Add the rest of the ingredients, toss, bring to a simmer and cook over medium-low heat for 35 minutes.
4. Divide everything between plates and serve.

Nutrition: Calories 241, Fat 12.6, Fiber 9.5, Carbs 15.6, Protein 34.1

1227. Pesto Chicken Mix

Preparation Time: 10 minutes
Cooking Time: 40 minutes
Servings: 4
Ingredients:

- 4 chicken breast halves, skinless and boneless
- 3 tomatoes, cubed
- 1 cup mozzarella, shredded
- ½ cup basil pesto
- A pinch of salt and black pepper
- Cooking spray

Directions:

1. Grease a baking dish lined with parchment paper with the cooking spray.
2. In a bowl, mix the chicken with salt, pepper and pesto and rub well.
3. Place the chicken on the baking sheet, top with tomatoes and shredded mozzarella, and bake at 400°F for 40 minutes.
4. Divide the mix between plates and serve with a side salad.

Nutrition: Calories 341, Fat 20, Fiber 1, Carbs 4, Protein 32

1228. Slow-Cooked Chicken and Capers Mix

Preparation Time: 5 minutes
Cooking Time: 7 hours
Servings: 4
Ingredients:

- 2 chicken breasts, skinless, boneless and halved
- 2 cups canned tomatoes, crushed
- 2 garlic cloves, minced
- 1 yellow onion, chopped
- 2 cups chicken stock
- 2 tablespoons capers, drained
- ¼ cup rosemary, chopped
- Salt and black pepper to the taste

Directions:

1 In your slow cooker, combine the chicken with the tomatoes, capers and the rest of the ingredients, put the lid on, and cook on Low for 7 hours.
2 Divide the mix between plates and serve.

Nutrition: Calories 292, Fat 9.4, Fiber 11.8, Carbs 25.1, Protein 36.4

1229. Yogurt Chicken and Red Onion Mix

Preparation Time: 10 minutes
Cooking Time: 30 minutes
Servings: 4
Ingredients:

- 2 pounds chicken breast, skinless, boneless and sliced
- 3 tablespoons olive oil
- ¼ cup Greek yogurt
- 2 garlic cloves, minced
- ½ teaspoon onion powder
- A pinch of salt and black pepper
- 4 red onions, sliced

Directions:

1 In a roasting pan, combine the chicken with the oil, the yogurt and the other ingredients, introduce in the oven at 375°F and bake for 30 minutes.
2 Divide the chicken mix between plates and serve hot.

Nutrition: Calories 278, Fat 15, Fiber 9.2, Carbs 15.1, Protein 23.3

1230. Paprika Chicken and Pineapple Mix

Preparation Time: 10 minutes
Cooking Time: 15 minutes
Servings: 4
Ingredients:

- 2 cups pineapple, peeled and cubed
- 2 tablespoons olive oil
- 1 tablespoon smoked paprika
- 2 pounds chicken breasts, skinless, boneless and cubed
- A pinch of salt and black pepper
- 1 tablespoon chives, chopped

Directions:

1 Heat up a pan with the oil over medium-high heat, add the chicken, salt and pepper, and brown for 4 minutes on each side.
2 Add the rest of the ingredients, toss, cook for 7 minutes more, divide everything between plates and serve with a side salad.

Nutrition: Calories 264, Fat 13.2, Fiber 8.3, Carbs 25.1, Protein 15.4

1231. Chicken and Sausage Mix

Preparation Time: 10 minutes
Cooking Time: 50 minutes
Servings: 4
Ingredients:

- 2 zucchinis, cubed
- 1-pound Italian sausage, cubed
- 2 tablespoons olive oil
- 1 red bell pepper, chopped
- 1 red onion, sliced
- 2 tablespoons garlic, minced
- 2 chicken breasts, boneless, skinless and halved
- Salt and black pepper to the taste
- ½ cup chicken stock
- 1 tablespoon balsamic vinegar

Directions:

1 Heat up a pan with half of the oil over medium-high heat, add the sausages, brown for 3 minutes on each side, and transfer to a bowl.
2 Heat up the pan again with the rest of the oil over medium-high heat, add the chicken and brown for 4 minutes on each side.
3 Return the sausage, add the rest of the ingredients as well, bring to a simmer, introduce in the oven and bake at 400°F for 30 minutes.
4 Divide everything between plates and serve.

Nutrition: Calories 293, Fat 13.1, Fiber 8.1, Carbs 16.6, Protein 26.1

1232. Creamy Peppercorn Ranch Dressing

Preparation Time: 10 minutes
Cooking Time: 10 minutes
Servings: 1
Ingredients:

- ¾ cup low-fat plain Greek yogurt
- ⅓ cup grated Parmigiano-Reggiano cheese
- ¼ cup low-fat buttermilk (see here for tip to make from scratch)
- Juice of 1 lemon
- 2 teaspoons freshly ground black pepper
- ½ teaspoon onion flakes
- ¼ teaspoon salt
- Post-Op
- 2 tablespoons

Directions:

1 In a blender or food processor, puree the yogurt, cheese, buttermilk, lemon juice, pepper, onion flakes, and salt on medium-high speed until the dressing is completely smooth and creamy.

Nutrition: Calories: 35; Total fat: 1g; Protein: 4g; Carbs: 2g; Fiber: 0g; Sugar: 1g; Sodium: 133mg

1233. Sweet Peach Jam

Preparation Time: 10 minutes
Cooking Time: 16 minutes
Servings: 10
Ingredients:

- 1½ lb. fresh peaches, pitted and chopped

- ½ tablespoon vanilla
- ¼ cup maple syrup

Directions:
1. Put all of the ingredients in the air fryer and stir well.
2. Seal pot and cook on high for 1 minute.
3. Once done, allow to release pressure naturally. Remove lid.
4. Set pot on sauté mode and cook for 15 minutes or until jam thickened.
5. Pour into the container and store it in the fridge.

Nutrition: Calories – 16 Protein 0.1 g. Fat – 0 g. Carbs – 3.7 g.

1234. Warm Peach Compote

Preparation Time: 10 minutes
Cooking Time: 1 minute
Servings: 1
Ingredients:
- 4 peaches, peeled and chopped
- 1 tablespoon water
- ½ tablespoon cornstarch
- 1 teaspoon vanilla

Directions:
1. Add water, vanilla, and peaches into the air fryer basket.
2. Seal pot and cook on high for 1 minute.
3. Once done, allow to release pressure naturally. Remove lid.
4. In a small bowl, whisk together 1 tablespoon of water and cornstarch and pour into the pot and stir well.
5. Serve and enjoy.

Nutrition: Calories – 66 Protein 1.4 g Fat – 0.4 g Carbs – 15 g.

16-Weeks
Meal Plan

Weeks 1-4	Recipe No.	Breakfast	Pages	Recipe No.	Lunch	Pages	Recipe No.	Dinner	Pages
DAY 1	5	Blueberry Banana Protein Smoothie	10	317	Rice with Chicken	84	386	Lush Moroccan Chickpea, Vegetable, and Fruit Stew	102
DAY 2	11	Sun Dried Tomatoes, Dill and Feta Omelet Casserole	14	323	Light Balsamic Salad	85	392	Pork Strips and Rice	104
DAY 3	25	Walnuts Yogurt Mix	12	337	Lime Shrimp and Kale	89	406	Fruited Quinoa Salad	108
DAY 4	14	Baked Cauliflower Hash	12	326	Cauliflower Lunch Salad	86	395	Kale Sprouts & Lamb	105
DAY 5	22	Seeds and Lentils Oats	11	334	Lemon and Garlic Fettucine	88	403	Orange and Garlic Shrimp	107
DAY 6	1	Italian Breakfast Sausage with Baby Potatoes and Vegetables	9	313	Creamy Chicken Breast	83	382	Black Bean Chili with Mangoes	101
DAY 7	6	Chocolate Banana Smoothie	14	318	Tomato Soup	84	387	Simple Pork Stir Fry	102
DAY 8	24	Lemon Peas Quinoa Mix	13	336	Coconut Turkey Mix	89	405	Tuna Sandwich	108
DAY 9	16	Bacon, Spinach and Tomato Sandwich	10	328	Quinoa and Scallops Salad	86	397	Pistachio-Crusted Whitefish	105
DAY 10	13	Greek Beans Tortillas	12	325	Leeks Soup	86	394	Pork with Couscous	104
DAY 11	10	Quinoa Bake with Banana	10	322	Easy Lunch Salmon Steaks	85	391	Pork and Greens Salad	104
DAY 12	2	Cauliflower Fritters with Hummus	14	314	Chicken, Bamboo, and Chestnuts Mix	83	383	Israeli Style Eggplant and Chickpea Salad	101
DAY 13	26	Stuffed Pita Breads	14	338	Parsley Cod Mix	89	407	Turkey Wrap	108
DAY 14	20	Cinnamon Apple and Lentils Porridge	12	332	Fruit Shrimp Soup	88	401	Speedy Tilapia with Red Onion and Avocado	106
DAY 15	4	Raspberry Vanilla Smoothie	13	316	Quinoa Chicken Salad	83	385	Lentil and Vegetable Curry Stew	102
DAY 16	15	Eggs, Mint and Tomatoes	12	327	Shrimp Cocktail	86	396	Shrimp with Garlic and Mushrooms	105
DAY 17	9	Mediterranean Egg Muffins with Ham	13	321	Lemongrass and Chicken Soup	85	390	Pork and Chickpea Stew	103

DAY 18	27	Farro Salad	14	339	Salmon and Cabbage Mix	89	408	Chicken Wrap	108
DAY 19	28	Cranberry and Dates Squares	14	340	Tofu & Green Bean Stir-Fry	89	409	Veggie Wrap	109
DAY 20	18	Salmon Frittata	12	330	Parsley Seafood Cocktail	87	399	Sauced Shellfish in White Wine	106
DAY 21	21	Lentils and Cheddar Frittata	13	333	Mussels and Chickpea Soup	88	402	Steamed Mussels in white Wine Sauce	107
DAY 22	17	Cottage Cheese and Berries Omelet	12	329	Squid and Shrimp Salad	87	398	Crispy Homemade Fish Sticks Recipe	106
DAY 23	23	Orzo and Veggie Bowls	13	335	Shrimp and Broccoli Soup	89	404	Roasted Shrimp-Gnocchi Bake	107
DAY 24	8	Greek Yogurt with Fresh Berries, Honey and Nuts	10	320	Sweet Potatoes and Zucchini Soup	85	389	Simple Braised Pork	103
DAY 25	3	Overnight Berry Chia Oats	9	315	Salsa Chicken	83	384	Italian Sautéed Cannellini Beans	101
DAY 26	19	Coriander Mushroom Salad	13	331	Shrimp and Onion Ginger Dressing	87	400	Pistachio Sole Fish	106
DAY 27	7	Moroccan Avocado Smoothie	10	319	Cod Soup	84	388	Pork and Lentil Soup	103
DAY 28	12	Breakfast Taco Scramble	11	324	Purple Potato Soup	86	393	Pork and Bean Stew	104

Weeks 5-8	Recipe No.	Breakfast	Pages	Recipe No.	Lunch	Pages	Recipe No.	Dinner	Pages
DAY 1	20	Cinnamon Apple and Lentils Porridge	13	332	Fruit Shrimp Soup	88	401	Speedy Tilapia with Red Onion and Avocado	106
DAY 2	7	Moroccan Avocado Smoothie	10	319	Cod Soup	84	388	Pork and Lentil Soup	103
DAY 3	2	Cauliflower Fritters with Hummus	9	314	Chicken, Bamboo, and Chestnuts Mix	83	383	Israeli Style Eggplant and Chickpea Salad	101
DAY 4	15	Eggs, Mint and Tomatoes	12	327	Shrimp Cocktail	86	396	Shrimp with Garlic and Mushrooms	105
DAY 5	24	Lemon Peas Quinoa Mix	14	336	Coconut Turkey Mix	89	405	Tuna Sandwich	108
DAY 6	6	Chocolate Banana Smoothie	10	318	Tomato Soup	84	387	Simple Pork Stir Fry	102
DAY 7	14	Baked Cauliflower Hash	12	326	Cauliflower Lunch Salad	86	395	Kale Sprouts & Lamb	105
DAY 8	8	Greek Yogurt with Fresh Berries, Honey and Nuts	10	320	Sweet Potatoes and Zucchini Soup	85	389	Simple Braised Pork	103
DAY 9	16	Bacon, Spinach and Tomato Sandwich	12	328	Quinoa and Scallops Salad	86	397	Pistachio-Crusted Whitefish	105

DAY 10	10	Quinoa Bake with Banana	11	322	Easy Lunch Salmon Steaks	85	391	Pork and Greens Salad	104
DAY 11	18	Salmon Frittata	12	330	Parsley Seafood Cocktail	87	399	Sauced Shellfish in White Wine	106
DAY 12	12	Breakfast Taco Scramble	11	324	Purple Potato Soup	86	393	Pork and Bean Stew	104
DAY 13	17	Cottage Cheese and Berries Omelet	12	329	Squid and Shrimp Salad	87	398	Crispy Homemade Fish Sticks Recipe	106
DAY 14	9	Mediterranean Egg Muffins with Ham	10	321	Lemongrass and Chicken Soup	85	390	Pork and Chickpea Stew	103
DAY 15	11	Sun Dried Tomatoes, Dill and Feta Omelet Casserole	11	323	Light Balsamic Salad	85	392	Pork Strips and Rice	104
DAY 16	23	Orzo and Veggie Bowls	13	335	Shrimp and Broccoli Soup	89	404	Roasted Shrimp-Gnocchi Bake	107
DAY 17	1	Italian Breakfast Sausage with Baby Potatoes and Vegetables	9	313	Creamy Chicken Breast	83	382	Black Bean Chili with Mangoes	101
DAY 18	26	Stuffed Pita Breads	14	338	Parsley Cod Mix	89	407	Turkey Wrap	108
DAY 19	19	Coriander Mushroom Salad	13	331	Shrimp and Onion Ginger Dressing	87	400	Pistachio Sole Fish	106
DAY 20	4	Raspberry Vanilla Smoothie	10	316	Quinoa Chicken Salad	83	385	Lentil and Vegetable Curry Stew	102
DAY 21	21	Lentils and Cheddar Frittata	13	333	Mussels and Chickpea Soup	88	402	Steamed Mussels in white Wine Sauce	107
DAY 22	28	Cranberry and Dates Squares	14	340	Tofu & Green Bean Stir-Fry	89	409	Veggie Wrap	109
DAY 23	27	Farro Salad	14	339	Salmon and Cabbage Mix	89	408	Chicken Wrap	108
DAY 24	3	Overnight Berry Chia Oats	9	315	Salsa Chicken	83	384	Italian Sautéed Cannellini Beans	101
DAY 25	5	Blueberry Banana Protein Smoothie	10	317	Rice with Chicken	84	386	Lush Moroccan Chickpea, Vegetable, and Fruit Stew	102
DAY 26	22	Seeds and Lentils Oats	13	334	Lemon and Garlic Fettucine	88	403	Orange and Garlic Shrimp	107
DAY 27	13	Greek Beans Tortillas	12	325	Leeks Soup	86	394	Pork with Couscous	104
DAY 28	25	Walnuts Yogurt Mix	14	337	Lime Shrimp and Kale	89	409	Fruited Quinoa Salad	108

Weeks 9-12	Recipe No.	Breakfast	Pages	Recipe No.	Lunch	Pages	Recipe No.	Dinner	Pages
DAY 1	5	Blueberry Banana Protein Smoothie	10	317	Rice with Chicken	84	386	Lush Moroccan Chickpea, Vegetable, and Fruit Stew	102
DAY 2	11	Sun Dried Tomatoes, Dill and Feta Omelet Casserole	14	323	Light Balsamic Salad	85	392	Pork Strips and Rice	104
DAY 3	25	Walnuts Yogurt Mix	12	337	Lime Shrimp and Kale	89	406	Fruited Quinoa Salad	108
DAY 4	14	Baked Cauliflower Hash	12	326	Cauliflower Lunch Salad	86	395	Kale Sprouts & Lamb	105
DAY 5	22	Seeds and Lentils Oats	11	334	Lemon and Garlic Fettucine	88	403	Orange and Garlic Shrimp	107
DAY 6	1	Italian Breakfast Sausage with Baby Potatoes and Vegetables	9	313	Creamy Chicken Breast	83	382	Black Bean Chili with Mangoes	101
DAY 7	6	Chocolate Banana Smoothie	14	318	Tomato Soup	84	387	Simple Pork Stir Fry	102
DAY 8	24	Lemon Peas Quinoa Mix	13	336	Coconut Turkey Mix	89	405	Tuna Sandwich	108
DAY 9	16	Bacon, Spinach and Tomato Sandwich	10	328	Quinoa and Scallops Salad	86	397	Pistachio-Crusted Whitefish	105
DAY 10	13	Greek Beans Tortillas	12	325	Leeks Soup	86	394	Pork with Couscous	104
DAY 11	10	Quinoa Bake with Banana	10	322	Easy Lunch Salmon Steaks	85	391	Pork and Greens Salad	104
DAY 12	2	Cauliflower Fritters with Hummus	14	314	Chicken, Bamboo, and Chestnuts Mix	83	383	Israeli Style Eggplant and Chickpea Salad	101
DAY 13	26	Stuffed Pita Breads	14	338	Parsley Cod Mix	89	407	Turkey Wrap	108
DAY 14	20	Cinnamon Apple and Lentils Porridge	12	332	Fruit Shrimp Soup	88	401	Speedy Tilapia with Red Onion and Avocado	106
DAY 15	4	Raspberry Vanilla Smoothie	13	316	Quinoa Chicken Salad	83	385	Lentil and Vegetable Curry Stew	102
DAY 16	15	Eggs, Mint and Tomatoes	12	327	Shrimp Cocktail	86	396	Shrimp with Garlic and Mushrooms	105
DAY 17	9	Mediterranean Egg Muffins with Ham	13	321	Lemongrass and Chicken Soup	85	390	Pork and Chickpea Stew	103
DAY 18	27	Farro Salad	14	339	Salmon and Cabbage Mix	89	408	Chicken Wrap	108
DAY 19	28	Cranberry and Dates Squares	14	340	Tofu & Green Bean Stir-Fry	89	409	Veggie Wrap	109
DAY 20	18	Salmon Frittata	12	330	Parsley Seafood Cocktail	87	399	Sauced Shellfish in White Wine	106

DAY 21	21	Lentils and Cheddar Frittata	13	333	Mussels and Chickpea Soup	88	402	Steamed Mussels in white Wine Sauce	107
DAY 22	17	Cottage Cheese and Berries Omelet	12	329	Squid and Shrimp Salad	87	398	Crispy Homemade Fish Sticks Recipe	106
DAY 23	23	Orzo and Veggie Bowls	13	335	Shrimp and Broccoli Soup	89	404	Roasted Shrimp-Gnocchi Bake	107
DAY 24	8	Greek Yogurt with Fresh Berries, Honey and Nuts	10	320	Sweet Potatoes and Zucchini Soup	85	389	Simple Braised Pork	103
DAY 25	3	Overnight Berry Chia Oats	9	315	Salsa Chicken	83	384	Italian Sautéed Cannellini Beans	101
DAY 26	19	Coriander Mushroom Salad	13	331	Shrimp and Onion Ginger Dressing	87	400	Pistachio Sole Fish	106
DAY 27	7	Moroccan Avocado Smoothie	10	319	Cod Soup	84	388	Pork and Lentil Soup	103
DAY 28	12	Breakfast Taco Scramble	11	324	Purple Potato Soup	86	393	Pork and Bean Stew	104

Weeks 13-16	Recipe No.	Breakfast	Pages	Recipe No.	Lunch	Pages	Recipe No.	Dinner	Pages
DAY 1	20	Cinnamon Apple and Lentils Porridge	13	332	Fruit Shrimp Soup	88	401	Speedy Tilapia with Red Onion and Avocado	106
DAY 2	7	Moroccan Avocado Smoothie	10	319	Cod Soup	84	388	Pork and Lentil Soup	103
DAY 3	2	Cauliflower Fritters with Hummus	9	314	Chicken, Bamboo, and Chestnuts Mix	83	383	Israeli Style Eggplant and Chickpea Salad	101
DAY 4	15	Eggs, Mint and Tomatoes	12	327	Shrimp Cocktail	86	396	Shrimp with Garlic and Mushrooms	105
DAY 5	24	Lemon Peas Quinoa Mix	14	336	Coconut Turkey Mix	89	405	Tuna Sandwich	108
DAY 6	6	Chocolate Banana Smoothie	10	318	Tomato Soup	84	387	Simple Pork Stir Fry	102
DAY 7	14	Baked Cauliflower Hash	12	326	Cauliflower Lunch Salad	86	395	Kale Sprouts & Lamb	105
DAY 8	8	Greek Yogurt with Fresh Berries, Honey and Nuts	10	320	Sweet Potatoes and Zucchini Soup	85	389	Simple Braised Pork	103
DAY 9	16	Bacon, Spinach and Tomato Sandwich	12	328	Quinoa and Scallops Salad	86	397	Pistachio-Crusted Whitefish	105
DAY 10	10	Quinoa Bake with Banana	11	322	Easy Lunch Salmon Steaks	85	391	Pork and Greens Salad	104

DAY 11	18	Salmon Frittata	12	330	Parsley Seafood Cocktail	87	399	Sauced Shellfish in White Wine	106
DAY 12	12	Breakfast Taco Scramble	11	324	Purple Potato Soup	86	393	Pork and Bean Stew	104
DAY 13	17	Cottage Cheese and Berries Omelet	12	329	Squid and Shrimp Salad	87	398	Crispy Homemade Fish Sticks Recipe	106
DAY 14	9	Mediterranean Egg Muffins with Ham	10	321	Lemongrass and Chicken Soup	85	390	Pork and Chickpea Stew	103
DAY 15	11	Sun Dried Tomatoes, Dill and Feta Omelet Casserole	11	323	Light Balsamic Salad	85	392	Pork Strips and Rice	104
DAY 16	23	Orzo and Veggie Bowls	13	335	Shrimp and Broccoli Soup	89	404	Roasted Shrimp-Gnocchi Bake	107
DAY 17	1	Italian Breakfast Sausage with Baby Potatoes and Vegetables	9	313	Creamy Chicken Breast	83	382	Black Bean Chili with Mangoes	101
DAY 18	26	Stuffed Pita Breads	14	338	Parsley Cod Mix	89	407	Turkey Wrap	108
DAY 19	19	Coriander Mushroom Salad	13	331	Shrimp and Onion Ginger Dressing	87	400	Pistachio Sole Fish	106
DAY 20	4	Raspberry Vanilla Smoothie	10	316	Quinoa Chicken Salad	83	385	Lentil and Vegetable Curry Stew	102
DAY 21	21	Lentils and Cheddar Frittata	13	333	Mussels and Chickpea Soup	88	402	Steamed Mussels in white Wine Sauce	107
DAY 22	28	Cranberry and Dates Squares	14	340	Tofu & Green Bean Stir-Fry	89	409	Veggie Wrap	109
DAY 23	27	Farro Salad	14	339	Salmon and Cabbage Mix	89	408	Chicken Wrap	108
DAY 24	3	Overnight Berry Chia Oats	9	315	Salsa Chicken	83	384	Italian Sautéed Cannellini Beans	101
DAY 25	5	Blueberry Banana Protein Smoothie	10	317	Rice with Chicken	84	386	Lush Moroccan Chickpea, Vegetable, and Fruit Stew	102
DAY 26	22	Seeds and Lentils Oats	13	334	Lemon and Garlic Fettucine	88	403	Orange and Garlic Shrimp	107
DAY 27	13	Greek Beans Tortillas	12	327	Leeks Soup	86	396	Pork with Couscous	104
DAY 28	25	Walnuts Yogurt Mix	14	337	Lime Shrimp and Kale	89	409	Fruited Quinoa Salad	108

Conclusion

The Mediterranean Diet Culinary Academy is the editor of this book, but this work would not have been possible without the help of our Chefs. We want to thank them a lot for their passion and contribution.

We hope you enjoy all of the recipes we have offered. The Mediterranean is an incredible experience. Dozens of different cultures, languages and cuisines blend. It's a gift for both the soul and the body, it fits for a peasant and for an emperor. Hopefully, this carried you to wherever you wanted to be – whether that was health, weight loss, tasty flavours or simple curiosity.

This cookbook was not intended to be the be-all-end-all publication on Mediterranean food. Still, it was structured to serve as a knowledge basis – to give you a complete idea of the basics of where to look when making choices for yourself—just the essentials and then enough to get you started, with enough to carry you in confidence. We also tried to give you a reliable, calorie-precise guide to what you'll be eating, not so you can obsessively track every calorie, but so you can start thinking about the food choices you make every day in hopes that it will encourage you to find your way to a healthy lifestyle.

Changing your diet isn't a simple thing, but hopefully, we have provided you enough examples to inspire you on this culinary journey. Cooking and eating is a fundamental part of existence, and it is also one of the most rewarding for the body and spirit.

We emphasize how the Mediterranean diet and slow cookers can be a beautiful combination if you want to try a healthier food version. However, once you get used to the genuine taste that great food can deliver through a slow cooker, you will quickly adjust your schedule.

Quicker and faster is not always better, especially when it comes to instant food or fast foods, which is unhealthy, as we have seen in an overweight society and harnesses several ailments. This book was also designed to learn what cooking can bring to your life, with a twist on Mediterranean cuisine.

Once you have this new form of cooking blended into your routine, you will find yourself switching to healthier foods, saving on groceries, and using less energy.

At the very least, we have enriched your life most slightly. Enjoy your Mediterranean meals with your friends and family to the best effect. Whatever you've gleaned from this cookbook, the one thing we must say is Bon appétit!

Index

FROSTY CHOCOLATE SHAKE............ 300

5-MINUTE HEIRLOOM TOMATO & CUCUMBER TOAST................................ 35

AIR FRIED CARROTS, ZUCCHINI & SQUASH.. 196

AIR FRYER BASIL TOMATOES........ 197

AIR FRYER RATATOUILLE................ 197

ALFREDO CHICKEN PITA PIZZA......... 272

ALMOND AND RIND CRUSTED ZUCCHINI FRITTERS....................... 187

ALMOND BREAD.................................. 78

ALMOND BUTTER AND BLUEBERRY SMOOTHIE.. 62

ALMOND BUTTER BANANA CHOCOLATE SMOOTHIE........................... 286

ALMOND COOKIES............................. 281

ALMOND-DATE ENERGY BITES......... 301

ALMONDS AND OATS PUDDING....... 285

AMARANTH TABBOULEH SALAD...... 44

ANASAZI BEAN AND VEGETABLE STEW... 231

APPLE & KALE SALAD....................... 45

APPLE AND BERRIES AMBROSIA...... 292

APPLE CRISP.. 304

APPLE CRUMBLE................................ 298

APPLE DATES MIX............................. 287

APPLE PUMPKIN SOUP..................... 250

APPLE QUINOA BREAKFAST BARS 27

APPLE RISOTTO.................................. 73

APPLES AND POMEGRANATE SALAD.. 218

APPLESAUCE....................................... 112

AROMATIC TILAPIA........................... 134

AROMATIC WHOLE GRAIN SPAGHETTI.. 97

ARTICHOKE FLATBREAD.................. 262

ARTICHOKE FRITTATA...................... 33

ARTICHOKE PIZZA............................. 279

ARTICHOKE SKEWERS...................... 66

ARTICHOKE SOUP............................. 254

ARTICHOKES AND CHEESE OMELET.. 16

ARUGULA AND CORN SALAD.......... 209

ARUGULA SALAD............................... 206

ASIAN-SPICED PORK LOIN.............. 166

ASPARAGUS SMOKED SALMON....... 144

ATHENIAN AVGOLEMONO SOUR SOUP... 243

AUTHENTIC GREEK RIZOGALO......... 291

AVOCADO AND APPLE SMOOTHIE.... 22

AVOCADO AND CUCUMBER SMOOTHIE.. 266

AVOCADO AND TOMATO WRAPS...... 55

AVOCADO CHICKPEA PIZZA........... 19

AVOCADO CUCUMBER SOUP......... 242

AVOCADO DIP.................................... 63

AVOCADO MAYO............................... 112

AVOCADO PEACH SALSA ON GRILLED SWORDFISH...................... 117

AVOCADO SAUCED CUCUMBER NOODLES... 192

AVOCADO SPREAD............................. 20

AVOCADO TOAST............................... 20

AVOCADO TOMATO GOUDA SOCCA PIZZA... 24

AVOCADO YOGURT DIP................... 79

AVO-ORANGE SALAD DISH............. 43

BABY SPINACH PIZZA WITH SWEET ONION.................................... 275

BACON & POTATO SOUP................. 253

BACON AND BRIE OMELET WEDGES... 31

BACON AND EGG WRAPS WITH SALSA... 54

BACON, SPINACH AND TOMATO SANDWICH... 13

BAKED CAULIFLOWER HASH.......... 13

BAKED COD CRUSTED WITH HERBS... 118

BAKED COD FILLETS WITH GHEE SAUCE.. 117

BAKED EGGPLANT ROUNDS.......... 188

BAKED FALAFEL................................. 97

BAKED OMELET MIX 11....................

BAKED RICOTTA & PEARS.............. 28

BAKED ROLLED OAT WITH PEARS AND PECANS..................................... 238

BAKED ROOT VEGETABLE CHIPS WITH BUTTERMILK-PARSLEY DIPPING SAUCE..................................... 261

BAKED SEA BASS.............................. 128

BAKED SHRIMP MIX......................... 130

BAKED TROUT AND FENNEL........... 133

BAKED WHOLE-GRAIN LAVASH CHIPS WITH DIP............................... 260

BAKED ZUCCHINI GRATIN.............. 179

BALSAMIC BEEF DISH...................... 145

BALSAMIC BRUSSELS SPROUTS..... 196

BALSAMIC BULGUR SALAD............. 208

BALSAMIC TURKEY BITES AND APRICOTS... 170

BALSAMIC-GLAZED PIZZA WITH ARUGULA & OLIVES........................ 273

BANANA AND QUINOA CASSEROLE 20

BANANA CHOCOLATE CUPCAKES.... 298

BANANA DESSERT WITH CHOCOLATE CHIPS....................................... 288

BANANA OATS.................................... 22

BANANA, CRANBERRY, AND OAT BARS... 292

BANANA, CRANBERRY, AND OAT BARS... 292

BANANA, PEAR AND COCONUT SMOOTHIE.. 265

BARLEY PORRIDGE........................... 31

BASIC MEATBALLS............................ 163

BASIC RECIPE FOR VEGETABLE BROTH... 239

BASIL & ARTICHOKE PIZZA........... 273

BASIL AND AVOCADO SALAD......... 47

BASIL SALAD...................................... 48

BASIL TURKEY AND ZUCCHINIS..... 173

BBQ CHICKEN PIZZA....................... 267

BEAN AND SUMMER SQUASH SAUTÉ... 227

BEANS AND CUCUMBER SALAD..... 211

BEEF & BULGUR MEATBALLS......... 148

BEEF & TAPIOCA STEW.................... 148

BEEF AND CHEESE GRATIN............ 155

BEEF BRISKET AND ONION SAUCE.. 113

BEEF CACCIATORE........................... 155

BEEF CORN CHILI............................. 145

BEEF KOFTA...................................... 154

BEEF PATTY IN MUSHROOM SAUCE... 113

BEEF PIZZA.. 148

BEEF ROASTED WINE SAUCE......... 112

BEEF TENDERLOIN WITH RED WINE REDUCTION........................... 164

BEEF, ARTICHOKE & MUSHROOM STEW.. 147

BEET SALAD DRESSING................... 112

BEET SALAD WITH PARSLEY DRESSING... 115

BELGIAN GOLD WAFFLES............... 302

BELL PEPPER AND TOMATO SATARA.. 190

BERRIES AND GRILLED CALAMARI.. 117

BERRY AND RHUBARB COBBLER...... 292

BERRY JAM WITH CHIA SEEDS....... 73

BERRY OATS....................................... 20

BEST EVER BEEF STEW.................... 154

BLACK BEAN BUDA BOWL.............. 224

BLACK BEAN CHILI WITH MANGOES... 102

BLACK BEAN STEW WITH CORNBREAD... 95

BLACK BEAN VEGGIE BURGER...... 177

BLACK BEAN WRAP WITH HUMMUS.. 222

BLACK-EYED PEA, BEET, AND CARROT STEW... 232

BLACK-EYED PEAS AND CORN SALAD.. 222

BLUEBERRIES QUINOA..................... 27

BLUEBERRY BANANA PROTEIN SMOOTHIE... 11

BLUEBERRY FAT BOMBS................. 67

BLUEBERRY GREEK YOGURT PANCAKES.. 37

LUEBERRY, HAZELNUT, AND LEMON BREAKFAST GRAIN SALAD......... 37

BLUEBERRY-BLACKBERRY ICE POPS... 289

BLUEBERRY-PIE SMOOTHIE........... 265

BOILED PEANUTS............................. 71

BOLD CHORIZO PAELLA.................. 161

BOLD FLAVORED HALIBUT............. 135

BLUEBERRY, HAZELNUT, AND LEMON BREAKFAST GRAIN SALAD............ 37
BLUEBERRY-BLACKBERRY ICE POPS............ 289
BLUEBERRY-PIE SMOOTHIE............ 265
BOILED PEANUTS............ 71
BOLD CHORIZO PAELLA............ 161
BOLD FLAVORED HALIBUT............ 135
BONELESS PORK CHOPS WITH SUMMER VEGGIES............ 156
BRAISED CREAM KALE............ 186
BRAISED SHORT RIBS WITH RED WINE............ 153
BREAD MACHINE PIZZA DOUGH............ 270
BREADED AND SPICED HALIBUT............ 117
BREAKFAST TACO SCRAMBLE............ 12
BRICK OVEN PIZZA (BROOKLYN STYLE)............ 271
BROCCOLI AND CAULIFLOWER MASH............ 184
BROCCOLI AND POTATO SOUP............ 246
BROCCOLI CHEESE............ 189
BROCCOLI CHEESE BURST PIZZA............ 277
BROCCOLI FENNEL SOUP............ 240
BROCCOLI RABE............ 202
BROCCOLI SALAD............ 194
BROCCOLI SOUP............ 249
BROCCOLI-PEPPER PIZZA............ 276
BROWN LENTILS SALAD............ 40
BROWN RICE PILAF WITH GOLDEN RAISINS............ 237
BROWN RICE PILAF WITH PISTACHIOS AND RAISINS............ 238
BROWN RICE PUDDING WITH PUMPKIN SPICE............ 69
BROWN RICE SALAD............ 42
BROWN RICE, CHICKEN AND SCALLIONS............ 307
BRUSSEL SPROUTS WITH SPICED HALLOUMI............ 181
BRUSSELS SPROUTS & CRANBERRIES............ 206
BUFFALO CHICKEN CRUST PIZZA............ 268
BUFFALO RANCH CHICKEN SOUP............ 251
BUTTERED CORN............ 201
BUTTERED PORK CHOPS............ 149
BUTTERED SHRIMP............ 137
BUTTERNUT SQUASH FRIES............ 57
BUTTERY SLOW-COOKER MUSHROOMS............ 75
CABBAGE AND PRAWN WRAPS............ 56
CAJUN GARLIC SHRIMP NOODLE BOWL............ 118
CANNELLINI BEAN LETTUCE WRAPS............ 234
CANTALOUPE SMOOTHIE............ 263
CARAMELIZED ONION AND GOAT CHEESE PIZZA............ 268
CARROT AND RED LENTIL SOUP............ 252
CARROT CAKES............ 96
CASHEWS AND RED CABBAGE SALAD............ 218
CATFISH FILLETS AND RICE............ 129
CAULIFLOWER POTATO SALAD............ 77
CAULIFLOWER AND THYME SOUP............ 250
CAULIFLOWER EGG BAKE............ 182
CAULIFLOWER FRITTERS............ 18
CAULIFLOWER FRITTERS WITH HUMMUS............ 10
CAULIFLOWER LATKE............ 205

CAULIFLOWER LUNCH SALAD............ 87
CAULIFLOWER POPPERS............ 67
CAULIFLOWER SOUP............ 192
CAULIFLOWER, LEEK & BACON SOUP............ 249
CELERY DILL SOUP............ 240
CHEESE AND HAM ROLL-UPS............ 150
CHEESE CHIPS AND GUACAMOLE............ 77
CHEESE PINWHEELS............ 279
CHEESE STUFFED MUSHROOMS............ 78
CHEESE STUFFED SPAGHETTI SQUASH............ 183
CHEESY CAULIFLOWER FALAFEL............ 180
CHEESY EGGS RAMEKINS............ 16
CHEESY KETO ZUCCHINI SOUP............ 248
CHEESY OLIVES BREAD............ 30
CHEESY STUFFED PEPPERS............ 184
CHEESY SWEET POTATO AND BEAN BURRITOS............ 50
CHEESY YOGURT............ 17
CHEESY ZUCCHINI TRIANGLES WITH GARLIC MAYO DIP............ 67
CHERRY TOMATO GRATIN............ 177
CHERRY-VANILLA RICE PUDDING............ 299
CHIA PUDDING WITH COCONUT AND FRUITS............ 303
CHIA-POMEGRANATE SMOOTHIE............ 37
CHICKEN AND APPLES MIX............ 308
CHICKEN AND ARTICHOKES............ 168
CHICKEN AND CASHEWS MIX............ 169
CHICKEN AND CELERY QUINOA MIX............ 309
CHICKEN AND GINGER CUCUMBERS MIX............ 307
CHICKEN AND MINT SAUCE............ 176
CHICKEN AND MUSTARD SAUCE............ 173
CHICKEN AND OLIVES............ 168
CHICKEN AND SAUSAGE MIX............ 310
CHICKEN AND SWEET POTATOES............ 169
CHICKEN BACON RANCH PIZZA............ 269
CHICKEN BAKE............ 168
CHICKEN BITES............ 65
CHICKEN CABBAGE SOUP............ 252
CHICKEN KALE SOUP............ 250
CHICKEN KALE WRAPS............ 65
CHICKEN KEBABS............ 168
CHICKEN PARMESAN WRAPS............ 49
CHICKEN PILAF............ 169
CHICKEN PITA............ 54
CHICKEN PIZZA............ 269
CHICKEN SALAD AND MUSTARD DRESSING............ 309
CHICKEN VEGGIE SOUP............ 250
CHICKEN WINGS AND DATES MIX............ 308
CHICKEN WINGS WITH ALFREDO SAUCE............ 115
CHICKEN WRAP............ 109
CHICKEN WRAPS WITH RICOTTA CHEESE............ 55
CHICKEN, BAMBOO, AND CHESTNUTS MIX............ 84
CHICKEN, CORN AND PEPPERS............ 169
CHICKEN-LETTUCE WRAPS............ 53
CHICKPEA AND SPINACH SALAD............ 224
CHICKPEA CAULIFLOWER TIKKA MASALA............ 92
CHICKPEA CURRY............ 98
CHICKPEA PATTIES IN PITAS............ 57
CHICKPEAS & QUINOA SALAD............ 46

CHICKPEAS, CORN AND BLACK BEANS SALAD............ 218
CHILI CHICKEN MIX............ 168
CHILI MANGO AND WATERMELON SALSA............ 66
CHILI PRAWNS............ 141
CHILLED AVOCADO SOUP............ 246
CHINESE CAULIFLOWER RICE WITH EGGS............ 183
CHIPOTLE TURKEY AND TOMATOES 170
CHIPOTLE, PINTO, AND GREEN BEAN AND CORN SUCCOTASH............ 194
CHIVES CHICKEN AND RADISHES............ 172
CHOCOLATE AND AVOCADO MOUSSE............ 293
CHOCOLATE BANANA SMOOTHIE............ 11
CHOCOLATE CHIP PECAN COOKIES 305
CHOCOLATE LAVA CAKE............ 290
CHOCOLATE MACAROONS............ 301
CHOCOLATE PEANUT BUTTER CRISPY BARS............ 297
CHOCOLATE PUDDING............ 301
CHOCOLATE RASPBERRY PARFAIT............ 74
CHOCOLATE, ALMOND, AND CHERRY CLUSTERS............ 292
CHORIZO-KIDNEY BEANS QUINOA PILAF............ 100
CHUNKY CHOCOLATE PEANUT BUTTER BALLS............ 296
CHUNKY TOMATOES............ 97
CINNAMON APPLE AND LENTILS PORRIDGE............ 14
CINNAMON DUCK MIX............ 174
CITRUS CRANBERRY AND QUINOA ENERGY BITES............ 292
CITRUS FLAVORED SALMON............ 134
CITRUS SALAD............ 48
CLAM CHOWDER............ 141
CLASSIC APPLE OATS............ 62
CLEMENTINE & PISTACHIO RICOTTA............ 61
COCONUT AND ALMOND TRUFFLES............ 301
COCONUT AND GRILLED VEGETABLE SOUP............ 239
COCONUT BLUEBERRIES WITH BROWN RICE............ 293
COCONUT BROWN RICE CAKE............ 74
COCONUT CILANTRO CURRY SHRIMP............ 139
COCONUT PORRIDGE............ 32
COCONUT PUDDING WITH TROPICAL FRUIT............ 71
COCONUT SALSA ON CHIPOTLE FISH TACOS............ 118
COCONUT TURKEY MIX............ 90
COD AND MUSHROOMS MIX............ 132
COD CHOWDER............ 142
COD SOUP............ 85
COD STEAKS AND PLUM SAUCE............ 114
COD TACOS WITH SALSA............ 51
COFFEE BBQ PORK BELLY............ 151
COFFEE FLAVORED PORK RIBS............ 146
COLD CUTS AND CHEESE PINWHEELS............ 68
COLORFUL PROTEIN POWER SALAD............ 221
CORIANDER AND COCONUT CHICKEN............ 161
CORIANDER MUSHROOM SALAD............ 14

CORN AND SHRIMP SALAD...... 16
CORN AND TOMATO SALAD........ 210
CORN COCONUT PUDDING........ 72
CORN SALAD........ 40
COTTAGE CHEESE AND BERRIES OMELET........ 13
COTTAGE CHEESE SALAD DRESSING........ 111
COTTAGE KALE STIR-FRY........ 184
COUSCOUS AND CHICKPEAS BOWLS........ 17
CRANBERRY AND DATES SQUARES........ 15
CRANBERRY AND PISTACHIO BISCOTTI........ 288
CRANBERRY BULGUR MIX........ 218
CRANBERRY ORANGE POUND CAKE........ 297
CRAZY CHOCOLATE CAKE........ 296
CRAZY SAGANAKI SHRIMP........ 119
CREAMED FRUIT SALAD........ 281
CREAMED GREEN PEA SALAD........ 227
CREAMY AVOCADO CILANTRO LIME DRESSING........ 82
CREAMY AVOCADO DRESSING........ 82
CREAMY AVOCADO SAUCE........ 78
CREAMY BACON-FISH CHOWDER.... 119
CREAMY CHICKEN BREAST........ 84
CREAMY CHICKPEA SAUCE WITH WHOLE-WHEAT FUSILLI........ 217
CREAMY CORIANDER CHICKEN........ 175
CREAMY CRAB DIP........ 79
CREAMY CURRY SALMON........ 132
CREAMY MUSHROOMS WITH GARLIC AND THYME........ 80
CREAMY PEPPERCORN RANCH DRESSING........ 310
CREAMY PUMPKIN PASTA........ 94
CREAMY RICE PUDDING........ 289
CREAMY SPINACH........ 185
CREAMY ZOODLES........ 177
CRÈME CARAMEL........ 284
CRISPED COCO-SHRIMP WITH MANGO DIP........ 119
CRISPY & SPICY EGGPLANT........ 196
CRISPY GREEN BEANS........ 196
CRISPY HOMEMADE FISH STICKS RECIPE........ 107
CRISPY PARMESAN CHIPS........ 67
CROCKPOT KETO CHOCOLATE CAKE........ 290
CRUMBLED FETA AND SCALLIONS. 29
CRUNCHY CHICKEN EGG ROLLS........ 53
CRUNCHY PORK RIND ZUCCHINI STICKS........ 76
CRUNCHY SESAME COOKIES........ 281
CUCUMBER AND ARUGULA SALAD. 48
CUCUMBER AND BASIL CLEANSING DRINK........ 265
CUCUMBER AND COCONUT SMOOTHIE........ 263
CUCUMBER DILL GAZPACHO........ 239
CUCUMBER HUMMUS SANDWICHES........ 261
CUCUMBER TOMATO CHOPPED SALAD........ 203
CUCUMBER-BASIL SALSA ON HALIBUT POUCHES........ 120
CUMIN GREEN CABBAGE STIR-FRY 185

CURRIED CAULIFLOWER WITH PINE NUTS........ 198
CURRIED EGGPLANT SLICES........ 197
CURRY CHICKEN, ARTICHOKES AND OLIVES........ 176
CURRY SALMON WITH MUSTARD..... 120
CURRY VEGETABLE NOODLES WITH CHICKEN........ 100
DAIKON CHIPS........ 81
DALMATIAN CABBAGE, POTATO, AND PEA SOUP........ 245
DALMATIAN POTATO SOUP........ 254
DANDELION AND STRAWBERRY SALAD........ 47
DANDELION GREEN SMOOTHIE........ 263
DANDELION SALAD........ 43
DATE AND NUT BALLS........ 289
DATE AND WALNUT OVERNIGHT OATS........ 33
DATE WRAPS........ 61
DELICATE COD DISH........ 136
DELICATE SQUASH SOUP........ 249
DELICIOUS BEEF CHILI........ 163
DELICIOUS CHICKEN ALFREDO DIP 78
DELICIOUS QUINOA & DRIED........ 50
DIJON MUSTARD AND LIME MARINATED SHRIMP........ 120
DILL BEEF BRISKET........ 162
DILL CHICKEN SALAD........ 110
DILL CHUTNEY SALMON........ 110
DILL RELISH ON WHITE SEA BASS. 121
DILL SALMON SALAD WRAPS........ 49
DRIED FIG TAPENADE........ 57
DUCK AND BLACKBERRIES........ 174
DUCK AND ORANGE SAUCE........ 307
DUCK AND ORANGE WARM SALAD. 175
DUCK AND TOMATO SAUCE........ 173
DUCK, CUCUMBER AND MANGO SALAD........ 175
DUO-CHEESE BROCCOLI CROQUETTES........ 190
EASY & PERFECT MEATBALLS........ 79
EASY AND HEARTY SHAKSHUKA........ 231
EASY BLUEBERRY AND OAT CRISP.. 293
EASY BROILED LOBSTER TAILS........ 122
EASY BUTTERNUT SQUASH SOUP.. 248
EASY CARROT DIP........ 81
EASY LUNCH SALMON STEAKS........ 86
EASY PIZZA WITH A PINCH........ 272
EASY PORK CHOPS........ 151
EASY RED LENTIL SALAD........ 233
EASY ROASTED BROCCOLI........ 80
EASY SEAFOOD FRENCH STEW........ 121
EDAMAME & GINGER CITRUS SALAD........ 222
EGG AVOCADO SALAD........ 204
EGG WHITE SCRAMBLE WITH CHERRY TOMATOES & SPINACH...... 37
EGGPLANT CHIPS........ 79
EGGPLANT PARMESAN STACKS........ 92
EGGPLANT PIZZA........ 278
EGGPLANT PIZZA WITH TOFU........ 267
EGGPLANT SALAD........ 41
EGGPLANT SOUP........ 247
EGGS WITH ZUCCHINI NOODLES..... 207
EGGS, MINT AND TOMATOES........ 13
EKMEK KATAIFI........ 286
ENDIVES, FENNEL AND ORANGE SALAD........ 27
ENJOYABLE SHRIMP........ 136

EXTRA CHEESY PIZZA........ 274
FALAFEL........ 61
FALAFEL BITES........ 216
FANCY BRAESIDE SHRIMP........ 136
FARRO CUCUMBER-MINT SALAD...... 100
FARRO SALAD........ 15
FAST CHEESY BACON AND EGG WRAPS........ 53
FAVORITE GREEK SALMON........ 134
FENNEL AVGOLEMONO........ 188
FENNEL-PARMESAN FARRO........ 177
FETA - AVOCADO & MASHED CHICKPEA TOAST........ 36
FETA & QUINOA EGG MUFFINS........ 35
FETA AND ROASTED RED PEPPER BRUSCHETTA........ 63
FETA CHEESECAKE........ 282
FETA CHICKEN AND CABBAGE........ 172
FETA FRITTATA........ 33
FIG & HONEY YOGURT........ 261
FIG & RICOTTA TOAST........ 262
FIG SMOOTHIE WITH CINNAMON.. 261
FIG WITH YOGURT AND HONEY........ 60
FISH AND ORZO........ 128
FISH AND TOMATO SAUCE........ 128
FISH CAKES........ 129
FISH CURRY........ 138
FISH STEW........ 143
FLANK STEAK WITH ORANGE-HERB PISTOU........ 153
FLAVORFUL BEEF BOURGUIGNON.... 162
FLAVORFUL BUTTERNUT SQUASH.. 196
FLAVORFUL SHRIMP CURRY........ 137
FLAVORFUL TOMATOES........ 198
FREEKEH, CHICKPEA, AND HERB SALAD........ 216
FRENCH VANILLA ICE CREAM WITH HOT FUDGE........ 301
FRESH AND NO-COOK OYSTERS........ 121
FRESH BELL PEPPER BASIL PIZZA.... 268
FRIED CABBAGE........ 185
FRIED RICE AND VEGETABLES........ 204
FRUIT KABOBS WITH YOGURT DEEP........ 282
FRUIT PIZZA........ 278
FRUIT SHRIMP SOUP........ 89
FRUIT SMOOTHIE........ 36
FRUITED QUINOA SALAD........ 109
FULL EGGS IN A SQUASH........ 30
GALAKTOBOUREKO........ 284
GARBANZO BEAN SALAD........ 41
GARDEN VEGETABLE STEW........ 242
GARLIC CHICKEN AND ENDIVES........ 172
GARLIC PULLED PORK........ 149
GARLIC ROASTED SHRIMP WITH ZUCCHINI PASTA........ 121
GARLIC SHRIMP........ 140
GARLIC SOUP........ 244
GARLICKY CAULIFLOWER FLORETS........ 197
GARLICKY MIXED VEGGIES........ 199
GARLICKY RED WINE MUSHROOMS........ 230
GINGER DUCK MIX........ 174
GINGER SCALLION SAUCE OVER SEARED AHI........ 122
GLAZED PEARS WITH HAZELNUTS.. 293
GNOCCHI HAM OLIVES........ 29
GNOCCHI WITH TOMATO BASIL SAUCE........ 94

GOAT CHEESE 'N RED BEANS SALAD........ 101
GOAT CHEESE EGGPLANT CASSEROLE........ 193
GOLDEN CABBAGE AND MUSHROOM SPRING ROLLS........ 52
GOLDEN CHICKEN AND YOGURT TAQUITOS........ 51
GOLDEN SPRING ROLLS........ 51
GOUDA CAULIFLOWER CASSEROLE........ 179
GRAHAM PANCAKES........ 302
GREEK BEANS TORTILLAS........ 13
GREEK BEEF AND VEGGIE SKEWERS........ 155
GREEK FARRO SALAD........ 101
GREEK FAVA........ 60
GREEK FROZEN YOGURT DESSERT 291
GREEK PARFAIT WITH MIXED BERRIES........ 283
GREEK QUINOA BREAKFAST BOWL 23
GREEK SALAD WRAPS........ 49
GREEK SHRIMP SAGANAKI........ 60
GREEK VEGETABLES........ 195
GREEK VEGGIE BRIAM........ 185
GREEK YOGURT PANCAKES........ 35
GREEK YOGURT SPINACH ARTICHOKE DIP........ 260
GREEK YOGURT WITH FRESH BERRIES, HONEY AND NUTS........ 11
GREEK YOGURT WITH WALNUTS AND HONEY........ 36
GREEK-STYLE CHOCOLATE SEMIFREDDO........ 283
GREEN BEANS GREMOLATA........ 225
GREEN CABBAGE WITH TOFU........ 191
GREEN CREAMY SOUP........ 245
GREEN SHAKSHUKA........ 26
GREEN SMOOTHIE WITH APPLE AND BLUEBERRIES........ 264
GRILLED AVOCADO WITH TOMATOES........ 223
GRILLED CAULIFLOWER........ 198
GRILLED FAJITAS WITH JALAPEÑO SAUCE........ 220
GRILLED KEFTA........ 160
GRILLED PORK CHOPS WITH TOMATO SALAD........ 156
GRILLED RATATOUILLE KEBAB........ 221
GRILLED ROMAINE LETTUCE SALAD........ 47
GRILLED SEITAN WITH CREOLE SAUCE........ 225
GRILLED STEAK WITH HERB SAUCE........ 164
GRILLED STEAK, MUSHROOM, AND ONION KEBABS........ 105
GRILLED TOFU WITH CHIMICHURRI SAUCE........ 223
GROUND MEAT PIZZA........ 279
GROUND PORK AND BEEF CHILI WITH TOMATO AND BASIL........ 157
GRUYÈRE CELERY BOATS........ 192
GUACAMOLE........ 201
HALIBUT AND QUINOA MIX........ 129
HALIBUT PAN........ 130
HAM MUFFINS........ 19
HARISSA BOLOGNESE WITH VEGETABLE NOODLES........ 99
HASSELBACK EGGPLANT........ 96

HEALTHY BASIL PLATTER........ 40
HEALTHY CHICKEN FRITTERS........ 80
HEALTHY CHICKPEA ROAST SALAD. 44
HEALTHY POACHED TROUT........ 122
HEALTHY ROASTED CARROTS........ 198
HEARTY BEEF RAGU........ 161
HEARTY BERRY SMOOTHIE........ 263
HERBED ALMOND TURKEY........ 173
HERBED CHEESE CHIPS........ 67
HERBED CHICKEN........ 171
HERBED EGGPLANT AND KALE BAKE........ 184
HERBED PORK MEATBALLS........ 166
HERBED QUINOA AND ASPARAGUS........ 39
HERBED SALMON LOAF WITH SAUCE........ 144
HOMEMADE APPLESAUCE........ 70
HOMEMADE BEET HUMMUS........ 71
HOMEMADE HUMMUS........ 72
HOMEMADE MUESLI........ 27
HOMEMADE THAI CHICKEN SOUP.. 250
HONEY ALMOND RICOTTA SPREAD WITH PEACHES........ 34
HONEY-CARAMELIZED FIGS WITH GREEK YOGURT........ 24
HUMMUS AND OLIVE PITA BREAD... 58
HUMMUS AND TOMATO BREAKFAST PITTAS........ 28
HUMMUS PEPPERS........ 258
HUMMUS, FETA & BELL PEPPER CRACKERS........ 60
IDEAL PIZZA DOUGH (ON A LARGE BAKING SHEET)........ 277
INDIAN CHICKEN STEW........ 84
INDIAN TOMATO AND GARBANZO STEW........ 224
INDIAN WHITE CABBAGE STEW........ 188
INDONESIAN-STYLE SPICY FRIED TEMPEH STRIPS........ 203
ISRAELI EGGPLANT, CHICKPEA, AND MINT SAUTÉ........ 235
ISRAELI STYLE EGGPLANT AND CHICKPEA SALAD........ 102
ITALIAN BREAKFAST SAUSAGE WITH BABY POTATOES AND VEGETABLES........ 10
ITALIAN FRIES........ 63
ITALIAN MUSHROOM PIZZA........ 275
ITALIAN SAUTÉED CANNELLINI BEANS........ 102
ITALIAN STUFFED PORTOBELLO MUSHROOM BURGERS........ 94
ITALIAN TOMATO AND CHEESE STUFFED PEPPERS........ 190
ITALIAN VEGGIE SALAD........ 227
JALAPENO CHEESE DIP........ 81
JALAPENO RICE NOODLES........ 219
KALE AND SPROUTS SALAD........ 47
KALE CHIPS........ 69
KALE DIP........ 81
KALE SPROUTS & LAMB........ 106
KATE'S WARM MEDITERRANEAN FARRO BOWL........ 217
KETO FRENCH ONION SOUP........ 250
KIDNEY BEAN SPREAD........ 66
KOHLRABI CHIPS........ 80
KOREAN BEEF AND ONION TACOS.. 50
KOSHARI........ 232
KOURABIEDES ALMOND COOKIES 285

LAMB SOUP........ 253
LEBANESE POTATO SALAD........ 223
LEEK, MUSHROOM, AND ZUCCHINI STEW........ 187
LEEKS AND EGGS MUFFINS........ 16
LEEKS SOUP........ 87
LEFTOVER SALMON SALAD POWER BOWLS........ 122
LEMON AND DATES BARRAMUNDI. 129
LEMON AND EGG PASTA SOUP........ 242
LEMON AND GARLIC FETTUCINE........ 89
LEMON AND WATERMELON GRANITA........ 296
LEMON AVOCADO SALAD DRESSING........ 82
LEMON BROCCOLI RABE........ 231
LEMON CAULIFLOWER COUSCOUS WITH HALLOUMI........ 180
LEMON CHICKEN SOUP........ 254
LEMON CROCKPOT CAKE........ 295
LEMON DILL HALIBUT........ 139
LEMON GARLIC CAULIFLOWER........ 195
LEMON PEAR COMPOTE........ 287
LEMON PEAS QUINOA MIX........ 15
LEMON PEPPER TILAPIA........ 140
LEMON RAINBOW TROUT........ 134
LEMON ZEST SOUP........ 253
LEMON-GARLIC BAKED HALIBUT...... 122
LEMONGRASS AND CHICKEN SOUP........ 86
LEMON-PEPPER CUCUMBERS........ 61
LEMONY BLACKBERRY GRANITA...... 93
LEMONY TURKEY AND PINE NUTS... 175
LENTIL AND TOMATO DIP........ 226
LENTIL AND VEGETABLE CURRY STEW........ 103
LENTIL AVOCADO TACOS........ 93
LENTIL BEET SOUP........ 257
LENTILS AND CHEDDAR FRITTATA... 14
LETTUCE FAJITA MEATBALL WRAPS........ 54
LETTUCE, BANANA AND BERRIES SMOOTHIE........ 266
LIGHT BALSAMIC SALAD........ 86
LIGHTER LASAGNA........ 259
LIME AND WATERMELON GRANITA.. 302
LIME IN THE COCONUT CHIA PUDDING........ 299
LIME SHRIMP AND KALE........ 90
LIME SPINACH AND CHICKPEAS SALAD........ 219
LIME TURKEY AND AVOCADO MIX.... 172
LINGUINE AND BRUSSELS SPROUTS........ 217
LIVELY FLAVORED SALMON........ 134
LOADED CAULIFLOWER MASHED POTATOES........ 77
LOADED MEDITERRANEAN HUMMUS........ 258
LOBSTER TAILS WITH WHITE WINE SAUCE........ 114
LOUKOUMADES (FRIED HONEY BALLS)........ 284
LOW-CARB BAKED EGGS WITH AVOCADO AND FETA........ 34
LUSH MOROCCAN CHICKPEA, VEGETABLE, AND FRUIT STEW........ 103
MACADAMIA HUMMUS........ 79
MAHI MIDSOLO AND POMEGRANATE SAUCE........ 132

MAHI TACO WRAPS...................... 137
MANGO & APPLE SAUCE.............. 111
MANGO & ARUGULA SALAD......... 45
MANGO AND ORANGE SMOOTHIE.... 264
MANGO CASHEW CAKE.................. 70
MANGO COCONUT CREAM PIE...... 299
MANGO PEAR SMOOTHIE.............. 36
MANGO SALAD............................. 48
MANGO SALSA............................. 82
MARGHERITA OPEN-FACE SAND-
WICHES...................................... 59
MARINATED BALSAMIC PORK LOIN
SKILLET...................................... 157
MARINATED VEGGIE SALAD......... 206
MARINATED VEGGIE SKEWERS...... 200
MASCARPONE AND FIG CROSTINI.. 280
MEAT CUP SNACKS..................... 150
MEATBALLS IN CREAMY ALMOND
SAUCE....................................... 152
MEATBALLS IN FRESH TOMATO SA
UCE... 158
MEATBALLS PLATTER................... 262
MEAT-FILLED PHYLLO (SAMBOOS
EK).. 64
MEATLOAF.................................. 162
MEATLOAF IN A PINCH................ 163
MEDITERRANEAN BAKED CHICK-
PEAS.. 215
MEDITERRANEAN BREAKFAST EGG
WHITE SANDWICH....................... 38
MEDITERRANEAN BREAKFAST
SALAD.. 42
MEDITERRANEAN EGG MUFFINS
WITH HAM.................................. 11
MEDITERRANEAN EGGS.............. 32
MEDITERRANEAN EGGS CUPS...... 34
MEDITERRANEAN EGGS WHITE-
BREAKFAST SANDWICH WITH
ROASTED TOMATOES................... 35
MEDITERRANEAN FETA AND QUI-
NOA EGG MUFFINS..................... 32
MEDITERRANEAN FRITTATA......... 23
MEDITERRANEAN LENTILS AND RI
CE... 235
MEDITERRANEAN POLENTA CUPS.. 66
MEDITERRANEAN PORK CHOPS.... 160
MEDITERRANEAN QUINOA AND
FETA EGG MUFFINS.................... 26
MEDITERRANEAN SALAD............. 206
MEDITERRANEAN SMOOTHIE........ 36
MEDITERRANEAN TOMATO SALAD
WITH FETA AND FRESH HERBS....... 285
MEDITERRANEAN TOMATO SOUP... 243
MEDITERRANEAN VEGGIES.......... 200
MEDITERRANEAN WHOLE WHEAT
PIZZA.. 278
MEXICAN CASSEROLE WITH
BLACKBEANS.............................. 178
MEXICAN-STYLE POTATO CASSE-
ROLE... 95
MIDDLE EASTERN CHICKPEA STE
W... 226
MIDDLE EASTERN ZA'ATAR HUM-
MUS.. 228
MIDWEEK DINNER HALIBUT......... 136
MINESTRONE CHICKPEAS AND
MACARONI CASSEROLE............... 236
MINI FRITTATAS.......................... 20
MINI NUTS AND FRUITS CRUMBLE. 20
MINI ORANGE TARTS................... 281

MINIATURE PIZZAS..................... 272
MINT AVOCADO CHILLED SOUP.... 248
MINT BANANA CHOCOLATE SOR-
BET... 294
MINT CHOCOLATE CHIP SORBET... 300
MINT CHOCOLATE FAT BOMBS..... 302
MINTED PEAS............................. 226
MINTY FRUIT SALAD................... 299
MINTY OLIVES AND TOMATOES
SALAD....................................... 211
MINTY WATERMELON SALAD........ 288
MINTY-CUCUMBER YOGURT
TOPPED GRILLED FISH................ 123
MINUTES VEGETARIAN PASTA...... 193
MISO-GARLIC PORK CHOPS......... 167
MIXED BERRIES SALAD................ 45
MIXED BERRY AND FIG COMPOTE.. 280
MIXED VEGETABLE MEDLEY.......... 194
MOIST SHREDDED BEEF.............. 161
MOROCCAN AVOCADO SMOOTHIE.. 11
MOROCCAN VEGETABLE STEW....... 241
MOROCCAN VERMICELLI VEGETA-
BLE SOUP.................................. 241
MOUTH WATERING TUNA............ 135
MOZZARELLA BEAN PIZZA........... 277
MOZZARELLA ITALIAN PEPPERS.... 187
MOZZARELLA ROASTED PEPPERS.. 190
MUSHROOM AND BELL PEPPER
OMELET..................................... 191
MUSHROOM CAKES..................... 97
MUSHROOM FLORENTINE............. 96
MUSHROOM GOAT CHEESE FRIT-
TATA... 23
MUSHROOM MÉLANGE................ 191
MUSHROOM RED WINE CHILI...... 193
MUSHROOM SPINACH SOUP........ 249
MUSHROOM STROGANOFF........... 183
MUSSELS AND CHICKPEA SOUP.... 89
MUSTARD AND ROSEMARY PORK
TENDERLOIN............................... 152
NAAN BREAD PIZZA.................... 267
NACHOS.................................... 63
NACHOS WITH HUMMUS (MEDI-
TERRANEAN INSPIRED).............. 58
NECTARINES WITH DRIED CLOVES 73
NETTLE SOUP............................. 255
NO-BAKE CHOCOLATE COCONUT
ENERGY BALLS........................... 306
NO-BAKE CHOCOLATE SQUARES... 283
NO-FUSS SARDINE...................... 135
NOURISHING ELECTRIC SALAD...... 43
NUGGET AND VEGGIE TACO WRA
PS... 54
NUTTY DATE PAPAYA SMOOTHIE... 263
NUTTY SEA MOSS SMOOTHIE....... 265
OAT AND FRUIT PARFAIT............. 288
OLD-FASHIONED CHILI................. 233
OLIVE AND FETA BURGERS.......... 163
OLIVES AND LENTILS SALAD........ 218
ONE-POT MEDITERRANEAN
SPICED BEEF AND MACARONI...... 154
ONE-POT SEAFOOD CHOWDER..... 123
ONE-SKILLET MEDITERRANEAN
PORK AND RICE.......................... 156
ONION DIP................................. 81
ORANGE & KALE SALAD.............. 45
ORANGE AND BANANA DRINK...... 66
ORANGE AND CUCUMBER SALAD.. 209
ORANGE AND GARLIC SHRIMP...... 108
ORANGE DUCK AND CELERY........ 174

ORANGE GLAZED BANANAS.......... 303
ORANGE HERBED SAUCED WHITE
BASS... 123
ORANGE ROSEMARY SEARED
SALMON..................................... 123
OREGANO CHICKEN AND ZUCCHI-
NI PAN....................................... 171
OREGANO TURKEY AND PEPPERS.... 176
ORZO AND LEMON CHICKEN SOUP 245
ORZO AND VEGGIE BOWLS.......... 14
OUTSTANDING SHRIMP MEAL...... 137
OVERNIGHT BERRY CHIA OATS..... 10
PAELLA...................................... 97
PAN FRIED TUNA WITH HERBS
AND NUT................................... 124
PAN-FRIED SALMON WITH SALAD... 98
PANKO TOFU WITH MAYO SAUCE...... 81
PAPAYA AND QUINOA SMOOTHIE...... 266
PAPAYA, JICAMA, AND PEAS RICE
BOWL.. 234
PAPRIKA CHICKEN AND PINEAPPLE
MIX... 310
PAPRIKA RICED CAULIFLOWER...... 186
PAPRIKA SALMON AND GREEN BEA
NS.. 124
PARMESAN AND PORK RIND
GREEN BEANS............................ 76
PARMESAN ASPARAGUS.............. 195
PARMESAN BRUSSELS SPROUTS..... 197
PARMESAN CHICKEN AND CREAM.. 170
PARMESAN CHIPS....................... 65
PARMIGIANO-REGGIANO CHEESE
BROILED AVOCADOS................... 191
PARSLEY AND CORN SALAD......... 209
PARSLEY COD MIX...................... 90
PARSLEY NACHOS....................... 65
PARSLEY SEAFOOD COCKTAIL...... 88
PARSLEY TROUT AND CAPERS...... 133
PASTA WITH CHICKPEA SAUCE..... 111
PASTRY-LESS SPANAKOPITA......... 32
PATBINGSU – IN MODERATION...... 74
PEA SALAD................................ 202
PEACH & CHIA SEED................... 62
PEACH AND RASPBERRY CRISP..... 303
PEACH CAPRESE SKEWERS.......... 261
PEACH-MANGO CRUMBLE............ 300
PEANUT AND CHIVES CHICKEN MI
X.. 307
PEANUT BUTTER AND CHOCOLATE
BALLS.. 295
PEANUT BUTTER BANANA GREEK
YOGURT..................................... 25
PEANUT BUTTER BANANA GREEK
YOGURT BOWL........................... 259
PEANUT BUTTER CHIP COOKIES... 305
PEANUT VEGETABLE PAD THAI..... 91
PEAR & STRAWBERRY SALAD....... 45
PEAR AND MANGO SMOOTHIE...... 33
PEAR CROUSTADE....................... 284
PEAR SQUARES.......................... 304
PEARL COUSCOUS SALAD............ 41
PEAS SOUP................................ 252
PEASANT STIR-FRY..................... 192
PECAN AND CARROT CAKE.......... 295
PECAN CRUSTED TROUT.............. 124
PECAN SALMON FILLETS.............. 131
PECAN-MAPLE GRANOLA............. 227
PENNE WITH VEGGIES................. 205
PEPPER MEDLEY......................... 228
PEPPER TOMATO SALAD.............. 205

PEPPERED PORK RACK..................... 151
PEPPERONI FAT HEAD PIZZA.............. 273
PEPPERS AND BLACK BEANS WITH
BROWN RICE................................. 231
PEPPERS AND LENTILS SALAD............ 218
PEPPERY BLACK BEANS.................... 228
PERFECT CUCUMBER SALSA.............. 78
PESTO AND LEMON HALIBUT............. 125
PESTO CAULIFLOWER STEAKS........... 76
PESTO CHICKEN MIX........................ 309
PESTO PEA SOUP............................ 240
PINEAPPLE & VEGGIE SKEWERS......... 201
PINTO AND GREEN BEAN FRY
WITH COUSCOUS............................ 203
PISTACHIO AND TAHINI HALVA.......... 291
PISTACHIO SOLE FISH...................... 107
PISTACHIO-CRUSTED WHITEFISH........ 106
PIZZA BIANCA................................ 267
PIZZA BUNS.................................. 270
PIZZA CRUST................................ 270
PIZZA DOUGH ON YOGURT............... 278
PIZZA DOUGH WITHOUT YEAST IN
MILK.. 277
PIZZA MUFFINS.............................. 271
PLANTAINS WITH TAPIOCA PEARLS 69
PLUM WRAPS................................ 65
POACHED SALMON.......................... 140
POLENTA WITH SAUTÉED CHARD
AND FRIED EGGS........................... 22
PORK AND BEAN STEW.................... 105
PORK AND CHEESE STUFFED PEP-
PERS.. 151
PORK AND CHICKPEA STEW.............. 104
PORK AND GREENS SALAD................ 105
PORK AND LENTIL SOUP................... 104
PORK BELLY.................................. 151
PORK CHOPS AND TOMATO SAUCE. 146
PORK LARB................................... 165
PORK MEDALLIONS WITH ROAST-
ED FENNEL.................................. 158
PORK POTATO............................... 146
PORK SOUVLAKI............................. 160
PORK STRIPS AND RICE................... 105
PORK TENDERLOIN WITH AP-
PLE-TARRAGON SAUCE.................... 166
PORK TENDERLOIN WITH ORZO........ 155
PORK TENDERLOIN WITH ROASTED
VEGETABLES................................ 157
PORK WITH COUSCOUS................... 105
POTATO AND PANCETTA BOWLS....... 39
POTATO CARROT SALAD................... 194
POTATO HASH............................... 19
POTATO LATKE.............................. 202
POTATO LEEK SOUP........................ 257
PREMIUM ROASTED BABY POTA-
TOES.. 59
PROVEN AL RATATOUILLE................ 190
PRUNE, GRAPEFRUIT, AND OR-
ANGE COMPOTE............................ 304
PUB PIZZA................................... 272
PUMPKIN AND CAULIFLOWER
CURRY.. 182
PUMPKIN PIE SQUARES................... 304
PUMPKIN SOUP............................. 253
PUMPKIN SOUP WITH RICE AND
SPINACH..................................... 254
PURPLE POTATO SOUP.................... 87
QUESO FRESCO AVOCADO SALSA 188
QUICK AND EASY PORK LOIN ROA
ST.. 150

QUICK VEGETABLE KEBABS.............. 216
QUICK ZUCCHINI BOWL................... 40
QUINOA AND CHICKPEA VEGETA-
BLE BOWLS.................................. 233
QUINOA AND EGGS PAN.................. 21
QUINOA AND EGGS SALAD............... 16
QUINOA AND SCALLOPS SALAD........ 87
QUINOA BAKE WITH BANANA........... 12
QUINOA BOWL WITH YOGURT,
DATES, AND ALMONDS.................... 286
QUINOA CHICKEN SALAD................. 84
QUINOA FLOUR PIZZA..................... 279
QUINOA GRANOLA.......................... 260
QUINOA MUFFINS........................... 21
QUINOA SALAD.............................. 40
QUINOA WITH ALMONDS AND
CRANBERRIES............................... 215
QUINOA, TOMATO & MANGO SAL-
AD... 46
RADISH AND CORN SALAD............... 209
RAINBOW MANGO SALAD................. 42
RAINBOW SOBA NOODLES............... 220
RASPBERRIES AND YOGURT
SMOOTHIE................................... 27
RASPBERRY & ARUGULA SALAD........ 45
RASPBERRY CHOCOLATE PARFAIT... 73
RASPBERRY VANILLA SOOTHIE.......... 11
RASPBERRY YOGURT BASTED
CANTALOUPE................................ 295
RASPBERRY, PEACH AND WAL-
NUTS SMOOTHIE........................... 262
RED CURRY.................................. 178
RED KIDNEY BEAN SALAD................ 229
RED LENTIL SOUP.......................... 239
RED PEPPERS & PINEAPPLE
TOPPED MAHI-MAHI....................... 125
RED SOUP, SEVILLE STYLE............... 244
REVANI SYRUP CAKE....................... 285
RICE DUMPLINGS IN COCONUT SA
UCE.. 74
RICE PUDDING WITH DRIED FIGS..... 282
RICE WITH CHICKEN....................... 85
RICHLY DELICIOUS TILAPIA.............. 135
RICOTTA-LEMON CHEESECAKE......... 289
RITZY FAVA BEAN RATATOUILLE....... 230
RITZY VEGGIE CHILI....................... 237
ROAST ASPARAGUS........................ 58
ROASTED ALMOND PROTEIN SAL-
AD... 232
ROASTED ASPARAGUS.................... 187
ROASTED BRUSSELS SPROUTS......... 206
ROASTED BRUSSELS SPROUTS
AND PECANS............................... 208
ROASTED CAULIFLOWER WITH
PROSCIUTTO, CAPERS, AND ALMO
NDS... 75
ROASTED CHICKPEAS..................... 260
ROASTED GARLIC DIP..................... 80
ROASTED HALIBUT WITH BANANA
RELISH.. 125
ROASTED POLLOCK FILLET WITH
BACON AND LEEKS........................ 125
ROASTED RADISHES WITH BROWN
BUTTER SAUCE............................. 75
ROASTED ROOT VEGGIES................ 207
ROASTED SHRIMP-GNOCCHI BAKE 108
ROASTED TOMATO SAUCE............... 83
ROASTED VEGETABLE ENCHILA-
DAS... 93
ROASTED VEGETABLE SOUP............ 243

ROASTED VEGETABLES AND ZUC-
CHINI PASTA................................ 208
ROASTED VEGGIE PANINI................ 59
ROASTED ZUCCHINI....................... 196
ROCKET TOMATOES AND MUSH-
ROOM FRITTATA........................... 29
ROMAINE LETTUCE BOATS.............. 192
ROMANTIC MUG CAKES.................. 290
ROSEMARY BEEF CHUCK ROAST..... 145
RUSTIC VEGETABLE AND BROWN
RICE BOWL.................................. 207
SAFFRON CHICKEN THIGHS AND
GREEN BEANS.............................. 161
SAGE TURKEY MIX......................... 308
SALMON...................................... 137
SALMON AND BROCCOLI................. 131
SALMON AND BULGUR SALAD.......... 39
SALMON AND CABBAGE MIX............ 90
SALMON AND COCONUT SAUCE....... 114
SALMON AND CORN SALAD............. 132
SALMON AND CREAMY ENDIVES...... 33
SALMON AND EGG MUFFINS............ 62
SALMON AND MANGO MIX.............. 133
SALMON AND PEACH PAN............... 131
SALMON AND RADISH MIX.............. 131
SALMON AND SAUCE..................... 114
SALMON FRITTATA........................ 13
SALMON WITH CAPER SAUCE.......... 144
SALMON WITH CREAMY LEMON SA
UCE... 138
SALMON WITH LEMON & DILL.......... 143
SALMON WITH LEMON-CAPER SAU
CE... 139
SALMON WRAP............................. 110
SALSA CHICKEN............................ 84
SALTED PISTACHIO AND TAHINI
TRUFFLES................................... 291
SATISFYING HALIBUT MEAL............. 135
SATISFYING SPRING SALAD............. 42
SAUCED SHELLFISH IN WHITE WIN
E.. 107
SAUTÉED CABBAGE....................... 219
SAUTÉED CITRUS SPINACH............. 230
SAUTÉED COLLARD GREENS............ 208
SAVORY FETA SPINACH AND
SWEET RED PEPPER MUFFINS......... 260
SAVORY PITA CHIPS....................... 65
SAVORY QUINOA EGG MUFFINS
WITH SPINACH............................. 24
SAVOY CABBAGE WITH COCONUT
CREAM SAUCE............................. 208
SCALLOPS IN WINE 'N OLIVE OIL..... 126
SCRAMBLED EGGS......................... 19
SEA BASS IN COCONUT CREAM SA
UCE... 142
SEAFOOD STEW CIOPPINO.............. 126
SEASONED BEEF KEBABS................ 159
SECRET INGREDIENT CHOCOLATE
BROWNIES.................................. 305
SEEDS AND LENTILS OATS.............. 14
SEMOLINA CAKE WITH ALMONDS.... 290
SERRANO-WRAPPED PLUMS............ 62
SESAME SHRIMP MIX..................... 132
SHAKSHUKA WITH FETA................. 25
SHAVED BRUSSEL SPROUT SALAD. 220
SHORT RIBS AND BEER SAUCE........ 112
SHORT RIBS AND SPECIAL SAUCE.... 112
SHRIMP & SAUSAGE GUMBO........... 143
SHRIMP AND BEANS SALAD............. 130
SHRIMP AND BROCCOLI SOUP......... 90

SHRIMP AND LEMON SAUCE............. 130
SHRIMP AND ONION GINGER
DRESSING.. 88
SHRIMP BOIL.. 143
SHRIMP COCKTAIL................................. 87
SHRIMP IN MARINARA SAUCE............ 140
SHRIMP PIZZA.. 269
SHRIMP SCAMPI...................................... 143
SHRIMP TACOS.. 138
SHRIMP VEGGIE PASTA SALAD.......... 202
SHRIMP WITH GARLIC AND MUSH-
ROOMS... 106
SIMPLE APPLE COMPOTE.................... 295
SIMPLE BAKED NAVY BEANS............... 224
SIMPLE BRAISED PORK......................... 224
SIMPLE COD PICCATA............................ 126
SIMPLE LEMON DAL............................... 205
SIMPLE PORK STIR FRY......................... 103
SIMPLE SPINACH DIP............................ 111
SIMPLY DELICIOUS TILAPIA................ 134
SKIRT STEAK FAJITAS........................... 164
SLOW COOKED BUTTERY MUSHRO
OMS... 208
SLOW COOKER BEEF WITH BELL
PEPPERS.. 165
SLOW COOKER CRANBERRY PORK
CHOPS.. 167
SLOW COOKER HONEY MUSTARD
PORK WITH PEARS................................ 167
SLOW COOKER MEATLOAF RECIPE.. 146
SLOW COOKER MEDITERRANEAN
BEEF HOAGIES....................................... 147
SLOW COOKER SHREDDED BAR-
BECUE BEEF.. 165
SLOW-COOKED CHICKEN AND CA-
PERS MIX... 310
SLOW-COOKED PEPPERS FRITTATA 22
SMALL PASTA AND BEANS POT 115
SMOKED SALMON AND POACHED
EGGS ON TOAST.................................... 33
SMOKED SALMON AND VEGGIES
MIX.. 132
SMOKED SALMON AND WATER-
CRESS SALAD... 131
SMOKED SALMON EGG SCRAMBLE
WITH DILL AND CHIVES....................... 22
SMOKED SALMON GOAT CHEESE
ENDIVE BITES... 258
SMOKED SALMON, AVOCADO AND
CUCUMBER BITES................................. 261
SMOKED TROUT TARTINE.................... 126
SMOKY LOADED EGGPLANT DIP........ 259
SMOOTHIE SNACK................................. 264
SMOOTHIE WITH NUTS........................ 264
SMOOTHIE WITH STRAWBERRIES
AND COCONUT...................................... 263
SNAP PEA SALAD................................... 202
SORREL SOUP... 256
SOUTHWEST STYLE SALAD................. 219
SOUTHWESTERN AVOCADO SALAD
DRESSING.. 82
SOY SAUCE BEEF ROAST.................... 145
SOY-GINGER BRAISED SQUID............. 142
SOY-GINGER STEAMED POMPANO.. 141
SPANISH PEPPER STEAK...................... 159
SPANISH STYLE SARDINE.................... 135
SPANISH-STYLE PIZZA DE JAMON... 274
SPANISH-STYLE SAFFRON RICE
WITH BLACK BEANS............................. 204
SPEEDY SWEET POTATO CHIPS 58

SPEEDY TILAPIA WITH RED ONION
AND AVOCADO....................................... 107
SPICED APPLE CHIA PUDDING........... 302
SPICED CAULIFLOWER CHEESE BA
KE.. 187
SPICED CHICKPEAS BOWLS............... 41
SPICED GREEN BEANS......................... 197
SPICED LENTIL BURGERS.................... 226
SPICED SOUP WITH LENTILS &
LEGUMES... 236
SPICED SWEET PECANS....................... 295
SPICY & SMOKY PIZZA.......................... 274
SPICY BARBECUE SHRIMP.................. 139
SPICY BEEF WITH OLIVES AND FET
A.. 154
SPICY CAULIFLOWER STEAKS
WITH STEAMED GREEN BEANS........ 180
SPICY DIP... 81
SPICY EARLY MORNING SEAFOOD
RISOTTO.. 29
SPICY ITALIAN BEAN BALLS WITH
MARINARA... 237
SPICY LENTILS WITH SPINACH........ 195
SPICY RED LENTIL DIP......................... 261
SPICY SWEET RED HUMMUS............. 102
SPICY SWISS CHARD............................ 232
SPICY TOFU BURRITO BOWLS
WITH CILANTRO AVOCADO SAUCE.. 91
SPICY VEGETABLE SOUP..................... 247
SPICY WAKAME SALAD......................... 43
SPINACH & DILL PASTA SALAD 225
SPINACH AND BUTTERNUT
SQUASH STEW....................................... 189
SPINACH AND KALE SOUP.................. 239
SPINACH AND MASHED TOFU SAL-
AD... 228
SPINACH AND ZUCCHINI LASA-
GNA... 180
SPINACH, FETA AND EGG BREAK-
FAST QUESADILLAS.............................. 26
SPRING SOUP WITH GOURMET GR
AINS... 235
SPRING SOUP WITH POACHED EGG
.... 248
SPROUTS PIZZA..................................... 278
SQUID AND SHRIMP SALAD............... 88
STEAMED MUSSELS IN WHITE
WINE SAUCE.. 108
STEAMED MUSSELS THAI STYLE..... 127
STEAMED SALMON AND SAUCE....... 114
STEAMED SQUASH CHOWDER.......... 209
STEAMED ZUCCHINI-PAPRIKA.......... 209
STIR FRIED BOK CHOY......................... 211
STIR FRIED BRUSSELS SPROUTS
AND CARROTS....................................... 210
STIR FRIED EGGPLANT......................... 210
STRAWBERRY AND RHUBARB
SMOOTHIE.. 31
STRAWBERRY FAT BOMBS.................. 69
STRAWBERRY RHUBARB COFFEE
CAKE.. 297
STRAWBERRY RHUBARB SMOOTH-
IE.. 287
STRAWBERRY STEW............................. 287
STRAWBERRY-LIME ICE POPS........... 290
STRAWBERRY-RHUBARB
SMOOTHIE.. 37
STUFFED AVOCADO.............................. 294
STUFFED BELL PEPPERS WITH
BEEF AND MUSHROOMS..................... 159

STUFFED CELERY.................................. 57
STUFFED DRIED FIGS........................... 282
STUFFED PITA BREADS........................ 15
STUFFED PORK LOIN WITH SUN-
DRIED TOMATO AND GOAT CHEESE 152
STUFFED SWEET POTATO................... 18
STUFFED TOMATOES............................ 21
STUFFED ZUCCHINI.............................. 199
SUMMER VEGETABLE SOUP............... 256
SUMMER VEGETABLES......................... 210
SUMMER VEGGIES IN INSTANT PO
T.. 211
SUMMERTIME VEGETABLE CHICK-
EN WRAPS.. 58
SUMPTUOUS TOMATO SOUP............. 212
SUN-DRIED TOMATOES OATMEAL.... 20
SUN-DRIED TOMATOES, DILL AND
FETA OMELET CASSEROLE................. 12
SUNNY-SIDE UP BAKED EGGS
WITH SWISS CHARD, FETA, AND
BASIL... 21
SUPER SUMMER SALAD....................... 230
SUPERFAST CAJUN ASPARAGUS....... 212
SUPERFOOD FONIO SALAD................ 44
SWEET AND NUTRITIOUS PUMP-
KIN SOUP.. 212
SWEET AND SOUR VEGETABLE
NOODLES... 100
SWEET AND SPICY BRUSSELS
SPROUT HASH....................................... 227
SWEET COCONUT CASSAVA................ 71
SWEET ONION DIP................................ 68
SWEET ORANGE AND LEMON BAR-
LEY RISOTTO.. 70
SWEET PEACH JAM............................... 310
SWEET POTATO AND SPINACH
BURRITOS.. 55
SWEET POTATO BALLS......................... 98
SWEET POTATO CAKES WITH
CLASSIC GUACAMOLE......................... 91
SWEET POTATO PUREE........................ 212
SWEET POTATO SOUP.......................... 253
SWEET POTATO TART........................... 30
SWEET POTATOES AND ZUCCHINI
SOUP.. 86
SWEET POTATOES OVEN FRIED........ 212
SWEET-AND-SOUR TEMPEH.............. 178
SWISS CHARD EGG DROP SOUP....... 249
TACO TEMPEH SALAD.......................... 222
TAHINI BEEF AND POTATOES............. 160
TAHINI PINE NUTS TOAST................... 36
TANGERINE AND POMEGRANATE
BREAKFAST FRUIT SALAD.................. 28
TARRAGON COD FILLETS..................... 131
TASTY AVOCADO SAUCE OVER
ZOODLES... 213
TASTY BEEF AND BROCCOLI.............. 149
TASTY BEEF STEW................................ 162
TASTY BLACK BEAN DIP....................... 64
TASTY TUNA SCALOPPINE.................. 127
TEMPEH SNACK..................................... 63
TEX-MEX QUESO DIP............................ 68
THE RAW GREEN DETOX SALAD........ 43
THIN CRUST LOW CARB PIZZA.......... 267
THIN-CRUST FLATBREAD..................... 258
THYME AND LEMON ON BAKED
SALMON... 127
THYME CHICKEN AND POTATOES..... 309
THYME SAGE BUTTERNUT SQUASH 198
TOFU & GREEN BEAN STIR-FRY........ 90

TOFU AND MUSHROOM SOUP............ 241
TOFU GOULASH SOUP.......................... 240
TOFU HOAGIE ROLLS............................. 221
TOFU SESAME SKEWERS WITH
WARM KALE SALAD................................. 181
TOFU WITH SALTED CARAMEL PEA
RLS 72
TOMATO & ARUGULA SALAD............ 46
TOMATO & BASIL BRUSCHETTA........ 60
TOMATO & OLIVE ORECCHIETTE
WITH BASIL PESTO................................... 93
TOMATO AND ALIMENTARY PASTE
SOUP 255
TOMATO AND AVOCADO SALAD........ 210
TOMATO AND CABBAGE PUREE SO
UP 243
TOMATO AND DILL FRITTATA............ 31
TOMATO AND LENTILS SALAD............ 17
TOMATO BASIL CAULIFLOWER RIC
E 213
TOMATO CHICKEN AND LENTILS....... 171
TOMATO CREAM CHEESE SPREAD... 63
TOMATO OLIVE SALSA.......................... 258
TOMATO PORK PASTE........................... 149
TOMATO SOUP.. 85
TOMATO TRIANGLES.............................. 66
TOMATO, AVOCADO, AND CUCUM-
BER SALAD.. 76
TOMATO-BASIL SKEWERS.................... 262
TORTELLINI AND SPINACH SOUP...... 247
TORTELLINI AND VEGETABLE SOUP 246
TORTELLINI IN RED PEPPER SAUCE 216
TRADITIONAL CHICKEN SOUP............ 251
TRADITIONAL INDIAN RAJMA DAL... 29
TRADITIONAL ITALIAN CAKE WITH
ALMONDS.. 283
TRADITIONAL KALO PRAMA............... 281
TRADITIONAL MEDITERRANEAN
LOKUM.. 280
TRADITIONAL OLIVE OIL CAKE
WITH FIGS... 280
TRADITIONAL OYSTER SOUP............. 247
TRAIL MIX... 68
TRIPLE BERRY BANANA SMOOTHIE 262
TROUT AND PEPPERS MIX.................... 119
TROUT AND TZATZIKI SAUCE............. 133
TUNA AND LETTUCE WRAPS............... 52
TUNA CROQUETTES............................... 85
TUNA IN POTATOES............................... 142
TUNA SALAD.. 39
TUNA SALPICAO....................................... 141
TUNA SANDWICH.................................... 109
TURKEY AND ASPARAGUS MIX........... 308
TURKEY AND CHICKPEAS..................... 172
TURKEY AND CRANBERRY SAUCE... 176
TURKEY AND SALSA VERDE................. 173
TURKEY PIZZA WITH PESTO TOP-
PING 275
TURKEY WRAP.. 109
TURKEY WRAPS WITH SAUCE............ 113
TURKEY, ARTICHOKES AND ASPAR-
AGUS 174
TURKEY, LEEKS AND CARROTS.......... 171
TURKISH-STYLE CHOCOLATE HAL-
VA 282
TURMERIC CHICKEN AND EGG-
PLANT MIX... 308
TUSCAN BLACK CABBAGE SOUP....... 256
VALENTINE PIZZA................................... 271
VANILLA APPLE COMPOTE.................. 287

VEGAN CHILI.. 97
VEGAN SANDWICH WITH TOFU &
LETTUCE SLAW.. 182
VEGAN SESAME TOFU AND EGGPL
ANTS 213
VEGETABLE NOODLES WITH BO-
LOGNESE 99
VEGETABLE OIL PIZZA DOUGH............ 278
VEGETABLE PASTA.................................. 99
VEGETABLE PATTIES.............................. 181
VEGETABLE SOUP MOROCCAN STY
LE 214
VEGETARIAN CHILI WITH AVOCADO
CREAM 207
VEGETARIAN COCONUT CURRY........ 213
VEGETARIAN KEBABS............................ 96
VEGETARIAN LASAGNA........................ 96
VEGETARIAN SPINACH-OLIVE PIZ-
ZA 268
VEGGIE BOWLS.. 44
VEGGIE GREEK MOUSSAKA................ 179
VEGGIE JAMAICAN STEW.................... 22
VEGGIE LO MEIN...................................... 213
VEGGIE MEDITERRANEAN QUICHE.. 25
VEGGIE PIZZA.. 270
VEGGIE QUICHE...................................... 18
VEGGIE RAMEN MISO SOUP.............. 214
VEGGIE SALAD.. 39
VEGGIE SALSA WRAPS......................... 54
VEGGIE VARIETY..................................... 98
VEGGIE WRAP.. 110
VERSATILE COD....................................... 136
VIETNAMESE BRAISED CATFISH...... 141
VINEGAR VEGGIES................................. 199
VINEGARY BLACK BEANS.................... 225
WALNUT & DATE SMOOTHIE............. 287
WALNUT TURKEY AND PEACHES... 170
WALNUT, COCONUT, AND OAT GRA-
NOLA 229
WALNUT-FETA YOGURT DIP................ 61
WALNUTS YOGURT MIX........................ 15
WARM AVO AND QUINOA SALAD....... 46
WARM BEEF AND LENTIL SALAD....... 258
WARM CAPER TAPENADE ON COD... 127
WARM PEACH COMPOTE...................... 311
WATERCRESS DETOX SMOOTHIE.... 264
WATERMELON PIZZA............................ 19
WATERMELON AND RASPBERRIES
SMOOTHIE 265
WATERMELON FETA & BALSAMIC
PIZZA 288
WATERMELON REFRESHER................ 264
WAX BEANS WITH TOMATO-MUS-
TARD SAUCE... 186
WHIPPED POTATOES............................ 219
WHITE BEAN AND TUNA SALAD....... 101
WHITE BEAN SOUP................................ 252
WHITE BEANS STEW............................. 96
WHITE MUSHROOMS SOUP............... 253
WHITE PIZZA WITH PROSCIUTTO
AND ARUGULA... 276
WHITE WINE-DIJON BRUSSELS SP
ROUTS 186
WILD MUSHROOM SOUP..................... 255
WILD RICE, CELERY, AND CAULI-
FLOWER PILAF.. 115
WRAPPED PLUMS.................................. 294
YOGURT CHICKEN AND RED ONION
MIX 310
YOGURT DIP... 294

YUMMY CAULIFLOWER FRITTERS.... 215
YUMMY SALMON PANZANELLA......... 128
ZA'ATAR CHANTERELLE STEW.......... 189
ZA'ATAR FRIES... 58
ZA'ATAR PIZZA... 276
ZESTY CITRUS SALAD........................... 46
ZESTY ORANGE-CRANBERRY EN-
ERGY BITES... 300
ZOODLES WITH BASIL & AVOCADO
SAUCE 111
ZUCCHINI & TOMATO SALAD............. 46
ZUCCHINI AND AVOCADO
SMOOTHIE 265
ZUCCHINI GARLIC FRIES...................... 215
ZUCCHINI HUMMUS WRAP................ 47
ZUCCHINI NOODLES WITH MUSH-
ROOM SAUCE... 193
ZUCCHINI PASTA SALAD..................... 203
ZUCCHINI PASTA WITH MANGO-KI-
WI SAUCE.. 215
ZUCCHINI STRIPS WITH MARINA-
RA DIP... 80
ZUCCHINI TOTS....................................... 79

Made in the USA
Middletown, DE
09 October 2021